VICTORY IN WAR

For millennia, policymakers and statesmen have grappled with questions about the concept of victory in war. How long does it take to achieve victory, and how do we know when victory is achieved? Also, as highlighted by the wars against Afghanistan and Iraq, is it possible to win a war and yet lose the peace? The premise of this book is that we do not have a modern theory of victory and that, in order to answer these questions, we need one. This book explores historical definitions of victory, how victory has evolved, and how it has been implemented in war. It also subsequently develops the intellectual foundations of a modern pretheory of victory and discusses the military instruments necessary for victory in the twenty-first century, through case studies that include the U.S. military interventions in Panama, Libya, the Persian Gulf, Bosnia and Kosovo, Afghanistan, and Iraq.

William C. Martel is Associate Professor of International Security Studies at the Fletcher School at Tufts University in Medford, Massachusetts. His research interests are in international security, technology, policy analysis, and governmental decision making. Martel received his A.B. from Saint Anselm College and his doctorate in international relations from the University of Massachusetts (Amherst), and he was a Post-Doctoral Research Fellow at the Center for Science and International Affairs at Harvard's Kennedy School of Government. He was formerly a Professor of National Security Affairs at the Naval War College in Newport, Rhode Island, and a member of the professional staff of the RAND Corporation in Washington. His publications include *Strategic Nuclear War* (1986), *How to Stop a War* (1987), *The Technological Arsenal* (2001), and articles in *Orbis, Strategic Review,* and the *Washington Quarterly.*

VICTORY IN WAR

FOUNDATIONS OF MODERN MILITARY POLICY

WILLIAM C. MARTEL
The Fletcher School, Tufts University

CAMBRIDGE UNIVERSITY PRESS
Cambridge, New York, Melbourne, Madrid, Cape Town, Singapore, São Paulo

Cambridge University Press
32 Avenue of the Americas, New York, NY 10013–2473, USA

www.cambridge.org
Information on this title: www.cambridge.org/9780521859561

© Cambridge University Press 2007

First published 2007

Printed in the United States of America

A catalog record for this publication is available from the British Library.

Library of Congress Cataloging in Publication data
Martel, William C.
   Victory in war : foundations of modern military policy / William C. Martel.
      p. cm.
   Includes bibliographical references and index.
   ISBN-13: 978-0-521-85956-1 (hardback : alk. paper)
      1. Military policy. 2. United States – Military policy. 3. Unitred States – History,
   Military – 21st century. 4. United States – History, Military – 20th century. I. Title.

   UA11.M36 2006
   355'.033573 – dc22

                                                                2006049158

ISBN-13 978-0-521-85956-1 hardback
ISBN-10 0-521-85956-5 hardback

To my parents,
Cyprien and Eunice Martel

Contents

Acknowledgments

I am indebted to a number of individuals who contributed on many levels to this work. First, a very special note of thanks goes to my editor at Cambridge University Press, John Berger, whose wise counsel and guidance were instrumental in bringing this work to fruition.

I would like to thank my colleagues at the Fletcher School at Tufts University, especially Professors Robert Pfaltzgraff Jr., Richard Shultz, and Matthew Kahn; the Academic Dean, Professor Laurent Jacque; and the Dean of the Fletcher School, Steven Bosworth, for the countless ways in which their wisdom and support contributed to my research.

Also, sincere thanks are owed to Theodore Hailes, David Kaiser, and William Pendley for their helpful comments and suggestions. Many students, too numerous to mention individually, have helped my thinking about the nature of victory.

I especially want to thank Andrea Dew, a doctoral candidate at the Fletcher School, who served so ably as research assistant for this study and whose wisdom and judgment made profoundly important contributions to this work.

A debt of gratitude is owed to the anonymous reviewers for Cambridge University Press whose constructive and incisive comments and suggestions helped to sharpen the arguments of this study.

My deepest appreciation goes to my copyeditor and production manager, Michael Gnat, whose unfailing attention to matters of logic, expression, and detail continues to astound me.

Many thanks go to Sarah Leonardi and the staff at the Amherst Town Library for their capable assistance with matters large and small.

I shall always deeply appreciate all that these individuals have done to make this work possible. It goes without saying that whatever shortcomings exist in this work are my responsibility alone.

1 | Introduction

ince the terrorist attacks on September 11, 2001, that killed some three thousand people, the United States has been waging a global war on terror, with campaigns in Afghanistan and Iraq. In an outline of U.S. policy for the war against the Taliban in Afghanistan in October 2001 and in the invasion of Iraq in March 2003 to remove Saddam Hussein, President George W. Bush declared that the United States would spend whatever resources are necessary to win this war on terror.[1] The outbreak of hostilities in the war against Iraq began on March 19, 2003, with a televised address to the nation in which Bush said that "we will accept no outcome but victory."[2] In January 2006, Bush said that the United States "will settle for nothing less than complete victory."[3]

Within several weeks of the start of Operation Iraqi Freedom, Saddam Hussein's military forces were decisively defeated, and U.S. forces began their occupation of Iraq. On May 1, 2003, President Bush declared from the deck of the aircraft carrier USS *Abraham Lincoln* that "major combat operations in Iraq have ended" and that "the United States and our allies have *prevailed*" in the war against Iraq. However, he emphasized that although "the battle of Iraq is one victory in a war on terror," the United States had not yet won the war on terror, and that "we do not know the day of final victory."[4] While many observers interpreted his words to mean that the United States had achieved victory, the question is how we should interpret this "victory." More than three years since the end of major hostilities, one hundred and fifty thousand U.S. troops are still deployed in the occupation of Iraq. Although power was transferred on June 30, 2004, to an interim Iraqi government, and the Iraqi people voted overwhelmingly on December 15, 2005, to establish a coalition government, the United States continues to fight against a Sunni insurgency that has killed thousands of U.S. troops and Iraqis. With casualties increasing daily, American society has been actively debating the costs, benefits, and risks of remaining in Iraq. It is no exaggeration to say that the

1

ferocity of the insurgency and the cost in lives has undermined the nature of the victory. It also has weakened the confidence of the American people in the ability of their political and military leadership to achieve victory.

With the wars against Afghanistan and Iraq so firmly established in American politics, it is inevitable that policymakers and military planners will find themselves asking some difficult and uncomfortable questions about war and victory. For example: Although President Bush said that the United States achieved victory in Iraq, exactly what does that mean? Does victory depend on capturing territory, or does it require the destruction of a society? How long does it take to achieve victory, and how do we know when victory has been achieved? Does the aftermath of a war influence what we mean by victory and how we judge that victory? Does the passage of time dilute what victory means? Did the United States achieve victory in Afghanistan and Iraq, and if so what kind? Does the insurgency weaken that victory, and is victory undermined if Afghanistan or Iraq fragments into civil war? Finally, is it possible for the state to achieve victory in war but lose the peace?

This war will be debated for generations, but the central questions are what happened and why. There is a natural temptation to frame this problem in purely political terms by assigning blame to or praising the efforts of the current group of policymakers in the Bush administration. But questions about what constitutes victory and how we know victory when we see it are actually long-standing and essentially bipartisan issues that generations of strategists and policymakers have confronted.

At a time when there is fundamental debate in international security about the desirability, costs, and risks of military intervention, the central and as-yet unresolved question addressed by this study is deceptively simple: What precisely does it mean when the state achieves victory in war? No realm of social, political, economic, or cultural affairs is immune from the use of the term "victory" to describe in general terms an outcome that for the individual or state is to some extent successful or consistent with its desires or goals. The evidence that there are analytical and methodological problems with the usage of "victory" is in part inferential: How could one term be used almost universally to describe such a wide range of outcomes without sacrificing its exactness? The problem, as we shall see, is that victory is used in the language of strategy, diplomacy, policy, business, and war to mean everything to everyone. From partial accomplishments to total successes, the term "victory" is employed almost reflexively as a synonym for outcomes that align with one's preferences. This usage of victory, however, is inadequate for describing the conditions and outcomes that are associated with the complexities and risks that are inherent in war. Thus, the question for this study is this: Can we add greater precision to the ways in which the scholarly and policymaking communities use the term "victory"?

There are two fundamental problems that this study must address. The first, as shown by the example of Iraq, is that there is no theory or precise language of victory that permits policymakers, military officials, and the public to agree on what "victory" means or when "victory" has been attained. The second is that humans have been waging war for the past six thousand years without a framework for victory, and yet have successfully waged wars. How can this be so? Is a theory of victory something distinct from a military strategy in war or a theory of war? What do we gain by developing one? How would such a theory fit into modern defense planning? This study seeks to provide preliminary answers to these and related questions.

The first step is to evaluate what we have in the context of systematic ideas or theories of victory. To begin with, we have thousands of years of ideas and practices about the configuration of military forces that are necessary to defeat an enemy. We also have voluminous writings in the field of military strategy for guiding how states or political organizations should conduct war to produce successful outcomes. In addition, for twenty-five hundred years there have been strategic thinkers who have sought to develop actionable concepts, perhaps even a theory of war, for helping political and military leaders understand how to conduct war. Finally, thousands of years of strategic thinkers searching for a theory of war, as well as discussing such broader concepts as tactical or strategic victory, have not organized a systematic framework beyond what war is and how the state should wage wars in order to win.

Generations of scholars and policymakers have written extensively about the nature of strategy in war and have produced a substantial body of literature, as reviewed in Earle, Paret, and Alger, among others.[5] This literature does discuss victory, but what is missing are fundamental organizing principles for, or a typology of, victory. The result is that we do not have a framework for victory beyond the implicit assumption that the unalloyed purpose of strategy is to achieve it. Nor do we have a systematic theory or literature of victory that by itself is distinct from and not implicit in the theories of war, strategy, and politics. Accordingly, the first step to resolve the gap that exists between the theory and practice of victory is to develop organizing principles for victory and to examine those with a series of qualitative case studies.

The central problem addressed in this study is that scholars and policymakers do not have and yet desperately need a coherent framework that answers our most fundamental questions about victory. Although policymakers, generals, and historians have grappled for millennia with these issues, the central dilemma involving victory is not principally *how* to win – what configuration of military and political resources should be marshaled, what is the proper balance between the offense and defense, or what are the proper tactics. Rather, there is a more fundamental issue for the state: *What precisely is the meaning of "victory"?* Without a systematic answer to the question of what it means to be victorious, scholars and policymakers cannot judge what interests are at stake, whether it is prudent for the state to go to war, and what resources the state should commit to war.

Most of the literature on strategy reduces the matter of victory to the conditions that produce either triumph or defeat. Wars, however, like all political phenomena, are a complex series of human and physical interactions that, except in the most extreme cases, do not readily reduce to categories of "winning" and "losing." While it is argued in this inquiry that the concept of winning means that the state has achieved some fraction of its strategic, political, military, territorial, and economic objectives consistent with the classic definition of limited war, the broader point is that the outcome of wars can be interpreted and expressed as a range of nuanced gradations that signal to what extent the state has achieved its objectives. The problem of the limits on the use of "victory" was expressed by the German strategist Carl von Clausewitz, who wrote in *On War* that "it is a want in our terminology that for a victory over the enemy tantamount to a rout, and a conquest of the enemy only tantamount to a simple victory, there is only one and same word to use."[6] The intent in this study is to improve this situation.

This brings us to the second key issue in the book, which examines what it means to *achieve* victory. Since we use "victory" synonymously with "winning," once the fighting stops and the war is "won," it would appear that victory has been achieved. However, as we have seen in Iraq recently, proclaiming the end of military operations does not mean that the state has successfully achieved its objectives in war – far from it. Historically, the concept of victory has been defined as achieving the basic political purpose of war, but victory more broadly means to achieve the state's tactical, political, military, and strategic goals and to manage consequences: how the war may alter the status quo, involve economic and social costs of mobilization, and impose postconflict obligations on the state.[7] In a strict sense, victory is meaningful only if it is interpreted as a distribution of outcomes that fall along a continuum.

If our understanding of victory is to be aligned with the social sciences, the literature on victory must be reinterpreted so that the results of wars can be categorized in more precise and nuanced terms to express the complex range of outcomes that naturally occur in war. What is missing from this literature on strategy is a systematic framework for analyzing victory in theoretical terms that is distinct from a theory of war or a military strategy for winning wars. Why would it be useful to have such a framework for debating the meaning of victory in war? It would have the advantage of forcing scholars and policymakers to discuss in a systematic and logical fashion what they mean by victory and are willing to invest to achieve it. It would clarify heated public debates about the wisdom of intervention because there could be some agreement about what the state plans to achieve, the extent of those achievements, and how to characterize that attainment in terms of victory. By better explaining the costs, benefits, and risks of intervention, it would help both policymakers and the public understand the nature and scale of the state's commitment. Finally, it would describe to foes and friends alike the state's plans and how it plans to accomplish them. There are, of course, functions that such a theory cannot provide. Foremost is that it could not predict the outcome of wars, given the uncertainties that surround all human endeavors. It could not provide a formula for ensuring that the state will be able to achieve its goals in the midst of the military, diplomatic, and economic intricacies that surround all wars. Most important, such a framework would not prevent policymakers from believing that they can approach the conduct of war in a formulaic or mechanistic fashion. In the end, we should not entertain any illusions that such a framework will eradicate the terrible uncertainties in all critical decisions about war.

Since it would be useful to develop a framework for understanding victory, where should we start in assembling this systematic structure? When one considers the difficulties associated with developing theories about problems in the realm of social science, of which the nature of victory in war is a classic example, the best place to begin is with what is known as *pretheory*. For social scientists, a pretheory describes the process of conceptual exploration that is designed to identify carefully and observe relationships in a field of inquiry, and subsequently to formulate organizing principles and testable theories. The advantage of pretheorizing is that it helps orient scholars or policymakers so that they can pick out the more important factors, evaluate their relative importance, and engage in systematic thinking about the area of investigation. The disadvantage to pretheory is that it illuminates why it is necessary to develop theory in the first place, given just how daunting it is to construct a theory of any political phenomenon. The most persuasive reason that pretheory is the right place to begin is eminently practical: Working along these lines will contribute to further scholarly research, greater emphasis on methodical deliberation among policymakers, and more informed public debates about the costs, benefits, risks, and uncertainties of achieving victory.

What, then, is the best way to proceed? In this study, we pursue two approaches. The first examines the works of the principal strategists and theorists who have labored since ancient times to understand how underlying human, political, military, economic, and psychological factors influence the nature of war and how victory has been interpreted. Since the means for waging war and analyses of its conduct have evolved over thousands of years, this search for pretheoretical ideas about victory examines the deliberations by those who have written about war since the time of ancient Greece and China. Standing on the shoulders of these historical giants affords a superior vantage and allows us to build our understanding of victory upon theirs. The second approach focuses on how modern developments have influenced these interpretations of victory, which has the benefit of focusing on wars and events whose influence and policy relevance is more obvious and immediate to the current generation of scholars and policymakers. This is not, however, a perfect method. Some scholars, for instance, may dismiss the idea that theory is relevant to policy, despite the fact that for two and a half thousand years military strategists and theorists have not hesitated to speak to princes and politicians about how they should conduct war and achieve victory. There is an argument that the least we can do now is to attempt to follow in their footsteps. A further advantage to focusing on how modern events influence a pretheory of victory is that vastly more information is available about contemporary wars. Such a focus also permits us to consider instances of war in which states used the most sophisticated weapons, technologies, economic power, and communications to achieve greater military capabilities than at any other period in human history. To balance these two contending approaches, this study examines the historical foundations of how military strategists and theorists have considered victory (Chapters 2 and 3), the historical origins of the American approach to war and victory (Chapter 5), and American experiences in several modern wars or military interventions (Chapters 6–11) so as to develop pretheoretical concepts or organizing principles of victory (Chapter 4).

What will be the product of this research? The intent is to build the foundations of a pretheory of victory, on the premise that such pretheoretical concepts will be useful for scholars who are interested in comprehending, in formal and systematic terms, the relationship between war and victory, and for policymakers who are responsible for making the supremely difficult decision of whether to take the state to war. This research reviews the writings of earlier generations of military strategists and theorists, relates their ideas to U.S. historical experiences with victory, and then uses pretheoretical concepts to examine instances of war or U.S. military intervention in the late twentieth and early twenty-first centuries. This framework, while by no means definitive, constitutes a preliminary attempt to define organizing principles for better understanding what victory is and what it means for the United States and other nations when they use military force.

What does a pretheory of victory have to do with a systematic theory of victory? Strictly speaking, the answer is largely unknown. The purpose of *pre*-theory is to develop organizing principles that may be useful in further debates about victory, rather than to propose a formal, systematic theory of victory. The most likely case with social-science inquiries is that the contest among the ideas generated – which often unpredictably produces new and better ideas and concepts – contributes, directly or indirectly, to future scholarship. It would thus be a perfectly reasonable and acceptable outcome for this or any pretheory to evolve into a formal, systematic theory of victory. The challenge for the scholarly and policymaking communities is, first, to accept, reject, or adapt this model as it relates to modern U.S. experiences; second, to do the same with respect to other historical periods for both the United States and other countries; and third, to understand whether these concepts hold true in general and, if not, what ideas might replace them. After all, while the intent here is to develop a pretheory of victory, this does not guarantee its relevance to either modern or historical wars. Whether and to what extent any of these pretheoretical ideas can be demonstrated to be relevant to theories of war and military strategy already extant in the literature are matters for future research.

Questions about the meaning of victory have arisen implicitly as a result of real-world cases of military intervention during the past decade. In the last thirty years, the United States alone has intervened with military force in Lebanon, Libya, Panama, the Persian Gulf, Somalia, Haiti, Bosnia and Kosovo, Afghanistan, and Iraq, among others. What emerged during all of these interventions was a subtle yet universal concern among policymakers and scholars: Did the state attain victory in these cases? Is victory based on the defeat of military forces, the capture of territory, the destruction of the state's government, economy, or infrastructure, or the occupation and rebuilding of the state, or all (or none) of the above? These matters and others like them are surrogates for the fundamental question about war that dates back to antiquity and is rarely answered with sufficient precision: What is victory, and how would we know when it has been achieved?

This question about victory also arises from the intersection of the literatures on security studies, international relations, and military history, which over the span of millennia have wrestled with the interrelationship of strategy, policy, diplomacy, and tactics. There is no paucity of literature on strategy and these fields: It is voluminous but has not focused with sufficient exactitude on the meaning of victory. Although authors have discussed victory and defined it in strategic, political–military, and tactical terms (see Chapters 2 and 3), their extensive deliberations have not produced a theoretical framework or language that permits scholars and policymakers to answer systematically what level of victory has been attained or how it relates to changes in the status quo, the extent of mobilization for war undertaken by the state, or to the victor's postconflict obligations. Thus, although there are many *ideas about* victory in the literature on strategy, its confluence with real-world interventions has not produced a set of theoretical propositions that represents a *framework for* victory. This is an important distinction. Victory is often defined as the desired outcome on many levels rather than in terms sufficiently precise to permit its analysis on *distinct* levels.

The elements of a framework for victory outlined herein may help policymakers, scholars, and the general public answer, via formal categories, what the state has accomplished when it uses force. This study preliminarily offers two broad answers to the question of what it means to achieve victory: First, it is more than a general desire on the part of the state to achieve its political objectives; second, it can be described in terms of discrete categories that relate to what the state has accomplished. Rather than define victory, as so many have before, in vague terms of "success," "decisiveness," "winning," or any other among a myriad of synonyms, this study proposes that three specific levels of victory be used in the lexicon of strategy and war: *tactical victory, political–military victory,* and *grand strategic victory.* As discussed in Chapter 4 and subsequently, each of these levels corresponds to specific objectives and outcomes in war. This framework also relates the level of victory to whether and to what extent a war changes the status quo, requires mobilizing the state's military and economic resources, and imposes postwar obligations on the state. By providing more precise language with which to describe the outcome of war, this study should help sharpen debate and make the nature of victory more transparent.

In the absence of a coherent theory or terminology, policymakers and scholars have used "victory" to cover an extraordinarily wide range of outcomes whose significance varies widely for different audiences. "Victory" carries such an array of meanings depending on the circumstances that it has imprecise and yet intensely emotional connotations. This contributes to confusion about the fundamental role of victory in guiding decisions to intervene militarily. In the end, everyone, from citizens to policymakers, must understand that the failure to develop a systematic theory of victory weakens the ability of the state to use force effectively and promotes political discord when societies debate whether to use force.[8]

With the emergence of nonstate wars, other conflicts with nonstate actors (intrastate and indirect interstate wars), the proliferation of weapons of mass destruction (WMDs), and the rise of ethnic, national, and religious sources of war and crises, it is imperative to develop organizing principles – a pretheory of victory – to help guide the deliberations of policymakers. Without concepts that permit policymakers to distinguish among various levels of victory, how can they reasonably seek to judge when to use force, what the state should achieve when it uses force, or whether the state has emerged victorious? And with the United States involved in the occupation of Iraq and fighting an insurgency, is there any more urgent time to study victory?

PURPOSE AND ORGANIZATION OF THE BOOK

To reach preliminary answers to such questions, this research is organized into several discrete arguments about the historical and contemporary origins of the concept of "victory," the various meanings of the word, and the ways in which it is used. This study seeks to formulate several organizing principles that enable scholars and policymakers to evaluate what it means to achieve victory in war and how to interpret the outcome of wars.[9] The first step in constructing this pretheory of victory is to study the ideas and principles of the major theorists whose writings since antiquity have formulated the foundations of strategy from the times of ancient Greece and China to the present.

This study begins in Chapters 2 and 3 with an examination of the writings of the principal European and Asian political and military strategists and scholars. This historical survey outlines the origins of the concept of victory, analyzes how each of these writers thought about victory, and focuses on how the concept has evolved in historical and philosophical terms in the literature of military strategy and diplomacy. Chapter 2 begins with strategists from ancient China, Greece, Rome, and the Renaissance; Chapter 3 continues with an analysis of strategists from the modern period of history who have shaped the concept of victory and its practice in war. What emerges from this review and analysis is that while many ideas about victory have been formulated, the term "victory" has been used routinely to describe an unmanageably wide range of outcomes in war. What is missing from this literature, then, is a coherent set of ideas that express unambiguously what it means for the state to achieve victory.

Chapter 4 begins with an examination of the many imprecise meanings associated with victory, showing how "victory" is effectively a synonym for a wide range of successful outcomes in war. It then discusses the meaning and nature of theory – what it means to have a theory, what a theory should accomplish – and presents the idea of a pretheory of victory as offering a preliminary framework of concepts for understanding what victory means. The fundamental reason why this study proposes a *pre*theory rather than a formal theory is addressed in the logic of social science, which holds that theories are elaborate, formal structures that rarely, if ever, come to fruition with any degree of exactitude. While we have many important organizing concepts in strategy and foreign policy, such as power and interests, the intent of this research is to describe those that may help guide scholars and policymakers to use the term "victory" with greater precision and clarity. It is in this structural domain that pretheories constitute a powerful analytic tool.

The chapter outlines several organizing principles for a pretheory of victory: the *level* of victory, the *change in the status quo* that results from war, the type of *mobilization* that the state must undertake, and the nature and extent of the state's *postconflict obligations* (see Figure 1 in Chapter 4). The first principle argues that victory can occur at three levels: *tactical victory*, such as winning either a specific battle or, as a result of the cumulative effect of many such battlefield triumphs, a war; *political–military victory*, entailing a state's achieving some of its political and military goals; and *grand strategic victory*, or the strategic successes that occur through the destruction of a society, its military, economy, and institutions of governance.

The second principle involves the kinds of change that victory in war may bring about. The use of force may modify an adversary's policies or defeat its ability to conduct war; it may even alter its institutional and economic foundations, or, in the extreme case, lead to regime change and a wholesale shift in its government and economy. In this study, the first two outcomes will be referred to as *limited changes* in the status quo, the latter two as more *comprehensive changes*.

The third principle addresses the resources that can be mobilized by the state for the conduct of war. In one case, the state can undertake a *limited* mobilization of its military forces or a mobilization of domestic public support; at the other end of the spectrum it can effect an *extensive* mobilization involving its economic and industrial sources of power, large numbers of ground forces, and its allies, in an international coalition.[10]

The fourth principle deals with *postconflict obligations,* the commitments imposed on the victorious state in the aftermath of war. Victory may require the victor merely to provide economic aid and developmental assistance, or to occupy the society of the adversary, or even reconstruct the infrastructure destroyed during the war – consider, for example, Germany and Japan after World War II or the more recent cases of Afghanistan and Iraq. In the more extreme cases, it may entail the obligation to establish a new governing structure, develop democratic institutions, and train new military and security forces to prevent the resurgence of opposition forces. As described in this study, the range of postconflict obligations runs from *limited* to *protracted*.

Again, while the principles outlined in Chapter 4 establish the broad outlines for analytic criteria for victory, they are not provided in order to derive a causal or predictive theory of victory. Instead, for reasons outlined in the social-science literature, the intent is simply to develop "reliable knowledge" in the form of organizing principles that will inform subsequent research on the nature and meaning of victory – a pretheory of victory.

Chapter 5 analyzes the forces that have shaped the U.S. approach to victory and how that thinking has evolved during the past two centuries. Since the inception of the republic in the late eighteenth century, a number of wars have decisively influenced the American theory of victory, including the Revolutionary War, the War of 1812, the Civil War, the First and Second World Wars, the Korean and Vietnam wars, and the cold war. In addition to presenting an overview of these conflicts and their effects, Chapter 5 also examines the concept of unconditional surrender and the extent to which that has played a significant role in American strategic thought, in how the nation conducts war, and in what it has sought to accomplish. What emerges is a set of

operating principles that have developed throughout American history and
whose application has been more or less consistent with how the society conducts its wars and attains victory.

To understand the relationship between the origins and evolution of victory and the value of a pretheory for developing a coherent framework for
victory, Chapters 6–11 present a series of qualitative case studies of U.S. military interventions conducted during the last two decades of the twentieth century and the first six years of the twenty-first. These represent methodologically and analytically a wide array of instances in which the United States used
military force to achieve varying levels of victory. In cases at the more destructive end of the spectrum, the United States used military force against Iraq
in the 1991 Persian Gulf War and again in the 2003 invasion of Iraq, both
of which represented classic high-intensity wars. In the case of lesser military
operations, the United States used force on a more selective scale in the 1986
raid against Libya, the 1989 invasion of Panama, the intervention against
Bosnia Kosovo in the 1990s, and the 2001 invasion of Afghanistan.

These six case studies are designed to highlight the organizing principles
of the proposed pretheory of victory and to test their ability to improve our
understanding of victory in systematic terms. These particular interventions
were selected because they occurred toward the end of and after the cold war,
involved conflicts at the high and low levels of destructiveness, were waged
in various regions, and produced different levels of victory. Each chapter is
organized into a discussion of the objectives that guided one of these interventions, a description and evaluation of the military operation and its impli
cations for victory, and conclusions about the long-term significance for the
development of a pretheory of victory.

Having by this point examined the evolution of the term "victory" and its
usage by the principal strategists, reviewed the nature of a pretheory of victory, and evaluated this framework for victory in the context of several cases
studies, this study turns in Chapter 12 to the question of the relationship between victory and the form of military power – land, maritime, and air. The
questions are whether various types of military force contribute differentially
to the development of a pretheory of victory, and whether certain forms of
military power are better suited to achieving specific levels of victory. The
principal arguments are that each instrument contributes in specific and fundamentally different ways to victory, and that some, such as ground forces, are
more relevant to attaining more strategic levels of victory than others. This
point is critical and yet hardly obvious in the midst of contemporary debates
about whether specific forms, notably air power, prove the most decisive for
winning wars. This discussion evaluates each instrument of military power,
considers its advantages and disadvantages with respect to victory, determines

whether various types of military force contribute to a pretheoretical discussion of victory, and concludes with thoughts on what military instruments are necessary for victory and whether the state has the right instruments to attain it.

Finally, Chapter 13 evaluates the implications of a pretheory of victory for our understanding of what it means to attain victory. As remarked by military historian Brian Bond, "All students of history must be struck by the ambivalence, irony, or transience of most military victories. . . ." And yet, "comparatively few historians have focused on the issues of victory and defeat in war."[11] Thus, if scholars and policymakers are to describe what it means for the state to achieve its political and military objectives, or to succeed (or fail) in foreign policy, the first step is to define victory in more precise terms. This final chapter explores the implications of the argument that, though victory remains an incomplete concept, fraught with multiple meanings, it is still the principal one by which men and women of state, in academia, and among the public discuss and evaluate the outcome of war. A viable pretheory of victory should permit greater transparency for the scholars who evaluate wars and for the policymakers who must decide whether to risk the credibility of the state and the lives of its people. It is immensely important for these policymakers to understand that victory involves a wide range of outcomes, that each outcome imposes different burdens on and risks for the state, and that formal thinking about victory may help them to evaluate more carefully the costs and risks of war.

AREAS OF FUTURE RESEARCH

This study provides only the first step toward broadening our understanding of the meaning of victory. It is *de*scriptive in examining the factors associated with victory, but it makes no attempt to be *pre*scriptive, at this preliminary stage of investigation, as to the conditions that may be associated with particular levels of victory. It uses an inductive approach to reason inferentially from general propositions about the nature of victory to how particular conditions in specific wars may relate to these propositions. As it examines how various strategists, theorists, and wars have contributed to the body of thought on what victory means, it uses the historical and case-study methods to analyze the data collected on wars to contribute some pretheoretical ideas about the nature of victory. As such, the present volume does not purport to be the final word on what we mean by the word "victory." Indeed, the hope is that this study will encourage those in the scholarly and policymaking communities who care about war to challenge and revise these interpretations.

Several areas of future research present themselves. The first is to evaluate whether there is a parametric relationship between the levels of victory and the extent of changes in status quo, level of mobilization for war, and the scale of the victor's postconflict obligations – although at first glance it might be more difficult to describe in parametric terms the status quo than the variables of mobilization and obligation. In any case, one aspect of this inquiry would be to evaluate whether and to what extent these organizing principles can be used to describe systematically how military and political theorists and strategic thinkers over the past several millennia have discussed, either directly or indirectly, the concept of victory in the literature on strategy and war. A second, but related, avenue for future research is to evaluate possible relationships among the organizing principles beyond the discussion in Chapter 13. A third is to broaden the analysis to include wars that were waged by nations other than the United States. Since the strategists in this study are drawn principally from Europe and the wars largely from American history, it would be useful to evaluate this pretheoretical framework for victory in the context of a richer array of cases.

Two final observations are in order. One is that the present study is likely to be quite controversial because it implies that prior research and earlier discussions in the fields of military strategy and policy have treated the problem of victory inadequately and failed to provide a systematic foundation for understanding it. Some will object that we already *have* theories of victory, as postulated by the works of such strategists as Sun Tzu, Clausewitz, Jomini, Lenin, and Douhet, all of whom have discussed what must be accomplished by the state in order to achieve it. Yet others will argue, as have theorists such as Clausewitz, that victory cannot be defined abstractly. My argument is this: Although the literature on strategy and war on which this analysis is drawn may be impressive in analytical and scholarly terms, we need to move forward toward a consensus on a proper language for discussing victory. This protean term has described everything from tactical victories in battle (in the writings of antiquity), to political–military victories in large-scale battles (principally among Continental strategists of the 1600s–1900s), to victory on a strategic scale (throughout history but mostly in modern times). At a time of active debate regarding the merits of present and future cases of military intervention, much greater clarity is needed.

The other observation is that this analysis did not develop in the linear fashion in which it is presented. What began in the 1990s as an inquiry into the meaning of victory, at a time when the United States was involved in numerous military interventions, soon led to ideas about the theoretical origins of victory as expressed by many of the strategists and theorists whose works are covered in Chapters 2 and 3. However, though the discussion of a pretheory of victory is presented in Chapter 4, much of the thinking therein was formulated iteratively, not only growing out of the historical review chapters but also deriving from my research on victory in American policy and on the case studies that are presented.

2 Historical Origins of Victory

n the annals of military strategy, policy, and diplomacy, there have been innumerable tomes written about the critical strategists and theorists of various eras. These books have dissected their every thought, the historical and political context within which they crafted their ideas, and, most important, their impact on how subsequent generations have contemplated and conducted war and diplomacy. Even a partial list of these individuals, which could easily number in the hundreds, does not do justice to the magnitude of their efforts or the span of history, quite literally thousands of years, that their thinking covered. Suffice it to say that countless individuals have labored to understand the central questions: why states fight wars, what it takes for them to win, and, paramount for the purpose of this study, what it *means* to win. Expressed differently, these are the fields of inquiry that govern theories of politics and war, military strategy, and victory, respectively.

This chapter treats some of the most important strategists and theorists of war, focusing specifically on how they have used the concept "victory" and how their ideas have contributed to the treatment and meaning of the word. Beginning with two of the greatest ancient strategic theorists, Sun Tzu and Thucydides, it proceeds to address the works of the major theorists of strategy and war through the late nineteenth century. (Chapter 3 continues the discussion through those of the late twentieth century.) While this survey is extensive, it is by no means all-inclusive. There are others whose works, while undoubtedly of historical significance, are not addressed in this study as a matter of economy and intellectual parsimony.[1]

The first criterion for inclusion here is whether an individual's works on strategy and war are consistently reviewed in the critical literature. This includes such principal works in the analysis of strategy and strategists as those edited by Edward Mead Earle and Peter Paret, as well as the analytical and interpretive works of John I. Alger, Azar Gat, and Michael I. Handel.[2] In addition there are the primary sources written by these theorists, several consulted in various editions. The purpose of this research was not to reanalyze or reinterpret their works or principal ideas, but simply to see how they used the term "victory," to note how their ideas about victory have been interpreted, and to understand their general contributions to the literature. Hence the general philosophy was to build on the conventional wisdom developed by military historians and students of strategy rather than to challenge their assumptions and conclusions about the role and influence of these renowned strategists and theorists.

The framework for the discussion of these individuals, including their thoughts on victory and related subjects, is an analysis of the ways in which their ideas have influenced how we in the modern age both think about victory and use the term to describe the outcome of wars or struggles. The intent is to outline the central arguments of those who have made the most significant contributions regarding the nature of victory as it relates to the problem of what strategy is and how it should be formulated and implemented. This is not, therefore, a work about the "how" of victory, an approach exemplified by John Alger in *The Quest for Victory:* "In order to gain victory, it is necessary to concentrate decidedly superior forces for the main effort by a regrouping of forces and combat means."[3] Nor is there any intention to reevaluate the theoretical, historical, and practical considerations raised by these ideas. Instead, the object of pursuit is the concept of victory: its definition in the works of the major strategic theorists and its evolution in historical and practical terms.

The analysis in this chapter and the next (which addresses more modern writers) centers on a series of questions asked about each theorist/strategist: Who is this individual? In what historical period did he write? What significant idea or ideas did he advance? What was his principal contribution to the evolution of military strategy and the matter of victory? As we shall see, most of these strategists and theorists focused on a discrete area of warfare, whether its tactical, operational, or strategic aspects.

The analysis also considers their writings on the extent to which a conflict may have altered the status quo, the ability of the state or political entity to mobilize itself for war, and the nature and scale of postconflict obligations on the victor – all concepts developed in Chapter 4 within the framework for a pretheory of victory. One question is thus how these theorists and strategists contribute explicitly to the pretheory that this study is building. Another is in what way their writings may combine arguments about three interrelated phenomena: the nature of military strategy (how to win battles and wars), a theory of war (why states fight), and a theory of victory – matters often discussed as almost interchangeable, rather than as the singularities each actually is. As will be seen, it is a complex undertaking to segregate these fields of inquiry and to focus specifically on victory rather than on the problems of strategic interaction among adversaries and the complex process of escalation that can dominate war.

The writings of many of these individuals roam widely and freely across the geography of strategy and tactics, with concerns that range from the development of a comprehensive and systematic theory of war, to better strategies for winning battles, to the imposition of Enlightenment approaches on the search for universal rules of war. Not every principle or idea they raise, not even about victory, will fit into the framework that is outlined in this study. Moreover, it is difficult to assign each individual a niche based on his precise ideas about the nature and meaning of victory. (These problems will be revisited in Chapter 13.) When theorists do seem to stand in similar places conceptually, it is partly that their ideas about victory reflect a certain range of tactical, operational, and strategic thought. It is hoped that this study will make those backgrounds and ideas more apparent.

ANCIENT STRATEGISTS

Sun Tzu

Writing in the third or fourth century B.C., the Chinese strategist Sun Tzu argued that war is the greatest concern of the state because failure in war can lead to the extinction of the state.[4] His observation was that the best way to achieve victory is for the state to avoid fighting when at all possible, relying instead on deception and intelligence so as to analyze methodically the range of possible outcomes in war and choose the best approach. Sun Tzu is one of the most prominent theorists among the ancient strategists with his suggestion that victory is not just a tactical event but involves outcomes and considerations that operate at the level of grand strategic victory.

The essence of victory for Sun Tzu is that it should be achieved as quickly as possible with the least expenditure of resources. Destroy the enemy in a total war if necessary, but avoid any war if at all possible. His reasoning was that states rarely benefit from war at any scale, particularly protracted wars.[5] He also argued that the element of surprise is of decisive importance.

Since all wars can result in outcomes that are decisive as well as catastrophic, Sun Tzu argued that it is prudent for the state to use the full range of its diplomatic *and* military instruments to achieve victory. However, the use of military operations should be the option of last resort because the risks involved in war are often so great as to be incalculable. Showing evidence of his Confucian heritage, he also observed that "Men all know the disposition by which we attain victory, but no one knows the configuration through which we control the victory." Implicit in this statement is the realization that the underlying nature of victory itself is elusive and not clearly understood.

Sun Tzu defined victory on two broad levels: one at the level of the outcome of battles or campaigns (tactical and political–military victory), the other at the level of the "disposition" of war, a reference to victory in strategic terms. Like many strategists throughout history, Sun Tzu used the phrase "victory" routinely in tactical terms to describe the outcome of military engagements, whether at the small unit level or in large-scale campaigns. For these engagements, he wrote in *The Art of War*, there are "five factors from which victory can be known," including knowing when to fight, how to employ large and small forces, shared "desires" (objectives) among the "upper and lower ranks," being prepared, and generals who are "not interfered with by the ruler."[6] As Sun Tzu wrote, "These are the Way (Tao) to know victory."[7]

Yet "victory" also expressed for Sun Tzu the broader and more subtle concept of outcomes that transcend the tactical details of battles and wars, as when he wrote about the abstract concepts of a "disposition" and "configuration" of victory. He framed victory in psychological terms with his comment that "if you know them (the enemy) and know yourself, your victory will not be imperiled."[8] Sun Tzu also argued that victory is a flexible concept: "[W]hen I have won a victory I do not repeat my tactics but respond to circumstances in an infinite variety of ways."[9]

Thucydides

The ancient Greek historian Thucydides (ca. 460–400 B.C.) wrote about his observations of the Peloponnesian Wars, which occurred in Greece between the city-states of Athens and Sparta.[10] (He had served Athens, unsuccessfully defending the colony Amphipolis, and was writing in exile.) Thucydides used the term "victory" to describe both the successful outcome of tactical battles and strategic successes against an enemy. He thereby firmly established the tradition – now more than two thousand years old and ongoing among strategists and policymakers – of using "victory" broadly in describing the wide and highly variable range of outcomes that can occur in war.

Thucydides used "victory" in his *History of the Peloponnesian War* to describe the tactical or political–military victories that can occur as the result of both land and cavalry fights and naval battles.[11] For Thucydides, victory should be viewed in terms of the tactical condition that exists when one force defeats another in battle. An important theme in his application of the word was the role of numerical superiority in permitting one side to prevail in battle over another (145); this was evident is his observation that "victory was with the Peloponnesians and the Athenian fleets destroyed" (147). In his discussion of the speeches of Pericles, Thucydides used "victory" to describe both favorable outcomes in military engagements and strategic successes

(83), which he observed would occur if the nation "put their might into it" (121).

Thucydides also used "victory" to describe a significant change in the status quo as, for example, when war led to the total destruction of another city-state. In the epilogue to Thucydides' *History*, Strassler observed that Sparta achieved a "total military victory" over Athens (550). He argued that Thucydides formulated a more sophisticated concept of victory by suggesting that there could be different degrees of change in the status quo, noting that, although Sparta had "initially contemplated the total destruction of her defeated adversary, it finally decided that Athens would be allowed to continue to exist as a city" (549). Alluding in Pericles' Funeral Oration to the high stakes involved in grand strategic victory, Thucydides warned that "a success against a detachment is magnified into a victory over the nation, and a defeat into a reverse suffered at the hands of our entire people" (113). However, Thucydides tempered his use of victory to describe strategic successes when he noted that Sparta's total military victory "gained little more than a short-lived supremacy in Greece."

Plato

Another classical thinker who contemplated the nature of victory was the Greek philosopher Plato (427–347 B.C.), who discussed the concept in general terms in *The Republic*. Writing in the fourth century B.C., his ideas about victory were shaped by the reality that warfare between states could involve the destruction of an opponent on a monumental scale, which he described as a "fight to the end."[12] In Book V of *The Republic*, Plato emphasized that war is an inherently risky undertaking because the fundamental nature of victory is to "gain the safety of the whole city" (126).[13] Since there is the risk that victory over a city-state will lead to its destruction and thereby make "it impossible for the rest of the city to recover" (127), Plato recognized that those who are defeated in war could be forced to sacrifice not only their own lives but those of their children as well.[14] The totality of war was expressed by his observation that "it is considered reasonable for the victors to carry off the harvest of the defeated" (131).[15]

Polybius

The Greek historian Polybius (201–122 B.C.) used "victory" to describe the product of a tactical defeat, which could be gained by "the superiority of [one's] position" and from the "advantages of ground."[16] Polybius advances the notion that victory can be absolute and, as demonstrated in the Roman defeat of Carthage, can lead to catastrophic results for the defeated.

For the Romans, the "pursuit of victory was relentless."[17] Victory in this context was defined as a largely tactical condition that exists when observers determine subjectively that "it is time to win a victory."[18] Since an important aspect of victory at that time was the occupation of the state or city-state, Polybius in his *Histories* emphasized the degree of change in the status quo that can be brought about by victory. For example, he cited the case of the treaty signed in 241 B.C. by Rome and Carthage, which stipulated that the Carthaginians should "evacuate the whole of Sicily" (56). Although arguing that Rome had, with this victory, taken the "most difficult and most essential step towards universal empire" (2), Polybius called upon Roman leaders to exercise caution when they achieve victory because it may impose significant postwar obligations upon the state. Given the level of obligations when a state totally annihilates its enemy, Polybius noted that the Romans used "their victory with mildness and generosity," in that, according to Scipio, "victory never made the Romans more severe than before" (368). Also, he acknowledged that although "It is no doubt a good thing to conquer on the field of battle . . . , it needs greater wisdom and great skill to make use of victory."[19]

Polybius emphasized the importance of strategic judgment in military leaders when he observed that a "good general not only sees the way to victory; he also knows when victory is impossible."[20] This ancient historian also used the word victory in strategic terms to describe "complete" or "final" defeat, as seen with Rome's victory over Carthage in the Third Punic War,[21] in which he referred to the "real consciousness of defeat" that exists when the parties in a war sign treaties.[22]

Titus Livius (Livy)

Two observers writing during the era of the Roman Empire, Vegetius and Livy, contributed to the concepts of victory that were developing in ancient times.[23] The first of these, Titus Livius (Livy), was a Roman historian who lived from 59 B.C. to 17 A.D. and authored the 142-volume *History of Rome* (*Ab urbe condita;* lit.: "From the Founding of the City"). Unlike the later Vegetius, Livy used the term "victory" to describe both tactical and strategic successes in war.

For Livy, "victory" principally meant prevailing in tactical engagements. He used the word to describe the outcome of such engagements on the battlefield when he wrote about "a famous victory . . . with cavalry"; soon after, he described the "expected victory" in the defense of a town.[24] In addition, he implied that victory has a moral quality with a discussion of those "who had right on their side" (33). When Livy described the condition that "was as good as victory – the admission, namely, that [Hannibal] was running away and refusing battle" (64), he established a connection between the way in

which one conducts military operations and its effect on achieving victory –
thus implying that "victory" can be used to describe the outcome of tactical
events other than battles.[25]

At the same time, Livy contrasted "the high hearts of victors" to the "de-
spondency of beaten men" and the need to restore "the morale of the
troops."[26] Livy also defined victory in broad strategic terms. For example, he
cited the example of discussions in the Roman Senate among senators who
proposed that "total war, by sea and land, should be undertaken" (29), and
on another occasion reported that the Carthaginian senators would "fight
[the war] to the end" (42). Observing that "Certain peace is better and safer
than anticipated victory," he argued that the pursuit of victory is a risky endeavor for the state.[27]

Flavius Vegetius Renatus

Flavius Vegetius Renatus (ca. fourth century A.D.), wrote *The Military Institutions of the Romans* to "collect and synthesize from ancient manuscripts and
regulations the military custom and wisdom that made ancient Rome
great."[28] Vegetius' ideas about victory were defined in terms of, and influenced by, the outcome of tactical battlefield engagements, as witnessed by his
statement that "victory depends much on the nature of the field of battle."[29]
With his argument that the enemy may not have good tactical options and
that the outcome of those battles can be described as "easy" or "immediate"
victories (102–3), Vegetius' ideas about victory had a distinctively and unquestionably tactical slant. For this Roman military strategist, victory – even
when defined in terms of "complete victory" (110) – was still a largely tactical matter.

Forming the basis of the ascendant scientific approach to military strategy,
Vegetius' ideas gained prominence during the Middle Ages, when his *De re
militari* – in particular in the twenty-six chapters of Book III – became a popular and influential study on the theory and practice of war. (Also known as
Epitoma rei militaris, his work remained popular throughout much of the Renaissance.) By analyzing the nature of tactical victory in war, his work concentrated on how the matter of discipline and organization in armies could
be managed to achieve victory.[30] His principal argument was that "Victory in
war does not depend entirely upon numbers or mere courage; only skill and
discipline will insure it" (13). In essence, Vegetius argued that victory depends on discipline, and that "He who aspires to victory, should spare no
pains to train his soldiers" (68). At the same time, he was critical of "unskilled
generals" who "think a victory incomplete unless the enemy . . . [is] so entirely surrounded by numbers as to have no possibility of escape." Thus, Vegetius
provided the equivalent of a territorial foundation of victory. As Delbrück

would later write in the *History of the Art of War* about Rome's influence on war, "However certain the victory was, the Romans still were accustomed to selling their lives dearly in every encounter."[31]

As this very brief discussion shows, for these classical theorists victory was, first and foremost, a tactical concept whose dimensions were defined in terms of the outcome of battle. Victory was the product of using military instruments to prevail in tactical engagements. There was some limited discussion among their writings of the implications of postconflict obligations (how the conquering force would rule the conquered) and the comprehensiveness of the change in the status quo (notably, whether the conquering force should annihilate the defeated and rule its territory). In the case of a victory against an adversary in a contest greater than any single tactical battle or skirmish, victory could have strategic significance. However, with the exception of Sun Tzu's *Art of War*, the ancient sources on military tactics and thinking devoted relatively little thought to the problem of grand strategic victory, and much less still to the foundations of a systematic theory of victory.

For a more comprehensive definition of victory, we turn to a series of Renaissance theorists who took the concept of war and victory to more complex levels.

SIXTEENTH- TO EIGHTEENTH-CENTURY STRATEGISTS

Niccolò Machiavelli

In the sixteenth century, the Italian political theorist and statesman Niccolò Machiavelli (1469–1527) wrote on the relationship among national policy, diplomacy, and military operations.[32] The primary expression of his thoughts about the nature and conduct of strategy was the book *Dell'arte della guerra* (*The Art of War*), which examined how rulers achieve and maintain power.[33]

The historical evolution of victory has been influenced by the writings of Machiavelli, who was perhaps the first modern thinker to advance the principle that the ultimate purpose of war is to dominate the enemy completely. As Gilbert argued, Machiavelli established the beginning of thinking strategically about war and victory.[34] He provided the intellectual foundation for a theory of victory that, when joined with advances in military technologies in the nineteenth and twentieth centuries, subtly shifted how thinking about strategy was related to the development of the concept of absolute war. Machiavelli's strategic analysis of victory was in direct contradiction to the prevailing fashion in the fifteenth century, which held that states managed military campaigns and wars as limited, almost procedural exercises, rather than events whose outcome had strategic consequences. In this way, Machiavelli's theories anticipated the modern developments that gave one state the technological ability and economic resources to defeat or annihilate another.

Influenced by Vegetius' ideas about the rules of warfare in ancient Rome, Machiavelli argued that a state could survive and prosper only if it possessed sufficient military power that it could use in a single-minded, disciplined fashion to support the ends of the state.[35] As he wrote in *The Prince,* published in 1513, the "Prince should therefore have no aim or thought, nor take up any other thing for his study, but war and its organization and discipline."[36]

Machiavelli viewed victory, as had other classical theorists before him, as the product of the tactical outcome of battles, and routinely used the word "victory" to describe the outcome of these tactical engagements. In his "General Rules for Warfare," Machiavelli urged that the leader "Never lead your soldiers to battle if you have not first made yourself sure of their courage and established that they are without fear and in order. Never make a trial of them except when you see that they expect to win."[37] For this theorist, the prevailing theory of war, and hence of victory, was influenced by the principle that individual battles might involve few or no casualties among the combatant armies. In addition to using "conquer" in the tactical sense to describe the outcome of military operations, Machiavelli alluded to the concept of grand strategic victory when he wrote that the Romans during the First Punic War "captured many Carthaginian cities and sacked many."[38] While Machiavelli realized that wars could last for years if not decades, this inherently strategic idea did not apparently influence his largely tactical view of victory.

The influence of psychological factors in victory was evident in Machiavelli's writings when he discussed in the *Discourses* (on Livy) those "little things . . . that hold the soldiers united and confident, which is the first cause of every victory."[39] He also had much to say about the conditions that make tactical victory possible, writing that an army will win battles when they are "so confident as to believe it will win in any case."[40] The German historian Hans Delbrück would argue that victory during the Renaissance depended on the number of soldiers in battle.[41] While Machiavelli assigned great significance to the courage of soldiers, he argued that attacking the enemy's expectations "will always cause you to gain the victory."[42] As he observed, "when a general wins, he ought with all speed to follow up his victory," using the example of Julius Caesar, who "after a victory never rested, but in pursuing his defeated enemies showed greater vigor and dash than in attacking them."[43] In his "General Rules for Warfare," Machiavelli noted that by "observing the intentions of his enemy" and undergoing the "most fatigue in training his own army [a leader] runs into fewer dangers and can better hope for victory."[44]

Machiavelli warned about the costs of victory and noted that the state can actually become weaker after one, because all victories involve losses on some scale.[45] He also warned that the tendency of statesmen and soldiers to become careless after a victory may increase the chances that the state will suffer a subsequent defeat. He implied that when war is necessary, victory should be guided by the principle that statesmen should expend the state's scarce resources carefully, because overestimating their power could weaken the state.[46]

Wars among city-states or dynasties during this period were deliberately limited in scope politically and militarily to ensure that defeat was not tantamount to the destruction of the state, which in turn was consistent with the limited economic and military resources available to fifteenth-century princedoms. These political units did not operate in terms of the principle of mass mobilization.[47] With regard to winning an *enduring* victory, Machiavelli noted that "victories are never so decisive that the victor does not have to maintain some moderation, and some show of justice."[48] In accordance with this principle, he argued that the all-out pursuit of victory was dangerous, that states should use moderation in their pursuit of victory, and that victory did not rest purely upon the ability to annihilate the enemy.[49] Machiavelli did not argue that states should *disavow* the principle of victory in military campaigns, but his warning that the costs of victory could overwhelm and risk impoverishing the victor state's society reflected the prevailing political consensus that the leader should not aspire to make warfare total. In effect, Machiavelli's theory of victory rested on the idea that the principal aim of war is unlikely to threaten the state's existence or its complete destruction. The proposition that total victory was *not* the ultimate reason for war led to a theory of war in which princes were discouraged from using all of their resources to defeat the enemy. With this line of argument one sees the origins of the rational calculus of war in which victories are deliberately limited but can still lead to victory on a strategic scale.

In the seventeenth century, a critical development in the theory of victory would be the shift to the system of modern states, and in the late eighteenth century to the development of the mass armies that, by the time of Napoléon and the French Revolution, would become the standard for modern warfare. Machiavelli was an early opponent of the idea of unregulated warfare, during a period when other theorists, including the legal scholar Hugo Grotius (1583–1645), argued that it is imprudent and unnecessary for states to fight wars for the purpose of inflicting maximum destruction.[50]

Raimondo Montecuccoli

One of the earliest architects of a general theory of war and the proposition that the ultimate objective of war is victory is Raimondo Montecuccoli (1609–80), an Italian soldier-prince who was the principal founder of the Austrian army, a field marshal in the service of the Austrian Habsburgs, a statesman, and the author of *Concerning Battle* (*Sulle battaglie*), *Treatise on War* (*Trattato della guerra*), and *On the Art of War* (*Dell'arte militare*).[51]

Why is the Renaissance thinker Montecuccoli an important figure in historical discussions of victory? The principal reason is that in the seventeenth century he was seeking to derive, as Gat argued, a "comprehensive and systematic presentation of war within a political framework"; this may be interpreted as a scientific study of the principles of war, whose importance would be based on the ability to "reduce experience to universal and fundamental rules."[52] Montecuccoli sought to develop a science of war based on the principle – condensed to its simplest form – that "War is an activity to inflict damage in every way [whose] aim is victory."[53] By promoting the idea that the very purpose of war is victory, he argued that victory was based on a range of competing objectives, from "seizing the initiative" and "annihilation" to the "necessity for systematic destruction" that one scholar described as an "energetic, wear-and-tear strategy."[54] His ideas also suggested that the use of violence by the state could be reduced to universal principles that would provide for Enlightenment thinkers a better understanding of the laws that govern warfare.

His approach to understanding war and victory, which sought to establish a scientific and inclusive theory of modern warfare based on principles and rules, is organized into several categories of argument about the wide-ranging nature of victory. The first is the *indeterminate nature* of victory, which can undermine the ability to know whether the state has truly achieved it. The meaning of victory can be unclear, as Montecuccoli wrote, because there will be occasions when a battle may be "hotly disputed," when the warring parties are "separated at dusk," or when a war or battle will simply end because both sides are either exhausted or distracted by other problems. In these cases, the problem is that "victory cannot be attributed to one side or another" (160). He understood that victory can be exploited in a public sense. For example, the *news* of a victory can be of decisive importance: "One hastens to spread news of a victory, the fame of which is always likely to be greater than the event itself." For Montecuccoli, "Publicity of this kind will frighten other foes, will make neutrals come over to the winning side, and will keep one's allies and subjects faithful and obedient" (164).

Second, Montecuccoli argued that, in tactical terms, victory has a *transient quality*, and should be exploited as quickly as possible. After victory has been achieved it is critical not to be distracted or, as he expressed it, "to become bogged down in front of some fortress" (163), because, as he reasoned, the victor must hunt down and annihilate the enemy forces that survived the battle. However, he cautioned that victory must be tempered with a measure of prudence toward the defeated, arguing that "Victory must be exploited with caution, compassion, and modesty" (165). He understood that after victory,

"Caution is demanded because success naturally gives rise to carelessness," observing that "It is possible to suffer certain reverses by being too confident" (165). As a measure of his appreciation for the relationship between victory and the postwar conditions within which states must operate, Montecuccoli noted that compassion is an essential postvictory attribute, arguing that "victory is inherently cruel" (167). The long-term strategy for the victor is to "control the enemy not by depriving him of all hope but . . . by pardoning him and by demonstrating the attractions of peace." In this case, a sense of prudence also dictates that one should "refrain from spilling civilian blood" (167).[55]

Third, the *ability* of the sovereign to achieve victory is influenced by various factors: *human* factors, which include the attributes of the "morale, age, and virtue of the soldiery"; *physical* factors, notably "an advantage in the type of weaponry, in artillery, in the number and kind of troops, in the elevated nature of the [battle] site or something else" (132); and the *historical record* of "past valor," "victories won earlier," or fighting the "very same enemies who were routed and beaten on a prior occasion" (132). In addition, he argued, using the case of the Battle of Wittstock in 1636 during the Thirty Years' War, that the "number[s] of prisoners and dead" constitute "sufficient indicators of victory" (161).

Sébastien le Prestre de Vauban and Maurice de Saxe

A prominent military engineer during the reign of Louis XIV, Vauban's (1633–1707) fame derived from his reputation as the foremost European builder of impregnable fortresses. Since the successful siege of a fortress was a central tenet of military strategy in the eighteenth century, Vauban is regarded as one of the foremost theorists of the doctrine of siege warfare that emerged as a principal component of military strategy.[56] He conceived of victory as a function of tactical success in battle, based largely on the successful development of fortresses that could not be breached.

At a time when war was conducted essentially as a progression of sieges, Vauban argued that states should be guided by the principle that victory should be based on avoiding unnecessary human and material losses in war.[57] Since siege warfare against fortified buildings produced extremely high levels of casualties among both attackers and defenders, Vauban proposed that states should exercise moderation in how wars are waged and the ends for which wars are fought. In the "Introductory Remarks" to *A Manual of Siegecraft and Fortification,* he observed that the "victor's gain . . . is always at a high cost," and contended that with "scattered territories and many strong fortresses" there is a "small advantage that accrues to the prince in winning [a battle]."[58] His general observation was that "only siege craft offers the means of conquering and holding territory." Furthermore, "a successful battle may leave the victor in control of the countryside for a while, but he still cannot become master of an entire area if he does not take the fortresses." Accordingly, "war that is conducted by sieges exposes a state to fewer dangers and holds forth better hope of victory." Vauban's thinking was significant because it contributed to the emerging debate on the value of limiting destruction in war, and later would influence the evolution of the concept of proportionality and its implications for limiting the means of war.

Writing in the wake of Vauban, Maurice de Saxe (1696–1750), the German-born marshal of France, defended in *Mes rêveries* the idea of avoiding "unnecessarily costly or useless battle" while vigorously pursuing the enemy after achieving victory in battle.[59] However, by the middle to late eighteenth century, military strategy was being harnessed to mobilize the state's immense human, economic, and industrial resources for war. Despite the prevalent desire to establish systematic rules or laws of strategy, de Saxe was highly skeptical of laying down laws or principles to govern the conduct of war.[60]

Starting in the late eighteenth century, from the time of Napoléon and the French Revolution, war was transformed into an enterprise that could indeed consume all of the state's resources. This was an age in which armies based on mass conscription began to replace the smaller professional armies that had dominated diplomacy and military affairs for centuries. It was during this time that the thinking about war shifted toward more aggressive strategies based on mobile combat and away from the more ponderous strategy of siege war.[61]

Frederick II of Prussia

Not surprisingly, the shift in the theory of war from siege warfare to mobile, industrial warfare would influence the development of the concept of victory. By using Machiavelli's ideas about the total nature of war and Vauban's scientific principles to broaden the technique of war, military strategists in the eighteenth and nineteenth centuries moved beyond the limits placed earlier on the permissible range of action in war. One strategist who had a decisive influence on the prevailing ideas about the nature of war, and hence about victory, was Frederick II of Prussia (1712–86), also known as Frederick the Great, whose most significant writings were his *General Principles of War* of 1746 and his *Military Testament,* composed in 1768 after the conclusion of the Seven Years' War. He contributed to thinking about the tactical nature of victory and the configuration of forces that were required to win. His principal contribution was to outline the precepts of what later became known as the strategy of blitzkrieg, which emerged as an instrument for achieving "quick victory" in war.[62]

Frederick the Great is an early architect of a more moderate notion of victory, though his ideas would be lost in the shift to total war that began with the French Revolution and continued throughout the twentieth century. In his time, victory was the product of cavalry charges in which armies attacked first in order to achieve victories that are so decisive that the enemy will be persuaded to negotiate.[63] In his "Military Instruction to His Generals," Frederick contended that the "most certain way of insuring victory is to march briskly and in good order against the enemy, always endeavoring to gain ground."[64] While the objective was the "entire destruction of your enemies," Frederick cautioned that "to shed the blood of soldiers when there is no occasion for it, is to lead them inhumanly to the slaughter," but that the failure "to pursue the enemy on certain occasions . . . is leaving an affair to future chance." When the "victory [has] been complete, we may send out detachments either to cut off the enemy's retreat, seize his magazines, or lay siege to three or four towns at the same time."

The argument that territory rather than combat losses is a more important determinant of victory was a significant theme in Frederick's writings: "victory is not decided by the number of slain, but by the extent of territory which you have gained."[65] Frederick's ideas about victory were also based in the defeat of armies, noting that "I am victorious . . . [when] one part of my army defeats the other [army]."[66] His approach to victory was shaped by the conclusion that "War is decided only by battles, and it is not finished except by them."[67] Despite his emphasis on offensive war, Frederick the Great opposed total war, rejecting any philosophy of victory that called for the annihilation of the enemy state. He also rejected the notion of protracted wars because these would exhaust Prussia's economic wealth and human resources – which is precisely what happened almost two centuries later to Germany during the First and Second World Wars.

His enduring contribution to the study of victory was the principle that battles are fought in order to achieve specific decisive results, rather than simply to obliterate an enemy. With that argument, Frederick indirectly influenced the idea that victory in war does not necessarily equate with the total destruction of a state. Finally, Frederick's emphasis on the role of surprise in military operations made an important contribution to the debate in the eighteenth century about the theory of war and the tactical foundations of victory.

Jacques-Antoine-Hippolyte, comte de Guibert, and Adam Heinrich Dietrich von Bülow

An influential theorist on the nature of victory, and a contemporary of Frederick II of Prussia, was Jacques-Antoine-Hippolyte, comte de Guibert (1743–90), who served France in the Seven Years' War and at Corsica.[68] Guibert's contribution to the literature on victory was his emphasis on the importance of distinguishing between limited and unlimited (or total) wars. In his *Essai général de tactique* (1770), Guibert correctly anticipated that the shift to mass armies, as a product of industrialization and mass mobilization in the nineteenth century, would compel strategists and statesmen to embrace a theory of total war. He understood that the shift to mass mobilization and mass armies would make it essentially impossible for states facing military defeat to shield themselves from the devastating consequences of revenge, including the wide-scale destruction of societies inherent in total war.[69] In effect, Guibert sought to produce a "definitive system of tactics, finally creating a science of war."[70] As will be discussed in Chapter 3, these ideas became considerably more relevant in the early decades of the twentieth century with the development and deployment of air power.

The late eighteenth-century Prussian soldier-strategist Adam Heinrich Dietrich von Bülow (1757–1807), argued that the development of mass armies and total war would end the era of small, limited, and decisive wars. His most significant contribution was his prescient principle that, with the advent of modern states, the strategy of war must reflect the total integration of war and politics.[71] Bülow's thinking about victory was consistent with the notion, increasingly dominant in politics and diplomacy during the nineteenth and twentieth centuries, that defeating the enemy is the fundamental objective of war. According to Gat, Bülow is important in terms of the historical development of victory because he provided "a thoroughly geometrical science of strategy" in which the conduct of war rested "on lines of operation" – a product of the development of firearms.[72] However, said Gat, Bülow's belief that victory could be won by means of a "brilliant strategic manoeuvre, without resorting to battle, was an absurd illusion."[73]

Thus the pre-Clausewitzian period of strategic thought, dominated by such thinkers as Vauban, Frederick the Great, Guibert, and Bülow, was characterized by evolving ideas about the relationship between war and victory. The most significant strategists were grappling with the concepts of total and limited war and with the influence of speed and tactics on achieving victory. While these thinkers still envisioned victory as a predominantly tactical concept, one defined as the measurable outcome of soldiers fighting soldiers in battles, some of them had begun to examine war in terms of strategic victory. For example, Machiavelli argued that war must be limited in its aims and required resources, and Bülow and Guibert held that it was becoming an all-encompassing event that would devour the assets and attention of the state. Not surprisingly, these men argued that war could be swift and decisive if states would seek to limit its devastation. It was the next generation of strategic thinkers, however, who pieced together the elements of total warfare in a series of conceptual developments that explored the tactical, strategic, and philosophical boundaries of war in the modern age.

NINETEENTH-CENTURY STRATEGISTS

The nineteenth century was a time of significant development for strategy and the ways in which states organized and prepared themselves for the conduct of war. As a result of the French Revolution and the reign of Napoléon, the strategy of war focused on unifying and coordinating the state's human and economic resources for total war. These developments led to the era of clashes between large-scale and well-organized national armies that fundamentally changed the nature of war and what it means to achieve victory.

Napoléon Bonaparte

Building on the precedents established by the National Convention's *levée en masse* (mass conscription) of August 23, 1793, Napoléon Bonaparte (1769–1821) significantly influenced the development and practice of the idea that states should use mass armies and societal mobilization to conduct total wars.[74] But he did far more than take advantage of such mass mobilization. Napoléon sought to articulate the fundamental principles of war, such as "unity of forces, urgency, and a firm resolution to perish with glory." Thus Napoléon argued, "To keep one's forces together, to bear speedily on any point, to be nowhere vulnerable – such are the principles that assure victory."[75]

While it can be argued that Napoléon defined victory in mechanistic terms, as a combination of armies and tactics, his ideas contributed to the concept of victory as the decisive outcome that occurs when the state harnesses all of its resources for war. Arguing that victory depended on being "stronger on one given point at one given moment," Napoléon defined victory largely in the tactical terms of how prevailing conditions on the battlefield translate into the total defeat of the enemy state.[76] As he wrote in his collection of maxims and precepts, "A rapid march exerts a beneficial moral influence on the army and increases its means of victory."[77] For Napoléon, human and psychological dimensions were an important component of victory: "[N]ever despair while there remain brave men around the colors. This is the conduct which wins, and deserves to win, the victory."[78]

Napoléon's principal contribution to the theory of victory was to delineate what led to successful battles at the end of the eighteenth century. His ideas about victory reflected the tactical nature of war, in which individual units can have a decisive effect on the outcome; for example, "It is a function of the cavalry to follow up the victory and prevent the beaten enemy from rallying."[79] Yet although he placed great emphasis on the relationship between tactical factors and victory, Napoléon also observed that "a victory always serves some good purpose."[80] Moreover, his strategic thinking established the idea that a state with mass armies will be able to attain victory on a scale that was historically unprecedented – even compared to Genghis Khan's conquests during the Middle Ages or the devastation inflicted on Europe during the Thirty Years' War. The strategy of war that was to emerge in the nineteenth century was based in part on Napoléon's precept that states use all of the human, economic, industrial, and technological resources at their disposal to win.

The shift from limited wars between ruling dynasties in the Renaissance to unlimited, national wars between modern European states in the nineteenth and twentieth centuries greatly complicated the achievement of "rapid, decisive victories."[81] The type of limited struggle that had prevailed since antiquity was transformed by the French Revolution and Napoleon's reign into the categorically different genre of total war between states – a new type that would culminate in the devastation of the First and Second World Wars.[82]

During the nineteenth century, sustained technological progress in weaponry and the ability to mobilize entire economies would spawn long and intense wars fought for unlimited objectives and the aim of annihilating the enemy state. For this new era, the principles of warfare needed to be redefined.

Antoine-Henri Jomini

Antoine Henri Jomini (1779–1869) of Switzerland served with the French army under Marshal Ney and, later, as a military adviser to Czar Nicholas of Russia. A prominent thinker who established many of the fundamental principles of the strategy for war, he is important in a study of victory because of his view that victory is both a strategic and tactical condition.

Emphasizing in his *Précis de l'art de la guerre* (*The Art of War*) the value of permanent principles whose "eternal validity can be comprehended and formulated by the human mind," Jomini redefined the concepts of war that had dominated strategic thought in the eighteenth century.[83] He held that determining the nature of war is a rationalist and scientific form of inquiry; that, as Gat put it, "War, like all fields of nature and human activity, was susceptible to a comprehensive and systematic theoretical study."[84] War had its own logic, based on rational, scientific laws; these provided rules for action, and when states follow those rules, victory would result. He organized his arguments into fundamental axioms governing the nature and conduct of war.[85]

Jomini encouraged "fighting battles in a truly scientific fashion."[86] "War," he wrote, "is always to be conducted according to the great principles of the art" (15). In particular, he defined the seizure of territory as a central postulate in his theory of war, whose twin objectives were "the secession of the territory by the enemy, and the means to threaten him in the heart of his own country" (16–17). This ability to occupy territory was of such critical importance in his theory of war that in "national wars the country should be occupied and subjugated, the fortified places besieged and reduced, and the armies destroyed" (27). In wars of all kinds, Jomini held that victory depends on "activity, boldness, and skill" (28). He noted that in "every battlefield [there is] a decisive point the possession of which . . . helps to secure the victory."[87] One of his most important principles was to apply, along "lines of operation" (which run from the base of operations to the objective), the largest possible number of forces at the decisive moment and place.[88]

Jomini's view of victory as determined by the ability to conquer an opposing state – or, at a minimum, to capture its territory[89] – was consistent with the nature of European warfare in the eighteenth and nineteenth centuries, which was based on campaigns fought within the geographic confines of the Continent. One of his most important contributions to strategy was the argument that victory entails destroying the military forces of the enemy, because only then is it possible for the state to conquer its opponent successfully.[90] His strengthening of the connection between territorial conquest and victory had a significant impact on prevailing theory in the nineteenth century. Though his approach lost some currency toward the end of that century – when, given the growth of centralized governments and industrialized economies, strategy slowly shifted toward the concept of total war[91] – his influence continues today. For example, U.S. Army doctrine and planning still adhere to the principle that war is governed by the objective of conquering territory.[92]

The universal theory of war Jomini espoused is the basis on which his contribution to victory is judged.[93] He argued that "victory does not always depend upon the superiority of the arm, but upon a thousand other things"; for instance, the "courage of troops, the presence of mind of the commanders, the opportuneness of maneuvers, the effect of artillery and musketry fire, rain, – mud, even – have the been the causes of repulses or of victories."[94] He argued that a "cherished cause and a general who inspires confidence by previous success are powerful means of electrifying an army and are conducive to victory."[95] Jomini emphasized the tactical nature of victory – "strategy directs armies . . . but tactics . . . gains victories" – and noted specific military configurations for achieving it: "The combination of . . . the attack in front by main force and the turning maneuver . . . will render victory more certain than the use of either separately."[96] He also stressed "[t]hat victory may with much certainty be expected by the party taking the offensive."[97]

The presumed universality of Jomini's military theory would be criticized by Clausewitz in *On War.*[98]

Carl von Clausewitz

The most significant military strategist in historical terms is unquestionably the Prussian army officer and war-college director Carl von Clausewitz (1780–

1831). He rightly has been heralded as the preeminent strategist of the nineteenth century for his work regarding the relationship between war and the state, often summed up in the well-known if sometimes misinterpreted phrase, "war is a mere continuation of policy by other means."[99] His approach to war and strategy was consistent with the prevailing trend in contemporary German philosophy of evaluating war in broad political and social terms.

Clausewitz established an intellectual framework for war in which the pursuit of clearly defined principles would lead to victory. By never deviating from the view that the fundamental aim of war is to disarm and overthrow the enemy in pursuit of political objectives, he promoted the idea that war is state-controlled violence pushed to its limits.[100] In effect, Clausewitz contributed to the burgeoning theory of total war that had been a theoretical possibility since Machiavelli's writings in the sixteenth century but had never been systematically implemented.[101] He believed that although war could be for either limited or unlimited objectives, victory is attained when the state achieves its political goals.[102] Hence, the key to victory is the achievement of political goals, not simply the acquisition of territory or the destruction of the enemy. Nevertheless, as French philosopher and political scientist Raymond Aron noted, Clausewitz "defines absolute victory in terms of the disarmament of the enemy."[103]

Clausewitz presented his ideas about the nature and conduct of war, as well as about the relationship between military affairs and state policy, in the three-volume work *Vom Kriege* (*On War*), published posthumously in 1832. The depth of his intellectual efforts to discover principles to guide how the state uses its resources and will to win in war is attested by the wealth of literature on Clausewitz and his influence on military strategy.[104] While he did not advocate the development of a universal theory of war or victory,[105] he did believe that such a universal theory was generally feasible.[106] In *On War*, Clausewitz wrote,

> Our purpose was not to assign, in passing, a handful of principles of warfare to each period. We wanted to show how every age had its own kind of war, its own limiting conditions and its own peculiar preconceptions. Each period, therefore, would have held to its own theory of war, even if the urge had always and universally existed to work things out on scientific principles.[107]

Despite the urge to develop scientific principles, Clausewitz defined war as a form of violence for the state, one whose central purpose is to achieve the state's political goals and perhaps, though not necessarily, to destroy another state. As Gat wrote, for Clausewitz, "The aims in the conduct of war are (a) to conquer and destroy the armed forces of the enemy; (b) to take possession of the resources of his army; and (c) to win public opinion. These aims . . . are intended to secure the complete defeat of the enemy."[108]

Clausewitz viewed victory on many levels. As already noted, he saw it as a political–military construct whose meaning involves attaining the state's political objectives rather than simply purely military ones. For this German strategist the natural objective of policy and of war was not victory alone but the ability of the state to attain and maintain peace,[109] which may be based on conquering enemy territory or overthrowing the enemy's government.[110] Fundamentally, he argued, "victory consists not only in the occupation of the battlefield, but in the destruction of the enemy's physical and psychic forces, which is usually not attained until the enemy is pursued after a victorious battle."[111] Yet for Clausewitz, "the destruction of the enemy cannot be the military aim,"[112] and "victory . . . is something beyond mere slaughter."[113]

Clausewitz also discussed victory in terms of both its tactical and strategic meanings. He distinguished between "knockout" victories, in which the winner imposes the terms of defeat on the enemy and destroys the state and its people, and less decisive forms of victory.[114] By implying that "victory comes to the one who holds out a moment longer than the other," because the turning point for victory occurs when the attacker loses superiority in battle, Clausewitz's concept of victory had mechanistic or procedural overtones.[115] Thus, "the chief aim is the certainty (high probability) of victory, that is, the certainty of driving the enemy from the field of battle."[116] In translation, these ideas suggest that victory is less relevant to success on the battlefield than it is to the "physical and moral" destruction of the enemy's military forces.[117] Writing at a time when Europe was dominated by interstate wars, Clausewitz realized that if war was not confined to the struggles between dynasties over essentially limited problems, it would evolve into conflicts between modern states that put their very existence at risk.[118] He, like many strategists, understood that offensive war in the nineteenth century could produce victory by destroying the reigning territorial, political, military, and social order of Europe.

In his writings, Clausewitz dealt extensively with the nature of victory and its implications for strategy. He began his "On the Theory of War" by defining victory in tactical terms as "the retirement of the enemy from the field of battle."[119] For Clausewitz, "the original means of strategy is victory – that is, tactical success."[120] As he wrote in Book IV, Chapter IV of *On War*, entitled "The Engagement in General," victory "arises from a preponderance of the sum of all physical and moral power," and his general theory of victory rests on three elements: "greater loss of the enemy in physical forces; greater loss of the enemy in moral forces; open admission of this by his renunciation of his intention [to fight]."[121] With the argument that the "only real evidence of victory" is the decision of one side to give up in combat, Clausewitz reaffirmed that victory relates in part to conditions on the battlefield.[122] He argued that the "surest way to victory" is to conduct "engagement[s] with the greatest economy of force," which makes the "most of the moral effect of strong reserves."[123]

His lasting contribution was to connect victory to an underlying political object. In arguing that the "greatness of a victory depends on the greatness of the masses over which it has been gained," he observed that the "importance of the victory depends on the importance of the object which it secures to us."[124] Although the numbers of forces were important to Clausewitz – "it is very difficult in the present state of Europe, for the most talented General to gain a victory over an enemy double his strength"[125] – he rejected the idea that the "magnitude of a victory" depends on the "number of vanquished forces."[126] On the grounds that "only great and general engagements produce great results," he contended that the "leading principle of war" is the "destruction of the enemy's force," which "is principally effected by means of the engagement."[127] Furthermore, he argued that "only great victories have led to great successes, on the offensive side."[128] While acknowledging that the ultimate purpose of war is "to conquer the enemy," he argued in his discussion of the "Strategic Means of Utilising Victory" that "unless pursued, no victory can have a great effect."[129] In effect, Clausewitz's argument was that the effectiveness of a victory depends on "the tactical form adopted as the order of battle; on the nature of the country; on the relative proportions of the three arms [i.e., infantry, cavalry, and artillery]; on the relative strength of the two Armies."[130] With these observations, he established the principle that victory is measured in part by conditions on the battlefield. He also outlined "three principles of victory": "surprise, advantage of ground, and the attack from several quarters."[131]

When reduced to its simplest form, the "aim of war should be the defeat of the enemy."[132] For Clausewitz, the "complete or partial destruction of the enemy must be regarded as the sole object of all engagements."[133] According to Brodie, Clausewitz saw "the conquest of the enemy's ground [as] a 'visible sign of victory'."[134] But as Clausewitz asked, "what constitutes defeat? The conquest of his whole territory is not always necessary, and total occupation of his territory may not be enough."[135] There are, however, "important indicators that signal the defeat of the enemy," including the "destruction of his army[,] . . . seizure of his capital if it is not only the center of administration by also that of social, professional, and political activity, [and] delivery of an effective blow against his principal ally if that ally is more powerful than he."[136] In its "pure" form, the aim of war is to "overcome the enemy and disarm him," which can be accomplished by "the destruction of the enemy's armed forces" and "the conquest of his territory."[137] In war, Clausewitz concluded, states can bring "about a gradual exhaustion of his [the enemy's] physical and moral resistance."[138]

As previously discussed, by the time of the French Revolution in 1789, states were gravitating toward a strategy of war based on using the preponderance of their military, economic, human, and technological resources. This development in military strategy heralded the age in which modern states had the means to conduct total war.[139] As war had now moved well beyond the limited dynastic aims that had dominated European politics since the Middle Ages, Clausewitz's analysis of victory distinguished between these two types of war, the one involving mere territorial conquests, the other the complete overthrow of the enemy – in modern terminology, limited and total war, respectively.[140] In the case of limited war, the intent is to wear down enemy forces through attrition; the intent in total war is to destroy enemy forces, as well as the opponent society's ability to support the war, through a campaign based on annihilation.[141]

Since a loss of territory theoretically weakens the ability of a state to mobilize its economy and military forces for war, that loss and the prospect of military defeat would weaken the will of the state.[142] This implies that once territory has been captured, victory on some level has been attained, signaling that the state has to some degree been disarmed and thus is less likely to be able to continue the struggle. For Clausewitz, this demonstrated that war between modern states need not be total. Since, in his view, war is defined by its political objectives, and since these do not necessarily call for the destruction of the enemy state, there is indeed a place for limited war.

Still, with his emphasis on annihilation and territorial conquest, Clausewitz canonized the principle that victory can entail (but is not necessarily equivalent to) the total defeat of a state. Yet victory, whether reached by a strategy of annihilation or of attrition, represents for Clausewitz more than the destruction of enemy forces or the capture of its sovereign territory. There is in his writings a political component to victory that the modern reader will find remarkably familiar.

His famous maxim, alluded to earlier – "war is a mere continuation of policy by other means" – implies (though it is only one side of his dialectic) that victory is defined at least partly in terms of the achievement of political objectives. Furthermore, Clausewitz defined war in political terms as "an act of force to compel our enemy to do our will."[143] In addition, he differentiated between the political and military objectives of war and gave the former priority: "Sometimes the political object and military object is the same. . . . In other cases the political object will not provide a suitable military objective. In that event, another military objective must be adopted that will serve the political purpose and symbolize it in the peace negotiations."[144]

Clausewitz also differentiated between tactics and strategy, and clearly attached the latter to the political aims of the combatant: "Tactics teaches the use of armed forces in the engagement; strategy, the use of engagements for the object of the war."[145] Lastly, he devised a metric for victory that relied on a rational calculus for evaluating all decisions about war: "To discover how much of our resources must be mobilized for war, we must first examine our own political aim and that of the enemy. . . . [S]ince war is not an act of senseless passion but is controlled by the political object, the value of this object must determine the sacrifices made for it in magnitude and duration."[146]

Thus, Clausewitz defines both defeat and victory in largely political terms and, like Sun Tzu and Machiavelli, warns policymakers that the costs of victory may outweigh its benefits.[147] Moreover, when he refers to the capture of territory, the enemy's capital, and the defeat of the enemy's army, he is merely pointing to indicators of victory, arguing that victory is not achieved until the state attains its political objectives. In the end, Clausewitz did not believe that the nature of war or victory should be reduced to "universal principles." The central theme of *On War*, according to Gat, was this: "War was affected by innumerable forces, dominant among which were political conditions and moral forces; it was saturated with the unknown and incalculable, and was changing throughout history."[148] It is on the basis of these arguments about the complexity of war that Clausewitz made significant and enduringly modern contributions to our understanding of victory.

When the theory of victory forged by Clausewitz and other German military strategists was coupled with new technologies that emerged in the mid-nineteenth century, this framework, at first flexible, solidified into a strategy for total war.[149]

Henry Wager Halleck

A contemporary of Jomini, Henry Wager Halleck (1815–72) – a Union major general during the Civil War and eventually Grant's chief of staff – focused on the role of offensive warfare in his *Elements of Military Art and Science*. Halleck's contribution to the theory of victory was to emphasize, as did many other nineteenth- and twentieth-century strategists, that the offensive had a dominant influence on military strategy. Strategy, for Halleck, was the "art of directing masses on decisive points,"[150] which is consistent with his argument that the objective of offensive war was to "keep your forces as much concentrated as possible," because this strategy for war will "secure victory."[151] While a strategist of relatively minor importance, Halleck used the term "complete and decisive victory" to describe the outcome of what were essentially tactical engagements.[152]

MID-NINETEENTH- TO EARLY TWENTIETH-CENTURY STRATEGISTS

Building on foundations established by Clausewitz, Jomini, and other theorists of military strategy, intellectual and philosophical discussions about the
nature of war were broadened during and after the mid-nineteenth century
to include the relationship between military power and economics. Some
thinkers argued that, given the development of national, trade-based economies in Europe beginning in the 1500s, victory in war is influenced by the
economic competition that exists within and among societies and that shapes
the underlying structure of international politics. This was particularly so in
that governments accumulated wealth in gold and silver bullion, which was
used to pay armed forces, including mercenaries, in wartime. Thus the balance
of trade could have an enormous impact on a state's ability to wage war.

In the late eighteenth century, Scottish philosopher-economist Adam Smith
(1723–90) advanced the concept of *mercantilism,* in which there is a close
connection between the state's economic resources, including its available
markets, and its military power.[153] Known primarily for his work on capitalism, Smith argued that the economic organization of the state directly contributes to the instruments of war available to it; thus the state's military power depends directly upon its economic substructure.[154] He wrote that, "a
civilized nation depends for its defence upon a militia . . . [which could] be
conquered by any barbarous nation," and described "victories which have
been gained by militias."[155] These ideas raised questions about the role of
government in making decisions about the conduct of war, and provided the
underpinning for the belief that governments guided by economic interests
are less inclined to involve the state in war.[156] However, some theorists, most
notably Alexander Hamilton (1757–1804), argued that economic competition
was itself a permanent source of wars between states.[157]

Although economic considerations have always been an important aspect of
war and military strategy, the unifying theme for wars conducted during the
eighteenth century was still the destruction of armies in the field. There had
certainly been wars whose object, at least in part, was to destroy the productive capacities of a state or principality – witness the devastation wrought in
what is now Germany during the Thirty Years' War (1618–48);[158] but the
theory that emerged in the mid- to late nineteenth century suggested that a
state could not achieve victory *unless* it destroyed the enemy's economic and
military power. This theory of victory was still governed by the strategic and
tactical objectives of destroying armies in the field, but it was the prospect of
damage to the civilian economy – whether intentional, as in General Sherman's
scorched-earth "March to the Sea" through Georgia, on behalf of the Union,
in the American Civil War; or inadvertent, as when missiles kill civilians by

mistake, as has been reported in recent U.S. interventions – that became an influential concept in the development of victory.

In view of this principle that victory is partly determined through the destruction of the enemy's civilian economy, theorists from the mid- to late nineteenth century who focused on the economic implications of war and strategy developed this central proposition: A state must possess significant industrial resources if it is to be a great military power and if it is to achieve victory over other states.[159]

Friedrich List

The German economist Friedrich List (1789–1846) broadened the idea of the relationship between victory and economics with the argument that the success of military operations depends, ultimately, on the state's ability to marshal overwhelming economic power.[160] He correctly anticipated that the time would come when the entire economic infrastructure of the state would be harnessed to support its war machine. An architect of the concept of total war, List showed that the railway system, for example, could convert the nation into an integrated and organized entity for the conduct of war.[161]

Since military power was seen as based on economic power, and the ability to achieve victory as determined in part by the ability to organize the state's economy efficiently to defeat the enemy decisively, the economic foundations of power were a critical focus of thinking about victory. Not surprisingly, List's ideas about the economic foundations of victory help establish the theoretical basis for the great wars of the twentieth century, when states mobilized their economy and military forces for total war.

Karl Marx and Friedrich Engels

In addition to the huge impact they had on philosophy, politics, and economics in the twentieth century, the nineteenth-century political theorists Karl Marx (1818–83) and Friedrich Engels (1820–95) considerably influenced the debate about war and victory. They not only had a profound effect on political and military affairs through their theory of socialism but also contributed to the concept of modern total war.[162]

For Marx and Engels, revolutions originated in the peasant classes, who have "nothing to lose but their chains. They have a world to win."[163] A common refrain in their writings was that the "final victory of the proletariat" would occur when the existing economic and political institutions of the state were destroyed.[164] Their philosophy of revolutionary action rested on the idea that a socialist insurrection would emerge from a general war or insurgencies, and armies of peasants would be victorious over the ruling classes. At that point, the vestiges of capitalism would be decisively destroyed. This ideology of revolution contained numerous references to victory in war; for instance, "a real victory of an insurrection over the military in street fighting, a victory as between two armies, is one of the rarest exceptions."[165] As Marx wrote in his essay "Alienation and Social Classes," the proletariat "wins victory only by abolishing itself and its opposite [i.e., private property]."[166] When that occurs, the "masses have gained a victory over property owners and financial wealth."[167]

Marx wrote of war as an essential feature of human existence: "Up till now violence, war, pillage, murder and robbery, etc., have been accepted as the driving force of history."[168] The notion of war based on the ideology of mass political revolutionary movements played a prominent role in Engels's philosophy of military strategy. When these ideological mass movements reached the stage where they could harness the technology of the modern state – notably the new railways and naval vessels that could traverse large geographic areas – this development, Engels believed, would profoundly alter how war was conducted.[169]

The theories of Marx and Engels are not commonly associated with victory theory, but they had a considerable effect on how societies and governments understood war and victory, and they accelerated the development of the concept of total victory, in which politics and war are seen as absolute endeavors by the state. In the face of capitalism's more oppressive characteristics during the nineteenth century, the theory of communism gained prominence for its suggestion that the complete destruction of governments is a historical inevitability and as such constitutes a moral imperative for the proletariat and their vanguard or elite. Twentieth-century revolutionaries, armed with this absolute mandate, would promote the idea that governments must be totally defeated, which was interpreted to mean that total victory included the destruction of existing political institutions.

Marx and Engels also advanced the theory, defined in terms of communist ideology, that all politics within societies is symptomatic of the absolute struggle between the forces of good and evil. The relationship between political and ideological struggles on the one hand, and the mantle of historical inevitability and revolutionary fervor on the other, legitimized the view that the revolutionary forces representing "good" must fight until total victory is achieved against "evil." Engels cautioned, however, that victory can have unusual consequences: "[I]n the long run the vanquished often gains more economically, politically and morally than the victor."[170] In the end, their ideas contributed to the burgeoning theory of total war, which took operational form in the first decades of the twentieth century. The possibility of total war would reemerge during the cold war, when the Soviet Union allocated the vast majority of its economic power and national wealth to the defense sector.[171]

Helmuth von Moltke

Helmuth Karl Bernhard, Graf von Moltke, the Elder (1800–91) significantly shaped ideas about military strategy and victory late in the nineteenth century. He is widely viewed as the architect of the series of Prussian military victories that permitted Prime Minister Otto von Bismarck to consolidate confederated German states into the German Empire in 1871, with Bismarck as chancellor and Moltke as a field marshal and parliament member.

As one of the founders of the German General Staff (Großer Generalstab) system that was developed, in part, to rationalize the new system of warfare, Moltke also is credited with the innovative idea of using railways to deploy, move, and supply armies efficiently in modern wars.[172] He articulated a strategy in which the proper application of economic and technological power (e.g., telegraphy), including the mobilization all of its human and economic resources for the conduct of war, would permit the state to achieve victory on a grand scale.[173] A corollary of his analysis was the argument that all of an enemy state's economic resources, including factories, cities, and people, are legitimate targets in war, because all of these are necessary for the state to organize itself to fight and win wars.

Friedrich Wilhelm Rüstow and Victor-Bernard Derrecagaix

The prolific German military writer Friedrich Wilhelm Rüstow (1821–78), who served in both the Prussian and Swiss armies and authored *The Art of Field Service in the Nineteenth Century* (1857), argued that tactical concentrations of military force are necessary for success in war. His statement that "victory is completed by pursuit" indicates his emphasis on the role of offensive operations in war.[174]

A contemporary of Rüstow was the French general and strategist Victor-Bernard Derrecagaix (1833–1915), who wrote in his *Modern War* (1885) that his own approach was to "analyze . . . and expound the methods which have given victory to our enemies."[175] The role of military history is to "develop . . . the intellectual and manly qualities which shall again lead us to victory" (19). To understand war and hence victory, Derrecagaix built "a treatise upon the art of war" that was designed to "constitute a body of doctrines" (1) for the proper conduct of war. His approach developed from the argument that if "wars have become absolutely national . . . [then] wars will then be rarer, more imposing, and more impassioned" (22).

Derrecagaix also emphasized the strategic nature of war and victory. In lengthy quotes from Clausewitz, he agreed that "War has only one aim: to overthrow the enemy and render him incapable of continuing resistance" (25). Like Clausewitz, Derrecagaix observed that war "should destroy [the enemy's] will, and make it submissive to ours by the annihilation of his moral power" (25). In tactical terms, to achieve this outcome it will be necessary to "render him incapable of defending himself," which suggests that the victor must be "stronger at the critical point" (243) in battle. In emphasizing the importance of pursuit in battle, Derrecagaix argued that "the victor has only to pursue" to "insure decisive results to the victory" (12).

Both of these strategists argued that there is a clear relationship between the offense, or pursuit, and victory in war.

G. F. R. Henderson

A prominent British strategist of the late nineteenth and early twentieth centuries was George Francis Robert Henderson (1854–1903), a lieutenant colonel in the Second Boer War, who argued that the ability to "move swiftly, strike vigorously, and secure all the fruits of victory is the secret of successful war."[176] In *The Science of War,* published posthumously in 1905, Henderson acutely observed that an "army may even be almost uniformly victorious in battle, and yet ultimately be compelled to yield" because of "strategical faults," such as the "failure to concentrate in sufficient numbers to reap the fruits of victory."[177] Henderson did not articulate any "specific formula for victory,"[178] but his ideas about victory emphasized the tactical nature of war. In view of his arguments that strategy is the "art of bringing the enemy to battle" and the "end of strategy is the pitched battle,"[179] the objective for the strategist, according to Henderson, was to secure "every possible advantage of numbers, ground, supplies, and moral . . . which shall end in his enemy's annihilation."[180] This idea of a nation's moral qualities relating to victory was addressed a few years later by the British military officer E. A. Altham, who wrote that "victory or defeat depends not so much on the size of armies and fleets as on their fighting efficiency, and that this efficiency is directly proportionate to the moral force of the nation."[181]

As an architect of tactical victory, Henderson observed that a superior army can be "defeated in detail" by relying on "more rapid mobilization . . . surprises, effected by hard marching, secrecy, feints, and the adoption of an unexpected line of operations."[182] The methods by which one can make "victory . . . very near," include "drawing the enemy into a trap . . . feigned retreat . . . spreading false information . . . changing the base" (42). On the other hand, he wrote, "Defeat . . . is far more often due to bad strategy than to bad tactics" (45). Henderson observed that the real reasons for victory can be illusive – quoting, for example, Wellington, who'd said, "'I have fought a sufficient number of battles to know that the result is never certain, even with the best arrangements'" (44). Building on the Clausewitzian argument that "War is assuredly no mechanical art" (45), he suggested that the exact nature of victory is highly uncertain. While Henderson's ideas about victory were clearly rooted in the tactical nature of events on the battlefield, he implied that it is far more complex than simply achieving success on the battlefield.

Alfred von Schlieffen

Another significant military thinker was Alfred Graf von Schlieffen (1833–1913), who served as the chief of the German General Staff three years after Moltke and whose "Schlieffen Plan" was the basis of the General Staff's strategic plan for the conduct of World War I.[183] Schlieffen contributed to the idea, increasingly popular at the time, that states have an obligation to organize themselves for total war. For supporters of this concept, victory would result when the state mobilized all its military and economic resources to defeat its enemy on a broad scale. According to Schlieffen's theory of victory, such a fully mobilized state must be prepared to destroy all sources of the enemy state's power.

Schlieffen's principal contribution to military strategy was to propose that modern war is primarily distinguished by the use of nineteenth-century industrialism to expand the ability of states to produce weapons, transport them to and around the theater of operations, and increase the speed of warfare.[184] In essence, his strategy proposed that the state rely on its industrial infrastructure for the weapons and supplies necessary for a strategy of annihilation.[185] Thus he emphasized utilizing the state's scientific and economic resources, in direct contrast to earlier generations of theorists who had viewed war as a principally military enterprise.

Although Schlieffen was not a "prophet of total war," annihilation was a critical element in his strategy of war.[186] For example, in considering how to deal with France as a military adversary, he argued that for Germany to win it must annihilate France's armed forces. Schlieffen believed in the primacy of crushing the enemy's military forces; destroying the civilian basis of the economy that sustains war was secondary. Thus his strategy, though focused on destroying armed forces, was also a product of his era.[187]

In his military writings, Schlieffen uses the term "victory" quite frequently to describe the outcome of battles – as when describing how "German arms won a victory in the Western theatre of war that forced the French to retreat behind their fortress line."[188] In arguing that armies may achieve "decisive victory" (34), Schlieffen emphasized the nature of success in war. For example, "The success of battle today depends more on conceptual coherence than on territorial proximity," and "one battle might be fought in order to secure victory on another battlefield" (185). Victory also could be achieved by the "annihilation of the enemy's army through envelopment" (188). Consistent with his tactical emphasis on victory, he described how a "decisive and annihilating victory requires an attack against two or three sides of the enemy" (200). He also articulated his belief that annihilation was central to achieving military victories in his "Cannae Studies," which analyzed a stunning defeat of the Romans by Hannibal in the Second Punic War.[189]

However, Schlieffen also used the term "victory" to describe broader strategic outcomes, including the ability of the leader to have "complete freedom . . . to do that which he believes must be done to win victory" (228). In his speech at the unveiling of the Moltke monument on the Königsplatz in Berlin on October 26, 1905, Schlieffen described "Not a victory like so many others which required another victory after some time had passed . . . but rather a victory that produced clarity" (228). Unifying these ideas was Schlieffen's argument that the ability to achieve decisive victory depends on mastering the "laws of strategy" (229).

Being a disciple of Clausewitz, victory for Schlieffen meant annihilating armies on the battlefield and destroying the industrial base of the civilian economy; yet his theory of victory did not rely heavily on the latter. He focused primarily on the military dimension of victory, rather than on smashing the civil society and killing civilians. For Schlieffen a state would achieve strategic victory when it quickly and decisively defeated the armed forces of another state, and this was the strategy that he advocated as the head of the German General Staff. However, Schlieffen realized that a strategy based on annihilation was consistent with modern political and social realities and preferable to one of attrition: It was long and costly wars of attrition that had undermined the social and economic order in Germany during his years of military service.[190] As it turned out, World War I was another long and painful war for Germany, whose defeat led, as Schlieffen had feared, to the destruction of its economic and social systems. It would also lead to what few had anticipated – the ascent of political radicalism in the form of Nazism fifteen years later.[191]

Ferdinand Foch

The military strategist Ferdinand Foch (1851–1929) served as the marshal of France and the commander of Allied forces during the last months of World War I. Foch's *The Principles of War,* whose ideas can be traced to Clausewitz, influenced the intellectual foundations of war adopted by French military officers in the early twentieth century. An enduring aspect of Foch's ideas was the belief that by using rational scientific principles to analyze the empirical conditions that govern war, we can understand its fundamental nature and thus the proper strategy for it. Foch enunciated permanent principles or laws that organized war's uncertainties and complexities on the basis of the proposition that "nothing ever repeats itself."[192] Arguing that we "must not conclude that, in the matter of warfare, there is no such thing as an absolute theory,"

Foch hightlighted the underlying nature of war, constant despite tactical conditions in continual flux.[193]

Although Foch's theories were shaped by the ideas of national warfare and absolute war, it is not clear that he comprehended the full implications of the idea that the development of absolute war in the late nineteenth and early twentieth centuries established the rationale for the total mobilization of a state's economy.[194] What Foch did observe was the emergence of wars waged by nations that used all of their resources to win.[195]

During Foch's time, the debate about the real meaning of victory resurfaced, couched in terms of limited versus unlimited war. Some theorists argued that victory exists when one state defeats another on the battlefield; others proposed that victory exists only after one state, using its overwhelming material wealth, destroys another's military and society. In an age dominated by state wars whose principal antagonists – England, France, Germany, Austria, and Russia – were the major economic powers in continental Europe, it was natural to believe that success would accrue to the side that produced the largest accumulation of supplies for war. But Foch deemphasized the use of empirical categories to determine whether states would win based on their ability to amass material resources. Nor did he argue that victory is achieved only with absolute destruction. To the contrary, Foch believed that when states marshal their resources to wage wars, victory – the outcome of battles fought among great armies on the battlefields of Europe – belongs to the side that can endure longer in a war of attrition.

Consistent with this view, Foch dismissed the idea of the shock approach to war, which held that victory could be achieved by the single, perfect, decisive military attack. For Foch, victory was the cumulative effect of many smaller successes in war, achieved when the state succeeds simultaneously on the strategic, tactical, and economic levels.[196] It was a "series of advantageous results," the "consequence of efforts, some of which are victorious while others appear to be fruitless, which nevertheless aim at a common goal . . . namely, at a decision, a conclusion which alone can provide victory."[197]

Foch was clear on what victory was not: "maintaining a position is not synonymous with being victorious," nor is "individual valor" sufficient for victory. Victory is not determined by "having sustained losses, still less a comparison between losses" (284). In contemporary war, wrote Foch, victory is achieved by "one means: the destruction of the organized forces of the enemy" (282); yet "defensive battle never brings about the destruction of enemy forces" because it "never allows one to conquer the ground held by the enemy (which after all is the only external sign of victory)" (283). Elevating the capture of territory, Foch emphasized the importance of tactical engagements to victory. Unless the state is able to gain territory in battle, it is "unable to create victory" (283). Victory thus has significant tactical foundations;

"Tactics, Order, Manoeuvre" (285) are the factors needed to provide it. Foch's emphasis on "material factors" contrasted with the "old theory" from the Napoleonic era, which rested on "superior numbers, better rifles, better guns, more skillfully chosen positions" (3).

Foch quoted another strategist who reasoned that "'It is not so necessary to *annihilate the enemy combatants* as to *annihilate their courage*'" (287). For Foch, then, "victory means [the] will [to win]" (293) – or to "break the enemy's will" (286–7). "Victory is ours as soon as the enemy has been brought to believe that his cause is lost," he wrote, and "An enemy is not to be reduced to impotence by means of complete individual annihilation, but by *destroying his hope in victory*" (287). Moreover, the "decisive victory, the true victory, is bound to be a moral victory" (287). Thus Foch held that victory, based on the "will to conquer," is established by the "moral superiority of the victors [and] the moral depression of the vanquished."[198] This emphasis on the moral force in war Foch derived from the thinking of Ardant du Picq.[199]

Overall, Foch possessed a highly integrated view of war, in which victory will occur when all of the state's human, military, and economic resources are properly combined.

Louis-Hubert Lyautey

The nature of colonial war and its relationship to a theory of victory was debated by French military strategists of the late nineteenth and early twentieth century. Prominent in the development of such a theory for colonial wars was Louis-Hubert Lyautey (1854–1934), who was the French resident-general of Morocco from 1912 to 1925, served as the French minister of war for three months during 1916–17, and was created a marshal of France in 1921.[200]

Classical military strategy and theories of victory are unsuited to the demands of colonial warfare. While the traditional objective in war is to defeat the armed forces of the enemy on the battlefield and destroy the civilian society, this has little relevance for colonial wars, in which victory involves both defeating the enemy militarily and preventing insurgencies from fighting successfully against the occupying power. The danger with using the concept of annihilation in fighting insurgencies is that this would generate public resentment and therefore greater resistance, thereby weakening the occupier's ability to subdue the state or conquer its territory.[201] In contrast with continental warfare, then, colonial wars seek not to destroy the enemy but to weaken the organization and stability of the native population and government.[202] The key to victory in colonial operations is to break their morale as part of a strategy for eroding their will to resist. The colonial power, consistent with the principles of psychological warfare, must destroy the ability and will of the local people to organize armies and to mobilize the economy.

The fundamental problem is how the state achieves victory when there are no obvious targets whose destruction would weaken the military power of the native government. The solution for Lyautey was to build relationships at a local level and to build the foundations of a society. Lyautey observed that, in colonial wars, "we should turn to destruction only as a last resort and only as a preliminary to better reconstruction."[203] In what is known as the Lyautey Doctrine, he proposed "reopening roads and market, restoring villages to life, recreating life."[204] More broadly, Lyautey sought to "investigate the internal politics of the country; to handle each tribe according to its own temper, to depend upon the most intelligent of the chieftains, to win over territory from the tribes successively without fighting – [like] the 'spreading stain of oil'."[205] Also, he suggested that "In dealing with the policing of native populations, one should always bear in mind the formula that *force should be displayed in order to avoid using it.*"[206]

Among his more general principles of war, Lyautey proposed that one's determination to win is crucial: "Faith in victory determines victory."[207] He also argued that "Complete success comes only to those who can control ideas, imagination, active minds and the initiative of the moment."[208]

The strength of Lyautey's influence on the doctrine for waging colonial wars derives from his rejection of absolute doctrines on any matter related to war.[209] However successful one deems his approach, Lyautey's ideas about such wars and his concept of victory are remarkably consistent with the types of conflict that may be prevalent in the twenty-first century: military interventions in which the enemy is neither defeated nor achieves victory in the classic sense.

Hans Delbrück

One thinker who influenced the emerging theory of victory in wars between states was the German military strategist and historian Hans Delbrück (1848–1929), who, having fought in the Franco-Prussian War, published the *History of the Art of War* in 1900.[210] Delbrück was described by English military historian John Keegan as the "pioneer of the modern 'scientific' and 'universal' approach" to military history.[211]

For Delbrück, "a victory that cannot be followed up has only a passing value."[212] Writing about victory in the Renaissance, he observed that "In the large battles . . . victory had evaporated without lasting effects" (107). Thus, "When one wins the battle, one must follow up the victory with all haste" (109). It is clear from this that victory for Delbrück involves more than tactical accomplishments. By writing that Napoléon's strategy rested on seeking to "complete his victory through politics" (434), Delbrück suggested that victory has a strategic component encompassing far more than success in battle.

With respect to war in the Napoléonic era, Delbrück proposed that the "natural principle of strategy is . . . assembling one's forces, seeking out the enemy's main force, defeating it, and following up the victory" (421). This approach emphasized an "overwhelming tactical victory" whose objective was to "put the enemy army out of action" (421). Thus the strategy of annihilation plays an important role in his analysis of war in that era. As he wrote, "victory does not depend on the 'point' where it is won or the 'strategic line' along which one moves," because the Napoleonic strategy of annihilation is designed to "destroy him [the enemy] as completely as possible" (432–3). He also discussed the role of material resources in such a victory, noting that "every resource would have had to be thrown into the battle in order to win the most complete possible victory" (435).

Delbrück's theory of war centered on the idea that there is a close relationship between the conduct of war and state policy. He is remembered for the argument, itself traceable to Clausewitz, that strategy is to be guided by the aims of the state. Delbrück outlined two main strategies of war, noting historical proponents of each. The first strategy – immensely popular during the nineteenth and twentieth centuries, as we have seen – was one of annihilation, which depended on fighting battles to defeat the enemy's armed forces decisively. Prominent examples of strategists of the annihilation school included Alexander, Caesar, and Napoléon.[213] Delbrück's second strategy of war involved weakening the enemy through the attrition of its armed forces and national economy. According to Delbrück, Pericles and Frederick the Great were prominent examples of commanders who favored a strategy of attrition.[214]

Given the efficacy of these competing strategies throughout history, Delbrück could find no justification for the belief that there is a unified theory of war that applies equally to all historical periods. In essence, he defended the principle, which owes its lineage to Clausewitz, that the prevailing ideas about war and strategy reflect the political environment of the given historical epoch.[215] Therefore, the strategy followed by the state should reflect the enemy it faces. This explains in part why Delbrück is described as a proponent of the "relativity of strategy" argument, which claims that the best strategy depends on the actions and strategies of the enemy.[216]

Once states came to possess the ability to annihilate one another, the prevailing theory of war embraced the principle that the purpose of war is to annihilate the enemy. This principle was demonstrated in World War I, when Germany's military objective was to crush France immediately and then turn its army toward Russia for the same purpose.[217] When the German offensive stalled, Delbrück argued for the reevaluation of any annihilation-based theory of victory. The problem, he suggested, is that overwhelming victories in war, as exemplified by Napoléon's triumphs, may strengthen the enemy's resolve and make wars even more destructive.[218] Wars based on annihilation will be transformed into total wars because the enemy state will oppose its own extinction with every means at its disposal. As Delbrück watched the Great War unfold, he may have believed that Germany's attempt to achieve victory through military annihilation of its enemies might lead to its defeat.

Friedrich von Bernhardi

The German strategist General Friedrich von Bernhardi (1849–1930), who authored *On War of To-day* and *The War of the Future*, defined "the will to victory" as a "fundamental" principle of success in war.[219] Bernhardi argued that the development of a "comprehensive doctrine of war" is necessary if we are to understand the "character of modern war."[220] He observed that we must have a "scientific structure of a doctrine of war" (*WT*, 18) if we are to understand the "permanent factors" or "certain organic laws" (*WT*, 43) that exist in military history. In *The War of the Future* (1920), he wrote that the "art of war moves between permanent laws and those which change periodically and are ever undergoing fresh development" (*WF*, 13). These ideas form a "doctrine for acting in the field – a law, as it were, of future victory" (*WT*, 19). While expressing concerns about the difficulties of developing "definite laws of acting and . . . binding rules for the practical conduct of war" (*WT*, 43), he warned that a doctrine of war is "not an exact science" and that the ability to successfully conduct war is "an art" (*WT*, 52).

For Bernhardi, "the will to victory" was one of his "great fundamental and vital principles" for success in war (*WF*, 19). For this theorist, the "determination to conquer . . . is an inexhaustible source of strength which leads to final victory in spite of every possible disaster" (*WF*, 180). He argued that victory can be the result of "particular circumstances . . . a happy coincidence of favourable conditions; a numerical or tactical superiority; a special kind of armament; a moral superiority inherent in the character of an army; or a superior principle of acting" (*WT*, 20). He also cited numerous examples from history that reaffirmed "the superior principle of acting" in war could be decisive, contending that such actions were decisive only "in reference to that of their opponent and to the totality of the conditions governing war in the time prevailing" (*WT*, 24–5).[221] The condition of the troops too can be a decisive factor in explaining why armies are "victorious on the battlefield" (*WT*, 21). Thus, Bernhardi wrote in *The War of the Future* about "annihilating" and decisive victories (which are "impossible without infantry") (*WF*, 222) and of a "victorious rupture of the enemy's front" (*WF*, 24). That his idea of victory was essentially tactical in nature is evident from his comment that "the main force of the attacker's fire and offensive power must be concentrated at one point, so that victory may be won at that point" in the hope that victory "will rapidly spread to the rest of the battle-front" (*WF*, 71).[222]

Bernhardi emphasized the importance of the offensive in war – "only the offensive can bring victory" (*WF*, 161) and "the offensive is the inevitable preliminary to a victorious decision in war" (*WF*, 163).[223] For him, "the chances of victory for the attacker . . . are very great" (*WF*, 81).[224] He was dismissive of defensive victories, which he observed are "never anything but a half victory"; "the hope that the enemy can be forced to make peace by attrition, i.e., the exhaustion of his forces, is in its nature a snare and a delusion" (*WF*, 161). Indeed, a state using a defensive strategy "renounces the prospect of military victory" (*WF*, 162).[225]

He also observed that "superior numbers under otherwise equal conditions should guarantee us victory at least in theory. Yet military history proves that it is not simply superior numbers that achieve victory but how those numbers are used and how the war is conducted" (*WT*, 89). Moreover, "Often it is the numerically weaker army which obtains the most decisive victory" (*WT*, 19), so numerical superiority may not produce the most successful outcomes. Bernhardi held that universal service helped Prussia to achieve victories (*WT*, 22), citing the example of the Romans, who "conquered the world with inferior numbers" (*WT*, 85).[226]

Looking for causes, Bernhardi attributed victory to "moral qualities," notably "[s]uperior resolution, boldness, daring, and steadfastness" (*WT*, 24). Though victory could be supported by diplomacy, ultimately it is the military that should guide the strategy and conduct of war.[227] Finally, victory depends on the efforts of the entire nation: "[Y]ears of ceaseless effort on the part of the whole nation are necessary to wage [war] to a victorious conclusion" (*WF*, 268).

CONCLUSION

The discourse on victory that has developed since the writings of Sun Tzu can be examined on the basis of two main theories of victory.

For the classical and premodern theorists, the central purpose of war was the ability of the state to conquer territory successfully. Thus, until the middle of the second millennium, strategists emphasized the conditions necessary to defeat armies in the field.

With the rise of the industrial age and its emphasis on mechanized warfare, societies could mobilize their total economic and industrial resources for war, increasing the capacity to wage wars animated by ideology and fueled by advanced technology. In this climate, the state that could marshal the largest and most technologically advanced forces was more likely to win. The theory of victory was therefore now characterized by the state's ability to assemble overwhelming resources for the purpose of defeating another state or coalition of states – to focus on "complete victory," to put an "end to war," rather than waste its resources on lesser objectives.[228] Societies began to head down this path, organizing the state for the conduct of the total wars that dominated strategy and war during the twentieth century.

The concept of victory prevailing in the late nineteenth and early twentieth centuries, which called for the annihilation of the enemy's military forces, would be reexpressed decades later, in remarkably consistent wording, in publications on Soviet military doctrine. The *Soviet Field Service Regulations* of 1936, for example, argued that the "principal objectives of the Soviet Union" in war were "decisive victory and the complete crushing of the enemy."[229]

For many prominent military strategists, Germany's defeat in World War I only reinforced the belief that the principal objective of war is victory through annihilation. The twentieth-century principle of victory, as practiced in World War II, would involve the wholesale devastation of a state's military, economic, and social institutions.

3 Modern Origins of Victory

his chapter examines the works of theorists of the late nineteenth and twentieth centuries to understand how their ideas influenced the development of the modern theory and practice of victory in war. In a practical sense, the theorists in this chapter have the closest connection to the modern concept of victory.

TOTAL WAR AND VICTORY

Systematic thinking about war, particularly total war, early in the twentieth century was shaped by two broad influences. The first was the relationship between the state's military organization and the sources of economic power.[1] The second was the ability of the state to conduct warfare on a devastating scale given the development of air power, nuclear weapons, and ballistic missiles. Despite the expansion of the economic foundations and technological instruments of war, the prevailing dogma held that conflict was the natural condition among states. With the development of these ideas, military strategists argued that the state's ability to mobilize its human, economic, and technological resources for total war was critical to victory. Some prominent military leaders dismissed economics as a lesser aspect of war.[2] Helmuth von Moltke the Younger (nephew to Graf von Moltke and chief of the General Staff early in World War I) was quoted as saying, "Don't bother me with economics, I am busy conducting the war." But by the next world war, Winston Churchill was commenting that "modern war is total" – that is, victory demands the ability to mobilize the total resources of the state to fight.[3]

In the first half of the twentieth century, strategists in the West were searching for broad principles governing how states fight and win wars. One theme that arose in this era was the "cult of the offensive," dominated by French and British military strategists. The idea, as expressed in the *U.S. Field Service Regulations* circa 1913, was that, "Decisive results are obtained only by offensive battles."[4] Field Marshal Bernard Montgomery (1887–1976) defined a set of principles of war in his 1945 *High Command in War*, in which he declared that, "A war is won by victories in battle. No victories will be gained unless commanders will sort out clearly in their own minds those essentials which are vital for success."[5] This debate about the development of total war and its dependence on the ability to mobilize the economy signaled a clear shift toward the notion that victory was achieved by the state that could energize its industrial power for offensive war.

Jean Colin

Jean Colin (1864–1917), who served with the French Ministry of War and on the faculty of the French War College, argued in *The Transformations of War* (1911) that, "Victory is above all a matter of force; that to win, we can never be too strong."[6] What Colin sought to understand was "if not the secret of victory, at any rate the causes that contribute to success or defeat."[7] While he did not expect the causes to be "very precise or formal," or for there to be a "hierarchy among the elements of war," the factors he deemed essential to victory include such "material" elements as "superiority in armament," "plentiful supply of munitions," "superiority in cavalry," "quality of troops in exercises," and "patriotic passion."[8] Arguing that the "strictest duty" of political authorities is "not to engage in a foolish war without hope of victory,"[9] Colin implied that in addition to the factors that contribute to victory, statesmen ought to rely on reason and analysis to achieve their military goals.

Erich Ludendorff

Erich Friedrich Wilhelm Ludendorff (1865–1937) contributed to the development of concepts of victory with his attack on the proposition that war is necessarily a total endeavor by the state. Described as a brilliant officer in the Germany Army, Ludendorff advanced the theory of total war (and, in addition, criticized Clausewitz's notions of absolute war), as expressed by five propositions.[10]

1. War is total because it involves the entire territory of the state.
2. Total war also involves the total population of the state, because to fight a total war it is necessary to mobilize the entire economy of the state.
3. The involvement of the people in total war implies that the state must actively strengthen the morale of the population.
4. A state must prepare for total war well before the start of hostilities.
5. Total war must be guided by one figure who has supreme authority over the military actions of the state.[11]

Ludendorff observed that the theory of total war is influenced by psychological factors that could affect the cohesion of the population when it faces the duress associated with the conduct of total war.[12]

Ludendorff understood, however, that victory is altered by total war, which puts at risk not only the military but the existence of the society as well.[13] Total war, therefore, is conceivable only when states are willing to achieve the destruction of the enemy on an unimaginable scale – which in modern times is without parallel in the history of military strategy. While these ideas predated the development of nuclear weapons by nearly fifty years, the underlying theme is that modern technology allows states to focus their resources to such an extent that total war becomes a logical and practical inevitability.

For Ludendorff, victory was defined as "action in the right place . . . followed up by a swift pursuit of the enemy."[14] He also stressed the role that the offensive plays in achieving victory, writing that "victory in the attack . . . is, and remains, the most effective method of war" (158).[15] With this emphasis on the offensive comes the "decisive victory" that "prevents the enemy from taking advantage of weakness" (161).

In his analysis of victory, Ludendorff addressed the role of the different military services, arguing that the "task of an Army in war is to beat the enemy . . . and strive for victory" (109–10). Comparing the roles of air power and land forces, he argued that victory is not possible "solely by the bombing of the enemy population," reasoning that the state's first priority is to "beat the enemy Army and then only will a victorious Army be able to act with its Air Force in the enemy country" (110).[16] For Ludendorff, the proper balance between air power and ground forces was one in which aircraft should "be used directly in the fight for victory but its firing force is only of secondary importance in comparison with that of the Army" (126). In practice, this meant that "victory over the enemy" would result from "attacking the enemy with superior numbers [of ground forces] and action of arms, at a weak spot" (25).

Thus, Ludendorff emphasized the nature of total war and the spirit of the offensive, particularly on the ground, as critical determinants of victory. In addition, he argued that the "final aim" of using military force is the "annihilation of the enemy" (132), which clearly was consistent with his theory of total war. Building on the principle that war "postulates the defeat of the enemy" (149), Ludendorff contended that victory is determined by the size of military forces: "It is a fact that victory 'goes to the big battalions'" (87).[17]

Finally, he also discussed the role played by psychological factors – notably the "psychical unity" (25) of the people and the will – in determining the outcome of wars. "Victory is created by the spirit" (101), he wrote, and "victory over the enemy's will . . . requires the highest quality of strength on the part of the Commander" (178).

Karl Haushofer

The concept of victory in the late nineteenth and early twentieth centuries was broadened by the work of several German geopolitical theorists, a prominent example being General Karl Haushofer (1869–1946).[18] The main contribution of the geopolitical school of thought was the principle that war involves not only the total physical resources of the state but also its geographical position and power relative to its adversaries and allies.

Germany's defeat in World War I, according to Haushofer, was attributable in part to that nation's lack of geographical and geopolitical understanding, which left it with inadequate alignments in that war. He later parlayed his years spent in Japan as a German military attaché into forging what looked to be a propitious alliance between the two countries for World War II.

According to Haushofer, since victory was not simply defeating armies but defeating the state and all that it represented, and therefore war is bound to be total, it is essential for the state to use all of its national resources as efficiently as possible to produce the goods needed for war. Such thinking about victory and the inevitability of total war encouraged the idea that there must be a supreme political authority to command the state's actions in war.[19] Haushofer argued that it was no longer practical for military authorities to do so because military organizations, although adept at the operational functions of war, are not well suited to managing a state's total resources.

REVOLUTIONARY IDEOLOGIES AND VICTORY

Vladimir Lenin, Leon Trotsky, and Josef Stalin

The development of revolutionary ideologies in the late nineteenth and early twentieth centuries had a significant effect on the theory of war and victory. Even before the establishment of Marxism as the official state ideology of the Soviet Union, such theorists as Vladimir Lenin (1870–1924), Leon Trotsky (1879–1940), and Josef Stalin (1879–1953) had considered the relationship between ideology and war.[20] Arguing that the political-economic organization of the state has a strong influence on how it conducts war, these thinkers reshaped the framework for war and victory in the modern age. Building on the work of Marx and Engels, who defined victory as the defeat of the capitalist classes by the proletariat and the triumph of socialism, Lenin, Trotsky, and Stalin understood victory in terms that were heavily dominated by the idea of political and economic revolution.

Vladimir I. Lenin's argument that war involves the entire society – in particular the working classes, who were to do the bulk of the fighting and dying to supplant capitalism with socialism – was a dominant theme in military strategy in the early twentieth century.[21] Lenin made frequent references to the "victory of socialism," arguing that the "complete victory of communism brings about the total disappearance of the state."[22] In a speech on September 12, 1918, Leon Trotsky read a telegram from Lenin who affirmed that the "alliance of the workers and revolutionary peasants will utterly smash the bourgeoisie, shatter any resistance on the part of the exploiters and ensure the victory of universal socialism."[23] By emphasizing that the concept of total war involves all of the people if the state is to achieve a "victory" in "a proletarian revolution," Lenin reaffirmed the principle that war can consume all of the human and material resources available to the state.[24] The objective of political and economic change, for Lenin, was to achieve the "ultimate victory of our [socialist] revolution."[25] Building on the Marxist principle that the world is divided into socialist and capitalist camps, he asserted that wars are fought ultimately for the ideological purpose of accomplishing the wholesale defeat and devastation of the enemy. For Lenin, the "soundest strategy in war is to postpone operations until the moral disintegration of the enemy renders the delivery of the mortal blow both possible and easy."[26] His thinking focused on the concept of total defeat of the enemy and the existing political order.

In formulating his ideas about victory in a message to the Bolshevik Central Committee written on October 8, 1917, Lenin reiterated Marx's ideas (which Lenin called "principal rules") about the use of force in an insurrection. As Lenin proposed:

1. Never *play* with insurrection, but when beginning it realize firmly that you must go all the way.
2. Concentrate a *great superiority of forces* at the decisive point and at the decisive moment, otherwise the enemy, who has the advantage of better preparation and organization, will destroy the insurgents.
3. Once the insurrection has begun, you must act with the greatest *determination,* and by all means, without fail, take the *offensive.* "The defensive is the death of every armed rising."
4. You must try to take the enemy by surprise and seize the moment when his forces are scattered.
5. You must strive for *daily* successes, however small (one might say hourly, if it is the case of one town), and at all costs retain "*moral superiority.*"[27]

With his discussion of using the offensive and surprise to destroy the enemy and the argument that "victory is impossible unless one has learned how to attack and retreat properly," Lenin emphasized the value of the offensive and the proper role of strategy in achieving "complete victory."[28] His reasoning was that "victory over the bourgeoisie is impossible without a long, stubborn and desperate life-and-death struggle which calls for tenacity, discipline, and a single and inflexible will."[29] As recounted by Josef Stalin, Lenin outlined three principles of victory: "The first thing is not to become intoxicated by victory and not to boast; the second thing is to consolidate the victory; and the third is to give the enemy the finishing stroke, for he has been beaten, but by no means crushed."[30] Thus, for Lenin victory had both immediate tactical qualities and longer-term strategic consequences for the success of the revolution.

Using ideas that are fairly consistent with Clausewitz's theory of total war, Trotsky, as people's commissar of war and supreme commander of the Red Army during the Russian Civil War, observed that a revolutionary ideology will destroy in the most complete sense the classes, society, and military organization of the old era.[31] In the same fashion as Lenin and Stalin, Trotsky used victory to describe the ultimate outcome of what he hoped would be the proletarian revolution. In the "Rough Outline for the Draft of a Programme of the Russian Communist Party," he argued that the "victory of the proletarian revolution requires total trust . . . of the working classes of all the advanced countries."[32] Trotsky also distinguished between "military victories" and "direct victories of the Revolution," the latter of which are of "a more or less spontaneous nature."[33] And he was concerned that some commissars who may be "lulled to sleep by victories" should be "removed and replaced by new Party workers of a critical turn of mind."[34] This revolution would be conducted in a ruthless fashion to achieve victory. Thus, in a telegram to Trotsky on May 26, 1919, Lenin argued that "swift victory in the Donbass" would require "the wholesale disarming of the population," and toward that end Trotsky was authorized to "apply shooting on the spot, without mercy, to every case of concealment of a single rifle."[35]

These revolutionary theorists had several significant consequences for the theories of war and victory that emerged in the early twentieth century. First, they codified the doctrine of total victory, which exists when the state and its resources are defeated in a total and comprehensive fashion – a formulation consistent with the category of grand strategic victory. As Lenin observed, "[W]e want to attain our goal . . . without any compromises, which only postpone the day of victory."[36] While these theorists argued that warfare is the product of "factors" that are independent of specific technological, social, and political forces, they also held that victory is shaped by complex political, economic, and ideological factors in a society.[37] The tendency of the Bolsheviks to think in terms of completely destroying their ideological and political opponents was consistent with arguing that anything less than total victory is meaningless.

A second principle of Marxist revolutionary ideology is that victory will be attained only if the state conducts military operations on the offensive. A prominent supporter of the importance of the offensive in war was Mikhail Tukhachevsky (see the section "Armored Warfare and Victory" below), who argued that for the state to prevail in war it must operate on the political and military offensive. He contended that since the object of victory is to destroy the enemy's forces through the ruthless application of offensive military operations, offense is the most effective strategy for producing victory in war.

A third influence of Marxist ideology on the theory of victory was the tendency to equate success in warfare with the destruction of the enemy's military forces and the seizure of the sources of its economic power.[38] Stalin, for example, combined these arguments into the idea that victory is produced when the state is on the offensive and thus when all of its full "economic and moral resources" are completely mobilized. In reality, this theory of victory was more absolute, comprehensive, and ruthless than many in the West understood in the 1930s.[39]

In the Marxist theory of victory, the fundamental objective of war is to destroy completely the enemy's military forces and economic means of power. From the principle developed by Clausewitz and earlier theorists of war – that victory exists primarily when the opponent's military forces are crushed in battle – a corollary is that victory is attained when the enemy can no longer offer any effective military resistance.[40] It is important to remember that Lenin and Stalin, who are the most prominent Soviet theorists on the nature of victory, are the products of an age in which victory was equated with destroying the political and economic organization of the state as part of a strategy for overthrowing the ruling classes who oppressed the working classes. These ideologists had a significant influence on the concept of victory that emerged early in the twentieth century because they increasingly legitimized the view of war as a total enterprise that leads to the defeat and annihilation of the state and its ruling classes. It is worth remembering that these theorists argued that "terrible struggles between capitalists and socialists before the final victory of the latter" are inevitable[41] – although the cold war did end without any such battles.

Mao Tse-tung

As the principal architect of the communist revolution in China, Mao Tse-tung (1893–1976) was responsible for the formation of the People's Republic of China in 1949. With his close intellectual and political connections to the Soviet Union, it is highly predictable that the ideas expressed in the ideology of Marxism–Leninism would be evident in Mao's thoughts about the nature of politics and war.[42] From an analysis of Mao's writings and pronouncements, his ideas about victory arguably fall into two broad but related categories – strategic and tactical.

The first, a more *strategic* conception of victory, is based on achieving success against the opponents of communism and socialism.[43] Mao, like many of his ideological contemporaries, viewed victory in terms of defeating his ideological enemies. Thus, he wrote that "victory or defeat in war is determined mainly by the military, political, economic and natural conditions on both sides."[44] However, whether the state actually achieves victory or defeat "is not decided by these [conditions] alone [because] these alone constitute only the possibility of victory or defeat."[45] Mao advanced an integrated view of victory in which the state or revolutionary cadres, depending on where one is in the revolutionary cycle, will be able to achieve victory only when they understand "the actual circumstances of war, its nature and its relations to other things."[46] The intellectual lineage of Mao's ideas in the writings of Lenin is clear from his observation that there can be "no victory for the revolution with armed struggle,"[47] and from his declaration of solidarity with the Soviet Union against the West and what he called the "People's Democracies."[48]

For Mao, understanding the "laws of war" is essential to being "able to win victory."[49] The term "victory" has a strategic quality for Mao that he uses in the context of "annihilation," albeit in the narrow case of defeating an enemy division.[50] Despite this military allusion, Mao apparently concluded that victory is a strategic phenomenon that is based on developing "a war of total resistance by the whole nation," because "[o]nly through such a war of total resistance can final victory be won."[51] This strategic conception of victory is evident from his declaration that "Victory or defeat in a war is decided . . . by the military, political, economic, and geographical conditions, by the character of the war, and by international support on both sides."[52] For Mao, victory can have a significant effect on the broad strategic situation, including the military engagements that may lead to victory.[53] In a line of reasoning consistent with strategic victory, Mao noted the relationship among different levels of victory, observing that "the accumulation of many minor victories [can] make a major victory" (159). What is interesting is his view that the ability to achieve victory is fundamentally related to the proper timing for military action: "We should strike only when the enemy's situation, the terrain and popular support are all in our favour and not in his and when we are positively certain of winning" (129). He warned that "if the battle harms rather than helps the campaign as a whole, such a victory can only be reckoned a defeat" (130).

Mao's reasoning for relating victory to military actions and strategy was that "For us, victory means chiefly victory in combating 'encirclement and suppression,' that is, strategic victory and victories in campaigns. . . . Until [such a] campaign has been basically smashed, one cannot speak of strategic victory or of victory in the counter-campaign as a whole, even though many battles may have been won" (98–9). But Mao also argued that there is a relationship between military and strategic victories: "In the history of war, there are instances where defeat in a single battle nullified all the advantages of a series of victories, and there are also instances when victory in a single battle after many defeats opened up a new situation" (82) – which can be interpreted as a strategic shift in the prevailing political conditions.

The second category of Mao's thoughts on victory involves the *tactical* military meanings that he associated with the state's ability to achieve victory. Mao's emphasis on the tactical quality of victory was evident from his guidance to the "winning side" (123) that in war it must exercise caution in the face of an early or apparent victory.[54] Throughout Mao's writings victory was defined as a largely military construct; for instance, victory cannot be achieved unless there is a "decisive battle between the two armies" (122). This emphasis on the relationship between battle and victory is an important theme in Mao's writings, as seen from his comment that "To accept battle in haste is to fight without being sure of victory" (107).

There was a pragmatic side to Mao's interpretation of victory. In the case of the relationship between the loss of territory and attaining victory, he was willing to accept the former if it meant that "we gain victory over the enemy, plus recovery and also expansion of our territory." Mao argued that "haste" in battle is to "fight without being sure of victory" (107), warning that "it is inadvisable to continue an engagement in which there is no prospect of victory" (139). He suggested that the belief that "strategic victory is determined by tactical successes alone is wrong" (88); rather, as noted earlier, it is determined by a range of military, political, and economic conditions. Thus, he argued that victory can be a cumulative phenomenon in which "many minor victories" can combine to "make a major victory" (159).

As one of the preeminent theorists of guerrilla warfare, Mao outlined six criteria that he argued provide a strategic guide to the successful conduct of guerrilla war: "the use of initiative, flexibility and planning in conducting offensives . . . co-ordination with regular warfare, establishment of base areas, the strategic defense and the strategic offensive, the development of guerrilla warfare into mobile warfare, and correct relationship of command"; these, he stated, are essential to "the winning of final victory" (56–7).[55]

For Mao, victory depended to a significant degree on the ability of the state to mobilize the population. Thus, he noted that "[a] national revolutionary war as great as ours cannot be won without extensive and thoroughgoing political mobilization" (228–9). "There are, of course, many other conditions indispensable to victory, but political mobilization is the most fundamental" (261). He stipulated that "the central task is to mobilize all the nation's forces for victory in the War of Resistance" (194), as the "key to victory in the war now lies in developing the resistance . . . into a war of total resistance by the whole nation" (194–5).

Mao expressed his view of the nature of a great victory when he wrote: "It dealt the enemy a heavy blow, created profound defeatism in the whole enemy camp, elated the people throughout the countryside and laid the foundation for the complete annihilation of the enemy by our army and for final victory."[56] Demoralizing an enemy, encouraging the people, and eventually annihilating the enemy – all are conjoined here in Mao's theory of victory.

ARMORED WARFARE AND VICTORY

There was an active period of debate after World War I about the future of warfare, in particular the development of the tank and its implications for land war. The principal architects of the argument that new technology, particularly armored forces, would alter the logic of war and change the conditions under which states achieve victory included the British theorists J. F. C. Fuller and B. H. Liddell Hart, the German generals Heinz Guderian and Erich von Manstein, and Marshal Mikhail Tukhachevsky of the Soviet Union.

J. F. C. Fuller

The British theorist J. F. C. Fuller (1878–1966) argued in the 1920s that victory is determined in part by the mechanisms or forces of technological progress. Advancing the view that "99 per cent. of victory depends on weapons, machinery placed in the hands of man so that we may kill without being injured,"[57] Fuller was a proponent of the view that science is the "backbone of victory."[58] For him, victory rests ultimately on having the right tools at one's disposal, and the rational strategy for the state is to use all of those tools to achieve "victory at the smallest possible cost."[59] It is the weapons that will permit the state to achieve victory, for "weapons form the direction in which victory must be sought."[60]

Fuller outlined his central precepts regarding the changing nature of war in *On Future War* (1928). He began by noting that the static warfare of the past, of which World War I is an exemplar, will be replaced by what he called a "war of movement" for which "all armies are organizing" (1). Most important, he argued that the "tank is the weapon of the future" (128) because it is "economical as a means of assisting in winning the war" (131). One reason for the importance of the tank is that it "protects the soldier" and has the ability to "safeguard and enforce that will to win which, as heretofore, must remain the driving power behind every battle" (151). Victory in a tactical sense will be determined by the extent to which tanks are employed: "[T]he side which can maintain the greatest number of tanks in the theatre of war will stand the best chance of winning" (148–9).[61]

Emphasizing the role of tanks in winning wars, Fuller argued that the essential condition in war is to occupy the enemy's country. The purpose of military action then, as Fuller proposed in *The Foundations of the Science of War*, is "to compel the enemy to accept the policy in dispute . . . by disarming the enemy and occupying his country."[62] The army must "gain command of the enemy's land," because "Occupation is, in fact, the attainment of this object."[63] En route to effecting this, the war's broader purpose is to "break the will of the enemy army command . . . and the will of the civil population."[64] But "the last and ultimate step is the occupation of the enemy's country, for without this occupation it is most difficult to assure his complete surrender."[65]

In *The Conduct of War, 1789–1961*, Fuller held that victory in war is gained by the ability to "pursue the enemy to the utmost of your power."[66] The use of new technologies was an important way of extending and amplifying that power. Writing in the aftermath of the high-casualty, trench-warfare World War I, Fuller contemplated the possibility that air forces might "replace armies and navies," make war less static and destructive, and "establish a new conception of war."[67] In this more mobile form of warfare, armies would use "fast-moving tanks, supported by aircraft" to defeat the enemy.[68]

What, then, is victory for Fuller? In essence, Fuller connected it with peace, arguing that the "true aim of war is peace and not victory [in which] peace should be the ruling idea of policy, and victory only the means toward its achievement."[69]

B. H. Liddell Hart

A prominent theorist in the interwar military debate was B. H. Liddell Hart (1895–1970), an officer in World War I who survived gassing, retired as captain a decade later, and spent the next fifteen years as a military correspondent, first for the *London Daily Telgraph,* then the *London Times.*

Liddell Hart was a strong proponent of the theory of the defense in war. Having witnessed trench warfare at first hand, he believed that direct attacks against a firmly positioned enemy rarely succeed. A strong defense, especially a mobile, elastic one, would be superior to the enemy's offense and inevitably prevail. Viewing such military forces conducting defensive operations as fundamentally invincible, Liddell Hart argued that focusing on the moral and economic aspects of war could then lead the enemy state to collapse. Although based in defense and attrition rather than offense and annihilation, this approach was still consistent with the idea of war as a total enterprise in which the state must use all of its resources to gain victory, which depends on defeating the enemy's military, economy, and society.[70] For Liddell Hart, though, it was important to note that "History shows that gaining victory is not in itself equivalent to gaining the object of policy."[71]

In contrast with many theorists, Liddell Hart was quite explicit about the nature of victory. In an operational sense, he reasoned that victory would be achieved by the state that, rather than attacking head-on, can use mobility, maneuver, and surprise – what he called the "indirect approach" – to put the enemy off balance and defeat it.[72] His thinking about tanks in warfare was that they should "be concentrated and used in as large masses as possible for a decisive blow against the Achilles' heel of the enemy army, the communications and command centres which form its nerve system."[73]

There is a cautionary tone in Liddell Hart's writings about the role of victory in war: "Victory is not an end in itself. It is worse than useless if the end of the war finds you so exhausted that you are defeated in the peace."[74] He observed that the more effort the state puts "to win victory, the less strength [it] will have to garner its fruits" (177). The implication is that victory should be interpreted in terms of the conditions that will prevail after the war: "It is the statesmen's responsibility . . . to look beyond the military victory, and to ensure that the steps taken for this purpose do not overstrain the fabric of the nation or damage its future" (156). Moreover, victory must in some respect entail the forwarding of the state: "Victory . . . implies that a nation's prospect after the war is better than if it had not made war" (43). Hence victory must be understood in the context of the state's long-term reasons for waging war in the first place. A corollary is that "Victory . . . is only possible if the result is quickly gained – for which only an aggressor can hope – or the effort is economically proportioned to the national resources" (43).[75]

Liddell Hart argued in terms of "keys" to the "lessons of history" that the fundamental purpose of war – as opposed to the "aim of all action in war," which, he concurred with Clausewitz, "is to disarm the enemy" – is to attain what he called a "better state of peace."[76] In this regard, he wrote that a "prosperous and secure peace is a better monument of victory than a pyramid of skulls."[77]

André Maginot

While it had been fashionable within military circles to believe that offensive military power would inevitably overwhelm the enemy, the concept of defensive operations received increasingly serious consideration, and even favor, as a strategy for victory in war, especially in the aftermath of the First World War. Liddell Hart was thus not the only twentieth-century thinker to emphasize the advantage of the defense in war.[78] A critical architect of the defensive strategy in France was André Maginot (1877–1932), who held elected office both before and after the war, received the Médaille Militaire for valor during it, and served on and off as France's Minister of War during the 1920s and early 1930s. Maginot feared that the Treaty of Versailles did not provide sufficient security for France against Germany. Responding to plans proposed by career officer and military engineer Marshal Joseph Joffre, Maginot decided that the way to strengthen France was to build a series of defensive fortifications along France's northeast, bordering on Germany.[79]

Construction of the so-called Maginot Line, with its more than a hundred forts, plus casements and bunkers interconnected by tunnels, took from 1929 to 1936 (with some hurried additions made in 1939–40). For the French these fortifications meant the ability to hold off an enemy attack for two weeks, by means of heavy artillery, providing France a window in which to mobilize fully for war.

The use of massive firepower directed against the enemy was key in defensive theories of war – both by artillery and, later, by military aircraft.[80] The idea was that victory could be achieved by a state that used sufficient firepower to destroy enemy forces before they could successfully overwhelm its defenses, thus preventing the attacker from conducting and winning wars through offensive actions. A successful defensive war depended on the ability of the state to assemble sufficient military and economic power to win while remaining on the defensive. For some military theorists, this was clearly the proper approach to victory.[81]

The Maginot Line of fortifications was the embodiment of French defensive theory. For Maginot and others who favored a strong defensive strategy, the proper use of firepower would decimate attacking military forces, defeat the enemy, and protect the French state. However, these forts and field positions, designed to forestall a German invasion, did not prove successful. In the Battle of France (May 10, 1940), Germany was able to make an end run around these defenses, driving a new generation of tanks (see next section) through the forests and hills of Ardennes – territory that had been deemed impassable for armored vehicles at the time Maginot's plans were being realized.

Erich von Manstein and Heinz Guderian

During the interwar period (1920s–1930s), two German officers in particular greatly advanced the concept of armored forces in the future playing a prominent role in achieving victory: Erich von Manstein and Heinz Guderian.

Field Marshal Erich von Manstein (1887–1973), who was credited by J. F. C. Fuller as the master of the blitzkrieg, defended the proposition that victories were won on the basis of the "self-sacrifice, valour and devotion to duty" of German soldiers.[82] He is best known for his promoting a highly mobile and flexible form of defense, in which armies willingly relinquish territory in order to encourage enemy forces to overextend themselves to the point where they would be vulnerable to counterattack. This position was in direct variance to Hitler's orders during the campaign on the Eastern Front against Russia, which advocated an attrition-based form of war. Overall, Manstein was a vocal supporter of the view that mechanized forces could achieve decisive results by attacking France by passing through the Ardennes.[83] (As we have just seen, he was proven correct.) He also was a prominent proponent of the idea that the use of armored forces more generally to conduct highly mobile land warfare would lead to victory.[84]

General Heinz Wilhelm Guderian (1888–1954) had seen how the collapse of mobile warfare in World War I had led to a stalemate that over four years produced millions of casualties.[85] In his influential book *Achtung Panzer!* (1937), which was very important in the development of tank warfare, he described how to translate the idea of mechanized warfare into the practical instrument of war known as the Panzer division.[86] In summary, his principal belief was that tanks "are today the best means available for a land attack."[87] In terms of the "significant characteristics of tanks," Guderian believed that their movement in battle is the most decisive. As he quoted the Army General Staff's *The Review of Military Science,* "'only movement brings victory'." Furthermore, "We believe that by attacking with tanks we can achieve a higher rate of movement than has been hitherto obtainable."[88] Ultimately, "'the architect of victory' is not the infantry but the tanks themselves, for if the tank attack fails, then the whole operation is a failure, whereas if tanks succeed, then victory follows."[89] With respect to the firepower of tanks, Guderian argued that "we intend to achieve victory . . . by carrying the attack quickly into the enemy's midst, [and] by firing our motorised guns with their protective armour direct into the target."[90]

Guderian's argument, which he acknowledged was derived directly from the writings of Fuller and Liddell Hart,[91] was that victory is achieved when mechanized armies of tanks, working in close coordination with air power and artillery, penetrate deep into enemy territory.[92] Armor advocates like Guderian argued strenuously that victory would depend on putting panzer divisions "in the forefront of the attack from the very beginning [because] they would thus achieve a deep and rapid break-through."[93] Guderian's revolutionary ideas of optimal tank deployment transcended the problems of positional warfare that had led to stalemate and overwhelming human losses on the battlefields of World War I. With his new theory of armored warfare, he rejected the emphasis on defense, position, and attrition that had dominated military operations during that war. In its place he envisioned armored forces able to conduct the highly mobile maneuver warfare that became known as blitzkrieg.[94]

Mikhail Tukhachevsky

An important interwar theorist of the nature of land war was Mikhail Tukhachevsky (1893–1937), who served as the Red Army's chief of staff, deputy commissar for defense, and later a marshal of the Soviet Union. His principal contribution to the literature on military strategy in the 1920s and 1930s was what became known as the theory of *deep operations,* in which the fundamental objective of armored formations was to attack deep behind enemy lines in order to disrupt the opposition's system of logistics. His ideas about deep operations were consistent with the blitzkrieg, used so successfully by the German Wehrmacht in World War II. Although executed in 1937 during Stalin's purges of the Red Army leadership, Tukhachevsky was nonetheless one of the principal architects of the system that combined highly mobile land warfare with armored forces to achieve victory.

Tukhachevsky's ideas about victory fall into three main categories. The first involves his emphasis on the principles of total war, urging the state to organize its planning and economy so as to win wars. As noted by Condoleezza Rice, "Tukhachevsky went on to suggest that to be really secure, industrial plans and war plans had to be coordinated."[95] The implication is that victory for the Soviet Union would depend on its ability to mobilize all of its economic resources with optimum effectiveness. Thus Tukhachevsky promoted the idea that victory may well depend on a state's willingness and ability to mobilize for total war.

The second is his argument that the most efficient way to achieve victory would be to fight offensive wars based on *combined-arms operations,* using "motorized rifle units, self-propelled artillery, and aviation to achieve breakthrough."[96] As Rice observed, the concept of combined-arms operations was attractive because of its embrace of the "concept of decisive and total victory and in its compatibility with the primacy of the offense."[97] In this sense, Tukhachevsky identified his ideological affiliation with the tenets of Marxism–Leninism, arguing in classic terms that "victory in the next war would depend on an offensive blow that would shock the weakened capitalist countries suffering from deep class divisions."[98]

The third critical idea that emerged in Tukhachevsky's work was the above-mentioned concept of deep operations, which dominated Soviet military planning as well as strategy during the 1930s and throughout World War II. When Stalin and his senior military commanders confronted Germany's invasion in June 1941, their fundamental strategy was based on the idea promulgated by Tukhachevsky that victory would depend on offensive, mobile operations conducted in depth as well as the total mobilization of the Soviet economy. As Rice argued, "Russia's victory in World War II was in many ways a victory for the concept of the whole country mobilized for war."[99]

Overall, Tukhachevsky greatly influenced the Soviet Union's approach to war through his principle that victory is based on the effective use of offensive operations by a society whose economy is totally mobilized.

In the end, these theorists, in particular Fuller and Liddell Hart, made significant contributions to the debate about land war as a result of their emphasis on the future role of tanks.[100] Fuller and Liddell Hart understood that "machines such as tanks would play an increasingly important part in future war" (601). Liddell Hart emphasized the role of infantry in mechanized warfare; Fuller argued that infantry played the lesser role of defending communications and bases (601–2). In positing that in the case of land warfare the defense is "superior to the attack" (612), Liddell Hart held that it was essential for states to develop mechanized forces that could conduct highly mobile operations. The purpose, for these two strategists, was to "restore mobility, minimize casualties, and secure a speedy victory by means of small, elite, professional mechanized armies" (622). In effect, they began the process of reconceptualizing the nature of land warfare, looking ahead to a time when states armed with tanks could pursue highly mobile warfare rather than the static, attrition based combat that dominated World War I – even if they did not fully comprehend the magnitude of the change that would be created by the combination of tanks and air power.[101]

Although the contributions of all these theorists were more about how to wage war and less about how to measure victory, their ideas helped shape the development of armored warfare as the new instrument for achieving victory.

MARITIME WARFARE AND VICTORY

Alfred Thayer Mahan and Julian Corbett

The American naval historian and strategist Alfred Thayer Mahan (1840–1914), who served as a Union officer in the Civil War, argued in his *Influence of Sea Power on World History* that strong naval and commercial fleets are critical to the nation's military power.[102] Mahan understood that the development of industrial power would increase a state's tendency to engage in wars over empire and global markets, leading to an expansion of state power.[103] But this also meant that states must be prepared to wage great wars in which the objective is to defeat the enemy on a grand scale.

Taking a Jominian approach, Mahan pursued the development of permanent principles that would guide maritime warfare, contending that "War has such principles [whose] existence is detected by the study of the past, which reveals them in successes and in failures."[104] Victory, he argued, "would, now as ever, result from the application of the principles which had led to the success of great generals in all ages."[105] Victory at sea entailed being able to control seaborne trade, possess greater force, and concentrate naval power at the right moment.[106] Yet he also understood the vital importance of nonmilitary political solutions: "Indeed, in peace [the state] may gain its most decisive victories by occupying in a country, either by purchase or treaty, excellent positions which would perhaps hardly be got by war."[107]

The prominent British naval historian and strategist Sir Julian Stafford Corbett (1854–1922) argued that the "one legitimate object [in war is] the overthrow of the enemy's means of resistance, and that the primary object must always be his armed forces."[108] Using the concept of "decisive victory," Corbett questioned current doctrine that victory is derived from defeating the military forces of the enemy. Although he rejected the idea that the purpose of naval warfare is to conquer territory (90) – the sea being something a state might be able to control but not to own – he argued that states should use victory at sea for the "capture or destruction of the enemy's property" (96), such as warships and merchant ships, so as to ensure free passage for the victor.

Admiral Alfred von Tirpitz

The German admiral Alfred von Tirpitz (1849–1930), commander of the Imperial Navy during the first half of World War I, agreed with Mahan's point when he held that a state could not be a great power unless it possessed naval forces and interests around the world.[109] As he wrote in his memoirs, "war could not be won, even in a military sense, without a sound policy which gave due weight to the naval position."[110] For Tirpitz, the "real aim" in war is "to strike at the heart of the Coalition" (5). More broadly, he argued that "Partial victories over lesser opponents are at best only means to the end"; and he lamented that states may be victorious in engagements, but "unable . . . to achieve any lasting political result" (29–30).

By implication, victory for Tirpitz is a strategic matter that rests on more than simply winning battles. In the case of World War I, he observed that "We ought to do more than just win battles, if we are to come out of this war with a prospect of rebuilding Germany" (234). In a subtle way, Tirpitz was arguing that the state has some obligations when the war is over. The conduct of war should therefore not be left to military authorities alone. The problem, as he argued, was that "The German Government had never approached the question how one should win a war, simply leaving the matter to the General Staff of the army, which in its turn was not competent to deal with the political, economic, and naval questions raised by a world-war" (26–7).

Admiral Raoul Castex

In his *Strategic Theories*, the French vice admiral Raoul Castex (1878–1968) defined "strategy" as that which "treats the totality of war, embracing war as a *whole* and, especially, its directing principles."[111] He continued by noting that, while Napoléon never used the word "strategy," preferring "grand tactics," Clausewitz argued that "strategy encompasses everything that happens on the battlefield" (3).

As a maritime theorist, it was natural for Castex to define victory in terms of sea power; however, he did not view victory solely through that lens, seeing a strong connection to what transpires on land. Discussing the concept of mastery of the sea, he stated that "Victory very frequently requires forcing a decision by more dynamic exploitation of sea power," which could be accomplished by "attacking or even invading the enemy's coasts" (43). Moreover, he noted that "Only victory on land permits the occupation of the enemy's territory. . . . Sea power is important to the extent that it contributes to victory on land" (43). While he argued that "only in exceptional cases does [sea power] achieve complete victory by itself" (43), Castex asserted that the "command of the sea again becomes a necessary condition for victory" (48).[112] Based on these comments about victory, it is clear that Castex distinguished between the concept of "complete victory" and lesser forms of victory that have occurred in wars (48).

The ideas of these land and naval theorists (and others) had important implications for the theory of victory. One is that the military and economic objectives of war are so intertwined that victory might entail the destruction of the state's armed forces as well as of the society itself. This means that victory belongs to the state able to annihilate the enemy's society and to destroy its military forces, not simply the latter. Previously, the foundations of victory had been based on the destruction of the enemy's armed forces, but with the advent of modern military technologies, policymakers and military officials could formulate victory as the product of both approaches. By the late nineteenth century ideas about victory had emerged that were consistent with the interpretation of a state's military forces and its economic foundations as legitimate and essential targets in war. The twentieth-century emphasis on targeting both military forces and society accompanied the development of military technologies, such as air power, that would permit the state to wage war with the intent of destroying both.

AIR WARFARE AND VICTORY

As already noted regarding the use of tanks, twentieth-century military strategists actively sought to understand the relationship between technology and victory. Perhaps the most significant technological development early in the century was the creation of viable aircraft. This led the strategic community, including the noteworthy figures of Giulio Douhet and Billy Mitchell, to propose that warfare conducted from the air represented a revolutionary development in military strategy and that air power would decisively change the nature of war. These ideas were amply demonstrated during the First World War, when states first had the opportunity to use aircraft in combat on a large scale.

Giulio Douhet

Of the earliest theorists of air power, the most prominent and influential was the Italian artillery officer Giulio Douhet (1869–1930), who led various Italian aviation efforts both before the First World War and again toward its end. He disagreed with the French General Staff, who were dazzled by the myth of the ground offensive, as expressed by their prewar philosophy of "Forward, and trust in victory."[113] By 1915, Douhet was propounding a theory of total war in which the state aimed to crush the morale of the civilian population by targeting people directly from the air. As a critical advocate of the idea of the "destruction of nations" from above,[114] Douhet is among the preeminent theorists of the influence of air power on modern war.[115] Author of *The Command of the Air* (1921) and *Probable Aspects of the War of the Future* (1928), he was a firm proponent of the importance of the air offensive in war, calling it "indisputable" that "wars [and victory] can be won only by offensive action" and noting that "by virtue of increased fire power, offensive operations demand a much larger force proportionately than defensive ones."[116] More important, he contended that "To be defeated in the air . . . is finally to be defeated and at the mercy of the enemy, with no chance at all of defending oneself, compelled to accept whatever terms he sees fit to dictate" (23). For Douhet, it was axiomatic that "To conquer the command of the air means victory" (25), given the newfound ability to "deprive the enemy of all means of flying, by striking him in the air, at his bases of operation, or at his production centers" (28).

Douhet's theory of air power rested on the proposition that air forces should achieve air superiority first, then focus on strategic bombing attacks against cities and industrial centers, while maintaining a defensive ground-force posture. By pursuing the simultaneous bombing of cities, industrial facilities, and railroads, he argued that it would be possible to defeat the enemy relatively quickly, perhaps in a matter of several days. As a contributor to the concept of total war,[117] he held that air power, then heralded as an exemplary modern technology of war, would radically transform the military power of states. Douhet established the intellectual basis for the argument that air power provided a unique instrument for achieving victory on a massive and perhaps global scale.

Douhet is famous for his aphorism that "Victory smiles upon those who anticipate the changes in the character of war, not upon those who wait to adapt themselves after the changes occur" (30). His explicit argument is that the development of air power coincides with a "new character of war," which "will surely make for swift, crushing decisions on the battlefield." In these "new" wars, victory will follow for those who "win with the fewest sacrifices and the minimum expenditure of means" (30). For this strategy to succeed, the nation must have an independent air force because this has been "shown to be the best way to assure victory." Such an air force must "be capable of winning the struggle for the command of the war," and "be capable of exploiting the command of the air, once it has been conquered, with forces capable of crushing the material and moral resistance of the enemy" (98).[118] The determinant of victory in this era of aerial warfare is the "fire power" that aircraft can deliver against targets at any location in a state (44). In operational terms, Douhet observed that aerial bombardment "will certainly have more influence on the realization of victory than a battle of the kind often fought during the last war [World War I] without appreciable results" (140). Arguing that victories with air power can be more decisive and efficient than those gained through attrition in land wars, Douhet postulated that the defeat of the enemy through the use of airborne bombs would occur on a scale and at a pace without historical precedent.

The strategist Bernard Brodie (see later in the chapter) argued in *Strategy in the Missile Age* that war for Douhet is by necessity total: "Every war *must* be a total war, regardless of the powers waging it, the causes of the conflict, or the original objectives of the statesmen who have let themselves be drawn into it."[119] "War must be total because the decision," according to Douhet, "must depend upon smashing the material and moral resources of a people . . . until the final collapse of all social organization."[120] As suggested by these ideas, Douhet's theory of war rests on two critical assumptions. The first was that aircraft created an offensive instrument in war against which the state cannot effectively defend itself; the second was that the bombardment of urban areas from the air will shatter the morale of the civilian population and lead to the state's defeat.[121] For a state embracing this strategy of aerial bombardment, victory would be inevitable,[122] as relentless annihilation from the air will drive the enemy society toward complete political, economic, and social collapse.[123] (This theory of war was translated almost directly into the U.S. strategic bombing campaign in World War II and later during the cold war into the nuclear war plans of the U.S. Strategic Air Command.)[124]

A further example of Douhet's influence on theories of victory was his argument that urban and industrial centers are the most critical targets in war, not the military targets that had dominated debates among earlier generations of strategists. His position was that using bomber forces to attack the state's vital political and industrial centers would lead to victory relatively quickly and without the need for large ground and naval forces.[125] While the objective of destroying cities in war was not new, for Douhet this line of thinking represented, according to one industrialist, "the center of a complete body of military doctrine."[126]

The principles Douhet advanced would have a decisive effect on the theory of victory in the decades preceding the outbreak of World War II.

General William "Billy" Mitchell

A contemporary theorist of Douhet, whom he met in 1922, General William "Billy" Mitchell (1879–1936) was one whose thoughts were of major importance in shaping U.S. defense policy. Mitchell argued that victory is shaped by the technology of air power and the ideology among policymakers and strategists that states should totally and permanently defeat one another. He proposed that if victory is to be permanent, "the hostile nation's power to make war must be destroyed – this means the factories, the means of communication, the food producers, even the farms, the fuel and oil supplies, and the places where people live and carry on their daily lives."[127]

Since his ideas were dominated by the technology of air power, Mitchell's framework for victory was based on Douhet's idea that total devastation, now accepted as a fundamental principle of war, could be accomplished by targeting the resources that are necessary for people to survive in a modern society. Mitchell argued that air power strengthened the emerging theory of victory because it gives states the power to "go straight to the vital centers [of a society] and either neutralize or destroy them," which inevitably "has put a completely new complexion on the old system of making war" (498). He argued for a theory of victory relying on air power because the "real objective" of war is to destroy "vital centers," by which he meant cities, factories, and human dwellings. Furthermore, he suggested that the "hostile main army in the field is a false objective." Thus, if the ultimate objective of war is to destroy population centers and resources, air power, according to Mitchell, will enable rapid victory by raising "such havoc or the threat of such havoc in the opposing country that a long-drawn-out campaign will be impossible" (498).

Mitchell's ideas shaped the theory of victory prevalent during the Second World War and into the subsequent nuclear age. He was hesitant, however, about developing a universal theory of war that would apply to all states in all instances.[128] For him, the critical objective was to simply describe the "best and most efficient way for our country to prepare for a probable future war" (500).

Alexander P. de Seversky

Born in Russian Georgia, the naval ace, aircraft designer, and theorist Alexander P. de Seversky (1894–1974) emigrated to the United States soon after the Russian Revolution, becoming a test pilot and aeronautical engineer with the U.S. Army Air Corps. He also served as a consultant and advisor to Billy Mitchell and was granted citizenship in 1927.

Seversky's thoughts about aviation's place in warfare had much in common with those of Mitchell and Douhet. In his 1942 *Victory through Air Power*, Seversky held that the "aim of total war is total destruction," and more generally that the development of air power had created a revolutionary instrument for achieving victory.[129] Air power, for Seversky, "has achieved primacy in modern warfare," and "those who do not grasp these elementary truths are unsuited to plan the strategy and the equipment for victory."[130] He contended that "air power must be the backbone of any successful strategy" in war, and that a "revolution in national thinking is essential before we can proceed to mobilize the men, the ideas, and the weapons for victory."[131] When a state's war machine can employ air power against its enemy, the state has at its disposal a "new approach to the problem of achieving victory under totally new conditions."[132] Seversky's ideas as to the transcendent importance of air power would resonate throughout military thinking and strategy over the course of the twentieth century.

The development of a concept of victory as achieved by means of air power, articulated by Douhet, Mitchell, and Seversky, further encouraged the trend toward total war. Meanwhile, the rise of the absolutist ideologies of totalitarianism, communism, and Nazism in the twentieth century reinforced the idea that victory exists when the enemy's society, government, military, and economy – the "total national life of the enemy" – are threatened with absolute defeat and destruction.[133] Total war was seen as a means to such a victory.

President Roosevelt reaffirmed the principle of total war when he asserted, in a fireside chat on May 2, 1943, "our determination to fight this total war with our total will and our total power" until the United States achieved "victory."[134] Yet while the United States embraced the concept, from a theoretical standpoint World War II was not a total war: Contrary to the classical definition, none of the combatants, with the exception of Great Britain, mobilized its total resources to wage the war; nor did any use all the weapons at its disposal (notably, chemical or biological ones). But these theoretical distinctions notwithstanding, World War II is rightly considered to be a total war because the combatants used every weapon that they believed necessary and appropriate to winning.[135] These were, of course, to include the atomic bomb.

COLD WAR AND NUCLEAR WEAPONS

After millennia spent trying to understand and identify the fundamental rules that govern victory, societies saw much of that thinking nullified by what transpired at the end of World War II and in its aftermath – notably the development and proliferation of nuclear weapons. This effectively shifted the meaning of victory from the historical one of winning a war to the cold-war principle of avoiding one. (See also Chapter 5's section on the cold war.)

Bernard Brodie

Writing soon after the attack on Pearl Harbor, the American military strategist Bernard Brodie (1910–78; at RAND 1951–66) noted Japan's "faith in victory" and observed that victory is a hollow concept if the state wins "simply by standing interminably on the defensive."[136] In that same work, *A Layman's Guide to Naval Strategy*, he wrote that, in the United States, the public elects "politicians whose policies may . . . greatly affect the price of victory."[137] By early August 1945, two atomic bombs had been dropped on Japan, dramatically altering that price.

Societies, after spending millennia trying to understand and identify the fundamental rules that govern victory, saw much of that thinking nullified by what transpired at the end of World War II and in its aftermath – notably the development and proliferation of nuclear weapons. "Following World War I it became axiomatic that modern war means total war";[138] but in the face of such weaponry, "no victory . . . would be worth the price,"[139] because of their "utterly revolutionary and potentially annihilistic effects."[140] The atomic bomb had changed the ultimate nature and purpose of war. What emerged in this postwar era was that victory in the presence of nuclear weapons was a concept largely without practical meaning or significance for policymakers.

For Brodie, in *The Absolute Weapon* (1946), what was eminently rational was the logic of *deterrence:* "The general idea is that if the enemy hits us, we will kill him."[141] Thus "the bomb may act as a powerful deterrent to direct aggression against great powers without preventing the political crises out of which wars generally develop."[142] Deterrence ultimately rests on the ability to "eliminate the cities of the other," which is "practically tantamount to final victory, provided always [one's] own cities are not similarly eliminated."[143] As Brodie observed, "Victory is the payoff, and therefore the confirmation of correct decision[s]" in war.[144] The only sensible principle for the nuclear powers was that "thermonuclear war between them is simply forbidden."[145] As he famously wrote in 1946, "Thus far the chief purpose of our military establishment has been to win wars. From now on its chief purpose must be to avert them."[146] Brodie also noted that "curtailing . . . our taste for unequivocal victory is one of the prices we pay to keep the physical violence, and thus the costs and penalties, from going beyond the level of the tolerable."[147]

Paul Kecskemeti

The Hungarian-born sociologist Paul Kecskemeti (1901–80), who lived in the United States as of 1942, defined the classic objective of total victory this way in his 1958 RAND analysis *Strategic Surrender:* "one side achieves a monopoly of armed strength and the other is reduced to defenselessness."[148] Arguing that the state can achieve total victory by either "disruption" (i.e., overcoming enemy resistance in pitched battle) or "siege or attrition," Kecskemeti suggested that military leaders would choose disruption when the enemy's "entire strength is concentrated in a field army," whereas attrition was more appropriate when the "enemy is entrenched behind a strong fortification" (6).[149] But with the development of nuclear weapons, he noted, theories of victory based on classic attrition strategies are now and perhaps forever obsolete (8).

Kecskemeti described surrender as "an agreement under which active hostilities cease and control over the loser's remaining military capability is vested in the winner" (5). In a *strategic* surrender, "What the loser avoids by offering to surrender is a last, chaotic round of fighting that would have the characteristics of a rout. . . . [The victor] can obtain his objective without paying the costs of a last battle" (8).

Building on these observations, Kecskemeti pointed out a fundamental feature of victory that many seem to have missed. "victory, defeat, and stalemate, when used to characterize the final outcome of wars rather than the outcome of military engagements, are not absolute, but relative, concepts" (20). He also noted that whether a state can be said to have achieved strategic victory is always bounded by uncertainty (208). Thus, although Germany suffered the defeat of total war and strategic surrender in 1918, the Allies' complete "victory" after World War I (232–4) had no permanent value for England and France, both of which had suffered extraordinary human losses in the course of "winning" (121–5). In World War II, Kecskemeti argued, the Allies sought total victory, which they achieved by mandating the terms of peace and refusing to negotiate with the Axis powers (215); yet theirs was a "hollow victory" (234), because their demand for strategic surrender forced the Axis powers to fight a war of attrition to the point where the Allies too were physically and economically exhausted.[150]

Raymond Aron

Nuclear weapons forced strategists and policymakers to wrestle with what it meant to achieve victory in a war fought with absolute weapons. The French philosopher, political scientist, and sociologist Raymond Aron (1905–83) concluded early in the nuclear age that "the only road to victory would be the avoidance of war," because the "spoils of victory could no longer be commensurate with the cost of battle." The obvious reason, for Aron, is that there are "ways of conquering that quickly transform victory into defeat."[151]

The broader point for Aron was that in the "pre-nuclear days it was rationally conceivable to aim at absolute victory in terms of disarming the enemy and thereafter to limit the fruits of victory"; but in the nuclear age it is "no longer necessary to disarm a country in order to annihilate it."[152] Aron also observed that the nuclear weapon "constitutes a supremely efficient instrument" for "imposing a Carthaginian peace" because the "extermination of the enemy can precede victory."[153]

Vasily D. Sokolovskii

One of the more influential works by Soviet strategists was *Soviet Military Strategy*, which was published in 1963 and edited by Marshal of the Soviet Union Vasily D. Sokolovskii (1897–1968), who had been a key figure in resisting and repelling the German invasion of 1941. Soviet strategists during the cold war subordinated all considerations to the conditions that are necessary to achieve "world-wide historical victories of the international revolutionary movement of the working class."[154] Sokolovskii argued that any war between the "opposing world social systems . . . will inevitably end with the victory of the progressive, communist social and economic system over the reactionary, capitalist social and economic system, which is historically doomed to destruction."[155] He distinguished between the principles of *partial victory* and *final victory:* The former involved "partial successes on various fronts and in various spheres of military operation,"[156] whereas the latter entailed the ability to "smash the enemy's armed forces completely, deprive him of strategic areas of deployment, liquidate his military bases, and occupy his strategically important regions" (71).[157] However, even final victory was at risk because states cannot be defeated by one attack. As Mikhail V. Frunze (1885–1925), a Bolshevik leader and revolutionary, was quoted in *Soviet Military Strategy*, "Even the complete defeat of an enemy army at a given moment does not assure final victory as long as the defeated forces are supported by an economically and morally strong rear" (230). Furthermore, Soviet strategists argued that "final victory will be attained only as a result of the combined efforts of all the branches of the armed forces" (313).

During the prenuclear age, the leaders of the Soviet state had equated victory with the total overthrow of the existing social and political structure of power within societies and throughout the international system. "Can the final victory of socialism be attained in a single country without the joint efforts of the proletariat in several advanced countries?" he asked. "No, it cannot."[158] Soviet-era strategists and ideologists remained uniformly consistent in relating victory to the triumph of socialism over capitalism. During the early decades of the twentieth century, Soviet strategic thinking about victory emphasized the "annihilation and total defeat of the enemy."[159] Thus, the purpose of Soviet military doctrine was to "defeat the enemy forces, occupy his territory, crush his will to resist, and achieve final victory" (235).

This position grew increasingly unrealistic given the development of nuclear weapons and the emphasis in the West on avoiding rather than waging wars. Writing during the nuclear age, Soviet strategists contended that a state could not necessarily "achieve a victory in a war with an opponent who did possess such [nuclear] weapons" (101). Yet such a war, if there was one, would be waged by "massive missile blows to destroy the aggressor's instruments for nuclear attack and, simultaneously, to destroy and devastate on a large scale the vitally important enemy targets . . . [so as] to attain victory within the shortest possible time" (313).

Although both numerical superiority and morale may contribute to a state achieving victory, neither can guarantee it. As *Soviet Military Strategy* notes, "Victory in war is determined not only by superiority in the military and technical sense . . . but also by the ability to organize the defeat of the enemy and make effective use of available weapons" (314–15). A related tenet in Soviet thinking was the importance of the "maximum mobilization of their [economic] resources and strength in order to gain victory," because as affirmed in *Soviet Military Strategy*, "Lenin showed that once it comes to war, everything must be subordinated to its interests" (274). In terms of the influence of morale, Sokolovskii cited Lenin's observation that "our proletariat, weak in numbers, exhausted by calamity and privation, was victorious because it was strong in morale" (123–4).

Henry Kissinger

The German-born Henry Kissinger (1923–) came to the United States in 1938 and gained citizenship five years later; he would eventually serve first as National Security Advisor and then Secretary of State during the Nixon and Ford administrations. In his *Nuclear Weapons and Foreign Policy* (1957), he formulated the basic argument about victory that would dominate strategic thinking during the nuclear age: "nuclear stalemate can be taken to mean that victory in all-out war has become meaningless."[160] As one of the principal architects of the postatomic theory of limited war, he observed that the quest for total victory can have paralyzing effects on the state.[161] The central problem for Kissinger was that the U.S. strategic doctrine governing the relationship between diplomacy and military matters "recognized few intermediate points between total war and total peace," principally because the prevailing theory of war was "based on the necessity of total victory."[162] In analytic terms, his argument was that the existence of nuclear weapons undermines the search for and the relevance of a practical theory of victory.

With the development of nuclear weapons, Kissinger argued that strategists, policymakers, and military officials – such as General Douglas MacArthur, who wanted to rain atomic bombs on China in retaliation for its direct involvement in the Korean War – denied "the existence of any middle ground between stalemate and total victory" (34). He contended that Americans were particularly resistant to renouncing total victory because the "destructiveness of modern weapons deprives victory in an all-out war of its historical meaning" (107), including such concepts as physical occupation. He thereby rejected the principle in U.S. strategy that equates victory with "breaking the enemy's will to resist and its reliance on the decisive role of industrial potential" (104). The danger for Kissinger was that "When the purpose of war became total victory . . . the result was a conflict of ever increasing violence" (106). For Kissinger, the core of the issue was that American strategic doctrine since World War I has rested on possessing "forces-in-being at the beginning of a war [that] need only be large enough to avoid disaster" because "mobilizing our industrial potential [would crush the enemy] after the outbreak of hostilities" (107).

As one would expect, the imbalance between victory and nuclear weapons represented a strategic problem of immense proportions for states seeking to manage diplomatic relations during the cold war. Central to Kissinger's work, therefore, is the recognition of the importance and difficulty of controlling escalation in crises, for the simple reason that nuclear-armed states will always seek to avert being drawn into a full-scale nuclear war (176–7). He argued that it is imperative for leaders to "understand that total victory is no longer possible" (143), given that the "search for absolute victory . . . paralyzes by the vastness of its consequences" (196).

VICTORY ALTERED

Believing that victory was not possible in the nuclear age on any traditional scale, some strategists defined victory in terms of political–military outcomes. In *On Thermonuclear War*, Herman Kahn (1922–83), a military strategist at the RAND Corporation, argued for a clear second-strike capability, to serve as a strong deterrent; for "when governments are informed of the terrible consequences of a nuclear war they will realize there could be no victors."[163] Kahn also used the phrase "prevail . . . if you cannot win," emphasizing the survivability of nuclear war in order to avoid distinguishing between the concepts of victory and defeat.[164] The economist and arms-control theoretician

Thomas C. Schelling (1921–) argued in *Arms and Influence* that nuclear weapons undermined victory as a practical principle of diplomacy because they could inflict "monstrous violence to the enemy without first achieving victory."[165] He also pointed out that "victory inadequately expresses what a nation wants from its military forces."[166] When the historical purpose of war for the United States was total victory – which the nation had experienced on a grand scale as recently as World War II – the state had gravitated toward policies calling for mobilizing all of the nation's economic capacity to produce weapons to destroy the enemy's will and ability to fight.[167] However, as Paul Kecskemeti warned, the "worst strategic outcome will no longer be defenselessness but utter destruction of the entire society."[168]

Policymakers soon realized that diplomacy in the nuclear age was fundamentally incompatible with any traditional definition of victory, such as a defeated government accepting the terms imposed by the victor. But though total war was no longer a useful instrument of national policy, victory might still be relevant if only in the limited sense of a state seeking to prevent the enemy from gaining victory.[169] As General Curtis LeMay remarked in a speech at the National War College in April 1956, "The most radical effect of the changes in warfare [i.e., nuclear weapons] is not upon how wars are won or lost, but upon how they will start."[170] The consensus among strategists and policymakers was that starting a nuclear war is an irrational objective for the state; victory would be such an impossibility as to persuade policymakers to avoid war in the first place. The alternative to peace, as Robert Oppenheimer wrote in *Foreign Affairs* in 1953, is war equivalent to "two scorpions in a bottle, each capable of killing the other, but only at the risk of his own life."[171] For Kecskemeti, nuclear weapons are so destructive that "the losses they cause must far outweigh any political advantage that might be derived from victory"; in practical terms, "strategic victory will be meaningful . . . only in wars that are non-total" – that is, wars that do not involve the use of nuclear weapons.[172] It is as a result of this debate that the theory and practice of deterrence entered the lexicon of the cold war as an instrument for managing the well-understood calculus of risks.[173]

Once strategists and policymakers understood that nuclear weapons had destroyed the practical relevance of the objective of grand strategic victory, the debate shifted to the development of the theory of limited war and the possibilities for limited victory.[174] One of the more prominent thinkers was the foreign-policy expert Robert E. Osgood (1921–86), whose *Limited War* focused on the nature of, and distinctions among, limited, unlimited, and total war. The American approach to war, he argued, has been to achieve "clear-cut, definitive" victories as effectively and quickly as possible and then to return to politics as usual.[175] As Osgood noted, "military victory, no matter how it comes about, at least provides the nation with the opportunity to solve its political problems later."[176] With this approach – a cycle of "unpreparedness, mobilization, overwhelming offensive, total victory, and demobilization" – the United States had shown by the late 1950s a remarkable potential for organizing itself to defeat a traditional enemy.[177] Yet despite its record of achieving overwhelming victories against its enemies, the United States was forced to alter its basic approach to war and victory once nuclear weapons entered the equation, since the constraints they imposed on action invalidated the concept of victory.

At the beginning of the nuclear age, the attempts of strategists and policymakers to manage the challenges for victory posed by nuclear weapons were dominated by theories of strategic bombardment. The debate began with the observation, drawn from the literature on air power, that the basis for victory in war is to attack political, economic, and military targets. But when it was grasped that nuclear weapons nullified these ideas, the foreign-policy establishment concluded that nuclear-armed warplanes could not produce victory in a meaningful fashion.[178] This view was expressed by Michael Howard, who observed that "It became almost impossible to visualize any political objective for which the use of such weapons would be appropriate."[179]

Once it was grasped that these weapons made victory impossible, the whole concept of victory was seen as an inherently irrational line of inquiry – except for a few spirited discussions among strategists.[180] Thus, early in the nuclear age, systematic discussions about victory rightly disappeared from the strategic literature, until eventually the idea of victory was no longer in vogue intellectually.[181] With nuclear weapons firmly embedded in strategic discourse, the principal conclusion among strategists and policymakers was that states have a profound obligation to deter their use. It was this concept that dominated how the administrations of all cold-war presidents – from Harry S. Truman to George H. W. Bush – translated the ideas of nuclear deterrence into policies that would allow the United States to defend its vital interests without engaging in a mutually annihilative war. Beginning with the concept of massive retaliation and proceeding through the various theories of nuclear strategy – mutual assured destruction, flexible response, limited nuclear war, and counterforce strategies – these ideas about deterrence rested principally on avoiding the use of this weaponry.[182]

Nuclear arms dominated defense planning during the cold war through debates about the role and importance of conventional military forces in helping states deter war and defend their interests.[183] Given the strategic stalemate that these weapons produced, some theorists argued that the way to manage political struggles was to shift the discussion to conventional war – as long as we understood that the prospect of defeat could instantly trigger the nuclear war that states sought to avoid in the first place.[184]

Thus, as societies grappled with the problems of total war, whether nuclear or conventional, victory as a practical option was not taken to be a serious point of contention among strategists and policymakers. Indeed, B. H. Liddell Hart argued in his 1950 *Defence of the West* that relying on nuclear weapons was dangerous because it rested on the risky assumption that victory in *any* form could emerge as the outcome of a struggle between nuclear-armed antagonists.[185]

Recall that Liddell Hart's principal argument about victory, formulated in the prenuclear age (see the section "Armored Warfare and Victory" above), rested on the proposition that "military victory is not in itself equivalent to gaining the object of war."[186] By this he meant that attaining military victory will not necessarily produce strategic victory. Moreover, when statesmen consider the advantages of victory, they must evaluate the "ultimate effect of the extra moral and economic loss suffered in reaching it" (44). Raising the question of the costs and benefits of war and victory, Liddell Hart warned about the "semblance of victory" that exists when the nation's efforts to win "cost them such a price, in moral and physical exhaustion, that they, the seeming victors, were left incapable of consolidating their position" (45). Liddell Hart contended that, for aggressors, the "pursuit of victory is likely to bring them more loss than gain" (177). These ideas as to the limits of victory are of interest particularly because they are still quite familiar despite having been voiced before 1945.

The cold war ideological struggle between democracies and totalitarian states also influenced the theory of victory, although to a lesser degree than the nuclear debate.[187] The concept of victory in a revolutionary war, which is interpreted to mean seizing political power within or against a state by force, was more meaningful at a time when states in Asia and Latin America were engaged in struggles that sought to achieve a victory, to use the language of communism, against the ruling classes. Contrary to the consensus that victory was not possible in the nuclear age, it *was* quite possible for revolutionary groups to achieve it, as did North Vietnam against South Vietnam and Fidel Castro in Cuba, to name but two instances. To complicate matters, revolutionary wars often involved states or factions within states that were allied with the major powers, which often played a supporting role in these struggles. The prospect that defeat by a faction supported by a major state might escalate into a crisis involving the great powers undermined the latters' credibility. This was not simply a theoretical distinction, as seen by active debates in the Johnson and Nixon administrations about whether the escalation of American involvement in Vietnam would pull the Soviet Union or China into the war.[188] Earlier, policies pursued by President Truman during the Korean War had been influenced by similar concerns about Soviet and Chinese involvement.[189]

CONCLUSION

The principle of total war, inherited from the late nineteenth century, dominated the first half of the twentieth. In two world wars, states marshaled extraordinary levels of resources to produce war machines capable of annihilating the societal, economic, and military forces of another state. What emerged as the prevailing concept of victory was the product of wars fought for strategic principles by states armed by industrial-level production that allowed them to pursue policies based on annihilation.

The principles for which wars might be fought included ideological ones – the struggle between freedom and totalitarianism in World War II being the classic example. As is discussed in Chapter 5, it was the perceived need for a clear victory over the totalitarian regimes of Germany and Japan that would lead to the policy of unconditional surrender underlying Allied strategy.

Also discussed in Chapter 5 is the development of the idea that the victor has postwar responsibilities toward the vanquished (see the section "Rebuild Economy and Infrastructure"). Even before World War II was over, President Roosevelt was talking about rebuilding the defeated enemy states on a grand scale, saying that the United States was obliged to prevent a resurgence of the political and military conditions that, left unresolved at the end of World War I, had directly contributed to the outbreak of hostilities in World War II.[190]

However, as we've seen, virtually all systematic thinking about victory came to a halt with the development of nuclear weapons and the realization that wars could lead to global annihilation within hours. The theory of victory was also buffeted by the emergence of intense ideological hostility between Washington and Moscow. At a time when civilian strategic thinkers and policymakers had significant input in the debate, systematic thinking about victory was dominated by nuclear weapons and the countervailing theories of limited and total war. The limits on victory in the nuclear age were expressed by political theorist Arnold Brecht, who had fled Hitler's Germany in 1933: "The fact that in war, even if victorious, many will be killed and mutilated . . . may not disparage war for him who is prepared to accept these implied evils."[191]

While the paralysis caused by the cold war and nuclear weapons reduced the value of systematic discussions of victory, the debate in the early twenty-first century is showing signs of a revival. With the end of the cold war and the emergence of the global war on terror, the concept of victory is ripe for reinterpretation. If, for the first time since the end of World War II, victory in war is being pursued in earnest – as evidenced by tentative, purported "victories" in Afghanistan and Iraq – it is clearly time to reopen systematic discussion of what "victory" is. This is all the more so now that U.S. wars against North Korea, Iran, and Syria must be counted as serious possibilities.[192]

4 Foundations of Victory

T he purpose of this study is to develop a pretheoretical framework based on several organizing principles to determine what it means for the state to achieve victory in war. This pretheory is not designed for predictive purposes, to forecast whether victory will occur under specific conditions or when to go to war. That said, this chapter discusses what constitutes a pretheory of victory and to what practical and conceptual uses it can be put. It begins with an examination of the language of victory, to define as precisely as possible the origins of the word "victory." It then explores what a theory is and should accomplish, and proceeds to define what it means to have a pretheory of victory, to explain what such ideas contribute to understanding victory, and to outline the components of a pretheory. Subsequent chapters apply this pretheory of victory to various wars fought by the United States, including six wars from the late twentieth and early twenty-first centuries.

LANGUAGE OF VICTORY

This chapter begins with a systematic search for a definition of "victory." Although the word is routinely used to describe the successful outcome of political, social, and economic events, this study focuses on cases that pertain directly to the realm of military strategy. As this review of the various meanings of "victory" in the context of strategy shows, its principal attribute is that it is associated with a wide range of outcomes of military actions and wars.

The word "war" comes from the Indo-European root *wers,* which is "to confuse or mix up"; in Old High German its root is *werra,* which translates as "a state of confusion or strife." For the past five hundred years or so, the word "war" has been defined along these lines: "state of open, armed, often prolonged conflict carried on between nations, states, or parties."[1]

A directly related term is "strategy," which since antiquity has been defined in the literature as the ways in which policymakers use political, military, and diplomatic instruments to achieve their nation's purposes.[2] Linguistically, the word "strategy" derives from the Greek *stratēgiia*, which refers to a "military leader" or the "leadership of troops."[3] In practical terms, "strategy" is defined as the "science and art of using all the forces of a nation to execute the approved plans as effectively as possible during peace or war," as well as the "science and art of military command as applied to the overall planning and conduct of large-scale combat operations."[4] For the past several centuries, the term "strategy" has been used to describe the political, economic, and military means by which policymakers, guided by a reasonable expectation that victory is possible, seek to defeat the enemy.[5]

In *Victory through Air Power*, the air-power theorist Alexander de Seversky defined strategy in nearly transcendental terms as the "expression of a man's mind, the embodiment of his whole military philosophy and convictions."[6] In *Strategy in the Missile Age*, the strategist Bernard Brodie observed that military strategy is "one of the most ancient of the human sciences," which "is at the same time one of the least developed."[7] The reason, for Brodie, is that we have not defined a "strategic theory" that is equivalent to a "theory for action."[8] In a synthetic sense, the purpose of strategy is to organize the state's policies and resources effectively for the purpose of achieving victory in war or nonmilitary endeavors.[9]

The problem immediately confronting a study of victory is that there is no formal theory of victory; the prevailing ideas about victory, developed over the millennia, are based on the loosely formed but universally held premise that the state organizes its strategy and resources to defeat and, ultimately in some cases, to annihilate another state in war. Yet there is no formal or analytic relationship between victory and strategy, and the concept of victory has been subordinated in the literature to the principles of strategy and the practice of diplomacy.

With this as background, this and subsequent chapters seek:

1. to elucidate the historical foundations of the relationships that exist between military actions and strategy;
2. to clarify the ideas about strategy that govern the actions of the state in war; and
3. to determine in analytic and theoretical terms what it means for a state to achieve victory.

Since the concepts of strategy and victory are so intertwined in the scholarly and policymaking literatures on strategy and war, the practical problem is how to establish a framework in which the term "victory" is not interpreted as a derivative of the language that is used to describe strategy and war.[10] At present, we have a theory of war that "explains how a particular war can be won" or how "a particular country or coalition can be beaten at a tolerable cost,"[11] but these theories of *strategy* and *war* do not provide a distinct and analytically based pretheory of *victory*. Before examining the foundations of a pretheory of victory, however, let us turn to the linguistic meanings and origins of victory itself.

The word "victory," which derives from the Latin *victoria,* "from *vinco, victus,* to conquer," is defined formally as "the defeat of an enemy in battle, or of an antagonist in any contest," or "the gaining of the superiority or success in any struggle or competition."[12] A critical aspect of its meaning is the "final defeat of an enemy or opponent," and it can imply a "moral or spiritual triumph of any kind."[13] Based on these definitions, victory is relevant to military endeavors in which the state defeats an opponent, "impos[es] one's will on the enemy," contributes to the final defeat of an enemy, or achieves some satisfaction with the outcome.[14] These distinctions contribute to the concepts of tactical victory, political–military victory, and grand strategic victory, presented later in this chapter as elements of a pretheory of victory.

One consequence of the wide range of meanings associated with victory is the diverse array of synonyms that are commonly used by policymakers and scholars to describe political and military outcomes. The words "conquest," "triumph," "vanquish," "subdue," "subjugate," and "overcome" are frequently used in contemporary English to describe the general outcome associated with victory, each communicating a slightly different meaning.[15] The fact that the concept of victory covers a broad range of interpretations and meanings has the unintended consequence of shaping and distorting how modern audiences interpret victory. Take, for example, the word "conquest," which describes the act of "subduing, subjugating, or achieving control over," the ability to "gain the victory," and "implies a mastery over or subjugation of the opponent."[16] "Conquer" also suggests "decisive and often wide-scale victory"; its root, the Latin *conquirere,* means "to procure," and the English verb is defined as "to gain or acquire by force" or "to defeat or subdue by military force."[17]

The related word, "triumph," is derived from the Latin *triumphus* and implies a "magnificent and imposing ceremonial performed in honor of a general who had gained a decisive victory over a foreign enemy."[18] The word "triumph" "suggests great acclaim or personal satisfaction accruing to the victor from a brilliant or decisive victory or an overwhelming conquest,"[19] denotes "a victory or success that is especially noteworthy because it is decisive, significant, or spectacular," and describes a "successful ending of a struggle or contest."[20] To "triumph" over an enemy is the most general form of achieving victory, whereas "vanquish" shifts the emphasis toward "total mastery."[21] The clear intent of "triumph" is a success that is celebrated ceremonially.

Another synonym for "victory" is "prevail," which describes the conditions associated with victory and is derived from the Latin *praevalere,* "to be strong," and means to "overcome; to gain the victory or superiority; to gain the advantage" as well as to possess greater strength or influence.[22] Perhaps the most common synonym for victory is "win," derived from the Anglo-Saxon *winnan,* to "strive [or] fight," and means to "gain the victory; to be successful; to triumph; to prevail."[23] At the same time, the word "victory" is influenced by "success," which comes from the Latin *successus* and means the "achievement of something desired, planned, or attempted."[24]

One conclusion from this review and analysis of related words is that victory encompasses such a diverse array of meanings as to obscure its real one. Its connotations range from the totality of "final defeat," "moral and spiritual triumph," and "overwhelming conquest" to the more moderate concepts of decisiveness, subjugation, and achievement. So as presently used, "victory" encompasses greater and lesser forms of success, which in practice tells very little about its precise nature. Not surprisingly, the subtle differences among these synonyms contribute to the confusion that surrounds the meaning of victory and our ability to use it to analyze the outcomes of war.

Since victory is characterized by overlapping and subtly different meanings, an alternative approach is to examine victory in terms of what it is *not.* The word most commonly used to describe the opposite of "victory" is "defeat," which as a verb means "to prevent the success of" or to "overcome."[25] Defined as the "failure to win" or "coming to naught," "defeat" is derived from the Medieval Latin *disfacere,* to "destroy, mutilate, undo."[26] When it is used to describe events that have a military context, "defeat" means "an undoing or annulling," "overthrow, as of any army in battle," or the "loss of a battle."[27] While "subdue" "suggests mastery and control achieved by overpowering," the word "subjugate" "more strongly implies reducing an opponent to submission."[28] A more decisive related verb is "rout," which "implies complete victory followed by the disorderly flight of the defeated force."[29] Since it is implicit in discussions of victory that a state or entity will subordinate itself to the victor, it is common to think in terms of "surrender," which is derived from the Old French *surrendre,* to deliver, and means to "relinquish possession or control of to another because of demand or compulsion," or to "give up one's self into the power of another."[30] Each of these related verbs, and those explored earlier, expresses different interpretations of victory.

In the present study, certain words or phrases have proven more useful than others in the hunt for "victory" in that they demonstrate that victory can occur on *different levels,* which they help to delineate. For instance, "conquest," "final defeat," "overwhelming conquest," and "moral or spiritual triumph" all describe victory in grand strategic terms. However, "triumph," "decisive," "acquire by force," "prevail,"[31] "subdue," and "achievement" express the notion of victory without clarifying its level, which might be anywhere in the range from tactical, in a given battle, to grand strategic.

If "victory" can be used to describe the outcome of wars as significant or conclusive yet also be used to interpret victory in lesser terms, what in fact does it mean? The only reasonable conclusion from this discussion of its origins and meanings is this: *"Victory" is an all-purpose word used to describe imprecisely the concept of a success in war.* As noted, that success may be at the tactical level, in which one unit defeats another; at the political or psychological level, when the state achieves some reasonable fraction of its objectives; or at the grand strategic level, when the state is able to impose its will on the most comprehensive scale.

It should be noted that all of these meanings and interpretations, all these competing and yet entirely plausible definitions of victory in the literature on strategy, not only relate to the outcome of political and military events but are consistent with the language of ordinary discourse.[32] Still, it is in recognition of this linguistic haze – a verbal fog of war, perhaps – that this study develops a pretheory of victory, whose purpose is simply to establish more formal, and thus more useful, meanings for the word.

FOUNDATIONS OF THEORY

What can a modern pretheory of victory provide, and why is it imperative to define victory so that it can be used with greater precision than is currently the case?[33] For one thing, without such a pretheory, policymakers and scholars cannot move beyond the systemic confusion in ordinary language that envelops the meaning of victory. Although one objective of this study is to generate workable concepts or principles regarding victory in war, this goal must be tempered by the realization that this or any inquiry is unlikely to produce a *comprehensive* theory of what victory means.[34]

The fields of analytic philosophy and political theory provide instruments that are helpful in instituting a pretheory of victory. The first steps on this journey, however, are to define what we mean by "theory," examine what constitutes a theory, and consider what it means to have a *theory* of victory. From there, the discussion turns to the foundations of a *pre*theory and proceeds to develop several organizing principles about victory.

The literature on theory in social science is well developed analytically.[35] A theory is defined as a series of "explanatory statements, accepted principles, and methods of analysis" that are used to understand the nature of events and relationships among those events, and ideally but often unattainably to predict the interactions among those events.[36] The political theorist William Bluhm related theory to the context of politics when he argued that "theory is an explanation of what politics is all about, a general understanding of the political world, a frame of reference." For Bluhm, theory permits individuals "to recognize an event as political, decide anything about why it happened, judge whether it was good or bad, or decide what was likely to happen next."[37] The political scientist David Easton defined theory as "any kind of generalization or proposition that asserts that two or more things, activities, or events covary under specified conditions."[38] In practical terms, "theory is a tool for evaluating what is happening and for guiding our political choices."[39] Ideally it can be used to "explain why an event occurred and to predict future events,"[40] but rarely do political theories attain this level of fidelity.

In practice, the term "theory" is most commonly used to describe the "fundamental conceptualization of a field," which can occur on "stronger" and "weaker" levels.[41] In the case of a stronger theory, the objective is to develop rigorous and scientifically demonstrable statements about reality; in its weaker form, theory is just a conceptual framework for understanding a problem.[42] For example, a "strong" theory of victory would develop explanatory principles that stipulate how actions translate into a specific form of victory, whereas a weaker theory – here, in the form of a pretheory – would provide organizing principles that form a framework for theorizing about victory in hopes of producing a stronger theory. In the present inquiry, the objective is to develop a weaker theory in order to identify those concepts that describe what it means for the state to achieve victory.

A theory, according to the political theorist Arnold Brecht, may be "scientific" or "nonscientific," and it is designed "to designate attempts to 'explain' phenomena."[43] A theory "may refer to some general 'law' in the sense of 'regularity,'" but a "'theory is never a 'law'; and while it refers to laws and may suggest the existence of several laws, it is not itself a law" (15). In his "What Is a Theory?" Brecht argued that the purpose of theory is to elucidate "propositions that try to 'explain' something" (501), or that "offer explanations" (502) for various political phenomena. A theory, furthermore, "may make use of either some 'law' already firmly established, or of some 'hypothesis'. . . . [It therefore] is not itself a 'hypothesis'; but it may make use of one, or propose one in the course of its own endeavour to 'explain' something" (522).

Theories rest on assumptions that are often "based on limited information or knowledge," and they are used to describe an "organized system of accepted knowledge that applies in a variety of circumstances to explain a specific set of phenomena."[44] A theory also may be defined as a "discussion of political values or the philosophy of politics," or as the "relation among political facts," useful for the "development of any science, social or physical, towards the attainment of reliable knowledge."[45]

For Easton, theory operates on three levels:

1. "singular generalizations, which . . . are statements of observed uniformities between two isolated and easily identified variables."

2. "synthetic or narrow gauge theory . . . [which] consists of a set of interrelated propositions that are designed to synthesize the data contained in an unorganized body of singular generalizations."
3. "broad-gauge or systematic theory, the conceptual framework within which a whole discipline is cast."[46]

Theory can even provide an "analytical model," although Easton warned that "the attainment of such advanced theory in social science is still in the distant realm of aspiration."[47] In *A Framework for Political Analysis,* he proposed the "need to argue for the construction of empirically oriented general theory."[48] He concluded, in *Varieties of Political Theory,* that "the task of theory construction is not of course to give substantive answers . . . [but] to formulate the appropriate questions and to devise appropriate ways for seeking answers."[49] As is discussed later, this is the principal function of a pretheory in the case of victory (see the section "Toward a Pretheory of Victory").

In the present study, formulating a pretheory of victory will help to *clarify* whether various levels of victory can be defined and compared, to *illuminate* the connections that exist among war, strategy, and victory, and to *distinguish* between victory on the one hand and its litany of synonyms (see the preceding section) that have long dominated discussions about strategy and war.[50] This search for a pretheory of victory is animated by the desire to develop greater precision not only in how we use the word, but also in how the state uses military force.[51]

British political theorist Bernard Crick defined theory in political terms as "attempts to explain the attitudes and actions arising from ordinary life and to generalize about them in a particular context; thus political theory is basically concerned with the relationships among concepts and circumstances."[52] Therefore, political theories are distinct from "*political doctrines* which state that something ought to be the case. . . . Political theories consider the relationships between concepts and circumstances; political doctrines assert a connection between thought and policy."[53] Crick describes "ideology as a particular type of doctrine,"[54] and thus beyond the realm of theory. For the purposes of this study, then, theory is intended to explain the relationships among political concepts and circumstances, as envisioned by Crick, and to guide policymakers in their deliberations about victory, as defined by Easton, Brecht, and Bluhm.

In the case of understanding victory, the purpose of a theory would be to guide or inform the behavior of scholars, who study the relationship between the use of force and strategy, and of policymakers, who make decisions in a political or military setting about whether to use force. When applied to the specific case of war, a theory of victory should ideally identify the critical attributes of war, describe the extent to which those attributes contribute to victory, and estimate their relative influence. The military strategist Carl von Clausewitz formulated this expansive definition of theory:

> If a theory investigates the subjects which constitute War; if it separates more distinctly that which at first sight seems amalgamated; if it explains fully the properties of the means; if it shows their probable effects; if it makes evident the nature of objects; if it brings to bear all over the field of War the light of essentially critical investigation – then it has fulfilled the chief duties of its province.[55]

When all of these conditions are met, and this is of course quite difficult, "It becomes then a guide to him who wishes to make himself acquainted with War from books." For Easton, theory should also provide "guidance to empirical research" by serving as an "incentive for the creation of new knowledge."[56] In practice, policymakers and scholars need a theory of victory if they are to understand when various factors and conditions in war might lead to the outcome that is generally known as victory.[57] For Brecht, theory is "one of the most important weapons in the struggle for the advance of humanity," because correct theories permit people to "choose their goals and means wisely so as to avoid the roads that end in terrific disappointment."[58] In the case of war, the worst alternative is to choose "roads" that lead to catastrophe for the nation and the world. The real test of a theory, for international relations theorist Hans Morgenthau, is for it to be "judged not by some preconceived abstract principle or concept unrelated to reality, but by its purpose: to bring order and meaning to a mass of phenomena which without it would remain disconnected and unintelligible."[59] Discussions about victory, based on "disconnected and unintelligible" interpretations of military and political events, clearly need some organizing principles.

In the language of analytic political theory, one problem with the term "victory" that has impeded efforts to formulate a theory is its "contested" nature, which means that scholars have not eliminated the vagueness, open-endedness, and ambiguity that surround it.[60] To say that the concept of victory remains contestable means that "criteria for its correct application embody [merely] normative standards," and that thus there is no agreement on what those criteria are or should be.[61] The purpose of *normative* statements, which employ the language of "ought" or "should," is to ascribe a value or preference to a condition, whereas *descriptive* statements use "is" or "are" to describe that which exists. In addition, normative and descriptive statements involve differing interpretations of events, including the matter of how cultural and historical experiences shape the ways in which individuals interpret victory differently. For example, a normative statement about victory might propose that "the full use of the instruments of power available to the state should produce strategic victory," whereas a descriptive statement of victory might say that "states rarely use the full range of instruments of power to achieve victory."

Since the concept of victory is heavily influenced by descriptive and normative standards of interpretation, it is unlikely that we will be able to formulate definitions for victory that transcend differing political ideologies and worldviews or that can achieve the standard of value-free inquiry.[62] To complicate matters further, "disputes about the propriety of these standards cannot be settled by rational argument alone."[63] In the absence of explicit criteria, discussions about victory will be mired in confusion by the "conceptual" and "cognitive relativism" of its meaning being "relative to anyone's value system or 'paradigm'."[64] Thus, despite its widespread use in politics and diplomacy, "victory" may always face barriers to its rigorous and systematic definition.

TOWARD A PRETHEORY OF VICTORY

A "pretheory" is a conceptual exploration designed to identify and observe relationships in a field of inquiry carefully, then to formulate organizing principles and testable theories. It may be used to develop new or rudimentary ideas regarding political phenomena or to classify procedures and methods of research and analysis.[65] The foundations of pretheory were established by James Rosenau, a scholar of international relations, who argued that the fundamental purpose of pretheory is to move beyond simple data collection and "render the raw materials comparable and ready for theorizing."[66] Theory cannot flourish "until the materials of the field are processed – i.e., rendered comparable – through the use of pre-theories" (129). In formal terms, a pretheory is designed to decide which sets of variables contribute to behavior or outcomes, and to assess their "relative potencies" (129) without assigning precise weights or influences.[67] These rankings, attached to the "main sources of external behavior" (130), "reflect the author's way of organizing materials for close inspection and not the inspections themselves" (132).[68]

Pretheory also facilitates "more systematic observation and more incisive comprehension of how international behavior is generated" (130), which in the end permits the formation of "consensuses" on the nature of empirical or political reality.[69] However, as Rosenau noted, a pretheory cannot "be so coherent as to account for the infinite variation that marks international life" (133). Initial efforts to formulate a pretheory will doubtless produce "crude formulations," Rosenau anticipated, "but the more one explicates, the more elaborate does one's pre-theory become" (135). This defense of the iterative nature of research is based on the fact that scholars seek progress in the field by first developing and later improving upon explanations of political behavior and outcomes by accounting for central tendencies.[70]

A pretheory of victory could assist the state and its policymakers in several ways. First, the scholarship on war will be more analytically rigorous and in-formative if it is guided by the coherent set of ideas. By defining appropriate language for describing the conditions or outcomes that constitute victory, based on a deductive analysis of historical cases of war, a pretheory should permit theorists to develop concepts and principles that more accurately de-scribe victory's connection to strategy and the conduct of war.[71] A pretheory will also help scholars investigate what factors appear to be related to victory and to test those relationships.[72] Armed with a clear conceptual foundation, theorists and scholars could help policymakers form sound decisions about military intervention, and have an agreed basis for validating or refuting ideas generated along the way.

Second, policymakers who can engage in deliberate discussions about the nature of victory will be more able to create successful policies for military intervention, policies based on a systematic definition of what the state is like-ly to achieve and the strategic, political, military, and economic implications of the attempt – the level of conflict required, the cost in lives and resources, and the consequences for the state's reputation. Policymakers guided by a more coherent framework for victory would better understand the costs and benefits of using military force and whether the state might actually achieve victory in light of them. Pretheoretical concepts about victory are likely to em-phasize the fact that victory at whatever level would probably impose costs and benefits on both the victorious and vanquished states. Policymakers will need to define clearly the outcomes of war in terms of what victory will mean to the victor and the defeated state alike if they are to determine meaningfully what objectives are to be achieved when the state uses military force and whether the resources available will suffice to achieve them. They must also consider the consequences if the objectives cannot be achieved and/or the necessary resources are not available. With this kind of rational calculus of war in place, policymakers could evaluate more clear-sightedly whether the per-ceived benefits of pursuing victory are worth the costs to the state. Such orga-nizing principles minimize the unnecessary risks that accrue when decisions about war are based on imprecise concepts. At the same time, it is also policy-makers who must decide how to invest in systems and technologies that will affect the state's chances of victory in wars yet to come. If the deliberations of defense planners responsible for developing and ensuring the maintenance of the state's future military capabilities and force structures are guided by systematic ideas about victory, political objectives can be translated into poli-cies consistent with what is achievable given the resources committed.

Third, a pretheory of victory could permit democratic societies to operate more effectively by allowing both a society and its policymakers to understand more fully the level of commitment and sacrifice that the use of military force will impose on the state. In view of the social compact that exists between the people and their government representatives, a pretheory's systematic ideas and formal language of victory are essential if citizens are to comprehend what sacrifices policymakers are asking them to make, what the state will gain from that commitment, why it is necessary for the state to use force, and the risks if the policy fails. Such theories may help policymakers mobilize public support for military intervention and thus shape public expectations about the consequences of war. After all, as used in ordinary language, "victory" implies a degree of completeness, finality, and totality that, historically, states have achieved only rarely. It requires a leap of faith to assume that people will support a war simply because they are told why it is being fought;[73] they also need to know its costs and risks.

However, certain limitations of any pretheory of victory are not easily overcome. Primary is the failure of efforts by theorists and practitioners to develop in social science what has been known for decades as a *causal* theory — the kind described earlier as geared to attaining "reliable knowledge" – with any degree of predictive qualities.[74] The same is true with victory. Since all events are interpreted through the lens of human cognition and perception, it is improbable that we could stipulate how or to what extent specific actions by the state will lead to victory in the theoretical sense. Without revisiting the well-rehearsed theoretical and methodological arguments about the difficulties with prediction, suffice it to say that any study of victory is inhibited by the fundamental constraint that applies to all forms of social-science inquiry. A social science inquiry cannot identify causal laws that define systematically and formally the relationship between political actions or interactions and their intended or unintended consequences, given the many imprecisely defined or weakly understood human variables that must be considered.[75]

Thus, the present study of victory is not designed to produce formulaic propositions that policy x or action y is related in a causal or predictive sense with victory. A pretheory of victory is only a framework for better analyses of possible costs, implications, and obligations – not a predictive tool for how to achieve victory at a particular price. Still, a pretheory should help policymakers better link their aims and means,[76] and thus determine whether what they hope for in victory is worth the potential cost.

In sum, a pretheory of victory is an instrument to help policymakers, scholars, and defense planners understand the political, military, technological, and economic conditions consistent with victory. Any pretheoretical ideas about victory matter only if they produce an organized approach to answering the vital questions that should arise when contemplating the use of military force: What does it mean to achieve victory? How likely is the state to achieve it? When would the state know if victory had been attained? What are the benefits, costs, and risks of victory? What resources are needed in its pursuit? And is the state – both government and populace – willing to pay that price?

PRETHEORETICAL CONCEPTS FOR VICTORY

This study of victory uses four concepts, or organizing principles, to describe in systematic terms the ways in which military and political theorists and other thinkers on strategy and war have employed, directly or indirectly, the idea of victory in their writings. These four concepts – the level of victory, change in status quo, mobilization for war, and postconflict obligations – jointly provide the foundation for a pretheory of victory. As shown in Figure 1, each of these can be expressed on a scale, ascending from left to right,[77] depicting varying degrees of activity and involvement in war. This typology is based on the judgment that surely not all victories are the same, just as the amount of destruction in war will differ. Several general observations about these organizing principles are in order before each is discussed in more detail.

The first observation is that these organizing principles represent not discrete "point solutions" but continua of effort, intensity, or achievement. Thus the terms that define levels of victory – "tactical," "political–military," and "grand strategic" – describe ranges, probability distributions, broad areas within which like events can be aggregated. Second, although there is no evidence that these organizing principles are related parametrically, this possibility will be considered as a venue for subsequent research in Chapter 13. Third, what is important is not whether individual scholars and policymakers examining specific points of analysis in this study draw similar conclusions, but that they be engaged in systematic discussions about military intervention and victory using the concepts outlined in this framework.

Levels of Victory

The first organizing principle in the proposed pretheory is the *level of victory*. In this framework, the outcome of wars can be placed along a continuum stretching across three levels, beginning with the simplest, tactical victory, proceeding through the broader political–military victory, and concluding with the most comprehensive level, that of grand strategic victory.[78] A word of methodological caution is in order: It is important to emphasize that this is a pretheory, that these are necessarily imprecise terms, and that much work lies ahead in the construction of more precise definitions. There are significant analytical challenges associated with categorizing victories – complex events involving thousands or millions of discrete individuals and events – as tactical, political–military, or grand strategic. The distinctions among these are not systematically addressed within the literature, except in the most general and loose sense. However, although the act of categorization can by itself reflect prejudicial tendencies, there are considerable analytic advantages to defining victories along a scale that ranges from purely tactical successes in bat-

Level of Victory

Figure 1. Pretheoretical concepts for victory.

tle to the wholesale defeat and destruction of another society.[79] This approach also has the benefit of being familiar in historical terms. When Clausewitz wrote in *On War* that there are "victories of different kinds and different degrees," some of which "have been preceded by very considerable efforts," he was pointing the way to distinguishing among victories.[80] Thus, although categorization on this scale is useful, it remains open to criticism and debate for reasons well argued in the literature on case-study analysis and analytic political theory.[81]

The first category, *tactical victory,* represents most of the historical thinking about the outcome of war and the purpose of strategy. In practice, tactical victory is equivalent to the outcome when the state or an army achieves victory in a battle or in a series of military engagements. This was the first category of victory to develop historically, as strategists and military commanders described as victory the rout of the enemy on the battlefield or in a series of military engagements.[82] The reason for the focus on battles, as military historian John Keegan argued, is that military history is "in the last resort about battle."[83] Realizing that understanding the nature of battle is key to achieving victory, strategists and historians have sought to "reduce the conduct of war to a set of rules and a system of procedures" and thus "make more orderly and rational what is essentially chaotic and instinctive" (18). Keegan noted that "a battle is something which happens between two armies leading to the moral and then physical disintegration of one or the other of them" (302).[84] For Keegan, battles can be categorized into "seven or eight types: battles of encounter, battles of attrition, battles of envelopment, battles of break-through and so on" (20–1).[85] A tactical victory is sometimes called a *decisive* battle, one that results in "clear-cut victory of one side over the other" (342). For Keegan, battles are decisive when "they kill some of these men and dissuade the rest, for a longer or shorter period, from wanting to fight any more" (342).

During the Enlightenment, military theoreticians who used the term "tactics" used it, according to war historian Azar Gat, to describe a "system of army organization and battle formation" in keeping with the original sense of the Greek *tà taktiká* (pertaining to arrangement). By the late eighteenth century, however, the term "tactics" was used more generally to describe "the art of war as a whole," and thus more broadly than how a state and its army are organized to fight and win battles and wars.[86] Given this transition in usage, much of our understanding about victory is based on "tactical victories" achieved in battle. This level of victory represents a disproportionately large share of the total number of victories in war.[87] As should be apparent in the ensuing discussions about the higher levels of victory, tactical victories in battle are integrated into the broader concepts of political–military and grand strategic victories.

The second and intermediate level of victory is *political–military victory*, in which the state has achieved a range of successes in war that are equivalent to and based on a sufficient number of tactical victories. Political–military victory covers everything from conquering territory and defeating armies to successes in limited wars. In analytic terms, this level encompasses the range of political and military outcomes that occur when force is used to defeat an adversary's military forces, and when that defeat compels changes in its political behavior or policies – when it "causes some real shift in the direction of human affairs far away from the battlefield," as Keegan (342) puts it. The nature of political–military victory was expressed indirectly by Clausewitz in *On War*, where he wrote that "The conqueror in a War is not always in a condition to subdue his adversary completely" – thus implying that victory in a military sense might have important political consequences yet not be sufficiently comprehensive to be equivalent to strategic victory.[88] A more recent thinker, Henry Kissinger, alluded to this concept with the observation that, "A military victory always has two components, its physical reality and its psychological impact . . . it is the task of diplomacy to translate the latter into political terms."[89]

The distinguishing feature of a political–military victory is that the state achieves some of its political and military goals through the cumulative effect of tactical victories in battle. Since there is agreement among strategists that the objective of war is to achieve the state's political ends as well as satisfy the policymakers' desire for prestige, the concept of political–military victory is consistent with the desire of policymakers to translate military intervention into improvements in the political environment.[90] The *military* component of political–military victory exists when the state uses force to destroy military targets or forces, which can range from the limited case of rendering antiaircraft defenses inoperative to the comprehensive case of completely destroying the adversary's military forces. For example, a state would attain a political–military victory if it successfully acquired the territory of another state through military conquest and compelled its subsequent defeat. The complementary concept is a *political* victory, which occurs when the state uses military force to defeat another state's policies, military capabilities, and governing institutions.[91] The problem, however, is that a military victory does not necessarily produce a political victory, and a political victory can be attained without victories in battle, say, if one side capitulates before hostilities.[92] Thus, a political–military victory could be achieved without defeating a nation's military capabilities – as, for example, in the case of the political–military victory attained by the United States when it launched an air strike against military and government targets in Libya in March 1986. On some levels, the concept of a political–military victory is analogous to the language of limited war that gained credibility during the cold war.[93]

A political–military victory occupies an intermediate position between victory on a tactical level, which has shorter-term and more focused effects in battle, and victory on the grand strategic level, which has wider and more significant implications for the state and the international system. A broader explanation of political–military victory would stress that the use of force permits policymakers to signal their resolve or warn an adversary that further action involves significant political risks. For example, the limited U.S. missile strikes against al-Qaeda training camps in Afghanistan in August 1998 were designed for the purely political purpose of signaling U.S. concern, yet ultimately the military consequences of those attacks had significant and long-lasting effects. The value of the concept of political–military victory is its ability to emphasize the relationship between the scale of destruction in war and its implications for the level of victory.[94]

The most transcendent and historically unusual concept is *grand strategic victory*.[95] This level is reached when a war, motivated by ideological or moral reasons, creates a victory of such magnitude that it leads to a profound reordering in the strategic foundations of international politics (see the section "Change in the Status Quo," below).[96] A grand strategic victory describes the case when the state imposes a strategic change in the international system by destroying the ideological and moral values of a society and then reestablishing the foundations of the enemy state, including its government, economy, and military power.[97] This uppermost level of victory refers primarily to hegemonic wars that are waged for significant reasons.[98] Furthermore, grand strategic victory describes the outcomes of wars in which the state defeats the economic, political, and military sources of power of another state, prevents it from using military power or posing a threat, and intends that those changes will have strategic consequences.

The concept of grand strategic victory has clear historical precedent as seen, for example, when Genghis Khan in the thirteenth century purportedly said that "The greatest happiness is to vanquish your enemies, to chase them before you, to rob them of their wealth, to see those dear to them bathed in tears, and to clasp to your bosom their wives and daughters."[99] The Swiss strategist Jomini, for instance, referred to the notion of victory on a grand strategic scale, and Clausewitz wrote about the nature of "great victory."[100] The relevance of grand strategic victory is evident in the cases of the destruction of Germany and Japan in World War II and the development there of new political, economic, military, and ideological foundations. Victory on this level is consistent with the concept of total war that emerged in the nineteenth and twentieth centuries to express the willingness of the state to devote all its resources to combating its enemy, as in Churchill's famous "Victory at all costs, victory in spite of all terror, victory however long and hard the road may be; for without victory there is no survival."[101]

When a state is involved in a struggle over great ideological and moral issues, which may lead it to frame the choice for war as a matter of survival, its objective is a grand strategic victory, one that will lead to a fundamental reordering of the international system. Such an objective has been implicit in the political lexicon since specific technological developments, notably aircraft and nuclear weapons, endowed the state with the power to achieve victory on an unprecedented scale.

The historical problem with respect to using "strategic" to modify victory is that the origins of the term "strategy" are open to debate.[102] Methodologically, the concept of grand strategic victory has an important connection with, and is closely linked to, the category of victory in this framework that yields significant changes in the regional or global status quo (see the next section). The vast majority of victories belong either at the tactical (the largest number) or political–military level; the instances of grand strategic victory are empirically rare. Interestingly, however, the current conflicts in Afghanistan and Iraq are consistent with an objective of grand strategic victory because the source of the war is ultimately the rise of Islamist terrorism and the absolute struggle between terrorist organizations and the West. It is not, therefore, inconceivable that grand strategic victory will become a more common objective in the twenty-first century, central to the lexicon of war, and the focus of instruments of power available to the state.

Change in the Status Quo

The second organizing principle in this pretheory of victory is the change in the status quo in the defeated state that the victor attains by the use of military power. This concept was evident in Hans Morgenthau's *Politics among Nations* when he addressed the relationship between "victorious war" and "inducements to imperialism." As he observed, "the nation which anticipates victory will pursue a policy that seeks a permanent change of the power relations with the defeated enemy. . . . It is the objective of this policy of change to transform the relation between victor and vanquished . . . [which can lead to] a permanent change in the status quo."[103] In this pretheory of victory, the change in the status quo can be located along a continuum that ranges from limited to comprehensive changes. At the *limited* end of the scale, the state uses force for limited aims to compel a change in the adversary's actual or declared *policies*. This can increase to the point where the state is able to use force for unlimited aims to defeat an adversary's *military* capability to conduct war. At the next level in this progression, the change in the status quo occurs when policymakers use force to transform the *institutional, constitutional, or economic* foundations in the state that contribute to the adversary's power and legitimacy. The most *comprehensive* degree of change in the status quo is the case of the occupation of the defeated state and *regime change*. At its most extreme, the change in the status quo could be a "Carthaginian peace," in which the state is annihilated and has no hope that its current government, leadership, and economy will survive.[104] A change in the status quo on this scale occurs when the state uses force to destroy the enemy's military chain of command, replace its political head of the state, demolish its existing system of governance, and in the extreme case occupy its physical territory.[105] Using a contemporary example, the U.S. invasion of Iraq in March 2003 (see Chapter 11) exemplifies a war that produced a comprehensive change in the status quo.

As might be expected, the relationship between the change in the status quo and the level of victory is analytically imprecise. The problem is that although higher levels of victory are likely to coincide with comprehensive changes in the status quo, this is not always true. Using the case of political–military victory, limited changes in the status quo are likely to occur when the state uses military force to compel another state to stop its practice of, say, supporting terrorist organizations. Largely as a result of U.S. military strikes against Libyan government facilities and military targets in March 1986 (see Chapter 6), the government of Muammar al-Qaddafi slowly but measurably (yet discontinuously – witness Lockerbie) reversed its policy of sponsoring terrorism.[106] This military intervention was at best a raid, but it sparked changes in Libya's willingness to support terrorism. A second example of a change in the status quo occurred in the late 1990s when the United States and the North Atlantic Treaty Organization (NATO) forced the Bosnian Serbs, as discussed in Chapter 9, to stop policies that were forcibly removing ethnic and religious minorities living in the province of Kosovo. To cite a recent example, the use of military force to remove the Taliban government from power in Afghanistan and destroy part of al-Qaeda's infrastructure, as discussed in Chapter 10, produced a comprehensive change in the status quo of that nation. The other contemporary example is the decision by the United States to use force in March 2003 to remove Saddam Hussein and his Baath Party regime. Though as of this writing it's too soon to tell, if the invasion of Iraq (see Chapter 11) ends up altering the fundamental system of governance in Iraq and shifting the political balance in the Middle East toward democratic societies, this use of force could effectively lead to a comprehensive change in the status quo and perhaps on a global scale.

Mobilization for War

The third organizing principle in a pretheory of victory is the scale of the state's mobilization of its political, military, economic, and social resources for war.[107] As with the other organizational elements in this study, the level of mobilization for war varies on a spectrum, ranging from limited to extensive. The scale at which states mobilize themselves for war is influenced, first, by the fact that significant resources are regularly spent on maintaining their capability for war and, second, that states can organize their military and industrial production for war with far greater efficiency in the twenty-first century than in previous ones.[108] In discussing this principle, we must distinguish between the mobilization of military resources and the mobilization of the civilian population.

During World War II the United States itself mobilized for war by organizing roughly one-third of its economic and human resources. Winston Churchill commented about the American penchant for large-scale mobilization, observing that, "In the military as in the commercial or production spheres the American mind runs naturally to broad, sweeping, logical conclusions on the largest scale."[109] World War II entailed a level of mobilization in the United States vastly greater than the limited mobilizations seen since in the late twentieth and early twenty-first centuries.[110] The effects of technological progress, sustained investments in defense capabilities, and (in the case of the United States) the shift to all-volunteer military forces in the post–Vietnam War era have all significantly reduced the effort that states must expend to mobilize for war.[111]

The *limited* end of the mobilization scale is strictly *military*, involving some combination of the state's standing air, maritime, and land forces, as well as existing stocks of military equipment available as a result of normal levels of industrial production in the military establishment. As discussed in Chapter 6, the 1986 U.S. air strikes against Libya were conducted entirely with standing air and maritime forces and thus did not require the wartime mobilization of industrial capabilities or of the civilian population. One of the features of the modern system of wartime production is that highly industrialized states can mobilize for war by relying on existing military forces and stocks of supplies. A parallel case is the 1989 invasion of Panama (see Chapter 7), which was based on the use of existing forces, notably a contingent of 23,000 soldiers.

As for more *extensive* mobilization – a topic explored in Chapter 2 in the context of Napoleonic mass mobilization and the trend toward total war – although state mobilization for war is often interpreted in the narrow terms of military and industrial production, a related concept is the mobilization of *public support* for war.[112] In democratic societies, for example, the state must be able to marshal and sustain public support if it is to expend the resources in blood and treasure that are necessary for victory. As these societies mobilize for war, there are public discussions of why it is important for the state to go to war, with the mass media – and the Internet in this age of global communications – used to disseminate that debate.[113] This is not just a democratic phenomenon, however; the ability to mobilize popular support for war influences not only the ability of democratic societies to use military power but also how well authoritarian and totalitarian states prepare their societies for war and sustain popular support.

One issue to be addressed under the rubric of mobilization for war is the relative importance of the various elements to be mobilized. In the case of postindustrial democratic societies, for example, public support may be a more critical factor than industrial and military mobilization.

In the end, the level of victory and change in the status quo are related to the state's mobilization for war. For example, a state may mobilize by calling up large numbers of reserve forces as part of its plan of operations – an action that might suggest a higher level of victory is being pursued. Relatedly, when policymakers seek to achieve greater levels of victory, they are more likely to use land forces to invade and occupy the enemy state, which in turn increases the level of mobilization required.[114]

Postconflict Obligations

The fourth organizing principle is the state's postconflict obligations, based on the idea that victory imposes a range of political and economic costs, or social-justice costs, on the victor. These costs, which include human and economic resources as well as political commitment, involve the decision to support or simply guide the efforts of the defeated society to rebuild itself after the war. Those efforts on the part of the victorious state can range from limited participation in its affairs to the protracted occupation of its territory and subsequent reconstruction of its political, military, and economic institutions.[115] Such obligations can be symmetrical, in that the defeated state has a reciprocal obligation to adhere to the terms of the agreement that brought the war to a conclusion. In the twentieth century, for example, the legal instruments of unconditional surrender to which both Germany and Japan agreed at the end of World War II established each state's obligation to follow the dictates of the Allied powers.[116]

Historically, the scale of postconflict obligations has varied quite widely. At the *limited* end of the scale, the state's *military* obligations include the destruction of the adversary's conventional and nonconventional (guerrilla) military forces in order to prevent any reversal of the victory gained by the war or any subsequent resurgence of the conflict. The postconflict obligations on the United States following the 1991 Persian Gulf War (see Chapter 8) were very limited, with the exception of enforcing the no-fly zones over northern and southern Iraq during the 1990s.[117]

There are many examples at the limited end of the continuum in which the victor has provided *economic aid* and development packages.[118] For example, in the early 1990s the United States provided limited assistance to help Panama rebuild its economy after Noriega's rule and the effects of the 1989 U.S. invasion (see Chapter 7). Likewise, the international community provided economic assistance to help rebuild Bosnia and the province of Kosovo after the NATO air campaign that was conducted in the spring of 1999 (see Chapter 9).[119] As the scale of postconflict obligations increases, the victor's responsibilities for providing economic aid toward the defeated's recovery become more *protracted*. Victorious states have established long-term plans for the *reconstruction* of the vanquished state's economic, communications, power, water, and transportation infrastructures that were damaged or destroyed by war. The implication is that the scale of postconflict obligations is related directly to the level of victory pursued and, thus, to the level of devastation wrought and the level of rebuilding necessary. It also is related, but inversely, to the postwar threat, in terms of what could happen if the nation were *not* rebuilt. The scale of obligations at the protracted end can be of monumental proportions, as seen, for example, with the post–World War II U.S. obligations to rebuild Germany and Japan. In this case, the United States assumed protracted postwar obligations when it established – along with the Soviet Union, Great Britain, and France – total control over and responsibility for the occupation and rebuilding of these defeated Axis powers.

Moving toward the more protracted end of the spectrum, the state's postconflict obligations can involve *nation building*.[120] In such cases, the victor's responsibilities can include establishing stable institutions of governance – which, in modern times, are essentially democratic in nature – providing for relatively free elections, training security forces to prevent a resurgence of opposition forces, and creating new military institutions.[121] The nature of protracted postconflict obligations was expressed by Josef Stalin, who reportedly remarked, "Whoever occupies a territory also imposes on it his own social system. Everyone imposes his own system as far as his army can reach. It cannot be otherwise."[122] In the twentieth century, the original post–World War II Morgenthau Plan called for returning Germany to a "preindustrial, pastoral state by taking away its industrial capacity," but political leaders in the United States decided to engage in a large-scale effort to rebuild the economic and political foundations of European societies.[123] The most significant example in which a state assumed protracted postconflict obligations is still the Marshall Plan, in which the United States provided $20 billion to Europe and Japan from 1947 to 1953 to rebuild the infrastructure and economic capacity that were destroyed during World War II. More recently, $18.4 billion was allocated by the United States to rebuild Iraq's infrastructure and economy after the 2003 war.[124]

CONCLUSION

This chapter has outlined the component elements of a pretheory of victory, designed to help scholars and policymakers organize the conditions historically associated with victory and to develop a more precise understanding of what victory is and what it means for the state, including its costs (before and after, for victor and vanquished alike). Each of the four components – level of victory, change in the status quo, mobilization for war, and postconflict obligations – is represented by a continuum. Thus, the level of victory proceeds from *tactical victory* to *political–military victory* to *grand strategic victory;* changes in the status quo range from *limited* to *comprehensive;* mobilization for war ranges from *limited* to *extensive;* and postconflict obligations range from *limited* to *protracted.*

Use of this framework requires policymakers to address several critical questions before committing the state to a military operation, whether it be a surgical air strike or an all-out invasion: Why have they decided to go to war? What kind of victory do they seek? What resources will be required to achieve it? and What will victory accomplish? The intent is to get them to consider, carefully and systematically, how the desired level of victory relates to the status quo, level of mobilization, and postwar obligations in the event that victory is attained.

5 America's Theory of Victory

The United States of America has an enviable record of strategic foreign-policy successes, one spanning more than two centuries. Just since the end of the Second World War and the emergence of the cold war in the late 1940s, the United States has conducted a highly successful foreign policy, including rebuilding Europe and Japan, mobilizing a global coalition against Soviet-style communism, and presiding over the collapse of the Soviet Union. By the late twentieth century it was American practice to interpret victory as the strategic equivalent of destroying another state in order to resolve a fundamental problem in international politics.[1] The problem, however, is that decisions to intervene with military force have been based on an understanding of victory that is incomplete, however successful its results may have been in the past.

The French philosopher and sociologist Jacques Ellul warned that societies should be cautious concerning the ideas that govern how their states conduct war: "The smallest error in the realm of war would cost countless lives and would be measured in terms of victory or defeat."[2] The question for policymakers and scholars is whether the prevailing "theory" of victory, honed during the middle of the past century, provides practical guidance for decisions about the use of force at present, when there is no ideological or geopolitical confrontation between great states, nor the looming prospect of war on a catastrophic scale as seen during World War II. The United States needs to ensure its notions of victory are relevant to modern challenges.[3] At a time when international security is being reshaped by the forces of Islamist terrorism, ethnic and national struggles, religion, and weapons of mass destruction, a systematic reconsideration of victory is in order.

Building on the foundations of the pretheory proposed in Chapter 4, this chapter examines the structure and content of the American concept of victory and outlines how it developed and evolved over the country's first two hundred years. The first section deals with the conflicts of the eighteenth and

104

nineteenth centuries: the nation-founding War of Independence, the War of 1812, and the Civil War. The second covers those of the twentieth century: the First and Second World Wars, its two most significant conflicts, as well the Korean War, Vietnam War, and the cold war. These case studies are followed by a look at the concept of unconditional surrender, which was important both in the Civil War and in World War II, and an analysis of American criteria for victory.

EIGHTEENTH- AND NINETEENTH-CENTURY WARS

War of American Independence (Revolutionary War)

The struggle of the thirteen American colonies for independence established the foundations of what would later emerge as the U.S. theory of victory.[4] Though the conflict's first battles are usually asserted to be those at Lexington and Concord on April 19, 1775, it is with the adoption and initial signing of the Declaration of Independence on July 4, 1776, that a War of Independence can clearly be recognized. From that point, the self-proclaimed "Thirteen United States of America" engaged Great Britain in a war that lasted five years and three months, until the fighting ground to a halt with General Charles Cornwallis's surrender at the Battle of Yorktown on October 19, 1781. The hostilities did not formally end, however, until the Treaty of Paris, which both parties signed on September 3, 1783.[5]

In the War of American Independence, the goal of the colonies was to impose a military defeat on Great Britain that would force it to withdraw, allowing them to establish formally their independence as a sovereign nation. Since Great Britain was an eighteenth-century superpower and could draw on resources from around the globe, it was absolutely necessary for the colonies to win decisively. Thus, their critical objective was to force Britain to recognize the sovereignty and independence of the "United States," withdraw from the colonies, end the political, economic, and military dependence of the "states" on London, and destroy Britain's power and influence in North America.

The colonists' strategy for achieving their goals was to fight a protracted guerrilla war. The colonies also cleverly brought in France, still aggrieved at their loss to Britain only a dozen years earlier in the Seven Years' War. Militarily, victory was achieved when Lord Cornwallis surrendered his forces to the combined armies of America and France at Yorktown.[6] As Field Marshal Montgomery would conclude in his 1968 *A History of Warfare,* the colonists' strategy against the British had been highly effective.[7] British human and material losses, though not catastrophic, were demoralizing. However, the price paid in human losses on the American side was extremely high: almost seven thousand killed in combat out of a population of three million.[8]

As the first of several wars in the formative stage of the American theory of victory, the War of Independence is significant on several levels. To begin with, it has been observed that the colonies' interest in "complete, total, absolute independence, and nothing less" established the foundations of the belief that victory should be attained in the purest and most absolute sense.[9] In the language of this study, what the colonies achieved against Great Britain was a political–military victory. Although the war clearly did have profound long-term consequences for the Americans, it is difficult to characterize the Revolutionary War as a "grand strategic victory": British land forces surrendered in the colonies, but Great Britain itself was not conquered, and its land armies and fleets were not defeated. At the end of the war Britain still possessed far greater military and economic power than did the United States. Moreover, in terms of Continental politics, the War of Independence was a sideshow for Britain, whose primary competitor and enemy was France. Finally, it should be noted that Britain returned to the Western Hemisphere to battle the United States in the War of 1812 in part to punish the newly independent states for the humiliating defeat imposed on London two decades earlier.

It is not surprising that the American theory of victory that emerged from the Revolutionary War involved absolutes. The nation's first experience with war was one in which failure was not an option; any outcome other than victory would have foreclosed the possibility of a successful movement toward independence. For the United States to exist as an independent, sovereign state, the colonists had an absolute requirement to defeat Great Britain. That the fledgling United States achieved a political–military victory in the War of Independence established the early basis for one American principle of war: Fight when necessary and ensure victory.

In terms of setting historical precedents, this war also established the principle, later codified in what became known as the Monroe Doctrine,[10] that the United States would not tolerate interference in the Western Hemisphere from other states. This principle of excluding European power from the American continents was expressed by George Washington in his *Farewell Address* on September 19, 1796, when he warned about "the insidious wiles of foreign influence." According to Washington, the nation was formed because of the colonists' abiding distrust of "external danger [and the prospect of] . . . frequent interruption[s] of their Peace by foreign [European] Nations."[11] The "Proclamation of Neutrality" that President Washington issued on April 22, 1793, declared that the United States would "adopt and pursue a conduct friendly and impartial" toward Great Britain, Holland, and Spain, who were united in their efforts against the French Revolution.[12] This reconfirmed the principle that had emerged from the War of Independence, which was now becoming a foundation of American thinking about victory; namely, that the only legitimate reason for the United States to wage war is when the nation finds it absolutely necessary to defend its interests and will achieve victory in the endeavor.[13]

When the Treaty of Paris was signed on September 3, 1783, Great Britain formally recognized the independence of the United States.[14] Although this was a political–military victory not a grand strategic one, the War of Independence did produce comprehensive changes in the status quo: Britain was no longer the controlling political and legal authority in the colonies, and the United States was established as a sovereign nation. These changes not only demonstrated the limits of Britain's power but began the trend toward democracy and the demise of colonial movements over the next two centuries.

In terms of the colonies' mobilization for war, the War of Independence is clearly at the middle of the spectrum. Although the budding nation simply did not have the economic wherewithal to mobilize itself in the strategic sense, the colonies did wage this war for over five years and invest some degree of their economic wealth in the endeavor. Finally, since the purpose of the war was to expel Great Britain from the colonies, eliminate London's imperial influence on their affairs, and separate American foreign policy from the machinations of the European power, the United States had no postconflict obligations toward their former rulers.

Thus, the first U.S. national experience with war was a political military victory with comprehensive changes in the status quo. It involved a moderate degree of mobilization for war, and ended with no postconflict obligations toward the enemy state.

War of 1812

The War of 1812, which is also known as the Second War of Independence, occurred at the same time that Britain was occupied with fighting France on the European continent in the Napoleonic Wars. The United States fought against Great Britain from June 18, 1812, to February 17, 1815, in a war that lasted two years and eight months.[15] The causes of the War of 1812 as well as the questions of who, actually, won the war continue to be debated by historians.[16] However, the consensus among historians is that the War of 1812 was provoked by Britain's violation of the sovereign rights of U.S. ships and London's policy of encouraging native Indian populations in the Northwest Territory to attack U.S. settlements and forts.[17] A broad interpretation of why the United States would declare war on Great Britain was presented by President James Madison in his "War Message" to the Congress on June 1, 1812. In that message he wrote that "the conduct of her [Great Britain's] Government presents a series of acts hostile to the United States as an independent and neutral nation."[18] The specific causes of the war for Madison were "impressments" of formerly British (now American) sailors to rejoin the British

Navy; the habit of British warships of remaining near U.S. ports to intimidate and harass commercial shipping; blockades conducted by British ships; the Orders in Council of 1807, by which Britain had declared a blockade of European ports; and the renewal of Indian wars in the west.[19]

The United States also went to war against the British in the War of 1812 as part of President Madison's desire to protect the new nation's territorial prerogatives and commercial interests,[20] and to confirm the principle of the sovereign authority of the United States. In military terms, there was a significant disparity in the size and capability of the U.S. and British military forces. As one scholar observed, as the world's most significant military power Britain possessed a navy with more than six hundred ships and an army with nearly a quarter of a million troops. The United States, by contrast, "could command little more than six thousand regular troops and a naval force consisting of sixteen vessels of all sizes."[21] In a war that lasted a little less than three years, the United States suffered casualties that included 2,260 deaths and 4,505 wounded.[22]

By what standards should we judge the implications of the War of 1812 for a pretheory of victory? First, because it was still to some extent a war of survival for the young United States, which managed to defend its political and territorial prerogatives successfully, this war too falls into the category of a political–military victory.[23] (A subtle point is that analyses of victory tend to emphasize what is at stake versus what is achieved, whereas one of the arguments in this study is that a theory of victory should place greater emphasis on the outcome rather than what is risked.) With this political–military victory, Washington demonstrated that London did not have sufficient power to destroy or call into question the independence and sovereign authority of the United States. This American victory reaffirmed the ability of its limited military force to defend the nation's existence against what was then the reasonable equivalent of a global superpower. Thus this political–military victory effectively both confirmed America's independence and enhanced its reputation among the states of Europe as a serious force to be reckoned with on the international scene.[24] The country, it should be noted, neither gained nor lost territory, and the same applies to the British Empire.

The second consideration is that in terms of the status quo, the War of 1812 did not materially improve the nation's ability to prosecute the war successfully or to mobilize itself.[25] The United States won a series of naval battles in the Great Lakes and several in the Atlantic Ocean, but the land campaign was an overall failure. The United States was unable to conquer Canada as many had initially hoped, and lost many significant battles throughout the war.[26] In military terms, the United States won the war with a series of last-minute victories, notably at the Battle of New Orleans on January 8, 1815 – fifteen days after the Treaty of Ghent was signed, but in advance of news of its signing.[27]

Yet despite the country's record of defeats, President Madison said in an address to the U.S. Senate that the war had been a "campaign signalized by the most brilliant successes."[28] Politically, one objective of the war had been to ensure that Great Britain did not encroach upon or reverse the strategic gains made three decades earlier in the War of Independence, and this was accomplished. In fact, the Treaty of Ghent that ended the war – signed December 24, 1814, but not ratified until February 16, 1815, and proclaimed two days later – essentially did so in terms of *status quo ante bellum,* effectively preserving the political and military conditions that existed before the onset of war.[29]

Third – although this is not one of the scales by which we are measuring victory – the war effectively strengthened the newly emerging sense of nationalism and unity in the United States. This victory in the country's first sizable war since the War of Independence contributed to America's sense that it possessed a distinctive political and cultural identity. For the United States to be able to best the world's greatest military power on land and sea, particularly in several decisive naval battles against an overwhelmingly superior British fleet, demonstrated that Great Britain had suffered a defeat of strategic importance.[30] Still, for reasons already discussed, the United States achieved neither a grand strategic victory nor any substantive change in status quo. Indeed, the fundamental question remains as to whether the United States accomplished what it set out to do in the war. Some argue that the War of 1812 "secured none of the objectives for which it was fought"; but this interpretation can be misleading because it fails to view this victory in strategic terms of the long-term establishment of the United States as a great power in competition with London.[31] However, a competing interpretation is that because the Americans knew "precisely what they wanted," which was to achieve "peace with no concessions," this victory gave them a strategic advantage over England.[32] As one observer in the nineteenth century wrote, the war "is pregnant with important lessons," primary among which is that "we have acquired a knowledge of our weakness and of our strength."[33]

In the end, the War of 1812 was a political–military victory for the United States and a strategic defeat for Great Britain in which neither state lost any of its territory nor saw the destruction of its form of government – despite the fact that British troops burned the White House.[34] The war produced a limited change in the status quo, reaffirming the United States as independent and as the dominant power in the region, thereby weakening Great Britain's strength in the Western Hemisphere. The United States did not engage in a significant mobilization for the War of 1812, but it did expend both human and economic resources during the war. Finally, because this was a war fought to defend political and territorial prerogatives rather than to defeat Great Britain strategically, the United States did not assume any postconflict obligations toward the British Empire.

American Civil War

In terms of its effect on the U.S. theory of victory, the most significant war of the nineteenth century was the Civil War (1861–5).[35] In the wake of tensions that had built for some time, South Carolina seceded on December 20, 1860, after Abraham Lincoln was elected president in 1860. It was followed shortly by Mississippi, Florida, Alabama, Georgia, Louisiana, and Texas. The Southern states decided on February 9, 1861, to establish the Confederate States of America, with Jefferson Davis as its president.[36] The Union North then fought Confederate forces for four years, from April 12, 1861, when its Fort Sumter was fired upon, to April 9, 1865, when General Robert E. Lee surrendered at the Appomattox Court House to General Ulysses S. Grant.[37] Historians still debate the causes of the war, but most agree that they included the widely divergent political, economic, and social views between the North and South on the matter of slavery, the principles of freedom established in the Constitution and the Bill of Rights, and the implications of these for the rights of individual states.[38]

During the Civil War, the prevailing theory of victory for the Union was to defeat the Confederacy and thereby nullify its secession from the republic as a separate sovereign and independent state. When Confederate forces fired against Fort Sumter in Charleston Harbor, President Lincoln ordered the use of military force against the states that had seceded. Between May and June, the states of Arkansas, North Carolina, Virginia, and Tennessee also seceded to join the Confederacy. The fact that North and South had diametrically opposing conditions for victory contributed to an intensely violent and destructive war in which the Union eventually achieved a political–military victory.

From the beginning, Lincoln's fundamental and nonnegotiable objective in the war was not only to abolish the institution and practice of slavery but also to restore the Union. Thus, for the Union, victory was defined in the absolute sense when the Confederacy had surrendered and was reintegrated into the United States. By contrast, victory for the leaders of the Confederacy was defined in terms of the ability of the Confederate States of America to establish their position as an independent and sovereign state. Thus, a critical component of the Confederacy's strategy was to engage the Union in battles whose overall objective was to inflict losses sufficient to demoralize the Union's government, military, and society in the hope that public opinion in the North would demand an end to war. For the South, the war would succeed only if the Confederacy could defeat Union forces in enough military campaigns to persuade the North that the costs of war were too great, so that it would accept Confederate sovereignty.

A decisive characteristic of the Civil War was the great disparity of the North and South in terms of their ability to mobilize economic resources and military capabilities. In contrast with the South's smaller population and essentially agrarian nature, the North's substantially larger population and vastly greater industrial base gave it a significant material advantage. Yet despite these asymmetries, both North and South mobilized for and conducted what became known in the nineteenth century as an exemplar of total war.[39] In terms of the economic and military resources the two sides committed, including the size of their fielded armies and human losses, as well as the long duration of the hostilities, the Civil War involved a significant degree of mobilization.[40] What remains notable was the sheer scale of the destruction and loss of life that both sides suffered. There were nearly a million casualties in that war, including an estimated five hundred and sixty thousand dead. The Civil War also firmly established the principle in the nascent American theory of victory that it is a legitimate aim of strategy to define victory in terms of destroying the enemy and rendering it unable to wage war.

Though it is unresolved to what extent the Union achieved the results that President Lincoln and his military commanders sought in the war, the unconditional surrender of Lee's armies at Appomattox – compelling the Confederacy to disband and its states to rejoin the United States, which therefore lost no territory – provided a clear political–military victory, perhaps as much of one as the War of Independence. It certainly accomplished Lincoln's strategic objective of ensuring that the United States would survive as a unified political and legal entity.[41] It demonstrated that the Confederacy would not be permitted to continue as an independent nation, and also that the institution of slavery, which had fueled the secessionist impulses that posed a threat to the nation's existence, would be brought to an end.[42] Lincoln had signed the Emancipation Proclamation on September 23, 1862, three months after Congress had outlawed slavery in U.S. territories, and the defeat of the Confederacy would soon lead to the abolition of slavery throughout the reunited country. Thus this political–military victory can be interpreted as a moral and ideological success for the Union.[43]

This victory showed that the country would use devastating military force, even against its own people, to defend its existence as a sovereign state. By the end of the war, a significant amount of Southern infrastructure was in need of reconstruction – a clear postconflict obligation for the North, notwithstanding debates about the effectiveness of postwar political and economic actions.[44] The level of destruction inflicted during the Civil War also indicated convincingly to the European powers that the United States might prove an important force in international politics. This in turn significantly bolstered the nation's reputation in Europe as a serious and potentially deadly adversary.[45]

To summarize in pretheoretical terms: The American Civil War represented a political–military victory for the Union because it destroyed the foundations of slavery as an institution and preserved the United States as a unified political and legal entity. The war did produce a comprehensive change in the status quo because the Union destroyed the Confederacy's government, military power, and economy. Both sides were forced to mobilize their economies and industrial resources, and the North prevailed principally because it had a vastly greater economic base to mobilize.[46] Finally, the Union inherited significant and protracted postconflict obligations for rebuilding the government and society of the South, which had been destroyed during four years of war.

The Civil War not only shaped the nation's distinctive political and cultural identity and its concept of victory; like the War of Independence and War of 1812, it also demonstrated that the nation was entering the ranks of the world's great economic, industrial, and military powers.[47] Though the Civil War ultimately increased the sense of national unity in the United States, some of the wounds it generated did not begin to heal until the process of national reintegration well into the twentieth century.

Defined by debates about the nature of fundamental human rights, involving immense levels of destruction, and governed by the demand for unconditional surrender (on which see a later section in this chapter), the Civil War demonstrated how deadly wars can be when animated by ideology. This destructive conflict established a nineteenth-century precedent for the total wars that were to come in the twentieth.

TWENTIETH-CENTURY WARS

The American theory of victory has been shaped by several wars during the twentieth century, notably the two World Wars, those in Korea and Vietnam, and the cold war. The victories gained or defeats suffered (in the case of Vietnam) reinforced the principle that the state should fight wars only when it has the political will and resources necessary to achieve victory. As will be discussed, the American experience in World War II has had a more profound and lasting effect on how American society defined victory than in any other war in its history.

World War I

As the first of the vast wars of the twentieth century, World War I (1914–18) established the modern foundations of how America approaches war and evaluates the conditions necessary for victory.[48] The United States officially joined the Great War when Congress declared war on April 6, 1917. The country quickly mobilized and was involved until the end of hostilities, November 11, 1918, when an armistice was signed by the newly declared German Republic (the kaiser having been forced to abdicate two days earlier).[49] The war in Europe had lasted four years; America's involvement, a year and seven months.

For three years President Woodrow Wilson's administration had acted in accord with the popular movement that supported isolationism and sought to avoid involvement in this European war. The isolationist movement lost momentum, however, in the wake of American deaths aboard merchant ships and other nonmilitary vessels torpedoed by German U-boats. These included the British luxury ocean liner *Lusitania,* whose sinking on May 7, 1915, left 128 U.S. dead. Wilson protested such actions as illegal, and Germany agreed to stop.[50]

In an address to the Senate on January 22, 1917 – one intended to foster a postwar League of Nations, with American participation, to preserve a peace once concluded – the president relayed European assurances that neither side in the war meant to "crush their antagonists." He interpreted this as meaning that what ended this war "must be a peace without victory" – that is, "a peace between equals" rather than "a victor's terms imposed upon the vanquished." However, he argued that only an international commitment to free and open seas, to arms control, and to avoiding "entangling alliances" would produce a permanent settlement of the issues that led to war and yield a "peace that is worth guaranteeing and preserving."[51]

Meanwhile, popular opinion in the United States had been slowly shifting to a consensus that war was necessary. However, the critical event propelling U.S. entry was Germany's announcement on January 31, 1917, that it would pursue a campaign of unrestricted submarine warfare.[52] In this climate President Wilson – who had campaigned for reelection in 1916 with the slogan "He kept us out of war" – supported plans that called for the mass mobilization of the U.S. economy and industry, ensuring that the nation's participation in the war would be on a massive scale.[53] Once the United States was finally drawn into World War I, there was broad political support in American society for achieving victory.[54]

Wilson framed the problem of preparing the nation to fight this war in a way that was consistent with the U.S. approach to victory. In his "War Message" delivered to both houses of Congress on April 2, 1917, the president asked that the "status of belligerent . . . thrust" on the United States by Germany's announcement be accepted.[55] He urged the United States to "exert all its power and employ all its resources to bring the Government of the German Empire to terms and end the war."[56] A few days later the United States formally chose to enter the war.

By 1917 the major European antagonists were already physically and psychologically exhausted from three years of attrition-style trench warfare, which had claimed the lives of millions of soldiers. The prevalent view among these weary and depleted states was that war had become a futile exercise, one leading to the utter devastation of societies and the slaughter of millions of young men.[57] Not so many years earlier, the idea that war had grown too destructive to be fought for rational reasons had been expressed by the Polish banker Ivan Bloch in his 1898 study of modern industrial warfare, *Is War Now Impossible?*[58] Now England, France, and Germany were losing millions of soldiers in combat over lines that would shift by only miles.[59] To imagine the scale of human slaughter, during August 4–25, 1914 – in the course of three weeks – the French alone suffered the loss of 260,000 military personnel.[60]

With his declaratory policy, however, Wilson had started the United States on a course leading to the massive mobilization of its economic and industrial resources. The infusion of U.S. military forces (thousands daily by the summer of 1918) and material resources into Allied efforts was sorely needed, and it clearly contributed to Germany's eventual downfall.[61] Germany, the symbol of authoritarianism in the early twentieth century, was decisively defeated, producing a political–military victory for the Allies. Yet despite America's late entry, some 126,000 U.S. troops were killed in World War I – its first significant human losses since the Civil War, fought half a century earlier.[62]

World War I influenced the American theory of victory, and the type of victory to be pursued, on several levels.[63] First and foremost, the political–military victory gained by the United States and its European allies would later be seen as having laid the foundations of World War II. Winston Churchill expressed this sentiment when he wrote in *The Gathering Storm* that, "in Europe and in Asia, conditions were swiftly created by the victorious Allies which, in the name of peace, cleared the way for the renewal of war."[64] The Great War had produced massive casualties and destruction on a large scale throughout Germany and France, but it did not lead to the rebuilding of the defeated Central Powers or to the conditions necessary to establish peace in the long term. When we consider the reparations imposed on Germany by the Treaty of Versailles, this political–military victory may indeed have contributed to the conditions that led to Germany's economic collapse and to the development of the radical ideology of National Socialism (i.e., Nazism), which gained power in the early 1930s.[65] The scale of devastation in Germany may have been equivalent to that of an Allied strategic victory; but the major European states, which had suffered extraordinarily high human and material losses in the war, could not translate that victory into long-term peace and stability.[66]

Second, Germany's armed forces had been defeated and its society wrecked by the combined forces of the United States, England, and France. One symbol of its military defeat was the scale of Germany's postwar demilitarization that was compelled by the Allies. As Churchill wrote in *The Gathering Storm*, "Germany was disarmed. All her artillery and weapons were destroyed."[67] It is estimated that some fifteen million people died in World War I all told, and as Churchill observed, "Wide regions had been systematically devastated by the enemy or pulverized in the encounter of the armies."[68] The Allies had achieved their political–military victory in part because they had successfully mobilized their economic and industrial resources for war; now they were determined that Germany not be able to mobilize again.

Third, the Allied political–military victory in World War I was consistent with the idea of victory that dominated American politics and war early in the twentieth century, and it legitimized the proposition that the central purpose of war is to achieve decisive results. These developments, however, would be short-lived. The end of World War I coincided with the rise of nationalism and the radical ideologies of National Socialism and Marxism–Leninism that would contribute significantly to the outbreak of World War II only twenty years later.[69] By the late 1920s, Adolf Hitler was making significant progress toward establishing National Socialism as the ideological foundations of modern totalitarianism in Germany.[70] Even before the Treaty of Versailles was signed on June 28, 1919, Vladimir Lenin had effected a communist revolution in Russia. In more ways than one, then, the aftermath of World War I provided a foundation for the radical ideologies that dominated the twentieth century and contributed to the outbreak of World War II and its historically unprecedented levels of devastation.

Fourth, the political–military victory in World War I signaled to the Continental powers that the United States, with its enormous financial resources and industrial might, had emerged in the twentieth century as a global power in its own right. Although entering the war in its later stages, America had made a decisive contribution, with its significant manpower and economic support, to the political–military victory attained in 1918.

As previously noted, the Allies' political–miltary victory could have been turned into a grand strategic one had their leaders looked past the utter defeat of Germany and felt an obligation to help rebuild its economy and industry after the war.[71] The economic, political, and military sources of power of Germany had been destroyed, and though it was to be thoroughly demilitarized to forestall future aggression, its government, economy, and society required reconstruction so as to foster regional stability. The concept of postwar obligations, however, had not been integrated into the victors' strategic lexicon. Thus the Allies failed not on the battlefield but at the neotiation table, by failing to implement humane economic policies after the war – policies that might well have averted the next war.[72]

The most destructive example of the Allies' failure to rebuild Germany's social fabric was the policy of reparations imposed by the Treaty of Versailles, whose terms and conditions effectively propelled Germany toward economic collapse in the late 1920s. The victorious parties agreed in the treaty that "Germany accepts the responsibility of Germany and her allies for causing all the loss and damage" of the war.[73] In his criticism of the economic clauses of the

Treaty of Versailles, Churchill described "the anger of the victors, and the failure of their peoples to understand that no defeated nation or community can ever pay tribute on a scale which would meet the cost of modern war."[74] By assigning blame for the war to Germany and imposing economic reparations that could only be described as draconian, the Allies effectively squandered their political–military victory.

The Allies did attempt to establish democratic norms in Germany; as Churchill observed, "The victors imposed upon the Germans all the long-sought ideals of the liberal nations of the West."[75] Yet although these ideals did take hold in Germany briefly, during the Weimar Republic, the economic harshness of the peace and the failure to rebuild Germany soon led to the economic conditions that, in turn, facilitated the collapse of democracy and the rise of fascism.[76] These conditions would likely have been avoided had the Allies rebuilt the defeated German society and treated the defeated population in a more humane fashion.

The lesson from thinking systematically about victory is this: World War I might have produced a grand strategic victory and long-term peace had the Allies possessed the judgment and humanity to spare Germany the economic pain it endured, above and beyond the humiliation it experienced as a nation defeated in war.[77]

Strictly from a pretheoretical standpoint, though, the United States in World War I achieved a political–military victory that produced an intermediate change in the status quo. This change, however, like the political–military victory itself, was undermined because of the Allies' actions (and inactions) at the end of the war and thereafter. In terms of mobilization, the United States had energized its economic and industrial base for the conduct of war, and by virtue of its enormous capacity had been able to outpace the war production of its allies. Finally, America had virtually no postconflict obligations – and this, as noted, would significantly contribute to the outbreak World War II.

World War II

With the possible exception of the Civil War, World War II (1939–45) had a more profound effect on America's theory of victory than any other war in U.S. history. Regardless of the measures used for analysis – the nature of the war, the objective measure of unconditional surrender, the global scale of hostilities, the total destruction of two belligerents by the end of the war, and the power of the atomic weapons that ended it – World War II firmly established for the American people and their leaders that victory on this scale provides the right model for how the nation conducts its wars. By historical standards, the United States not only achieved grand strategic victory in World War II but also redefined the term "victory" for Americans and their policymakers.

In World War II the Allied strategy was to fight until Germany and Japan were unable to offer any effective military resistance.[78] For the Allies, the war could not end until these totalitarian states either were destroyed as functioning societies or agreed to accept the terms of unconditional surrender, whichever came first. In a message congratulating senior military officers for the success of the air campaign against Germany on October 11, 1943, Churchill emphasized the nature of Allied policy as one of "beating the life out of Germany."[79] When the three leaders of the Allied coalition, President Franklin D. Roosevelt, Prime Minister Winston S. Churchill, and General Secretary Josef Stalin, met in Southeast Ukraine on the Black Sea at the Yalta Conference in February 1945, they reiterated that Allied policy was to prosecute the war until Germany and Japan accepted the terms of unconditional surrender.[80] The object of war was expressed more bluntly by General Curtis LeMay, who was one of the principal architects of the air war against Japan and the first commander of the Strategic Air Command. As he said regarding the firebombing of Japanese cities, the object of war is "to kill people, and when you've killed enough they stop fighting."[81] This strategy was rooted in the stark language of the Atlantic Charter, signed by Allied leaders on August 14, 1941. In that, Roosevelt and Churchill had cited as their fifth objective the "final destruction of the Nazi tyranny," or as Churchill said, "until victory is won."[82]

One element of the American and Allied political strategy for the war was the moral dimension to their notions about the nature of diplomacy and war.[83] The view in the United States and England was that they had an obligation to obliterate the brutal, repressive, and expansionist regimes of Germany and Japan to prevent them from pursuing the aggressive diplomatic and military policies that they had instituted in the 1930s. Using the rhetoric from Washington and London in the Atlantic Charter, the Allies declared that there was no choice but war if they were to defend the principles of democracy, freedom, and self-determination.[84] This political strategy successfully guaranteed that the Allies' strictly military objectives during the war were subordinated to the broader political objectives of the destruction of the totalitarian regime in Berlin and the authoritarian one in Tokyo.[85] This approach legitimized the American view that a meaningful form of victory is most likely to result when, in contrast to World War I, the enemy state has been totally and unambiguously defeated.

The objective of destroying the political and military capabilities of the Axis powers in World War II was based on the supreme objective of war, which was to mobilize the military, economic, and technological resources necessary to annihilate the enemy and weaken its ability to wage war. Henry Kissinger would later say that, in this war, "we had brought to bear our superior resources and inflicted a terrible retribution. The enemy had been utterly defeated by a strategy of attrition unencumbered by political considerations."[86]

Furthermore, the sheer scale of America's victory in the Second World War strengthened the consensus among policymakers and the public that it is legitimate and rational to use all necessary means to defeat another state when it threatens U.S. interests.[87]

The effect of World War II on the American theory of victory can be examined on several levels. First, by any historical standard the United States achieved a grand strategic victory in World War II: It defeated Germany and Japan militarily, destroyed the roots of National Socialism in Germany and of militarism in Japan, demolished their economies and societies on an unprecedented scale, and after the war rebuilt both societies, established democratic governments, and laid the foundations of societies that remain stable and prosperous six decades later. This, in turn, strengthened the argument that success in war should be equivalent to "ultimate victory."[88] Moreover, President Truman articulated a new dimension to this ultimate victory in his Oval Office remarks on August 14, 1945, saying that, "No nation in the history of the world had taken such a position [wanting neither territory nor reparations] in complete victory."[89] The American theory of ultimate victory by whatever means necessary thus acquired the added dimension of extreme postconflict restraint.

Second, World War II affirmed for the United States that the principal reason for war is to defeat the enemy totally in order to remove the threat to peace. That the most meaningful type of victory would be the absolute, total, and final defeat of Germany and Japan was evident in the policy of unconditional surrender (see later section) articulated by the Allies. In a telegram to President Roosevelt on December 10, 1941, three days after Pearl Harbor, Churchill referred to "final victory," in which he noted that with U.S. entry into the war, "All the rest was merely the proper application of overwhelming force."[90] General Dwight Eisenhower also talked about "final victory" to the troops involved in the Allied invasion at Normandy on June 6, 1944.[91]

Third, the conduct of the military campaigns in World War II was consistent with unambiguous conditions regarding the nature of the enemies, their treatment of other nations, and their policies of conquest and subjugation, most notably the alleged repressive and evil nature of the German and Japanese governments.[92] The vilification of the German and Japanese governments, which were described as cruel, repressive, and evil, went beyond the usual war propaganda: The Allied leadership believed they were fighting a war of good versus evil. When combined with the intensity of the emotions that influenced the policies of Allied governments – which "base[d] their hopes for a better future for the world . . . [on the] the right of all peoples to choose the form of government under which they will live"[93] – these political circumstances contributed to ideas about victory that were defined in terms of defeating evil. This jibed with the trend in the American theory of victory to base victory on unconditional surrender or some similar and equally absolute measure of success.

Fourth, victory was influenced by the military, technical, and economic means that were available to the modern state for waging war. In addition to its military and economic resources, the United States also conducted the secret scientific research of the Manhattan Project, which produced the atomic bombs whose use against Hiroshima and Nagasaki brought the war to an unequivocal conclusion. The development of atomic weapons was consistent with the notion that the state is entitled to use whatever instruments are necessary to win a war. The war's framing in moral terms strengthened the principle that it is rational and proper to use overwhelming military power to defeat evil regimes. When the United States and the Allied powers achieved grand strategic victory against the expansionist tendencies and militaristic policies of Germany and Japan, this was seen as a rational and moral outcome. Their victory reaffirmed the principle that when the state is forced to fight, it is legitimate to impose total defeat on its aggressors. World War II thus represents the pinnacle of success in war: From it emerged the proposition that the "good wars" are those in which the state achieves grand strategic victory when there is no alternative but to fight.

In conclusion, the United States and its allies in World War II achieved grand strategic victory against Germany and Japan on a scale that effectively redefined the meaning of victory. Victory in that war coincided with a comprehensive change in the status quo both in terms of the victors and the vanquished, but also in terms of the structure and nature of international politics in the postwar era. To achieve this victory, the United States engaged in industrial and military mobilization on a scale that had not been seen in American history and remains the exemplar of the nation's efforts to mobilize itself for total war. Finally, in what became a historical precedent, the United States established a level of postconflict obligations unlike any before. For nearly a decade after the defeat of Germany and Japan, the United States provided the resources that permitted them to recover from the devastation of war.

The Cold War

The U.S. theory of victory that emerged from World War II did not provide concepts useful during the cold war, that period of strategic hostility between the United States and the Soviet Union in which for nearly fifty years neither fought the other directly. One would think that a theory of victory should not be altered by a time of relative peace, but in fact the cold war was a time of great strategic ferment for policymakers and scholars who sought to understand what victory means when states possess nuclear weapons. The cold war began shortly after the end of World War II and became formally enshrined in the late 1940s by the Truman Doctrine[94] as a period of intense strategic hostility and ideological competition between the United States and the Soviet Union. The American theory of victory was thus necessarily reshaped by the development of atomic weapons and the theory of limited war as a cardinal principle of American foreign policy.[95]

During the cold war, the American theory of victory confronted a historically unique problem; namely, there are few, if any, circumstances in which the United States would risk war with the Soviet Union, which had its first atomic-bomb test in 1949.[96] The first event to demonstrate that there are limits placed on the theory of victory during the cold war was the Korean War. Predictably, these and other events slowly led to the collapse of the modern concept of victory, as strategists and policymakers concluded that a strategy of victory was not rational or practical when it could promote a nuclear war involving nuclear-armed states and their allies.[97] In effect, it slowly dawned on the post–World War II generation of strategists and policymakers that for the first time in history a form of weaponry – both fission-based atomic bombs, like those used on Japan, and the later fusion-based (thermonuclear) hydrogen bombs – may have rendered the concept of military victory totally meaningless. (See "Cold War and Nuclear Weapons" in Chapter 3.)

One of the principal architects of strategy in the early years of the nuclear age was Bernard Brodie, who argued that nuclear weapons made it imperative for states to link tightly their national policy and military aims. The reason was that strategy had shifted from the historical basis of waging wars in order to achieve peace to the avoidance of wars altogether.[98] Thus at first blush nuclear weapons altered many historically derived conclusions about victory. Another strategist, Henry Kissinger (later a U.S. secretary of state), concurred, noting that "Many familiar assumptions about war, diplomacy and the nature of peace will need to be modified before we have developed a theory adequate to the perils and opportunities of the nuclear age."[99] Using this line of reasoning, arms-control theoretician Thomas C. Schelling directly addressed the problem for victory when he observed that military strategy is no longer equivalent to a science of military victory because nuclear weapons are more useful for coercion and intimidation than for victory in the traditional sense.[100] Not surprisingly, America's policymakers, military leadership, and intellectuals concluded that the U.S. theory of victory that had been consistent with the unconditional surrender of Germany and Japan was neither credible nor meaningful when states are armed with nuclear weapons.

In response to the development of long-range, nuclear-armed bombers and ballistic missiles, strategists developed theories postulating that all wars – whether local, unconventional, or nuclear – must be limited in nature and scope because governments could not defend their citizens against nuclear attack or reasonably guarantee any outcome even remotely consistent with "victory."[101] The prevailing military conditions destroyed the idea that the theory of victory could provide any basis on which policymakers could make rational decisions about whether to use military force, given the likely outcome of war – even if the state was defending its vital interests. In effect, the debate about limited war was stimulated by those who sought to preserve credible military options for seeking "partial victories," rather than victories that would completely defeat the enemy.[102]

However, it was widely if grudgingly understood by the late 1940s and certainly by the early 1950s that the combination of nuclear weapons and the ideological struggle between democratic and totalitarian states had effectively destroyed the theory of victory reified by the success of World War II as the fundamental doctrine governing how states conduct war.[103] Given the technology of atomic and, later, hydrogen bombs, the theories that governed the use of military force slowly evolved into an instrument of last resort, to be used only in the most unusual and therefore unlikely circumstances.[104] Once policymakers and citizens understood by the 1950s that any use of nuclear weapons against a similarly armed state would lead to mutual annihilation, the principle of using force to achieve victory was no longer a legitimate option for the state.[105] If the use of force against a nuclear-armed state was not a practical instrument of national policy, then victory was not a practical or meaningful concept. Indeed, the only rational "use" for nuclear weapons was to *deter* war and preserve peace rather than to fight in order to win.[106] This logic was evident to President Eisenhower, who observed that with nuclear weapons "there is no alternative to peace."[107] By the late 1950s and early 1960s, then, the consensus in the American government was that the objectives of deterrence, punishment, and limited wars were more rational than any competing theory of victory because any direct confrontation among nuclear-armed states – even if begun indirectly, by a conflict between allies of such states – would produce mutual suicide rather than victory.

Several conclusions arise from this discussion of the influence of the cold war and nuclear weapons on victory. The first is that, as noted previously, before nuclear weapons were introduced as an instrument of national strategy at the end of World War II, the American theory of war had espoused the principle that it was morally and politically necessary to use any and all required military means to achieve total victory.[108] As strategic theorist and defense analyst Colin S. Gray wrote, an American should understand that the "only kind of war his county can fight and fight very well, is one where there is a clear concept of victory."[109] However, even early in the cold war, strategic thinking in the U.S. defense establishment was governed by the idea that this kind of military total victory cannot be attained against states that possess nuclear weapons and ballistic missiles. As Brodie argued, "Under those circumstances no victory, even if guaranteed in advance . . . would be worth the price."[110]

A second observation is that the U.S. theory of victory had proven itself inadequate in those cases when it is not necessary or, in the nuclear age, practical to impose total defeat or destruction. The problem, as Kissinger argued, is that states need "a strategic doctrine which gives our diplomacy the greatest freedom of action."[111] The conceptual high tide of World War II, on one hand, and the paralysis of the cold war, on the other, leave much to be desired in terms of what constitutes victory for an America facing less extreme circumstances. The legacy of the cold war – and the argument in this book – is that America needs a flexible theory of victory to help policymakers and military leaders plan for different circumstances by clarifying what victory means and what credible alternatives to grand strategic victory must be available to the state. Given such a theory, policymakers ideally will be guided by criteria that permit them to judge whether and when it is prudent to intervene with military force – although, of course, there is never any guarantee that intervention will achieve the goals sought.

The conduct and eventual outcome of the cold war point to several conclusions involving the American theory of victory. The first is that if a viable objective of conflict is to ensure that one state's fundamental political and economic ideas prevail over those of an enemy state, then the cold war can be interpreted as a grand strategic victory for the United States. With the Soviet Union's political and economic collapse and gradual military deterioration, the prevailing ideas promoted by the United States about democratic values and free markets were seen to have won, and thus to have been legitimized. Victory in this case included the establishment of democratic governments, the development of free-market economies, and the emergence of foreign policies on the part of Russia and other former Soviet republics that are less hostile toward U.S. interests. Thus, the United States subsequently contributed to the reorganization of political and economic institutions in Europe and Asia on an unprecedented scale. All of these outcomes are consistent with the idea of grand strategic victory.

Second, since victory in the cold war was not derived from military combat against the Soviet Union, nuclear weapons having deterred conflict between Washington and Moscow, this was a historical anomaly – a rare example of a grand strategic victory that was not the result of military victory on the battlefield. In a climate dominated by nuclear weapons, any strategy based on military victory could have led to the destruction of both societies, plus those of their respective allies. Thus, from its beginnings in the Truman Doctrine, the U.S. cold-war strategy had been one of *containment:* preventing the spread of Marxism–Leninism and totalitarianism rather than destroying the Soviet Union's government, economy, and society. Yet as President Ronald Reagan predicted in a speech in 1981, "The West won't contain Communism. It will transcend Communism."[112]

Third, since nuclear annihilation was the likely outcome of direct military confrontation between the two superpowers, a number of indirect, proxy wars were fought by the *allies* of the superpowers. However, even in these wars there were severe constraints on victory: An ally serving as proxy could not be fully defeated without diminishing the credibility of its superpower ally, which could lead to the very war that was actively being avoided.[113] Thus, the cold-war era produced an intellectual paralysis about what victory, if even possible, means for the state.

Of course, the irony of the cold war, insofar as America's theory of victory is concerned, is that the United States did achieve the grand strategic victory against the Soviet Union that many believed was unattainable, or at least highly unlikely, and did so *without* direct hostilities or war. This grand strategic victory, which radically reordered the international system, produced a comprehensive change in the status quo for the states involved in the struggle. It had involved the mobilization of U.S. economic, industrial, and technological resources on a limited scale, over several decades, as part of a strategy designed to marshal enough military power to deter war, not to engage in it.[114] Moreover, with the end of the cold war the United States had quite limited postconflict obligations, largely involving economic assistance to the states of the former Soviet Union and of Eastern Europe.

The Korean War

From the 1950s throughout the 1970s, the United States was involved in two localized wars in Asia. The first was the Korean War that began on June 24, 1950, when the military forces of the Democratic People's Republic of Korea (PRK; North Korea) launched a surprise invasion of the Republic of Korea (ROK; South Korea), and ended with the signing of a U.N.-negotiated armistice at Panmunjom on July 27, 1953.[115] In this war, the North Korean–Chinese armies of roughly one million troops fought against the numerically comparable forces of the United Nations.

This war began when North Korean forces invaded South Korea without warning; within two months they had almost reached the southern tip of the Korean Peninsula. The United Nations requested support for the defense of South Korea, which led to the formation of an international force commanded by General Douglas MacArthur. These forces stabilized a defensive perimeter around Pusan, in the southeast corner of the peninsula, and then conducted an amphibious landing behind North Korean lines at the port of Inchon, halfway up the west coast. U.N. forces, which were largely manned by U.S. troops, pushed North Korean forces back to the Yalu River, which forms the boundary between the People's Republic of China and North Korea. The United States hoped, with U.N. backing, to reunify the Korean Peninsula under the control of South Korea. On October 1, 1950, General MacArthur warned the North Korean capital, Pyongyang, that "the early and total defeat and complete destruction of your armed forces and war-making potential is now inevitable,"[116] and the city fell to U.N. forces on October 19. However, a Chinese counterattack in support of North Korea pushed U.N. forces back to the thirty-eighth parallel – the line where Korea had been divided into Soviet (North) and American (South) occupations zones after World War II (it having been part of the Japanese Empire since 1910). Chinese and North Korean forces captured Seoul, the capital of South Korea, on January 4, 1951, but U.S. forces recaptured it on March 14, 1951.[117] The next two years were largely a stalemate; then the armistice set up a demilitarized zone around the thirty-eighth parallel.

This war had several important consequences regarding the American theory of victory. Despite its success only five years earlier in World War II, the United States was just beginning to grasp the enormous effect that the cold war could have on what victory means and whether the state can pursue it, in the absolute sense that victory had come to represent, when Soviet nuclear weapons were a factor.[118] As Weigley observed, "Any strategy other that the now familiar strategy of annihilation proved so frustratingly at variance with the American conception of war."[119]

Stalin had concluded that North Korea would be defeated and was determined to avoid war with Washington. Meanwhile, American policymakers believed that they must avoid confrontation with the Soviet Union or its allies – including, at that time, the People's Republic of China, which supported the North Korean regime in Pyongyang.[120] The risks of nuclear war thus imposed profound limits on the range of permissible actions available to the United States. The Korean War was to demonstrate that America could no longer afford to pursue a grand strategic victory.

Once American strategists and policymakers internalized that they could not hope to achieve such a victory in Korea, what emerged was the cold-war strategy of military actions that sought neither to defeat a client state nor to lose any direct military confrontation. In effect, the United States pursued policies and military actions that were consistent with political–military victory (e.g., pushing North Korean forces north of the thirty-eighth parallel) but not with grand strategic victory (e.g., destroying the regime that provoked the war and occupying its territory). For example, although the United Nations waged a large-scale ground and air campaign against North Korea for several years, until the 1951 negotiations led to a hiatus in bombing targets along the Yalu River, there was never any serious discussion of occupying North Korea (as opposed to reunification), given fears in Washington that it would lead to direct confrontation with Moscow and Beijing.[121] Moreover, North Korean forces may have been driven back or defeated, but the government itself was not to be destroyed, nor its territory occupied. This was not a reality that was widely welcomed in the field, nor one accepted by the U.S. commander, General MacArthur, who rebelled at President Truman's decision to limit the range of options available to U.S. military commanders and thus reduce the risk of nuclear war with the Soviet Union. Truman ultimately relieved MacArthur of his command in part over these limits on U.S. military options and the type of victory that could be achieved.[122] However, even if it seemed that full-blown victory was beyond reach, defeat was not a realistic possibility for the United States.[123]

Several conclusions about victory can be drawn from this review of the Korean War. First, the United States and its U.N. allies achieved a political–military victory based on the defeat of the combined military forces of North Korea and China on the peninsula, but grand strategic victory was precluded and they were unable to attain a comprehensive change in the status quo. North Korea itself was not defeated militarily and its totalitarian government was not removed; fifty years later the boundary between the two Koreas remains the same, and the relationship between Pyongyang and Seoul remains mostly hostile.[124] Although it is easy to hypothesize that grand strategic victory would have avoided this, it might well have also drawn Moscow or Beijing into direct war with the United States.

A second conclusion is that when other nuclear-armed states are involved, it is prudent to abide by the logic of escalation control and limited war, since political–military victories are vastly preferable to defeat or annihilation. It was possible to achieve a political–military victory in the case of the Korean War: North Korean forces would be forced back to above the thirty-eighth parallel and deterred from future invasions. However, the end of the Korean War signaled that success was being interpreted in the United States as any outcome that did not involve either of two extremes: the conventional military defeat of its forces or escalation into nuclear war. The logic behind political–military victory in Korea was that the United States had defeated aggression, protected South Korea, and demonstrated its resolve to defend allies; likewise, China and the Soviet Union had protected *their* ally and demonstrated *their* resolve. The problem, however, was that this U.S.–U.N. political–military victory was so pale in comparison with the recent U.S.–Allied victory in World War II that it seemed to undermine the credibility of victory as an organizing principle for action. Nevertheless, this revised theory of victory gained currency and credibility during the cold war because it was the only practical alternative between the extremes of annihilation and capitulation.

In conclusion, the theory of victory that emerged from the Korean War was demonstrably a product of the nuclear stalemate between Washington and Moscow that prevented either side from achieving strategic victory – or even exercising the military power that historically had led to it. The Korean War is perhaps best described as a political–military victory that produced a moderate change in the status quo. To prepare for this war, the United States engaged in a limited mobilization of its military and economic power. Later, it assumed relatively limited postconflict obligations, principally support for rebuilding South Korea after the hostilities and maintaining a long-term military presence on the Korean Peninsula.

Vietnam War

The Vietnam War reaffirmed for American policymakers, theorists, and military leaders the principal conclusion that had emerged during the Korean War: Victory is not possible in war when the state faces nuclear-armed enemies.[125] At a time when the effects of the cold war on victory had been fully inculcated into American strategy and policymaking, these conclusions about victory are significant in terms of their impact on the American theory of victory and how the United States conducted the Vietnam War.[126] Indeed, the combination of hostile relations with Moscow and growing discontent in American society about the futility of defeating insurgencies in the nuclear age had weakened the intellectual consensus on what it meant to achieve victory. Finally, the Vietnam War stands alone as the only significant defeat in American military history. While the reasons are debated, one scholar observed that "The key to U.S. defeat was a profound misunderstanding of enemy tenacity and fighting power . . . a failure to appreciate the fundamental civil dimensions of the war, and preoccupation with the measurable indices of military power and attendant disdain for the ultimately decisive intangibles."[127] To this list of explanations for the U.S. defeat should be added the failure to understand and take into account the demise of practical concepts for victory in the late twentieth century.

The Kennedy, Johnson, and Nixon administrations pledged publicly to protect South Vietnam against aggression from North Vietnam, but the surrender of Saigon, the South Vietnamese capital, on April 30, 1975, signaled that the United States had been defeated by North Vietnam in a decadelong insurgency. According to the original intent of American policymakers in the Kennedy and Johnson administrations, U.S. officials defined victory in the territorial and political terms of preventing North Vietnam from using its military to force South Vietnam into aligning with the communist bloc. U.S. victory was to be based on preventing the annexation of South Vietnam by Hanoi (capital of the North). Thus the consensus in American society was that the United States had lost the war: It had failed to prevent North Vietnam from conquering the South and transforming it into a communist state.[128]

Unlike the other American wars in this study, then, the Vietnam War is a war lost by the United States. In military terms, the United States lost the war because its military campaign was designed to prevent the loss of territory rather than prevent the spread of an insurgency that was based on communist ideology. However, for one official, Assistant Secretary of Defense John McNaughton, the principal objective for the United States was "to avoid a humiliating defeat" and thus regional loss of prestige, whereas the public position was that the United States could and would win the war.[129]

As one of the more complex, confusing, and polarizing wars of the twentieth century, the Vietnam War has important implications for the theory of victory. The first is that, despite the consensus that it is extremely difficult for traditional military forces to achieve victory in guerrilla wars, the logic of the cold war required the United States to fight guerrilla forces in Vietnam.[130] In the more than three decades since the end of that war, there has been little enthusiasm in American society for fighting insurgencies that are based on ethnic, national, and religious forces, given the difficulties in attaining victory in such wars.[131]

Second, the Vietnam War contributed to uncertainty in America about the state's ability to achieve victory and its willingness to tolerate casualties in war. In Vietnam, mounting U.S. casualties contributed to the collapse of public support for the war by fostering the perceptions that victory was not a realistic outcome and that intervention was not worth the costs. As discussed in Chapter 8, there is a relationship between the state's willingness to tolerate casualties and the likelihood that it has a reasonable chance of achieving victory.[132] The notion of "casualty avoidance" gained prominence during the 1990s, when the United States intervened with military force in Somalia, Haiti, Bosnia, and Kosovo in what are regarded as strategically insignificant wars in which the chance of attaining victory was believed to be relatively low.[133] More recently, senior U.S. military officials were hesitant to conduct cave-by-cave searches for the Taliban and al-Qaeda in Afghanistan in late 2001 because they feared that this tactic would produce significant U.S. casualties and undermine public support for the war.[134] At the time of this writing (early 2006) there is growing public dissatisfaction with the daily casualties being sustained by U.S. forces that are occupying Iraq.[135]

A third point relates to the ways in which policymakers and scholars think about victory. The Vietnam War coincides with an era in which policymakers used the concepts of *systems analysis*, with its emphasis on measuring cost and effectiveness, to determine the right strategy for victory. Under the guidance of Robert McNamara, who was secretary of defense in the Kennedy and Johnson administrations, the Department of Defense evaluated whether military operations were successful or victorious on the basis of quantifiable factors.[136] As McNamara wrote in his memoir, "I see quantification as a language to add precision to reasoning about the world."[137] In this climate, the question was whether some optimal allocation of resources would increase the probability of victory in the Vietnam War. Quite the opposite proved true because detailed analyses of strategy and operations could not easily be translated into concrete achievements. In effect, the tools of systems analysis did not help the United States achieve victory but effectively diverted attention away from more serious analyses of victory in that war.[138]

In the case of the Vietnam War, in which 58,000 Americans died, the United States deliberately did not fight the war to *achieve strategic victory* but to demonstrate that it had the resolve to *contain communism*. From the beginning, U.S. policymakers did not believe that victory was possible. President Lyndon Johnson, in discussing strategy for the Vietnam War with Secretary of Defense Robert McNamara, said on February 26, 1965, "I don't think anything is going to be as bad as losing, and *I don't see any way of winning*."[139] On June 21, Johnson reaffirmed the conclusion that the United States could not win when he told McNamara, "I don't see any . . . plan for a victory – militarily or diplomatically."[140] Furthermore, on July 2, Johnson confided to McNamara that "We cannot win with our existing commitment";[141] and on July 25, presidential advisor Clark Clifford said in Johnson's tape-recorded diary, "he [Johnson] doubted that America could win the war."[142] The problem was that the United States could not marshal the political will to use the instruments of power at its disposal to achieve victory because it was stalemated by the risks of nuclear war with North Vietnam's sponsors, the Soviet Union and the People's Republic of China.

A final observation about the relationship between the Vietnam War and the American theory of victory is that Vietnam was a war in which many American policymakers manifested signs of strategic paralysis. Fearing the risks of confrontation with nuclear-armed communist nations, U.S. policymakers were hamstrung by the dilemma in which victory was unobtainable and defeat was unacceptable.[143] Moreover, America's gradual withdrawal from the Vietnam War would contribute to the idea that, if no real victory is possible, given the threat of nuclear annihilation, it is futile to intervene. Like the stalemate of the Korean War, the U.S. defeat in Vietnam contributed to the intellectual impairment in American policymaking that lasted until the 1980s and 1990s, when U.S. military successes against Libya, Panama, and Iraq demonstrated that the United States had moved beyond the Vietnam syndrome. One sign that the defeat in Vietnam had continued to haunt American statesmen was evident when the first President Bush wrote in his memoirs that doubts about victory raised by the Vietnam War "had been put to rest and American credibility restored" by the success in the Persian Gulf War.[144]

The central questions about the Vietnam War for this study are just what was achieved by the United States in terms of (non)victory and how did the war influence the American theory of victory. Since three U.S. administrations had all pledged publicly to protect South Vietnam against aggression from the communist North, the April 1975 surrender of Saigon clearly signaled a defeat for the United States. However, although for the rest of the decade and into the 1980s the Vietnam War was certainly considered an American strategic and military defeat, this perception has been eroded outside of U.S. strategic circles. For example, many of the nations in Southeast Asia do not believe that the Vietnam War was, in retrospect, a strategic defeat for the United States: After the military defeat in South Vietnam, such states as Singapore, Malaysia, Thailand, and Indonesia managed to consolidate their independence. In fact, Vietnam's recent shift toward political and economic integration with the West, including cooperation on defense and security issues with the United States, suggests that a defeat can, over time, evolve into a victory.[145]

Also, the Vietnam War reaffirmed for a generation of U.S. policymakers and scholars that America's theory of victory was irrelevant given the geopolitical realities of the cold war. This line of reasoning contributed to the decision by the Kennedy administration to develop the doctrine of flexible response.[146] The enduring legacy of the Vietnam War for the American theory of victory is that if large-scale wars are to be avoided, and if guerrilla and proxy wars are difficult to win, then victory is not a meaningful concept.

Using the pretheoretical framework from Chapter 4, the Vietnam War can be categorized as a defeat for the United States that produced a comprehensive change in the status quo from the perspective of the leadership in North Vietnam. The United States did not engage in a significant program of mobilization for the war, preferring instead to fight using peacetime economic and fiscal policies, though also using a conscription-based military. Moreover, because of its hostile relationship with Hanoi, the United States was banished from involvement in Vietnam for several decades and thus did not have any postconflict obligations.

UNCONDITIONAL SURRENDER

Perhaps no concept or policy more effectively communicates how American policymakers and citizens think about the nature of victory than "unconditional surrender," which expresses in absolute terms that the fundamental objective of a U.S. war is total victory for the United States and total defeat for the enemy.[147] Yet in terms of modern history, rarely has a state demanded that another state submit to unconditional surrender. As one scholar concluded, between the end of the sixteenth century and 1943, or for a period of about three and a half centuries, not one of Great Britain's fifteen wars ended on the basis of unconditional surrender.[148] Unconditional surrender, though otherwise only rarely used as a criterion for victory, played a significant role in both the Civil War and World War II – and later, as we shall see, in the U.S.-led wars in Afghanistan and Iraq.

Even without the modifier "unconditional," the word "surrender" has the nearly absolute meaning of the act of giving up or abandoning, or to "give up one's self into the power of another."[149] Although surrender is thus essentially an unqualified act, the use of the term "unconditional" means "absolute," and should be interpreted to mean that the state surrenders "without conditions or limitations."[150] As defined by one observer, unconditional surrender is interpreted as "an old military formula applied when an enemy lays down his arms and leaves the consequences to the mercy of the conqueror."[151] In practical terms, the phrase "unconditional surrender" establishes an absolute condition for how wars will end.

The historical origins of unconditional surrender are unclear, but there have been occasional instances in which states or armies demanded that a military fort or garrison surrender unconditionally. An example from the distant historical past is Rome's demand in the Third Punic War that Carthage surrender unconditionally. When the Carthaginians refused to surrender their territory, cities, and people, the Roman legions destroyed Carthage in 146 B.C.[152] The Italian legal scholar Grotius, who was an early architect of international law, described the surrender of Carthage in *Three Books on the Law of War and Peace* as a case of "pure surrender." For Grotius, unconditional, pure, or "absolute" surrender bestows on the victor the "full authority, legal and actual" to treat the defeated without any constraints.[153] But, as he wrote, "The same sense of justice bids that those be spared who yield themselves unconditionally to the victor."[154] The problem, as Grotius observed, is that "After the surrender there is nothing that the vanquished may not have to suffer . . . he is in such a position that everything can be taken from him – his life, his personal liberty, and the property not only of the state but also of individuals."[155] In his analysis of the question, "What is the duty of the victor toward those who make an unconditional surrender?" Grotius concluded, "it is always the part of honour to incline to clemency and generosity," but, "The fact remains, that the victor becomes absolute master."[156]

In the case of the United States, the origins of unconditional surrender as an object of state policy can be traced to the Civil War and President Abraham Lincoln's demand that the Confederacy surrender unconditionally to the Union.[157] After two days of attacks on Fort Donelson in Tennessee, with the advantage seesawing between North and South and with Union reinforcements now arriving, Major General Ulysses S. Grant on February 16, 1862, insisted on the "unconditional and immediate surrender" of Confederate Brigadier General Simon Bolivar Bruckner, who accepted what he called these "ungenerous and unchivalrous terms."[158] When U.S. Grant, now nicknamed Unconditional Surrender Grant, captured a Confederate army at the Battle of Vicksburg in 1863, he initially demanded that Lieutenant General John C. Pemberton submit to these terms; but he relented, offering parole instead.

After the Battle of Shiloh in 1862, Grant concluded that the only way to save the Union was by the "complete conquest" of the Confederacy through a policy of total war.[159] The necessity for unconditional surrender was evident in the war plans of President Lincoln, the architect of the overall strategy for the war. Although at first Lincoln sought to suppress an insurrection rather than to conquer Confederate territory or to overthrow the Confederate government, he eventually concluded that this struggle between two belligerent states must end with the total defeat of one side. Ultimately, he demanded that the Confederacy agree to the terms of unconditional surrender. Thus, Lincoln's strategy for the defeat of the Confederacy, which was based on unconditional surrender and was analytically similar to a strategy of total war, provided the intellectual foundation for three military campaigns: Grant's destruction of Lee's army at Petersburg, General Philip H. Sheridan's decisive defeat of General Jubal A. Early in the Shenandoah Valley, and General William T. Sherman's advance through Georgia and the Carolinas.[160] By contrast, there is no evidence that the concept of unconditional surrender was relevant or meaningful to the South's strategy for the war. However, the leader of the Confederacy, President Jefferson Davis, proposed that victory might be based on dispersing the South's armies as part of a strategy for waging a guerrilla war that would last for decades.[161]

Although Lincoln never called directly for unconditional surrender, his war aims – which included "The restoration of the National Authority throughout all the States. . . . No receding by the Executive of the United States on the Slavery question. . . . No cessation of hostilities short of an end of the war, and the disbanding of all forces hostile to the Government" – amounted effectively to a policy of unconditional surrender. Lincoln's belief that a Confederate surrender was the only way to stop the war was interpreted by Southern officials to mean that Lincoln would accept "nothing less than unconditional surrender."[162] In effect, Lincoln's strategy eliminated any hope among Confederate officials that Washington might trade its demand that the South put an end to slavery in exchange for a negotiated end to the war.[163] In the end, Lincoln's guidance to Grant rejected the prospect of any negotiations with Lee except to discuss the terms of surrender.[164] The day before the surrender at Appomattox on April 9, 1865, General Grant wrote to General Lee that "there is but one condition I would insist upon – namely that the men and officers surrendered shall be disqualified for taking up arms against the Government of the United States until properly exchanged."[165]

In contrast to the American Civil War, World War I afforded a relatively minor role for the policy of unconditional surrender. When the German High Command asked about negotiating peace on the terms established in President Wilson's Fourteen Points, Wilson replied that the United States would demand "not peace negotiations but surrender."[166] Although Generals Hindenburg and Ludendorff expressed the view that Wilson's response was equivalent to a demand for unconditional surrender, in the armistice signed on November 11, 1918, formally bringing World War I to an end, the only use of this phrase was that Germany agreed to the "Unconditional surrender of East Africa."[167] The terms set by the Allied powers – released by the German government and published that same day – included the "surrender" of cannon, machine guns, trench mortars, and planes; the "surrender" of locomotives, railway coaches, and trucks; the "surrender" of U-boats, light cruisers, and Dreadnoughts; and other restrictions.[168] Thus the hostilities of World War I were ended with highly detailed, procedural conditions, rather than with unconditional surrender.

By far the most prominent and significant case in which the United States established unconditional surrender as prerequisite to the end of war was World War II.[169] As early as Roosevelt's declaration of war against Japan before the U.S. Congress on December 8, 1941, the idea of unconditional surrender, though not expressed directly, was in the air when he pledged, "the American people in their righteous might will win through to absolute victory."[170] In his declaration of war against Germany on December 11, Roosevelt stated that "Rapid and united effort . . . will insure a world victory of the forces of justice and of righteousness over the forces of savagery and of barbarism."[171] With these statements, Roosevelt expressed the quintessentially American ideal that the purpose of victory is a "moral" one, in which it is imperative that the sources of evil are vanquished through the total defeat and punishment of the states that started the war. The consensus among U.S. and British leadership was that the war should be fought – as stated in the United Nations Declaration, which was signed by twenty-six countries on January 1, 1942 – until "complete victory over their enemies" is achieved.[172]

In practical terms, the demand for unconditional surrender was enshrined as the fundamental objective of the war at the Casablanca Conference in 1943, when President Roosevelt and British Prime Minister Winston S. Churchill co-chaired a meeting of American and British political and military planners. At that meeting, the wartime leaders of the United States and Great Britain decided to demand the unconditional surrender of Germany, Italy, Japan, and their allies.[173] The phrase formally entered the lexicon of the Allied powers at noon on January 24, 1943, when President Roosevelt told the press after that conference that the United States and Great Britain "were determined to accept nothing less than the unconditional surrender of Germany, Japan, and Italy."[174] As Roosevelt also said that day, "The elimination of German, Japanese and Italian war power means the unconditional surrender of Germany, Japan, or Italy. That means a reasonable assurance of future world peace. It does not mean the destruction of the population of Germany, Italy or Japan, but it does mean the destruction of the philosophies in those countries which are based on conquest and the subjugation of other people."[175] (Churchill initially said that he had first heard unconditional surrender proposed at the Casablanca press conference, but he later amended the record to say that the British Cabinet had been asked earlier by the Americans for their views on a policy of unconditional surrender.)[176] In a speech in Cyprus on February 1, 1943, Churchill spoke about fighting "until unconditional surrender is extorted from those who have laid the world in havoc and ruins."[177] In a February 12 address to the White House Correspondents' Association, Roosevelt said our policy entailed "fighting hard on all fronts and ending the war as quickly as we can on the uncompromising terms of unconditional surrender."[178]

On June 6, 1944, President Roosevelt reiterated that Allied policy remained the "total conquest of the Axis."[179] Just over a year later, a declaration issued by three heads of state – Truman, Churchill, and Chiang Kai-shek – warned about the "inevitable and complete destruction of the Japanese armed forces and just as inevitably utter destruction of the Japanese homeland."[180] (Although Stalin was an active participant at Potsdam, the Soviet Union did not declare war against Japan until after the atomic bomb was dropped on Hiroshima.) Throughout the war, the policy of unconditional surrender was quite popular in American society. In his first address to the Congress, the day after FDR's burial, President Truman declared, "America will never become a party to any plan for partial victory! . . . Our demand has been, and it remains – Unconditional Surrender!"[181] As he later wrote, "when I reaffirmed the policy of unconditional surrender, the chamber rose to its feet."[182] And in his Memorial Day message of June 1, 1945, Truman "threatened Japan with 'the kind of ruin which they have seen come to Germany' if it did not surrender promptly and unconditionally."[183]

At the end of the war, both Germany and Japan agreed to the terms of unconditional surrender. To cite the words of Germany's surrender on May 7, 1945: "We the undersigned, acting by authority of the German High Command, hereby surrender unconditionally to the supreme command of the Allied Expeditionary Force and simultaneously to the Soviet High Command all forces on land, sea and in the air who are at this date under German control."[184] Likewise, the Japanese surrender signed aboard the USS *Missouri* on September 2 proclaimed "the unconditional surrender to the Allied Powers of the Japanese Imperial General Headquarters and of all Japanese armed forces and all armed forces under the Japanese control wherever situated."[185] Germany and Japan's decisions to surrender contributed to the American theory of victory; but decades later there is still a lively scholarly debate about the precise reasons that compelled these states to surrender unconditionally, and whether the demand for unconditional surrender extended the war.[186]

In the American experience of war, the United States used its entire military and economic power in the two wars in which the U.S. objective was to defeat the enemy totally. In both cases, the United States was willing to make significant sacrifices to defend its interests until the aggressor was unable or unwilling to continue the war.[187] In U.S. military strategy, this concept is consistent with total war, in which the supreme principle of war is to achieve victory by annihilating the enemy. Once the United States defined its strategy in World War II as the unconditional surrender of the Axis powers, U.S. strategy was to marshal all of the resources necessary to destroy the armed forces and economy of the enemy. The only option for the enemy, from the American perspective, was to surrender unconditionally before the process of annihilation was completed. As stated in the *United States Strategic Bombing Survey, Summary Report, European War,* "In January 1942, at Casablanca, the objective of the strategic air forces was established as the 'destruction and dislocation of the German Military, industrial, and economic system and the undermining of the morale of the German people to the point where their capacity for armed resistance is fatally weakened.'"[188] A policy of unconditional surrender, which is consistent with grand strategic victory and the desire for permanent peace, is based on the proposition that the war will produce a comprehensive change in the status quo and that the successful prosecution of the war will involve extensive mobilization. Moreover, a U.S. decision to seek unconditional surrender implies that the victory is likely to require extensive postwar obligations toward the defeated.[189]

Articulating a policy of unconditional surrender has several consequences for how the nation organizes itself for war. First, it transforms the conflict into total war, and thus virtually guarantees that the state is obligated to mobilize considerable resources to destroy the enemy's political, economic, and military means for waging war. In World War II, for example, the United States mobilized its domestic economy into a war machine whose production levels of aircraft, tanks, and ships vastly exceeded the production capacities of Germany or Japan or the number of weapons that these states could destroy, shoot down, or sink.[190]

Second, a policy of unconditional surrender is likely to have a significant deterrent effect on potential U.S. adversaries. Although this objective has been the exception rather than the rule in wars fought by the United States, the rhetoric of unconditional surrender signals to potential adversaries that the state's policy could shift to *total* war, thus implying that America is prepared to wage war until the enemy is so psychologically and economically exhausted that it can no longer fight. By indicating that the United States views a war as an absolute struggle against an enemy, whether it be a state, such as Iraq, or the forces of terrorism, this rhetoric can limit the enemy's ability to end the war before it is too enfeebled, militarily and otherwise, to continue.

Third, the principle of unconditional surrender raises the prospect, which involves considerable risks for the enemy, that the United States may seek to completely reshape the enemy state and its institutions so that it will never again be able to threaten the United States or any other democracies. President Roosevelt used this logic when he said that Germany, Japan, and Italy "must be disarmed and kept disarmed, and they must abandon the philosophy which has brought so much suffering to the world."[191] To defeat Japan, the U.S. Joint Chiefs of Staff approved on May 8, 1943, the "Strategic Plan for the Defeat of Japan," which promulgated the objective of unconditional surrender and raised the possibility that it might be necessary to invade the Japanese home islands.[192] Furthermore, the Joint Chiefs of Staff issued a directive on May 25, 1945, named Operation Downfall, for a planned invasion designed to bring about Japan's unconditional surrender. These plans established the basis of the U.S. strategy for defeating Japan in World War II.[193]

Fourth, the decision to implement a policy of unconditional surrender shows that the state is pursuing grand strategic victory, although whether it can succeed depends on many factors, including the ability of a democracy to maintain public support. President Lincoln during the Civil War and President Roosevelt during World War II faced similar problems with maintaining public support for a total war.[194]

The policy of unconditional surrender raises several analytic problems. One is that its comprehensive nature makes it more difficult to define the term precisely or to develop gradations in the policy. This issue was raised by General George C. Marshall, the chief of staff of the U.S. Army, on June 9, 1945, in a memorandum to Secretary of War Henry L. Stimson, when he suggested that the United States should change the objective of the war against Japan from "unconditional surrender" to "complete defeat and permanent destruction of the war making power of Japan." His reasoning was that since the term unconditional surrender is "difficult to define," "we should cease talking about unconditional surrender of Japan and begin to define our true objective in terms of defeat and disarmament."[195] Marshall's argument was evidence of a deeper debate at the highest levels of the U.S. government as to whether the demand for unconditional surrender might so limit Germany and Japan's options that the war might be prolonged and thus vastly more destructive.[196]

To sum up: The decision to impose unconditional surrender represents one of two contending American approaches to, or strategies for, war. The first involves wars of conquest or the defense of territory, which can translate into a political–military victory and negotiated conclusion; the second seeks to overthrow the antagonist's political and economic system in a form of grand strategic victory.[197] From this review of American military history, it is clear that the vast majority of U.S. wars fall into the category of political–military victories. The obvious exceptions are the Civil War, World War II, and the cold war. In the first two of these, the United States waged a total war governed by the policy of unconditional surrender and ended with the destruction of the adversary's political, economic, and military systems. The cold war, however, remains an anomaly: Although the United States achieved grand strategic victory, it did so without hostilities, the level of mobilization consistent with total war, or the reorganization of the enemy's political and economic system of governance. Furthermore, the language of unconditional surrender was not used during the cold war – and would have had little practical meaning in that nuclear context. In terms of the relationship between unconditional surrender and the American theory of victory, the fundamental U.S. approach toward war remains highly sympathetic to the principles outlined in unconditional surrender even if it remains the case that this objective has rarely been sought in American military history. American culture celebrates its winners by consecrating their accomplishments and memories, and victory on the scale represented by unconditional surrender remains as central to the American ethos of war as the ideals of freedom and prosperity are to its politics and economics.

AMERICAN CRITERIA FOR VICTORY

Building on the foregoing review of American wars, this discussion examines several criteria used to define what victory means, whether and at what level the state has achieved it, and its political, military, and economic costs. Before evaluating these criteria for a pretheory of victory, it is important to understand precisely what *criteria* are. At the simplest level, a "criterion" is defined as a "standard, rule, or test on which a judgment [in this case, victory] or decision can be based"; a fuller definition is "a standard of judging; any approved or established rule or test, by which facts, principles, opinions, and conduct are tried in forming a correct judgment respecting them."[198] In the *Dictionary of Philosophy,* a criterion is defined thus: "Broadly speaking, any ground, basis, or means of judging anything as to its quality. . . . [It may be] either assumed or derived."[199] So the objective is to produce rules or standards for judging what victory is and the conditions that exist when the state is said to have attained it. However, the process of describing and understanding these criteria involves several analytic problems.

First, as dicussed in Chapter 1, there is no precise agreement on what victory means or even whether victory can be defined in exact terms. Considering the complex nature of war and the imprecise nature of the language associated with victory, there may be several criteria for victory that apply equally well to any specific outcome.[200] Second, the fact that states achieve widely different outcomes in war, ranging from tactical to strategic victory and partial to total defeats, greatly expands the range of possibilities that must be addressed by criteria for victory. Third, the prevailing belief in American society is that any outcome that falls short of defeating the enemy in strategic terms is often interpreted as equivalent to defeat or failure. Although for historical and cultural reasons American society is not comfortable with what could be described as partial or incomplete victories, the fact is that since 1945 – and indeed throughout most of the nation's history – U.S. military interventions have yielded political–military victories rather than grand strategic ones. In this sense, then, criteria for victory are likely to be weighted toward more significant victories. With these thoughts in mind, this discussion represents an initial effort to define how to translate *actions the state may implement* when it seeks to win into criteria for understanding victory.

1. Defeat Enemy Military Forces and Its Economic Infrastructure

The first action used as a criterion is defeating the enemy's military forces and the economic infrastructure that supports its ability to wage war. The ability to accomplish this determines whether it is possible for the state to continue to prosecute a war and whether victory has been attained. General Eisenhower reaffirmed this principle after Germany's surrender on May 7, 1945, when he said, "The Allied forces which landed on the continent on June 6, 1944, have utterly defeated the Germans on land, sea and in the air."[201] When this criterion is satisfied, victory is achieved because the enemy is no longer able to support hostilities and its military forces are unable to offer further resistance. However, this condition can occur even when large numbers of enemy military forces are still *deployed*, whether in a theater of operations or globally. For example, at the time that Colonel General Alfred Jodl signed the surrender instrument on Germany's behalf, millions of German soldiers were deployed throughout Europe. Nevertheless, on that day, Germany relinquished control over "all forces on land, sea and in the air who are at this date under German control."[202]

Pursuing the defeat of the enemy state's military forces and economy, so that it cannot offer effective military resistance, may lengthen the duration of the war and increase the level of destruction. For example, Allied political and military leaders in World War II worried that the objective of unconditional surrender was likely to increase the resistance of the German and Japanese governments and populations. As outlined in numerous studies written in the aftermath of that war, the concern was that this policy would make the war more destructive and costly and ultimately prolong it.[203] If the state pursues victory on a strategic scale, which represents a more ambitious and time-consuming objective than lesser forms of victory, it can motivate the enemy's military forces and civilian population to offer greater resistance.[204] If the objective is grand strategic victory, the enemy has little to lose from adopting a policy of maximum resistance. In conceptual terms, there is some relationship between the criterion of defeating military forces and the level of victory required to achieve this outcome.

The decision to defeat the enemy's armed forces and economic capability does increase the human and material demands on the state's economy and industrial base. During World War II, for example, American planners did not assume that simply producing more military equipment than Germany would ensure the defeat of German armed forces; rather, they concluded that victory would emerge only if the United States could fight Germany as part of a strategy whose ultimate objective was to destroy Germany's military power.[205] In the case of Japan, even after the first atomic bomb was dropped on Hiroshima on August 6, 1945, President Truman warned Tokyo, "We are now prepared to obliterate more rapidly and completely every productive enterprise the Japanese have above ground in any city. . . . Let there be no mistake; we shall completely destroy Japan's power to make war."[206] Tokyo's ministers announced on August 10, 1945, that "the Japanese Government is ready to accept the terms enumerated in the joint declaration which was issued at Potsdam on July 26, 1945";[207] they ratified that decision on August 14, and Japan formally surrendered on September 2.

The United States had inflicted considerable destruction on Japan's military forces and cities; but rather than allow Japan to endure the physical and economic deprivation that would greatly prolong its suffering and slow the pace of political recovery, America took on the postconflict obligation of rebuilding Japan's government, constitution, economy, and political culture in the years to come.[208] However, there is no guarantee that a victorious state will assume responsibility for the fate of a militarily and economically defeated enemy. For example, the policies pursued by the Soviet government toward the German people in the Soviet-controlled zone were brutal in contrast with the policies adopted in the American zone, suggesting that Moscow planned to take control of Germany and to punish the populace to the extent permitted by the Allied powers.[209] The Soviet plan to impose reparations on Germany and generally effect retribution was discussed by Josef Stalin, who defended, according to President Truman, the "moral right of the Soviet Union to reparations . . . based on the fact that for three and a half years its territory had been occupied and much devastation caused."[210]

Finally, there are serious consequences when a state does *not* defeat the enemy's armed forces but leaves those forces intact. The destruction of a state's military power puts its survival entirely at the discretion of the victor. As discussed in Chapter 8, the decision by the United States and its coalition partners to allow Iraqi military forces, including its Republican Guard units, to survive Iraq's defeat in the 1991 Persian Gulf War was interpreted by some in the long term as a failure. Iraq's political and military position was left unresolved by the war; this, in turn, diminished the level of the victory achieved by the coalition. A decade later the United Nations faced a resurgent Iraq, whose alleged programs for developing weapons of mass destruction were used as a basis for the U.S.-led invasion in March 2003, as discussed in Chapter 11.[211]

2. Control the Enemy State

The second action serving as a criterion of victory is establishing and maintaining complete control over the enemy state and its institutions. Often taking the form of occupation, this more comprehensive form of victory exists when the victor exercises sovereign control over the defeated state and its territory. (A related criterion, rebuilding a government – whether along democratic lines, as in West Germany, or totalitarian ones as in East Germany – is covered in the next section.)

At the end of hostilities in World War II, the United States and its allies used their overwhelming power to establish complete control over the territories and governments of defeated Germany and Japan. (The Allied sphere of influence extended to those states that had initially been conquered by the Axis powers but were reestablished as sovereign states by the end of the war.) On June 5, 1945, the United States, Soviet Union, United Kingdom, and France assumed supreme authority in Germany. The "Protocol of the Proceedings of the Berlin (Potsdam) Conference," signed on August 1, 1945, gave the victorious powers effective sovereign control over all facets of civil society and government in Germany, which the Allies had earlier divided into zones of influence.[212] In the "Proclamation Defining Terms for Japanese Surrender," which was signed on July 26, 1945, and known as the Potsdam Declaration, the Allied powers established a similar degree of control in postwar Japan: "[U]ntil there is convincing proof that Japan's war-making power is destroyed, points in Japanese territory to be designated by the Allies shall be occupied. . . . We call upon the government of Japan to proclaim now the unconditional surrender of all Japanese armed forces. . . . The alternative for Japan is prompt and utter destruction."[213] As stated in a presidential policy statement issued days after Japan's formal surrender, "There will be a military occupation of the Japanese home islands to carry into effect the surrender terms and further the achievement of the ultimate objectives."[214] All of these actions were consistent with Roosevelt's declaration in his Fourth Inaugural Address on January 20, 1945, that "In the days and in the years that are to come we shall work for a just and honorable peace, a durable peace, as today we work and fight for total victory in war."[215]

As a result of the grand strategic victory over the Axis powers in 1945, the United States and the Allies gained the legitimate right and authority to exercise complete control over all political and governmental activities of Germany and Japan.[216] The practical effect was that the Allied political and military officials responsible for the occupation dominated virtually every facet of life in the defeated German and Japanese societies, including their physical territory and government as well as military forces and economy. The occupation authorities that were imposed by the Allies lasted for four years in Germany and more than six years in Japan, whereafter full sovereign authority was returned to these states.[217] The criterion of controlling the enemy state implies that the victor destroys or nullifies those individuals, institutions, and norms that initially led to war. In the case of World War II, President Roosevelt had proclaimed that a fundamental objective of the war was "smashing the militarism imposed by [German and Japanese] war lords upon their enslaved peoples."[218] The first of President Truman's two "ultimate objectives" was to "insure that Japan will not again become a menace to the United States or to the peace and security of the world"; as one means of accomplishing this, "Japan will be completely disarmed and demilitarized."[219]

The Allies' high degree of control over Germany and Japan was moderated by their view that the purpose of victory was not to abuse or enslave those who are defeated in war. For example, President Roosevelt had declared in 1942 that the "United Nations have no intention to enslave the German people," and British Prime Minister Churchill said that "Our inflexible insistence on Unconditional Surrender does not mean that we shall strain our victorious arms by a wrong and cruel treatment of whole populations."[220] The Potsdam Declaration affirmed that "We do not intend that the Japanese shall be enslaved as a race or destroyed as a nation."[221] From this interpretation it follows that the victor should use the opportunity presented by victory not to punish the defeated society but to reform those elements that pushed the enemy state toward war. Citing the Potsdam Declaration: "There must be eliminated for all time the authority and influence of those who have deceived and misled the people of Japan into embarking on world conquest."[222] However, there is no guarantee that this strategy for victory will be shared universally by other states. A case in point is Moscow's policies and actions during the Red Army's occupation of states in Eastern and Central Europe after World War II.[223] Likewise, the Soviet Union's strategy after World War II was to punish the German population and install a totalitarian government under Moscow's tight control.

3. Political and Governmental Reform

The third action-as-criterion, related to the second, is reforming the defeated state's political and governmental system. In his January 6, 1942 State of the Union address, President Roosevelt had outlined the principle behind this criterion for victory when he'd proposed "establishing and securing freedom of speech, freedom of religion, freedom from want."[224] In the aftermath of World War II, the United States assumed responsibility for implementing programs that were designed to build democratic governments in Germany and Japan.[225] After their respective surrenders in May and August 1945, the United States began the process of helping these states adopt the democratic governments that have endured for more than half a century. Having gained absolute control over the Japanese government and shared responsibility with the Allies for Germany's fate, the United States instituted programs that formally established the procedures by which these societies moved toward democratic governance. In (West) Germany, the United States reorganized the government in order to "destroy the roots of aggression" and impose a "social, legal, and economic revolution."[226] In Japan, the governmental reforms, however democratically inclined, were controlled authoritatively by the Supreme Commander for the Allied Powers (SCAP), General Douglas MacArthur.[227]

In Japan, the U.S. policy was to build a democratic government while encouraging the nation to change its "feudal and authoritarian tendencies."[228] The occupation, according to the U.S. Initial Post-Surrender Policy for Japan (September 6, 1945), was designed to "bring about the eventual establishment of a peaceful and responsible government which will respect the rights of other states and will support the objectives of the United States as reflected in the ideals and principles of the Charter of the United Nations" (45). It was also intended to "shape the machinery of government in such ways as will increase the responsiveness of the great powers of government to the will of the mass of the Japanese populace" (64). Furthermore, Article 9 of Japan's new constitution went so far as to declare that "the Japanese people forever renounce war as a sovereign right of the nation and the threat or use of force as a means of settling international disputes" (39). The policy of building a democracy in Japan was based on four objectives: "To eliminate the political power of the Emperor. To make the executive power responsible to the people or their representatives. To establish a legislative body directly responsible to an electorate of all adult citizens. To develop a political party system in which democratically controlled parties can be held responsible by the nation for the conduct of the government" (64). This program of democratic government reform included a representative government elected by the populace, an independent judicial system, and the new constitution, which went into effect on May 3, 1947. The constitution – a Japanese rewrite of an American draft – moved the political power of the Emperor to the people, granting him a symbolic role. It also included provisions for its amendment, though these require a two-thirds majority in both houses of the Diet, followed by a referendum (64–72).

The decision to rebuild the governments of Germany and Japan along democratic lines was essential to harmonizing their political, military, and economic policies with the strategic interests and policies of the United States. For policymakers in Washington, a pragmatic reason for rebuilding the government of Germany in this way was so it would assist in the effort to prevent the Soviet Union from dominating postwar Europe.[229] By the 1950s Germany and Japan had made significant progress toward establishing free, stable, and prosperous societies, and by the 1960s both states were able to support the U.S. strategy of building a coalition of states to bolster Washington's policy of containing the Soviet Union and the ideology of communism.[230] As a result, the criterion of political and governmental reform that was established as a fundamental condition of victory also strengthened collaterally the policy of containing Soviet-style communism. A corollary benefit of reforming these societies was this policy would significantly reduce the risk of Germany or Japan reverting to the militarism or totalitarianism that could lead to another war.[231]

4. Rebuild the Economy and Infrastructure

The fourth action to operate as a criterion of U.S. victory is rebuilding the defeated states' physical infrastructure and economy, which ranges from feeding and clothing the defeated population to rebuilding its transportation, energy, and food production and distribution systems. This criterion stands in stark contrast to the historical pattern, in which victorious states largely ignored the plight of the vanquished state, which was permitted to suffer the pain, deprivation, and starvation that are the products of military defeat. Perhaps the most vivid example from history is that of Rome, which utterly devastated Carthage at the end of the Third Punic War – selling its people into slavery, burning the city, and razing what was left.[232] In an example from the twentieth century, Truman noted in his memoirs that Stalin had defended the principle of punishing the defeated: "Stalin remarked that that we should appreciate the position in which the Poles found themselves. They were taking revenge on the Germans, he said, for the injuries that the Germans had caused them in the course of centuries."[233]

The post–World War II policy of boosting the economy – at first, agriculturally and through humanitarian relief efforts, but eventually even by encouraging the rebuilding of industry in Germany and Japan – was in reaction to the fact that the war, particularly the air war, had reduced both economies to a state of absolute ruin. Both had undergone several years of strategic bombing; Germany had also endured an invasion. To understand the scale of the commitment to rebuild, it is estimated that the war had destroyed roughly half of the total economic capacity of Germany and Japan.[234] Facing a historically precedented level of devastation, the Allies were forced for humanitarian reasons to organize a massive effort to feed, clothe, and shelter the German and Japanese populations, who otherwise would have died by the millions from starvation and exposure to the elements. However, the U.S. postwar policy for rebuilding was guided by the principle that the German and Japanese people must assume primary responsibility for providing the manpower and technical talent necessary for their economic and industrial reconstruction.

In Germany, World War II had destroyed or rendered uninhabitable 40 percent of the housing; millions were homeless, and the average consumption of food was fewer than a thousand calories per day. To prevent mass starvation, the United States and United Kingdom together starting spending one billion dollars a year to provide food and shelter.[235] To implement this criterion of victory, the United States in July 1947 proposed the Marshall Plan to provide billions of dollars in economic assistance for helping (West) Germany and other societies in Western Europe, especially Britain and France, rebuild after the war; it was signed into law on April 3, 1948, and began disbursements in July.[236] The intention of the architects of the Marshall Plan, which expressed their overall approach to economic recovery, was to provide Germany (except the Soviet-controlled sector) with the financial resources necessary for rebuilding its economy and infrastructure but to leave the work and responsibility for rebuilding to the German people.[237]

In the case of Japan, the scale of destruction from the air war had similarly disabling effects on its economy. To imagine the devastation, consider the fact that five months before the atomic bombs destroyed Hiroshima and Nagasaki and killed several hundred thousand people, the firebombing of Tokyo on March 10, 1945, had killed an estimated hundred thousand people.[238] As articulated in the Initial Post-Surrender Policy, "The Japanese people shall be afforded opportunity to develop for themselves an economy which will permit the peacetime requirements of the population to be met. . . . The plight of Japan is the direct outcome of its own behavior, and the Allies will not undertake the burden of repairing the damage."[239] U.S. policy for the occupation therby placed the overall responsibility for economic reconstruction on the Japanese people and their new government. Japan was seen as having less economic or strategic importance than Germany to the United States, and the rebuilding of its economy was slow; still, those modest U.S. efforts were supplemented with imports of food to "prevent complete collapse or starvation."[240]

U.S. policymakers did assume primary responsibility for providing monies that permitted those devastated societies to engage in postwar reconstruction. They understood, as had Roosevelt, that the failure to respond would lead to human misery on a massive scale in Europe and Japan – and perhaps to another war. The consensus in Washington was that the failure to provide financial assistance after World War I had directly contributed to the German economic collapse of the 1920s, which in turn had led to National Socialism and Hitler in the early 1930s; World War II had been a product of the militarism that ensued.[241] Moreover, American policymakers pragmatically understood that their ability to contain the Soviet Union would be strengthened by a coalition of democratic, free-market states in Europe and Asia.

An implicit consequence of this criterion is the ability to control how and toward what ends the defeated society reconstructs its economy. The United States used its economic resources, military power, and political authority – including the imposition of martial law in Germany and Japan immediately after the war[242] – to direct how Germany and Japan managed their economic renewal. Enforced demilitarization was central to Allied plans, of course. In Germany, however, the United States also soon urged economic integration of the various Allied zones and encouraged German exports, needed by the rest of Europe, in hopes of promoting financial stability.[243] In Japan, as noted, General MacArthur's peremptory authority governed how Japan rebuilt its postwar government, economy, and civil society.[244] For example, Japan became a vital supplier for the U.S.–U.N. Korean War effort, with the moribund Toyota providing over five thousand vehicles (and thus revitalizing itself). Such instruments of control notwithstanding, the United States did accept significant economic costs, designed to prevent the then-hated Germans and Japanese from suffering undue pain once the war was over.[245] This policy of economic reform, based on the investment of vast resources to rebuild and thereby modernize destroyed industrial facilities, eventually permitted Germany and Japan to become serious economic competitors of the United States.

Nearly sixty years since the United States proposed the Marshall Plan for rebuilding war-ravaged societies in Europe, the decision to rebuild a severely defeated enemy's economic institutions and infrastructure has become a fundamental criterion of victory. It was as a result of this criterion, however, that the United States refrained from attacking transportation, communication, government, and economic systems when it intervened with military force during the 1990s. The dilemma is that the United States would have felt obligated to reconstruct these targets after the war; and yet these are precisely what must be destroyed in order to achieve victory according to the American theory. Later, the coalition air campaign against Iraq in 2003 destroyed significant sectors of the Iraqi society, but there was a systematic effort to spare the bridges, roads, infrastructure, and industries that would otherwise have to be rebuilt.

5. Realign the Enemy State's Foreign Policy

The fifth action-as-criterion is reorganizing the defeated state's foreign policy in order to prevent threats to the victor's strategic interests. When we consider the economic and human resources, as well as materiel, that the state might expend in war, it is prudent to take steps that will prevent the vanquished state from developing an independent foreign policy that might be hostile to the victor's interests. Recall that one U.S. postwar objective (quoted in section 3) was to set up a new Japanese government that specifically would "support the objectives of the United States" and the U.N. Charter.[246]

In pragmatic terms, the principal reason for realigning the defeated state's foreign policy is to make it more supportive of the victor's interests and thereby reduce the chance of future wars.[247] This reasoning was contained in the language of the Atlantic Charter in 1941, which affirmed that the objective of the alliance was to prevent Germany from threatening international peace and security.[248] In a memorandum for President Truman, Secretary of War Henry Stimson declared that the United States has a "national interest in creating, if possible, a condition wherein the Japanese nation may live as a peaceful and useful member of the future Pacific community."[249] The broader reason for the military occupation of Japan was to "permit [Japan's] eventual admission as a responsible and peaceful member of the family of nations."[250]

When Germany and Japan surrendered unconditionally to the Allied powers, the United States and its allies assumed control over all aspects of their foreign and security policies. The reasoning for policymakers in Washington was that with the expenditure of national blood and treasure and the large-scale devastation in Europe and Asia after World War II, the nation would not accept any German or Japanese policies or actions that threatened the U.S. desire to promote peace and prosperity after the war. Thus any approach that did not include total control over these state's foreign policies would likely have generated significant domestic and diplomatic problems for the Truman administration.[251]

The challenge for the victor is to ensure that the defeated state does not revert to the antagonistic and destabilizing foreign policies that compelled the victor to wage war in the first place. However, this criterion does not guarantee that the vanquished state will support the interests of the victor forever. For example, although Germany has pursued foreign policies that are largely supportive of the United States, it did directly challenge Washington by opposing the Bush administration's decision to attack Iraq in March 2003.[252]

6. Build a New Strategic Relationship with the Defeated State

The final action serving as a criterion of U.S. victory is forging close ties with the vanquished state. Once an enemy's military and economic instruments of power have been destroyed, there can be significant political and humanitarian pressures to build a new strategic relationship with the defeated state, with the victorious state becoming its guardian. There were many instances in the twentieth century of the United States using victory as an opportunity to build new relationships with the states it had defeated; Germany, Japan, and Panama are prominent examples. How effective such revised relationships could be was manifested in the coalition organized by Washington to support the policy of Soviet containment.

One reason for building new relationships is to establish a political and social order that contributes to international stability. Ignoring the plight of the defeated state might, at its extreme, lead to mass starvation in the defeated society, threatening the foundations of international security. Such neglect, by violating the norms of civilized behavior, would also tarnish the victor's reputation and thus weaken its power. The punitive reparations demanded of Germany by the Allies after World War I exemplify another kind of failure to construct a new strategic relationship – in this case, as already noted, precipitating a second war.

A final observation is that this criterion tends to impose significant post-conflict obligations on the victorious state, as seen not only in Germany and Japan but more recently with the wars against Afghanistan and Iraq. The decision to build strategic relationships with defeated states is an expensive and long-term undertaking whose magnitude cannot be ignored when considering how (or even whether) to intervene militarily so as to achieve victory.

CONCLUSION

This chapter has reviewed two hundred years of the nation's experiences with war, from 1776 to 1975. All of these conflicts, from the War of Independence to the Vietnam War, have left their indelible marks on the American theory of victory. By relating these wars to the organizing principles of a pretheory of victory, the intention was to develop a more systematic understanding of what victory in fact means to the United States.

The development and application of a U.S. theory of victory can be divided into three distinct historical phases. The first, as exemplified by the experiences in the Revolutionary War and Civil War, is characterized by the concept of *political–military victory,* in which wars can be fought for reasons of territory and ideology. Without success in these wars, either the United States would never have existed as a sovereign state, independent of Great Britain, or it would have split into two separate nations – industrial and increasingly antislavery in the North, agricultural and slavery-dependent in the South – and likely would have fought another, perhaps even more destructive war later. For the Civil War the United States mobilized itself economically and industrially on a massive scale, producing death and destruction in epic proportions.

In the second period, victory was defined by the concept of *total war,* war fought without any serious attempt to limit the use of military power and to achieve ends proportionate to the resources consumed. In World War I, the European states pursued a strategy of annihilation without any evident conscience for the human casualties and economic losses engendered in four years of war waged by industrial-age, mass-mobilized armies. The United States, joining late, marshaled its economic and industrial bases in order to win that war decisively. Yet even this war's outcome is consistent only with political–military victory, as neither the United States nor any of the Allied powers sought to rebuild or reform the government of Germany or to preclude the conditions that had led to war. Thus changes in the international status quo were transitory, not fundamental; no foundation was laid for long-term peace. In World War II – the most significant U.S. war and the most influential on its theory of victory – the combatants laid waste to nations on several continents and killed tens of millions. The ideological objective was to defeat totalitarian militarism in Germany and Japan; the military objective, to force the Axis powers to surrender unconditionally. After the war, America helped to rebuild the economics of the defeated states as part of a strategy to prevent a resurgence of Berlin and Tokyo's expansionist policies. The conduct and outcome of World War II were thus consistent with *grand strategic victory*. The principle that such high-level outcomes entail significant postconflict obligations joined the American theory of victory in this second period.

The theory and practice of grand strategic victory that emerged during the second period were rendered ineffective in the third by the development of nuclear weapons and long-range ballistic missiles. Given the prospect of mutual assured destruction during the cold war, victory was not viewed as a practical concept.

With the end of the cold war and the onset of new risks from global terrorism – policymakers and scholars must now consciously decide what it means to achieve victory, what level of victory is desired, what changes victory should or must bring, and what costs of war are acceptable, both for victor and vanquished.

A Note on the Case Studies (Chapter 6–11). The following six chapters examine a series of conflicts, from the end of the cold war through the beginning of the twenty-first century, in which the United States used military force to achieve varying levels of victory. These wars represent a diverse array of situations in which America intervened militarily to defend vital interests and/or lesser ones: from a classic, high-intensity war like that in the Persian Gulf in 1991 or the 2003 invasion of Iraq, to smaller military operations like the 1986 raid against Libya, the 1989 invasion of Panama, and intervention in Bosnia and Kosovo during the late 1990s. One reason for studying multiple conflicts is to evaluate how well the pretheory of victory proposed in Chapter 4 helps to develop a systematic framework for understanding the nature of victory.

In some of these cases, the United States used military force to achieve decisive victory; in others, the nature of victory may be ambiguous, as in the case of the 1991 Persian Gulf War (which heightened debates in 2002–3 as to whether the United States should remove Saddam Hussein's regime in Iraq). At the more limited end of the military scale, the 1986 raid against Libya and the 1996–9 intervention in Bosnia are important examples of America's selective use of force to punish states for actions that threatened U.S. interests and to coerce these states into changing their policies – all without attempting to achieve victory in the grand strategic sense.

These cases studies, which span four presidential administrations, are presented chronologically, each beginning with background on the strategic, political, and military reasons for intervention. Each then discusses the nature of the operation, whether and in what ways the action should be evaluated as a victory, and how the particular case has influenced, or may yet be influencing, the American theory of victory.

6 1986 Raid on Libya

On the evening of April 15 and the morning of April 16, 1986, the United States launched a military raid using air strikes to destroy several political leadership and military targets in the Libyan cities of Tripoli (the capital) and Benghazi. These were selected because of their direct connection to the Libyan government which was directly and actively supporting terrorist activities against the United States and its allies.[1] The specific provocation for this raid was to retaliate against Libya for its involvement in a terrorist attack in West Berlin that killed one U.S. serviceman and wounded several other Americans. This military raid was conducted with about a hundred Air Force and Navy aircraft, including bombers, electronic countermeasures (ECM) aircraft, air defense, and tankers for aerial refueling. This chapter discusses this close series of air strikes, known as Operation El Dorado Canyon, in terms of its implications for victory.

Operation El Dorado Canyon is unique among the case studies in this book because it was essentially a small-scale military raid. Yet this intervention, conducted toward the end of the cold war, contains important lessons regarding the use of military power against a so-called rogue state and its implications for theories of victory.[2] Since this military attack against Libya was conducted largely in retaliation for terrorist attacks that had been launched against the United States and its allies, this raid has significant implications for what it means to achieve victory at a time when America is involved in the global war against terrorism. In the aftermath of the attacks of September 11, 2001, the 1986 attack against Libya highlights the use of military power to achieve victory when the state is restrained (as it was during the then-ongoing cold war) from using military force on a massive scale. The U.S. decision to attack Libya in April 1986 was designed to persuade Muammar al-Qaddafi that further support for terrorism against the United States and its allies could lead to military reprisals. The raid on Libya illustrates how America used its armed forces in the 1980s to achieve a quasi-political–military victory against terrorism, dem-

149

onstrating that it could achieve a form of victory, without risking nuclear war, and still produce significant changes in the behavior of other states.

BACKGROUND

Before turning to the specific case of Libya, the broad strategic nature of terrorism must be considered. The purpose of terrorism is to create chaos and fear that undermines the will and morale of societies by implying that the state cannot protect its citizens and homeland.[3] Since the objective is to create fears that the state is losing control and is unable to prevent such crises, the ultimate target of terrorism is less the specific victims of an act than the credibility and resolve of the government itself.[4] Often, at least in the case of suicide terrorism, the longer-term objective is the withdrawal of the targeted nation's military forces from territory deemed as homeland by the terrorists.[5]

The traditional approach for terrorists was to select "soft" or undefended targets for their shock value rather than to inflict a mortal wound against the state. While we cannot discount the possibility that terrorists might be able to disrupt an individual power plant or cause some economic dislocation and psychological discomfort, the consensus is that it is difficult for terrorists successfully to attack the extensive electrical, banking, or telecommunications infrastructures in modern societies.[6] Even the worst case of a premeditated terrorist attack that killed civilians or soldiers would be unlikely to affect seriously a targeted nation's capacity to fight (though its resolve might be subject to internal political pressures).[7] For example, the nearly simultaneous attacks against U.S. embassies in Kenya and Tanzania in August 1998 led to a significant military response by the United States in the form of cruise-missile attacks against al-Qaeda training camps in Afghanistan.[8]

One problem with combating terrorism is the clandestine identity of those who are responsible. Even if the likely perpetrators are known and their guilt is clear, the state may not have the proof that is politically necessary for retaliation. Also, after a terrorist attack, the state is forced to search for clearly defined targets against which to direct political, economic, and military reprisals, but these rarely exist: Terrorist organizations often disperse their forces so as not to present a definable target for military attack. Such organizations use small cells of individuals to operate secretly within societies by blending into the local population, and these are difficult to find and destroy even in the best of cases; moreover, they do not possess an immediate or recognizable center of gravity that can be attacked easily with conventional political, economic, and military instruments of power. When terrorists are identified and located, they will often move from one sovereign state to another that provides sanctuary from reprisal.[9] It is thus partly the shadowy nature of these groups that hampers the ability of the targeted states to retaliate. Another issue is the question of scale: Until the attacks of September 11, 2001, the architects of terrorism and their sponsors had tended to keep terrorist actions below the threshold at which states would respond aggressively with military force, much less reorganize their national-security strategy to fight a global war against terrorism.[10] For many state sponsors of terrorism, the list of which has included Iran, North Korea, and Syria, the ability to keep a low political profile helped to avoid direct reprisals from the West.[11]

It is in the context of challenges to the United States created by the development of state-sponsored terrorism in the 1980s that the raid on Libya in 1986 must be understood.[12] The arguments made in support of Operation El Dorado Canyon against Libya at the time remain quite familiar from the present post-9/11 perspective. Today, however, the risk posed by terrorism may be even more acute, given evidence that such terrorist organizations as al-Qaeda have actively sought to acquire weapons of mass destruction, including nuclear weapons, a danger highlighted in the 2002 U.S. *National Security Strategy*.[13] In the 1980s, however, the cold war still significantly constrained the ability of the United States to apply military force persuasively against terrorist organizations or states that sponsor terrorism, because of fears that aggressive counterterrorism policies would provoke crises with the Soviet Union, which actively supported a variety of revolutionary groups, some of which used terrorist tactics.[14] Although the United States itself was largely insulated from the spate of terrorist attacks that occurred in the 1980s, terrorists had attacked American citizens abroad.[15]

While the number of terrorist incidents was on the rise in the mid-1980s, U.S. officials had credible reports that Libyan officials were seeking to escalate their campaign of terror with strikes against innocent civilians and assassinations of government officials in the West.[16] Perhaps more than any other incident, the event that changed the logic of U.S. counterterrorism policies was when American diplomats were taken hostage at the American embassy in Tehran, Iran, in November 1979, during the Carter administration. That event effectively elevated fears that state sponsors of terrorism were willing to threaten the West and the United States. Ronald Reagan's position during the 1980 presidential campaign and throughout the transition in the late fall of that year was that the United States must take decisive action against state sponsors of terrorism. The problem was that America lacked clear terrorist targets against which to strike with the appropriate military instrument of power.

Libya had become a focal point for international terrorism soon after Colonel Muammar al-Qaddafi gained power in 1969, and since then it has been implicated in numerous acts of terrorism.[17] Qaddafi used terrorism to weaken the role of democracies in the Middle East, support those (e.g., the PLO) who wished to destroy Israel, and increase Libya's power and influence in the region. The Qaddafi regime's open support for terrorism had prompted the

State Department on December 29, 1979, to include Libya on its very first list of state sponsors of international terrorism, and by April 1986, the possibility of attacking Libya had emerged as a serious option for the Reagan administration.[18]

The immediate origins of the military crisis began with Libya's involvement in the bombing of a discotheque in West Berlin on April 5, 1986, in which more than two hundred people were injured, of which sixty-three were American servicemen, one of whom died.[19] Publicly presenting evidence of Libya's involvement, American intelligence officials claimed that they had intercepted a message from Qaddafi in which he ordered an attack against Americans that should "cause maximum and indiscriminate casualties."[20] Senior officials in the Reagan administration resolved that the United States would no longer brook Libya's support of terrorism.[21] President Reagan made the decision to conduct military attacks to punish Libya for the bombing and, in the longer term, to persuade Qaddafi (and other states) that a policy of supporting terrorism carried significant risks and penalties.[22] Public support in the United States for this attack against Libya would prove quite high, with 77 percent of the American people supporting the raid, as well as further attacks should those be needed.[23]

The administration's decision, however, had presented some difficulties for policymakers. First, the traditional instruments of military power would not necessarily be effective instruments for undermining Libya's support for terrorism. Second, U.S. officials must abide by domestic and international law, for which they are held publicly and legally accountable, whereas terrorists and state sponsors of terrorism are under no such obligation. Yet by choosing to retaliate against Libya, the United States changed the rules of engagement: This demonstrated that America would use military force, even in "preemptive action," to punish Libya – and perhaps others – for supporting international terrorism.[24]

U.S. OBJECTIVES

There were several strategic objectives that guided the U.S. raid on Libya. One, already noted, was to deter Qaddafi from supporting international terrorism by demonstrating that such support would involve significant penalties: As President Reagan said, "We believe that this preemptive action . . . will not only diminish Colonel Qadhafi's [sic] capacity to export terror, it will provide him with incentives and reasons to alter his criminal behavior."[25] Another was to show rogue states and terrorist organizations alike that Washington was committed to fighting state-sponsored terrorism.[26] (A parallel consideration was Washington's desire to send a message to Syria, which was culpable in its support for terrorism but harder to target, given its more amicable relationship with Moscow.)[27] Yet another objective, as President Reagan reportedly said, was "to punish the right people"[28] – supporters of terrorism – yet "to minimize casualties among the Libyan people, with whom we have no quarrel."[29] In addition, U.S. government officials hoped that military action would build broad international support for dealing aggressively with terrorism, including support for military intervention.[30]

On January 27, 1981, one week after the hostages held in Iran had returned to America, President Reagan had announced, "Let terrorists be aware that when the rules of international behavior are violated, our policy will be one of swift and effective retribution."[31] Reagan had furthered U.S. policy toward terrorism on April 3, 1984, two years before the Libya raid, by signing the classified National Security Decision Directive 138, which (among other things) established preemptive strikes as part of the U.S. policy for dealing with terrorism.[32] Now there were serious frictions between the United States and Libya: terrorist attacks against American citizens, an escalating war of words, and growing military confrontation over freedom of navigation for U.S. maritime forces in the Gulf of Sidra.

Colonel Qaddafi's increased vitriol toward the United States contributed to the already poisonous political atmosphere between Washington and Tripoli. The crisis intensified as Qaddafi called for attacks against the United States, praised terrorist acts as great acts of heroism, aligned himself and Libya with organizations committed to radical revolution, and directly threatened the American people with "exporting terrorism to the heart of America."[33] Although few observers believed that Qaddafi had the ability to carry out his more outlandish threats, his public calls for such attacks reinforced the impression that diplomacy would not suffice to defuse the situation. With his inflammatory rhetoric, Qaddafi effectively closed the Libyan–U.S. diplomatic channel and made it easier for the United States to resort to coercive military force in dealing with Libya.

In the months leading up to April 1986, there had been a significant increase in the number of terrorist acts in which Libya's direct involvement could be demonstrated. In the hijacking of EgyptAir Flight 648 in November 1985, two Israeli citizens and three Americans were shot and thrown from the aircraft onto the tarmac (two died); fifty-eight passengers perished in the subsequent attempt to rescue the hostages on board.[34] One month later, Libyan-sponsored terrorists were implicated in brutal, near-simultaneous attacks with hand grenades and automatic weapons against El-Al passengers at airport terminals in Rome and Vienna.[35] In the absence of formal evidence of ties between Libya and these acts of terrorism, Libyan officials implicated themselves with their open praise for these attacks, publicly stating their willingness to provide sanctuaries for rebels and terrorist teams and calling for suicide squads to strike "U.S.–Zionist" facilities.[36]

The Reagan administration publicly condemned these terrorist incidents and by late 1985 privately began planning to use military action against Libya to stem the tide. There was a debate within the government about whether the United States had exhausted all diplomatic options, whether economic sanctions would be more effective than military action, whether the United States should attack Libya directly, and whether Qaddafi would respond to American military action. On January 7, 1986, the U.S. government froze Libya's financial assets, severed economic relationships, and ordered Americans to leave Libya. The growing consensus among policymakers was that, since Qaddafi was one of the "prime movers" behind the rise in global terrorism in the 1980s, it was time for the United States to respond militarily against Libya's government and military.[37] Even so, President Reagan did have some doubts as to whether military intervention could eliminate terrorism.[38]

The Reagan administration decided to demonstrate U.S. resolve without acting in ways that would provoke Libya to support further acts of terrorism. Specifically, the United States conducted naval FON (freedom of navigation) exercises in the Gulf of Sidra – the warmest part of the Mediterranean, on the northern coast of Libya – in international waters, beyond Libya's recognized territorial limit of twelve miles. (Libya sometimes claimed the whole gulf for itself.) These military exercises thus permitted the United States to deploy military forces near Libya, and thus force Qaddafi, as President Reagan observed, "'to go to sleep every night' wondering what the United States might do," thus deliberately – but only indirectly – provoking Libya.[39]

The U.S. policy decision to conduct a military raid on Libya was shaped by a number of objectives. One was to demonstrate that Washington was willing to use force to attack terrorism at its source. Although a number of terrorist attacks had been conducted against targets outside the United States, by the mid-1980s senior officials in the Reagan administration believed that America was the ultimate target of these attacks, that diplomacy had proved ineffective, that it was time to take responsibility for solving this problem, and that Washington could no longer avoid overt action.[40] The administration's decision to conduct Operation El Dorado Canyon was based on the hope that Libya's support for terrorism would weaken if Qaddafi could be made to see that abetting terrorist actions against the United States and its allies would cost him dearly in political and military terms.[41]

The second objective of Washington's policy was to deflate Qaddafi's reputation as an antagonist of the United States. Libya had gained notoriety as a fervent supporter of the radical ideologies and groups that in the 1980s had been waging a war of terrorism against the United States and the West. Qaddafi's active sponsorship of these groups had enhanced his status in anti-West circles. In the months prior to the attack, the Reagan administration had tried diplomatic approaches, including the severing of economic ties, to moderate

Qaddafi's increasingly erratic behavior; but this policy had failed. By the spring of 1986, Washington believed that the most promising option, the only one likely to create a significant change in Libya's behavior, was a military intervention[42] – one that weakened Qaddafi's power and prestige, and perhaps even destroyed it.[43]

A third objective of U.S. policy was to reinforce President Reagan's image as a decisive leader in foreign policy, one who was willing to use military force against states that support terrorism. An important consideration in debates in the White House was that American credibility would be strengthened if Reagan was willing to confront state sponsors of terrorism forcefully. Ever since the taking of American hostages in Iran in November 1979, terrorism had remained a sensitive issue for the American public. Noting the positive public reaction when those hostages had been released on the day of Reagan's 1981 inauguration, officials in the administration concluded that there would be political benefits to dealing with terrorism aggressively.[44] As the president would note in his address to the nation about his reasons for the attack, President Reagan referred to the lessons of appeasement in the years before World War II, when he said that "Europeans who remember history understand better than most that there is no security, no safety, in the appeasement of evil."[45]

A fourth objective was to bolster the public's faith in the U.S. government – particularly, its ability to defend American citizens.[46] It was common for terrorists to attack U.S. interests, allies, and citizens in other countries, as exemplified by the bombings against American servicemen in Germany. The belief among military, intelligence, and law-enforcement officials was that visible action to protect innocent civilians from terrorist attacks was necessary to maintain public faith. As Vice President George H. W. Bush, chair of the task force on terrorism, said at a press conference on March 6, 1986, "We should reiterate the willingness of our Administration to retaliate and retaliate swiftly when we feel we can punish those who were directly responsible."[47]

For these reasons, then, senior policymakers in the Reagan administration concluded that a victory against such a prominent sponsor of terrorism as Libya would have significant benefits. A military strike would show that the United States had the political will and military capability to retaliate against states or groups that attack Americans or even actively support such attacks. For years the United States had relied on political, economic, and diplomatic pressure in its attempts to sway Qaddafi, but it was clear from the historical record that this had not produced adequate results. Intelligence reports indicating that he was preparing to respond to what he saw as the provocative actions of the U.S. Sixth Fleet in the Mediterranean reinforced the view in the White House that the United States had to take direct action against him.[48]

The United States now had a viable target for demonstrating its resolve to strike back against terrorism and its state sponsors. The decision to intervene militarily would demonstrate Washington's willingness to take overt action and, ultimately, improve the effectiveness of counterterrorism policies.[49]

DESCRIPTION OF OPERATION

The planning for military strikes against Libya started late in 1985, but the United States had begun to exert military pressure against Libya in the preceding years, principally by the deployment of three U.S. carrier task forces of the Sixth Fleet to the Mediterranean Sea. For instance, on August 19, 1981, while conducting maneuvers as part of an FON exercise, two F-14 Tomcat fighter aircraft from the Sixth Fleet had shot down two Libyan Soviet-designed Sukhoi Su-22 fighters after dodging an air-to-air missile that one had fired.[50] In response to Qaddafi's repeated declaration that Libya had jurisdiction over the Gulf of Sidra, the United States conducted a series of FON exercises, known as Operation Attain Document, during January–March 1986 to demonstrate that those waters were not subject to Libyan control.[51] On March 24, 1986, Libya conducted a missile attack against U.S. ships in international waters.[52]

On the evening of April 15, 1986, and the following morning, the United States launched military air strikes against targets in Libya.[53] The attacks, codenamed El Dorado Canyon, struck five targets, four of which had a direct connection to Libyan support of terrorism: the Aziziyah Barracks, which served as the headquarters for Libyan terrorist activities; military facilities and especially transport planes at the main airport in Tripoli; Murrat Side Bilal base, which was used for training terrorists in underwater attacks; and the Jamihiriyah Guard military barracks in Benghazi, a command post for terrorists. The fifth target, the Benina air base southwest of Benghazi, was hit in order to prevent Libyan fighter aircraft from attacking U.S. bombers.[54]

Since the plan involved attacking these targets simultaneously at night and with a high degree of precision, the raid consisted of strike packages of Navy A-6 and Air Force F-111 aircraft. (The aircraft carriers *America* and *Coral Sea* in the Mediterranean carried A-6 aircraft, but not in sufficient numbers, so Air Force F-111 bombers were included.) The strikes were conducted with roughly a hundred aircraft: from the Air Force, five EF-111 electronic countermeasures aircraft, twenty-four FB-111 strike aircraft, and twenty-eight KC-10 and KC-135 tankers for refueling; from the Navy, 14 A-6E strike aircraft, 12 A-7E and F/A-18 electronic warfare and jamming aircraft, F-14 aircraft for combat air patrols (CAP), and 4 E-2C Hawkeye airborne command and control aircraft. For comparison, the number of aircraft in this strike, small as it may seem, was larger than Britain used during the entire Falklands War.[55]

When the strike began, Navy A-6 aircraft attacked the air base and military barracks in the Benghazi area, while Air Force F-111's struck military targets

and government facilities near Tripoli. The reason for this allocation of aircraft
was to minimize the complexities of "deconflicting" the aircraft routes and
delivery times of the dozens of aircraft that were launching weapons against
multiple targets. The rules of engagement that governed the strike were quite
strict, stipulating that before any weapon could be released aircrews could
make only one pass over their assigned target, the weapon system must be
fully functional, and the targets positively identified.[56] The actual raid lasted
roughly twelve minutes and involved the use of sixty tons of munitions. While
the Libyan military did not mount any effective resistance, one FB-111 aircraft and two American aviators were lost during the strike.[57]

Operation El Dorado Canyon involved a wide range of capabilities, including a large tanker force for refueling the F-111 bombers that flew round-trip
missions from air bases in England. The fact that France refused to give these
aircraft permission to fly through French airspace increased the round-trip
flight by about 2,600 nautical miles, which added six or seven hours of flying
time.[58] Additional aircraft in the vicinity of the targets were assigned to suppress Libya's ground and air defenses, protect aircraft while they were over targets in Libya and during their return to the aircraft carriers and bases in Great
Britain over the Mediterranean Sea, provide command and control, and conduct search and rescue missions if necessary.

Libya's military capabilities were far below those of the United States, and
the raid was successful. The targets destroyed during the attack included Qaddafi's home and headquarters in the Aziziyah Barracks compound. In an address to the nation, President Reagan said that these targets represented the
"headquarters, terrorist facilities, and military assets" that were critical to Libya's terrorist behavior. Laser guided munitions that exploded within fifty feet
of his residence not only produced significant damage but killed his fifteen-
month-old adopted daughter and injured two of his sons.[59]

Qaddafi, in an underground bunker, escaped the attack; but in the months
that followed he was described as "shaken, confused, and uncharacteristically
subdued," allegedly suffering from severe paranoia.[60] Though the number of
terrorist attacks increased in the months immediately after the strike, in the
long term Libya's support for terrorism was significantly reduced. According
to the U.S. State Department, the number of terrorist events involving Libya
decreased from nineteen in 1986 to six in both 1987 and 1988. However, the
bombing of Pan Am Flight 103 over Lockerbie on December 21, 1988, may
well have been conducted in retaliation for the El Dorado Canyon strike.[61]

EVALUATING U.S. INTERVENTION

The U.S. attack against Libya produced a quasi-political–military victory because its narrow purpose was to use military force to dissuade Colonel Qad-

dafi from continuing his policy of actively supporting and sponsoring international terrorism.[62] The Reagan administration had no interest in destroying or even inflicting significant harm on Libya's political system, economy, or military forces: The United States was not attempting to achieve a grand strategic victory and fell short of a political–military one. Rather, the objective of the military strike was simply to impose enough pain on Qaddafi to compel him to realize that it is highly dangerous for him to support terrorism.[63] In this sense, the attack was successful because, according to a Department of Defense study, following the strike – though not in its immediate wake – Qaddafi did finally reduce his support for subversive and terrorist groups.[64] Thus, the Libya raid represents a quasi-political–military victory in which the United States used coercive force on a relatively small scale to change the behavior of a state that had actively supported terrorism, and achieved more than a tactical victory.

In the political and military context of limited objectives, it was prudent for the Reagan administration to reject any options that involved any larger-scale use of military force, including that of ground forces. Although an invasion of Libya might have produced a strategic victory on some level, such a use of ground forces would have been politically unacceptable and strategically untenable for the Reagan administration. There is little doubt that U.S. ground forces could have militarily defeated Qaddafi's military and thus compelled him to change his behavior; but this path was so laden with the risks of entanglement, casualties, and diminished U.S. prestige and credibility that it never emerged as a practical option. Since the primary goal was to change Libya's terrorism policy, while demonstrating Washington's willingness to use military force against leaders like Qaddafi who support terrorism, the United States employed air power to achieve a quasi-political–military victory.[65]

U.S. military planning was influenced by several factors. First, since there was evidence that Qaddafi was planning to conduct further terrorist attacks against the United States or American citizens abroad, the decision was to use military force that could act immediately and achieve decisive results. The second was to select forces that would allow the United States to achieve its objectives quickly. Had U.S. operations against Libya lasted for days or weeks, the United States would have confronted an array of diplomatic problems with allies and enemies alike. Since Libya was an ally of the Soviet Union – though relations were somewhat strained by Qaddafi having used (and lost) Soviet-supplied weaponry against Chad in the early 1980s[66] – the strike might have brought Moscow into the conflict and thus violated the cold-war rule of avoiding any direct involvement of the superpowers in a crisis. There was also the possibility that a sustained campaign against Libya might persuade other states that were hostile to the West to take advantage of U.S. involvement through the use of terrorist attacks or military action. Third, once officials in the Reagan administration understood that France was reluctant to support their plans, as seen by its decision to deny U.S. aircraft permission to fly through French airspace, the administration concluded that unilateral action would free America from the political complications of coordinating with allies whose support for U.S. military action was uncertain. So though the failure to gain French support was a temporary setback for U.S. diplomacy, President Reagan and his military leadership had even greater flexibility in planning and execution: The raid remained under U.S. control.[67]

Fourth, the decision to attack Libya's political leadership put enormous pressure on the U.S. military, in particular the Air Force, to ensure that its strikes hit only the assigned targets.[68] Since many of the targets in the raid were located in Tripoli's urban areas, there was a definite risk that innocent civilians who lived near potential targets yet did not directly support Libya's terrorist activities might be killed or injured. It was for this reason that President Reagan stipulated to his military commanders that they were to bomb military targets as precisely as possible, in order to avoid collateral civilian casualties, and to exclude targets whose proximity to civilian targets might unintentionally kill or injure civilians.[69] Finally, the raid sought to minimize both American losses and the overall exposure of U.S. personnel – including the risk of them being held hostage – by keeping the number of U.S. military personnel who would be placed at risk in this operation as small as possible.[70]

By most measures, Operation El Dorado Canyon, by using F-111 bombers based in England as well as carrier-based aircraft, satisfied these political and military objectives. It demonstrated that the United States had the political will to attack states that sponsor terrorism and to conduct military operations with absolutely minimal support from third parties. It also minimized the risks of entanglement by avoiding the use of ground forces and the subsequent occupation of enemy territory, and limited the risks to U.S. military personnel and innocent Libyan citizens. The decision to use military force in a limited strike sent a clear message to Qaddafi and the leaders of other state sponsors of terrorism.

INTERPRETING VICTORY

As noted, the military strike against Libya represented a quasi-political–military victory because the United States accomplished its principal foreign-policy goal: demonstrating that states supporting terrorism or engaging in actions that threaten American interests face considerable risks. In so doing, the United States used military force successfully and effectively to achieve an important victory in the war against terrorism.[71]

This case raises other considerations that are relevant to the relationship between victory and the conduct of foreign policy. First, the operation produced a victory that did not and still does not equate with how America traditionally defines victory. Rather than measuring victory in terms of the number of targets destroyed or people killed, the quasi-political–military victory in Libya was defined by the objective of achieving a policy change: compelling Qaddafi to stop supporting terrorism. The response of the Libyan government to the U.S. military raid was a brief spike in activity followed by a gradual decrease in, and apparent curtailment of, its support for terrorism.[72] This quick series of coordinated strikes provides a model of how to organize and execute a military operation, one widely interpreted as having attained the results sought by policymakers.[73] In view of reports that Qaddafi was "depressed" afterward, it can be inferred that the raid shattered his sense of personal safety and security by showing that he was highly vulnerable to a military strike.[74] Given the stated primary objective, this operation produced results halfway between a tactical victory and a political–military one, as defined in Chapter 4.

The raid on Libya also reaffirmed the principle of the advantages associated with using relatively small forces to achieve significant military results. Although the United States had positioned large naval forces in the region, the actual raid used relatively few bombers to destroy with some precision a small number of targets. This minimized the risk that Libya would be able to shoot down American aircraft and use captured pilots as leverage, putting pressure on policymakers in Washington. The attack did lead to the loss of one F-111 bomber and its two pilots, but the United States successfully avoided the political complications that occur when protracted military operations create the impression that the state has not achieved victory. Although at times the use of large-scale military forces is desirable – as, for instance, in the 1991 Persian Gulf War against Iraq (see Chapter 8) – this increases the pressure on the state to achieve a grand strategic victory or run the risk that its actions will be interpreted as a failure. An important conclusion for policymakers, therefore, is that their chance of realizing victory may be better served by the strategic surprise possible with smaller raids. Since the current generation of U.S. stealth aircraft and uninhabited air vehicles (drones) are so technologically superior to anything most other potential adversaries have to offer, the United States has the ability to use military force with nearly total surprise.

The U.S. definition of victory is influenced by its military capabilities, which increasingly rely on the use of highly reliable and precise munitions, the standard for which was established during the Persian Gulf War. However, there are limitations on the ability of precision munitions to work successfully: In Operation El Dorado Canyon, several assigned targets were missed, and collateral damage was not completely eliminated. Many targets were located in such heavily populated areas that senior officials in the Reagan administration took active measures to minimize the number of innocent civilians who might be killed. In fact, F-111 bomber crews were instructed not to release their weapons unless they were certain that their munitions would hit the designated targets.[75] Not surprisingly, this stipulation substantially constrained the ability of the aircrews to destroy their assigned targets. The rules of engagement in the Libya raid made the bombing more difficult by requiring that aircrews identify their targets clearly and be certain that the computers controlling the delivery of munitions would operate without errors. In a normal mission, the crews would choose among several options for delivering weapons against a target; but as a result of these political restrictions on the use of force, aircraft passed through target areas without being authorized to drop their bombs.[76] The consequence for victory is that technological constraints influenced the actions of policymakers, who feared that operational problems could undermine the level of victory attained by the United States.

The raid on Libya also demonstrated that the unilateral use of military force can produce significant political benefits. Although there are instances when it is essential to marshal the political support of other nations before engaging militarily, the raid suggested the advantages to unilateral action when it is difficult to achieve a consensus among states that action should be taken. At the time, many U.S. allies agreed privately that direct action against Libya was necessary but were unwilling to express publicly their support for U.S. military intervention. The best-known case was the decision by French President François Mitterrand to deny U.S. bombers the use of French airspace, even though French public opinion strongly supported the American attack against Qaddafi. Defending his refusal to grant these overflight rights, Mitterrand said, "I don't believe that you stop terrorism by killing 150 Libyans who have done nothing."[77] A related observation is that even though the raid on Libya occurred toward the end of the cold war, it was unlikely that Soviet President Mikhail Gorbachev, had he been involved in any multilateral discussions, would have supported U.S. military action or allowed Washington to compromise either Moscow's relations with Libya or his nascent program of political and economic reform.

Finally, Operation El Dorado Canyon reaffirmed the value of using military force without the need to attain victory on the grand strategic level. Such limited strikes are beginning to dominate U.S. defense planning; *small-scale contingencies,* as they're now called, seek primarily to change the behavior of a state and not necessarily to impose grand strategic victory.[78] In Libya, victory was defined in terms of limited political and military objectives: The raid effectively punished Qaddafi for actions that exceeded the bounds of what U.S. policymakers were willing to accept. Just as important, the case of intervention against Libya highlights the need for a theory of victory in which the use of military force is not governed by a requirement that victory occur at the highest level in order to produce meaningful results. This operation, then, not only yielded a U.S. quasi-political–military victory but contributed to a reshaping of the very language of victory.

Longer-term signs of the significance of this political–military victory occurred seventeen years later. In March 2003, Qaddafi admitted in a conversation with a German diplomatic aide that "he had abandoned terrorism and seeks the opportunity to make Libya's new position known."[79] In August of that year, the government of Libya formally accepted responsibility for the bombing of Pan Am Flight 103, which had killed 270 people. In the settlement, Libya agreed to pay $2.7 billion dollars into a fund for the families of the victims.[80] Still, the United States continued to maintain economic sanctions against Libya because of its ongoing involvement in programs for developing weapons of mass destruction and "other activities," presumably related to terrorism.[81] Perhaps the most significant long-term effect of the raid occurred in December 2003, when the Libyan government admitted that it indeed had programs for developing WMD but that those programs would be submitted to full inspections and dismantlement by the United States, Great Britain, and the United Nations.[82] Thus, limiting the proliferation of weapons of mass destruction may prove an indirect result of the U.S. political–military victory achieved by air strikes in 1986 – though Libya's decision was certainly encouraged by the April 2003 toppling of Saddam Hussein's regime in Iraq.

CONCLUSION

The U.S. raid on Libya has several critical consequences for victory. First, with its near-simultaneous strikes against government and military facilities in Libya, the United States effectively attained a quasi-political–military victory, as its objective was to demonstrate to the government of Muammar al-Qaddafi and, more broadly, to other governments that might support terrorism that such policies will have painful consequences. In analytic terms, this strategy was successful once the government of Libya concluded that the costs of abetting terrorism were likely to significantly exceed the possible benefits. Although this victory has evolved over the span of two decades, the evidence is that Libya's support of terrorism had been significantly reduced even by the late 1980s.

Thus the raid led to a limited change in the status quo: Libya's support for terrorism clearly ebbed during the years after the raid, but there were no comprehensive or significant changes in the government of Libya, and Gaddafi is still its leader.

The United States conducted the raid with no significant preparations or military mobilization because it used standing military forces on a limited scale to conduct a "surgical" strike against a handful of government facilities and military targets. The raid was carried out with air forces launched from airfields in Great Britain and from local aircraft carriers; it required no ground forces. In operational terms, a small number of bombers were involved in a raid on Libyan territory that lasted only minutes. Mobilization was also limited in that the Reagan administration did not expend much political capital to build public support: Afterward, there would turn out to be significant public support in the United States for the raid – and for future raids if necessary.

Regarding the nature and extent of postconflict obligations for the United States: Since the raid, intended to dissuade Qaddafi from supporting terrorism, did not lead to the removal of the government of Libya or to a change in its governing institutions, in practical terms the United States had no post-raid obligations to Libya. However, had Qaddafi been killed in the raid – which, purportedly, was not an intended result, although both his home and headquarters were hit – Reagan administration officials believed that his death would have been welcomed by the Libyans, who presumably would have dealt with the aftermath on their own.[83]

A reasonable summation, then, is that the raid on Libya in 1986 involved a quasi-political–military victory, limited change in the status quo, limited level of mobilization, and no postconflict obligations. For these reasons, Operation El Dorado Canyon is a perfect example of what it means for the state to use limited military force selectively, or even "surgically," to achieve an outcome that can fairly be characterized as a victory.

7 | 1989 Invasion of Panama

I n a resolution issued on December 15, 1989, the National Assembly
of Panama declared that a state of war existed with the United States.
Shortly after, members of the Panama Defense Forces (PDF) shot three
American officers, one of whom died. On December 17, 1989, President
George H. W. Bush ordered the invasion of Panama, called Operation Just
Cause, which began on December 20, 1989. The stated purpose of this military action, which involved 22,000 soldiers, 3,400 airmen, 900 Marines, and
700 sailors, was to remove General Manuel Antonio Noriega, who was the
head of the PDF, and restore a democratic government to Panama. As Secretary of State James Baker said, the United States took military action because
it has an "inherent right of self-defense" in matters that affect the security of
the Panama Canal and the region.[1]

Under the leadership of General Noriega, Panama had been plagued in the
1980s by massive corruption that was related to the government's active involvement in drug smuggling in Central America, which had progressively disrupted ordinary economic activity and fostered a climate of fear and anxiety
in Panama. On December 20, at 1 A.M. local time, the U.S. military attacked
key targets in Panama to destroy the authoritarian and brutal regime of Noriega. As President Bush explained in an address to the nation on the morning of the invasion, the goals of the United States were "to protect the lives
of American citizens in Panama and to bring General Noriega to justice in the
United States."[2] While this "war" was over within hours, it took almost two
weeks to capture Noriega.

The 1989 invasion of Panama is an important military operation for a discussion of a pretheory of victory, for several reasons.[3] First, in this invasion
the United States won what is roughly consistent with a political–military victory. This brief action against Panama illustrates how the United States used
military force on a small but relatively overwhelming scale to end the chaos
in Panama that threatened Washington's vital interests in the region, both re-

garding the Panama Canal and Central America generally. Although this was not a total war in any practical sense – neither the United States nor Panama was fully mobilized – General Colin Powell, then the chairman of the Joint Chiefs of Staff, reportedly argued that the operation must be "total" to ensure that the United States can successfully "capture or drive out the entire leadership."[4] This chapter examines how the invasion of Panama contributed to the evolution of American thinking about how military force can be used to achieve victory, as well as to what victory means.

BACKGROUND

The U.S. vital interest in the affairs of the Western Hemisphere traces back to President James Monroe, who declared in his seventh annual message to Congress, on December 2, 1823, "the American continents, by the free and independent condition which they have assumed and maintain, are henceforth not to be considered as subjects for future colonization by any European powers. . . . [W]e should consider any attempt on their [Europe's] part to extend their system to any portion of this hemisphere as dangerous to our peace and safety."[5] The clear intention behind this so-called Monroe Doctrine was to prevent the European powers from expanding their sphere of influence in the Western Hemisphere and drawing the United States, whose sovereignty was not yet even fifty years old, into their disputes.

Beyond President Monroe's policy consideration, the United States has a strategic interest in the Panama Canal, whose construction under U.S. auspices began during the administration of Theodore Roosevelt.[6] Since it opened for business in 1914, the canal has been a vital American interest because of the enormous volume of military and commercial traffic that passes through it. Bisecting the Western Hemisphere at its narrowest point, the canal significantly reduced the transit time between the coasts of the United States and provided an easy connection between the Atlantic and Pacific Oceans. It has been a conduit for vast quantities of natural resources and manufactured goods that are exported from the United States or imported from Europe and Asia. According to State Department reports in the mid-1990s, approximately 4 percent of the total world trade and 13 percent of U.S. maritime commerce passed through the Panama Canal each year.[7]

Though its economic importance has since waned, the canal still is viewed as a U.S. strategic asset, one whose implications had been clearly understood even in early discussions about its construction. For instance, the naval strategist Alfred Thayer Mahan wrote in 1890 that such a canal would constitute "a strategic centre of the most vital importance" to the commerce of the United States.[8] The canal is significant militarily because it allows U.S. Navy forces to move rapidly between the Atlantic and the Pacific: A ship unable to cross through the canal must go around the tip of South America, taking an extra two weeks to get from one coast to the other.[9] As James Baker would observe, "America's overriding interest in Panama has been to maintain a stable environment for the operation of the Panama Canal and U.S. military installations."[10]

It has been America's strategic interest to preserve peace and security in Panama as well as uninterrupted access to the canal. As expressed nearly two centuries ago by Monroe and as demonstrated on numerous occasions, the United States seeks to ensure that its power and influence in the region are not undermined or challenged by other states or groups. Since Panama occupies a vital position along the major trade routes that connect states in the industrialized world, successive generations of American policymakers have vigorously defended the idea that conditions in Panama contribute to peace and stability in the Western Hemisphere. By the late 1980s, though, U.S. policymakers were deeply concerned about the deteriorating conditions in Panama and the risks these posed regarding access to U.S. bases and facilities, implementation of the canal treaties, support for anticommunist military forces in Nicaragua and El Salvador, and the operation of intelligence-gathering facilities that focused on Cuba and the rest of Latin America.[11]

The U.S. commitment to the security of the canal is formalized by treaty obligations with Panama that are designed to keep the canal open to both commercial and military traffic. In 1964 the United States renegotiated its treaty rights to the canal as a result of pressure put on the Johnson administration by the Panamanian government to end what were described as America's sovereignlike rights in the Canal Zone. The eventual result of these negotiations was the 1977 Panama Canal Treaty, and shortly thereafter the Treaty Concerning the Permanent Neutrality and Operation of the Panama Canal, which was signed during the Carter administration and ratified in 1979.[12] U.S. policy toward Panama became a contentious issue in the late 1970s when President Carter's decision eventually to cede primary control of the canal to Panama effectively diminished U.S. rights in that country. Not surprisingly, there was intense opposition to this decision from those who argued that the United States was abrogating its responsibilities toward Panama.[13] Nevertheless, according to the terms of the 1977 treaty, the United States maintained its legal obligation to intervene in Panama if the canal's security and integrity were at risk.

During the 1980s, Panama's society underwent significant changes as a result of the influence of drug money on the government and the military. The Panamanian leadership was becoming increasingly involved in the trafficking of illegal drugs, notably cocaine, which flowed from South America through Panama to markets in the United States. By the mid-1980s there was credible evidence that both General Manuel Noriega and members of the Panama Defense Forces were active participants in a Colombian drug cartel's efforts to ship cocaine to the United States. By 1989, the first year of the Bush administration, it had become apparent that the United States could not successfully contain the drug trade as long as Panama's leadership was actively participating in it. At the same time, such corruption had contributed to the general disintegration of Panamanian society. Given the evidence of growing corruption and violence, and the long-standing U.S. commitment to preserving access to the canal and stability in the entire region, there were mounting pressures in the United States to intervene. It was thus increasingly likely that Washington would at some point move to reverse the destruction of the social and economic order in Panama.

Senior officials in the Bush administration argued that the progressive deterioration of Panamanian society threatened American interests.[14] By virtue of the obligations expressed in the Panama Canal Treaty, the United States had the right of self-defense to preserve the integrity of Panama and the canal.[15] In this climate, the decision by the Bush administration to invade Panama was motivated by the desire to reestablish political and military security and control in Central America. Senior officials in Washington were concerned that allowing Panama to slide further into authoritarianism and corruption would represent a strategic and economic failure for the United States.[16] Indeed, the worst case scenario for government policymakers was that the progressive deterioration of Panama's society would spread to weaken neighboring Central American states just when significant progress was being made toward the development of democratic societies and free-market economies in the region.[17] Finally, in the waning days of the cold war, the disintegration of Panama would raise embarrassing questions about whether the United States had the political will to maintain security in the Western Hemisphere.

The long-standing political and economic grievances of societies in Central America with regard to U.S. policies also influenced the Bush administration's decision to use force against Panama.[18] U.S. relations with Latin American states, including those of Central America, have historically engendered the sentiment that the United States, as the rich and powerful neighbor to the north, is essentially indifferent to the needs and interests of the states in the region. There is much sympathy in Latin America for the view that the United States has been too willing to interfere in the internal affairs of Latin American societies. The decision to invade was thus complicated by the belief that regional states would interpret the use of force, even if to protect Panama's security and economic interests, as another case of U.S. interference in the affairs of states south of its borders.[19] Military intervention in Latin American states was an intensely emotional issue, and the U.S. invasion of Panama had important political implications. The use of force by the United States in the Western Hemisphere would raise the specter of great-power intervention

in the internal affairs of weaker states and therefore be interpreted as a violation of their legitimate sovereign rights. Although an invasion by a member
of the Organization of American States would further inflame popular sentiment in the region, some members of the OAS (headquartered in Washington) loosely supported the United States because they believed that Panama
had failed to manage its own internal affairs, and that the stability of Central
America itself was at risk.[20] Many Latin American leaders reportedly believed
that it was time to eradicate the problems that were leading to the disintegration of democratic institutions in Panama. Still, a U.S. military action would
reinforce the popular belief that the United States held essentially imperial
attitudes toward the region, and it was feared that Washington could not forge
a positive relationship with the states of Latin America in the aftermath of an
invasion.[21]

The geopolitical realities of relations with the Soviet Union late in the cold-
war era were another factor in the Bush administration's decision to invade.
The late 1980s had brought growing signs that the USSR and its satellite states
were in the early stages of political and economic collapse, and American foreign policy was committed to strengthening the emerging Latin American democracies. Now, barely one month after the fall of the Berlin Wall, the Joint
Chiefs of Staff were concerned that Panama, in Noriega's unfriendly hands,
could become a wartime base for Soviet or Cuban attacks against U.S. maritime operations.[22] Thus, many U.S. government officials believed in the use
of force to protect American interests and to demonstrate the nation's resolve
and credibility. News of General Noriega's involvement with the Medellin drug
cartel was gaining prominence in the media; if in addition to disregarding U.S.
diplomatic efforts he could harass the United States, with no evident pain or
retribution, it would undermine America's reputation in the region – at the
very moment when the tapering cold war presented opportunities for states
to settle old scores. The strategic calculation for the Bush administration, then,
was that the use of military force against Panama to remove Noriega was consistent with American interests, because it showed that Washington was unwilling to tolerate transgressions within its sphere of influence. The invasion
was thus intended also to dissuade the leaders of states in Latin America and
elsewhere from attempting to take advantage of the shifting cold-war conditions to attack their neighbors and undermine regional stability.

U.S. OBJECTIVES

The U.S. military invasion was designed to protect the 30,000 Americans living in Panama, protect the Panama Canal and U.S. defense sites, help the Panamanian political opposition build a democracy, destroy the Panama Defense
Forces, and bring Noriega to justice.[23]

In practical terms, the principal American objective was to remove General Manuel Noriega from power without assassinating him.[24] In his position as the head of the Panama Defense Forces, Noriega effectively held full political, military, and economic power. Since the government, military, and society were controlled hierarchically, he and his subordinates had a complete monopoly on power in Panama. Senior officials in the Bush administration understood the strategic implications of this emerging authoritarianism, and how it threatened U.S. access to the canal as well as regional stability.[25]

The second objective of the U.S. military operation was to disarm and neutralize the Panama Defense Forces, which were under Noriega's effective control, to prevent them from inflicting casualties on U.S. military personnel both during and after military operations. Before the invasion, the PDF comprised nineteen companies and six platoons – roughly fourteen thousand troops (of whom some four thousand were deemed combat-ready) – twenty-nine armored personnel carriers, twelve patrol boats, and twenty-eight light transport aircraft. Although the PDF was thus a small and only marginally capable military force, senior U.S. officials feared that Noriega might retreat with his forces into the countryside and mountains to wage a protracted guerrilla war against U.S. forces and the canal.[26] Indeed, the immediate concern for the Bush administration was that the U.S. military operation would be jeopardized if the PDF were able to conduct reprisals against facilities, individuals, and civil institutions in Panama.

A related, longer-term objective was to transform the PDF from a political arm of the state, used to terrorize the public and direct the drug trade, into a constabulary force whose principal function would be to maintain peace and order in Panama.[27] Senior officials in the Bush administration argued that Operation Just Cause would succeed only if the PDF could be refashioned into a constabulary force for protecting a restored, democratic social order; that Panama could evolve into a free, stable, and prosperous society only if the United States ended Noriega's authoritarian rule and reversed the deterioration that had begun to accelerate in the months before the invasion.[28] In part, it was the growing anarchy in Panama – a banking system corrupted by the infusion of drug money, rapidly increasing street crime – that persuaded President Bush it was time to "save American lives, bring Noriega to justice, and restore Panamanian democracy."[29] The influx of large amounts of drug money, having already corrupted Panama politically, was also weakening its economic and social fabric, as well as the overall security of the Panama Canal.

Finally, the Bush administration hoped that destroying the Noriega regime would weaken Panama's role in the drug trade and help stanch the flow of drugs into the United States. There is no evidence that U.S. officials believed that his removal and imprisonment would *stop* Central American drug traffic;

the hope was that replacing Noriega with officials who were neither sympathetic to nor benefiting financially from such trade would complicate operations for the Colombian cartel.

In the month preceding the invasion, General Noriega's regime was employing progressively authoritarian tactics against American citizens who resided in Panama. The murder of a U.S. Marine and the alleged physical attack and psychological harassment of an American military officer and his wife by members of the PDF on December 16, 1989, captured the public's attention and galvanized support within American society and the Bush administration for armed intervention against Panama.[30] The fact that such attacks could occur in Panama, which for decades had been a quiet and orderly society, persuaded a majority of the American people that the situation in Panama had gone beyond the limits of what the United States could countenance.[31]

For all these reasons the Bush administration risked U.S. relationships with friendly OAS member nations in order to crush Noriega's military dictatorship as quickly, decisively, and surgically as possible.[32]

DESCRIPTION OF OPERATION

The design and implementation of Operation Just Cause were based on several considerations. First, it was decided to use overwhelming military force so as to defeat the Panama Defense Forces in the shortest possible time.[33] Bush administration officials argued that to avoid the destruction of life and property in Panama that would occur in a protracted campaign, it was prudent to employ overwhelming force against Noriega and the PDF in a brief but intense military campaign.[34] An additional motivation, as noted earlier, was to prevent Noriega from using the invasion as an opportunity to initiate a guerrilla war.[35] The danger was that if he established guerrilla bases, the United States would be forced to wage costly and frustrating military operations to find and destroy the PDF, and these could last for weeks, if not months. If the PDF could escape into the mountains and countryside to form an insurgency, it is likely that vastly greater physical devastation would result and the benefits of an invasion greatly diminish. Furthermore, such a campaign would have revived memories of the quagmire in the Vietnam War and eroded U.S. public support for the invasion.

For these reasons, then, U.S. policymakers concluded that they must use overwhelming force in a quick and decisive fashion to defeat the Panama Defense Forces and reestablish political and economic order in Panama. These principles constituted the foundations of the political–military victory against the regime in Panama that the Bush administration achieved in late 1989 and early 1990.

Land Campaign

The U.S. Southern Command (SOUTHCOM) had principal responsibility for planning and executing the operation. Though it involved forces from all branches of the military services, the success of the U.S. military operation would depend on using ground forces. In effect, Operation Just Cause was a land war that sought to capture PDF military targets as well as economic ones, including the electrical distribution center at Cerro Tigre, the Madden Dam, and the canal locks, as part of a strategy to destroy the PDF's ability to offer any effective military resistance.[36] The conclusion by American policymakers that General Noriega's capture was a crucial part of the operation compelled the United States to conduct military operations designed to defeat Panama's armed forces, as the general was known to use the PDF to protect himself. A clear defeat of the Panama Defense Forces, one precluding any guerrilla option, could be effected only by ground forces, and U.S. military commanders would direct their initial forces against PDF units guarding him. Moreover, by successfully defeating the PDF in combat and capturing Noriega, the United States would have the option of prosecuting him in the criminal justice system.[37] The U.S. land campaign alone entailed 22,000 Army forces.[38]

For the United States to remain faithful to the underlying reason for the invasion – to protect Washington's strategic interest in Panama and ensure the integrity and security of the Panama Canal as a vital waterway in the global economy – it was essential to prevent the PDF from waging protracted operations that destroyed the physical infrastructure in Panama.[39] Not only would an organized campaign of resistance against U.S. forces threaten the integrity and security of the canal and lead to large-scale destruction; it would also have tarnished America's reputation for decisive and effective military action, have dangerous implications for U.S. foreign policy, and possibly weaken neighboring states as well.[40]

A critical objective of the land campaign was to gain control of the command and control facilities that supported Noriega and his PDF commanders.[41] The decision to capture these sites and render them useless to the PDF dictated that Operation Just Cause comprise an invasion with ground forces whose objectives were to occupy Panama, end Noriega's ability to control the PDF, and eliminate the PDF's ability to resist American forces. A related objective for U.S. ground forces was to prevent PDF units from using other ground lines of communication, such as roads, to move around the countryside to conduct military operations. Once PDF units nationwide were isolated from their commanders and could neither maneuver nor communicate, their military defeat would be inevitable.[42]

Finally, U.S. military commanders understood that successfully defeating the PDF militarily would support the political objective of preserving civil so-

ciety in Panama. Since by the late 1980s General Noriega and his military authorities effectively controlled all political, military, and economic activities
in Panama, the PDF was the only institution providing any semblance of a
police function.[43] U.S. military commanders and planners determined that,
once the PDF was destroyed, civil society in Panama would reemerge as soon
as law-enforcement mechanisms were reestablished. After the invasion, U.S.
military forces were temporarily given the job of supplementing the police
functions that had been administered by the PDF, in order to minimize the
risk that Panama would descend into political, economic, and social chaos.[44]

Air Power

The function of air power in Operation Just Cause was to destroy PDF centers of gravity. Of the more than two hundred aircraft that were involved in
the deployment to Panama, the Air Force provided two EF-111 aircraft for
jamming, six EC-130 aircraft, eight AC-130 gunships, six F-117A Nighthawk
stealth fighter-bombers, and other aircraft from the First Special Operations
Wing for a total of thirty-four hundred personnel.[45] In theory, the most significant advantage associated with using air power was tactical: U.S. military
forces achieved nearly complete but not, as it turned out, total surprise against
the PDF leadership and units in the field.[46] Planning had placed a premium
on surprise because of the need to overwhelm PDF units before they could
disappear into the countryside to conduct a guerrilla war. In an attack with all
six F-117A fighters, two one-ton bombs were dropped near the PDF's 6th
and 7th Rifle Company barracks in order to stun and confuse the Panamanian soldiers. With this and similar strikes, the United States successfully destroyed the PDF's command and control facilities before it had any effective
warning that a military attack was under way.[47]

Air power also provided a new capacity for conducting precise strikes against
critical military targets. The operational concept for U.S. aircraft was to use
precision-guided munitions to destroy command and control sites at the outset of the invasion without unnecessarily harming military personnel and civilians. The actions of U.S. policymakers were guided by the desire to shield Panama's civilian population from the lethal effects of the war, prevent damage
to military and economic facilities critical to Panama's economic recuperation,
and maintain the support of those Panamanian civilians who believed that the
United States was trying to remove a corrupt leadership and reestablish social
order.[48]

A further contribution of air power was to airlift essential operational supplies. From the onset of the operation, aircraft formed the primary means for
moving U.S. Army troops, weapons, and supplies into Panama. These Mili-

tary Airlift Command (MAC) craft were refueled by Strategic Air Command KC-10's and KC-135's, and SAC tankers were employed in refueling deploying and covering aircraft as well.[49]

In addition, air power served to deter Cuban and Nicaraguan interference in the operation.[50] The United States flew combat air patrols with F-15 and F-16 fighters to protect the aircraft that were ferrying people and equipment between the United States and Panama. Although the risk posed by the Cuban Air Force was minimal for technical and (geo)political reasons – and any threats to U.S. forces would expose Cuba to military retaliation on a scale against which it could not possibly defend itself – U.S. military commanders still wanted to ensure that Cuban fighters could not attack or otherwise interfere with U.S. aircraft flying in and out of Panama.

U.S. Air Force units deployed various platforms to maintain command and control relationships between the air, ground, and maritime forces of the operation. To ensure that the United States successfully established and maintained communications "superiority" in the region, E-3 AWACS aircraft and other airborne platforms were used for communications. It also supported the operation with satellites that are part of the U.S. global command and control network. At the same time, air power provided direct support for ground forces that were engaged in combat against PDF units, including U.S. Air Force AC-130 aircraft armed with machine guns and cannons, and U.S. Army helicopters that were used to destroy PDF units and facilities. These elements of air power gave the United States a distinct operational advantage because it could direct fire against PDF units in heavily congested and populous urban areas in a precise fashion without generating significant levels of collateral damage. It is important to emphasize that one reason for the success of the invasion was that U.S. military forces were able to insulate Panama's civilian population from the effects of the war. The prospect of large numbers of civilian casualties would have undermined popular support for the United States and strengthened support for the Noriega regime. Thus, the success of the operation depended partly on the ability of U.S. military forces to focus their lethal effects on PDF units, which were viewed by the civilian population as largely responsible for the dismal state of political and economic affairs in Panama.

Since American air power was able to destroy physical facilities and target individuals with virtually complete surprise and almost "surgical" precision, U.S. forces were able to weaken the military ability and psychological resolve of the PDF to fight. As the invasion progressed, it was apparent to U.S. military commanders that PDF units were not enthusiastic about fighting because they understood that further resistance would mean their immediate destruction at the hands of superior U.S. military forces. Air power had proven key in lowering PDF resistance to the American invasion.

Maritime Forces and Special Operations Forces

The principal function of the maritime forces involved the use of a carrier battle group to interdict the air and sea lines of communication, thereby ensuring that Cuban military forces would not attempt to assist the PDF. U.S. Navy units provided some seven hundred men from the Naval Special Warfare Group TWO, members of special warfare units, SEAL teams, and an amphibious task force for the invasion.[51] In addition, General Maxwell Thurman, the commander of SOUTHCOM, used a joint task force of special operations forces, assigned from the U.S. Special Operations Command, to conduct simultaneous military strikes against a number of targets, including airfields and command and control facilities that were associated with the leadership of the PDF. Various units of special operations forces were also given the responsibility for rescuing hostages, conducting reconnaissance operations, and, most important, with locating and seizing Manuel Noriega.[52]

INTERPRETING VICTORY

The U.S. invasion of Panama, whose purpose was to destroy Noriega's regime and restore political, social, and economic order in that country, produced a political–military victory for the United States. The outcome of the operation against Panama was never in doubt: America brought such disproportionate power to bear against Panama, and the PDF, deprived of a guerrilla option, could not possibly resist. Thus, while there are several features of Operation Just Cause that are relevant to how the United States might achieve victory, it is prudent to be cautious when drawing conclusions as to how this invasion influences thinking about victory.

First, the United States invaded because U.S. policymakers concluded that conditions in Panama posed a threat to vital American interests that could be resolved only by defeating the PDF and reorganizing that country's political, economic, and social systems.[53] The stakes of the decision to intervene were quite high: Any outcome that produced less than the total defeat of the PDF would have preserved Noriega's rule, perpetuated authoritarian rule in Panama, unleashed an insurgency, and weakened the credibility of the United States. More than a decade later, the consensus in Washington is that the military defeat of the Noriega regime was the only realistic option for normalizing politics in Panama.[54]

Another observation is that the U.S. military invasion of Panama reaffirmed the principle that success in military operations depends on precisely defined military objectives. This responsibility for these falls entirely on the president, the only person with the constitutional and political authority to approve how the government defines the political and military objectives that will guide the use of military force. President Bush communicated that his narrow objectives were to capture Noriega, disarm the PDF, and preserve the security of Panama and its canal. Such precision increases the likelihood that this operation will be seen by future generations as a model for intervention.[55]

Operation Just Cause demonstrated that the United States could apply overwhelming military force, decisively and quickly, to achieve a political–military victory based on removing a tyrant, reshaping politics in Latin America, and restoring democracy, while inflicting minimal casualties on both sides. Ultimately, American casualties in the operation were 23 killed and 324 wounded. Overall, 450 PDF members and 200–300 civilians died in the operation.[56]

The military invasion of Panama has several important consequences both for U.S. national security and the American theory of victory. First, the United States helped to rebuild Panama's government, society, and economy for the explicit purpose of reestablishing a democracy, which led to a significant change in the status quo and established some postwar obligations on the United States. Ending a speech to the nation on January 3, 1990, President Bush observed that "[a] free and prosperous Panama will be an enduring tribute" to the efforts to "restore democracy to Panama."[57] The decision to conduct stabilization operations with civil affairs units, which was known as Operation Promote Liberty, permitted the United States to reestablish law and order, foster stability, and rebuild the government of Panama. By assisting with public safety, health, and population control, the United States and Panama's new government promoted political and economic reform while restructuring the PDF.[58]

Second, the military invasion of Panama involved some political risks for the United States internationally. Although there was support among OAS members for U.S. intervention, given Noriega's involvement in the drug trade and Panama's gradual disintegration, some discontent among individuals and governments is always to be expected when the United States intervenes militarily. With regard to cold-war geopolitics, however, this invasion affirmed that the United States, despite the myth prevailing in the 1980s, now had the political will to use military force to achieve victory in a decisive fashion.[59]

The decision to apprehend Manuel Noriega and remove him as the head of the government complicated the operation and imposed considerable difficulties (including diplomatic ones) for the United States; but it also reaffirmed the principle that it is legitimate for the state to capture government leaders.[60] It is problematic, however, for military forces to locate and capture one individual among the millions in a state, or even among the thousands in the military command and control establishment, to be brought before an international court or military tribunal.[61] Coercive military force is not a surgical instrument. When the government leader who is to be isolated and captured is directing his own military through its command and control system, the risk is that mixing military objectives (e.g., destroying facilities with precision air and ground attacks) with political ones (e.g., capturing the leader) can muddy the nature and level of victory that the state seeks to attain.

In the end, Operation Just Cause is also, like the earlier Operation El Dorado Canyon (see Chapter 6), an important example of the small-scale contingencies that are increasingly dominating the conduct of American security policy.[62] The invasion did not employ the full range of coercive instruments of power that were available to the United States; but it demonstrated that there are occasions when it is necessary to use military force to remove from power a leader whose influence represented a significant threat to peace and security. The success of this intervention helped establish the foundations for the theory of victory that was beginning to emerge toward the end of the twentieth century.

CONCLUSION

In the invasion of Panama the United States achieved a political–military victory by destroying the government of Manuel Noriega and reorienting Panama toward the gradual development of a peaceful and prosperous political and social order. In so doing the United States deprived other states in the Western Hemisphere from taking advantage of Panama's situation to foment chaos and instability.

This invasion produced a comprehensive change in the status quo, in that the United States replaced the military regime in Panama, leading to significant alterations in the nature of Panama's policies and actions. Removing General Noriega and his government allowed the United States to impose a new institutional and economic basis of power in Panama; in part, this was because it greatly diminished the ability of the Medellin drug cartel to dominate political and economic affairs, which had radicalized Panamanian society. Operation Just Cause also likely suggested to other leaders in the region that the influence of drugs and the emergence of radical politics could provoke military action by the United States.

By any scale, the extent to which the United States mobilized itself for the invasion of Panama was relatively limited. This joint operation involved a small number of U.S. conventional military forces, including ground forces, air power, and limited maritime forces, and lasted for only a few days, until the PDF was defeated. What is significant in scale, though, is the popular support that the Bush administration enjoyed, ostensibly because of the American public's concern that U.S. military personnel and Panamanians were being brutalized by members of the PDF.

After the invasion, the United States was obligated to help Panama rebuild its government, military, economy, and society. Although Just Cause had destroyed military resistance in Panama, it had produced only slight collateral damage; thus U.S. economic assistance necessary to rebuild facilities in Panama was minimal. As part of its limited postconflict obligations, the United States also supported Panama in rebuilding a legitimate and democratically elected government. Initially, this included using the U.S. military to stabilize Panama, but it later shifted to limited economic support to help Panama restore its society and economy, which had been weakened by neglect during Noriega's years in power.[63] In fact, at the end of 1999, control of the canal was ceded to Panama, in accord with the Panama Canal Treaty that had been signed in 1977 by Presidents Carter and Torrijos.

What can we conclude from this invasion in terms of a pretheory of victory? First, as in Libya, the United States had achieved a political–military victory through a small-scale military operation, rather than with a massive, society ending use of force. The realization that fewer than thirty thousand troops could still produce highly significant results – including, in Panama, a change in regime – strengthened the foundations of victory. This was the first time since World War II that the United States had achieved such a significant victory without the costs that are normally associated with decisive victories, and without the need to attain a grand strategic victory.

Second, coming toward the end of the cold war, Operation Just Cause was seen as allowing U.S. policymakers to move beyond the decades of paralysis in which victory had been held to be unachievable, given fears of nuclear escalation.[64] This clear victory against a small and weak state was a strong contrast to the longer, inconclusive wars of that era, notably in Korea and Vietnam but also in lesser raids, which produced more ambiguous results. With this invasion, in which combat lasted only several days, the Bush administration renewed confidence in the nation's ability to be victorious. In effect, the U.S. policymaking community learned that attaining a political–military victory that could have significant results for the state was a legitimate and practical objective.

A final point is that the invasion of Panama, though waged against an insignificant military opponent, strengthened the argument that the combined use of air, ground, and maritime forces may be a prerequisite for victory. Operation Just Cause was the first significant military operation to be conducted since the passage of the Goldwater–Nichols Act of 1986, which emphasized the importance of joint military operations as U.S. military services learned to integrate more completely and effectively how they used military force.[65] However, the value of joint military operations would soon be challenged, during the Persian Gulf War of 1991, by the argument that air power is the preeminent tool of military power and can decisively win wars.

8 1991 Persian Gulf War

fter Iraqi forces invaded Kuwait on August 2, 1990, the United States deployed more than five hundred thousand troops to the Persian Gulf region throughout the fall and early winter to encourage Iraqi withdrawal and to prevent it from invading the oil-rich Kingdom of Saudi Arabia (Operation Desert Shield). In the predawn hours of January 17, 1991, two days after a U.N. deadline for Iraqi withdrawal, U.S.-led forces attacked Iraq in what became known as the Persian Gulf War. The five-and-a-half-week air campaign (Operation Desert Storm) was followed on February 24 by an invasion with ground forces (Operation Desert Sabre) that led to the complete collapse of Iraqi military forces and their subsequent withdrawal into Iraq. The purpose of this military invasion, which involved a broad coalition of nations, was to remove Iraqi military forces from Kuwait forcibly and thereby prevent the destabilization of the region under Iraqi hegemony.

The Persian Gulf War is an important example of the development of the theory of victory and its influence on American security policy in the late twentieth century.[1] Responding to a threat to U.S. national interests in the region, the United States used force to achieve a decisive political–military victory; it was not intended to be on the scale of a grand strategic victory attained by the Allies in World War II.[2] This chapter examines the conduct of the 1991 war against Iraq and its implications for the development of a pretheory of victory.

BACKGROUND

The fundamental American policy in the Persian Gulf War was to use military coercion to preserve the balance of power in the region, oppose wanton international aggression, and prevent a hostile state such as Iraq from controlling the world's oil supplies.[3] The Bush administration sought to prevent any state in the region from imposing hegemony over the other states, to strengthen the political and military stability in the Persian Gulf by establishing alliances with friendly states, to deter or defeat threats to the United States and its allies by protecting the free flow of oil, and to prevent the spread and use of weapons of mass destruction. This policy is consistent with the broad outlines of U.S. diplomacy: Since the end of World War II, American presidents have held that international peace and security depends on events in the Middle East. In his August 8, 1990, address to the nation, President Bush acknowledged that "my administration, as has been the case with every President from President Roosevelt to President Reagan, is committed to the security and stability of the Persian Gulf."[4] Since the Persian Gulf contains the world's largest known reserves of petroleum, and therefore provides the fuel that drives the global economy, oil reserves in the Middle East by necessity elevate the region to a place of central prominence in American foreign policy. What animated the policy of the Bush administration was the concern that any attempt to interfere with oil supplies or attain regional hegemony could cause severe economic dislocations that would have catastrophic consequences for markets in the United States and around the globe. These considerations had influenced U.S. defense planning during the cold war; a principal concern of the Carter administration had been a Soviet invasion into the Persian Gulf.[5]

Almost two years before the war, President Bush had written: "Access to the Persian Gulf oil and the security of key friendly states in the area are vital to U.S. national security. The U.S. remains committed to defend its vital interests in the region, if necessary and appropriate through the use of U.S. military force."[6] This policy, articulated in National Security Directive 26 on October 2, 1989, also held that "Normal relations between the United States and Iraq would serve our longer-term interests and promote stability in both the Gulf and the Middle East."[7]

Thus, the immediate focus of Bush administration policy following Iraq's invasion of Kuwait was to prevent oil supplies to the industrialized economies from falling under Iraqi control. Having invaded Kuwait, President Saddam Hussein now effectively controlled over 20 percent of the world's oil reserves; had he moved to invade Saudi Arabia, he would have controlled an additional 20 percent of the reserves, not to mention Saudi Arabian Gulf ports.[8] Meanwhile, the United States received roughly 20 percent of its crude oil imports from the Persian Gulf; Japan and Europe imported approximately 70 and 40 percent, respectively, of theirs from the region. Given this level of international dependence on the area's oil, there were widespread fears that Hussein would be able to impose an economic stranglehold on the United States and its allies by raising oil prices, which would increase inflation, or withholding oil altogether.[9] The central motivation of the international community in joining the U.N. coalition against Iraq was therefore to prevent him from threatening, much less controlling, oil supplies in the Persian Gulf region.[10]

Although oil was an important consideration in shaping the U.S. decision to respond militarily to Iraq's invasion of Kuwait, other political factors also motivated the United States and the international community to fight Iraq, including the desire to preserve Kuwait's sovereignty and to punish Iraq for its violations of international law. From the beginning of the crisis, when a hundred thousand Iraqi forces invaded Kuwait on August 2, 1990, the United Nations affirmed that the attack on Kuwaiti sovereignty violated the U.N. Charter and various principles of international law. In the United States, President Bush and other government officials argued that there could not be security in the Persian Gulf if Iraq could freely annex Kuwait without suffering any reprisal from the international community. As the president said in his address of August 8, 1990, "If history teaches us anything, it is that we must resist aggression or it will destroy our freedoms."[11] Thus, for the United States it was essential to respond aggressively with military force against Iraq if the international community was to maintain the confidence of other states in the region. The United States could not accept Iraq's annexation of Kuwait because of its consequences for peace and security in the Middle East.

An additional objective for U.S. policymakers was to demonstrate the credibility of America's commitments to friends and allies in the Gulf region. Had the United States ignored its obligation to defend an ally against outright aggression, the fact that other states might entertain doubts about America's trustworthiness would have serious consequences for U.S. policy. As one commentator observed, "Contempt is contagious. When you act weakly in one place, you are presumed to be weak elsewhere."[12] Since Iraq's attack against Kuwait ultimately challenged U.S. security guarantees to Saudi Arabia, Israel, and other states in the region and around the world, defending Kuwaiti sovereignty with military force was important to preserve U.S. credibility in the region. The economic and political implications of the invasion for Saudi Arabia, which was an important ally of the United States, also influenced the U.S. decision to take military action.[13] The strategic objectives of the Saudi government were to contain Iraqi hegemony without provoking Hussein, while also maintaining oil prices and the free flow of oil.

Iraq's motivations for invading Kuwait despite U.S. and international diplomatic reactions are not totally clear, since the invasion involved extraordinary risks for Baghdad.[14] The desire to establish regional hegemony through an invasion of Kuwait and the overt threat that it posed to Saudi Arabia were the likely motivations. In the face of declining oil prices and diminished revenues, Iraq confronted the increasingly serious prospect of cash-flow problems: For one thing, as a result of the protracted and costly Iran–Iraq War (1980–8), Iraq owed more than $37 billion to its Arab neighbors (including Kuwait and Saudi Arabia).[15] Since that war, Iraq had spent enormous resources to build up its conventional military forces. Though its army was now smaller than it had been, it was still the largest army in the Persian Gulf.[16] With its increased military spending (including on nuclear, biological, chemical, and missile programs) and declining oil revenues, Iraq, despite significant oil reserves, could not match the wealth of such neighboring OPEC partners as Kuwait or Saudi Arabia, or afford lavish domestic spending programs for modernizing its society. Its status as a debtor nation was construed as an insult by Iraq's leadership, who argued that Iraq's economic problems were the result of the Iran–Iraq War, which, they claimed, had been fought on behalf of all Arab nations.[17]

Iraqi grievances and hostility toward Kuwait were fueled by disagreements over oil that was being extracted from Kuwaiti oil fields. For one thing, Iraqi officials accused Kuwait of "slant drilling" into Iraq's portion of the Rumaila oil field; for another, they argued that the revenue generated by Kuwait's oil exports did not adequately support Baghdad, and that the resulting economic imbalance justified the decision to ameliorate Iraq's finances by seizing Kuwait.[18] Indeed, many Iraqi citizens and government officials made precisely this latter argument in the months following the August 1990 invasion. These circumstances suggest that Iraq's strategic ambition was to reverse its position as one of the less economically privileged members of OPEC.

Finally, it is important to consider whether, as some observers have argued, U.S. policy may have encouraged Iraq to invade Kuwait. The unanswered question is the overall consistency of that policy in the months leading up to the invasion.[19] The debate has focused on whether comments made to Saddam Hussein and his deputy prime minister by the U.S. Ambassador to Iraq, April Glaspie, inadvertently signaled acceptance of Iraqi aggression.[20] The argument is that Glaspie unwittingly created two false impressions: first, that American interests were not threatened by Iraqi designs on Kuwait; second, that the United States would not necessarily respond militarily if Iraq moved against Kuwait. However, the countervailing argument is that, although the United States did not communicate as precisely as it might have that Iraq's invasion of Kuwait would threaten U.S. interests and provoke a U.S. military response, it was unrealistic for Saddam Hussein to believe that the United States would ignore his attempts to annex one of the critical producers of oil in the Middle East.[21]

U.S. OBJECTIVES

On August 20, 1990, eighteen days after Kuwait's invasion by Iraq, President Bush noted four fundamental objectives of U.S. policy in the Persian Gulf: "the immediate, complete, and unconditional withdrawal of all Iraqi forces from Kuwait; the restoration of Kuwait's legitimate government to replace the puppet regime installed by Iraq; a commitment to the security and stability of the Persian Gulf; and the protection of the lives of American citizens abroad."[22] A few days after Kuwait's territorial integrity was violated by Iraqi forces, President Bush declared that Iraq's actions clearly represented a violation of international law that neither Washington nor the United Nations would tolerate.[23] When the United States and members of the U.N. coalition declared that Kuwait's sovereignty had been violated, and that the situation in Kuwait must return to the *status quo ante bellum,* these public declarations established the condition that Iraq must withdraw from Kuwait or be forcibly removed.[24] In addition, on October 1, 1990, the U.S. House of Representatives passed a nonbinding resolution that supported Bush administration policies while urging the president to use diplomacy to resolve the crisis.[25] Since it was in America's strategic interests to defend Saudi Arabia and its oil reserves, the United States was committed to defending the sovereignty and territorial integrity of Saudi Arabia against Iraqi intimidation or encroachments.[26] Moreover, the Bush administration argued that any failure of political will might encourage other regimes that have similar hegemonic ambitions.

When diplomacy, U.N.-imposed economic sanctions,[27] and even the buildup of U.S.-led international military forces in Saudi Arabia did not remove Iraq from Kuwait – in short, as war became increasingly likely – the intent behind U.S. policy was to force Iraq to withdraw while ensuring that the United States was not drawn into a quagmire in the Middle East. As will be discussed, victory for the United States meant restoring Kuwaiti sovereignty while avoiding any permanent involvement by the United States in Iraq; that is, only a political–military victory was sought.[28]

The primary short-term objective in the decision to wage war was to remove Iraq from Kuwait; a longer-term objective of U.S. policy, consistent with U.S. and Arab interests in the Persian Gulf, was to ensure that Iraq did not emerge as the dominant power in the Middle East.[29] The scale of Iraq's military modernization program in the 1980s had made it the largest and most significant military power in the Persian Gulf, though its military and economic might, as already noted, had been weakened by the war with Iran and the effects of declining oil revenues.[30] By the time of the invasion of Kuwait in 1990, Iraq had established the reputation among its Middle Eastern neighbors as a significant regional power whose territorial and strategic ambitions posed a threat to stability in the region. Iraq's military capabilities also affected the regional strategic objectives of the United States, which therefore sought to diminish Iraq's military power and effectively contain Baghdad.

The second U.S. objective was to eliminate Iraq's nuclear weapons program, but it must be noted that its precise extent and status were unclear to U.S. planners going in. Although the United States expended considerable efforts to target nuclear facilities, the true magnitude of Baghdad's nuclear complex (in which Iraq had invested $10–20 billion) was not known until the end of the war.[31] A postconflict Department of Defense study reported that the program had included nonnuclear testing to "ensure the viability of a nuclear device," which had led U.S. war planners to assume that Iraq could have a "rudimentary nuclear weapon by the end of 1992, if not sooner."[32] The majority of the evidence suggested that Iraq's program for developing nuclear weapons could have produced a primitive nuclear arsenal by the mid-1990s. Postwar analyses have questioned the wisdom of Iraq's decision to invade Kuwait several years before it could possess nuclear weapons; clearly, such devices would have proven a significant deterrent to states considering intervention against Iraq.[33] As one observer noted, Iraq could "build the weapons that would blackmail into impotence any power daring to unseat Saddam."[34] The possibility of Iraq threatening its neighbors with nuclear blackmail was so serious that many states supported efforts to destroy its facilities. As a nuclear-armed Iraq could also inhibit the deployment of U.S. military forces to the Middle East, the destruction of Iraq's nuclear potential was seen as one of the most important goals of the Gulf War.

As the U.S. military began actively planning for war, defense planners and intelligence analysts put Iraq's military, economic, and technological assets under intense scrutiny. The targets receiving the closest attention were facilities for developing weapons of mass destruction – not only nuclear but also chemical and biological weapons, as well as ballistic missiles for their delivery. At the start of the six-week air war, Iraqi nuclear facilities were subjected to heavy bombardment. After the war, all known or suspected facilities for developing WMD were placed under the jurisdiction of the United Nations Office of Special Inspections for dismantlement.[35]

A third objective of the war was to demonstrate to other states that the United States is a reliable ally and that, as President Bush said, "American leadership remains absolutely indispensable."[36] A critical objective of U.S. policy in the Persian Gulf since the 1979 Islamic Revolution in Iran had been to strengthen the moderate states, including Saudi Arabia, in this oil-rich region. In the end, the United States and Saudi Arabia spent billions of dollars on the Saudi military infrastructure and reserves of equipment and supplies, so as to bolster the credibility of U.S. promises to defend Saudi Arabia in the event of a threat to the security of the kingdom.

Part of the U.S. strategy leading up to the war was to assemble an international coalition to respond to Iraq's invasion of Kuwait. The United Nations Security Council Resolution (UNSCR) 678, which was approved on November 29, 1990, authorized "Member States co-operating with the government of Kuwait . . . to use all necessary means to uphold and implement [all relevant resolutions] and to restore international peace and security in the area."[37] The fact that such diverse states as Japan, Niger, the Soviet Union, Argentina, China, and Greece denounced Iraq's invasion of Kuwait was evidence that a broad international consensus held Iraq accountable for its aggression.[38] The coalition involved roughly fifty states, including thirty-eight that jointly contributed more than 200,000 troops as well as 1,200 tanks, 750 aircraft, and 60 naval vessels.[39] This "grand coalition," as the centerpiece of the Bush administration's policy, was designed to remove Iraq forcibly from Kuwait, show the importance of multilateral action and thus the limits of unilateralism, and reinforce the credibility of U.S. policy by demonstrating broad international support for the war.[40]

The longer-term U.S. intention was to deter future Iraqi aggression.[41] The invasion of Kuwait had surprised those observers who understood that the United States placed a high priority on security in the region. Some asserted that America had failed to communicate its resolve to the Iraqi government, which in turn had fostered doubts in Baghdad about U.S. willingness to respond to an invasion of Kuwait. Congress, for example, never formally declared war, although it did vote to support President Bush's policy of using military force to remove Iraqi forces from Kuwait.[42] Iraq, however, is not easily deterred by what might be interpreted as ambiguous U.S. policies, as witnessed by the litany of bellicose actions taken by Iraq *since* the 1991 Persian Gulf War: the movement of Iraqi forces to the Kuwaiti border in October 1994, growing Iraqi assertiveness against weapons inspections,[43] the failure of the inspections regime,[44] and the hundreds of occasions in which Iraq's integrated air defense radars have targeted U.S. and coalition aircraft flying the northern and southern no-fly zones.[45] The fact that in 1991 Saddam Hussein was allowed to remain in power has thus been interpreted as a fundamental cause of further problems in the region. (See Chapter 11 regarding the 2003 U.S. invasion of Iraq.)

The Desert Shield military buildup in the fall of 1990 was thus intended to convey, unambiguously, that the United States would not tolerate Iraqi attempts to intimidate or attack its neighbors. The military campaign of January and February 1991 (Desert Storm and Desert Sabre)[46] was intended to prove that America would respond with devastating force if Iraq violated this "rule." Its objectives were to restore Kuwait's territorial integrity and sovereignty, protect Saudi Arabia from aggression by Iraq, destroy Iraq's military forces and WMD programs, deter future Iraqi aggression and hegemony, and demonstrate that the United States had the capacity and will to win.

DESCRIPTION OF OPERATION

The manner in which the United States decided to use its conventional military power to defeat Iraq was influenced by several factors.[47] The first was the absolute military superiority of U.S. forces. Although many nations contributed military troops and equipment, the United States provided most of the military manpower and weapons, deploying over half a million troops, thousands of aircraft, tanks, and ships. Neither its NATO allies nor Kuwait nor Saudi Arabia possessed anywhere near the human or material resources that were necessary to defeat Iraq militarily.[48] The members of the U.N. coalition understood that the United States would provide most of the military forces for the campaign, and it was presumed, although hardly discussed in public, that American forces would bear the greatest burden in casualties.

The prospect of casualties, however, did not have a dramatic influence on the debate in American society, during U.S. war preparations, as to the potential price of victory in the Persian Gulf. Moreover, studies conducted prior to the Gulf War radically overestimated the level of U.S. casualties that might occur.[49] On the basis of public-opinion research, the American people seemed prepared to accept large numbers of casualties in defending Kuwait and the Gulf States.[50] In early January 1990, in an ABC News–*Washington Post* poll, 66 percent approved of Bush's handling of the crisis thus far, and 65 percent believed that the United States should fight if necessary to expel Iraq from Kuwait.[51] This suggests that prior to the war the American people were willing to risk significant human and material resources. Even after evidence was presented that Iraq might use chemical weapons to cause thousands of American and coalition casualties, the Bush administration was able to maintain broad public support throughout the military campaign.[52]

A second factor influencing the American campaign was the decision to define the mission narrowly and to defeat the Iraqi military only to the extent necessary to achieve that. When former President George H. W. Bush later defended this strategy in the war, he observed:

> If I had told General Schwarzkopf to send the 82d Airborne Division rolling into Baghdad, we would have become an occupying power in an Arab land. The coalition would have shattered instantly; only a handful of nations would have stayed. We would have made a hero out of a brutal dictator. . . . Some argue that if we had kept going only twenty-four hours more, we could have wiped out another, say, fifty thousand Iraqis fleeing on the "highway of death." . . . [We] do not measure success by how many people are killed, but by whether the mission has been completed.[53]

A third factor was the idea that the United States should use its extreme advantage in military technology to defeat Iraq's military as quickly and decisively as possible, with minimal U.S. and coalition casualties.[54]

During the five months of Desert Shield, the United States assembled an overwhelming military coalition of ground, naval, and air forces, one that was fueled by "mountains" of supplies in the desert.[55] The operational strategy was to begin the war with air attacks to destroy the Iraqi air force and weapons of mass destruction, surprising and confusing Iraqi forces by demolishing their command and control systems. The air campaign would be followed by a ground war to surround and destroy the Iraqi units occupying Kuwait.

Air Campaign

The air campaign was designed to be consistent with the principle that the strategic use of air power will contribute decisively to winning a war.[56] The coalition air campaign, Operation Desert Storm, was organized into four distinct phases. Phase I was simultaneously to establish air superiority, paralyze the Iraqi leadership and its command system, attack the Iraqi national command authority, destroy its nuclear, biological, and chemical weapons facilities, and weaken units of the elite Republican Guard. Phase II was to suppress or destroy Iraq's ground-based air defenses deployed in the Kuwaiti theater of operations. Phase III was to conduct air attacks against Iraqi ground units, in particular the Republican Guard Forces Command. Phase IV involved air and sea bombardments against Iraqi ground forces.[57] Over the forty-three days of the war, there were 109,876 sorties against 1,200 targets.[58]

The United States launched its large-scale air campaign in Iraq on January 17, 1991, thirty-eight days before the start of the ground campaign. Including a wide range of targets, its principal objective was to destroy the ability of the Iraqi military to oppose the coalition military effectively. First, B-52 bombers launched cruise missiles and U.S. warships launched Tomahawk land attack missiles, both targeting power facilities and military communications sites, the latter in and around Baghdad; the B-52s also targeted airfields.[59] Meanwhile attack helicopters took out early-warning radars in southern Iraq. From the beginning, the air campaign achieved complete air superiority throughout the theater. Overall, coalition air forces flew roughly 18,000 sorties to destroy or disrupt twelve sets of strategic targets, dropping 85,000 tons of bombs – and of those, only 3 percent were precision-guided munitions.[60] Important strategic targets were the thirty-three national-level leadership bunkers and facilities located in Baghdad and throughout Iraq, which were targeted to prevent Iraq's national leadership from directing and coordinating its military establishment.[61] The fact that the air campaign forced Iraq's leadership to relocate to bunkers to avoid being killed inhibited their ability to control and direct Iraqi military forces in the field.[62]

The air campaign's target sets included electrical production facilities, command sites, air-defense systems, air forces and bases, naval forces and port facilities, oil refining and distribution facilities, railroads and bridges, military storage and production facilities, and weapons-related sites.[63] Once the coalition had quickly destroyed Iraqi aircraft, ground warning sites, and a significant fraction of Iraq's command and control network, complete air superiority was achieved. This meant that coalition forces could conduct air strikes with nearly complete impunity for the duration of the war. Moreover, coalition aircraft were free to fly throughout Iraqi airspace secure in the knowledge that Iraq's ability to know how the war was proceeding or to respond effectively with military action had been destroyed.

The destruction of three categories of target in particular had a significant effect on the outcome of the war. The first was the complex of nuclear, biological, and chemical facilities that Iraq had started to build in the 1980s. As noted earlier, U.S. intelligence estimates had predicted that Iraq would produce a nuclear weapon by 1992 at latest, so these facilities were high-priority targets for planners.[64] Roughly 5 percent of the aircraft and cruise missile sorties that attacked strategic targets in Iraq were targeted against nuclear, biological, and chemical (NBC) weapons facilities. These attacks included extensive strikes against the Baghdad Nuclear Research Facility that was devoted to developing nuclear weapons.[65] In the end, this part of the air campaign arguably had the greatest effect on the postwar balance of power because it significantly delayed Iraq's efforts to acquire nuclear weapons. (In view of evidence that Iraq continued to pursue its program for developing NBC weapons as well as ballistic missiles for their delivery, a United Nations Special Commission [UNSCOM] was established in April 1991, allowing weapons monitoring and verification that significantly delayed Iraq's program for developing WMD until these inspections ended in December 1998.)[66]

The air campaign also attacked facilities associated with the development, production, and storage of short-range ballistic missiles of a type known as Scuds. Iraq had both conventional, Soviet-design Scuds and its own modified versions.[67] After Iraq fired Scud missiles against Israel and Saudi Arabia in January 1991, the air campaign shifted to the "Great Scud Hunt," in which aircraft conducted twenty-five hundred missions searching unsuccessfully for Scud missiles to prevent their use against Israel or other coalition members.[68]

Finally, in Phase IV of the air campaign, the U.S.-led coalition employed a significant array of combat aircraft in various roles to weaken Iraqi ground forces (infantry, armor, and artillery) deployed in the Kuwaiti theater of operations (KTO).[69] In gradually escalating attacks during the weeks before the ground campaign, coalition aircraft, flying more than 35,000 sorties, dropped thousands of tons of bombs on both conscript and elite (Republican Guard) army divisions in order to destroy their morale, cohesion, and combat effectiveness.[70] These forces, which had dug into heavily fortified and protected positions, were nonetheless quite vulnerable to the effects of a precise air campaign. Although initial estimates claimed Iraqi military casualties as high as 100,000–250,000, many commentators believe that the real number of soldiers who died during these air raids, conducted principally by B-52 bombers, is closer to 25,000.[71] Nevertheless, the almost immediate collapse of Iraqi ground forces during the ground campaign was based in part on the air campaign having significantly weakened the ability of Iraqi forces to resist the coalition ground forces of Operation Desert Sabre.[72]

Overall, the air campaign destroyed Iraq's air defenses, established air superiority, demolished enemy command and control centers, depleted Iraqi ground forces, and effectively disrupted Iraq's ability to fight the war. Desert Storm also destroyed (for instance) 30 percent of the Iraqi tanks, significant numbers of which were also destroyed during the ground campaign. Perhaps the most important *failure* of the air campaign was its inability to locate and destroy Iraqi Scud missile launchers and the remaining facilities used to produce nuclear, chemical, and biological weapons and ballistic missiles.[73]

Ground Campaign

The overall objective of the ground campaign was to isolate and destroy elite Republican Guard units, forcibly remove Iraqi military forces from Kuwait, and return the government of Kuwait to its legitimate leaders.[74] During Operation Desert Sabre, a force of roughly two hundred thousand coalition soldiers penetrated Iraqi defenses, cut Iraqi lines of communication, and destroyed Iraqi forces in Kuwait. The four-day ground war turned into a rout, as the tens of thousands of Iraqi soldiers who attempted to escape from Kuwait could not offer coordinated resistance.[75]

From the outset of the crisis in August 1990, many senior American officials had believed that air power alone could not defeat Iraq, since only ground forces could force Iraq to withdraw from Kuwait. President Bush also had expressed concerns when he observed, "Air power could do only so much."[76] Bob Woodward reported in *The Commanders* that "[Defense Secretary] Cheney had become an absolute believer in the need for ground power" because he "saw ground power as the key back-up to airpower."[77]

When the ground campaign began on February 24, 1991, its strategic purpose was to surround and destroy Iraqi army units in a massive sweeping motion that would extend throughout Iraq and Kuwait. After thirty-eight days of aerial bombardment that had knocked out enemy command and control facilities and hobbled their communications, the Iraqi leadership was effectively prevented from understanding the nature of the tactical campaign. This permitted coalition ground forces to envelop those of Iraq in Kuwait almost without incident.[78]

To support the ground offensive, the United States deployed seventeen heavy brigades, six light-infantry brigades of airborne and air-assault units, and Marine Corps regiments and amphibious brigades. In addition, the United Kingdom, Egypt, France, and Syria contributed tens of thousands of ground forces and military equipment.[79] Arab–Islamic forces, which were organized into Joint Forces Command-North and -East, included troops from Egypt,

Syria, Kuwait, and Oman, among other states.[80] Since the coalition needed an extensive logistics base to support the hundreds of thousands of ground troops engaged in massive combat operations, U.S. forces developed a logistics infrastructure of bases and an extensive transportation system in Saudi Arabia to provide offensive operations with fuel, ammunition, food, and water.[81]

It is not surprising that the ground offensive was a military victory for U.S. and coalition forces. The United States had assembled a technologically advanced military force that simply overwhelmed the ability of the Iraqi political leadership and its military to maintain effective combat operations. Before the ground offensive even began, the combat effectiveness of Iraqi units had been reduced by half or more by the long air campaign. In its wake, Iraqi forces simply could not mount or sustain any effective resistance to coalition ground attacks. At the same time, in addition to coalition forces' superior training and preparedness, coalition battlefield commanders had such sophisticated technology available that they could receive tactical intelligence and retarget Iraqi forces much more rapidly than Iraqi commanders could estimate what was happening on the battlefield and move their forces.[82] Finally, the Iraqi armed forces disintegrated almost immediately during the ground war, leading some to refer to the main Iraq–Kuwait highway, now strewn with Iraqi military equipment in retreat from Kuwait, as the "Highway of Death." The scenes of devastation led U.S. policy and military leaders to end the war after four days of ground combat.[83] At that point, it was estimated that coalition forces had destroyed or captured 3,847 tanks, 1,450 armored personnel carriers, and 2,917 pieces of artillery since the beginning of Desert Storm.[84]

Maritime Campaign

The fundamental purpose of the maritime campaign was to control all sea-lanes in the vicinity of Iraq, destroy Iraqi naval forces, and support military efforts to restore the territorial sovereignty of Kuwait.[85] The rapid movement of maritime pre-positioning ships (MPS) to Saudi Arabia was coordinated with troops flown in directly from the United States. The concept was to allow U.S. ground forces to join more rapidly with their heavy equipment than would normally be the case. This consideration was important given concerns that Iraqi forces might invade Saudi Arabia.

The purpose of the sea-control campaign was to project power in the sea-lanes that surround Kuwait. More than 165 ships were used to isolate Iraq economically, help destroy Iraqi naval forces, and secure the coalition's sea lines of communication through which 95 percent of their supply cargo was delivered. The U.S. campaign against surface warfare ships destroyed or damaged 143 Iraqi naval vessels, damaged all Iraqi naval bases and ports, put all oil platforms in the northern Persian Gulf under coalition control, and prevented

Iraqi naval vessels from attacking coalition forces. Within three weeks, coalition forces had destroyed Iraq's Navy and eliminated Iraq's ability to conduct maritime operations in the Persian Gulf.[86] At the same time, sea control allowed U.S. carrier battle groups to strike targets in western Iraq with cruise missiles launched from surface ships and submarines, and to conduct strikes with aircraft launched from aircraft carriers in the Mediterranean Sea and the northern Persian Gulf. Finally, it was necessary to control the sea before coalition forces could mount an amphibious operation against the Iraqi military in Kuwait. Although such an attack never proved necessary, maritime forces assembled along the coast established a credible amphibious capability, effectively pinning Iraqi troops into defensive positions.[87]

Although Iraq's contact mines (based on a Russian pre–World War I design) did pose a threat to naval operations during the Gulf War, the greater danger was the more advanced magnetic and acoustic mines that Iraq had acquired from the Soviet Union and Italy. As a result of these capabilities, ongoing mine countermeasures were required, and coalition maritime operations were significantly affected. In fact, Iraq's mines damaged two U.S. naval vessels, the USS *Tripoli* and USS *Princeton*.[88]

Still, having now gained control over the sea as well as the air, the United States and its coalition could maintain the supply of vital equipment to support the war, enforce a blockade of Iraq, conduct cruise missile strikes, and deceive the Iraqi leadership into believing that they faced an amphibious attack into Kuwait. Each of these operations contributed to the political–military victory that the United States achieved in the Gulf War.

Intelligence and Command

The Gulf War demonstrated that the United States had an unparalleled ability to integrate events on the battlefield into military operations and yet deny that information to the adversary. The capacity of U.S. military forces to collect and disseminate information during the campaign was without historical precedent. Furthermore, U.S. intelligence capabilities decisively helped the coalition defeat Iraqi forces while incurring minimal casualties. With its knowledge of the precise nature and timing of events on the battlefield and the means to apply that knowledge to the prosecution of the war, the United States had an absolute strategic advantage that ultimately defeated Iraqi forces. The war did, however, highlight several areas in which the United States could improve its ability to gather intelligence and disseminate it to the fighting forces, most notably its use of space-based surveillance and communications.[89]

From August 1990 until the end of military hostilities in February 1991, the United States was guided by two exceptionally clear military objectives: removing Iraqi forces from Kuwait – by force if necessary – and restoring Kuwait to its prewar borders. These objectives helped the United States and its coalition partners organize and execute a campaign that dismantled Iraq's occupation forces in six weeks. Although Iraq had considerable strengths – notably, its large ground forces and chemical weapons – the coalition effectively exploited Iraq's weaknesses – a highly centralized command and control system, military experience limited to a frontal war against a regional power, rigid political and military decision making, and dependence on other nations for spare parts.[90] The devastation inflicted on Iraqi military forces, communications facilities, and industrial sites was so overwhelming that Iraqi troops were barely able to limp home from Kuwait. In fact, so many Iraqi forces were destroyed while withdrawing that commentators referred to the "mother of all retreats" along the "highway of death" from Kuwait to Iraq.[91] Although some parts of the Iraqi military did survive – notably, units of the Republican Guard as well as Iraqi Air Force units that had flown to Iran at the very start of the war – it would prove a shell of its former self, in terms of its overall size and composition, in 2003.[92] Since 1991, Iraq's military forces have been so focused on internal defense that they no longer constitute the expeditionary force that once had been able to threaten its neighbors.

Operation Desert Shield/Desert Storm established a new precedent for conducting military operations: gaining support from the United Nations to create an international coalition to defend peace and security against transgressions by rogue states. In effect, the Gulf War established the principle that states violating the norms of internationally acceptable behavior may face military reprisals from a U.N. coalition. The coalition formed to combat Iraq contributed military forces and tens of billions of dollars in financial assistance to help cover the so-called *incremental costs* of the operation, that is, anything the United States would not normally have had to spend on its investment in force structure and baseline operating costs. These were estimated to be $61 billion, and a number of states, including Saudi Arabia, Kuwait, United Arab Emirates, Japan, Germany, and South Korea, contributed nearly $53 billion in a financial burden-sharing agreement with the United States.[93]

INTERPRETING VICTORY

The initial interpretation was that the United States had used its technological and economic strengths to trounce Iraq and achieve a significant victory. From this interpretation emerged a view of the Persian Gulf War as a model victory, in which the United States used decisive weapons, information and communication technologies, and an international coalition to defeat a regional power overwhelmingly.[94] President Bush had contributed to this interpretation when he stipulated that the U.S. strategy was "the immediate, unconditional, and complete withdrawal of all Iraqi forces from Kuwait," because "anything less than total withdrawal from Kuwait of the Iraqi forces . . . will not be acceptable."[95] The U.S. plan for victory was to defeat Iraq as quickly as possible and then withdraw, thus avoiding protracted military operations and/or an occupation, as well as the loss of public and international support that might accompany either one.[96] In practical terms, the war was viewed as a victory of strategic dimensions because the United States defeated Iraq swiftly, minimized the loss of American and coalition soldiers, and avoided entanglement in a postwar quagmire.

Strategic victory dominated how U.S. policymakers defined the outcome. For example, Secretary of State James Baker wrote that "Within hours of the launch of the ground war, it was apparent to all of us that victory would be swift and total."[97] In the long term, Baker observed, the war was successful because "Iraq's military had been so weakened that Saddam's ability to threaten his neighbors in the future was clearly, substantially diminished."[98] Though there had been concerns that the war might be very costly – in the fall of 1990, General Colin Powell had argued unsuccessfully that, rather than fight, the United States should impose economic sanctions until Iraq withdrew from Kuwait, because a war might last for years and require great patience on the part of the United States – these concerns faded once it was obvious that the United States would decisively defeat Iraq militarily.[99] According to a Department of Defense report, "The combined Coalition forces . . . had won one of the fastest and most complete victories in military history."[100]

The interpretation of the war as a decisive victory was based on the fact that the United States had avoided both a protracted war and the significant casualties that could have undermined the will of the American people to win. The U.S. strategy had succeeded in minimizing American casualties, which were described by one senior U.S. official as "gratifyingly light."[101] Yet the Gulf War had demonstrated that the American people could support a military engagement even in the face of estimates that casualties might be significant.[102] However, the broader lesson about victory for senior U.S. officials was derived from their views of the Vietnam War. As President Bush noted, "In this war – unlike Vietnam – we had a defined mission, and we carried it out."[103] For Secretary Baker, "the Persian Gulf crisis would establish in rather convincing fashion that our country's long and oftentimes debilitating post-Vietnam hangover had at least temporarily run its course."[104]

The consensus that the war had produced a significant victory was influenced by President Bush, who wrote about "prevailing" in the Gulf War and the "importance of winning." Confident late in the war that the United States would achieve victory, he described a "greater feeling of surety that the campaign would be a swift success."[105] When the war was over, Bush spoke in a televised address to the nation on February 27, 1991, about a "victory quick, decisive, and just. . . . No one country can claim this victory as its own. It was not only a victory for Kuwait but also a victory for all the coalition partners. This is a victory for the United Nations, for all mankind, for the rule of law, and for what is right."[106] His use of language on this scale conveyed the message that the United States had prevailed in a strategically significant fashion, and that it was permissible to use the more grandiose interpretation of victory. Though the war's outcome was considerably less than grand strategic victory, this language about victory contributed to how policymakers and the public initially interpreted the war.

However, a debate would soon emerge as to whether this victory was being properly interpreted. As early as December 1991, 80 percent of Americans polled believed that the United States had not finished what it had started and that victory was "far from complete."[107] President Bush seemed to understand that we had not achieved a grand strategic victory when, the day after the war ended, he wrote in his diary that "It hasn't been a clean end – there is no battleship *Missouri* surrender. This is what's missing to make this akin to WWII, to separate Kuwait from Korea and Vietnam."[108]

The initial rhetoric and analyses of the war may have interpreted the outcome as a grand strategic victory, but that interpretation is not supported by the facts. It is imperative that scholars and policymakers understand that, in terms of the present study's pretheoretical language, what the Persian Gulf War produced was no more than a political–military victory.

There are several reasons for this important reclassification. The first is that the United States used overwhelming force based on clearly defined, limited, and militarily achievable objectives to which it strictly adhered during the conduct of the war. Even in the waning days of the war, when the United States and the coalition could have seized Iraq, reorganized its government and leadership, and attempted to realign the Middle East strategically, the firm U.S. objective was only to force Iraq to withdraw from Kuwait. Thus, although the United States did expel Iraq from Kuwait, it did not *strategically defeat* Iraq.[109] Even the political–military victory achieved was slowly eroded in the 1990s by a regular series of military confrontations with and responses against Iraq: the southern no-fly zone established in August 1992; the U.S. cruise-missile attacks against a nuclear complex in January 1993 (on President Bush's last day in office) and on Iraqi intelligence headquarters in June 1993; the deployment of 54,000 U.S. troops to the region in October 1994 in response to Iraqi troop movements toward Kuwait; further U.S. retaliatory missile attacks in September 1996 (Operation Desert Strike); and the standoff over arms inspections between November 1997 and February 1998.[110]

Second, the United States did not remove Saddam Hussein and his Baath Party, deciding instead that the Iraqi people rather than an occupying power should determine Iraq's postwar political situation. As President Bush wrote in his memoirs, "We were disappointed that Saddam's defeat did not break his hold on power."[111] In response, in May 1991 Bush approved a covert "lethal finding" that authorized spending a hundred million dollars "to create the conditions for the removal of Saddam Hussein from power."[112] This decision alone confirmed the Gulf War victory as political–military, because it signaled that Saddam Hussein was still very much in power and that the political balance in Iraq and the Gulf region remained the same. The Bush administration argued that if the United States had defeated Iraq comprehensively, it would be drawn into a quagmire involving the reorganization of the territory of Iraq among Iran, Turkey, and the Kurds, as well as disputes among Sunni, Shiite, and Kurdish groups. The argument advanced by policymakers in the Bush administration was that imposing a more significant victory would have commanded a heavy price in lives and political credibility in a region where the balance of power is historically shaped by a complex array of national and religious forces. The risk for Washington was that states in the Persian Gulf would see U.S. intervention as an excuse for pursuing imperial policies that are hostile to Islamic societies.[113]

Third, although Iraq was defeated militarily by coalition forces, Iraq's leadership survived. The war did not remove Saddam Hussein from power, and his control over Iraq gradually increased. It has been suggested that Saddam Hussein defined victory in terms of standing up to the United States and that surviving would strengthen his power and weaken U.S. power and influence in the long term.[114] In a January 17, 2001, speech marking the tenth anniversary of the 1991 Persian Gulf War, Saddam Hussein declared that Iraq had achieved "victory over enemies" of the Arab world because it had been "unyielding to exploitation."[115] In an August 2001 televised address to the Iraqi people, Saddam said that "the proud and loyal people of Iraq and their valiant armed forces will win victory in the final results of the immortal Mother of All Battles."[116] Taken at face value, these words suggest that Saddam might hold entirely different ideas of what victory means, or that he might have been persuaded that he could take on the United States again and win.[117] To cite the words of Iraq's Deputy Foreign Minister Tariq Aziz, "Victory can be achieved through the strategic results of any confrontation, and we are confident that we gained victory in that struggle, which lasted 10 years and is still going on."[118] Thus, for some observers, Saddam Hussein emerged with a victory from the Gulf War because he survived to consolidate his hold on political power in Iraq. As expressed by one Eastern European diplomat, "Victory is when the ruler stays in power, no matter how many people he kills, no matter how much the country is ravaged."[119]

For these reasons, the Gulf War is best seen as a political–military victory. The coalition forced Iraq to leave Kuwait by inflicting sufficient destruction on Baghdad for Iraq to capitulate; but it neither replaced the government nor rebuilt Iraq's economy, military, or society. The objective had been to force Iraq out of Kuwait, and so the Bush administration and the coalition members explicitly avoided a strategy that could produce grand strategic victory. In fact, the United States had stopped the war at precisely the point when further operations would have led to the dismemberment of Iraq and conditions equivalent to grand strategic victory: occupying Iraq, disarming its military, capturing or killing Saddam Hussein, putting a new regime into power.[120] Instead, Iraq's political leadership survived the war, consolidated its power, reasserted Iraq's role as a powerful state in the Middle East, and continued to threaten its neighbors.[121] Saddam Hussein's decision to ignore various U.N. resolutions regarding weapons of mass destruction and to continue, until the late 1990s, programs for developing nuclear, chemical, and biological weapons and delivery missiles confirms that the coalition's political–military victory was not sufficiently compelling to make him rethink his basic policies.[122] Nor was there any serious debate in the United States about whether to broaden this victory until the terrorist attacks on September 11, 2001, amid a contentious debate about Iraqi support for terrorism (see Chapter 11).

CONCLUSION

In terms of a pretheory of victory, the war against Iraq produced a political–military victory in which the U.S.-led coalition destroyed the foundations of Iraq's military power and its facilities and program for building WMD and ballistic missiles. Despite the United States having used its conventional military power in a large-scale campaign, the war's outcome was limited by the political objective of restoring the *status quo ante bellum*. Simply put, the United States forced Saddam Hussein to withdraw from Kuwait and prevented Iraq from threatening the oil supply in the Middle East. In the end, it did not accomplish much more than that.

Neither the United States nor the members of the U.N. coalition sought to change the regime in Baghdad or to alter the balance of power in the region, except in the general hope that Saddam Hussein might be removed from power by his disgruntled generals. For these reasons, the Persian Gulf War produced a limited change in the status quo rather than regime change or significant changes in the nature of the Iraqi government and its policies and actions.

The United States and its coalition members mobilized extensively for the war, including the formation and organization of that coalition and the logistics of amassing and delivering the forces and supplies necessary for waging a major theater war. This large-scale military campaign involved most elements of U.S. conventional military forces, including air, land, and sea forces, entailed the ability to sustain those forces, and necessitated procedures by which allied forces could communicate and operate together. The United States, beginning in August 1990, engaged in extensive mobilization for a thirty-eight-day air campaign and four-day ground campaign that successfully destroyed significant numbers of government facilities and military targets throughout Iraq and led to a rout of Iraqi forces. There was also extensive political mobilization: From the first, and up to the start of the air campaign, the Bush administration's diplomatic strategy relied on building broad support from within the international community. The fact that the coalition remained intact throughout the war is still interpreted as a significant diplomatic accomplishment. The Bush administration simultaneously, and perhaps with somewhat less success, established strong domestic support for the war; with the exception of contentious votes in the U.S. Senate, it enjoyed broad public support throughout the brief war.

The last consideration is how the nature and extent of U.S. postconflict obligations shaped the nature of victory. After the war, the United States helped Kuwait rebuild itself from the damage inflicted by Iraqi military forces during its occupation, including oil fields set ablaze by Iraqi forces in retreat. Kuwait had sufficient wealth from oil revenues to finance rebuilding any infrastructure that had been destroyed by Iraq; the United States provided technical assistance. Iraqi society, meanwhile, had suffered enormous devastation during the war, was crippled by the U.N. economic sanctions that continued thereafter, and was by virtue of those sanctions unable to control its economic affairs; yet the U.S. victory did not establish any postconflict obligations toward Iraq, principally because Iraq had not been defeated on a strategic level. In practice, though, the United States was burdened with postwar obligations, though of a military kind: the creation and enforcement of no-fly zones in Iraq, the decision to maintain forces in Saudi Arabia and Kuwait, and the deployment of U.S. forces to the region several times when it appeared that Iraq might be marshaling forces to invade Kuwait again.

In summary, the United States in the Persian Gulf War achieved no more than a political–military victory; it had rejected the option of grand strategic victory, both to ensure international cooperation and to avoid a quagmire. Although the war involved an extensive level of mobilization, it produced a limited change in the status quo, and created limited postconflict obligations in the form of military operations that were designed to contain Iraq.

The hope was that this victory would teach the leadership in Baghdad to avoid reckless actions that might encourage U.S. intervention. However, just the opposite occurred. Iraq's series of provocative actions throughout the 1990s showed that Saddam Hussein did not fear the United States, nor personally suffer the consequences of the political–military victory that Washington had gained at great expense. The U.S.-led coalition's failure to impose grand strategic victory may have been interpreted by Saddam Hussein as signs of weakness in the Bush and Clinton administrations: If the United States was not willing to destroy Iraq's government and engage in postconflict, nation-(re)building obligations, then it must not have been serious about resolving the Iraqi problem.

Finally, policymakers' highly inflated expectations regarding the victory – the first U.S. victory in a major conflict in decades – contributed to the mistaken belief that they had achieved grand strategic victory. American expectations thus exceeded what was accomplished by the war, as Iraq's leadership, government, and economic priorities survived intact. Unless debates among policymakers and scholars make more precise distinctions between types of victory, there will be confusion in Washington and among the public as to whether and how the state achieves victory.

Washington's reluctance to defeat Iraq on a grand strategic level – in essence, its tacit agreement to permit Baghdad's government and military leadership to continue their prewar policies – eventually eroded the political–military victory that had been achieved.[123] It was against this backdrop that the administration of President George W. Bush decided to invade Iraq in 2003 (see Chapter 11).

9 | Bosnia and Kosovo, 1992–1999

During 1991–2, several territories of the Socialist Federal Republic of (SFR) Yugoslavia declared independence. Though Macedonia and Slovenia managed to gain autonomy quickly and relatively peacefully, ethnically driven wars resulted in Croatia (1991–5) and Bosnia–Herzegovina (1992–5). U.N. forces were installed in Croatia in February 1992, and the focus shifted in April to Bosnia–Herzegovina, with the outbreak of civil war among its ethnic Croats, Serbs, and Bosniaks. The United States and its NATO allies became involved in a protracted debate about whether to intervene in the civil war in Bosnia[1] to stop ethnic "cleansing" and genocide. During these various Yugoslav (also known as Balkan) wars, which stretched to include Kosovo during 1996–9, the United States, United Nations, and members of the international community watched as "ethnically based criminal violence" by "the majority population – Muslim, Serb, or Croat – cleansed its community of now unwanted minorities."[2]

The U.S. decision to intervene in Bosnia involved several discrete phases: protecting U.N. humanitarian relief efforts as of July 1992; bolstering NATO no-fly zones as of April 1993; campaigning in May 1993 for the selective lifting of a U.N.-imposed arms embargo and the conducting of air strikes; deciding later that month to pursue a policy of containment; pushing for a negotiated settlement through a diplomatic "endgame strategy" developed in the summer of 1995 (while Congress was in recess after voting to break the embargo);[3] and participating in the two-week NATO air campaign that began late that August.

Facing a deliberate campaign of genocide against Bosniaks, the mounting killings of civilians (eventually some 25,000–60,000), and fears that the entire Balkan region would disintegrate into ethnic, national, and religious chaos, the strategy of the United States – first under George H. W. Bush's administration, then, as of January 1993, that of Bill Clinton – began on a diplomatic note and gradually shifted toward military intervention.[4] This strategy would culminate in several military actions involving the United States: notably the NATO air campaign against Bosnian Serbs in the summer of 1995 and the one in March 1999 against Serbia in response to the massacre of ethnic Albanians in the formerly autonomous province of Kosovo.[5] During the three years before its military intervention, the United States had conducted humanitarian relief operations in Bosnia to alleviate some of the suffering in the region, but these efforts had done little to stop the devastation that was being inflicted by the warring parties.

This chapter focuses on the humanitarian relief operation and air campaigns that were conducted in Bosnia throughout the 1990s, as well as the later action in defense of Kosovo, in terms of how these operations contribute to and can be interpreted by a pretheory of victory.

BACKGROUND

Since the start of SFR Yugoslavia's disintegration in the 1990s, policymakers in Washington actively debated the risks and benefits of coming to the aid of victims of civil war.[6] Yugoslavia is a case study of how long-suppressed and historically based ethnic and religious antagonisms can lead to civil wars and the breakup of states; and some question whether victory is even possible in such wars.[7] With its history of ethnic, national, and religious frictions, the former Yugoslavia was the first state to shatter the general peace and order that prevailed in Europe at the end of the cold war.[8] In the early months of 1992, the relative harmony among ethnic and religious groups in Bosnia disintegrated into a war whose brutality and carnage is reminiscent of the destruction that had occurred in Yugoslavia during World War II.[9]

Although the United States did not intervene militarily in the former Yugoslavia until mid-decade, the proper course of action had been debated in the Bush and Clinton administrations. At a time when free societies were emerging throughout the former Soviet Union, Eastern Europe, and the Balkans, policymakers in the Clinton administration sought to encourage these and to prevent post–cold war ethnic fissures from escalating into wars.[10] Meetings on the ongoing Balkan crisis, characterized by Clinton's Secretary of State Madeleine Albright as "rambling and inconclusive," focused on whether and how the United States should intervene in Bosnia's civil war.[11]

In strategic terms, the war in Bosnia is significant for a discussion of victory because it involved highly divisive ethnic, religious, and national differences between the Serb and Croat peoples, whose animosities stretch back more than a thousand years, and between each of them and Bosniaks.[12] The strong religious affiliations among the Bosnian population – Serbs were largely Orthodox Christian, Croats predominantly Roman Catholics, and Bosniaks mostly Muslim – exacerbated the divisions among ethnic and national groups, po-

larizing Bosnian society into virulently opposed factions.[13] The origins of the
Bosnian civil war are openly debated: Some say it was caused by Serb aggression and expansionist policies; others, that it resulted from forces of nationalism and political opportunism, with all sides sharing responsibility.[14] The
broader interpretation is that many groups, animated by fundamentally different visions of the past and radically different interpretations of historical grievances, destroyed Bosnia's ability to exist as a peaceful society.[15] With no sense
of shared values and norms – and lacking the strict oversight of SFR Yugoslavia – it was unlikely that a unified political culture would develop in Bosnia.
In this climate, profound ethnic and national hostilities ultimately divided the
population into warring factions, each of which violated the principles of human rights as established in international law.

The question for American foreign policy was this: If a multiethnic state
like Bosnia was likely to be in a state of perpetual chaos, should the United
States intervene militarily in crises that plunge societies into civil wars? When
we consider that many states in Europe, Asia, the Middle East, and Africa may
be plagued by the forces that led to war in the former Yugoslavia, the strategic problem for the United States is whether the war in Bosnia was a harbinger of future decisions about what it means to achieve victory when the state
intervenes militarily in civil wars.[16]

A critical aspect of the response to the war in Bosnia was systemic indeci-
sion in Washington and European capitals about the risks of intervention.
Since late 1992, Washington policy had been confused as to whether it was
prudent for the United States to become involved in this civil war.[17] These
disagreements involved members of the Congress, whose criticism of policies
toward Bosnia led members of the Congress, most notably Senate Majority
Leader Bob Dole, to condemn Clinton policy.[18] The confusion in administration policy also was evident in disagreements among the members of the
NATO alliance. The different degrees of resolve among the United States and
its European allies were based on the fact that these states had radically different views about the threat posed by the collapse of SFR Yugoslavia.[19]

From the European perspective, as the former Yugoslavia crumbled into
warring ethnic and religious factions, with tens of thousands being killed and
hundreds of thousands fleeing the carnage of several regional conflicts, its disintegration was producing millions of refugees that threatened to create social
and political chaos.[20] Many European policymakers feared that the spillover into Europe of refugees from the Bosnian civil war would overwhelm their governments and transplant ethnic and religious frictions into societies that, with
the end of communism, were now experiencing the social pains of political reform and economic reorganization.[21] In Hungary, for example, many people
believed that a migration of disaffected Slavic and Muslim peoples from a society already experiencing frictions with the Magyars was a recipe for societal

disaster. Germany, which was home to millions of foreign workers and would be spending hundreds of billions of deutsche marks on reunification, could not risk that refugees from Yugoslavia would provoke social and economic unrest.[22]

Policymakers in Europe and the United States feared that the civil war in Bosnia could weaken Europe at precisely the time when the end of the cold war provided an opportunity to establish political freedom and economic prosperity in post-Soviet societies. As Secretary of State Warren Christopher warned, "If this conflict continues – and certainly if it spreads – it would jeopardize our efforts to promote stability and security in Europe as a whole."[23] If Europe's southeastern corner was allowed to be ravaged by a brutal and repressive civil war in which hundreds of thousands were murdered in genocidal campaigns, without apparent fear of reprisal, then Europe's future as a pillar of freedom and security would be at risk.[24]

Policymakers in the Clinton administration shared concerns similar to Europe's about the dangers posed by the civil war in Bosnia, notably that the outbreak of religious animosities and ethnic slaughter was symptomatic of global instability.[25] Senior officials in both the Bush and Clinton administrations at first agreed with the European argument that the crisis in the Balkans was a "European problem" that should be resolved by the Europeans.[26] The prevailing view in the Clinton administration was that Bosnia's war represented a problem for European security that the United States could not ignore.[27] Unless the countervailing forces of reason and order were brought to bear against the perpetrators of these crimes against humanity, the civil war in Bosnia would undermine the principles established by World War II and the U.N. Charter.[28] As President Clinton would state after the Bosnian war had ended, "if you look at the results from Bosnia . . . it proves once again that American leadership is indispensable, and that without it, our values, our interests, and peace itself would be at risk."[29]

U.S. policy in the 1990s was designed to discourage rogue states or nonstate actors from taking actions that would undermine international legal and humanitarian values. U.S. policymakers warned that if the West countenanced such acts of barbarism and treachery, they would spread and eventually undermine the moral fiber of civilized societies.[30] Washington also worried that a failure to resist the war in Bosnia might persuade future aggressors that the United States and the West are unwilling to resist these depredations. Senior officials in the Clinton administration who were responsible for policy toward Bosnia believed that ignoring the slaughter in Bosnia would undermine the credibility of the United States, Europe, and NATO.[31] In an address on September 21, 1999, that summarized these policy concerns before the United Nations, Clinton argued that we must "strengthen the capacity of the international community to prevent and, whenever possible, to stop outbreaks of mass killing and displacement."[32]

Since U.S. foreign policy in general relied on America's willingness to re-inforce talk with action, and thus dissuade rogue states or groups from using violence and brutality to realign the balance of power, the war in Bosnia might have been seen as a central element of a strategy for establishing internation-al peace and stability in Europe into the twenty-first century. Yet both the Bush and Clinton administrations were not initially persuaded that events in Bosnia affected the nation's vital interests.[33] For James Baker, the Bush administra-tion's first secretary of state, national interests did not compel the United States to intervene militarily.[34] According to Clinton's secretary of state, "The Bush team had concluded that our national interests were not sufficiently engaged to justify U.S. military action," but "that premise became increasingly unsus-tainable."[35] Early in the Clinton administration, policymakers found it difficult to define whether and to what extent American vital interests were being harmed by the Bosnian civil war, but they did define a "middle category" of interests.[36] Senior policymakers in the State Department and Defense Depart-ment argued in 1994–95 that U.S. interests were so limited that it did not merit the risks of military intervention.[37]

While policymakers and the public believed that the carnage of the war was reprehensible, there was no evidence that the American people associated the war with the nation's vital interests. For example, public-opinion polls con-ducted in February 1993 showed that although a majority would support mil-itary intervention in Bosnia, only 15 percent said that U.S. national-security interests would be the main reason for such involvement.[38] A year later, 59 percent said that American involvement in Bosnia was not in the self-interest of the United States.[39] In June 1995, just months before the start of Oper-ation Deliberate Force, 63 percent of Americans polled said that though Bos-nia represented a human tragedy, it did not threaten the country's vital inter-ests.[40] Moreover, between 1995 and 1997 more than 50 percent of Americans polled disapproved of the presence of U.S. troops in *postwar* Bosnia.[41] One problem for the United States, also well documented in public-opinion polls, was that deploying U.S. military forces in Bosnia might lead to a quagmire from which it would be difficult to extricate itself without embarrassment.

What, then, convinced senior U.S. policymakers to intervene with military power? The principal reasons were to prevent genocide and to preserve the credibility of the United Nations and NATO.[42] A fundamental component of U.S. policy was the maintenance of international norms, as embodied in these two entities. U.S. policymakers sought to ensure that the United Nations could play a key role in building and preserving the foundations of cooperative se-curity in international politics, much as it had done in Iraq (see Chapter 8); any failure to do so would be detrimental to American efforts to build inter-national consensus.[43] In the case of Bosnia, the United Nations placed its cred-ibility on the line when it established the United Nations Protection Force

(UNPROFOR) and deployed twenty-five thousand U.N. troops to protect civilians and urban enclaves in Bosnia. When it became apparent that U.N. forces would fail to contain the violence, the United States intervened: The prospect of U.N. forces being ignored or, worse, captured as hostages by the Bosnian Serbs would undermine the credibility of the United Nations.[44]

Another consideration that shaped the U.S. decision to intervene in Bosnia was the desire to "confirm NATO's central role in post–cold war Europe,"[45] preserving its preeminence as a military institution. The argument was that NATO could not remain a credible instrument of European security if it ignored the genocidal plight of a southeastern European state in the throes of social and political disintegration. There was concern that this chaos could spread throughout the former Yugoslavia and beyond, contributing to political instability in the industrial democracies in Europe.[46] Efforts to preserve NATO's centrality through intervention in Bosnia might backfire if it could not stop the carnage; yet its credibility had already been weakened when it initially failed to respond and again when it allowed the capture of U.N. forces. In May 1995, for example, hundreds of UNPROFOR peacekeepers had been blockaded near weapons collection sites around Sarajevo and held hostage by Bosnian Serbs.[47]

Finally, in successive diplomatic missions, American policymakers, notably Secretary of State Christopher, were informed that the Europeans would provide only limited support to the U.S. policy of dealing with the crisis in Bosnia. When Christopher visited a string of European capitals on May 2, 1993, to request European support for "lift and strike" – lifting the U.N. arms embargo to get weapons to the outgunned Croats and Bosniaks and conducting air strikes – he was informed by officials in London, Paris, Moscow, Brussels, Bonn, and Rome that they would not support such American policy.[48] The thrust of Continental diplomacy during 1993 was that Europe could manage the crisis, although Washington could chose to play a peripheral role.[49]

By 1995, as Secretary Christopher put it, "the President decided that the United States should take a stronger hand, diplomatically and militarily" in Bosnia.[50] Yet General Colin Powell, then Chairman of the Joint Chiefs of Staff and seen as a "formidable presence" by senior members of the Clinton administration,[51] argued strenuously against U.S. military intervention in Bosnia. He observed that the wooded and hilly terrain in Bosnia was ideally suited to waging a guerrilla war against foreign troops and would lend itself to concealing ammunition dumps, artillery, and supplies. He warned that "faced with limited air strikes, the Serbs would have little difficulty hiding tanks and artillery in the woods and fog of Bosnia or keeping them close to civilian populations."[52] Serb inhabitants of the former SFR Yugoslavia had established their ability in the Chetnik resistance during World War II, inflicting significant losses on the Wehrmacht.[53] The lesson that Bosnia was an extremely difficult place in which to conduct military operations against determined defenders was not lost on policymakers in the Clinton administration. Moreover, Bosnian forces had already demonstrated, in both world wars, the will and ability to inflict great losses – and were doing so again in this conflict. The use of military force by the United States to restrain the civil war in Bosnia would become a strategic failure if U.S. ground forces suffered such losses.

Yet air strikes alone would not suffice, as Powell emphasized: "[N]one of these actions was guaranteed to change Serb behavior. Only troops on the ground could do that. Heavy bombing might persuade them to give in, but would not compel them to quit."[54] The United States would need as many as a quarter of a million troops and a long bombing campaign to defeat the Bosnian Serbs and subdue the region.[55] Policymakers worried that the forces required would be so large as to constitute a permanent occupation. Given all these factors, the Clinton administration's decision to intervene led to a complex war plan. Military planners needed to devise a way to strike targets that weakened the military without creating heavy civilian losses. The ability of the international news media to cover events in Bosnia extensively increased the pressure on the United States to ensure that only military targets were destroyed and to limit collateral damage – not only to civilians but to economic facilities, such as power plants.

A related problem was how to determine who precisely the enemy was, or even which ethnic or religious groups should be punished with military force. The common interpretation was that the Bosnian Serbs were the main aggressors in this civil war, in part because of the atrocities they committed. Yet there was considerable evidence that the Croats had committed their own share of atrocities. Thus any decision to use military force entailed the United States having to resolve the crisis in Bosnia at the risk of appearing to take sides in a conflict whose origins were a millennium old. (This issue would gain even greater significance at the U.S.-mediated peace talks held in Dayton, Ohio, in the fall of 1995.)[56] Nevertheless, certain events – such as the seizure by Bosnian Serbs of the eastern Bosniak enclave of Srebrenica while it was protected by U.N. forces – had considerably fueled doubts as to the ability of the United Nations to intervene effectively in this civil war. At stake was whether and to what extent American ground forces might be drawn into the war.[57]

A final consideration about military intervention was that, as Powell had indicated, the effectiveness of U.S.-initiated air strikes against targets in Bosnia, on their own, was highly uncertain.[58] (The clearly optimistic case was that military intervention would provide an opportunity for the warring groups to resolve their civil war, rebuild their society, and restore social harmony.) The level of uncertainty was increased by the fact that Clinton administration officials did not know how long U.S. forces should remain involved in what was to be the largest military operation in Europe since World War II.[59]

For these reasons, the Bosnian crisis is a significant case study that exemplifies the problems with victory in crises that are fueled by nationalism and escalate into an insurgency or civil war.[60]

U.S. OBJECTIVES

The objectives of U.S. policy outlined in the Clinton administration's 1995 *National Security Strategy* were to achieve a political settlement that preserved Bosnia's territorial integrity and sovereignty, prevent the fighting from spreading into a "broader Balkan war" that could endanger stability in Central and Eastern Europe, halt the "destabilizing flow of refugees" from the war, stop the "slaughter of innocents," and preserve "NATO's central role in post–Cold War Europe."[61]

The first and most important objective for the administration was to stop the genocide in war-torn Bosnia. As President Clinton said in August 1992, "We cannot afford to ignore what appears to be a deliberate and systematic extermination of human beings based on their ethnic origin."[62] In addition to numerous instances in which military forces under the command of Serb and Croat political authorities engaged in genocide, there was evidence that a number of less organized groups also were guilty of atrocities. Perhaps the worst example occurred in Srebrenica, where thousands of civilians were lined up alongside open-earth pits and machine-gunned to death.[63] Not only the Clinton administration but the American people as well were appalled at the collapse of Bosnia's civil society, which led its citizens to wage a war of genocide against one another. This strong humanitarian impulse in American politics was a compelling reason for becoming involved in Bosnia, despite the belief of most observers that U.S. vital interests were not at risk. In public-opinion polls conducted in May 1993, 63 percent said that the United States had a moral obligation to use military power to stop the atrocities in Bosnia.[64]

A second objective in the U.S. decision to intervene was the reaffirmation of state sovereignty as an inviolable principle in international politics. As the infiltration of extranational Serbian and Croatian military forces progressively weakened Bosnian sovereignty, officials in the Clinton administration believed that the United States must preserve the integrity and credibility of Bosnia's sovereignty and the individual rights of its populace.[65] They also feared that ignoring these Serbian and Croatian military efforts would encourage other states to shift their territorial boundaries or destabilize their neighbors.[66] As Clinton's 1995 *National Security Strategy* noted, "Nations should be able to expect that their borders and their sovereignty will always be secure."[67] Administration officials were concerned that international security would be weakened if Bosnia's fate were determined by states or groups using force and genocide to destroy social and political systems of governance. Generations

of government policymakers had sought to demonstrate that all states benefit from an international system based on rules, laws, and norms that reinforce
the rights of sovereign states. Thus, stating that the price of inaction was to
abandon the hope for global stability, Clinton administration officials argued
that preserving Bosnia's sovereignty was essential to stability in the Balkans
and southeastern Europe and to a stable balance of power in Europe.[68]

The consensus in the administration in the mid-1990s was that the most
immediate impediment to regional stability was Serbia's expansionist policies,
which were designed to establish a Greater Serbia encompassing most of Bosnia and Croatia.[69] In retrospect, Serbia's power and influence was clearly on
the rise during the 1990s until the United States intervened militarily to stop
it. Based on the battlefield successes enjoyed by Croatia's military forces, the
losses suffered by Serbia in the summer of 1995, and the effects of Operation
Deliberate Force (examined later in this chapter), American military power
simultaneously weakened Serbia and strengthened other states in the region.

A third objective of U.S. intervention was to stanch the flow of refugees in
Europe. As the Bosnian population witnessed genocide and the crumbling of
civil society, hundreds of thousands migrated to the relative peace and safety
of other European states. Since the outbreak of Bosnia's civil war in 1992, it
was estimated that by 1994 several hundred thousand people had migrated
to the major industrialized countries in Europe.[70] The concern among these
Europeans, as noted earlier, was that the influx of Bosnian refugees from disparate national and religious groups would weaken Europe's political, economic, and social stability by carrying into recipient nations the rifts that were
already destroying Bosnia. Thus, a critical U.S. objective was to address the
massive movement of refugees into Western Europe.

Many U.S. officials believed that Europe could not be secure as long as there
was a civil war in the former Yugoslavia – a region where events had already
triggered one world war.[71] Moreover, officials in the Clinton administration
believed that events in Bosnia would reaffirm one of the major principles of
twentieth-century history: A conflict in the Balkans that is allowed to fester
will spread throughout Europe and eventually drag the United States into
war.[72] In language that reminded many of U.S. policy during the Vietnam War,
American policymakers used the domino theory of aggression to suggest that
a spasm of ethnoreligious carnage in Bosnia might spread to other states along
the Adriatic Sea and eventually engulf the Balkans in war.[73] In polls conducted in January 1993, 41 percent of Americans believed that sending troops to
Bosnia would be reminiscent of the situation in the Vietnam War.[74] Using language similar to that of the Bush administration's policy toward Iraq in the
months before the Persian Gulf War, policymakers in the Clinton administration argued that a failure to contain the Serbs today would guarantee further

violence in Europe because it would suggest to other states or groups that the West does not have the resolve to resist these actions.[75]

In the end, the fundamental objectives of American policy were to resolve the humanitarian crisis in Bosnia, restore peace and security in this volatile state, prevent the alienation of European allies, avoid the need for deploying U.S. troops to Bosnia, and achieve victory in the process.

DESCRIPTION OF OPERATIONS

The use of military force by the United States in this Balkan region was organized into five distinct phases, the first four of which were in Bosnia: Operation Provide Promise, which involved humanitarian relief operations (July 1992–March 1996); Operation Deny Flight, comprising a no-fly zone, *close air support* (i.e., air strikes on behalf of and directed by ground forces) for NATO troops, and air strikes (April 1993–December 1995); Operation Deliberate Force, which was an air campaign against Bosnian Serb military targets (August 29–September 14, 1995); Operations Joint Endeavor and Joint Guard, which deployed American ground forces – first as part of NATO's Implementation Force, beginning late in the fall of 1995, then among its Stabilization Force – to supervise the Dayton Peace Accords, signed in December 1995, until the deadline for withdrawal in June 1998; and Operation Allied Force, which involved an air campaign over Kosovo (March 24 to June 10, 1999).[76] Each of these military operations is discussed in this section.

Operation Provide Promise

The purpose of the U.N.-run Operation Provide Promise, which ran from July 2, 1992, to January 9, 1996, was both to deploy peacekeeping forces and to provide humanitarian supplies of food, medicine, and relief supplies to the besieged population of Sarajevo and other ethnic enclaves.[77] The relief part of the operation was conducted, under U.N. command, by the U.S. Air Force Europe 435th Airlift Wing located at Rhein–Main Air Base in Germany. It involved distributing humanitarian supplies both by truck convoy and by transport aircraft flying out of Rhein–Main and from Falconara Air Base near Ancona, Italy, to drop supplies into isolated Bosnian cities and towns – mostly Sarajevo but also others, such as Goražde and Žepa.[78] In addition to U.S.-operated C-130, C-141, and C-17's, aircraft operated by France, the United Kingdom, Canada, and Germany participated in the airdrops. The more than one hundred sixty thousand metric tons of food, medicine, and supplies flown into Bosnia in 12,895 sorties helped prevent mass starvation and death.[79]

A number of problems were encountered during this operation. The first was the threat posed by Serb antiaircraft fire and surface-to-air missiles

(SAMs).[80] Political and military authorities in Washington and European capitals worried about losing aircraft to hostile fire; although the United States was unscathed, Italy lost a G-222 in September 1992.[81] A second was the classic problem of communicating among units and platforms from various nations. This reaffirmed the challenges that NATO faces when it conducts military operations with nations whose organizations, communications systems, and weapons are not standardized.[82] A third problem was that weather conditions in Bosnia significantly hampered the ability to deliver humanitarian supplies to the intended cities and towns with a high degree of accuracy. A fourth and admittedly less significant problem was that the intense pace of operations conducted over several years eroded the morale of U.S. and NATO military personnel.[83]

In addition to these operational concerns, a strategic problem for Provide Promise was the failure to articulate criteria that could be used to evaluate whether the operation could be considered a victory. As both American and NATO policymakers learned, it is difficult to establish clear measures of success for an operation designed to provide humanitarian relief to the victims of a civil war. The fact that people continued to starve, despite extensive efforts to provide food and clothing, may not demonstrate that the operation was a failure; but it clearly raised difficult political questions for senior U.S. and European officials asked to defend this expenditure of military and economic resources and the risk to military personnel. One lesson from this operation is that humanitarian uses of military force do not produce unambiguous measures of victory.

Operation Deny Flight

The second phase in the pattern of escalation in the use of force in Bosnia was Operation Deny Flight. It was implemented on March 31, 1993, by United Nations Security Council Resolution (UNSCR) 816, and gave authority to shoot down aircraft that violated the no-fly zone previously established over Bosnia–Herzegovina.[84] The purpose of this operation, which was in effect from April 1993 to December 1995, was first to enforce the no-fly zone for all fixed- and rotary-wing aircraft, to prevent the Serbs from conducting air attacks. The United Nations and NATO later expanded the operation to include close air support (CAS) strikes against tanks, artillery, and other military facilities and supplies throughout Bosnia – for instance, in defense of the *safe area* (U.N.-protected refuge) Goražde – in response to increased aggression by Serb ground forces. Eventually, it was expanded to include air strikes against Bosnian Serb forces, to prevent their siege tactics from destroying the capital city of Sarajevo and other areas in Bosnia. The roughly fifty to a hundred NATO fighter and reconnaissance aircraft involved in Operation Deny Flight flew from bases in Italy and from aircraft carriers in the Adriatic Sea. A final point is that this U.N.–NATO operation was conducted under a "dual-key" system: U.N. and NATO military commanders had to approve the use of force jointly.[85]

The following discussion briefly reviews the decisions made after the initial commitment to establish a no-fly zone in Bosnia. These show the escalation in U.N.–NATO involvement in this civil war and other conflicts in what used to be SFR Yugoslavia, and demarcate the steps by which Washington and its European allies gradually increased their military participation.

On May 6, 1993, UNSCR 824 established safe areas in Bosnia and authorized the conduct of offensive air operations.[86] On June 4, 1993, UNSCR 836 declared that NATO aircraft would provide close air support against ground forces in Bosnia. Nine months later, on March 31, 1994, the United Nations declared in UNSCR 908 that NATO aircraft were authorized to attack Bosnian Serb divisions nearby. This decision was also implemented to provide CAS in Goražde on April 10–11 after personnel from the U.N. High Commission for Refugees (UNHCR) were attacked by heavy-weapons fire. Eleven days later, on April 22, 1994, UNSCR 913 established an *exclusion zone* (i.e., one intended to remain free of heavy weapons) around the town of Goražde. Close air support attacks were launched on July 11, 1995, against Bosnian Serb tanks en route to Srebrenica, a safe area that had already been besieged and then breached, its Dutch U.N. forces held hostage. On October 9, 1995, CAS attacks were conducted in retaliation for similar Bosnian Serb attacks launched against U.N. personnel in Tuzla.[87]

The next step in the escalation of U.N.–NATO involvement in the former Yugoslavia was the decision to conduct (non-CAS) air strikes. In February 1994, NATO's North Atlantic Council (NAC) condemned the siege of Sarajevo and proceeded to bomb artillery and mortars in the region surrounding the city. At the request of UNPROFOR, NATO aircraft struck a facility in the Sarajevo Exclusion Zone on August 5 (after Bosnian Serbs captured weapons from a collection site near the capital) and a Bosnian Serb tank on September 22.[88] On November 19, 1994, the United Nations declared in UNSCR 958 that NATO could extend air operations against military targets and facilities into Croatia; two days later, NATO aircraft attacked that nation's Udbina airfield. In 1995, NATO air strikes in Bosnia included attacks against the ammunition depot in the town of Pale, on the outskirts of Sarajevo (May 25–26) and against air defense radars, communications centers, ammunition dumps, and bridges and barracks in Serb-held positions on September 7.[89] (UNSCRs 981 and 982 had extended U.N.–NATO cooperation in Bosnia and Croatia to the end of November.)[90] In a move to deter further NATO air strikes, Serb forces handcuffed U.N. soldiers near potential bombing targets. This complicated NATO's strike plans, created tensions in the organization, and signaled a need to escalate its involvement.[91]

In effect, Operation Deny Flight was conducted because Bosnian Serb military forces had killed and wounded large numbers of civilians throughout Bosnia. Its principal military objective was to prevent their aircraft from conducting attacks, and it was successful against their fixed-wing fighter aircraft: Serb commanders apparently understood that flying in Bosnian airspace carried a significant risk of being shot down by NATO fighters. However, Deny Flight was not a model of success against violations by Bosnian Serb helicopters. The problem was that NATO forces detected literally hundreds of violations by helicopters, which would typically land when warned by NATO fighters, wait until those left the area, and then resume flight. Worse yet, some violations in the no-fly zone were caused by U.N.-operated helicopters, which often were wrongly identified as enemy aircraft.[92]

Operation Deliberate Force

The next phase in the use of the U.S. military in Bosnia was Operation Deliberate Force, a military operation against Bosnian Serb forces. The culmination of three years of involvement by the United Nations and NATO, this operation helped to usher in peace negotiations at Wright–Patterson Air Force Base in Dayton, Ohio.[93]

The timeline for Operation Deliberate Force began with a meeting at the London Conference on July 21, 1995, that was designed to organize NATO's responses to Bosnian Serb attacks. This meeting, which fostered the subsequent air campaign, was precipitated by the fall of Srebrenica on July 11. At that time, the principal policymakers in the United Nations and NATO outlined a plan for conducting air strikes against Bosnian Serb targets as well as preemptive attacks to suppress their air defense radars and missiles. A few days later, on July 25, the North Atlantic Council decided to use NATO air power both to protect the city of Goražde and to defend the principle that NATO would escalate its military strikes in response to Serb aggression.[94] When the safe area in Žepa fell to Bosnian Serb forces on July 26, the NAC extended protection to the other safe areas (Bihać, Goražde, Sarajevo, and Tuzla) as of August 1, 1995. During that month, NATO prepared plans for an air campaign against Bosnian Serb targets. The decisive event that started the air campaign was the artillery shelling of a Sarajevo marketplace on August 28, 1995, which killed thirty-eight civilians and wounded eighty-five.[95] Intelligence sources confirmed that the attack had been conducted by forces under the control of the Bosnian Serb Army (BSA). Two days later, in the early morning of August 30, NATO approved air attacks against Bosnian Serb targets in retaliation for Serb shelling of Sarajevo.[96] According to a statement by NATO's Secretary General on September 5, 1995, "The air operations [against Bosnian Serb military targets in Bosnia] were reinitiated after United Nations and NATO military commanders concluded that the Bosnian Serbs had failed to demonstrate their intent to comply with U.N. demands to remove military threats against Sarajevo."[97]

NATO warned that air strikes would be launched against Bosnian Serb military targets if any of the safe areas in Bosnia were attacked. For NATO, the explicit mission of Operation Deliberate Force was "deterring attacks on safe areas and employing, if necessary, the timely and effective use of airpower until attacks on or threats to these areas had ceased."[98] Its political objective was to conduct air strikes until Serb forces no longer threatened the safe areas that were established to protect civilians. The United Nations and NATO mandated that air attacks would be triggered by the following two kinds of event: "(1) Any concentration of forces and/or heavy weapons, and the conduct of other military preparations which . . . presented a direct threat to the remaining U.N. safe areas [i.e., Bihać, Goražde, Sarajevo, and Tuzla] or (2) Direct attacks (e.g., ground, artillery or aircraft) on the designated safe areas."[99]

The Joint Targeting Board, which coordinated the selection of all approved targets and comprised representatives from NATO and the United Nations, chose targets based on achieving military damage with sophisticated targeting systems on aircraft, notably precision munitions that minimize collateral damage. One reason for minimizing collateral damage was the belief among NATO authorities that the air campaign would not be politically sustainable if innocent people were being killed or maimed.

The military strikes conducted during Operation Deliberate Force were directed against five specific categories of target, in descending order of priority. First and foremost was the Bosnian Serb military's integrated air defense system (IADS), which included electronic warfare and target acquisition radars for guiding surface-to-air missiles against NATO aircraft. The Serb ground forces, notably such heavy weapons as tanks, artillery, and troop concentrations, were second. Third were Serb command and control centers, military headquarters, and communications sites; fourth, lines of communication, which involved the transportation infrastructure of bridges, roads, and tunnels. The final target category focused on direct and essential military support targets, which included ammunition and supply depots that support the stationing of military equipment.[100] During the air campaign roughly sixty aircraft from several NATO nations operated from bases in Italy and from the U.S. aircraft carrier USS *Theodore Roosevelt*, stationed in the Adriatic Sea.[101]

Operations Joint Endeavor and Joint Guard

In what was known as Operation Joint Endeavor (from December 5, 1995, to December 20, 1996), forces from the United States and its NATO allies deployed twenty thousand peacekeeping forces to Bosnia to implement the military terms of the Dayton Peace Accords.[102] This operation represented the first "out-of-area" deployment of NATO forces and the first time that U.S. and Soviet soldiers were involved in a joint military mission.

The purpose of Joint Endeavor was to provide peacekeeping forces to supervise the ceasefire that was organized by NATO in the Balkan civil war. As soon as the Dayton Accords were signed on December 14, 1995, the United States deployed its 1st Armored Division to Bosnia–Herzegovina. The functions of the Implementation Force (IFOR) were to enforce the ceasefire, establish boundaries for the zone of separation between the hostile parties, and ensure that their troops withdrew to barracks and moved their heavy weapons to storage sites. IFOR was also designed to supervise democratic elections in the country. Although there were challenges to this military force by the antagonists, the operation successfully enforced the Dayton military protocols.

With the completion of the IFOR under Operation Joint Endeavor, the U.S. military forces then remained in Bosnia to serve as the Stabilization Force (SFOR) in Operation Joint Guard (December 20, 1996–December 20, 1998). Like the IFOR before it, SFOR was to supervise the activities of the military forces in Bosnia and to contribute to stability in the country.[103]

Operation Allied Force

On March 24, 1999, military forces under the command of NATO launched an air campaign against Serbia in response to human-rights abuses against ethnic Albanians in Kosovo, a southern and formerly autonomous province of SFR Yugoslavia but, since the breakup, part of the Federal Republic of Yugoslavia (FRY).[104] The bombing campaign, code-named Operation Allied Force, lasted seventy-eight days, until the FRY president, Slobodan Milošević, withdrew the Serbian army and paramilitary forces from Kosovo.[105]

The origins of the Kosovo crisis are found in early 1998, when widespread fighting among ethnic groups led to the displacement of three hundred thousand Albanian Kosovars.[106] Although a ceasefire in October 1998 avoided a humanitarian disaster in the winter, fighting resumed with the collapse of a peace conference in Paris on March 19, 1999, when the Serbian government in Belgrade would not agree to a peaceful resolution. Serbian officials reportedly believed that they could defeat the Kosovar Liberation Army (KLA) within a week in "Operation Horseshoe" (*Potkova*) and *then* negotiate a peace agreement. They also believed that NATO would not intervene militarily, but that if NATO did intervene, the effects would be insignificant.[107]

In response to the collapse of talks, NATO launched Operation Allied Force, designed to force the Yugoslavs to comply with U.N. Security Council Resolution 1199, which predated the failed ceasefire.[108] The operation, involving an air campaign that lasted from March 24 to June 10, thus sought to force

Belgrade to accept the following conditions: the withdrawal of Serbian forces, the demilitarization of Kosovo, the deployment there of an international military force, the return of all refugees and displaced persons, and the establishment of a provisional administration in Kosovo under international control.[109]

This campaign, which has been described as an example of the optimal use of air power to achieve victory, employed a significant amount of such power.[110] This was the largest combat waged in the history of NATO, involving some thirty-eight thousand combat sorties during twenty-four-hour operations over seventy-eight days. This air campaign, which involved the use of 829 aircraft from fourteen nations, three aircraft carriers, and the use of twenty-eight thousand munitions, did not involve the loss of any aircrews.[111] Its purpose was to target and destroy three categories of Serbian target. The first were military targets, notably the fielded forces of the Serbian military, which included command and control nodes, artillery, maneuver forces, logistics nodes, headquarters, air defenses, lines of communications, naval forces, surface-to-surface missiles, and training areas. The campaign began with cruise-missile strikes, principally against air defenses.

Serbia's modern integrated air defense system greatly influenced the pace and nature of NATO air strikes throughout the campaign. For example, in its efforts to neutralize Serbia's air defenses while minimizing its own casualties, NATO had to fly at night and at altitudes above fifteen thousand feet, which significantly reduced the effectiveness of the air campaign.[112] In addition, because Serbia's IADS was so highly redundant, it suffered relatively little degradation during the air war. Moreover, targeting ground forces was hampered by the ability of Serbian forces to hide and camouflage targets with a remarkable degree of effectiveness; arguably, this forced NATO to increase attacks against economic and industrial targets in the area of Belgrade.[113]

In addition to military targets, the air campaign at the same time targeted the political leadership and infrastructure, notably Milošević, members of the civil and military leadership, information systems, and higher headquarters. For its third type of target, as just referenced, the air campaign expanded to target infrastructure upon which the Serbian civilian population depended: A NATO Summit meeting on April 23, 1999, authorized attacks against such "sustainment targets," including the oil supplies, electrical power, rail lines, bridges, and roads that constitute centers of gravity for the civilian economy.[114] (Though all of Serbia's fuel production was reportedly eliminated, FRY was able to import fuel through Montenegrin ports.)[115] NATO's decision to bomb critical economic and industrial facilities in the area of Belgrade directly affected the citizenry and is believed to have significantly weakened popular support for Serbia's political leadership, including Milošević – ultimately contributing to his electoral defeat in 2000.[116]

The overall political and military effectiveness of the air campaign in Operation Allied Force can be evaluated along several lines. First, it was designed to destroy fixed installations of military value to the Serbs while minimizing American and civilian casualties. Initially, at least, it was also designed not to destroy infrastructure that would be needed for the postwar reconstitution of the society. Thus Operation Allied Force did not begin with the massive, overwhelming, and often surprise strikes against strategic centers of gravity, such as occurred in the Gulf War, that systematically paralyze the enemy. Rather, the air campaign was so "deliberately restrained," with its attacks escalating gradually, that its overall military effectiveness was compromised.[117] As a consequence, the air campaign was not as politically effective as it could have been, and probably took longer than it should have.[118]

The second issue is its effectiveness in destroying Serbian military targets and persuading Milošević to surrender control of Kosovo.[119] The initial claims were that the air war had destroyed 9 percent of Serbia's ground forces, 42 percent of its aircraft, 25 percent of its armored vehicles, 22 percent of its artillery, and 9 percent of its tanks.[120] However, there were conflicting reports from various U.S. military groups that quite small percentages of Serbian combat systems had actually been destroyed, and a subsequent analysis by the Allied Force Munitions Assessment Team reinforced doubts about the air campaign's effectiveness.[121] In effect, three thousand aircraft sorties by NATO – dropping fourteen thousand weapons, 90 percent of which were precision-guided munitions – had destroyed a mere fourteen tanks, eighteen armored personnel carriers, and twenty artillery pieces or mortars.[122] This poor record was partly due to the strict conditions imposed by U.S. and NATO officials on the conduct of the air campaign (e.g., the high-altitude, nighttime sorties mentioned earlier) in order to avoid the capable Serbian air defenses; however, weather also played a part.[123] Although a dismal failure in terms of destroying Serbian ground forces, the air campaign did prove highly effective against civilian targets ("turning off the lights in downtown Belgrade") and "highly accurate against fixed targets, like bunkers and bridges."[124]

Finally, the target-approval process employed during Operation Allied Force was tightly controlled by senior military and Executive officials, an approach reminiscent of that followed by the Johnson administration during the Vietnam War. Reportedly, President Clinton, Secretary of Defense William S. Cohen, Chairman of the Joint Chiefs of Staff Hugh Shelton, and Allied Force commander General Wesley Clark personally reviewed potentially sensitive target photographs before they selected the weapons to be used and granted approval for air strikes, removing facilities from target lists if they were deemed too close to civilian buildings.[125]

For these reasons, the overall conclusion is that Operation Allied Force was not as militarily successful as the campaign conducted eight years earlier in the Persian Gulf War.[126] Nevertheless, the air campaign did ultimately compel President Milošević's government to agree on June 3, 1999, to a withdrawal from Kosovo, with terms (and a NATO ultimatum) delivered by envoys from the European Union and Russia.[127] Subsequently, and with U.N. authorization on June 10, 1999, NATO ground forces deployed into Kosovo.[128]

INTERPRETING VICTORY

The original U.S. strategy for intervention in the disintegrated SFR Yugoslavia was based on containing the forces of ethnocentric nationalism that had produced two civil wars in the region, first in Croatia, then in Bosnia. A series of varyingly effective military interventions resulted. It was only after several U.S.–NATO air campaigns, the last of which ended in June 1999, that a modicum of peace and stability emerged. There have been positive developments regarding the future of Bosnia, but it remains an international protectorate.[129] In the intervention in Kosovo, the United States achieved a clear political–military victory, one with important lessons for American policymakers.[130]

The initial intervention in the Bosnian civil war allowed the United States, the United Nations, and NATO to provide humanitarian supplies to people who otherwise would have starved to death or died from exposure during the harsh winter months. In narrow terms, then, the humanitarian resupply operation was a success in that the Bosnian Serb military forces did not manage to obstruct it. In fact, the three military operations in Bosnia – Provide Promise, Deny Flight, and Deliberate Force – represent a political–military victory for the United States and NATO.

The use of military force in the Bosnian civil war has significant implications for U.S. policy because this case is representative of crises that involve a volatile combination of ethnonational and religious frictions. As we have seen as recently as 2004 in the Darfur region of Sudan, there is no shortage of antagonisms leading to genocide and humanitarian crimes.[131] Such crises may raise questions about the credibility of the United States, NATO, and the United Nations.[132]

The Clinton administration's criteria defining U.S. military intervention in Bosnia were that it "must advance U.S. interests, risks to U.S. personnel must be 'acceptable,' personnel and funding must be available, participation must be necessary for the mission's success, the roles, objectives and duration of participation must be clear, public and congressional support must exist or be 'mustered,' and command and control arrangements must be 'acceptable'."[133] The purpose of U.S. policy, as expressed by President Clinton, was to "limit the conflict to Bosnia, to try to restore humanitarian conditions, to see that a bad example is not set, and to limit the refugee outflow."[134]

There were numerous debates between the Departments of State and Defense – mirroring public debate – as to whether U.S. interests were at risk, whether the United States should intervene to protect any such interests, and whether to intervene even if U.S. interests were not at risk.[135] The policy reviews conducted by the Clinton administration between 1993 and 1995 reinforced the perception that the White House did not have the political will either to intervene fully or to stay out of the war altogether.[136] In fact, until Operation Deliberate Force forced the Serbs to enter war-ending negotiations, American involvement in Bosnia had been interpreted as a political failure. There had been general pessimism about the ability of the United States to prevail because it was believed that the Serb leadership was politically tougher and more determined than its counterparts in NATO, the United Nations, or Washington. There had also been concern as to whether the Bosnian civil war would spread throughout the Balkans. However, the ultimate outcome of U.S. intervention in Bosnia demonstrated – at least, for Madeleine Albright – the value of using limited force and maintaining allied unity.[137]

The Clinton administration's initial plans for intervention appeared to reflect the idea that military force should be used only to achieve grand strategic victory. Officials seemed unclear about how to plan for a lesser type of victory, perhaps believing that military action, especially involving ground forces, could lead to a long-term commitment from which it would be difficult to withdraw. There was confusion about the risks of using force to achieve an outcome, not guaranteed, that was less than decisive.[138] The concern was that the United States could not "produce an enduring solution with military force – air or ground."[139] In this context, air power was seen as the least unacceptable option because it demonstrated the state's willingness to use force.[140] In terms of Chapter 4's organizing principles for victory, this limited use of air power afforded the United States both a political–military victory and a significant change in the status quo: It compelled Bosnian Serbs to stop their strategy of genocide and intimidation against non-Serb peoples. Thus it did accomplish a critical objective of the Clinton administration, even if some senior officials may have privately hoped for grand strategic victory.

In analytic terms, then, Washington had moved beyond the cold-war theory in which the United States would intervene only when it could achieve a significant victory without risking war with nuclear-armed adversaries. The decision to conduct air strikes in Bosnia signaled that the United States was willing to use deadly force to compel a state to alter its behavior without the requirement of a U.S.-imposed grand strategic victory. One consequence of Operations Deliberate Force and Allied Force was to shift the debate in the United States to a more pragmatic discussion of what it means to achieve victory, with the sense that it is permissible for the United States to use force to achieve justifiable ends even if no grand strategic victory will result.

In any event, some critical requirements for a grand strategic victory were missing from the Bosnia campaign. One was a credible U.S. military threat; this had been weakened by the long debate about the risks of intervention, or what has been called the "lack of follow-through on earlier threats of military action." Another was the failure to demonstrate how an "objective can be achieved decisively" through the use of force. In such cases, wrote one administration official, "the actual use of force becomes problematic."[141]

The debate preceding military intervention in the Balkans had been between policymakers who sought to contain the conflict and prevent genocide and others who were skeptical about the ability to achieve victory against ethnic and religious antagonisms, let alone in the face of lukewarm public support.[142] It was evident from the beginning that the Clinton administration's initial interest in deploying American ground forces to Bosnia was systematically being resisted by sustained congressional opposition. Although this struggle was fueled by partisan differences, it also demonstrated that the administration had failed to persuade the Congress that it had a credible plan for victorious intervention in Bosnia.[143] The implication is that the efforts of policymakers to commit the United States to use military force may face considerable congressional resistance unless framed in terms of a coherent and realistic plan for victory that links the ends, ways, and means.

An important issue is the relationship between victory and the use of air power and/or ground forces. Employing air power does not mean that the state must also use ground forces, and the proper balance between these is a key issue in the modern American theory of victory. It is still an open question as to whether grand strategic victory is possible only when air power is used, and whether air power is a more attractive option that can also achieve victory in strategic terms.[144] With regard to Bosnia, however, the consensus is that the use of air power compelled the Serbs to cease their campaign of genocide and persuaded the warring factions to negotiate. Operation Deliberate Force clearly afforded a U.S. victory in that it moved a troubled part of the former SFR Yugoslavia toward relative peace and stability, and the Clinton administration was satisfied with its political–military victory.[145]

Later, in response to the oppression of Kosovo, the United States used air power to destroy a wide range of Serbian strategic and tactical targets, inflicting punishment sufficient to persuade Milošević to enter peace negotiations.[146] Operation Allied Force demonstrated that the United States and NATO would use military might to force the Serbians to change their behavior. It showed too that American resolve would not weaken even when faced with inadvertent civilian casualties (minimized by the campaign's insistence on a high degree of precision).[147] Finally, it decisively destroyed the myth of Serbian invincibility that had emerged after several years of U.S. and European vacillation.

One of the lessons from the Bosnian civil war is that the international community needs to develop a theory of victory that is relevant to crises fueled by ethnic and religious tensions – and that includes a faster timetable for involvement.[148] U.S.–NATO intervention in Bosnia was intended to separate the warring Serb, Bosniak, and Croat factions, creating a breathing space and giving the Bosnian people a chance to rebuild their society. Victory in this context entailed the cessation of hostilities among ethnic and national groups, and ending a civil war with horrific genocidal overtones.

A second observation is that the policymaking community must accept that the state may use force even if it does not intend to achieve victory on a grand strategic scale. Significant political changes have indeed been effected in Bosnia since 1995, as well as in Kosovo since 1999; but those are the result of subsequent developments rather than the immediate product of government-destroying military action. Thus these conflicts, which never became the quagmires for the U.S. military that many observers feared, helped to transform how American society conceives victory because, in the end, U.S. policy had not been driven by the desire to achieve grand strategic victory.[149]

In a poll conducted in December 1997, fifteen months before the U.S.–NATO air campaign against Serbia, 60 percent of respondents believed that the Clinton administration did not have a "clear and well-thought-out policy on the Kosovo situation."[150] However, the gap between public opinion and U.S. policy would narrow considerably. By March 1999, when Operation Allied Force got under way, 53 percent of Americans polled were favoring a military campaign against Serbian military targets that would produce victory.[151] (In addition, 67 percent believed that the Serbian government was responsible for the exodus of refugees from Kosovo, and 58 percent that Serbia was using mass killing to eliminate Kosovar ethnic Albanians.)[152] Here too the United States and its allies achieved a political–military victory; as one study argued, Kosovo is "a much better place today than it would have been absent NATO intervention."[153] This victory did not, however, lead to a strategic realignment in international politics.

The fragile peace established in the Balkans is showing signs of erosion. In March 2004, after an upsurge of ethnic violence in the province of Kosovo, NATO increased the number of its troops in the region.[154] This development indicates that the political and nationalist problems that led to violence and war in Kosovo during the mid- to late 1990s have not yet been resolved. As one diplomat expressed the situation, "we froze an insurgency in 1999" with military power and yet "did nothing to solve the political reasons" for it.[155] As of this writing, there is no schedule for withdrawing international forces or any decision on the final status of Kosovo – still a U.N.-administered part of Serbia and Montenegro – though talks have commenced.[156] It remains to be seen whether the political–military victory attained in the Balkans will hold.

CONCLUSION

The interventions in the wars in Bosnia and Kosovo in the 1990s achieved political–military victories by compelling the cessation of Serb military aggression against the various other ethnic and religious groups in these regions (and vice versa). These interventions began as a strategy by the United States and its European allies to achieve what for all intents and purposes was to be a political–military victory in Bosnia: to intervene with the minimum number of troops required to stop the Serbs' campaign of genocide and humanitarian abuses without entangling the United States and its allies in a Balkan quagmire. Later, however, when the United Nations sought to establish autonomous governments in Bosnia and Kosovo and rebuild the foundations of political, economic, and military security in the region, the nature of the intervention shifted subtly in the direction of grand strategic victory to support U.N. and NATO efforts.[157] This shift in the nature of the victory sought – from political–military toward grand strategic and back again – contributed to the erosion of credibility of U.S. policy during the 1990s as the United States wavered between intervention for humanitarian reasons and a long-term, strategic realignment of the governments of Bosnia and Kosovo to foster peace and security in the region.

Second, interventions in the Balkans did produce comprehensive changes in the status quo. In policy terms, NATO's military intervention successfully forced FRY President Slobodan Milošević to end his alleged policy of destroying and displacing non-Serbian peoples in Bosnia (through active, extranational support of and influence over the Bosnian Serb army, or VRS) and Kosovo (through Serb paramilitary units and the Yugoslav army, or VJ). This in itself reflected a comprehensive change in the political–military balance in the Balkans. Militarily, the campaigns that were conducted in 1995 and 1999 did destroy some Serb military capabilities, though subsequent analyses of Operation Allied Force suggest that the Serbian military suffered far fewer losses of significant equipment than initially estimated. Although it is thus debatable whether the air campaign actually led to a comprehensive change in the *military* status quo, if it did not, it was certainly not for lack of effort.

In political terms, the military campaigns in Bosnia led to Dayton, where Bosnian Serb interests were represented by Milošević. The Dayton Accords established two interlocked political subdivisions – (Serb) Republika Srpska and (Croat and Bosniak) Federation of Bosnia and Herzegovina – and a three-member presidency, one from each ethnic group, with a rotating chairman.[158] This dual-entity system remains in place, though there have been some efforts to create statewide agencies. The 1999 air campaign against Serbian forces led to regime change: The regime of Milošević was destroyed and many senior government officials were removed from office. (This de facto regime change is important because it was interpreted in terms of avoiding a potential quagmire rather than those of deliberately defeating the leadership of a state that was engaged in crimes against humanity.)[159] Milošević was brought before the International Court of Justice at The Hague on charges of war crimes and crimes against humanity. He died in prison on March 11, 2006, just months from when his long trial was expected to end.[160] In overall terms, then, Operations Deliberate Force and Allied Force comprehensively changed the status quo in the Balkans.

Third, although there was some limited mobilization of allied-coalition personnel to conduct operations, the larger focus was ensuring sufficient supplies of munitions, since the 1995 and 1999 campaigns relied predominantly on air power. The NATO air campaign in 1999 consumed such large numbers of cruise missiles that the United States depleted its stocks and was forced in the spring to accelerate the production of replacements to refill war stocks.[161] In terms of public support, the debate in the United States about whether, how, and why it was prudent to intervene against Bosnia never produced a clear consensus or any popular basis of political support. However, by the time that evidence of Serbian atrocities against Kosovo was mounting in late 1998, there was clear political support in the United States for an air campaign against Serbian forces. Still, it was difficult to build the case for a ground war in view of concerns that the United States and its allies would be drawn into a Balkan quagmire.

The fourth aspect is the nature and extent of postconflict obligations on the United States, NATO, and the United Nations. Since the civil wars in the Balkan states had significantly damaged their economic and social infrastructures, the United States and members of the international community assumed a long-term obligation to help rebuild those societies. Politically, the United States and its allies sought to limit strictly their postconflict obligations, to avoid the entanglements associated with "nation building"; but their obligations became far more protracted than was originally planned, and this is precisely what has evolved in the region. Since one of the consequences of intervention was the destruction of Milošević's regime in Serbia, America and its allies were compelled to become involved in rebuilding the governmental institutions that had led to humanitarian abuses in the first place and the economic facilities that had been damaged in the course of military operations. The government of Kosovo has been administered since June 1999 by the United Nations Interim Administration Mission in Kosovo (UNMIK).[162]

The United States and its allies also had a postconflict obligation to retain military forces in the region, in order to maintain peace and security. In Bosnia, the NATO-led SFOR gave way to the European Union Force (EUFOR), which not only enforces the Dayton Accords but serves to police organized crime.[163] The Kosovo Force (KFOR), led by NATO, has been in Kosovo since

June 1999 to ensure both the withdrawal of Serbian forces from the area and the demilitarization of the KLA; it also serves to support UNMIK.[164] Economically, the international community retained a long-term obligation to help Bosnia and Kosovo rebuild infrastructure; in the latter, efforts are led by the European Union[165] and include people on the ground to administer direct economic aid to support the reconstruction of damaged facilities, though not necessarily to engage in wholesale nation building.

For these reasons, the interventions in Bosnia and Kosovo in the 1990s can be described as political–military victories that led to comprehensive changes in the status quo, involved limited mobilization for war, and protracted postconflict obligations for the United States and its allies. But how should these victories be interpreted?

One answer is that since the decisions to intervene were motivated by ideological and moral outrage at the systematic campaigns of genocide that were being conducted, these interventions in the Balkans legitimized the principle that it is acceptable to rely on these reasons for going to war. Another is that intervention in Bosnia reacquainted the political and military leadership in the United States and NATO with the concept of victory: For the first time since the end of the cold war, the United States achieved victory in an ethnic and/or religious war, which has been interpreted as a particularly difficult type of war in which to intervene successfully. The campaigns in Bosnia and Kosovo not only changed the political balance in the region but also reaffirmed the value of human rights as an international standard.

However, though these interventions were designed for political–military victories, the regime in Serbia was in fact changed and the international community has long been engaged in rebuilding Bosnia and Kosovo and reconfiguring their institutions of governance. Thus it may seem that the United States and its allies, though achieving political–military victories, may have hoped to attain grand strategic ones without having to commit to higher levels of mobilization and to muster greater public support. It is likely that the debacle in Somalia and the unraveling of Haiti – both highlighting how the credibility of the United States can be undermined if things go wrong – had imbued U.S. policymakers with a healthy respect for the political risks of intervention. Perhaps the United States had wanted a grand strategic victory but had been unwilling to declare publicly that it was committed to the destruction of the Milošević regime and would accept whatever postconflict obligations were required to cement that victory.

It wasn't until the ongoing humanitarian excesses in the Balkans made action necessary that U.S. and European policymakers responded, if somewhat tepidly. In the case of Bosnia, the United States and its NATO allies accepted what turned out to be a legitimate and useful case of political–military victory; however, this strengthened support in Serbia for Milošević at a time when

Washington was trying to undermine his position. In analytic terms, the United States had demonstrated that it was averse to accepting risks in managing the problem of Serbia, whose influence was extending across the region, and this weakened its ability to intervene effectively.

The broad conclusion that emerges from this analysis is that the state must consciously choose from the beginning between political–military and grand strategic victory, and that if the objective is to achieve the latter, its plans for military intervention must include regime change. Even though the intervention in Kosovo led to regime change after all, it should not be interpreted as a grand strategic victory: The policy of the United States and Europe had been to manage the problem rather than to alter the strategic balance in Europe fundamentally. It is as a result of disparity between the stated level of victory pursued and the level achieved that U.S. intervention in the Bosnian civil war is not viewed in public-policy debates as the important victory that it turned out to be. After all, the campaign in Kosovo led to a political–military victory in which the Serbian regime of Milošević was destroyed and Serbia was eliminated as a major threat in the Balkans, and it did so at reasonable cost. It is difficult to improve upon this outcome; perhaps at least Kosovo should be interpreted as a quasi-strategic victory.

10 2001 Invasion of Afghanistan

On September 11, 2001, four airplanes were hijacked by al Qaeda operatives, who deliberately flew two aircraft into the World Trade Center towers in New York City and one, about half an hour later, into the Pentagon in Washington, D.C. The fourth plane crashed into a field in Pennsylvania, short of its intended targets in Washington, which are believed to have been the Capitol or the White House.[1] Since some attacks were directed against the political leadership in Washington, many senior officials in the U.S. government believed that al-Qaeda had planned to decapitate the government by destroying the Pentagon and the White House or Capitol, thereby killing its most senior officials.[2] Those attacks – the first on American soil since the raid against Pearl Harbor on December 7, 1941 – killed nearly three thousand people.[3]

While the American people and their leaders still reeled from the enormity of the terrorist actions and mourned their dead, the political and military leadership in the administration of President George W. Bush had already begun planning to launch a counterstrike against al-Qaeda's leaders, who operated with impunity in Afghanistan under the protection of the repressive Taliban regime.[4] In an event that marked a historic change in the nature and conduct of American foreign policy, on October 7, 2001, just three and a half weeks after the attacks on Washington and New York, President Bush ordered the invasion of Afghanistan in what was called Operation Enduring Freedom.[5] The invasion began with an air campaign to attack facilities used by al-Qaeda to train its cadres of terrorists. As President Bush explained in an address to the nation on Sunday, October 7, the purpose of this military operation, which involved relatively few soldiers but the large-scale use of air power, was to strike "al-Qaeda terrorist training camps and military installations of the Taliban regime in Afghanistan. These carefully targeted actions [were] designed to disrupt the use of Afghanistan as a terrorist base of operations, and to attack the military capability of the Taliban regime."[6]

The invasion of Afghanistan was the first phase of the Bush administration's "global war on terrorism."[7] President Bush described this war in no uncertain terms in an address to a joint session of Congress on September 20, 2001: "Our war on terror begins with al-Qaeda, but it does not end there. It will not end until every terrorist group of global reach has been found, stopped, and defeated." As a signal of the commitment of the government, Bush said that, "We will direct every resource at our command – every means of diplomacy, every tool of intelligence, every instrument of law enforcement, every financial influence, and every necessary weapon of war – to the disruption and to the defeat of the global terror network."[8]

The conduct of Operation Enduring Freedom (officially still ongoing) is highly significant to the development of a theory of victory for several reasons. First and foremost, the invasion of Afghanistan by the United States marked a change in the strategy for dealing with terrorism. In the 1990s, Washington had viewed terrorism predominantly as a law-enforcement issue and not the business of the Department of Defense.[9] The attacks of 9/11 radically altered this perception and made the Operation Enduring Freedom the first phase of American military operations whose purpose is destroy terrorist organizations and the regimes that support them. Moreover, in two months the United States achieved regime change in Afghanistan. The success of this invasion, coming while the U.S. was still in shock from the events of 9/11, began some of the first serious discussions on the nature and cost of victory; equally important, it reintroduced the concept of grand strategic victory, as an attainable prospect, into the policy and military lexicon. The invasion demonstrated that the United States was willing to use military force selectively to destroy regimes that support terrorism. This chapter examines how the U.S. military intervention against the Taliban regime has affected the way in which U.S. policymakers think about using military force to achieve victory.

BACKGROUND

The U.S. decision to launch Operation Enduring Freedom against the Taliban must also be viewed in the context of U.S. long-term interests in the region. In the late 1970s and throughout the 1980s, the principal focus of U.S. policy toward Afghanistan was to counter the invasion launched by the Soviet Union on December 27, 1979.[10] The legacies of the decade-long Soviet–Afghan War, which ended on February 15, 1989, are more than one million civilian deaths, the destruction of Afghanistan's economy and lasting economic problems, enduring political and tribal divisions, and the rise of the Taliban regime in 1996. During that war, the principal U.S. role was to supply money, weapons, and training to the Afghan "freedom fighters," or Mujahideen (lit.:"ones who engage in the struggle"), who operated freely in the mountainous regions of Afghanistan to attack Soviet forces.[11] Of perhaps greatest impact was the decision of the Reagan administration to provide the Stinger surface-to-air missiles that were credited with successfully preventing Soviet air forces from operating effectively during the war. These weapons proved to be so effective that Soviet forces were unable to conduct daylight helicopter flights, which negated the Soviet Union's technological edge over the rebel forces.[12]

In the aftermath of the Soviet invasion and the subsequent stalemate that was imposed on Soviet forces by the Mujahideen, overall political and economic conditions in Afghanistan were a shambles. That decade of struggle against Soviet forces in Afghanistan had fueled the emergence of a global Islamic fundamentalism and created a power vacuum in the early 1990s from which the Taliban movement originated.[13] At first, under the leadership of Mullah Mohammed Omar, the Taliban (lit.: students) was just one of many armed factions operating around Kandahar. These original Taliban, many of whom were orphans of war, were united by their loyalty to Mullah Omar and his vision of a society based on the strict application of Islamic law.[14] As the movement gained strength politically in Afghanistan, it benefited from military help provided by Pakistan. By 1996, the Taliban had captured large numbers of arms, which it used to seize control of the capital city of Kabul on September 26 of that year.

The Taliban regime that was subsequently established in Kabul became one of the most oppressive fundamentalist regimes in the world.[15] The basis for the Taliban's power was its enforcement of a strict interpretation of Shari'ah using the brutal Department for Promoting Virtue and Preventing Vice. The Taliban regime was never officially recognized by the United States, but it received extensive political and economic support from the government of Pakistan. Under the rule of the Taliban, Afghanistan became a state sponsor of terrorism with its support of the formation of the al-Qaeda terrorist organization led by Saudi-born Osama bin Laden, a veteran of the Mujahideen's *jihad* (lit.: struggle) to drive the Soviet Union out of Afghanistan.[16] During the first several years, bin Laden had run al-Qaeda from Sudan; but as Sudan came under pressure from the United States and other governments to cease its support for terrorist organizations, bin Laden moved his center of operations to Afghanistan in 1996. As the Taliban strengthened their grip on power, he and al-Qaeda were protected by them in exchange for financial support.[17]

After building his organization during the 1990s, in 1992 bin Laden issued a *fatwa* – a ruling on Islamic law, "normally . . . by a respected Islamic authority" – calling for a jihad against the West because of its "'occupation'" forces in Saudi Arabia, "specifically singling out U.S. forces for attack."[18] The strategy was to force the U.S. to leave Saudi Arabia, overthrow the Saudi government, liberate Mecca and Medina, and support revolutionary groups around the world.[19] As part of this fatwa, al-Qaeda conducted bombings of the U.S. embassies in Kenya and Tanzania on August 7, 1998: The former killed some two hundred Kenyans and twelve Americans, injuring thousands; the latter killed eleven people, none American.[20] In retaliation, on August 20, 1998, the Clinton administration launched a cruise-missile strike against terrorist bases in Afghanistan and Sudan. Known as Operation Infinite Reach, the strike was targeted against terrorist camps and training bases in Afghanistan, where bin Laden was thought to be in a meeting, and against a pharmaceutical plant in Khartoum, Sudan, believed to have been involved in producing nerve gas and connected to bin Laden.[21] Some seventy-five cruise missiles hit Afghanistan, more than twenty people were killed, and bin Laden subsequently vowed to take revenge against the United States.[22] In announcing the attacks in a tel-evised address, President Clinton said that the target was bin Laden and his terrorist organization.[23] The Taliban condemned the attacks in Afghanistan, and there were massive protests staged around the world, mostly in Muslim countries, that denounced U.S. aggression.

As background, al-Qaeda had been implicated in several acts of terrorism well before the 9/11 attacks, notably the 1993 bombing of the World Trade Center towers, the bombing of the Khobar Towers in June 1996 (which killed nineteen U.S. servicemen), and attacking the USS *Cole* in Yemen in October 2000; it was also purportedly arming and training Somali warlords when U.S. forces arrived in Somalia in December 1992 to support U.N. humanitarian efforts.[24] Just two days before the September 11 attacks, al-Qaeda repaid its Taliban hosts for their protection by assassinating Ahmed Shah Massoud – the military leader of the anti-Taliban Afghan forces, Mujahideen groups known in the West as the Northern Alliance – through a special unit organized to target enemies of the Taliban.[25]

The arguments made for the attack on Afghanistan are similar to those ad-vanced by the Reagan administration when it launched Operation El Dorado Canyon against Libya in April 1986.[26] In strategic terms, the goal of terror-ism is to undermine the will of societies and their support for the state and its leadership.[27] In essence, its central objective is to weaken a government by using terrorist attacks to create conditions that suggest that the state cannot protect its own people.[28] Although scholars and policymakers contest how to define terrorism and who should be classified as a terrorist, the Title 22,U.S. Code, Section 2656F(d) U.S. Code defines it thus: "Terrorism is premedi-tated, politically motivated violence, perpetrated against noncombatant targets by sub-national groups or clandestine agents, usually intended to influence an audience."[29] One scholar takes this argument a step further by suggesting that terrorism is an act of violence whose political motive or goal is perpetrated against innocent persons and is played before audiences whose fear produces the desired result.[30] Terrorism has been a strategic problem for modern societies for decades, but the risks have dramatically increased: There is evidence that, for the past decade, terrorist organizations have actively sought to acquire weapons of mass destruction.[31] This danger was emphasized in a report issued in 2003:

> [D]espite a number of new initiatives to strengthen and accelerate international efforts to keep WMD out of terrorist hands launched by the Bush Administration since September 11, there remains an enormous gap between the seriousness and urgency of the threat, and the scope and pace of the U.S. and the international response. . . . [Bin Laden's] al-Qaeda terrorist network has made repeated attempts to buy stolen nuclear material from which to make a nuclear bomb, and has also tried to recruit scientists to help them with the task of weapon design and construction. Al-Qaeda has attempted to get all types of weapons of mass destruction: chemical, biological, and nuclear.[32]

Indeed, it was grave concerns about al-Qaeda's attempts to acquire nuclear weapons that influenced many of the Bush administration's fundamental decisions about war in the aftermath of the 9/11 attacks.[33]

During the 1990s, the U.S. and its citizens were increasingly the targets of terrorist attacks. With the exception of the 1993 garage bombing of the World Trade Center (a symbol of multinational corporations and wealthy nations), these were generally overseas – the Khobar Towers, the embassies in Kenya and Tanzania, the *Cole*. Many involved attacks on U.S. military personnel; some were made with the support of al-Qaeda.[34] Still, officials in the Clinton and Bush administrations worried that the U.S. homeland might be the target of a significant attack.

Throughout 2001, the intelligence and law enforcement agencies were "receiving frequent but fragmentary reports about threats."[35] As noted in *The 9/11 Commission Report,* there was a surge in threat reports that July and August, but these threats were believed to involve states in the Middle East and Europe. Director of Central Intelligence George Tenet, in the President's Daily Brief (PDB), routinely informed President Bush on the threat posed by al-Qaeda: There were forty intelligence briefs on terrorism in the PDBs between January 20 and September 10, 2001 (254). A prominent example of these warnings was the PDB of June 30, 2001 – headlined "Bin Ladin [*sic*] Planning High-Profile Attacks" – which argued that Osama bin Laden, as the leader of al-Qaeda, was planning attacks described as having "dramatic consequences of catastrophic proportions" (257–8).[36]

However, two systemic problems undermined the ability of U.S. intelligence agencies to combat international terrorism. The first was a failure of imagination: Although U.S. officials were well informed about al-Qaeda, its capabilities, and its desire to attack the United States, the evidence suggests that those officials never believed an attack of the magnitude of 9/11 was possible; and such an attack on U.S. soil by international terrorists was without precedent. The second failure, as noted in the *9/11 Commission Report*, was organizational: The attacks on September 11 "fell into the void between the foreign and domestic threats. . . . No one was looking for a foreign threat to domestic targets. The threat . . . was foreign – but from foreigners who had infiltrated into the United States" (263). Al-Qaeda was able to exploit "deep institutional failings within our government" (265) to escalate the war against the United States by flying commercial airliners into high-rise buildings specifically to kill Americans in their homeland.[37]

In response to al-Qaeda's 9/11 attacks, the United States radically reorganized its counterterrorism strategy and the governmental organizations that are designed to combat terrorism. A central component of that response was to create the Department of Homeland Security as part of a large-scale restructuring of the intelligence community.[38]

U.S. policy was to achieve grand strategic victory in the war against terrorism; but senior U.S. policymakers realized that the United States could not successfully destroy al-Qaeda as long as the Taliban controlled the government and military in Afghanistan and provided a sanctuary for these terrorists. This thinking was reflected in the 2002 *National Security Strategy,* which declared that the United States must be "prepared to stop rogue states and their terrorist clients before they are able to threaten or use weapons of mass destruction against the United States and our allies and friends."[39] The more controversial aspect of this Bush Doctrine was its declaration that the United States will use force preemptively if necessary to deal with these threats.[40] As President Bush said in his 2002 State of the Union Address, "Our nation will continue to be steadfast and patient and persistent in the pursuit of two great objectives. First, we will shut down terrorist camps, disrupt terrorist plans, and bring terrorists to justice. And, second, we must prevent the terrorists and regimes who seek chemical, biological or nuclear weapons from threatening the United States and the world."[41] Moreover, as the Bush Doctrine states, "We make no distinction between terrorists and those who knowingly harbor or provide aid to them."[42]

Senior officials in Washington realized that allowing the Taliban regime to remain in power in Afghanistan, where it could continue to provide sanctuary and training grounds to al-Qaeda, represented a long-term strategic threat to the United States. This was a particularly acute danger in an era when terrorist organizations actively sought to acquire weapons of mass destruction. In view of the warning in the *9/11 Commission Report* that "al-Qaeda has tried to acquire or make nuclear weapons for at least ten years,"[43] the worst-case scenario for senior officials was a terrorist organization that used a nuclear weapon to kill hundreds of thousands of Americans in a major urban area.[44]

In planning the invasion of Afghanistan, officials in the Bush administration were concerned with three issues: first, the message that the invasion would send to other potential state sponsors of terrorism; second, the message the invasion would send to other Muslim countries in Southwest Asia and the Middle East; and third, the nature of U.S. responsibilities to the people of Afghanistan once the Taliban regime had been removed. Administration officials were aware that the failure of the West to engage in Afghanistan, by rebuilding its government and society after the Soviet Union withdrew in 1989, had contributed to the power vacuum that had eventually led to the rise of the Taliban.[45] This thinking was evident during the debate among senior officials in late September and early October 2001 about the long-term consequences of an invasion of Afghanistan for the credibility of U.S. policy. Said the president, "What we do in Afghanistan is an important part of our effort . . . [because it will] signal to other countries about how serious we are on terror."[46] Bush held the view that kicking the terrorists out of Afghanistan might "persuade other countries that had supported terrorism . . . to change their behavior."[47]

The unequivocal message the administration wanted to send was that if any state supports the activities of terrorism, the U.S. will hold it responsible for its actions. In the case of Afghanistan, the U.S. first wanted the Taliban regime to hand over Osama bin Laden – to surrender him unconditionally to the United States. Once it became clear that the Taliban would not give up the al-Qaeda leader in the manner specified or meet additional U.S. demands, the administration launched Operation Enduring Freedom with the explicit purpose of regime change in Afghanistan.[48]

Since Afghanistan is a Muslim state, U.S. policymakers were concerned that the military invasion might suggest that Western states were prone to intervene in the internal affairs of Islamic ones.[49] If an attack on Afghanistan was interpreted as an attack against Islam, it would weaken the ability of the United States and other states to combat terrorism. The fact that such nations as Pakistan supported the United States would, it was hoped, minimize the odds that military action would inflame popular Islamic sentiment against the American intervention. On September 23, CIA Director Tenet relayed to senior U.S. officials this policy recommendation from a field agent: "underscore that the U.S. had no desire for territory or permanent bases in the region."[50] For the Muslim world, then, the administration's message would be straightforward: Once the Taliban was gone and Afghanistan stabilized, the United States was not planning to remain there. Equally important was the need to persuade Muslim countries to become full members of a "coalition of the willing" (a phrase now usually applied to the war in Iraq). This strategy was not intended only to prevent the invasion from igniting into a regionwide conflict: U.S. policymakers also knew that support from the predominantly Muslim Pakistan would be vital in tracking down al-Qaeda and Taliban operatives.

Finally, in planning Operation Enduring Freedom, policymakers in Washington publicly declared their commitment to support the efforts of the people of Afghanistan to develop a post-Taliban government.[51] By signaling its commitment to the Afghan people and to avoiding another political vacuum, the United States established a basis for the postconflict reconstruction phase – which, on another level, demonstrated that Washington was committed to achieving grand strategic victory in the war against the Taliban.

U.S. OBJECTIVES

Though many factors influenced the U.S. decision to attack Afghanistan militarily, the fundamental objective of U.S. policy was to destroy al-Qaeda and the Taliban regime – "to disrupt the use of Afghanistan as a terrorist base of operations, and to attack the military capability of the Taliban regime."[52] These objectives were consistent with the demands to the Taliban outlined earlier in Bush's address to a joint session of Congress on September 20, 2001:

> Deliver to United States authorities all the leaders of al-Qaeda who hide in your land. Release all foreign nationals, including American citizens, you have unjustly imprisoned. Protect foreign journalists, diplomats and aid workers in your country. Close immediately and permanently every terrorist training camp in Afghanistan, and hand over every terrorist, and every person in their support structure to appropriate authorities. Give the United States full access to terrorist training camps, so we can make sure they are no longer operating. These demands are not open to negotiation or discussion. The Taliban must act and act immediately. They will hand over the terrorists, or they will share in their fate.[53]

As Secretary of Defense Donald Rumsfeld outlined in a press briefing at the Pentagon, the central U.S. objective was to demonstrate that the Taliban could no longer harbor terrorists without fearing the risk of war. The U.S. strategy was to develop alliances with anti-Taliban groups that would do the fighting and ultimately destroy the Taliban regime.[54]

The consensus in the Bush administration was that the Taliban's support for al-Qaeda represented a transcendent threat to U.S. interests and security. Although U.S. policy up until the September 11 attacks had been to oppose the Taliban regime diplomatically, senior officials agreed after 9/11 that it was time for decisive action.[55] For the administration, a primary objective of the war was to destroy the foundations of power that sustained the Taliban and permitted them to provide an effective sanctuary for al-Qaeda. Once the Taliban was disabled – a de facto regime change – the U.S. strategy was to support the anti-Taliban resistance movements that had emerged since the mid-1990s, set up an interim government run by such Afghans, and, eventually, establish a democratic government in Afghanistan.

Beyond destroying the Taliban's infrastructure and attacking al-Qaeda facilities, Operation Enduring Freedom was intended to demonstrate the will of the United States to eradicate terrorism. Senior officials in the Bush administration argued that the United States could not ignore the Taliban regime without sending the signal that Washington's new policy of destroying terrorism lacked resolve. An unambiguous message to state sponsors of terrorism was included in various speeches by the president and senior administration officials, echoing what was said in Bush's address before Congress: "[W]e will pursue nations that provide aid or safe haven to terrorism. Every nation, in every region, now has a decision to make. Either you are with us, or you are with the terrorists. From this day forward, any nation that continues to harbor or support terrorism will be regarded by the United States as a hostile regime."56 The U.S. policy with respect to achieving victory in the war against terrorism was equally explicit: "We will direct every resource at our command – every means of diplomacy, every tool of intelligence, every instrument of law enforcement, every financial influence, and every necessary weapon of war – to the disruption and defeat of the global terror network."57 Policymakers in the administration called this a "total war on terrorism."58

From the earliest planning stages, the Bush administration presented the attacks against the Taliban and al-Qaeda as the beginning of a long-term war against terrorism and the states that sponsor it. The duration of U.S. strategy was evident when President Bush told Congress, "This war will not be like the war against Iraq a decade ago, with its decisive liberation of territory and its swift conclusion. It will not look like the air war above Kosovo two years ago, where no ground troops were used and not a single American was lost in combat."59 He emphasized that the U.S. "response involves far more than instant retaliation and isolated strikes. Americans should not expect one battle, but a lengthy campaign, unlike any other we have seen."60 And Secretary of Defense Rumsfeld "counseled caution to anyone who thinks a military victory in Afghanistan will be easy or swift."61

The process of planning the attack against Afghanistan began on September 12, 2001, when Rumsfeld ordered General Tommy Franks, commander of the U.S. Central Command (CENTCOM), to prepare "credible military options" for dealing with the problem of terrorism in Afghanistan.62 On September 21, General Franks presented a plan to President Bush whose central objective was to "destroy the al-Qaeda network inside Afghanistan along with the illegitimate Taliban regime which was harboring and protecting the terrorists."63 CENTCOM's plan was designed to attack al-Qaeda and the Taliban leadership, and capture or kill Osama bin Laden; defeat and destroy the Taliban military infrastructure, starting with its air defenses; and target al-Qaeda training camps.[64] At the same time, this military operation involved a significant degree of humanitarian aid that was designed to help rebuild the government and society of Afghanistan.[65] With this policy, the United States established a commitment to rebuild Afghanistan by focusing on "post-Taliban reconstruction" to stabilize the country after the Taliban regime was destroyed, and not to occupy the country. As Rumsfeld observed in a meeting with senior administration officials who were planning the operation, "We're not invading, we're not going to stay."[66]

CONDUCT OF OPERATION

Operation Enduring Freedom was designed to employ unconventional (notably, special operations) forces for reconnaissance, targeting, and direct action, working alongside local Afghan forces in the Northern Alliance.[67] The operation began with an air campaign that required the military cooperation of the former Soviet Socialist Republics of Uzbekistan, Tajikistan, and Turkmenistan.[68] A fundamental principle of the operation was that it involved working with an international "coalition of the willing," one that would eventually grow to include the efforts, albeit quite limited in most cases, of sixty-eight nations.[69] This U.S. strategy sought to pressure Pakistan both to withdraw its considerable support for the Taliban and to provide information and support for U.S. forces who were tracking Osama bin Laden and Mullah Omar, the head of the Taliban.[70]

The strategy in Operation Enduring Freedom was to coordinate the use of U.S. military power with anti-Taliban forces in Afghanistan to defeat the Taliban and al-Qaeda in the shortest possible time without destroying Afghanistan's infrastructure or causing significant civilian casualties. Policymakers in the Bush administration argued that the ability to minimize the destruction of the economy and infrastructure would depend on using overwhelming force in a brief but intense military campaign. However, the Taliban and al-Qaeda had few centers of gravity – significant targets for massed military attack – on which U.S. military forces could focus. Since the enemy retreated to cave complexes and mountainous areas, it was quickly understood that to root out Taliban and al-Qaeda forces the U.S. would need to conduct search and destroy operations, known to be difficult and lengthy, throughout Afghanistan.

The war plans consisted of two distinct elements: an air campaign and ground operations conducted by U.S. special operations forces and CIA paramilitary forces. Operation Enduring Freedom began on October 7, 2001, with air strikes on al-Qaeda training camps and Taliban military installations.[71] The initial air campaign used a variety of weapons systems: land-based B-1, B-2, and B-52 bombers, F-14 and F/A-18 fighters based on aircraft carriers in the Indian Ocean and Arabian Sea, and Tomahawk cruise missiles launched from U.S. and British submarines and surface combatant ships.[72] The first day of the air campaign employed fifteen bombers, twenty-five carrier-based aircraft, and fifty cruise missiles to attack a total of thirty-one al-Qaeda and Taliban targets. These included early warning radar sites, command facilities, Taliban military aircraft, airports, and runways, terrorist training camps used by al-Qaeda, and Afghanistan's surface-to-air missile facilities.[73] Senior policymakers were adamant about keeping civilian casualties as low as possible, and the Defense Department had produced a "no-strike" list that included power plants, schools, hospitals, and mosques; this, according to one observer, was meant to "show it was not an attack against the Afghan population."[74] It would also simplify the postwar rebuilding of Afghanistan.

By late October, U.S. air strikes had destroyed most of Afghanistan's air defenses. At the same time, U.S. special forces units had coordinated with Northern Alliance leaders to conduct ground attacks against a number of targets. Taliban forces were quickly put on the defensive.[75] By mid-November, the provincial capital Mazar-i-Sharif had fallen, followed by the provincial capitals Herat, Kabul, and Jalalabad. Extensive searches for senior members of the Taliban and al-Qaeda continued in the cave complexes in the vicinity of Tora Bora and along the Afghan–Pakistani border.[76] By December 7 the last Taliban stronghold, Kandahar, had fallen to U.S. Marines and Northern Alliance forces, and by mid-December Afghan militias were claiming victory.[77] At the start of Operation Enduring Freedom, Taliban forces had controlled 80 percent of the territory of Afghanistan and the nation's political, military, and economic activities. Seventy-eight days later, General Tommy Franks was visiting Kabul to represent the United States at the inaugural ceremony for the new interim government.[78]

On May 1, 2003, Secretary of Defense Donald Rumsfeld declared major combat operations ended: U.S. forces would now work on stabilizing and rebuilding Afghanistan.[79] The United States maintained an active program for detaining members of the Taliban and al-Qaeda so that they could be interrogated about the structure and nature of that terrorist organization, including its efforts to acquire weapons of mass destruction.[80] Moreover, the hunt for the principal architects of the Taliban and al-Qaeda, including Mullah Omar and Osama bin Laden, has continued ever since.[81]

Military operations in Enduring Freedom were dominated by U.S. forces working in conjunction with the Northern Alliance; but the international coalition assembled by the United States in the aftermath of 9/11 also played an important role, assisting in the political and economic reconstruction of Afghanistan. Although this coalition is not on the scale of that of the Persian Gulf War, twenty-one states among the "coalition of the willing" have contributed "nearly 8,000 troops to Operation Enduring Freedom and to [NATO's] International Security Assistance Force in Kabul."[82]

Several factors increased the complexity of Operation Enduring Freedom. The first challenge for those planning the war was the difficulty of locating the Taliban and al-Qaeda leadership. Despite efforts in December 2001 to kill enemy leaders in the vicinity of Tora Bora, the most senior ones, including Mullah Omar and Osama bin Laden of al-Qaeda reportedly escaped into the western reaches of Pakistan. U.S. policymakers had been concerned even before the war began with the political problem that would result if the United States was not able to capture or kill Osama bin Laden: Knowing that victory would be judged on the fate of bin Laden, President Bush hoped to separate the credibility of the military campaign from whether the United States found or killed the top Taliban and al-Qaeda leadership.[83] Instead, victory was to be measured by regime change and the establishment of a new stable government founded with democratic ideals. Second, it was difficult for U.S. military planners to find critical facilities and infrastructural elements that could be targeted during the air campaign. This was attributed to the relative primitiveness of the Afghan economic infrastructure after more than two decades of war. The frustration caused by this so-called deficit in targets was voiced by Secretary of Defense Rumsfeld: "How do you win a war if the enemy can't be hit?"[84]

Air Campaign

The central planning of the highly effective air campaign, including the development of target lists and the deployment of aircraft, was conducted in the air operations center located at Prince Sultan Air Base in Riyadh, Saudi Arabia. However, in operational terms, the air campaign was conducted from a number of bases throughout the region. At the same time, U.S. naval aircraft were flying missions from aircraft carriers operating in the Arabian Sea, which produced thousand-mile round-trip missions against targets in Afghanistan. In addition, U.S. bomber aircraft that were based in Diego Garcia in the Indian Ocean flew missions that lasted eight or nine hours.[85] Other U.S. aircraft, notably tankers and combat search and rescue, flew missions from air bases in Uzbekistan, Tajikistan, and a French air base in Djibouti (in east Africa, between Eritrea and Somalia, on the Red Sea and the Gulf of Aden).[86]

Why did the U.S. rely so heavily on air power in the first phase of the military operation in Afghanistan? One reason is that its principal advantage is the element of surprise; this kept Taliban and al-Qaeda forces either on the run or pinned down in caves and other facilities. Another is its effectiveness: The air campaign was able to destroy much of the Taliban's forces and military infrastructure before the U.S. military conducted joint ground operations. Analyses of this campaign concluded that Operation Enduring Freedom established a new post–Persian Gulf War standard for conducting precise strikes against military targets.[87] U.S. aircraft used GPS-guided Joint Direct Attack Munitions

(JDAMs) to destroy air defense, command and control, and other military facilities while greatly limiting unnecessary harm to civilians. During the campaign, U.S. aircraft flew only about two hundred sorties per day, an order of magnitude lower than the twenty-five hundred sorties flown daily in 1991 during Desert Storm (see Chapter 8 on the Persian Gulf War); and yet, remarked CENTCOM's General Tommy Franks, U.S. aircraft were hitting roughly the same number of targets with that much lower number of sorties.[88] Between October 7 and December 23, U.S. aircraft conducted some 6,500 strike missions (U.S. naval aircraft handled 75 percent, or 4,900) with roughly 17,500 munitions against 120 targets and 400 vehicles and artillery pieces in Afghanistan. By November 20, more than 60 percent of the 10,000 bombs and missiles delivered by U.S. aircraft had been precision guided. That percentage held steady for December 10, by which time 12,000 munitions had been used.[89] General Franks noted that 10,000 of the 18,000 devices used by February 7, 2002, had been precision in nature, about half of those guided by laser and half by global positioning. By mid-September, GPS was accounting for three-quarters of the precision-guided bombs and missiles employed to date.[90]

As mentioned earlier, U.S. policymakers had stipulated from the outset that casualties among the Afghan civilian population were to be minimized. The consensus in the Bush administration was that high civilian casualties would undermine any popular support for the United States and strengthen support for the Taliban. The "rule of low collateral" also applied to protecting economic facilities that would be critical to the long-term task of rebuilding Afghanistan and maintaining the tolerance and goodwill of the Afghan people.[91] In the end, U.S. military forces largely insulated Afghanistan's civilian population from the effects of the air campaign. Though the number of civilian deaths remains uncertain, it is reported that, by the summer of 2002, some 375 Afghan civilians had been killed in U.S. air strikes.[92]

Maritime Forces

The role of U.S. maritime forces was to support the air campaign against the Taliban and al-Qaeda by destroying military and terrorist facilities and to support the efforts of units of U.S. special operations forces and the anti-Taliban Northern Alliance. From the beginning of the operation, the United States had as many as three carrier battle groups launching strike aircraft. The Enterprise Battle Group operated from the Arabian Sea, where it was relieved by the Carl Vinson Battle Group. The Theodore Roosevelt Carrier Battle Group supported the operation from its patrol in the Mediterranean Sea. In addition, the Kitty Hawk Battle Group and John Stennis Battle Group contributed strike aircraft to Operation Enduring Freedom. The maritime forces also included an Amphibious Ready Group, which comprised two thousand Marines.

The Marines established a forward operating base, called Camp Rhino, near the city of Kandahar, from which to conduct military operations.[93]

The other important component of the maritime operations was the early use of cruise missiles, which were launched from U.S. and British surface ships and submarines. These missiles provide an effective means of attack when surprise is necessary and military planners want to minimize the risk to pilots of attacking heavily defended targets. Such strikes were important in the early stages of the war, when the air campaign was attacking fixed targets: Some eighty-eight cruise missiles were launched on five of the first nine days of the operation. As the campaign shifted toward more tactical strikes, cruise missiles became less useful.[94]

Land Campaign: Special Operations and CIA

As President Bush stated, "Conventional warfare is not going to win this, this is a guerrilla struggle."[95] Operation Enduring Freedom was therefore governed by two imperatives: First, use special operation forces, working with the Northern Alliance, to conduct unconventional warfare against enemy forces. Second, keep the number of U.S. troops in Afghanistan to a minimum so that the war would not be interpreted as a U.S. assault on an Islamic nation. The latter was particularly important in the immediate post-9/11 context, when the United States deliberately framed its military operations as a war on terror rather than a war against Islam or Islamic nations. Moreover, given the success of the Mujahideen in their long guerrilla war against Soviet forces, it was also essential to prevent the conflict from being interpreted as a war against Afghanistan and its people.[96] Policymakers in Washington had no desire to ignite an Afghan jihad against the United States while U.S. units were hunting down Taliban and al-Qaeda forces.

The land campaign was conducted by U.S. special operations and CIA paramilitary forces whose principal function was to organize the Afghan opposition, primarily the Northern Alliance, against the Taliban and al-Qaeda. The intention, as stated by CIA Director George Tenet in a meeting with Bush's war cabinet, was that "the tribals were going to do the bulk of the ground fighting and not the U.S. military."[97] The strategy of the special operations forces was to organize and support military strikes against a number of targets, including the airfields, command and control facilities, and military facilities connected with the Taliban and al-Qaeda. The cooperation between U.S. special operations and Northern Alliance forces dramatically changed the strategy of air strikes. Instead of concentrating on the Taliban infrastructure, the air war became a campaign that used tactical strikes against insurgent forces that were operating in the field. The flexible use of air power, which required the close cooperation between small units on the ground and air forces, eventually became the antecedent of the highly successful use of these tactics by U.S. forces in the 2003 Iraq War.

Technological Considerations

There are several technological considerations that decisively shaped Operation Enduring Freedom. First, the war was run by U.S. Central Command from Tampa, Florida, using operation centers in Kuwait and Uzbekistan. This was the first large-scale campaign fully to use what are known as "reachback" operations, in which forces were organized and controlled from facilities that are thousands of miles away from the battlefield.[98] This development, which relies on advanced command and control systems, satellites, and Internet and Web-based systems, lowers the number of U.S. forces deployed in the region and reduces their vulnerability to attack. Minimizing the presence of American forces in Afghanistan was important when one considers that al-Qaeda justified its jihad against the United States and the West on the basis of U.S. forces deployed in Saudi Arabia after the 1991 Persian Gulf War.

Operation Enduring Freedom also employed a number of advanced surveillance and targeting systems.[99] For the first time, Predator unmanned aerial vehicles (UAVs) were used extensively for surveillance and targeting purposes, and Hellfire antitank missiles were launched from Predator UAVs to destroy members of al-Qaeda. The Afghanistan campaign, as already noted, also used an unprecedented number of precision-guided munitions. The combination of surveillance and precision gave U.S. forces an unprecedented ability to find and destroy targets over a large area of operations.

INTERPRETING VICTORY

There are several lessons from the U.S. invasion of Afghanistan that pertain to our understanding of victory.

The first objective of the war, which developed early in the deliberations of the Bush administration, was to remove the Taliban regime – the only serious option for destroying the base of operations from which al-Qaeda had operated with impunity since 1996. The practical solution for these policymakers was to destroy the Taliban regime, reorganize the country's political and economic system, nullify al-Qaeda's ability to operate terrorist camps there, and in the end develop a stable, democratic, and secure Afghanistan.[100] The plan was to implement a policy of political change in Afghanistan that leads to rebuilding the government and restoring civil authority.[101] To support this policy, Bush declared that the United States was willing to work with the United Nations to create a post-Taliban government in Afghanistan.[102]

In the end, regime change in Afghanistan was both a tactical tool for eradicating the Taliban and al-Qaeda and a strategic tool for demonstrating to other potential supporters of terrorists that the United States has the resolve to destroy them. "The ideal result from this campaign, the president said, would be to kick terrorists out of some places like Afghanistan and through that action persuade other countries that had supported terrorism in the past, such as Iran, to change their behavior."103

Second, how the U.S. military conducted the invasion of Afghanistan reaffirmed that the necessary first steps toward victory are to define precisely what one means by "victory" and then to adhere to a strategy to achieve that. President Bush's announcement of the initiation of air strikes stated that they were intended "to disrupt the use of Afghanistan as a terrorist base of operations, and to attack the military capability of the Taliban regime."104 When judged by these criteria, and in view of subsequent elections that arguably represent the beginning of an Afghan transition to democracy, the military campaign against the Taliban regime may be seen by future generations as a model for how the state should organize to achieve victory.105

What is clear in this case is the idea that the concept of victory defines the military campaign and in a strict sense provides overall guidance for the operational conduct of the war. This relationship between victory and military force was outlined when Bush said that "We will win this conflict by the patient accumulation of successes."106 Thus, once the Bush administration identified its goals as the destruction of al-Qaeda and of any regime that supports terrorism, this translated directly into the strategy of removing the Taliban.

For U.S. policymakers, the objective of regime change was consistent with America's willingness to assume the postwar responsibilities of nation rebuilding, a topic discussed by senior administration officials in many planning sessions before the bombing began. Their principal questions were, "Who would rule Afghanistan if the Taliban were deposed? What was the mechanism for some kind of democracy in a country dominated by tribal factions?"107 At one point, the president expressed concern that, in planning for the campaign, "There's been too much discussion of post-conflict Afghanistan."108

The last time the United States had used military force specifically to demonstrate its unwillingness to acquiesce to the actions of regimes that support terrorism had been the 1986 raid on Libya (see Chapter 6), an intervention governed by limited political and military objectives. Policymakers in the Bush administration, however, unambiguously demonstrated in Operation Enduring Freedom that terrorism was no longer a peripheral matter: They believed strategic change was necessary to avert the danger posed by terrorism to the nation's vital interests. The decision to wage war against the Taliban affirmed that terrorist events would henceforth be interpreted not as "crimes" but as "acts of war": as military attacks requiring the state to respond with "all tools of national power," as Defense Secretary Rumsfeld put it in "Campaign against Terrorism: Strategic Guidance for the U.S. Department of Defense," rather than as problems to be handled through law-enforcement measures or covert action.[109]

Thus far, the outcome of the ongoing Operation Enduring Freedom seems consistent with the grand strategic victory intended (although U.S. policy-makers did not use that phrase directly) in that the United States has achieved its objectives – with the exception of capturing (or killing) the top leadership of al-Qaeda and Taliban, Osama bin Laden and Mullah Omar. The president had stated in his October 7 address that "Our military action is also designed to clear the way for sustained, comprehensive and relentless operations to drive them [the terrorists] out and bring them to justice."[110] When the objective is to isolate and capture the head of a government who also is directing the military through the command and control system (as was accomplished in Panama; see Chapter 7), there is a real risk that the state will fail. It is diffi-cult for the state to pinpoint individuals among a population of millions (or even the thousands in the military and government), capture them, and bring them before an international court or military tribunal (as has since been achieved in Iraq; see Chapter 11). Nevertheless, the ability of these two lead-ers to evade capture will influence how scholars and policymakers interpret the outcome in Afghanistan. Another development affecting judgments about victory in Afghanistan is the ongoing insurgency: As of late June 2006, 156 U.S. soldiers had been killed by insurgent attacks in Afghanistan.[111]

Still, by killing, capturing, or otherwise displacing the Taliban leaders who controlled the government and actively supported al-Qaeda, the Bush admin-istration demonstrated that the United States was willing to use overwhelm-ing military force in a decisive manner to destroy a regime that supports terror-ism. Moreover, although the campaign attacked the full complement of the Taliban's military and political centers of gravity, the war was organized so as not to lay waste to cities throughout Afghanistan.

CONCLUSION

One day after September 11 and several weeks before the invasion of Afghan-istan, Bush declared, "Now that war has been declared on us, we will lead the world to victory."[112] Warning that the war "will not be short . . . [and] the course to victory may be long," Bush declared that the "United States will do what it takes to win this war."[113]

As discussed in the previous section, the United States sought from the be-ginning to achieve a grand strategic victory against the Taliban and al-Qaeda. President Bush left little room for any other interpretation. The nature of this victory was described by Secretary of Defense Rumsfeld in December 2002 when he said, "They have elected a government. . . . The Taliban are gone. The al-Qaeda are gone. The country is not a perfectly stable place, and it needs a great deal of reconstruction funds."[114] However, this victory does not fit neatly into the model of well-defined historical moments. As Rumsfeld observed, "It [victory] is more like the Cold War than World War II. . . . The Cold War ended kind of with a collapse internally, because of constant pressure over a sustained period of time."[115]

The invasion of Afghanistan produced a comprehensive change in the status quo by removing the Taliban government and thereby displacing the al-Qaeda organization. Militarily, destroying the regime was essential to prevent it from providing a sanctuary for al-Qaeda's terrorism. Politically, it was the necessary first step toward demonstrating that the United States would respond forcibly to the attacks of 9/11. Operation Enduring Freedom signaled the credibility of the post-9/11 Bush administration policy focused on attacking "terrorist organizations, state sponsors of terrorism, and nonstate sponsors . . . [in the context of] weapons of mass destruction."[116] The invasion thus demonstrated to the leaders of other states that support for terrorism could invoke U.S. military action.

The other dimension of the change in status quo is the U.S. commitment to establishing democratic governance in Afghanistan.[117] In what is now officially known as the Islamic Republic of Afghanistan, the people voted to select delegates to establish a constitution that was approved in January 2004. It includes equal rights for men and women, a president who will be elected by the Afghan people, and a national assembly with two houses, among other provisions.[118]

By any standard, the extent of the U.S. mobilization for the invasion of Afghanistan was limited. Exactly a month after 9/11, President Bush promised the Pentagon, "In the missions ahead for the military, you will have everything you need, every resource, every weapon, every means to assure full victory for the United States and the cause of freedom."[119] However, even when one includes the initial air campaign, the attack represented a small fraction of U.S. conventional military power. In addition to the air strikes and their maritime support, all that proved necessary was the U.S. deployment of a very small number of ground forces and paramilitary units. As one study observed, the "U.S. commitment to overthrow the Taliban had been about 110 CIA officers and 316 Special Forces personnel, plus massive airpower."[120] Using only an exceedingly small fraction of its overall military power to achieve a grand strategic victory, the United States was able to destroy the Taliban's government and prevent it from supporting the terrorist organization al-Qaeda. Within seventy-eight days, the Taliban regime had collapsed and been replaced by an interim government. This limited use of U.S. force, however, did not reflect low public support for the war. For example, a *Washington Post* poll conducted in March 2002 "found that nine in ten Americans continue to support military action in Afghanistan."[121] Of course, one reason the U.S. action in Afghanistan received broad public support at home was that it occurred quite soon after the 9/11 attacks.[122]

With the end of active combat in May 2002, the United States and members of the international community committed themselves to a large-scale program of rebuilding the political, economic, an social institutions of Afghanistan.[123] The United States alone promised to provide more than a billion dollars in postwar aid.[124] The U.S. overthrow of the Taliban regime implied that America would assume the postconflict obligation of helping the Afghan people rebuild their society and create a stable state – one that would not allow al-Qaeda or similar organizations to resume terrorist activities. For the Bush administration, this meant reconstructing the Afghan state along the lines of a legitimate, democratically elected government. The Taliban's rule from 1996 to 2001 had left much of Afghanistan's infrastructure in a state of chaos; fortunately, the war had done comparatively little to damage it further, as the U.S. military campaign had been designed to minimize collateral damage to facilities as well as to civilians.

After several decades in which previous U.S. governments had launched campaigns against states that sponsored or supported terrorism (Operation El Dorado Canyon against Libya; Operation Infinite Reach against Sudan and Afghanistan), policymakers in the Bush administration demonstrated that new rules were in effect when they used military force to destroy a regime, signaling that other governments might likewise be attacked. The destruction of the Taliban regime in Afghanistan should be interpreted in the new context that engendered these new rules: the so-called the global war on terrorism.

As noted, the immediate outcome of Operation Enduring Freedom is consistent with grand strategic victory. Although past victories on such a scale have resulted from great wars between states, the war in Afghanistan shows that grand strategic victory is possible even in small-scale wars and is not necessarily a historical anomaly. However, there is a question as to whether the concept of grand strategic victory is meaningful in the case of nonstate actors, such as al-Qaeda and the Taliban (a group that persists in diminished form). Such entities complicate the meaning of victory for states because, lacking rigid, statelike facilities, they are free to engage or disengage from war for months or years at a time. Strictly speaking, then, in wars against insurgents or terrorists, as in Afghanistan, the concept of grand strategic victory may seem somewhat inadequate, however complete the victory that is attained. Yet for U.S. policymakers, grand strategic victory exists when the fundamental ideas of the opponent, whose contested ideas provide the underlying source of war, are defeated.[125] So perhaps the only practical way to measure success in the war on terror is in terms of regime change: In this war of ideologies, what other metric is there for success than the destruction of regimes that foster a climate of radical beliefs, engender terrorism, and/or provide material support and comfort to terrorist organizations? It is difficult to imagine how else victory in a war on terror would look – unless one could eradicate the conditions within societies that produce individuals whose sense of alienation attracts them to terrorism in the first place.

Guided by this logic, regime change is bound for the foreseeable future to remain the condition used to measure success in a war whose objective is to defeat the sources of terrorism. Such measures as territory gained, the defeat of the opponent's military, or the destruction of its economy and infrastructure would be inadequate. Regime change is a critical determinant of victory when it can deter the balance of power on a global scale – as does the destruction of the Taliban regime in Afghanistan. Victory in an essentially ideological war entails removing the opponent and its ideology from power.

What factors or conditions might diminish what has been described here as the grand strategic victory achieved by the United States in the invasion of Afghanistan? The foremost is the insurgency being waged by former members of the Taliban. This insurgency has thus far been successfully resisted, but it is persistent, and some regions of the country are more vulnerable than others, especially outside of the cities.[126] Another factor would be the failure of governmental reform or of the presidency of Hamid Karzai.[127] The animosities that historically have dominated politics in Afghanistan could rise again to undermine the development of a democratic government and practices. Thus far, however, these forces have not been able to derail the grand strategic victory that the United States has usually attained in the war in Afghanistan.

11 · 2003 Invasion of Iraq

O n Wednesday, March 19, 2003, President George W. Bush ordered the invasion of Iraq. As he explained that night in an address to the nation, the purposes of this military operation, known as Operation Iraqi Freedom, were "to disarm Iraq, to free its people and to defend the world from grave danger."[1] To accomplish these objectives, the United States and its coalition partners used military force to strike "selected targets of military importance to undermine Saddam Hussein's ability to wage war."[2] By demonstrating that the same strategy of regime change that the U.S. had used in Afghanistan in 2001 was still an option that the U.S. was willing to exercise, the invasion marked a new era in U.S. foreign policy in which the Bush administration is committed to destroying regimes that support terrorism. In the case of Iraq, the strategy is to wage a counterinsurgency campaign against remnants of the Baath Party regime and foreign jihadists who seek to establish a base of operations in Iraq for war against the West.[3] As President Bush declared, "The return of tyranny to Iraq would be an unprecedented terrorist victory."[4] Since the United States will be waging a global war against terrorism to destroy regimes that support terrorism or terrorist organizations, this chapter discusses the implications of the 2003 invasion of Iraq for the development of a pretheory of victory.

The initial outcome for the United States in Operation Iraqi Freedom is broadly consistent with grand strategic victory, but there are significant doubts about what victory will look like and how long it may take to achieve it, while others openly suggest that the United States may be defeated.[5] In November 2005, democratic Congressman John P. Murtha called for the immediate withdrawal of U.S. forces from Iraq on the grounds that it is a "flawed policy."[6] In framing U.S. objectives for the war, President Bush did not use the term "grand strategic" in a formal sense, but in an address to the nation on March 19, 2003, he said that the United States "will accept no outcome but victory." This language is, however, synonymous with victory on a scale that seeks to realign the international system in strategic terms.[7] During the war, senior U.S. officials explicitly linked the decision to destroy Saddam Hussein's regime with the broader objective of destroying weapons of mass destruction (WMD) and encouraging the development of democratic values and institutions in the Middle East. President Bush declared in his March 19 address that "helping Iraqis achieve a united, stable and free country will require our sustained commitment."[8]

The war in Iraq confirms four key elements in U.S. foreign policy: a commitment to a strategy of regime change; the permissibility of using military force to attack alleged state sponsors of terrorism; the introduction of democratic values into the Middle East; and grand strategic victory as the organizing principle in the global war against terrorism.

BACKGROUND

The reasons for the decision to invade Iraq can be traced to concerns about the possible intersection between weapons of mass destruction and terrorism in Iraq. The consensus among policymakers in the Bush administration was that the terrorist attacks on September 11 warned of the possible devastation if terrorists ever possessed WMD. Senior military officials began the early phases of planning for an invasion of Iraq in the fall of 2001 at approximately the same time that the United States launched the invasion of Afghanistan.[9] The chronology of events prior to the invasion is significant because it reaffirms that senior Bush administration officials had based the necessity of invading Iraq on the 9/11 attacks, arguing that eliminating Iraq's weapons of mass destruction and destroying the Iraqi regime were essential to winning the global war against terrorism. These officials were unwilling to accept any risk that Saddam Hussein's regime in Baghdad might possess WMD. As early as October 11, 2001, Bush had argued that Saddam was actively developing biological and chemical weapons of mass destruction and sought to acquire nuclear weapons.[10] On November 21, 2001, President Bush directed Defense Secretary Donald Rumsfeld to begin developing war plans for Iraq; by July 2002 he had reportedly decided to use military action to remove Saddam Hussein.[11]

As already noted in Chapter 10, in 2002 Bush and his administration declared that the United States must be "prepared to stop rogue states and their terrorist clients" – to "prevent the terrorists and regimes who seek chemical, biological or nuclear weapons" – from using WMD against the United States and its allies.[12] In his 2002 State of the Union Address, Bush said that Iraq, Iran, North Korea, "and their terrorist allies, constitute an axis of evil, arming to threaten the peace of the world."[13] Senior officials from the Bush administration accused Iraq of possessing WMD and of violating its obligations as established by the United Nations to cease all such programs. In a speech delivered late in August 2002, Vice President Dick Cheney accused Saddam Hussein of seeking chemical and biological weapons of mass destruction as part of a strategy for dominating the Middle East.[14] In the buildup to war in late 2002 and early 2003, U.S. policymakers warned that Saddam must comply with U.N. Security Council Resolutions, which mandated that Iraq must fully reveal and dismantle those programs under United Nations supervision.[15] On November 8, 2002, the U.N. Security Council, acting at U.S. urging, adopted Resolution 1441, which declared that Iraq had one last opportunity to comply with its existing obligations to disarm or face serious consequences.[16] In a speech on March 17, 2003, President Bush declared that, with its unanimous passage of Resolution 1441, the U.N. Security Council had found "Iraq in material breach of its obligations [and vowed] serious consequences if Iraq did not fully and immediately disarm."[17] Thus U.S. plans for an invasion of Iraq were actively being developed at the same time that U.S. patience with Iraq's failure to comply with inspections of WMD was being exhausted.

What complicated the Bush administration's decisions about whether to remove Saddam Hussein's government was the widespread belief within U.S. and foreign intelligence services that Iraq had possessed weapons of mass destruction both before and after the Persian Gulf War. To make matters worse, Baghdad's behavior throughout the fall and winter of 2002–3 suggested to many observers that Iraq likely still possessed WMD.[18] This presumed presence of WMD was the principal argument influencing the U.S. decision to wage war against Iraq.[19] The problem is that no evidence has been found that Iraq still had significant programs for developing biological, chemical, and nuclear weapons as well as ballistic missiles. Even studies and inspections conducted after the declared end of major combat (May 1, 2003) failed to produce any evidence that Iraq possessed WMD; this not only provoked a debate about whether the Bush administration had falsified the intelligence for war but also energized a debate about the need for the United States to reorganize its intelligence community.[20] In the end, the victory attained in the 2003 Iraq War will be interpreted historically at least in part on the basis of the failure of postinvasion efforts to discover weapons of mass destruction.

In parallel with diplomatic efforts to develop support for an international "coalition of the willing"[21] that would join with the United States, the U.S. Congress passed a resolution endorsing the administration's efforts to obtain prompt U.N. Security Council action to ensure Iraqi compliance with U.N. resolutions and authorizing the use of force against Iraq.[22] In remarks in January 2003 with Polish President Aleksander Kwaśniewski, President Bush said that his policy was to force Iraq to comply with international arms inspections: "What I have in mind for Saddam Hussein is to disarm. The United Nations spoke with one voice. We said, we expect Saddam Hussein, for the sake of peace, to disarm."[23]

Despite the accelerating pace of diplomatic efforts in the winter of 2002–3 and the failure to develop broad allied support, there was growing evidence that the United States was moving toward using military force against Iraq.[24] On March 17, 2003, President Bush issued an ultimatum to Saddam Hussein insisting that he "and his sons must leave Iraq within 48 hours. Their refusal to do so will result in military conflict, commenced at a time of our choosing."[25] Once those diplomatic moves failed, the first strike of Operation Iraqi Freedom occurred on March 19, 2003, at 9:33 P.M. (5:33 A.M. in Iraq), with an attack by F-117 stealth fighters against a location where the Iraqi president and his top advisors were mistakenly believed to be meeting.[26]

U.S. OBJECTIVES

The fundamental objectives of the Bush administration in Operation Iraqi Freedom were to destroy Saddam Hussein's regime and end its alleged support for international terrorism,[27] find and destroy presumed weapons of mass destruction, preserve Iraq's ability to supply oil, and create a stable and peaceful democratic society that would not threaten its neighbors in the Middle East. The foundations of this U.S. policy against Iraq were established in a top-secret National Security Presidential Directive (NSPD) entitled "Iraq: Goals, Objectives and Strategy." Its guidance to military commanders was to "Free Iraq in order to eliminate Iraqi weapons of mass destruction. . . . End Iraqi threats to its neighbors. . . . And liberate the Iraqi people from tyranny, and assist them in creating a society based on moderation, pluralism and democracy."[28]

A key element of this strategy was that U.S. policymakers saw destroying the regime of Saddam Hussein as the only way to achieve its other objectives.[29] For instance, in a speech on February 26, 2003, President Bush emphasized that overthrowing Saddam Hussein would promote democracy and stability in the Middle East.[30] In his March 19 address announcing the U.S. invasion, Bush said one objective was to "restore control of that country to its own people"; three days later, he reaffirmed that our mission was partly "to free the Iraqi people."[31] Nor was the U.S. policy of regime change in Iraq a new one; an earlier incarnation dates from 1998, when President Clinton signed a law providing $97 million to opposition forces in Iraq "to remove the regime headed by Saddam Hussein" and "to promote the emergence of a democratic government."[32] Five years later, senior officials in the Bush administration were likewise defining success in terms of removing Saddam Hussein and destroying his government.[33] Because of concerns among these officials that the removal of Saddam's regime would produce a political and economic vacuum that might lead to civil war in post-Saddam Iraq, the United States planned to occupy the the country after the war and establish an interim administration and then government run by Iraqis as soon as possible.[34]

The Bush administration framed its policy of regime change to a significant extent on the presumption that Baghdad possessed WMD that could be used against the United States or its allies and that raised the risks attached to alleged Saddam Hussein's support of terrorist organizations.[35] In an interview given on April 4, 2002, the president said that "The worst thing that could happen would be to allow a nation like Iraq, run by Saddam Hussein, to develop weapons of mass destruction, and then team up with terrorist organizations so they can blackmail the world. I'm not going to let that happen."[36] This policy toward Iraq was consistent with the administration's earlier decision to invade Afghanistan and threaten other states that were believed to support or sponsor terrorism.[37] As Bush stated on March 17, 2003, "Terrorists and terror states do not reveal these [WMD] threats with fair notice, in formal declarations. . . . The security of the world requires disarming Saddam Hussein now."[38] However, although the administration declared that operational linkages between Iraq and al-Qaeda operatives indicated a significant threat to U.S. interests, no compelling public evidence of any viable linkage between the two ever emerged in the public debate.[39]

Since the beginning of the debate in the U.S. government about the broad strategy for dealing with terrorism after 9/11, senior officials in the Bush administration had argued that Iraq's presumed WMD-development programs posed a significant threat to the United States and its allies in the Middle East.[40] Although international inspectors from the United Nations Special Commission (UNSCOM) had been conducting inspections of purported Iraqi WMD facilities since the end of the Persian Gulf War in 1991, the consensus in the international nonproliferation community and among intelligence agencies throughout the 1990s was that Saddam Hussein likely possessed significant WMD programs yet had successfully hidden these from the inspectors.[41] Senior government officials were also aware that Saddam in 1998 had forced the U.N. inspectors to leave Iraq, which further heightened suspicions that Iraq continued to possess weapons of mass destruction.[42] Although some of these facilities had been dismantled, the consensus among senior policymakers was that Iraq remained a potential source of biological, chemical, and possibly nuclear weapons.[43] Thus a second objective of Operation Iraqi Freedom was to destroy Iraqi programs for developing weapons of mass destruction.

A third objective that governed the conduct of operations was to protect the vast oil fields in the Middle East, notably those in Iraq and Saudi Arabia. The Bush administration sought to preserve the flow of oil from the region and to keep oil prices stable while militarily preventing Iraq's oil fields from being sabotaged.[44] In planning for the war, Defense Secretary Rumsfeld and the commander of U.S. Central Command, General Tommy Franks, were specifically worried that Saddam's forces would set Iraq's oil fields on fire, as they had done to Kuwaiti oil fields in 1991 during their retreat in the Persian Gulf War (see Chapter 8).[45] Although the oil issue was less important than concerns about terrorism and weapons of mass destruction, President Bush and his senior advisors understood the dire implications if the flow of Iraqi oil to the industrialized economies was interrupted at a time when Iraq's oil infrastructure was decaying.[46]

U.S. policy on the nature of the victory sought against Saddam Hussein's regime and terrorism was quite direct. In his address to the nation on March 19, 2003, President Bush declared that this war against Iraq "will not be a campaign of half measures, and we will accept no outcome but victory."[47] Although the precise formulation of victory remained elusive, the policy declarations by senior policymakers used a "language of war" that was dominated by the principle that the United States would achieve victory.[48] As shall become evident, the Bush administration's goal was to achieve a grand strategic victory (although that phrase was not used explicitly).

DESCRIPTION OF OPERATION

The central argument of a 1996 study entitled *Shock and Awe: Achieving Rapid Dominance* was that the application of overwhelming military power would destroy the enemy's will to resist.[49] Following this reasoning, the Bush administration's strategy in Operation Iraqi Freedom was to employ overwhelming U.S. military power in such a rapid and highly mobile fashion that it would destroy Iraqi military and security forces yet avoid significant civilian casualties and preserve Iraq's economic infrastructure.[50] In practical terms, the objectives of the campaign were to destroy the military foundation of Iraq's power, remove the regime of Saddam Hussein, and thereby establish a new democratic political and economic order in Iraq.

The first strike against the regime of Saddam Hussein occurred on March 19, 2003, with a combined air and ground campaign.[51] Although the initial plan was to begin the war on March 20, intelligence sources suggested on the day before combat operations were planned to commence that Saddam Hussein and his two sons had been located in a leadership bunker at the Dora Farm compound.[52] These air strikes were conducted with deep-penetration "bunker buster" bombs; the broader war began with strikes using F-117 and F-15 aircraft against Iraqi air defense sites, Scud missile sites, and artillery forces that could be used against coalition forces. At the same time, a number of strikes were conducted with Tomahawk cruise missiles launched from U.S. warships.[53]

Even before these air strikes began, however, several dozen teams of CIA and special operations forces had been deployed into the Kurdish region in northern Iraq and into the Iraqi desert region (west and southwest of the Euphrates River) to destroy Scud missiles, biological and chemical weapons, and Iraqi observation sites scattered along the borders of Jordan, Kuwait, and Saudi Arabia, as well as to protect Iraq's oil fields from sabotage.[54]

The guidelines from the Afghanistan campaign about avoiding civilian casualties applied with equal force to U.S. military operations in Iraq, and the president specified that "coalition forces will make every effort to spare innocent civilians from harm."[55] Before the war, General Franks had produced an "Iraq Targeting Primer" listing four considerations that would govern targeting: Minimizing collateral damage and civilian casualties was outlined in its third criterion.[56] Senior Bush administration officials reaffirmed this principle throughout the war. Early in the campaign, many significant targets were "off limits to attack" because of the "pervasive fear of civilian casualties" among U.S. policymakers.[57]

The military operations in Operation Iraqi Freedom were dominated by the United States, which by March 20 had deployed roughly 241,000 troops in the region. In addition to U.S. troops, 41,000 British, 2,000 Australian, and 200 Polish troops were involved. A total of 183,000 troops participated in the ground invasion.[58] After major combat operations were over on May 1, 2003, these coalition forces were used to support the process of rebuilding the political system and economy of Iraq. In any event, the overall conduct of the war was managed almost entirely by the U.S. military, and CENTCOM had overall responsibility for military planning and execution.

Senior political and military planners decided against following the pattern of the prolonged air campaign and brief land campaign that had been used in the Persian Gulf War, for several reasons. First, a lengthy air campaign would allow Iraq's leadership both time and opportunity to build support in the Middle East and globally against the U.S.-led coalition. Second, it would give Baghdad a chance to set fire to the oil fields, because there would not yet be any ground forces to put pressure on Iraqi forces.[59] Third, it would grant Iraq's political and military leaders time to prepare its military to wage a more effective war against coalition forces. Finally, the decision to wage the ground war after the air campaign would have presented Iraqi military planners with a wide array of coalition military targets that could be attacked during the air phase of the war.[60]

U.S. military planning thus shifted from the kind of air–land war involving a six-week air campaign followed by a four-day land war to a newer construct, based on "lines of operation," in which land and air operations are conducted "independently and often simultaneously."[61] The plan was thus not to conduct separate air and ground campaigns but to develop and execute one integrated campaign against the full range of Iraq's military forces.[62] Air power, armored forces, special operations forces, and maritime power were to be totally integrated into a coherent instrument whose objective was to destroy Saddam Hussein's government and "inflict a massive and sudden defeat on a large traditional army."[63] In essence, Franks and Rumsfeld sought to transform radically how the United States conducted war by building on the concepts articulated in the study *Shock and Awe.* This approach to war moved beyond the precision strikes of earlier campaigns to magnify the disruptive effects caused by combining precision strikes with fast-paced combat operations and tightly integrated air and ground forces.[64]

Designed to weaken the ability of the Iraqi military to conduct operations and to interfere systematically with its supply lines, reinforcements, and overall command and control apparatus, Operation Iraqi Freedom had "three imperatives": (1) Locate and destroy any weapons of mass destruction possessed by Iraq and prevent their use in the war; (2) prevent Iraq's leadership from either igniting the nation's oil wells or pumping oil into the Persian Gulf; and (3) kill the political and military leaders of the Iraqi government while limiting damage to the civilian population and economic infrastructure.[65]

Leadership Attack and Ground War

As already noted, on March 19 U.S. military forces attacked what was known as the Dora Farms complex, a leadership target believed to contain Saddam Hussein, his sons Uday and Qusay, and senior military officials. The purpose of this attack, which used stealth aircraft and cruise missiles, was to "decapitate" the regime, break the link between the Iraqi leadership and its military forces, and thus significantly reduce the overall effectiveness of the Iraqi military. Though this strike was not successful, it demonstrated that the United States was intent on regime change, beginning with the removal of Saddam.

In the ground war the principal axis of attack for U.S. Army and Marine Corps units was into southern Iraq, where U.S. and British ground forces launched a large-scale invasion without the expected precursor attack from air power.[66] One of the first steps in this invasion occurred in the al-Faw peninsula when units of British and U.S. special operations forces secured the Rumaila oil fields. In roughly four days U.S. Army forces had advanced as far as an-Najaf, just sixty miles from Baghdad, while U.S. Marines had reached the city of al-Kut. From early reports, these armored penetrations of Iraq were highly successful; but as the fighting intensified and U.S. forces took casualties on March 23, the prospects of an easy advance toward Baghdad dimmed. At this point in the war, the media reported that the overall military campaign had run into difficulties, and more worrisome still, that early reports of the coalition's overwhelming success in the war were misleading. Many commentators described this period as one in which the U.S. war plan might be failing.[67]

One reason for the interpretation that the war was not proving as successful as originally planned was that the Iraqi population did not form a popular uprising in support of the U.S. military operation. That the Iraqi people did not rise up against their government represented a significant strategic surprise for U.S. policymakers and war planners, who still continue to debate why this problem occurred and what it means for planning future wars.[68]

The broad purpose for the air campaign was to weaken Saddam Hussein's regime, minimize the ability of the Iraqi military to control the movement of its ground forces, ensure that Iraqi forces could not use WMD (notably chemical or biological weapons), and protect coalition ground forces with close air support.[69] Thus, in contrast with Operation Desert Storm, the air campaign waged during the Persian Gulf War, the air component of Operation Iraqi Freedom relied heavily on the use of precision-guided munitions to attack the enemy psychologically rather than on the brute-force approach of methodically destroying thousands of political, military, and economic targets throughout Iraq. Despite its successes, the principal flaw in this air campaign was the failure of military planners to estimate adequately the considerable political control that Iraqi officials would still exercise over the people.[70] As one study concluded, "the 'shock and awe' portion of the air campaign appears to have done little to weaken Saddam's grip on Iraq's population."[71]

During the first three days of the war and in conjunction with the ground war, U.S. military forces conducted a large-scale air campaign in which roughly twenty-five hundred precision-guided missiles and bombs were dropped. In the early phase of the operation, targets included Iraqi air defenses, command and control facilities, the leadership of the Iraqi regime, and sites believed to be associated with weapons of mass destruction; this impeded the ability of Iraq's military forces to offer resistance during the war. In addition, close air support was provided for special operations forces, and combat air patrols and strikes were designed to prevent Iraq from using its air power. In this early phase, U.S. military forces conducted more than seventeen hundred sorties with aircraft and fired roughly six hundred cruise missiles, of which five hundred were sea-launched from thirty coalition ships and submarines; the other hundred were air-launched from U.S. Air Force bombers.[72]

The air campaign was significant in its own right both in terms of the absolute number of munitions used and in the historically unprecedented number and percentage that were precision guided. Like the October 2001 invasion of Afghanistan, the war in Iraq provided an opportunity for U.S. military forces to use precision-guided munitions, including laser- and GPS-guided JDAMs, against military targets, thus keeping civilian casualties as low as possible. By the end of the war, U.S. and coalition military forces had conducted some 47,600 sorties and dropped on the order of 19,000 unguided munitions and

9,750 precision munitions in strikes throughout Iraq.[73] Of the twenty thousand bombs or missiles that were dropped by U.S. aircraft, roughly 65 percent or thirteen thousand of those were precision guided, the bulk of which being GPS-guided weapons.[74]

The war plan was consistent with the principle of minimizing damage to Iraqi society. The overall list of targets in the air campaign, which were known as "aim points," was decreased by many hundreds so that electric power plants, bridges, and other elements of the economic infrastructure that would be necessary to Iraq's reconstruction would not be destroyed. Within the initial days of the war, it was apparent to senior political and military officials that the success of the land campaign was not going to hinge on the ability to destroy civilian targets.[75]

It is, however, misleading to conclude that the operation was dominated by air power; rather, it relied on large-scale ground operations that were closely integrated with the use of air power. In terms of land operations, the initial efforts by U.S. Marines and the British Royal Marines were designed to protect elements of the infrastructure that were critical for the operation of the Iraqi economy. The central objective was to use a force of 219,000 U.S. Army, Marine, and coalition land forces to advance northward to Baghdad. Almost immediately, however, these began to meet significant resistance from Iraqi forces. As U.S. forces began to attack units of the Iraqi Republican Guard, units devoted to what was called "regime support" (e.g., the paramilitary Fedayeen Saddam), and other targets with precision munitions during the next several days, U.S. and coalition units encountered threats to their forces and lines of supply, including sandstorms that hindered military operations to some extent. Despite these impediments, by late March the scale, agility, and pace of U.S. military operations, with their integrated use of land forces and precision strikes, had effectively destroyed the ability of Iraqi forces to offer any significant military resistance (69–75).

One explanation for the success of coalition military operations was the decision by military commanders to destroy the "regime's center of power" rather than to defeat all Iraqi forces on the battlefield. As one study noted, coalition forces "did not attempt to occupy or secure rear areas" but relied instead on precision strikes to "disrupt and paralyze enemy operation" (76). This strategy allowed coalition forces to destroy military units and their lines of communication without having to wreck Iraq's economic infrastructure or strike urban areas where Iraqi forces were hiding. Late in March, the course of military operations was significantly hampered by weather conditions, in particular sandstorms and rain. However, with technological advances in sensors, U.S. forces were able to conduct integrated land and air operations, including roughly fourteen hundred air missions against ground-forces targets and air defense sites throughout Iraq (77).[76] The essence of this military plan, as outlined by General Franks, was to "surprise the enemy by attacking at all times of day and night all over the battlefield" (83). By the end of March coalition forces were moving toward Baghdad, which was to be the decisive military engagement of the war.

By early April 2003, U.S. and allied military forces were attacking "strategic regime" and other targets in Baghdad, including as well as the Medina, Baghdad, and Hammurabi units of the Republican Guard. In what was known as the Battle of Baghdad, the objective of U.S. forces was to destroy the regime of Saddam Hussein without inflicting widespread damage on the city and its five million inhabitants. This battle involved many smaller battles but not the one, great battle that many expected would occur. For one observer, the initial attack on the international airport "exposed the overall weakness of the remaining Iraqi forces . . . and enabled the coalition to launch deep armored penetrations and raids into Baghdad" (94).[77] Given the speed and lethality of coalition operations, Iraqi military forces were unable to offer any effective military resistance, which demonstrated that Saddam's regime could not marshal the military resources or popular will to wage the urban warfare that many feared would immediately engulf the capital city.

By early in the second week of April, the government of Iraq had lost its ability to govern or to control its military forces, but why Iraq's military forces disintegrated as quickly as they did remains unexplained (116). One conclusion is that a "tightly centralized dictatorship, with no convincing popular ideology and support, is inherently vulnerable to a strike at its center of power" (96). That is precisely the result that U.S. military forces were able to achieve with the use of highly integrated air and land operations against Iraq. However, members of the Iraqi regime did attempt to organize a popular uprising against U.S. and allied forces. Although this opposition never emerged during the war, by the fall of 2003 it had evolved into a serious insurgency that would inflict thousands of casualties on U.S. forces (96).[78]

The central purpose of maritime forces in Operation Iraqi Freedom was to support the land and air campaigns, and in many senses they contributed significantly to the victory achieved against Iraq.[79] Maritime forces were important because of the firepower that aircraft flying from carriers and cruise missiles launched from ships and submarines brought to the war. By the war's end, on May 1, 2003, roughly sixty thousand naval personnel and 140 ships were deployed in the region, including four aircraft carrier strike groups deployed in the Mediterranean Sea and the Persian Gulf, providing support principally by means of air strikes. Seven thousand sorties were flown from aircraft carriers operating in the Persian Gulf or Indian Ocean. In addition, U.S. and British ships and submarines over the course of the campaign launched eight hundred cruise missiles against a variety of targets in Iraq. At the same time, patrol and reconnaissance missions of maritime aircraft, notably P-3's, contributed to the broad intelligence picture of Iraq's military and intelligence capabilities both on the battlefield and throughout the nation.

During the air and land campaign, the United States employed special operations forces to conduct military strikes against a number of targets, including possible launch sites in western Iraq for Scud missiles as well as a wide range of airfields, command and control facilities, and military sites integral to the operation of Iraq's military and government. Analysts agree that these forces played a significant role in the outcome of the war.[80] Such units from the United States, Britain, and Australia conducted operations in the western deserts to prevent Iraq from launching Scud missiles at Israeli cities. Joint Special Operations Task Forces (JSOTFs) were also used to conduct "interdiction missions" against the supply lines that stretched from Syria to Iraq; to help organize the Kurds in the northern areas of Iraq into more effective fighting forces; to organize attacks against the facilities of the largely Kurdish, Islamic separatist, terrorist group Ansar al-Islam; and to assist with the capture of the northern cities of Mosul and Kirkuk.[81] In the southern areas of Iraq, Special Forces units were used primarily to preclude the Iraqis from destroying the oil fields that constitute an important source of Iraq's national wealth. Overall, an important aspect of the role of these units in Operation Iraqi Freedom was the unprecedented extent to which CENTCOM's General Franks insisted on integrating and coordinating special and conventional forces at all levels in the war.[82]

Once the Iraqi military lost the ability to fight, U.S. military forces moved to dominate the rest of Iraq, while coalition forces started to reestablish some semblance of security in Iraqi cities and towns. These actions represented the first steps in the formidable process of rebuilding the nation, government, and economy of Iraq after weeks of war and years of neglect under U.N.-imposed sanctions.[83] The first formal step in nation-building activities began with the call in late April 2003 by the Saudi foreign minister for U.S. and British forces to establish an interim government in Iraq.[84]

By May 1, 2003, when the end of major combat operations was announced, 139 American soldiers had died in Operation Iraqi Freedom; some twenty-three hundred more have since died in the conflict in Iraq.[85] By late June 2006, total deaths are 2,524.

INTERPRETING VICTORY

The outcome of Operation Iraqi Freedom illustrates the complexities that surround the concept of victory and its implications for policymaking and scholarship. This analysis of the invasion of Iraq in 2003 is organized on the basis of several factors, beginning with the strategic goals that were established by the Bush administration.

From the beginning the Bush administration consistently adhered to the policy of destroying the regime of Saddam Hussein and sons and establishing a democracy in Iraq. From the perspective of senior policymakers in Washington, this was absolutely vital to achieving victory. The top-secret "Iraq: Goals, Objectives and Strategy" directed a U.S. policy of working "with the Iraqi opposition to demonstrate that we are liberating, not invading, Iraq, and give the opposition a role in building a pluralistic and democratic Iraq, including the preparation of a new constitution."[86]

A related reason for the U.S. invasion was to destroy a regime that in the aftermath of 9/11 was believed to possess weapons of mass destruction and a potential willingness to share those weapons with terrorist organizations. The solution was to install a government in Baghdad that would not support such activities. As is made clear by the record of deliberations in the Bush administration from late 2001 to the outbreak of hostilities on March 19, 2003, the consensus among policymakers was that failing to remove Saddam Hussein and his sons from power would produce an incomplete victory. This consensus was influenced by senior policymakers' belief that the political–military victory achieved in the Persian Gulf War had been diminished by the failure to change the Iraqi regime in 1991.[87] Given this line of reasoning, policymakers concluded sometime late in 2002 that it was time for the United States to take action against Saddam's regime once and for all.[88] Only decisive military action would put an end to the inconclusive debate about whether Iraq possessed WMD, might provide such weapons to terrorists, and would continue to ignore the demands of the international community to disarm.

The strategy of regime change in Operation Iraqi Freedom involved significant risks for the Bush administration because "victory" depended directly on capturing or killing Saddam Hussein and other senior officials and replacing their government. The strategy for victory involved first using local political organizations and groups to remove Saddam Hussein's regime, and then encouraging various political, religious, and national groups to participate in the building of democratic governance in Iraq.[89] The success of this strategy will thus depend on the ability of U.S. political and military officials to work closely not only with Iraqi antigovernment groups but with the Shiite and Sunni (Islamic sect) communities generally, as well as with the ethnic Kurds (concentrated in the north), to develop the foundations of a new government once Saddam's Sunni-favoring Baath Party regime was removed. In a critical sense, victory would be defined not in the tactical sense of capturing or holding territory or defeating Iraq's military but in the strategic sense of replacing a dictatorial regime with a democracy that would be hostile to terrorism. These aspects of regime change demonstrate that U.S. policymakers were thinking in terms of grand strategic victory, even if they did not use that expression.

A second factor that determines whether the United States will be able to achieve grand strategic victory is the problem posed by the Iraqi insurgency that formed in the wake of the declared end of major combat operations.[90] As the insurgency has demonstrated so vividly, a successful case of regime change involves much more than simply removing the head of state. The insurgency is dangerous precisely because it undermines the ability of the United States to achieve stability in postwar Iraq and detracts significantly from any U.S. declaration of victory on whatever level.[91] Thus, more than any other factor, the Iraqi insurgency raises fundamental doubts about the ability of the United States to achieve victory – whether grand strategic or the lesser forms – in the war in Iraq. The problem for analyses of victory is that how policymakers and scholars interpret the outcome of the war in Iraq and its effects on democratic reform and stability in the Middle East will depend partly on the duration and intensity of this Iraqi backlash.

The third factor is whether the process of democratic reform in Iraq will succeed in the long term. With elections on January 30, 2005, to elect a constituent assembly to write a constitution, the constitutional referendum on October 15, 2005, and the elections for a full Iraqi parliament on December 15, 2005, Iraq is in the early stages of a radical political transition that may lead to a democracy. The January 30 assembly elections were welcomed as a positive sign that political and social reform in Iraq would lead to the emergence of a democratic government and stable society.[92] The elections held on December 15, 2005, represented a significant development in Iraq because the overall 70 percent voter turnout among the Shiite, Sunni, and Kurdish groups signaled an unparalleled degree of popular support for Iraq's new political system.[93] The long-term hope is that the successful development of democratic institutions after the invasion of Iraq might become the model for future generations of policymakers who seek as a matter of deliberate policy to build a democracy in a state that once contributed to instability and war.[94]

The fourth factor that influences how to interpret victory in Iraq is the failure of the United States to anticipate the nature of the postinvasion environment and to develop the appropriate military and political plans. From the start, the Bush administration expressed its willingness to assume responsibility for rebuilding postwar Iraq.[95] However, although the military campaign successfully minimized the destruction of the civilian economy, the complexities of nation building are daunting in a country, such as Iraq, where intense religious and political differences complicate efforts at reconciliation. The most serious consideration involves postinvasion planning. By most accounts, senior policymakers in the Bush administration were surprised by the failure of the Iraqi people to rise up spontaneously in support of the U.S.-led invasion.[96] These same policymakers incorrectly concluded that the models of occupation established by the United States for dealing with postwar Germany and Japan would apply equally well to Iraq. On some levels, this case of "strategic surprise" relates to the failure of the United States to defend Iraqis who revolted after the 1991 Persian Gulf War against the Saddam Hussein regime and who were subsequently suppressed in a brutal fashion – in some cases with chemical weapons. The failure to plan adequately for the insurgency,[97] coupled with the fact that thousands more in the U.S. military have died in Iraq since May 1, 2003, the declared end of major combat, raises significant questions about whether the United States has attained victory in this war.[98]

There are other considerations that influence how to evaluate any victory in Operation Iraqi Freedom. For example, during the initial invasion, U.S. military forces suffered extraordinarily limited casualties: In a campaign that lasted six weeks and involved more than two hundred thousand troops, by the end of major combat operations, U.S. losses of 139 deaths are historically small. However, any evaluation must take into account the casualties suffered by U.S. military forces in the three-plus years since May 2003: An additional twenty-three hundred U.S. troops had been killed in postwar operations in Iraq by June 2006, which means that almost seventeen times as many Americans have died since the invasion than in Operation Iraqi Freedom itself.[99] As the number of U.S. casualties in the postinvasion phase continues to increase, a legitimate question is how long the United States can sustain these losses without diminishing the scale of victory that might be achieved.

It is equally likely that whether the United States achieved grand strategic victory will be judged in light of the incorrect conclusion that Iraq possessed weapons of mass destruction. In the aftermath of the 9/11 attacks, there was consensus within the White House, Congress, and much of the intelligence community that Iraq possessed WMD and that the United States could not accept the risks that Iraq might make these weapons available to terrorist organizations. Though no evidence of WMD programs was discovered in the postinvasion inspections, the fact remains that American policymakers believed after 9/11 that the mere possibility justified military action. By most accounts, there was a disparity between what was reported in the National Intelligence Estimates, which are designed to summarize the consensus view in the intelligence community, and the subsequent analysis and investigation, which has failed to find any evidence of Iraqi WMD programs. The fact that no such programs were discovered has undermined a key reason given for the war, and this is bound to affect perceptions of victory.[100]

It is worth noting that, although the extraordinary level of dependence of the United States and its allies on oil supplies from the Middle East suggested that Iraq's influence in the region threatened the global economy, there is no evidence that the war was fought directly or even primarily over oil. In comparison with other considerations, oil exerted far less influence on the deliberations of the Bush administration than purported weapons of mass destruction or Iraqi support for terrorism.[101] In the plans for war, the United States and its coalition partners disavowed any intention of retaining Iraqi territory or seizing its oil wealth. Instead, their declared plan was to ensure that Iraq's oil contributed to the global oil supply and – once the petroleum industry was restored to production – that its revenues were used to finance the costs of rebuilding Iraq.[102]

Finally, there are also several technological considerations that influence the interpretation of victory in Iraq.[103] First, the Iraq War is the truly first precision war in modern times. As noted earlier, military planners were able to use unprecedented numbers of precision-guided munitions – some 65 percent of the total used during the invasion. Moreover, Predator unmanned aerial vehicles were used extensively for surveillance and targeting purposes, and Hellfire antitank missiles were launched from MQ-1 Predators to destroy improvised explosive devices (IEDs) and attack insurgent positions.[104] The second is that U.S. military commanders were able to take advantage of an extraordinary degree of transparency of events on the battlefield by using advanced command and control systems, satellites, and Internet and Web-based systems. The intention was partly to reduce the presence of forces in the region, since the presence of American forces in Saudi Arabia after the first Persian Gulf War arguably contributed to the development of al-Qaeda and its hostility toward the West. Third, military commanders were able to conduct the war at a rapid pace largely because of the close integration between air and ground operations. Despite the remarkable technological capabilities that were brought to bear by U.S. military forces, it remains difficult to judge the precise relationship between the use of ground forces and strikes with air power.[105] In the end, however, judgments about victory are only partly determined by technology.

OBSERVATIONS

The U.S. policy toward victory in Iraq evolved over the span of several years. Early in the process of making decisions about the costs and benefits of conducting an invasion of Iraq,[106] senior policymakers in the Bush administration actively debated what would need to be accomplished to achieve victory and how we should interpret whatever victory emerged. From the beginning of these deliberations in late 2001 and throughout 2002, President Bush was discussing the "strategic implications to a regime change in Iraq."[107] His decision to use military force against Iraq was designed to bring about the "end of the current regime – nothing short of that" (230). The tone of Bush's rhetoric was evident from his remark that "one year from now we will be toasting victory" (260). The strategic purpose of the invasion was expressed by Vice President Cheney, who defined the president's goals as "democracy in

Iraq and trying to transform the region." At a final briefing from his military commanders at the start of hostilities, Bush encouragingly said, "Let's win it" (379). But what did he mean by winning, and how should we interpret his language and the guidance given to policymakers and military officials?

In the debate among the principal policymakers prior to the war, Secretary of State Colin Powell raised the question of how we should define success in this war (150), while Cheney and his advisor Scooter Libby emphasized in their discussions with policymakers the "importance of winning decisively" (402). The critical challenge for the Bush administration, as described by Woodward in *Plan of Attack*, was to be certain that "there would be no ambiguity about victory" (402) if Iraq was defeated militarily.[108] The broad framework for victory was established by President Bush within the first week of the war with two clear decisions. The first was his statement in a meeting of the National Security Council that "Only one thing matters: winning"; the second was his guidance that the "big picture" is not "a matter of timetable [but] it's a matter of victory" (405–6).

More detail about the nature of the Bush administration's construct for victory emerged after the war. Nearly three years after the invasion of Iraq, in a speech on February 1, 2006, President Bush defined his "plans for victory in Iraq," which are based on three conditions. The first is that whenever the United States puts its military forces "in harm's way we got to go in with victory in mind." But what does that victory involve? Specifically, Bush said, "[T]he victory is for Iraq to be a democracy that can sustain itself and govern itself and defend itself, a country which will be an ally in the war on terror, a country which will deny safe haven to the al-Qaeda, and a country which will serve as a powerful example of liberty and freedom in a part of the world that is desperate for liberty and freedom."[109]

The second condition for victory focuses on reform of the Iraqi economy, which as Bush said is designed "to make sure their economy is able to function as good as possible so that people see the benefits of democracy." The third condition relates to the question, "[H]ow long will we be in Iraq?" As to the matter of timetables and withdrawals, Bush said that it is "a mistake to have a definite timetable for withdrawal" because the insurgency will react. For Bush, the only option in this war is "victory in Iraq"; but when that occurs and how it will be determined will depend in large measure on the judgments of U.S. military commanders. As he noted, "now it's up to the commanders on the ground to help us achieve that victory."[110]

A review of the language used by Bush both before and after the war to describe the "path to victory" demonstrates that the U.S. strategy was consistent with what is described in this study as grand strategic victory. Although the final outcome will remain unknown for some time as Iraqis work out the details of new political, economic, and social arrangements, the explicit intent

of U.S. policymakers was to use military force to alter the fundamental political and economic foundations of Iraqi society and simultaneously to reorient
Iraq's foreign policy. What remains unknown at this writing is whether signs
that Iraq will continue along a trajectory that accords such a U.S. victory. It
is equally uncertain how whatever results will be interpreted, given the wide
array of forces that continue to shape events in Iraq. As was noted in Chapter 1, this is the central problem with victory: We do not have a clear idea as
to what these purposeful words actually mean in concrete reality, and therefore we need a systematic framework for translating words into policies.

Though it is clearly still too early to make a definitive judgment, a tentative
interpretation is that Operation Iraqi Freedom may produce a grand strategic
victory for the United States, based on the framework for a pretheory of victory outlined in Chapter 4.

First, as discussed previously, although President Bush did not specifically
use the term "grand strategic victory," he implied that as a goal when he said
at the start of hostilities, "this will not be a campaign of half measures."[111]
Six months later he declared in incontrovertible terms that the U.S. "will do
what is necessary, we will spend what is necessary, to achieve this essential victory in the war on terror," including rebuilding Iraq as a bastion of freedom.[112]
A reasonable interpretation is that administration officials decided to wage the
war on a scale commensurate with grand strategic victory. The Bush administration chose to destroy the Saddam Hussein regime, disarm Baghdad militarily, eliminate its ability to support terrorism, and promote the development
for the first time in decades of a democratically elected government in Iraq.
Senior administration officials argued that regime change would lead eventually to a free, stable, and prosperous society in Iraq.[113] As President Bush
declared on the deck of the aircraft carrier USS *Abraham Lincoln* on May 1,
2003, "The tyrant has fallen, and Iraq is free."[114]

The second observation about victory is that the war against Saddam Hussein's regime produced the foundation for a comprehensive change in the status quo in Iraq, although it is still too early to tell whether that change is likely
to last. The campaign did lead to the collapse of the Baath regime and the
destruction of the Iraqi military; but the insurgency that soon developed challenges the argument that the war produced a comprehensive change in the
status quo. As one observer noted, the war was a "stunning military victory
[but] the aftermath soon became a continuum of violence and uncertainty."[115]
Still, there is a nascent democratic government and a possibility that Iraq might
contribute to peace and stability in the Middle East. The U.S. exit strategy is
to help the Iraqis organize, train, and equip their reconstituted military while
reducing the extent to which U.S. forces provide security.[116]

One significant change in the status quo is the capture of Saddam Hussein, whose trial is ongoing as of this writing.[117] With its decision to topple Saddam, the Bush administration demonstrated once again that it was willing to destroy regimes perceived as supporting terrorism. However, as long as observers debate whether it was necessary to invade Iraq to prevent it from becoming a sanctuary for al-Qaeda or other terrorist organizations, and in the absence of credible evidence that Iraq actively supported such organizations that threatened the United States, the Bush administration's actions will be enshrined in controversy – one that contributes to doubts as to whether victory was attained.[118]

The third observation about victory concerns the extent of American mobilization for the war against Iraq. In contrast to the smaller-scale preparations for Operation Enduring Freedom against the Taliban in Afghanistan, the United States engaged in a lengthy mobilization of the military and the defense industry for the Iraq War, which was initially estimated to cost several hundred billion dollars.[119] With a relatively large contingent of more than two hundred thousand military personnel[120] – a force less than half the size of that used a twelve years earlier in the Persian Gulf War – the United States combined air and land campaigns to destroy the Iraqi regime and end major combat operations in six weeks. Total forces in the region number more than two hundred thousand, including troops from coalition partners. In terms of public support, throughout the invasion, two-thirds or more of Americans polled believed that the decision to invade Iraq was the right one.[121] According to one poll, a majority continued to believe so through early October 2004, though another has the scales tipping the other way in February of that year, then remaining fairly even through September.[122] Since then, there has been a statistical dead heat on the issue of rightness, according to the one poll, but a clear majority holding that the war was not worth fighting in the other.[123]

The fourth observation that raises the greatest uncertainties about victory is the nature and extent of U.S. postconflict obligations in Iraq. The Bush administration declared that Washington was obliged to ensure that Iraq evolved into a democratic and stable society. Before the war, senior political and military officials had been engaged in postwar planning for the occupation of Iraq and rebuilding its political system and economy. Bush's aforementioned National Security Presidential Directive included in its strategy "to demonstrate that the United States is prepared to play a sustained role in the reconstruction of a post-Saddam Iraq."[124] On December 28, 2002, in a teleconferenced meeting that included the president and Secretary Rumsfeld, General Franks listed the establishment of a postwar provisional government as one of twelve critical conditions that would determine whether the war would be adjudged a success.[125] The analysis that led to these conclusions was presented to the president in early March 2003 by Undersecretary of Defense Douglas Feith,[126] who briefed the National Security Council on a plan for the war in a paper entitled "U.S. and Coalition Objectives." The strategy outlined was to maintain Iraq's territorial integrity, move toward democratic institutions, rebuild Iraq with support from the international community, and do so with popular support from the Iraqi people, so as to indicate that this was a legitimate undertaking in the eyes of the Iraqis.[127] In the "Phase Four Stability Operations," the objective was to develop a comprehensive plan for establishing democratic institutions and rebuilding the infrastructure in Iraq. In that plan, the State Department was to be responsible for promoting the "creation of a broad-based, credible provisional government" (62).[128] Moreover, the process of rebuilding the government was to begin with a "Baghdad conference" (342) to name interim leaders for establishing a new democratic government.

In terms of rebuilding Iraq's political system, the plan called (among other things) for a Governing Council, elected city councils and mayors, free political parties, and free elections. It was understood that a corollary to rebuilding Iraqi society successfully was establishing the rule of law.[129] This strategy for reconstructing Iraq's political institutions also involved specific plans for dealing with individuals who worked in Iraq's military or intelligence organizations or in the Iraqi Foreign Ministry. High-ranking officials in the Bush administration estimated that roughly twenty-five thousand senior government and Baath Party personnel would have to be removed before the Iraqi government could be successfully remade (339). Some of these institutions, such as the Foreign Ministry, were to be "purged" (342–3); others, like the intelligence services and the military, were to be "dismantled" (343) and reorganized. (The remnants of the dismantled Army, who had withdrawn into the countryside, undefeated in battle, unfortunately provided a recruitment base for the insurgency that quickly began – and included Baath Party officials, many of whom are Sunni, in its ranks.)[130] With regard to the economy, the U.S. strategy was to emphasize privatizing Iraq's state-owned firms, modernizing its stock exchange, and reforming its central bank and tax code.[131]

In practice, the process of rebuilding the government and economy of Iraq was determined by three conditions. One was the invasion's military campaign, designed explicitly by U.S. policymakers to limit damage to the Iraqi economy and minimize civilian deaths.[132] The second was that the Office of Reconstruction and Humanitarian Assistance (ORHA), created by presidential directive on January 20, 2003 (NSPD 24), was established under the aegis of the Department of Defense.[133] According to ORHA's mandate, the United States was committed to helping Iraq rebuild its society on the basis of a democracy. In the months leading up to the invasion, ORHA staff focused on how the critical oil, water, food, electrical, and medical-care components of the Iraqi economy would be rebuilt, using Iraqi officials as much as possible to staff this process. The third was the overall cost of reconstruction plans: Initially budgeted at $21 billion, these were designed to deal not only with the direct effects of war but also with the widespread neglect of the Iraqi infrastructure that had lately occurred under Saddam Hussein's rule.[134] Ultimately, the pace of these reconstruction plans would be slowed considerably by the economic damage inflicted by the Iraqi insurgency, which was actively resisting the U.S. occupation.[135]

VICTORY DESTABILIZED

The removal of Saddam Hussein and his regime and the move toward democracy of Iraq represent a watershed moment in Middle East politics. Whether the forces of democratization take hold in Iraq[136] will influence judgments about a U.S. victory, as will the length and violence of the postinvasion occupation[137] and the timing and conditions of the U.S. withdrawal.[138] Paramount in any evaluation of the potential for victory is the success of the bloody insurgency waged by former Baath Party officials, ex-military officers, regional jihadists, local Islamic militants (Sunni and Shia), and criminal gangs, that kills hundreds of Iraqi civilians weekly.[139]

Despite initial indications that the United States achieved a significant victory in Iraq, there is a sense that something has gone wrong with the war.[140] The most evident counterindication of victory has been the insurgency, whose objective is simply to make the costs of occupation greater than the United States will accept. On the very day of President Bush's triumphant announcement aboard the USS *Abraham Lincoln*, seven U.S. soldiers were wounded in Falluja by the initial insurgent attack. How can the United States achieve grand strategic victory in the face of this backlash?[141]

As noted in the Conclusion to Chapter 10, a war waged against nonstate actors raises problems for grand strategic victory, in that victory seems incomplete by comparison to victory against another state. In this sense, the nature of a victory against the insurgency in Iraq is more difficult to categorize. A related problem is whether to measure grand strategic victory in Iraq in terms of regime change and the eventual successful rebuilding of its society and economy. Since GSV is defined in part as the ability to impose regime change, it is unclear what other metric would suffice. While we could describe victory in Iraq on the basis of classic measures of defeat, such as territory lost or gained, defeating the opponent's military forces, or destroying its economy and infrastructure, these measures would be inadequate here because this war is being waged on ideological grounds. In wars that are animated by ideology, there seems to be no other viable measure for victory than changing the regime of the opponent in order to destroy at the source the hostility that can lead to state support of terrorism. And this involves a long-term commitment.

Although the Iraqi people are slowly building the basis for a democratic government, they and U.S. occupation forces face considerable difficulties on a daily basis. For now, much depends on how the earlier "de-Baathification" of the Iraqi administration and military plays out, and whether the nascent Iraqi government is able in the long term to establish stability by co-opting and incorporating the various factions, including Baathist Sunnis, that have supported the insurgency.[142] It would be premature to conclude that governmental reform in Iraq is failing: The successful elections in January 2005, selection of a government in April, and the approval of the constitution that October are indicators of ongoing success. By most accounts, the government of Iraq is also making steady progress in drawing the Sunni population into the political process: Having largely boycotted the January 2005 elections, Sunni voters made a strong showing in those of December.[143]

A final factor that would influence judgments about victory is whether the Iraq War ends up contributing to transnational terrorism in the long run. Could Iraq become the new center of terrorist activity in the Middle East?[144] Both Iran and Syria have allowed, and perhaps encouraged, foreign terrorists to enter Iraq to support the insurgency; this contributes to instability and raises the specter of civil war. Though perhaps the risk is low if sufficient U.S. military forces remain, Iraq slipping into chaos and civil war would destroy whatever victory the United States achieved – and, more important, represent a calamity for the Middle East.[145]

12 Military Power and Victory

For hundreds of years of military history, and certainly since the mid-nineteenth century, the formula for victory has been to use overwhelming firepower, technologically advanced weapons, and economic production to overcome and defeat the enemy decisively. In the case of the American "way of war," the objective was to use these economic and technological foundations to achieve victory while minimizing the cost in lives and societal destruction.[1] The emphasis in U.S. defense planning on minimizing the loss of life was expressed by the authors of the *Strategic Bombing Survey*, who asked in 1946 whether "the weakness of the United States as a democracy would make it impossible for her to continue all-out offensive action." This question was raised during the debate about whether the United States could withstand the human losses that would occur from an invasion of the Japanese home islands.[2] This logic of war was altered during the cold war, when U.S. policies shifted toward the principle that the United States would do better to develop, deploy, and sustain smaller and more technologically advanced forces than to compete directly with the Soviet Union in numbers of weapons or troops.[3]

Beyond the scale of war or the extent of preparations for war, the unifying theme in analyses of the nature of war is how and to what extent military forces contribute to the state's ability to achieve victory. In debates about winning a war, the classic twentieth-century assumption among policymakers and defense planners is that the various forms of military power – ground, maritime, and air – all contribute in different but equal ways to the state's ability to achieve victory. What is missing from this well-practiced argument, however, is an analysis of whether all forms of military power are equally effective in producing victory. As this study is concerned with understanding the meaning of victory, policymakers and defense planners must comprehend that some types of military force are more appropriate to the kinds of victory that the nation is likely to attain. This chapter considers how the various instruments of military power contribute in different and distinct ways to victory, evaluates the advantages and disadvantages associated with each instrument in terms of a pretheory of victory, and examines whether the type of military force is relevant to the level of victory achieved by the state.[4] It concludes with the argument that there is a relationship between the level of victory that the state seeks and the right military instrument for those conditions and, furthermore, that some types of military force are better suited to achieving different levels of victory than others.

The discussions below provide idealized models of how each type of force contributes to victory. In practice, however, they would not serve as isolated forms of military power: No modern state would use ground forces without also using air power and maritime forces.

EVALUATING GROUND FORCES

Ground forces dominate how states define victory, conduct war, and survive when the war is over. Their fundamental purpose is threefold: to defeat and destroy armies;[5] to create a presence and conquer territory as part of a strategy of establishing a significant degree of control over a state;[6] and to defeat another state in the comprehensive sense of the term.[7] A dominant theme in historical analyses of war and strategy is the argument that ground forces, whether involving cavalry on horses or mechanized tank armies, are central to the state's ability to achieve victory. Rome used its armies to besiege and then completely destroy Carthage, slaughtering or enslaving its entire population to emerge victorious in the Third Punic War.[8] Nearly twenty-two centuries later, the United States employed more than two hundred thousand ground forces to defeat Iraq's military forces, remove Saddam Hussein's regime, and occupy the country (see Chapter 11). Ground forces dominate how states define victory, conduct war, and survive when the war is over.

Ground forces are the principal and most invasive instrument by which a state can coerce, defeat, destroy, or occupy another state. The strategy behind their use is to find and destroy opposing forces, seize and establish control over the enemy's territory, and regulate its society. Simply put, ground forces enable the state to occupy another's territory and impose its will on the defeated society: to "achieve dominance on the ground."[9] More important, the decision to use ground forces – notably, in the case of the United States, the Army and Marine Corps – demonstrates to the targeted nation, as well as to the international community, that the state seeks a comprehensive victory, one at least on the scale of political–military victory if not a grand strategic one.[10] Thus the use of ground forces signals the state's political and military commitment to defeat its opponent, to achieve victory in a significant sense, rather than merely to punish or deter it.

For instance, the Clinton administration's intervention in Bosnia was preceded by several years of domestic debate in which observers argued that the turbulent history of hostility among ethnic, national, and religious factions raised significant doubts about the ability of the United States to achieve victory – unless it was willing to put its ground forces between the warring factions in the Bosnian civil war.[11] It was the decision to intervene with ground forces, the most decisive form of military power, that indicated the administration's commitment to success on a significant level.[12]

The essential argument in this chapter is that the concept of victory is ultimately based on a state's ability to destroy the military foundations of another state and capture its territory.[13] The state is most likely to attain grand strategic victory when it uses ground forces to conquer territory, destroy the military, defeat the state, and establish control with what is known as "boots on the ground."[14] This section discusses the advantages and disadvantages of ground forces in terms of their ability to contribute to victory.

Advantages of Ground Forces

The first and most significant advantage of ground forces is that they are inherently flexible: They can provide drinking water and other humanitarian assistance, destroy tanks and armored vehicles, and/or kill enemy soldiers. The use of ground forces permits the state to accomplish an extraordinarily wide range of military and political effects, ranging from defeating the enemy's military forces to destroying its government and occupying the society.[15]

Since the state can employ ground forces for a wide range of purposes, including full-scale combat, it can not only coerce and defeat adversaries but also create order in societies that are torn apart by civil strife or war. These objectives are particularly significant at a time when the United States is waging a war against terrorist organizations that seek to disrupt states by wreaking havoc on their population, economy, and government. As of this writing (2006), there are significant U.S. ground forces deployed around the world, including in Europe, the Middle East, and Asia – most notably thirteen thousand troops in Afghanistan a hundred and sixty thousand in Iraq.[16] In Iraq, U.S. Army and Marine Corps forces have been actively engaged in the rebuilding of infrastructure, weakened by decades of neglect and destroyed during the 2003 war. This includes electrical power, water supplies, oil production, transportation, communications, health care, housing, and more.[17]

The second advantage to ground forces is their operational endurance.[18] U.S. ground forces are designed based on an extensive infrastructure of logistics, transportation, communications, intelligence, and command and control so as to be able to operate in a theater for months if not years.[19] Their operational endurance is the product of significant investments over the decades in such underpinnings. Given its economic, industrial, and technological resources, the U.S. military can maintain overseas operations with ground forces almost indefinitely[20] – with the caveat that public support for such deployments will not last forever.[21]

We should note that the technological "revolution in military affairs" of the past couple decades has significantly increased the precision and lethality of ground forces.[22] A new generation of advanced weapons and platforms has been developed with vastly greater killing power.[23] These advances have drawn upon advances in information and computer technologies, notably the U.S. military's global positioning system (GPS) of satellites for navigation, government reconnaissance satellites, and commercially owned satellites that provide imagery and communications both in peace and war.[24] This emphasis on technology was noted in the U.S. Army's *Field Manual 100-5: Operations,* which held that leaders must be able to "assimilate thousands of bits of information to visualize the battlefield, assess the situation, and direct the military action required to achieve victory."[25] Such new technologies and their application have significant implications for how ground forces conduct military operations and on the nature of the victory that can be attained.

Ground forces, then, provide the most effective military instrument when the state seeks to achieve significant results against the traditional components of an enemy state. They are a more permanent form of military power (compared, e.g., to air and maritime forces), and their deployment in significant numbers both demonstrates that significant interests are at stake and enables the state to achieve necessary political–military or grand strategic victories.

Disadvantages of Ground Forces

As just noted, ground forces are an effective and enduring instrument against an enemy state, such as the Taliban in Afghanistan and Saddam Hussein in Iraq. Their effectiveness is less certain – though their use may still be deemed necessary – against nonstate actors, such as the terrorist groups operating along the Afghan–Pakistani border region or the insurgent groups in post-invasion Iraq (see Chapters 10 and 11). Moreover, there are several distinct disadvantages associated with the use of ground forces.

To begin with, the decision to use ground forces dramatically increases the risks that the state will find itself entangled in a war and unable to withdraw until victory has clearly been achieved. As we've seen, victory can be particularly elusive and difficult to define in the case of civil wars or insurgencies. During the debate in the 1990s about how best to intervene against ethnic cleansing and genocide in Bosnia, many observers warned that U.S. ground forces, once deployed, would be extraordinarily difficult to withdraw until the civil war ended and peace was restored.[26] Thus the Clinton administration, in deciding to use ground forces in Bosnia, publicly committed itself to achieving victory by ending the campaign of genocide. However, as senior officials learned from the cases of Somalia, Haiti, and Bosnia, ground forces are such a highly visible tool of foreign policy that policymakers cannot extract them until victory is achieved: If a successful conclusion to the war is prevented, by an insurgency or otherwise, policymakers will pay a heavy political price. In 1993 the Clinton administration withdrew American forces after images of the deaths of eighteen soldiers in Mogadishu, Somalia, were transmitted globally. That withdrawal was interpreted as a defeat, raising doubts as to the credibility of U.S. foreign policy that lasted throughout the Clinton presidency.[27] Even after a military victory, however, postconflict activities conducted by U.S ground forces can increase the risk that the American military will be drawn willy-nilly into nation building, a course initially criticized by senior officials in the administration of George W. Bush. As then–National Security Advisor Condoleezza Rice observed in 2001, "There's nothing wrong with nation building, but not when it's done by the American military."[28] As we've already seen, though, the Bush administration has had to engage in extensive postconflict obligations in Afghanistan and Iraq, including the fostering of democratic political systems – clearly, a form of nation building. The debate in 2004–6 about the wisdom of maintaining ground forces in Iraq was based in part on fears that the United States might find itself entangled in Iraqi politics for years (see Chapter 11).[29]

A second disadvantage is that the deployment of ground forces increases the risk that the United States will lose control of the political agenda that first produced the decision to intervene. Once large numbers of troops are on the ground, there are practical difficulties for policymakers of how to declare that it is time to withdraw those forces without implying that the initial strategy for intervention was wrong or misguided. There are several prominent instances when the United States expanded its initial strategy and objectives for intervention in what has come to be known as "mission creep."[30] An important case (though predating the expression) is the Vietnam War, in which Johnson administration policymakers dramatically increased the number of ground forces despite growing suspicions among some senior government officials that there was no realistic strategy for victory.[31] This war remains an important historical example of the state's failure to maintain control over intervention. Although this problem is not confined to ground forces alone, their highly visible nature increases the odds that the state will then pursue victory on a significant scale simply because it took the step of deploying them.

A third disadvantage is that ground forces are so unwieldy that they cannot be used in a timely or responsive fashion. Realistically, it can take many months before the state can deploy militarily significant numbers of ground forces to a theater.[32] To fight the Persian Gulf War, it took the United States from August 1990 to January 1991 to move half a million troops from Europe and elsewhere into Saudi Arabia, and it did so without any active military opposition from Iraqi forces.[33] Furthermore, it required months to build up U.S. forces for the March 2003 invasion of Iraq. The important exceptions to this rule are the 101st Airborne Division, 82nd Airborne Division, and special operations forces, whose logistical infrastructure is designed so that they can move to a theater rapidly: Deploying the 101st or 82nd Airborne Division is estimated to take several weeks, as these are relatively light and numerically smaller forces. Still, the fact that ground forces are large, ponderous, and complex organizations whose movement to a theater requires weeks if not months has driven the U.S. Army to develop new doctrines and technologies, under the rubric of *transformation,* to increase its ability to move significant numbers of forces from the United States to a theater of operations within days or weeks.[34] The U.S. Army chief of staff, General Peter Schoomaker, said that the goal is to transform the Army so that it can deploy and be ready to fight more quickly and with increased lethality in combat.[35] If successful, this development will improve the ability of ground forces to contribute to victory, particularly victories on the lower end of the scale, and thus to become a more flexible instrument of power.

One reason for the slow deployment and readying of ground forces is that they are dependent on a significant system of logistics to sustain military operations.[36] To counter this dependency, the United States pre-positions supplies and equipment in Europe, Southwest Asia, and the Pacific, creating the capability to conduct military operations without having to wait months for logistical support to be in place. Though this pre-positioning reduces the time it takes for ground forces to prepare for sustained combat, it does not change the fact that they are not highly mobile. This problem was understood in the late 1970s by the Carter administration, which created rapid deployment forces early in the 1980s to remedy this operational shortcoming in U.S. military capabilities.[37] For example, since the stability of the Persian Gulf is critical to U.S. interests, it was necessary to be able to respond quickly and decisively in that region. As President Carter said in his State of the Union address, "an attempt by any outside force to gain control of the Persian Gulf region will be regarded as an assault on the vital interests of the United States. And such an assault will be repelled by any means necessary, including military force."[38]

In conclusion, the use of ground forces does not necessarily lead to a significant victory. Their use can entangle the state in operations that policymakers view as political disasters, interventions from which it is difficult to withdraw much less emerge as victors, as is clear from Vietnam and Somalia. Moreover, modern conventional ground forces are so large, unwieldy, and dependent on logistics that they cannot respond as quickly in a crisis as other forms of military power, principally that of air power.

Ground Forces and Victory

Only ground forces can establish the physical presence needed for the occupation and reorganization of a society, which are prerequisites for grand strategic victory. Thus if the state is committed to imposing military defeat, occupation, and reform of its enemy's political, economic, and legal institutions, the use of ground forces is imperative, and will signal that commitment to neighboring nations as well as to the international community.[39]

The decision to use ground forces does not, however, mean that grand strategic victory is inevitable, or even being pursued. With ground forces, the state might destroy an enemy's governmental, military, and economic institutions, and thereby achieve a political–military victory, yet not resolve the underlying problems that had been caused by (say) civil war, insurgency, or the destructive behavior of a state's leadership. Resolving those is in fact one of the goals of grand strategic victory. One important example of this distinction is Iraq: The political–military victory attained in the 1991 Persian Gulf War, when President George H. W. Bush decided not to invade Iraq, left Saddam Hussein's authoritarian government intact. This "incomplete victory" would contribute to the reasons for intervention against Iraq in 2003 (see Chapters 8 and 11). Policymakers should understand that ground forces neither guarantee grand strategic victory nor even preclude failure (see the section on Vietnam in Chapter 5).

When the strategy is to shatter a society's military, governmental, and economic foundations and institutions on a devastating scale, no instrument of national power is more effective than ground forces in defeating the enemy's military forces and establishing control over the society. The dilemma is that even when policymakers do not consciously adopt a policy based on grand strategic victory – say, if all they mean to achieve is a political–military one – their decision to use ground forces tends to propel the state toward pursuing a victory at the higher level. This is because, having used ground forces to destroy the constituent parts of a society, America may well have to choose between occupying and rebuilding the defeated enemy state or allowing it to disintegrate into chaos and humanitarian disasters. The United States proposed the Marshall Plan in 1947 because the Truman administration confronted precisely these choices.[40] Thus although the Bush administration argued in 2001 that it is not legitimate or practical for the United States to use the military for nation building, it is for this precise purpose that ground forces are presently being used in Iraq.

The inescapable conclusion is that when policymakers rely on ground forces they must understand that, in practice, the costs of victory may exceed the benefits. The pursuit of grand strategic victory, whether by initial design or as a result of unfolding events, puts considerable pressure on policymakers and the public to make an unambiguous declaration of their commitment to victory once ground forces are deployed. Policymakers must understand that the decision to use ground forces signals to the international community that they have declared the state's commitment to victory – and to a grand strategic one if need be. Moreover, as noted in the case of Bosnia (see Chapter 9), it is difficult to build and sustain public support for the use of ground forces when policymakers do not precisely define the level of victory that they seek.

In sum, there is no better instrument than ground forces for attaining grand strategic or political–military victory: They allow the state to destroy most forms of military power, occupy the defeated state, and rebuild its institutions of governance. However, the costs of using ground forces can be considerable given the political risk of being stuck in a quagmire, a situation that compromises the state's ability either to win or to withdraw without undermining its credibility. The implication is that the use of ground forces can lead as easily to grand strategic or political–military victory as to outright failures.

EVALUATING MARITIME FORCES

The purpose of maritime forces – the inclusive term for naval ships (carrier strike groups, surface and submarine forces), aircraft and missiles, and ground forces that conduct amphibious landings – is to project power and intervene militarily on a global basis against targets on the land, sea, and air.[41] For the U.S. military, the term "maritime" is used quite broadly to include the "oceans, seas, bays, estuaries, islands, coastal areas, and the airspace above these, including the littorals."[42] For some observers, maritime forces are essentially designed to fight at the tactical level of war.[43] Whereas ground forces are designed to conquer and control territory, the function of maritime forces is to permit the state to project military power, which is known by defense planners as the "presence" that contributes to "blunting an initial attack and, ultimately, assuring victory."[44] *Presence* is an instrument of influence that translates into the ability to respond initially with military power. As defined in the 1994 *National Security Strategy*, "presence demonstrates our commitment to allies and friends, underwrites regional stability, gains U.S. familiarity with overseas operating environments, promotes combined training among the forces of friendly countries, and provides timely initial response capabilities."[45] In support of this strategy, "[n]aval forces have five fundamental and enduring roles: projection of power from sea to land, sea control and maritime supremacy, strategic deterrence, strategic sealift, and forward naval presence."[46] The relevant concept here is *forward presence,* "robust and credible naval expeditionary forces present forward where our vital interests – economic, political, and military – are most concentrated."[47] Forward presence is the basis of *maritime power projection,* "a broad spectrum of offensive military operations to destroy enemy forces or logistic support or to prevent enemy forces from approaching within enemy weapons' range of friendly forces," including "amphibious assault operations, attack of targets ashore, or support of sea control operations."[48] When reduced to the simplest terms, the raison d'être of maritime forces is to project "power and influence in peace, crisis, and conflict" on a global scale.[49]

For various reasons, maritime forces are the instrument most compatible with maintaining a global military presence. In historical and practical terms, maritime power projection has been integral to how states extend their military reach where and when they choose.[50] Not surprisingly, maritime forces often provide the weapon of choice when American policymakers want to project power while minimizing the risk of the state being drawn into a crisis or an eventual entanglement.

This section discusses the advantages and disadvantages associated with maritime power, using the concepts of geographic mobility, responsiveness, operational endurance, commitment, and flexibility. The central argument of this analysis is that maritime forces are uniquely well suited to the attainment of political–military victories.

Advantages of Maritime Forces

The first and foremost advantage of maritime forces is that they are geographically mobile, which translates as their ability to maneuver in an unrestricted fashion.[51] In the lexicon of defense planners, *mobility* is the "quality or capability of military forces which permits them to move from place to place while retaining the ability to fulfill their primary mission."[52] It is their intrinsic mobility that explains why maritime forces historically have played a dominant role in military strategy and operations.[53] In ancient Greece, the Athenians used their maritime capabilities to dominate the Aegean, and later the Carthaginians used it to control the Mediterranean.[54] For thousands of years, maritime power has contributed to the ability of the state to apply military power on a broad geographic scale. Nowadays, since "[s]eventy-five percent of the Earth's population and a similar proportion of national capitals and major commercial centers lie in the littorals," maritime power is likely to be involved when the state uses military power.[55]

In contemporary terms, the ability of maritime forces to maneuver is central to the military strategy of projecting power globally to defend the state's interests. As stated in the U.S. Navy's "Sea Power 21" – a "new operational construct . . . to meet the requirements of this new century" – maritime forces have the relative freedom of movement to allow the state to project its sovereignty and "conduct combat operations anywhere, anytime without having to first ask permission."[56] The Navy's "Vision . . . Presence . . . Power," published in 2000, notes that maritime forces are "relatively unconstrained by legal, political, and military restrictions that may be imposed on ground-based forces by host nations."[57] This conclusion was evident in the "bottom-up review" conducted in 1993 by the Clinton administration, in which Secretary of Defense Les Aspin noted that "maritime forces have the operational mobility and political flexibility to reposition to potential trouble spots by unilateral U.S. decision."[58] Relieved of the political restrictions on action that are often imposed by states and international organizations – constraints tied to a need for basing rights on the sovereign territory of other states – maritime forces provide an unparalleled degree of mobility and freedom of movement for modern military forces.[59] They are of significant value when policymakers seek a flexible instrument of military power.

The second advantage of maritime forces, one closely related to mobility, is the concept of *responsiveness,* which means that these forces can be moved whenever and wherever it is necessary. As expressed in the U.S. Navy's "Forward . . . From the Sea," the intent is for the state to be "capable of responding quickly and successfully."[60] By their nature, maritime forces are inherently capable of reacting quickly in a crisis, perhaps in hours or days depending on the circumstances. For example, during the Taiwan Straits crisis in March 1996, when China conducted test firings of short-range ballistic missiles toward Taiwan, the United States deployed two carrier battle groups to persuade China that taking military action in the direction of Taiwan might lead to war with the United States.[61] An additional benefit related to their responsiveness is that maritime forces can be maintained on alert for weeks or months while sustaining a credible capability if it is necessary for the state to respond immediately during a crisis. For example, the United States kept an aircraft carrier on patrol in the Persian Gulf in 1998 to deter Iraq from violating United Nations resolutions. The fact that maritime forces allow the state to maintain military forces on alert almost indefinitely explains in part why the United States has developed a military strategy that calls for deploying significant naval forces in the Atlantic, Pacific, Mediterranean, and Persian Gulf regions.

A third benefit of maritime power is its *operational endurance* (though this is not as high as that of ground forces).[62] Maritime forces can conduct operations in an area as long as they have access to supplies of fuel, ammunition, spare parts, and other consumables. Thus the endurance of maritime forces is a direct function of providing the materials that are required for sustaining peacetime and combat operations.[63] Although maritime forces do not have the operational endurance of ground forces, the trade-off is that they can provide the first and sometimes the only immediate military power that is available to the state. They thus provide important capabilities for policymakers when the state needs to move military forces, use military power quickly and decisively, and sustain those forces almost indefinitely.

The fourth advantage is that maritime forces allow the state to make an overt statement of its intention and *commitment* to defend its interests in the region. As noted in the 1993 *Report on the Bottom-Up Review*, "The peacetime overseas presence of our forces is the single most visible demonstration of our commitment to defend U.S. and allied interests."[64] To be sure, the use of maritime forces involves relatively low risks because these forces can be shifted easily from one region to another as circumstances demand. Politically, it is useful for policymakers to be able to have a naval task force operating along the coast of a potential adversary as part of a strategy for demonstrating that the state is prepared to use military force.[65] In terms of avoiding events that could lead to political and military entanglements, maritime forces are an ideal instrument for threatening adversaries without the need to deploy ground forces to the region. Defense planners understand this relationship. As noted in "Vision . . . Presence . . . Power," maritime forces "can sustain combat-credible presence in forward areas without the need for expensive and inherently vulnerable land-based regional support infrastructures."[66] Because the movement of maritime forces does not involve basing rights, their use minimizes the risk that the presence of military forces at over seas bases might exacerbate local hostilities.

Fifth, maritime forces permit the state to exercise greater *flexibility* when it is necessary to initiate hostile acts and influence the direction and pace of events in a crisis. In part, this is because the use of maritime forces, as already mentioned, is partially insulated from the political considerations that govern the use of ground forces and air power. One measure of flexibility used by defense planners is *flexible response:* The "capability of military forces for effective reaction to any enemy threat or attack with actions appropriate and adaptable to the circumstances existing."[67] The combination of surface and submarine vessels, amphibious ground forces, and naval air power within maritime forces gives policymakers a very effective and flexibly responsive military instrument. For example, in the military operations conducted against Afghanistan during late 2001–early 2002, aircraft flying from carriers operating in the Indian Ocean conducted the vast majority of the air attacks that were launched against the Taliban and al-Qaeda.[68]

In summary, the overall advantage to maritime forces is that they are an inherently flexible instrument of national power.[69] At a time when the United States must manage the dangers associated with terrorism, nuclear weapons, various regional problems, and the prospect of crises that could escalate into large-scale wars, including a confrontation with Iran or North Korea, policymakers must have flexible instruments of military power at their immediate disposal. Maritime forces provide an effective instrument that lets the state respond flexibly, rapidly, and easily to threats to the state's interests, all while minimizing the political burdens associated with military intervention. Another way to put this is that maritime forces contribute significantly to the state's ability to achieve victory in a wide range of circumstances and geographic regions.

Disadvantages to Maritime Forces

There are, however, several disadvantages to maritime forces that affect their contribution to victory. The first is that they are profoundly expensive to build, operate, and maintain. Currently, the United States possesses twelve carriers, with estimates that each new nuclear-powered aircraft carrier costs roughly $2.5 billion to develop and $7.5 billion to procure, for a total cost of $10 billion apiece. Moreover, since these costs will likely only increase, many studies have suggested that aircraft carriers are a prohibitively expensive way for the state to project military power.[70] For similar reasons, it costs roughly $2 billion to procure a nuclear-powered submarine, another prominent and expensive maritime platform. The estimated cost for building the thirty submarines authorized in the fiscal year 2006 defense budget was $80.4 billion.[71]

The billions of dollars that the United States will invest in building and operating fleets of aircraft carriers and submarines represent an enormous expenditure of the nation's resources. Known as *high-value assets*, carriers and submarines represent a significant investment in military systems. Carriers also have a highly visible presence when deployed in a region – more so than submarines, given the differences in how these weapon systems operate – and represent significant concentrations of people (with crews of five thousand) and military power. Thus, although it would be extremely difficult for most states to destroy an American aircraft carrier, the destruction of one in a war would have significant political and military implications.[72]

A second disadvantage of maritime forces is that the technological superiority enjoyed by the United States for decades could be threatened by the proliferation of advanced military technologies and weapons.[73] In view of the proliferation of nuclear, biological, and chemical weapons, ballistic and cruise missiles, and advanced guidance and sensor technologies, many third-tier states and nonstate actors, such as terrorist organizations, will possess modern weapons that once belonged only to the most advanced states. While these potential adversaries cannot prevent the United States from winning a conventional war or achieving its fundamental military objectives, they might be able to use these advanced military capabilities to put U.S. maritime forces at risk. For example, the Exocet missile, which is easily available on the international arms market, can inflict devastating damage on modern ships. On May 17, 1987, an Iraqi fighter aircraft launched two French-built Exocets at the American destroyer USS *Stark* in the Persian Gulf. The damage from these antiship missiles – "one of which detonated near berthing spaces, resulting in heavy loss of life" – was substantial, though the ship remained afloat and was able to return home for repairs under its own power.[74] Another example of this technological risk was the sale by Russia in the late 1990s of several diesel submarines and advanced versions of antiship cruise missiles to Iran; these pose a threat to U.S. naval forces in the Persian Gulf.[75]

Since maritime forces include many significant targets, including aircraft carriers and Aegis-class guided missile cruisers, their destruction can produce significant losses of equipment and personnel – and possibly create the perception that the state's willingness to achieve victory is being undermined. The proliferation of advanced military technologies could thus effectively weaken the state's ability actually to achieve victory. Also, because maritime forces can no longer operate with the degree of impunity that they once possessed, intervention with maritime forces may now involve significant political risks.

A third disadvantage is that the effective use of maritime forces depends on maintaining a significant logistics infrastructure on a theater and global basis.[76] The nature of the logistics system means that it may be weeks or months before the forces and supplies needed to conduct a significant maritime operation can be repositioned to the theater. For example, if the United States wanted to move a carrier battle group and its support structure from the Atlantic to the Pacific theater of operations – say, to the Taiwan Straits – a reasonable estimate is that it would require at least a month. To move one aircraft carrier from the East Coast to the Indian Ocean would require at least two weeks.[77] Although, as a general principle, U.S. military forces are deployed so that significant numbers of units are available in each geographic region, the time required to move aircraft carriers from one theater of operations to another lessens the overall flexibility of maritime forces, at least for planning purposes. In the case of aircraft carriers, the counterargument to their diminished flexibility is the fact that more than one carrier can be kept on station in a critical area. Thus, even if it takes a month to redeploy a carrier, another carrier is almost always available. However, if the carrier on station is damaged in battle – say, as a result of a Silkworm antiship cruise missile strike that damages the catapult and puts a temporary halt to flight operations – the time needed to shift a carrier between theaters becomes a significant impediment to conducting military operations in a flexible and responsive fashion.

Finally, while maritime forces enable the state to cover the geographic areas where the vast majority of the world's population resides, not all potential military threats lie within range. In fact, there are strategically significant areas that cannot be reached by maritime forces, including vast tracts in Russia and China for traditional military operations, or in the states of central Africa (e.g., the Democratic Republic of the Congo), where it might be necessary to support humanitarian operations.

The principal conclusions from this analysis, then, are that maritime forces are constrained by basic economic, technological, and operational factors, require significant resources, depend heavily on logistics, are threatened by the proliferation of advanced technologies, and cannot be moved as quickly as one might wish. These limitations, though similar to those that affect the other forms of military power, do affect the nature and scale of the victory that the state can hope to attain.

Maritime Forces and Victory[78]

What maritime forces do well, and perhaps better than the other forms of military power, is to project decisive military power throughout multiple geographic regions.[79] These forces have an unparalleled ability to project power across the oceans quickly and decisively, intervening with a range of military instruments on a global scale and with an element of surprise that strengthens their military value to the state. They thus serve to persuade adversaries that they are permanently vulnerable to military attack.

Also, since victory in war was, for thousands of years, determined by the ability of seafaring states to impose their will across broad geographic regions through their navies,[80] the notion of using maritime forces to *signal intent* became a prominent part of diplomacy. This was especially pronounced during the cold war, when the United States relied heavily on its maritime forces to provide a global presence in its ideological and geopolitical struggle with the Soviet Union. At a time when both U.S. and Soviet actions were tightly constrained by fears that a crisis could escalate into nuclear war, maritime forces provided a critical tool for demonstrating the state's presence and thereby deterring military action against oneself and one's allies. In view of the tensions and hostilities that marked the cold war, these forces evolved into a convenient tool used by American policymakers to demonstrate their political resolve, indicate a willingness to take action, and warn that the state's vital interests were being threatened. In this era the aircraft carrier battle group was a preferred military instrument that, diverted from routine patrols throughout the globe, could signal that the United States was prepared to take military action. To cite but one example, President Nixon ordered an aircraft carrier, the USS *Enterprise,* to proceed into the Bay of Bengal in support of Pakistan during the Indo-Pakistani War of 1971.[81] However, some observers argue that signaling with maritime forces is actually an indecisive and "time wasting" response, one that suggests the state wants to create the appearance of being resolute but is unwilling to take truly decisive action.[82]

Finally, because maritime forces offer an unparalleled tool for projecting ground, sea, and air power globally, they are highly relevant to how policymakers think about victory. These flexible, mobile, and responsive forces can destroy military targets with great efficiency while maintaining a military presence over large areas. However, maritime forces cannot as a practical matter destroy a society and occupy it unless the war also involves, in joint operations, the use of ground forces.[83] That is to say, the state can use maritime forces to achieve political–military victory but not grand strategic victory; the latter belongs distinctively to ground forces and, on a lesser scale, to air power. There is no doubt that maritime forces can bomb an enemy state into submission, but the mere destruction of targets is not equivalent to grand strategic victory.[84] Maritime forces are simply not well-suited to changing an enemy state's underlying political and economic institutions.

That there are significant limits on the ability of the state to use maritime forces to achieve victory was demonstrated in Afghanistan. During Operation Enduring Freedom, aircraft operating from U.S. carriers in the Indian Ocean conducted thousands of attacks against military targets throughout the country and destroyed many military facilities. Yet although maritime forces played an important role in applying military power quickly and decisively against targets that could be bombed from the air, the United States could not have achieved what could arguably be called a grand strategic victory until ground forces were deployed. Nor is there any evidence that American policymakers believed they could defeat the Taliban with maritime power alone.[85]

One lesson is that policymakers should be hesitant to define concepts for grand strategic victory that depend primarily on the use of maritime forces. (There is, of course, the possibility that a political–military victory achieved by maritime forces could be converted into a grand strategic victory through the subsequent deployment of ground forces.) Maritime forces *are* well-suited, however, to achieving conditions consistent with victories that are less than grand strategic in significance.

EVALUATING AIR POWER

Throughout the twentieth century and as recently in the 1990s, scholars and policymakers have debated whether air power is a radically different form of military power that makes a unique contribution to victory. The argument that the state can achieve political–military victories in war by destroying military forces and societies on a broad scale via air power is highly controversial within the defense establishment.[86] The principal argument in the present discussion is that air power, though having unique qualities that can make decisive contributions to victory, is unlikely to win wars by itself to the exclusion of other instruments of military power.

Advantages of Air Power

Since its beginnings in the early years of the twentieth century, when strategists in Europe and the United States had hoped it would transform the nature of warfare, air power has rapidly evolved to the point where it is arguably the most flexible and technologically prominent instrument of military might available to the state.[87] Some definitional clarity is in order here, as "air power" encompasses far more than combat aircraft.[88] Defined more precisely, it also includes missiles and ballistic missiles with ranges from tens to thousands of kilometers.[89] According to one military aviation specialist, air power is also "inseparable from battle space information and intelligence" and includes all of the military services.[90] To understand how it contributes to victory, this discussion examines the concepts of speed, range, mobility, flexibility, and precision as those shape air power as an instrument of war.[91]

The first and perhaps most important advantage of air power is that aircraft and missiles operate at vastly higher speeds than their ground or maritime counterparts (with the obvious exception of aircraft or missiles launched from the latter). In modern terms, *speed* is highly beneficial because increasing the pace or "tempo" of war allows the state to achieve its political and military objectives more quickly and decisively. By virtue of their speed and range, aircraft and missiles can "strike targets across the entire depth and breadth of an enemy country," achieving a level of surprise that can significantly affect the outcome of a war.[92] Thus, a principal advantage of air power is that it can operate at higher speeds, covering greater distances relatively quickly and thereby changing the fundamental pace and nature of warfare. Its proponents argue that it is air power's speed that produces victory on radically shorter time scales. States once required months if not years or decades to achieve victory in military campaigns and wars; but the development of modern air power makes possible (though not certain) the decisive defeat of an enemy state within days or weeks. The 1991 Persian Gulf War is often cited as the first example of such newfound effectiveness.[93] In the first hours of that war, the speed of air power allowed U.S. forces to destroy command and control systems and thus to prevent the Iraqi leadership from directing and coordinating its military establishment.[94] When used in this way, air power can severely limit the ability of enemy military forces to know what is happening and to respond to military attacks effectively. Thus whereas armies and naval forces may take months to conduct operations that lead to victory, air power can be applied almost immediately and with comparative decisiveness; in fact, air strikes can occur so quickly that they overwhelm the adversary's ability to respond.

The second advantage of air power, and related to speed, is the *range* of aircraft and missiles. In the nuclear era, air power provided the instrument for delivering nuclear weapons anywhere on the globe with little or no warning – thereby altering the nature of warfare and a state's willingness to engage. As a result of technological developments during the latter half of the twentieth century, a bomber, modified transport aircraft, or missile can now be targeted against virtually any spot on the earth, hit that target within eighteen hours (far fewer in the case of missiles), and destroy it with one weapon on the first shot. In practical terms, the range of air power provides unrestricted access to military or urban targets anywhere on the planet, uniquely circumventing natural obstructions, such as oceans, mountains, and other physical boundaries, with relatively few constraints. It can even reach targets that were buried deep to avoid detection and to increase their ability to withstand destruction.[95]

The range of air power extends to its defensive applications. Whereas the United States once positioned troops on the ground or fleets along coasts to create a military presence and warn of attack, technological advances have made it possible to create military presence not only with manned aircraft but with unmanned aerial vehicles, drones, and cruise missiles. For example, the modern counterpart of the nineteenth-century naval fleet cruising along the coast to warn of enemy attack is an Airborne Warning and Control System (AWACS) aircraft. Deployed at a base or flying well beyond the reach of hostile air forces, this can warn of attack by aircraft, covering large areas.

A third advantage of air power, and related to range, is its *mobility*. Air power can be stationed at great distances from potential crises yet still allow the state to apply military power quickly and accurately. In the military operations against Kosovo in March 1999, B-2 bombers launched from Whiteman Air Force Base in Missouri conducted bombing runs against targets in Kosovo.[96] The mobility of air power means that it can be used without necessarily deploying forces to the theater of operations, and that any forces deployed can be withdrawn once the objective has been achieved – thereby minimizing the risk that the state will become entangled in a quagmire. Part of its importance as an instrument of national policy, then, is that air power permits quick and decisive action while minimizing the duration of the state's involvement.[97]

A fourth advantage is its inherent *flexibility*. Air power has been described as a "highly versatile coercive instrument . . . [that can] attack strategic, operational, and tactical targets . . . resupply friendly forces and provide essential intelligence."[98] In theory as well as practice, air power can be used "across the entire spectrum of crises and conflicts."[99] In addition, it can be used for a diverse array of military missions, delivering anything from pallets of food or propaganda leaflets to laser-guided bombs or nuclear weapons. The use of air power in Operation Enduring Freedom against the Taliban in Afghanistan (see Chapter 10) is a recent example of the wide range of purposes to which air power can be employed in war.

A fifth advantage of (modern) air power is that it is capable of applying military force with great *precision*. Although all services of the U.S. military have made significant progress in developing weapons that can be delivered with greater accuracy, including computer-controlled naval gunfire as well as radar- and GPS-guided artillery, air power was the first prominent beneficiary of this technological revolution. Recent military operations, notably the Persian Gulf War in 1991, Operation Enduring Freedom in Afghanistan in 2001–2, and Operation Iraqi Freedom against Iraq in 2003, refined the concept of precision to the point where one guided missile launched from an aircraft or ship has a greater than 90 percent chance of destroying the intended target. This technological development is all the more remarkable when one considers the ineffectiveness of air power during World War II, when the ability to destroy even one industrial facility with air power, according to the *Strategic Bombing Survey,* "was a formidable enterprise demanding continuous attacks to effect complete results."[100] To illustrate the problem of strategic targeting in World War II, the ability to "destroy a target the size of a small house" required "a force of 4,500 heavy bombers carrying a total of nine thousand tons of bombs."[101] Thus what now requires one modern precision weapon dropped from an aircraft would have required dropping literally thousands of weapons during World War II. To use the example of one attack conducted in that war, on August 17, 1943, two hundred B-17 bombers dropped three thousand bombs against a concentration of ball-bearing factories in Schweinfurt, Germany.[102]

Note that the development of highly accurate munitions increases the demand for accurate and timely intelligence. To be effective, military planners require highly detailed intelligence so that they know specifically what to target, when to hit it, and the precise effect sought – all of which is known in the language of modern defense planning as "effects based warfare."[103] Though there is little doubt about the ability to destroy a target once it has been identified and selected, the more significant problem is to know not only which building to hit but through which window the bomb should pass and at what precise moment to achieve the desired effect as efficiently as possible.

These advantages of air power combine to grant the state two noteworthy capabilities. One is the ability to identify and destroy the adversary's military forces, bases, and supply centers with little or no warning – and once the enemy's air defense system is destroyed, no practical warning is possible. Furthermore, leadership facilities as well as command and control systems are also vulnerable to attack with air power. When its military leadership is destroyed or at least significantly weakened by air power, the enemy is likely to suffer defeat.[104] What remains uncertain, however, is whether this military capability will translate into grand strategic victory or some lesser form of victory (see the upcoming section "Air Power and Victory").

Air power also allows the state to destroy an enemy's economic capacity.[105] In the U.S. air campaign in World War II, air power was used successfully to attack the economic infrastructure that sustained the German and Japanese war machines.[106] The fundamental objective of the air war, as outlined at the 1943 Casablanca Conference, was to "fatally weaken[]" Germany's "capacity for armed resistance."[107] The air attacks conducted in World War II against German cities and industries were part of a strategic plan whose objective was to prepare for an invasion by ground forces.[108] And as part of efforts to destroy the society, these air attacks sought to weaken the morale of the enemy population. As the authors of the *Strategic Bombing Survey* concluded, the "morale of the German people deteriorated under aerial attack" to the point where the "people lost faith in the prospect of victory" (11–12). Although this conclusion about the effects of air attacks on the morale of an enemy population is subject to active debate and interpretation, what is not debated is that air power can be designed to focus the effects of war on a society through a deliberate strategy of inflicting unprecedented levels of devastation. By virtue of its speed, range, mobility, and flexibility – as well as lethality – air power represents a modern form of warfare that can overwhelm enemy forces and destroy the economic foundations of modern societies. It is uncertain, however, whether this capability suffices to allow the state to achieve grand strategic victory.

Finally, it is worth noting the conclusions derived by the authors of the *Strategic Bombing Survey* about the "results achieved by Allied air power" (37). These include the following: "even a first class military power . . . cannot live long under full-scale and free exploitation of air weapons over the heart of its territory" (37–8). It continued by noting that the "Germans were unable to prevent the decline and eventual collapse of their economy" (38). More important, "whatever the target system, no indispensable industry was permanently put out of commission by a single attack. Persistent re-attack was necessary" (39). In the contemporary debate about air power it is prudent to keep these experiences in mind when discussing its contributions to victory.

Disadvantages of Air Power

There are several disadvantages associated with the use of air power.[109] The first is its sporadic nature. Although air power can hit targets in a rapid and decisive fashion, it does not possess the considerable operational endurance associated with the comparatively slow ground and maritime forces, each with its large supporting infrastructure. In effect, air power has always been suited to "hit and run" operations whose objective is to disarm the enemy's military forces in preparation for ground operations if the state seeks to achieve victory on a significant scale. This was the model of war that was applied in the 1991 Persian Gulf War, when a five-and-a-half-week air campaign preceded a ground campaign that lasted four days. However, this relationship between air power and ground forces was altered in the 2003 war against Iraq, when air strikes initiated the war – because U.S. officials believed (incorrectly, as it turned out) that they had located Saddam Hussein and his leadership cadre.[110]

A second disadvantage to air power, one related to its sporadic nature, is its dependence on a network of bases that are extremely vulnerable to attack from aircraft, ballistic missiles, or cruise missiles.[111] To maximize the military effectiveness of its air power, the state must have access to bases in the region where military operations will occur. In the case of the Persian Gulf War, U.S. military commanders argued that the United States could not effectively defend Saudi Arabia against Iraqi ground forces unless significant numbers of forces were based in that country.[112] This dependence on marshaling significant military forces is a limit to the earlier argument that air power can be deployed anywhere at a moment's notice. In truth, air power does not translate into the robust and mobile military capability described earlier unless and until it is deployed on a large scale at bases in the theater of operations.

To increase the endurance of its air power, the United States invested billions of dollars over decades to build a global infrastructure of bases, runways, and logistics for resupplying such forces. During the cold war America established agreements with many nations to create bases on their sovereign territory in order to increase U.S. capabilities for projecting power. The dilemma for defense planners is that air power cannot create a significant degree of endurance unless it has global presence, which in turn is likely to generate hostility based on perceptions of U.S. hegemonic ambitions. The presence of U.S. military personnel and bases in the Saudi homeland not only fueled anti-Americanism among some Saudi citizens but also is believed by many observers to have influenced the rise of al-Qaeda.[113]

A further disadvantage is that the use of hosted military bases significantly limits the inherent flexibility of air power because the state must consider the demands and interests of the host nation. For instance, in January 2003 Turkey – a coalition landing and staging ground in the 1991 Persian Gulf War – declared that it was concerned about allowing the United States to use its bases for a new invasion of Iraq because it feared hostile reactions throughout the Arab world.[114] Turkey eventually rejected the use of its bases by U.S. and British forces but allowed coalition overflights in its airspace.[115] This limited the freedom of the United States to use military force and arguably influenced the effectiveness of the campaign.

A third disadvantage is that air power is an extremely expensive instrument of military power.[116] The increasing cost of advanced military technologies, including air power, requires such significant investments that it constrains the ability of the state to maintain technologically superior forces.[117] The enormous costs associated with research, development, and production for technologically advanced weapons limit the ability even of the wealthiest nations to afford such weapon systems. For fiscal year 2006, the total spent by the United States on the procurement of all military programs by the three services was $78 billion; of that, $25 billion or 32 percent was spent on aircraft programs.[118] The United States spends vastly more on defense than the other major powers, highlighting the fact that advanced weapons programs, including those for aircraft, are inordinately expensive; for instance, the unit cost of a B-2 stealth bomber is $1.157 billion.[119] Though the Bush administration has increased defense spending significantly, there are doubts whether the nation can afford to buy as many of the extraordinarily expensive aircraft as the military says it needs.[120] A related problem is that the value of air power is limited when U.S. policymakers debate whether it is prudent to put such highly expensive weapons at risk. For example, policymakers will certainly debate whether to put the Airborne Laser–carrying aircraft at risk in lesser contingencies, since each aircraft will be worth several billion dollars.[121]

The final disadvantage to air power relates to doubts about its relevance in lesser contingencies. For most of the twentieth century, the value of air power was obvious. For example, the United States used air power during World War II to achieve grand strategic victories against Germany and Japan; more recently, air power played a decisive role in the political–military victory in Iraq in 1991 and in the tentative GSVs in the invasions of Afghanistan (2001–2) and Iraq (2003). What is uncertain, however, is whether air power will be decisive in lesser contingencies that include humanitarian and peacekeeping operations. Meanwhile, the focus in U.S. defense planning has shifted decisively toward more significant military operations, which include not only Afghanistan and Iraq but the possibility of a war on the Korean Peninsula.

Air Power and Victory[122]

It is fair to say that air power has been a critical instrument of warfare since its development in the twentieth century and will remain so for the foreseeable future.[123] A dramatic example is World War II, in which 35 percent of all U.S. war production was devoted to air power, which played a significant role in virtually all aspects of the war in the European theater, including sea control, ground battles, reconnaissance, supply, and attacks against German industrial facilities.[124] It also helped turn the tide against Japan, beginning with the Battle of the Coral Sea in 1942.[125] The destruction wreaked by air power was devastating. In Germany only, some 3.6 million homes were destroyed, three hundred thousand civilians were killed and nearly eight hundred thousand wounded, and virtually all cities were reduced to ruins.[126]

More recently, the Persian Gulf War in 1991 and the air campaign against Kosovo in 1999 persuaded the current generation of U.S. policymakers and the public that air power is a unique, selective, and war-winning instrument.[127] Such experiences with air power during the twentieth century have clearly shaped the theory of victory in war and given American society an idealized notion of what air power can accomplish. However, a more complete analysis of the relationship between air power and victory raises several points worth noting, all leading to the same conclusion: The use of air power alone can be highly effective in terms of achieving the conditions necessary for, at best, political–military victory, by destroying the enemy's military and economic bases of power; however, it cannot by itself attain the grand strategic victory that is possible when ground forces occupy and rebuild the enemy state.

Even this moderate conclusion, though, is contentious for the proponents of air power. Since the early years of the twentieth century, air-power theorists, including such notables as Billy Mitchell and Giulio Douhet, have argued that air power is a decisive weapon that the state could use to attack the enemy's "vital centers" and thus achieve a strategic form of victory.[128] As Douhet reasoned, the ability of air power to destroy vital centers would lead to the collapse of the state.[129] Later theorists posited that "air power now possesses the wherewithal for neutralizing an enemy's military means . . . through the functional effects achievable by targeting his key vulnerabilities and taking away his capacity for organized military action."[130] The point remains, however, that air power by itself does not lead to victory on a strategic scale.

In fact, there is no evidence that the use of air power *by itself* has ever forced an enemy state to surrender, much less attained a grand strategic victory.[131] In the case of World War II, Germany's defeat occurred after Allied ground forces invaded that nation, destroyed its armies and society on a massive scale, and occupied its territory. The use of air power against Japan, notably the bombing campaign against its home islands – and especially the dropping of atomic bombs on Hiroshima and Nagasaki by B-29's early in August 1945 – led to Japan's formal surrender. The case of Japan is interesting because it did surrender before the Allies could conduct an invasion of the Japanese home islands.[132] However, Japanese forces had already been subjected to significant military attacks by U.S. ground and maritime forces in the Pacific theater of operations. Moreover, by the time of its surrender, Japan itself had weathered strategic bombardment for more than a year. Arguably, then, its surrender was precipitated not by attacks with conventional air power but by two massively destructive atomic blasts.[133] Nuclear weapons had such a decisive effect on the nature of war in subsequent decades that there are analytically legitimate questions about whether it is correct to treat atomic bombardment as equivalent with victory in wars waged with conventional weapons.[134]

In the case of the 1991 Persian Gulf War, the U.N. coalition used thousands of aircraft during a five-and-a-half-week-long bombing campaign against Iraq (see Chapter 8). Although Iraqi forces were compelled to leave Kuwait, their withdrawal and subsequent defeat occurred only after a force of half a million soldiers invaded Kuwait and threatened to invade Iraq.[135] For many observers, Iraq's defeat was hastened by the effective use of air power, but the point remains that it was only when the ground campaign began that Iraqi forces withdrew from Kuwait and Baghdad agreed to cease hostilities. Another case is the air campaign against Serbian forces in Kosovo in 1999 (see Chapter 9): Though the seventy-eight-day air campaign clearly was instrumental in persuading the Serbs, led by President Slobodan Milošević of the Federal Republic of Yugoslavia, to stop committing human rights abuses against ethnic Albanians living in that province, what ultimately led to to victory was NATO's threat that it would deploy ground forces against the Serbs.[136]

The problem with any theory of victory that elevates the influence of air power above that of maritime and ground forces is that policymakers might mistakenly conclude they can win wars by smashing societies from above. In 2002 Deputy Defense Secretary Paul Wolfowitz alluded to this line of reasoning, admitting that "some people in the Rumsfeld circle believe that 'air power is now so accurate that you don't need armies.'"[137] Yet, as we have seen, grand strategic victory is possible only when armies conquer territory or are believed to be imminently capable of doing so. Air power can contribute to victory by persuading the enemy that its political, economic, and military institutions will be destroyed, thereby weakening or destroying its will to continue fighting; but it cannot independently achieve the "strategic effects" of military action on the ground.[138]

In broad terms, air power is not sufficient to achieve grand strategic victory principally because it is unlikely to persuade a state to surrender. The more cogent argument is that using multiple forms of military power (i.e., joint military operations), even if one form is predominant, is consistent with theories of military power that reject the idea of victory as the product of singular explanations.[139] Even the most prominent proponents of air power did not argue that air power by itself would lead to victory.[140] In fact, in the first half of the twentieth century, theorists argued simply that air power would allow states to avoid costly land wars, such as those of the two world wars – which is quite another matter than winning, let alone a high-level victory.[141]

In conclusion, if victory is based on destroying military, governmental, and economic targets from a great distance, air power is better suited than other forms of military power and is unquestionably a decisive instrument for the state. By virtue of its ability to destroy military forces and societies, rather than to occupy them, air power helps create the precursor conditions for grand strategic victory but does not itself provide such a victory. In the vast majority of cases – and barring the special case of nuclear warheads – air power is at best an immensely important form of military power that leads to smaller-scale (e.g., political–military) victories. Still, any overarching conclusions as to the relationship between victory and air power will remain incomplete until we can evaluate the extent to which the expensive and highly specialized forms of air power contribute in the future to victory in lesser contingencies (i.e., humanitarian and peacekeeping operations).

CONCLUSION

The conflicts examined in the six case studies (Chapters 6–11) used varying combinations of the forms of military power. The military intervention in Libya and those in Bosnia and Kosovo were largely based on air power (with some maritime involvement in the first case and some ground forces in the latter two); these produced political–military victories. The operations in the remaining cases – Panama (a small-scale conflict), the Persian Gulf War, Afghanistan, and Iraq (larger-scale wars) – were conducted with the full range of air, ground, and maritime forces; the first two yielded political–military victories, the latter two (at least, arguably) grand strategic victories. Thus, although it might be assumed that political–military victories use less than the full complement of military power whereas grand strategic victories use all the above, this analysis suggests that there is no such strict correspondence. The relationship between the forms of military power used and the exact level of victory achieved is inconsistent. A political–military victory can be achieved in a mere twelve minutes with limited air strikes (Libya) or in six weeks with air, maritime, and ground forces (Persian Gulf War). The ability of the state to achieve victory is based less on the type(s) of military force used than on its broader objectives.

That said, there is *some* relationship between the types of military power used and the level of victory: As discussed in the preceding section, the state can achieve tactical or political–military victories without ground forces, but these are necessary to attaining grand strategic victory. There is also a correlation between using multiple forms of military power and achieving *higher* levels of victory. This is because the state gains flexibility when it mixes instruments of power in varying combinations: It can thereby choose the best military instrument(s) for the particular conditions faced and the level of victory sought.

Similar lines of inquiry can be applied to examine the relationship (if any) between the instrument(s) of military power used and the three other factors of the pretheoretical framework outlined in Chapter 4: change in status quo, mobilization for war, and postconflict obligations. Regarding changes in the status quo, the use of air power produced both limited (Libya, Persian Gulf War) and comprehensive (Panama, Bosnia and Kosovo, Afghanistan, and Iraq) changes in the prevailing conditions in the enemy society, and even globally. As we've also seen, the use of all forms of military power combined might produce either limited (Persian Gulf War) or comprehensive (Panama, Afghanistan, and Iraq) changes in the status quo. There is thus apparently no clear relationship between joint military operations and the extent of such changes.

As one would expect, the level of mobilization *is* related to the type(s) of military power used by the state: A heavy reliance on air power coincided with limited mobilization for war. The conflicts in Libya and the former Yugoslav regions of Bosnia and Kosovo involved little real mobilization. However, even in cases when all forms of military power were used, there were both limited (Panama) and extensive (Persian Gulf War, Afghanistan, Iraq) levels of mobilization. This makes sense, in that states confront greater and lesser conflicts.

Finally, the type(s) of military power used does not relate to the nature and extent of postconflict obligations. On the one hand, when the state relied primarily on air power, it produced both limited (Libya) and protracted (Bosnia) obligations for the victor. On the other, using all forms of military power led both to limited postconflict obligations (Panama, Persian Gulf War) and to protracted ones (Afghanistan, Iraq).

As noted earlier, the United States used varying combinations of military power to achieve some level of victory, either political–military or grand strategic, in all six of the conflicts examined in depth. It should by now be clear that this study is not attempting to provide a formulaic interpretation in which one form of military power is more likely to attain a specific level of victory. The danger with this "school solution" is that policymakers could be persuaded that certain forms of military power – in particular, air power – are more likely to lead to victory. The 1990s saw a debate in the defense establishment as to whether air power was uniquely suited to winning wars. Some argued that air power, when combined with precision weapons and an integrated command and control system that permits precision munitions to be used at a tactical level, represented a fundamentally new development in the nature of war and the state's ability to attain victory.[142] The corollary to this argument was that the state should rely primarily on air power to achieve victory when it must intervene – as it did in the Persian Gulf War in 1991 and the air campaign against Kosovo in 1999.

The one clear exception to the general noncorrespondence between type(s) of military force used and level of victory is the requirement of ground forces for grand strategic victory. Recently, ground forces have been used in innovative and nonconventional ways, with a reliance on a rapid pace of operations and the deployment of special operations forces for winning modern wars. The invasion of Iraq in 2003 (see Chapter 11) is an example of the ways in which modern ground forces can change the nature of war.[143]

Here are several concluding thoughts about where the various instruments of military power fit in a pretheory of victory. To begin with, air power is unique in terms of its capability to conduct deep strikes against enemy territory on a sustained and highly accurate basis. Maritime power has a unique ability to project military power and to establish and maintain a sporadic military presence. The value of air power is its ability to move people, material, and weapons relatively quickly; maritime forces can move larger amounts of material and weapons, albeit more slowly. The strength of both air and maritime power rests in part on their mobility and unrestricted access to military or urban targets, which in turn derives from the speed and range of aircraft or missiles. Ground forces, however, have a distinct ability to occupy territory and, if necessary, to destroy the fundamental political and economic institutions of a society – and to establish the basis for reorganizing them.

As we have seen in various wars and military operations, each instrument of military power by itself has the ability to contribute to victory. The principal framework for organizing the military services in the post–World War II era was established by the Key West agreement of April 21, 1948, which stipulated that each service was responsible for defeating its enemy counterpart and that the synergy among the three services would give the United States a powerful military instrument of its foreign policy.[144] What emerged from the Key West agreement was the principle that "it is the mission of the Air Force to dominate the sky, of the Navy to control the seas, and of the Army to defeat the enemy's ground forces."[145] The corollary expressed by the 1946 *U.S. Strategic Bombing Survey* was that "The role of air power cannot be considered separately . . . from the roles of ground and naval forces nor from the broad plans and strategy under which the war was conducted."[146] Even in the case of air power armed with nuclear weapons, the other forms of military power are not insignificant.[147]

The U.S. military continues to modernize itself technologically to be more relevant to the kinds of war that the state may confront. For example, the U.S. Marine Corps is designed to provide highly mobile forces for a range of operations, including those other than war.[148] At the same time, the U.S. Army has "lightened" many of its divisions so that it can move forces more quickly and thus conduct a wide array of operations, ranging from peacekeeping to full-scale war against a significant military power.[149] The U.S. Navy has expanded from a blue-water (deep ocean) force to include green- (littoral) and brown-water (river) capabilities, partially in response to the threat posed by the submarine and missile forces possessed by such smaller navies as Iran and China.[150] To mention one case, Iran's growing naval capabilities in the Persian Gulf, which are based on its purchases of Russian submarines, could inflict damage on U.S. maritime forces.[151] Finally, we are seeing a shift in the U.S. Air Force toward the use of air power in precise, selective attacks against elusive targets, and potentially in urban areas, in a timely fashion, all of which suggests that the Air Force is altering its approach to war.[152]

13 Conclusions

This chapter explores the implications of the argument that prior research has not provided a coherent and systematic framework for understanding what it means for the state to achieve victory. The discussion is divided into two sections: The first addresses the implications for scholarship – which general arguments it calls into question and which it reinforces, the second focuses on the implications for policy and the policy prescriptions that follow from this analysis. Some consideration in each of these sections is given to the implications suggested by this study for further research.

IMPLICATIONS FOR SCHOLARSHIP

A discussion of the implications of this research for scholarship begins with the argument that prior formulations of victory have been inadequate. At the risk of oversimplification, the framing argument in this study may be recapitulated as follows: We do not have a precise theory of victory that is evident from the writings of the prominent military strategists and theorists about the nature of strategy and war in the history of Western civilization. As discussed at length in Chapters 2 and 3, many have written extensively about victory, but the principal focus has been on the "how"; that is, what needs to be done in a mechanical sense to achieve victory. To complicate matters, despite the vast literature on strategy and war, we do not have any clearly defined theory, set of concepts, or language for victory. Although the problem of victory is of immense importance, the language used to describe victory consists largely of terms whose usage is imprecise.

How might we demonstrate that the previous assertion is correct? One way would be to ask the following question: By what standard definition or usage of victory could we array the principal theorists, whose writings span several thousand years of history? This question raises many methodological problems, but the foremost are that no one concept of victory is likely to provide sufficient explanatory power and that no such standard, whether based on strategic, operational, or tactical concepts, is available. The evidence for this statement is the extraordinary difficulty that surrounds efforts to array military strategists and theorists in terms of standard conceptions of victory. Their comments about victory are scattered among tactical, political–military, and grand strategic victories. Theorists routinely use the word "victory" to refer to the full range of outcomes that coincide *on some level* with what victory is generally assumed to mean. Take, for example, the case of Sūn Tzu, whose writings in *The Art of War* defined victory on the level of the outcome of tactical battles or campaigns, which correspond to tactical or even political–military victories. However, he also described victory in terms of the "disposition" of war – an elegant reference to victory in a strategic sense.

Given the slippery nature of the concept, Clausewitz's intent, according to John Keegan, was to formulate a "theory of victory that would ensure it [the Prussian army] victory in the future."[1] The same desire for certainty and repeatability holds for virtually all of the prominent historical strategists and theorists of war, who have understood correctly that victory is a complex, multivariate phenomenon for which singular definitions, much less formal unified theories, have been difficult to formulate. These are legitimate methodological difficulties: Scholars (and policymakers) need a more coherent framework for discussing the meaning of victory. It is not sufficient to write "victory" in the expectation that the literature provides answers or that others will know what it means.

This same fuzziness has attached to the U.S. experience with war, which often is described using the language of victory or defeat. There has been a wide array of outcomes of American wars (see Chapters 5–11), including some classifiable as "incomplete" or even defeats, but no earlier attempt at systematic categorization into a unified framework. Wars as disparate in scale, significance, cost, and outcome as World War II and the 1991 Persian Gulf War are described as victories. How can such an approach be adequate, much less justified, when the former represented a cardinal event in human history, whereas the latter was a prelude to the invasion, occupation, and democratization of Iraq in 2003? As a matter of record, scholars, policymakers, and publics use the term "victory" to describe what is generally known as success in war; but the "victories" enjoyed by the United States in these two examples have very little in common.

The central problem for scholars is to sharpen the language that governs what victory is and what it has come to mean for the current generation of policymakers, so that discussions of war can be conducted with much greater rigor and clarity. To do so, scholarly inquiry must deal with three fundamental points: (1) The current thinking about victory is inadequate; (2) a theory of victory is missing from the literature on strategy and war; and (3) contemporary theorists and strategists have failed to theorize about victory in systematic and analytic terms. Let us begin with the first point.

A fundamental argument of this study is that current thinking about victory is inadequate despite the considerable (yet imprecise) emphasis it receives in the literature on strategy and war. One explanation has to do with the nature and practice of strategy, in whose literature and language the meaning of victory is enveloped. According to the logic of strategy, victory is the outcome when the state uses the mechanism of war or armed intervention to accomplish its policies. Strategy is the path toward the outcome that is based on what the state seeks to accomplish, and victory is expressed in terms of that outcome. Given the implicit connection between the state's strategy for war and victory, it is easy to elide the ends (victory) and means (strategy); yet it is essential to emphasize the quality of victory as a distinct and separable issue if discussions of victory are to be put on a sounder basis.

In this debate it is useful to consider what earlier theorists, such as Clausewitz, Sun Tzu, and others, have contributed to the analysis of victory. As a general proposition, they advanced the idea that victory is a state or condition that exists when the state has achieved its objectives. This idea has worked quite well in a nonspecific sense because there is a broad consensus that the term "victory" is a synonym for varying degrees of success in war. Thus "victory," despite its failure to define precisely the range of outcomes possible in war and how these relate to what the state seeks to achieve, had the virtue of unanimity as a useful descriptor of success whenever the state used military force.

It is then easy to see why there has been no theory of victory or coherent theoretical framework that governs the use of the term in recent centuries. "Victory" became a convenient shorthand for generations of strategists, scholars, and policymakers who learned that victory is used universally for positive outcomes in war. It did not matter whether military intervention produced a strategic or tactical success because "victory" symbolized for all concerned that the state had achieved an outcome generally in accord with its desires.

Why, then, the failure to develop one? Given the challenges associated with developing a more precise framework for using the term "victory," it seems that generations of scholars have allowed the status quo to prevail – that as a synonym for success in war, victory would remain the preferred choice for describing military accomplishments by the state positively. We might even continue to use "victory" to mean many things to many audiences: States certainly have been able to fight and win wars without a more systematic language of victory. On the basis of precedent alone, and as demonstrated by the large number of wars that have been fought and won throughout history, we can argue that the traditional approach to victory has worked quite well and has yielded a number of defeats. It is difficult to dismiss this argument,

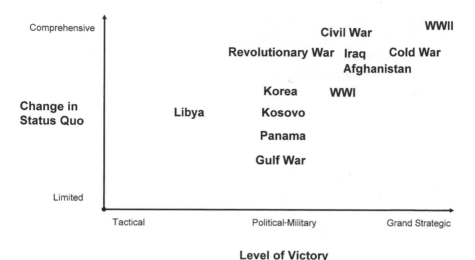

Figure 2. Change in status quo versus level of victory.

given the weight imposed even by the number of U.S. military successes in history. The problem with this argument, however, is the fact that modern societies appear entrapped in divisive political debates about whether and when the state should intervene with military force. In the end, such debates often hinge directly and unavoidably on the questions in which this study is grounded: What does victory mean, and what are its costs, benefits, and risks for the state?

The pretheory of victory presented in Chapter 4 is a preliminary framework for discussion among scholars and policymakers of the factors that apparently are related to what we mean by the term "victory." Although not definitive or final in any analytical or methodological sense, it highlights factors that may prove helpful in examining the concept of victory. To advance beyond these general observations, one approach is to use a two-dimensional matrix to describe the unique conditions associated with specific levels of victory and their relationship to either change in status quo, mobilization, or postwar obligations (see Figures 2–4).

Of the twelve American wars included, four (World War II, cold war, Iraq, and Afghanistan) can be classified as grand strategic victories, with the caveat that judgments as to the level of victory attained in Afghanistan and Iraq must remain tentative for now. Of these four wars, the first two occurred in the twentieth century and the latter two in the first decade of the twenty-first. The remaining nine wars, from the eighteenth through twentieth centuries, can be classified as political–military victories: the Revolutionary War, War of 1812, Civil War, World War I, Korean War, Libyan raid (*nearly* a PMV), invasion of Panama, Persian Gulf War, and the interventions in Bosnia and Kosovo.

Figure 3. Scale of mobilization versus level of victory.

Interestingly, political–military victories that are distributed historically likely constitute the norm for victory; grand strategic victories are rarer and more significant events, and in this sample have a contemporary focus.

What general observations can be drawn about the relationship between the level of victory and the other organizing principles for victory? Figure 2 outlines the relationship between the level of victory and the extent to which the war altered the status quo for the state or states involved in war. The change in status quo tends to be clustered in the middle to high end of the scale, which ranges from limited to comprehensive. As one would expect, every war produced some degree of change. The extent of the relationship generally appears to be linear: Increasing the level of victory tends to produce correspondingly greater changes in the status quo. For example, grand strategic victories tend to produce more comprehensive changes in the status quo, as seen for World War II and the cold war. Indeed, radical change in the status quo is one criterion of grand strategic victory. However, the extent of the change in the status quo can vary even within the same level of victory. For example, the Korean War, invasion of Panama, Persian Gulf War, and the interventions in Bosnia and Kosovo are all classified as political–military victories yet produced different degrees of change.

Figure 3 portrays the general relationship between the level of victory and the state's level of mobilization for war. For this sample of wars, the level of mobilization tends to be clustered in the middle to low end of the scale, which ranges from limited to extensive. Somewhat predictably, the level of victory is *not* related linearly to the extent of mobilization: Increasing the level of victory does not necessarily lead to greater levels of mobilization. For instance,

Iraq and Afghanistan, which may yet prove to be grand strategic victories, both involved mobilization on rather limited scales. World War II is the classic example of the state achieving grand strategic victory after extensively mobilizing its economy and society for war. In the cold war, however, the United States achieved grand strategic victory with relatively low to moderate levels of mobilization. The range of wars that produced political–military victories (Revolutionary War, 1812, Civil War, WWI, Korea, Libya [*near*-PMV], Panama, Persian Gulf War, and Bosnia–Kosovo) illustrates that the level of victory may not be necessarily related to the level of mobilization.

Figure 4 addresses the relationship between level of victory and postconflict obligations. For the wars in this sample, postconflict obligations tend to be clustered in the low end to middle of the scale, which ranges from limited to comprehensive. A general observation is that grand strategic victory may be related to comprehensive postwar obligations, with the contemporary exception of the cold war, in which the victor's obligations were quite limited. World War II, however, produced significant postconflict obligations, as did Iraq and Afghanistan. The group of wars that yielded political–military victories shows that such cases do not necessarily create comparable postconflict obligations. There is thus some question whether the state can achieve grand strategic victories in active conflicts without creating significant postconflict obligations.

The use of these matrices to analyze the relationships that may exist among the organizing principles for a pretheory of victory should be tempered by several caveats. One is that these scales are notional or illustrative, and how these organizing principles are measured strongly depends on the scales that are chosen. It is left to subsequent research to produce more precise scales for measuring how various concepts relate to victory. Another is that this model does not describe *causal* relationships among these victory-related concepts or imply that there is causal relationship between level of victory and the rest.

In analytic terms, what should this framework or pretheory of victory tell us, and what are its strengths and weaknesses? To begin with, a pretheory should provide the basis on which scholars (and/or policymakers) carefully identify and observe relationships in a field of inquiry and subsequently formulate organizing principles and testable theories. Its most important function is to help develop new ideas for formulating definitions about political phenomena and classifying procedures and methods of research and analysis.[2] In a formal sense, the decision to build this analysis on pretheorizing is based on Rosenau's recognition that theory by itself cannot flourish "until the materials of the field are processed – i.e., rendered comparable – through the use of pre-theories."[3] What this means is that a pretheory is designed to help the scholar decide which variables contribute to a particular behavior or outcome and assess their relative potencies without necessarily *specifying* their relative weights or influ-

Figure 4. Postconflict obligations versus level of victory.

ences. Preliminarily, a pretheory of victory should thus tell us which variables are more important in explaining what victory is and what it means for the state; at a later stage of inquiry it should improve our understanding of the relative importance (i.e., weight) of each variable.

Such a pretheory also ought to help orient the analyst to examine the salient factors that account for victory, as well as outline the requirements for building a pretheory. Pretheorizing ought to encourage "more systematic observation and more incisive comprehension" of the factors that may constitute the foundations of victory, and permit the formation of "consensuses" on the nature of empirical or political reality. Over time, predicted Rosenau, unrealistic pretheories will be weeded out, most likely leaving not one but "several major schools of thought."[4] This is consistent with the broader purpose of a pretheory of victory: to help scholars and policymakers relate political and military actions to victory in a systematic and orderly fashion, thus moving the discourse beyond the imprecise or inchoate.

A pretheory is particularly well suited for dealing with the poorly defined concepts and definitions that abound in inquiries into political phenomena. The nature of victory in war is thus a perfect candidate for the application of pretheoretical methodology. In view of the widespread failure to use the term "victory" precisely – though there is apparent unanimity that it means something *positive* – pretheorizing is likely to help scholars (and policymakers) develop concepts that provide greater analytical and descriptive power for understanding the meaning and consequences of victory.

The final strength of a pretheory is its influence on the intellectual debate about victory in war. In the end, discussion of a pretheory should provoke a spirited and perhaps intense debate about the nature of victory, why certain organizing principles were selected, and the relationships that exist between and among these factors. If Rosenau is correct that a single pretheory of victory is unlikely to emerge triumphant, then we should expect contentious debates about what the central organizing principles of victory are, how victory ought to be expressed and the proper language for describing it, and how victory relates to such factors as change in the status quo, mobilization for war, and the state's postwar obligations toward the defeated. There is no illusion that the particular pretheory proposed in this study will end the debate; rather there is a hope that it will focus and encourage it. As Rosenau warned, "To think theoretically one must be constantly ready to be proven wrong."[5]

The foremost weakness of a pretheory of victory is methodological: Not designed to have predictive power, it cannot forecast whether victory will occur under specific conditions. Nor does a pretheory establish a causal model or theory of the relationships between and among these principles.[6] Other weaknesses are that pretheories cannot account for the "infinite variation" of international politics (and thus will produce "crude formulations") and that their analytic power is limited by the fact that "the more one explicates, the more elaborate does one's pre-theory become."[7] At some point the research must deal with the limits imposed by what is known in science and philosophy as "Occam's razor," which stipulates that we should prefer simpler workable explanations, those with fewer variables, to unnecessarily complex explanations.[8] The risk is that more elaborate pretheories may needlessly multiply the number of factors, produce less not more rigorous explanations of political phenomena, and in the end fail to move the field beyond the present level of understanding. Thus, an important weakness with the search for pretheories is that it can lead to the endless proliferation of ideas and the subsequent erosion of knowledge.[9]

Although the function of a pretheory is to place events into a systematic framework and relate them to similar events, there are conditions that a pretheory may never handle well and events that do not fit. The case studies in this volume focus on the larger and more significant wars or interventions conducted by the United States toward the end of the twentieth and at the beginning of the twenty-first centuries. This span of time and range of contingencies is admittedly rather narrow. What about wars or conflicts at the lesser end of the scale? What about purely tactical victories? What about various cases of intervention conducted in the 1990s, of which Somalia, Haiti, and to a lesser extent Rwanda are noteworthy examples? Rwanda is an anomaly: an instance requiring humanitarian intervention to which the international response was virtually nonexistent. Could humanitarian interventions be classified as victories on the scale of tactical, political–military, or grand strategic, or are these cases better left aside in building a typology of victories? Would their absence weaken the framework or make it more useful for dealing with significant events? If all political and military events can be described as successes or failures, should one language of victory be used to classify all cases of intervention? These considerations are here reserved for future research.

What other criticisms can be levied against this pretheory of victory? One is that this framework for victory may be too general, and that more precise measures are needed of victory and its relationship to changes in the status quo, levels of mobilization, and postwar obligations. For example, one might argue that a good surrogate for the mobilization of a state for war is the nature of public opinion in crises and wartime – though democratic societies may have a more difficult time mobilizing for war without widespread popular support,[10] and public opinion may be impossible to measure in regimes that control the press. Alternatively, one could study the extent of economic preparations for war as a more precise measure of mobilization.[11] There is no intent to dismiss such considerations out of hand; but since a pretheory is meant simply to provide a preliminary schema to foster better understanding in advance of attempting to formulate an actual theory, such weaknesses are consistent with and endemic to the nature of the inquiry.

A second criticism relates to the feasibility (or even necessity) of the present approach, reflecting the skepticism that properly should attend any theoretical framework or approach to a problem, particularly one as intensely debated as the nature of victory. To resolve some of these methodological problems, the next step should be to conduct parametric analyses to elucidate the nature of the relationships, thus far defined as ordinal (i.e., ranked), between and among these organizing principles. Whether there are more analytically rigorous and parsimonious ways to organize these and perhaps other principles into a more effective framework for understanding the nature of victory should be the subject of future inquiry.

One general argument reinforced by this study is that victory is not simply a mechanical extension of the state's strategy for war. The term "strategy" connotes no more than the paths or alternatives that define a means to a specified end. Clausewitz wrote in *On War* that "Strategy is the use of the engagement for the purpose of the war," whereas for Jomini, "Strategy is the art of making war upon the map. . . . Strategy decides where to act."[12] In essence, strategy provides the linkage between means and ends, in which victory is presumably the end that the state seeks to achieve through the use of military force. As normal as it may be to consider the former as a means of achieving the latter, that should not be construed as evidence of a logical or necessary linkage between strategy and victory: A "good" strategy will not necessarily produce victory, nor a "bad" strategy necessarily lead to defeat – unless, of course, they are described as such after the fact and with the benefit of hindsight.

The present research clearly calls into question the nature of victory itself. For too long "victory" has been a catchall used to describe outcomes that are varyingly positive or at least in accord with the state's interests or objectives. It should by now be painfully obvious that the term "victory" must be used with greater precision, and the landscape of possible successful outcomes needs to be mapped in some detail. Wars end not with the binary condition of victory or defeat but with a complex scale of outcomes that cannot be reduced to so simple an end state. Thus the language of victory employed in this study includes specific levels of victory. A related point is that simply modifying the term "victory" without some systematic foundation in place merely confuses the debate about war and strategy and weakens the ability of scholars, policymakers, and the public to discuss and agree upon what precisely the state is seeking to accomplish.

IMPLICATIONS FOR POLICYMAKING

Since the audience for this study includes both scholars and policymakers, let us turn to the implications of this research for the policymaking community. This discussion focuses on how to interpret the case studies (Chapters 6–11) through the lens of pretheoretical ideas about victory, what the implications are for policymaking from the lessons learned in these cases, and what policy prescriptions follow from this analysis. It concludes with general observations about the relationship between pretheoretical concepts of victory and the conduct of policy. The central question is this: How useful is a pretheory of victory for understanding these and other cases of military intervention?

First, however, it is essential to consider the nature of these case studies – in particular, how representative they are of what might be encountered in future crises. There are several dimensions in which these case studies are perhaps less than representative. First, they reflect a relatively narrow *time frame*, from the late twentieth century to the early twenty-first. Second, this analysis focuses on the *United States* as the principal antagonist and thus excludes the experiences of other states with war. (Although the Persian Gulf War, the interventions in Bosnia and Kosovo, and the recent invasions of Afghanistan and Iraq involved coalition forces, the fact still remains that these cases represent actions predominantly of the United States, which largely forged the coalitions.) Moreover, the emphasis on the military successes of the United States – the *single dominant* military power, at this peculiar time in history, and finally rid of the cold war and its daunting effects – may distort the appearance of victory. Subsequent studies might therefore do well to include the wartime experiences of other states. Also clearly to be included in any expansion are conflicts that are *less localized* and cases in which the principal intervening state actually suffered *defeat*.

Other criteria that guided the selection of these cases, however, increase their representativeness. These cases are fairly representative, for instance, of the *types* of military actions that states can conduct: from raids (Libya) to air campaigns (Bosnia and Kosovo) to classic military invasions (Panama, Persian Gulf War, Afghanistan, and Iraq). Turning to the matter of *scale,* these interventions include small-scale operations (Libya, Afghanistan), other medium-sized contingencies (Panama, Bosnia–Kosovo), and large-scale enterprises (Persian Gulf War, Iraq). The *duration* of the military operations examined ranged from hours (Libya) to weeks (Panama), to months (Persian Gulf War) if not years (Bosnia–Kosovo, Afghanistan, Iraq). In terms of the *regions* involved, these interventions occurred in the Middle East (Libya), Latin America (Panama), Eastern Europe (Bosnia–Kosovo), and Southwest Asia (Persian Gulf War, Afghanistan, and Iraq).

Since the intent was to develop pretheoretical ideas about victory based on recent cases of U.S. military intervention, there are inevitably ways in which the representativeness of these case studies can be debated. The question remains, How useful is a pretheory of victory for understanding these and other cases? Based on this review, what should policymakers infer about the relationship between these cases and a pretheory of victory?

Despite the brevity of the intervention against Libya in 1986, the United States achieved more than just a tactical victory and less than a PMV — hence a quasi-PMV. If we ignore the extremely limited nature of the raid and focus on the fact that this use of military force altered Libya's policy of supporting terrorism, then this intervention met an important criterion of a political–military victory: compelling changes in the political behavior or policies of the enemy state. Libya's attitude toward terrorism was ultimately tempered at an exceptionally low cost to the United States, including no postconflict obligations. With respect to the pretheory of victory, what remains of interest in the case of Libya is the ability of decidedly lesser forms of intervention, notably based on air power, to achieve important results. Although this observation may seem intuitively obvious, the tendency to focus on large-scale interventions in the global war on terrorism can obscure the relevance of brief, highly focused, almost surgical strikes on attaining results that are consistent with victory.

In the invasion of Panama in 1989, the United States achieved a political–military victory that destroyed the ability of the Noriega government to collude with the Medellin drug cartel and use Panama (and its strategically important canal) as a conduit for drug trafficking. Far more extensive militarily than the raid on Libya, this invasion had important regional and strategic consequences. It demonstrated that the United States was willing to take decisive military action during the cold war, when the prospect of nuclear annihilation weighed heavily on victory, and it helped the United States reassert the idea that it can fight and win limited wars for lesser degrees of victory.

The invasion of Panama in 1989, like the earlier raid on Libya, expanded the range of envisionable U.S. victories. With an effect on the status quo arguably comparable to that in Libya, but with higher-level mobilization and significantly greater postconflict obligations, the intervention in Panama shifted the nature and scale of American victory toward more significant levels. In one sense, the invasion of Panama is conceptually similar to that of Afghanistan in October 2001: A primary goal was the removal of a severely destabilizing force (a drug cartel; al-Qaeda) in a region of strategic importance. A key difference, however, is that whereas in Panama the objective was to restore the government and society to the pre-Noriega days, the invasion of Afghanistan may arguably produce a grand strategic victory because it seeks to change the nature of the government. The important observation for policymakers is that the political–military victory against Panama foreshadowed the development of an era when it was permissible for the state to achieve significant victories.

The invasion of Kuwait in the Persian Gulf War to force Iraqi forces to withdraw is an illustration of the difference between political–military and grand strategic victories. America unquestionably achieved a political–military victory against Iraq, but certainly no more than that. What has dominated postwar analyses of the Gulf War is the U.S. failure to achieve victory on a strategic scale, owing to fears among policymakers in the administration of George H. W. Bush that the United States would be drawn into a quagmire as ethnic, religious, and national groups vied for power. What emerges from an analysis of this 1991 war is that the United States was unwilling to shoulder the risks inherent in postconflict obligations toward Iraq: There was an implicit understanding among that administration's policymakers that the pursuit of grand strategic victory produces significant postconflict obligations (as the administration of George W. Bush has learned from March 2003 invasion and subsequent occupation of Iraq). These factors effectively excluded grand strategic victory from U.S. policy. Thus, though mobilization for the Persian Gulf War vastly exceeded that for the raid against Libya or the invasion of Panama, and despite the larger-scale, overwhelmingly decisive military operations against Iraqi forces in the air campaign and ground war, the United States achieved a political–military victory – a result less satisfying than the effort expended should have produced.

In the military interventions against Bosnia and Kosovo, the United States also attained political–military victories but might well have achieved a grand strategic victory, at least in Kosovo, given the great change in the status quo (the Milošević regime removed) and high postconflict obligations. The military operations against Bosnian Serb and Serbian forces led to international confusion about what the United States and its NATO allies were trying to accomplish and what resources they were willing to commit before, during, and after the conflict. American and European policymakers, fearing entrapment in a Balkan quagmire, never resolved for themselves and articulated publicly what victory was worth to them, in lives and credibility.

These actions in the Balkans, with relatively limited mobilization, produced significant changes in the regional status quo but entailed significant postconflict obligations for the United States, its NATO allies, and other international organizations. These states and organizations will for years retain in Kosovo significant numbers of military and civilian personnel who are responsible for helping develop a stable and peaceful democratic order. This is reminiscent of the nation building that is routinely associated with the establishment of new forms of government in grand strategic victory. Yet the military interventions in the Balkans did not produce such a victory. The intent from the beginning was to quench the fires of genocide while avoiding any suggestion that the United States would rebuild Bosnia and Kosovo or remain involved in the long term.

A further point is that the political–military victories in the Balkans are consistent with the level of victory that states are likely to attain in the normal conduct of foreign policy, since moderately sized military interventions are more representative of how they are likely to use force than are such large-scale military operations as the Persian Gulf War. The operations and outcomes in Bosnia and Kosovo share certain parallels with those in Panama in terms of the level of victory, change in status quo, and level of mobilization; yet they differ in terms of postconflict obligations, which were vastly greater in the Balkans.

The invasion of Afghanistan in 2001 is interesting analytically because the United States is positioned to achieve grand strategic victory. The decision to wage a "global war on terrorism" reintroduced the idea, for the first time since World War II, that such a victory is a practical option. The Afghanistan policy rested on the removal of the Taliban government, the destruction of al-Qaeda, and the development of democratic processes and institutions. On the basis of the Bonn Agreement of December 2001, Afghanistan has produced the country's first democratically elected parliament, with 102 members in the upper house and 249 in the lower.[13]

Why this shift to grand strategic victory, and what are its implications for policy? The 9/11 attacks on the United States appeared to U.S. policymakers to be a harbinger of possibly even worse strikes to come: The vital interests of the United States, including the safety of its people, were at risk. It was this confluence of events and beliefs that triggered the decision by President Bush in September 2001 to raise victory to the highest possible level. As a result, U.S. policymakers revisited the concept of grand strategic victory, which had lain dormant since President Roosevelt's declarations in the Atlantic Charter of August 14, 1941, and Yalta Agreement of February 11, 1945, that the Axis powers would be defeated totally.[14] With victory in Afghanistan defined by the removal of the Taliban regime, which had granted safe haven to al-Qaeda, it was clear that the United States must be willing and prepared to assume significant postconflict obligations.

What remains interesting about the outcome in Afghanistan is its relationship to the pretheory of victory. In addition to being a putative case of grand strategic victory, the invasion and subsequent occupation produced a comprehensive change in the status quo, including regime change, and established protracted postwar obligations on the level of nation building.[15] Yet the invasion required a minimal level of mobilization and was conducted with several hundred Special Forces troops and thousands of air strikes over a period of months. Thus, once again, the scale of military operations is not necessarily proportional to the scale of victory. Implicit here is the argument that, in the postindustrial United States, the cost of victory is measured less in terms of the scale of mobilization than in the cost of the subsequent obligation to rebuild the defeated state. Indeed, the small mobilization required and the decision to assume substantial postconflict obligations fundamentally shaped U.S. planning for this war from the beginning.

Finally, the invasion of Iraq in March 2003 raises the possibility of another U.S. grand strategic victory, although a highly effective insurgency has been conducted in Iraq since that May, when combat operations ended and the occupation began. There is evidence that U.S. policy from the outset was to achieve grand strategic victory. The position of the Bush administration, however contested, has been that the reason for the invasion was the judgment that Saddam Hussein might contribute support in the form of WMD to terrorist organizations, such as al-Qaeda, that seek to attack the United States and its allies (see Chapter 11). This reasoning was reiterated in a speech by President Bush on December 18, 2005: "Our coalition confronted a regime that defied United Nations Security Council resolutions, violated a cease-fire agreement, sponsored terrorism, and possessed, we believed, weapons of mass destruction. After the swift fall of Baghdad, we found mass graves filled by a dictator; we found some capacity to restart programs to produce weapons of mass destruction, but we did not find those weapons."[16]

However one interprets this reason for war, the pretheory provides a means for examining this outcome. As outlined by President Bush, the intent was to "do everything it takes to win,"[17] a phrase that is evidence of the intent to achieve grand strategic victory. As to the extent of change in the status quo, events in Iraq, provided they stand, can be interpreted only as comprehensive. Since the invasion and subsequent occupation, the United States and its coalition partners have provided the political, military, economic assistance needed to help the Iraqi people develop the foundations of democracy. A series of national elections was held in 2005 and, despite early signs of a split between Islamist and secular groups, there is evidence of broad agreement on a coalition government that will be based on the participation of Shiites, Sunnis, and Kurds.[18] These events signal the emergence of an Iraq that is quite different from the old one, both governmentally and politically.

The United States engaged in a moderate level of mobilization for this war: More than a year before the invasion, forces were being readied for combat operations and gradually shifted to the theater. However, when we consider the scale of the war, the level of mobilization was roughly comparable to that of the Persian Gulf War and by all measures a mere fraction of the preparations for, say, World War II. In terms of postconflict obligations, the United States assumed historically significant responsibilities for Iraq. The U.S. strategy was to "help the Iraqi people build a new Iraq with a constitutional, representative government that respects civil rights and has security forces sufficient to maintain domestic order and keep Iraq from becoming a safe haven for terrorists."[19] U.S. policy emphasized what are called "important metrics" in the realm of economic reconstruction, which includes gross domestic product, per capita GDP, inflation, electrical power production, oil production, and the number of new businesses. In some of these categories, such as increases in GDP, oil production, and the rate of new business starts, there are measurable signs of progress in the economic reconstruction of Iraq.[20]

Despite positive political and economic signs, judgments about the fate of Iraq and the nature of victory in that war must of necessity remain tentative. Should political reforms, economic reconstruction, and the development of security forces that can maintain peace and stability truly transform Iraq from a dictatorship into a constitutional democracy, the invasion of Iraq will have been an unqualified success – in the language of prethcory, a grand strategic victory. However, if Iraq continues to be plagued by insurgent attacks against its citizens and U.S. and coalition forces, this will undermine its ability to "establish the institutions of a unified and lasting democracy,"[21] eventually overwhelming efforts to move Iraq toward reform and reconstruction. A protracted insurgency that leaves ordinary Iraqis feeling pessimistic about the future could degrade the outcome from grand strategic to political–military victory or worse. Thus a most dangerous possibility is of an ongoing insurgency weakening Iraqi morale and encouraging radical elements that seek to dominate Iraqi politics. This could lead to civil war – either religiously based, between Shiite and Sunni groups, or among regional groups, including the Kurds. A parallel danger is that a coalition of al-Qaeda operatives and insurgents could establish control and turn Iraq into a safe haven for terrorists seeking to export an Islamic revolution to neighboring states.[22] Such an outcome, equivalent to Afghanistan under the Taliban, is a vision not of victory on any level but of strategic failure at the highest level – what the Bush administration has termed a "decisive victory over the United States."[23]

For now, there are some positive signs as to Iraq's future. Perhaps foremost is the turnout in the elections for a full Iraqi parliament, held December 15, 2005, which preliminary analyses suggested was 70 percent (10.9 million of 15.6 million registered voters).[24] Although there were some reports of voter fraud, the head of the U.N. election coordination effort declared the election results overall to be "transparent and credible."[25] If the Iraqi people are increasing their level of participation in politics, perhaps efforts at political and social reconstruction are beginning to gain greater legitimacy. In late June 2006, there are reports that Iraqi insurgent groups are seeking to negotiate some form of reconciliation with the Iraqi government. (See "Some Insurgents are asking Iraq for Negotiations," *New York Times,* June 27, 2006, p. A1.)

There are two other critical considerations regarding the war in Iraq and its implications for pretheoretical ideas about victory. One is the matter of politics and policy in the United States: Will U.S. policymakers and the American public, wearying of the strains of war and reports of U.S. soldiers being killed daily, decide to withdraw from Iraq or to establish a timetable for withdrawal? President Bush has specifically rejected a timetable for withdrawal, arguing that "Withdrawing on an artificial deadline would endanger the American people, would harm our military, and make the Middle East less stable."[26] In June 2006, the Republican-controlled Senate voted down a call to start withdrawing U.S. troops by the end of the year.[27] As to withdrawing from Iraq as a result of pressure from the insurgents, President Bush has said, "that is not going to happen so long as I'm the Commander-in-Chief."[28] With such language emanating from the Bush administration, it is improbable that the United States will step back from the high point of a perceived victory in Afghanistan to accept an outcome in Iraq that could be interpreted as less significant or momentous. Nevertheless, in a democracy, public opinion can produce unexpected turns in policy.

The other consideration is whether the experience in Iraq establishes a precedent for grand strategic victory that imposes excessively burdensome expectations on policymakers. When next they confront a decision of whether to intervene militarily, there will be enormous political pressures to have a clear plan for achieving victory on a significant scale. How likely are policymakers to run the risk of defeat or failure in the face of such a precedent? Does the war against Iraq reaffirm or erode their willingness to assume significant post-conflict obligations, knowing that those may be essential to attaining grand strategic victory yet pose the greatest political challenges?

Several final observations are in order about the implications of this analysis for policymaking. The first is that the six case studies, comprising most of the U.S. conflicts waged between 1986 and 2006, were presented chronologically so as to outline the evolution of victory in the waning years of the cold war and the emergence of the new international order. These two decades, during which long-standing constraints on victory were removed by the cold war's end, produced both political–military and grand strategic victories. Though this limited sample of conflicts includes interventions both large and small, the question remains whether these wars are sufficiently representative to provide a basis for a pretheory of victory. This sample of war is not all-inclusive,[29] but it represents the most important cases of intervention that were conducted by the United States and some of its allies in recent decades. Moreover, it includes those conflicts that are likely to dominate how current and subsequent generations of policymakers think about intervention, in much the same way that Vietnam, World War II, World War I, and the Civil War influenced how receding past generations of policymakers balanced the risks of war and the meaning of victory. (In fact, one might consider these and other wars addressed in Chapter 5, regarding the evolution of American thinking about victory, as further case studies on a small scale.)

In the end, this study – whose purpose is not to end but to encourage debate about victory – challenges the following traditional, commonly cited arguments:

Considerable military writing has already focused on victory, which is principally a synonym for success, and everyone knows what victory is.

It has proven difficult to make theoretical advances beyond these ideas about victory.

One cannot express victory in generic terms because of the wide range of conditions in war.

What we know as the principles of war represent a "toolbox" for policymakers and military commanders who seek to achieve victory.

Nuclear weapons undermined the concept of victory.

Prominent military strategists, of which Clausewitz is a prominent example, criticized attempts to characterize victory in abstract terms

A categorical approach to victory is logically and conceptually flawed.

Victory is a symbolic expression that cannot be calculated because its components are unknown.

Policymakers cannot choose to achieve victory because what happens in war is fundamentally uncertain.

A pretheory is of dubious value because the nature of victory and how we interpret it is altered by time, and we must therefore wait before decisive judgments about victory are possible for any given war.

Whatever judgments about victory have been gleaned from the history of

war and strategy, including recent American experiences, are not sufficiently representative of war.

However, none of these provides a structured framework for understanding
victory, advances our knowledge of the meaning of victory, or provides a
foundation for criticism.

What policy prescriptions follow from this analysis? First, policymakers must
define precisely what victory is to mean in a particular situation. It is not
enough to say that the state seeks victory, that "we must win" and are "committed to winning": Debate must focus on what kind of victory is sought and
why, how it will change the status quo, what level of mobilization (political,
economic, military) is required, and what postconflict obligations are to be accepted by the victor.[30] Such discourse can only improve how well societies understand the nature of intervention, and will permit policymakers to formulate what they need to achieve and to evaluate whether those requirements are
important, relevant, and worthwhile. It is worth wondering, however, whether policymakers might be concerned that using a precise language of victory
would limit their flexibility.

Victory is determined by what policymakers both say and do; it is as much
a matter of precise language as it is of precise action. Stating clearly and precisely what policymakers intend to achieve will not necessarily produce victory on whatever level unless those words are matched by equally precise action.
The 1991 Persian Gulf War (see Chapter 8) is a case in point: Strong language
was not followed by actions sufficient to produce grand strategic victory, and
this ultimately led to another invasion to resolve the matter. Conversely, clear
military actions will not guarantee victory unless policymakers declare precisely what level of victory they intend to achieve. The 1999 U.S.–NATO air campaign to punish the Serbians for their actions against Albanian Kosovars (see
Chapter 9) was not accompanied by a resolute declaration as to the level of
victory sought, and the strategic consequences of the political–military victory it produced have never been properly recognized. Although victory, not
surprisingly, is not inevitable even if policymakers ensure that the language
of victory employed jibes with the military force used, both these wars might
have yielded more significant and perhaps strategic results had policymakers'
words and actions been more consistent.

Second, any decision by policymakers to use military force must be deliberately and self-consciously based on an analysis of the benefits, costs, and risks
of victory. Although the benefits of victory often appear obvious in terms of
the state's interests, the prospect of postwar obligations can influence how the
public and policymakers interpret victory. It remains to be seen whether these
observations apply generally to all postindustrial societies or are unique to the

United States when it goes to war, but grand strategic victory will almost certainly entail comprehensive postconflict obligations, whereas political–military victory is likely to involve lesser (though perhaps still significant) postwar responsibilities for the victorious state. Occupied Iraq is a contemporary exemplar of the significant costs and risks likely to be encountered even after major combat operations are complete.

Third, policymakers (and scholars) must contemplate whether there is indeed a direct linkage between victory and the technological means of warfare. One of the precepts of the revolution in military affairs is that technological change is altering how states conduct warfare.[31] Notwithstanding the discussions of technological advances herein, this study has avoided any suggestion that the state's ability to achieve victory is determinatively influenced by its technology of war. Rather, a preliminary premise might be that victory inheres more in *what* the state accomplishes and less in *how* it does so – a judgment to be sharpened by future research. Given these limitations, perhaps one of the first issues that should be examined in future research is whether victory inheres more in *what* the state accomplishes and less in *how* it does so.

Finally, systematic thinking about the meaning of victory will have implications for force structure and defense-budget priorities and can be used to create a better relationship between military forces and the state's political and military requirements. Are some forces better suited to achieving victory in certain contingencies? Are others better suited in general? A deeper understanding of victory in all its forms, and with all its relevant factors, will help policymakers and defense planners make more informed trade-offs among the various elements of force structure (see Chapter 12).

Notes

N.B.: Web sources cited herein were all accessible as of mid-2006 via the URLs provided.

1. Introduction

1. President George W. Bush, "Full Text of the State of the Union Speech," January 20, 2004, www.msnbc.msn.com/id/4012231/: "And my Administration, and this Congress, will give you the resources you need to fight and win the war on terror."

2. "President Bush Addresses the Nation," March 19, 2003, at www.whitehouse.gov/news/releases/2003/03/20030319-17.html.

3. See David E. Sanger, "In Strong Words, Bush Defines Terms of Debate on Iraq," *New York Times*, January 11, 2006, p. A12.

4. See "Bush Makes Historic Speech aboard Warship," *CNN*, May 1, 2003, at www.cnn.com/2003/US/05/01/bush.transcript/ (emphasis added).

5. For a critical analysis of strategy, which encompasses discussions of victory in a theoretical and historical sense, see Peter Paret (ed.), with Gordon A. Craig and Felix Gilbert, *Makers of Modern Strategy: From Machiavelli to the Nuclear Age* (Princeton: Princeton University Press, 1986); John I. Alger, *The Quest for Victory: The History of the Principles of War* (Westport, CT: Greenwood, 1982); Edward Mead Earle (ed.), with Gordon A. Craig and Felix Gilbert, *Makers of Modern Strategy: Military Thought from Machiavelli to Hitler* (Princeton: Princeton University Press, 1973); Raymond Aron, *The Century of Total War* (Garden City, NY: Doubleday, 1954); Colin S. Gray, "Nuclear Strategy: The Case for a Theory of Victory," *International Security* 9.4 (Summer 1979), pp. 54–87; Gray, *War, Peace,* *and Victory* (New York: Simon & Schuster, 1990); Paul Kecskemeti, *Strategic Surrender: The Politics of Victory and Defeat* (Stanford: Stanford University Press, 1958); Henry A. Kissinger, *Nuclear Weapons and Foreign Policy* (New York: Harper & Brothers, 1957).

6. Carl von Clausewitz, *On War*, ed. and intro. Anatol Rapoport (Baltimore: Penguin, 1971), p. 315.

7. See Michael I. Handel, *Masters of War: Classical Strategic Thought*, 3d ed. (London: Frank Cass, 2001), pp. 155–94; Bradford A. Lee, "Winning the War but Losing the Peace? The United States and the Strategic Issues of War Termination," in Bradford A. Lee and Karl F. Walling (eds.), *Strategic Logic and Political Rationality: Essays in Honor of Michael I. Handel* (London: Frank Cass, 2003), pp. 249–73, at p. 249.

8. There should be no illusions that a pretheory of victory could eliminate the fundamental discord about war and politics that exists in all political systems, particularly those that embrace democratic values.

9. William T. Bluhm, *Theories of the Political System*, 2d ed. (Englewood Cliffs, NJ: Prentice–Hall, 1971), p. 8, who observes that "Every author of a political theory has aspired to be the guide both of statesmen and of citizens."

10. Rarely do states mobilize *all* of their capacity for war. In the case of World War II, the United States mobilized roughly one-third of its total economic capacity.

11. Brian Bond, *The Pursuit of Victory: From Napoleon to Saddam Hussein* (New York: Oxford University Press, 1996), p. 1.

2. Historical Origins of Victory

1. To remedy these inevitable gaps, a subsequent study on theorists and strategists who have contributed to our understanding of victory will address some of the individuals who are omitted from the present research.

2. Edward Mead Earle (ed.), with Gordon A. Craig and Felix Gilbert, *Makers of Modern Strategy: Military Thought from Machiavelli to Hitler* (Princeton: Princeton University Press, 1973); Peter Paret (ed.), with Gordon A. Craig and Felix Gilbert, *Makers of Modern Strategy: From Machiavelli to the Nuclear Age* (Princeton: Princeton University Press, 1986). Other works included John I. Alger, *The Quest for Victory: The History of the Principles of War* (Westport, CT: Greenwood, 1982); Azar Gat, *The Origins of Military Thought: From the Enlightenment to Clausewitz* (Oxford: Clarendon Press, 1991); Michael I. Handel, *Masters of War: Classical Strategic Thought*, 3d ed. (London: Frank Cass, 2001).

3. Alger, *Quest for Victory*, p. 134.

4. Sun Tzu, *The Art of War*, trans. and intro. Samuel B. Griffith (New York: Oxford University Press, 1971); Handel, *Masters of War*, pp. 19–32.

5. Sun Tzu, *Art of War*, trans. Griffith. See Michael Carver, "Conventional Warfare in the Nuclear Age," in Paret (ed.), *Makers of Modern Strategy*, pp. 779–814, at p. 800, who described the tenets of Sun Tzu: "one should seek victory in the shortest possible time, with the least possible effort, and at the least cost in casualties to one's enemy."

6. Sun Tzu, *The Art of War*, trans. Ralph D. Sawyer (Boulder, CO: Westview, 1994), pp. 178–9.

7. Ibid.

8. Ibid., p. 215.

9. Handel, *Masters of War*, p. 31.

10. Robert B. Strassler (ed.), *The Landmark Thucydides: A Comprehensive Guide to the Peloponnesian War* (New York: Simon & Schuster, 1996); Thucydides, *History of the Peloponnesian War*, trans. Rex Warner (Harmondsworth: Penguin, 1972). See also Donald Kagan, *The Outbreak of the Peloponnesian War* (Ithaca, NY: Cornell University Press, 1969), esp. chaps. 19 ("The Causes of the War") and 20 ("Thucydides and the Inevitability of the War").

11. Strassler (ed.), *Landmark Thucydides*, pp. 32, 33, 198, 235. Subsequent citations are given in the text.

12. *Plato: The Republic*, trans. G. M. A. Grube (Indianapolis, IN: Hackett, 1974), p. 45. Subsequent citations are given in the text.

13. What's more, "the victor's crown they and their children receive is their nurture and all the necessities of life" (p. 126).

14. "[T]here is considerable danger that, if they [i.e., anyone] are defeated, as happens frequently in war, they will lose their children's lives as well as their own" (p. 127).

15. He continued (p. 131): "They should, however, keep in mind that they will not always be at war, and that peace will return."

16. *The Histories of Polybius*, text F. Hultsch, trans. Evelyn S. Shuckburgh (London: Macmillan, 1889), p. 163.

17. See Adrian Keith Goldsworthy, *Roman Warfare* (London: Cassell, 2000), p. 19. Also, R. M. Errington, *The Dawn of Empire: Rome's Rise to World Power* (Ithaca, NY: Cornell University Press, 1972).

18. *Polybius on Roman Imperialism: The Histories of Polybius*, text F. Hultsch, trans. Evelyn S. Shuckburgh (South Bend, IN: Regnery/Gateway, 1980), p. 56. Subsequent citations are given in the text.

19. Quoted in Chas. W. Freeman Jr., *The Diplomat's Dictionary* (Washington, DC: National Defense University Press, 1996), p. 395.

20. Quoted in Robert Debs Heinl (comp.), *Dictionary of Military and Naval Quotations* (Annapolis, MD: United States Naval Institute, 1988).

21. See *Polybius on Roman Imperialism*, p. 8; *Histories of Polybius*, p. 175.

22. *Histories of Polybius*, p. 176.

23. For a discussion of Roman attitudes toward imperial expansion and war, see William V. Harris, *War and Imperialism in Republican Rome, 327–70 B.C.* (Oxford: Clarendon, 1979).

24. Livy, *The War with Hannibal: Books XXI–XXX of the History of Rome from Its Foundations*, trans. Aubrey de Selincourt (London: Penguin, 1972), pp. 31, 78. Subsequent citations are given in the text.

25. See Hans Delbrück, *History of the Art of War within the Framework of Political History*, 4 vols., trans. Walter J. Renfroe Jr. (Westport, CT: Greenwood, 1975–85), vol. I: *Antiquity*, p. 343, for comments about "final victory" for Rome in the Third Punic War against Carthage.

26. Livy, *War with Hannibal*, pp. 65, 78.

27. Quoted in Freeman, *Diplomat's Dictionary*, p. 393. As Cicero wrote: "The only excuse for going to war is to be able to live in peace undisturbed. When victory is won we should spare those who have not been bloodthirsty or barbarous in their warfare" (ibid.).

28. Vegetius, "My Reveries on the Art of War," in T. R. Phillips (ed.), *Roots of Strategy: The Five Greatest Military Classics of All Time* (Harrisburg, PA: Stackpole Books, 1985), p. 68.

29. Vegetius, *The Military Institutions of the Romans*, ed. T. R. Phillips, trans. John Clark (Harrisburg, PA: Military Service Publishing, 1944), p. 93. Subsequent citations are given in the text.

30. For this argument, see Alger, *Quest for Victory*, pp. 5–6.

31. Delbrück, *History of the Art of War*, vol. I, p. 355.

32. For analyses of Machiavelli, see Felix Gilbert, "Machiavelli: The Renaissance of the Art of War," in Paret (ed.), *Makers of Modern Strategy*, pp. 11–31; Gat, *Origins of Military Thought*, pp. 1–9. Alger, *Quest for Victory*, pp. 6–7, observed that "Machiavelli's writings marked the beginning of nearly three centuries of military thought that was strongly influenced by classical thought, that reflected an interest in the search for principles, fundamentals, general rules, or any of the variety of synonyms used to define such basic concepts" of war.

33. See Gat, *Origins of Military Thought*, p. 6: "*The Art of War* is Machiavelli's positive and complete scheme for the building of armies, and reflects the full scope of his military outlook."

34. Felix Gilbert, "Machiavelli: The Renaissance of the Art of War," in Edward Mead Earle (ed.), *Makers of Modern Strategy: Military Thought from Machiavelli to Hitler* (Princeton: Princeton University Press, 1973), pp. 3–25, at p. 24, makes the argument that Machiavelli established the beginning of strategic thinking about war and by extension victory.

35. See Charles R. Schrader, "The Influence of Vegetius' *De re militari*," *Military Affairs* 45.4 (December 1981), pp. 167–72, at p. 167.

36. Gilbert, "Machiavelli," p. 3.

37. Niccolò Machiavelli, *The Art of War*, in *Machiavelli: The Chief Works and Others*, 3 vols., tran. Allan Gilbert (Durham, NC: Duke

University Press, 1965), vol. II, pp. 563–726, p. 718.

38. Niccolò Machiavelli, *Discourses on the First Decade of Titus Livius*, in *Machiavelli: Chief Works and Others*, vol. I, pp. 175–529, at p. 502 (bk. 3, chap. 33).

39. Ibid., p. 503. Machiavelli wrote about "mentioning many reasons through which they [the soldiers] could hope for victory, that he could in addition tell them certain things that were good, and from which they could see that victory was certain" (ibid., p. 504).

40. Ibid., p. 502.

41. Delbrück, *History of the Art of War*, vol. IV· *The Modern Era*, p. 63, who in writing about the "Organization of Mercenary Armies," observed that "only a large number of soldiers gave the prospect of victory."

42. Machiavelli, *Art of War*, p. 654.

43. Ibid., p. 655.

44. Ibid., p. 718.

45. Machiavelli, *Discourses*, p. 380.

46. Sheldon S. Wolin, "The Economy of Violence," in Niccolò Machiavelli, *The Prince: A New Translation, Backgrounds, Interpretations*, trans. and ed. Robert M. Adams (New York: W. W. Norton, 1977), p. 187.

47. See Garrett Mattingly, *Renaissance Diplomacy* (Baltimore: Penguin, 1964), for a review of politics and diplomacy during this era, esp. pp. 140–6.

48. Machiavelli, *Prince*, pp. 64–5.

49. Gilbert, "Machiavelli" (Earle version), pp. 13–14. As Machiavelli wrote, "That cannot be called war where men do not kill each other, cities are not sacked, nor territories laid waste."

50. Hugo Grotius, *Commentary on the Law of Prize and Booty* (Oxford: Clarendon, 1950); Grotius, *The Law of War and Peace*, trans. Francis W. Kelsey (New York: Bobbs–Merrill, 1963), p. 577.

51. The best studies on Montecuccoli from which this study draws are Thomas M. Barker, *The Military Intellectual and Battle: Raimondo Montecuccoli and the Thirty Years War* (Albany, NY: SUNY Press, 1975); Gat, *Origins of Military Thought*, pp. 13–24; Günther Rothenberg, "Maurice of Nassau, Gustavus Adolphus, Raimondo Montecuccoli, and the 'Military Revolution' of the Seventeenth Century," in Paret (ed.), *Makers of Modern Strategy*, pp. 32–63, at pp. 55–63.

52. Gat, *Origins of Military Thought*, pp.

16, 20. Also: "These [rules] can then be applied to particular times and experiences by means of skillful judgement" (p. 20). Thus, "His universal science of war was obviously simply a reflection of the warfare of his day . . . [the] rise of the centralized state, the monetary economy, and the growing professional armies" (p. 22).

53. Ibid., p. 22. Gat also observed (ibid., p. 29) that "The military thinkers of the Enlightenment maintained that the art of war was also susceptible to systematic formulation, based on the rules and principles of universal validity which had been revealed in the campaigns of the great military leaders of history."

54. Barker, *Military Intellectual and Battle*, p. 60, described how Montecuccoli's teaching evolved chronologically: "As for strategy, in the first period the emphasis is upon seizing the initiative . . . alongside this plan for a war of annihilation, Montecuccoli admits that there are times when one's forces are so small that they permit only a war of attrition. . . . In the second period . . . there is reference to the necessity of systematic destruction. . . . In the third period . . . what predominates is a minutely described, energetic, wear-and-tear strategy." Subsequent Barker citations are given in the text.

55. Furthermore (ibid., p. 167), "The most signal victory is one illuminated by clemency rather than darkened by cruelty. The Romans not only pardoned their defeated enemies but also took them as comrades."

56. See Sébastien le Prestre de Vauban, *A Manual of Siegecraft and Fortification*, trans. and intro. George A. Rothrock (Ann Arbor: University of Michigan Press, 1968).

57. For an excellent analysis of Vauban's influence on military strategy, see Henry Guerlac, "Vauban: The Impact of Science on War," in Earle (ed.), *Makers of Modern Strategy: Military Thought*, pp. 26–48, who advances the notion that Vauban had a decisive effect on strategic thinking during his age.

58. This and the following quotations in this paragraph are all from Vauban, *Manual of Siegecraft*, p. 21.

59. Bernard Brodie's words, in his *War and Politics* (New York: Macmillan, 1973), p. 247.

60. See Heinl (comp.), *Dictionary of Military and Naval Quotations*, p. 343: "War is a science replete with shadows in whose obscurity one cannot move with assured step. Routine and prejudice, the natural result of ignorance, are its foundation and support. All sciences have principles and rules. War has none. The great captains who have written of this give us none. Extreme cleverness is required merely to understand them."

61. See R. R. Palmer, "Frederick the Great, Guibert, Bülow: From Dynastic to National War," in Earle (ed.), *Makers of Modern Strategy: Military Thought*, pp. 49–74, for a discussion of the changes in how the state organized and employed armies.

62. Ibid., p. 58. In practice, blitzkrieg translates into a short and lively war.

63. Dennis Showalter, *The Wars of Frederick the Great* (New York: Longman Group, 1996), pp. 356–7. The purpose of armies during Frederick's time was to "win victories, then to demonstrate the state's readiness and capacity to defend its interests." This was "an age when battles were decided by the firepower of linear formations and victory was completed by cavalry charges." Furthermore, "Victory offers at least the promise of cutting the Gordian knot of agreements, expectations, and premises that sustain any system involving sovereign powers."

64. This and the following quotations in this paragraph are all from Frederick the Great, "Article XXII, Of Combats and Battles," in "Military Instructions, The King of Prussia's Military Instruction to His Generals," www.sonshi.com/frederickthegreat1-22.html. The present quotation continues: "It is the custom to allow fifteen yards of interval between squadrons in a difficult, intersected country, but where the ground is good and even, they form in a line entire."

65. Ibid.

66. "The Instruction of Frederick the Great for His Generals 1747," in Phillips (ed.), *Roots of Strategy*, pp. 301–400, at p. 380. "The general who has already gained these premonitory signs of victory can then boldly bring up the infantry which covers his wing and the infantry on his flank, to outflank the hostile infantry, take them in the flank and envelop them, if he is able" (p. 388).

67. Ibid., p. 391.

68. James N. Wassen, *Innovator or Imitator: Napoleon's Operational Concepts and the Legacies of Bourcet and Guibert* (Ft. Leavenworth, KS: School of Advanced Military Studies, U.S. Army Command and General Staff College, 1998).

69. Palmer, "Frederick the Great, Guibert, Bülow," p. 67.

70. Gat, *Origins of Military Thought*, p. 44; thus, "it was the comprehensive expression that he gave to the ideas of the Enlightenment."

71. For a review of Bülow's influence on the strategy of war, see ibid., pp. 79–94; Palmer, "Frederick the Great, Guibert, Bülow." Also, Brodie, *War and Politics*.

72. Gat, *Origins of Military Thought*, p. 79. Jomini's concept of *lines of operation*, picked up by Clausewitz, is still in use today. As originally defined, it refers to linking military forces with decisive points, centers of gravity, and objectives, as a tool for planning military campaigns. See Philipp Eder and Johann Fischer, "A Solution for the Confusing Application of Lines of Operation," *Campaigning (JAWS)* (Spring 2006), pp. 50–60, at pp. 53–6.

73. Ibid., p. 204.

74. Michael Howard, "Jomini and the Classical Tradition in Military Thought," in Howard (ed.), *The Theory and Practice of War: Essays Presented to B. H. Liddell Hart on His Seventieth Birthday* (New York: Praeger, 1966), pp. 3–20; Baron de Jomini, *The Art of War* (New York: G. P. Putnam, 1854); Archer Jones, "Jomini and the Strategy of the American Civil War: A Reinterpretation," *Military Affairs* 34 (December 1970), pp. 127–31; Crane Brinton, Gordon A. Craig, and Felix Gilbert, "Jomini," in Earle (ed.), *Makers of Modern Strategy: Military Thought*, pp. 77–92.

75. Quoted in John I. Alger, "Napoleon and the Birth of Modern Military Thought," in his *Quest for Victory*, pp. 17–50, at p. 17.

76. See Marshal Ferdinand Foch, *The Principles of War*, trans. Hilaire Belloc (New York: Henry Holt, 1920), p. 294.

77. "The Military Maxims of Napoleon," in Phillips (ed.), *Roots of Strategy*, pp. 389–557, at p. 410.

78. Ibid., p. 412.

79. Ibid., p. 423.

80. Delbrück, *History of the Art of War*, vol. I, p. 355, observed that this maxim "is still subject to exceptions and limitations."

81. Brian Bond, *The Pursuit of Victory: From Napoleon to Saddam Hussein* (New York: Oxford University Press, 1996), p. 2.

82. John J. Mearsheimer, *Conventional Deterrence* (Ithaca, NY: Cornell University Press, 1983), p. 30. See Palmer, "Frederick the Great, Guibert, Bülow," p. 49, who argues that since the French Revolution, war "has become increasingly a clash between peoples, and hence has become increasingly 'total'."

83. Bernard Brodie, *Strategy in the Missile Age* (Princeton: Princeton University Press, 1959), p. 78, quoted Mahan, who said of Jomini that his "methods change but principles are unchanging." See Alger, *Quest for Victory*, pp. 17–50; Brinton et al., "Jomini," pp. 84–5.

84. Gat, *Origins of Military Thought*, p. 139.

85. Brinton et al., "Jomini," pp. 87–8: "Jomini believed that the practice of warfare could be reduced to a set of general rules which could be learned and applied in all situations."

86. Baron de Jomini, *The Art of War: A New Edition, with Appendices and Maps*, trans. G. H. Mendell and W. P. Craighill (Westport, CT: Greenwood, 1971), p. 182. Subsequent citations are given in the text.

87. See "Jomini's *Art of War*," in *Roots of Strategy, Book 2: 3 Military Classics* (Harrisburg, PA: Stackpole Books, 1987), pp. 389–557, at p. 498.

88. Gat, *Origins of Military Thought*, p. 110: "Jomini gave theoretical expression to the new military reality and ideal raised to prominence by Napoleonic warfare: concentration of forces."

89. As Brinton et al. observed (ibid., p. 89), for Jomini the "purpose of warfare is to occupy all or part of the enemy's territory."

90. Gat, *Origins of Military Thought*, p. 115: "The destruction of the enemy's field armies was the new military aim."

91. In terms of the influence of Jomini on modern strategy, Brinton et al., "Jomini," p. 92, argued that the "progressive totalitarianism of warfare has effectually destroyed the validity of purely geographical campaigns and has made limited war impossible."

92. The matter of the relationship between conquering territory and victory is of contemporary interest. See "Chapter 3: The Army in Military Operations," *FM-1 The Army* (Washington, DC: Headquarters, Department of the Army, June 14, 2001), which cites Army doctrine: "The primary functions of The Army, as outlined in Department of Defense Directive 5100.1, are to organize, equip, and train forces for the conduct of prompt and sustained combat operations on land. Accordingly, The Army must possess the capability to *defeat enemy land forces and seize, occupy, and defend land areas*" (chrishaase.com/aa/FM1/ch3.htm; emphasis added). For the argument that victory is based on ground forces that occupy territory, see David T. Zabecki, "Landpower in History:

Strategists Must Regain an Understanding of the Role of Ground Forces," *Armed Forces Journal International* 140.1 (August 2002), pp. 40–3, which observes that "Only ground forces can take and hold territory. . . . Occupation to defend territory signals that a nation is willing to spend its blood and treasure for that particular piece of ground and the resources contained therein." See T. R. Fehrenbach, *This Kind of War*, as cited in "Chapter 1: The Army and the Profession of Arms" (at chrishaase.com/aa/FM1/ch1.htm): "[Y]ou may fly over a land forever; you may bomb it, atomize it, pulverize it and wipe it clean of life – but if you desire to defend it, protect it, and keep it for civilization, you must do this on the ground."

93. Gat, *Origins of Military Thought*, pp. 128, 130–1: "Jomini always stressed that he did not believe in a military 'system', certainly not in a complete geometrical system such as that of Bülow. Instead, he believed in 'principles', or, in other words, in a much more flexible and less pretentious theoretical framework." Thus, Jomini will be "judged not so much from the point of view of its success in analyzing the warfare of its time but rather for its claim to be a universal theory of war." (H. Lecomte, whose father was a contemporary of Jomini, wrote that Jomini had attempted only to deduce several principles that "would not assure victory, but would make it more probable." Quoted in Alger, *Quest for Victory*, p. 129.).

94. Jomini, *Art of War: New Edition*, p. 282.

95. "Jomini's *Art of War*," pp. 554–5. Yet "[t]he same general may, on the other hand, be at once a good tactician and strategist, and have made all the arrangements for gaining a victory that his means will permit. In this case, if he be only moderately seconded by his troops and subordinate officers, he will probably gain a decided victory. If, however, his troops have neither discipline nor courage and his subordinate officers envy and deceive him, he will undoubtedly see his fine hopes fade away."

96. Ibid., pp. 494, 510.

97. Jomini, *Art of War: New Edition*, p. 326.

98. For an analysis of Jomini, see Gat, *Origins of Military Thought*, pp. 106–31. As Gat explained (p. 123), "Jomini's abstract principles, he [Clausewitz] argued, ignored the living

reality of war, the operation of moral forces, and the unique conditions of every particular case." And again: "In *On War* he [Clausewitz] again argued that principles like those of Jomini which were abstracted from the real conditions of particular cases could never be universally valid." In "Jomini's *Art of War*," p. 494, Jomini was critical of Clausewitz: "Clausewitz commits a grave error in asserting that a battle not characterized by a maneuver to turn the enemy cannot result in a complete victory."

99. Carl von Clausewitz, *On War*, ed. and intro. Anatol Rapoport (Baltimore: Penguin, 1971), p. 119.

100. Hans Rothfels, "Clausewitz," in Earle (ed.), *Makers of Modern Strategy: Military Thought*, pp. 93–113, at p. 102.

101. To be explicit, the concept of "total war" is not the same as "grand strategic victory" because the latter refers to the destruction of the existing political, economic, and military order within a society, whereas the former refers to the use of the complete range of instruments of war.

102. Michael I. Handel, *Masters of War: Sun Tzu, Clausewitz and Jomini* (London: Frank Cass, 1992), p. 24.

103. See Raymond Aron, "Introduction," in Herman Kahn, *Thinking about the Unthinkable* (New York: Avon Books, 1962), pp. 1–15, at p. 14. In the nuclear era, "it [disarmament] is no longer necessary to take away all the enemy's weapons from him; it will suffice to take away his means of retaliation to hold him at your mercy." Aron continued with the argument that, "in pre-atomic days it was rationally conceivable to aim at absolute victory in terms of disarming the enemy and thereafter to limit the fruits of victory" (p. 199).

104. Of the vast literature on Clausewitz, see Carl von Clausewitz, *On War*, ed. and trans. Michael Howard and Peter Paret (Princeton: Princeton University Press, 1976); Peter Paret, *Clausewitz and the State: The Man, His Theories, and His Times* (Princeton: Princeton University Press, 1976); Paret, "Clausewitz," in Paret (ed.), *Makers of Modern Strategy*, pp. 186–213; Paret, "Clausewitz: A Bibliographical Survey," *World Politics* 17.2 (January 1965), pp. 272–85; Gat, *Origins of Military Thought*, esp. pp. 156–254; Christopher Bassford, *Clausewitz in English: The Reception of Clausewitz in Britain and America* (New York: Oxford University Press, 1994); Alan D. Beyer-

chen, "Clausewitz, Nonlinearity, and the Unpredictability of War," *International Security* 17.3 (Winter 1992–3), pp. 59–90; Michael I. Handel, *Clausewitz and Modern Strategy* (London: Frank Cass, 1986); Handel, *Masters of War;* Michael Howard, *Clausewitz* (Oxford: Oxford University Press, 1983). Rothfels, "Clausewitz," p. 94, notes that *On War* was divided into eight books, which focused on the nature of war, the theory of war, strategy, combat, military forces, defense, the attack, and the plan of war.

105. Gat, *Origins of Military Thought,* p. 123: "That the conduct of war could not be reduced to universal principles was the general message of *On War.*"

106. Ibid., p. 198: "Clausewitz argued for the feasibility of a universal theory of war, citing a long list of propositions." And again: "One would agree, and abandon the attempts, were it not for the obvious fact that a whole range of propositions can be demonstrated without difficulty: . . . that victory consists not only in the occupation of the battlefield, but in the destruction of the enemy's physical and psychological forces, which is usually not attainable until the enemy is pursued after a victorious battle; that success is always greater at the point where the victory was gained."

107. As quoted in ibid., p. 189.

108. Ibid., p. 205.

109. Raymond Aron, *Clausewitz: Philosopher of War* (Englewood Cliffs, NJ: Prentice Hall, 1985), pp. 97, 100. In Clausewitz's words, "By the medium of victory, strategy attains the end which it has devised for the combat. . . . A victory which aims to weaken the armed forces of the enemy is something other than a victory which only enables us to occupy a position" (p. 97).

110. Ibid., p. 101. See also James M. McPherson, "Lincoln and the Strategy of Unconditional Surrender," in Gabor S. Boritt (ed.), *Lincoln, the War President* (New York: Oxford University Press, 1992), pp. 29–62, at p. 38: "The first usually means a limited war ended by a negotiated peace. The second usually means a total war ending in unconditional surrender by the loser."

111. See Clausewitz, *On War,* ed. Howard and Paret, p. 71. See also Richard E. Beringer, Herman Hattaway, Archer Jones, and William N. Still Jr., *Why the South Lost the Civil War* (Athens: University of Georgia Press, 1986),

p. 115, for its discussion of the challenges of pursuit in battle.

112. See Clausewitz, *On War,* ed. Howard and Paret, p. 566. "The end is either to bring the enemy to his knees or at least to deprive him of some of his territory. . . . This culminating point in victory is bound to recur in every future war in which the destruction of the enemy cannot be the military aim."

113. Carl von Clausewitz, *On War,* trans. J. J. Graham (New York: E. P. Dutton, 1918), p. 250.

114. Aron, *Clausewitz: Philosopher of War,* p. 57.

115. Ibid., pp. 129, 156.

116. See "Clausewitz's *Principles of War,*" in *Roots of Strategy, Book 2,* pp. 301–88, at p. 326: "For it is easy to change an indecisive victory into a decisive one through energetic pursuit of the enemy." And, "Next to victory, the act of pursuit is most important in war" (p. 337).

117. Aron, *Clausewitz: Philosopher of War,* p. 194.

118. Rothfels, "Clausewitz," p. 96, argued that wars "involved the very existence of the nations concerned and, as in the religious wars of the sixteenth century, they involved opposing principles, opposing philosophies of life."

119. Clausewitz, *On War,* ed. Rapoport, p. 192.

120. Clausewitz, *On War,* ed. Howard and Paret, p. 143.

121. Karl von Clausewitz, *On War,* trans. O. J. Matthijs Jolles (Washington, DC: Infantry Journal Press, 1950), p. 182.

122. Ibid. There are other "essential" parts of victory: "the lowering of the flag" and the "element of humiliation and shame" (p. 182).

123. Ibid., p. 190.

124. Ibid., pp. 245–6.

125. As quoted in Bassford, *Clausewitz in English,* pp. 29–30: "an important superiority of numbers but which need not be over two to one, will be sufficient to ensure the victory, however disadvantageous other circumstances may be."

126. Clausewitz, *On War,* trans. Jolles, p. 203.

127. Ibid., p. 208.

128. Ibid., p. 210.

129. Ibid., pp. 213, 585–93.

130. Ibid., p. 211.

131. Clausewitz, *On War,* trans. Graham, pp. 138–9.

132. Clausewitz, *On War*, ed. Howard and Paret, pp. 595–600.

133. Ibid., pp. 227.

134. Brodie, *Strategy in the Missile Age*, p. 53.

135. Clausewitz, *On War*, ed. Howard and Paret, pp. 595.

136. Ibid., p. 596.

137. Ibid., pp. 90–1.

138. Ibid., pp. 93.

139. See Rothfels, "Clausewitz," p. 99, in which war is "an affair of the whole nation."

140. Clausewitz, *On War*, ed. Howard and Paret, pp. 617–37, for a discussion of the conduct of "total war."

141. For Clausewitz's analysis of the concept of "major victory," see Clausewitz, *On War*, ed. Howard and Paret, pp. 253–70.

142. Rothfels, "Clausewitz," p. 107.

143. Clausewitz, *On War*, ed. Howard and Paret, p. 75.

144. Ibid., p. 81.

145. Clausewitz, *On War*, ed. Howard and Paret, p. 128.

146. Ibid., p. 92.

147. Ibid.: "Once the expenditure of efforts exceeds the value of the political object, the object must be renounced and peace must follow."

148. Gat, *Origins of Military Thought*, pp. 123–4.

149. For a discussion of German military thinkers, see Antulio J. Echevarria II, *After Clausewitz: German Military Thinkers before the Great War* (Lawrence: University Press of Kansas, 2000).

150. Henry Wager Halleck, *Elements of Military Art and Science* (New York: D. Appleton, 1862), p. 37.

151. Ibid., p. 40.

152. Ibid., pp. 52–3.

153. See Robert Gilpin, *The Political Economy of International Relations* (Princeton: Princeton University Press, 1987); Stephen D. Krasner, "State Power and the Structure of International Trade," *World Politics* 28.3 (April 1976), pp. 317–48.

154. See Edward Mead Earle, "Adam Smith, Alexander Hamilton, Friedrich List: The Economic Foundations of Military Power," in Earle (ed.), *Makers of Modern Strategy: Military Thought*, pp. 117–54, at p. 122.

155. See Adam Smith, *An Inquiry into the Nature and Causes of the Wealth of Nations* (London: George Routledge & Sons,

Ltd., 1898), pp. 552–3, who argued that "A well-regulated standing army is superior to every militia. Such an army, as it can best be maintained by an opulent and civilized nation, so it can alone defend such a nation against the invasion of a poor and barbarous neighbor."

156. A late twentieth-century form of this argument, the *democratic peace theory*, suggested that the rise of democratic governments would decrease the chance of war. For a discussion of these arguments, see Michael C. Desch, "Democracy and Victory: Why Regime Type Hardly Matters," *International Security* 27.2 (Fall 2002), pp. 5–47, esp. the section "Do Democracies Really Win Wars More Often?" (pp. 9–25). See also these consecutive articles in *International Security* 28.1 (Summer 2003): Ajin Choi, "The Power of Democratic Cooperation," pp. 142–53; David A. Lake, "Fair Fights? Evaluating Theories of Democracy and Victory," pp. 154–79; Michael C. Desch, "Democracy and Victory: Fair Fights or Food Fights?" pp. 180–94.

157. See Earle, "Adam Smith, Alexander Hamilton, Friedrich List," p. 136.

158. See [Bernard Law Montgomery,] Viscount Montgomery of Alamein, "European War in the Seventeenth Century," in *A History of Warfare* (New York: William Morrow, 1983), pp. 263–89.

159. See Earle, "Adam Smith, Alexander Hamilton, Friedrich List," p. 143, who argued that the "greater the productive power, the greater the strength of the nation . . . and the greater its independence in time of war." This often translates into the notion that the "ability of a nation to wage war is measured in terms of its power to produce wealth."

160. Ibid., p. 143. As List put it, "all warlike operations depend so much on the condition of the national revenue."

161. Ibid., p. 149. "List foresaw that the network of railway lines . . . would enable the army of a unified Germany, in the event of an invasion, to move troops from any point in the country to the frontiers in such a way as to multiply many fold its defensive potential."

162. See Sigmund Neumann and Mark Von Hagen, "Engels and Marx on Revolution, War, and the Army in Society," in Paret (ed.), *Makers of Modern Strategy*, pp. 262–80, at p. 263.

163. Karl Marx and Friedrich Engels, "Communist Manifesto," in Robert C. Tuck-

er (ed.), *The Marx–Engels Reader* (New York: W. W. Norton, 1972), pp. 331–62, at p. 362.

164. Friedrich Engels, "The Tactics of Social Democracy," in Tucker (ed.), *Marx–Engels Reader*, pp. 406–23, at p. 410.

165. Ibid., p. 417.

166. Karl Marx, "Alienation and Social Classes," in Tucker (ed.), *Marx–Engels Reader*, pp. 104–6, at p. 105.

167. Karl Marx, "On the Jewish Question," in Tucker (ed.), *Marx–Engels Reader*, pp. 26–52, at p. 31.

168. Karl Marx and Friedrich Engels, "The German Ideology, Part I," in Tucker (ed.), *Marx–Engels Reader*, pp. 110–64, at pp. 115–16. As Marx and Engels wrote in their "Communist Manifesto" in 1888, "Thus the whole historical movement is concentrated in the hands of the bourgeoisie; every victory so obtained is a victory for the bourgeoisie" (p. 342).

169. See Sigmund Neumann, "Engels and Marx: Military Concepts of the Social Revolutionaries," in Earle (ed.), *Makers of Modern Strategy: Military Thought*, pp. 155–71, who noted that "Engels regarded ["movements of armed mobs"] as a 'drama without parallel in the annals of military history'" (p. 166).

170. Friedrich Engels, "Letters on Historical Materialism," in Tucker (ed.), *Marx–Engels Reader*, pp. 640–50, at p. 645.

171. See James Noren, "CIA's Analysis of the Soviet Economy," in Gerald K. Haines and Robert E. Leggett (eds.), *Watching the Bear: Essays on CIA's Analysis of the Soviet Union* (Washington, DC: CIA, Center for the Study of Intelligence), at www.cia.gov/csi/books/watchingthebear/article02.html.

172. Helmuth Karl Bernhard, Graf von Moltke, *Strategy – Its Theory and Application: The Wars for German Unification, 1866–1871* (1896; rpt. by Westport, CT: Greenwood, 1971); Arden Bucholz, *Moltke, Schlieffen, and Prussian War Planning* (Providence, RI: Berg, 1993).

173. Ibid. (both works).

174. See Alger, *Quest for Victory*, pp. 58–9, who notes that "In the early twentieth century, French doctrine continued to reflect conclusions drawn from the victories attained a century earlier." Also, Stephen Van Evera, "The Cult of the Offensive and the Origins of the First World War," *International Security* 9.1 (Summer 1984), pp. 58–107.

175. See Victor-Bernard Derrecagaix, *Modern War*, trans. C. W. Foster (Washington, DC: James J. Chapman, 1888), p. viii. Subsequent citations are given in the text.

176. Alger, *Quest for Victory*, pp. 78–9. Henderson attributed these principles to the American Civil War general "Stonewall" Jackson. See G. F. R. Henderson, *Stonewall Jackson and the American Civil War, Volumes I and II* (London: Longmans, Green, 1898); G. F. R. Henderson, *Stonewall Jackson and the American Civil War* (New York: Grosset & Dunlap, 1904).

177. G. F. R. Henderson, *The Science of War: A Collection of Essays and Lectures, 1892–1903*, ed. Neill Malcolm (London: Longmans, Green, 1905), p. 45.

178. See Jay Luvaas, "The Henderson Legacy," in G. F. R. Henderson, *The Civil War: A Soldier's View – A Collection of Civil War Writings by Col. G. F. R. Henderson*, ed. Luvaas (Chicago: University of Chicago Press, 1958), pp. 301–14, at p. 307.

179. Henderson, *Science of War*, p. 39. In addition see Henderson, *Civil War: A Soldier's View*.

180. Henderson, *Science of War*, p. 39.

181. See E. A. Altham, *The Principles of War, Historically Illustrated* (London: Macmillan, 1914), p. 35.

182. Henderson, *Science of War*, p. 41. Subsequent citations are given in the text.

183. See Alfred von Schlieffen, *Alfred von Schlieffen's Military Writings*, trans. and ed. Robert T. Foley (London: Frank Cass, 2003); Terence Zuber, *Inventing the Schlieffen Plan: German War Planning, 1871–1914* (New York: Oxford University Press, 2002).

184. Montgomery, *History of Warfare*, pp. 459, 463; Spenser Wilkinson, *The Early Life of Moltke* (Oxford: Clarendon, 1913); Hajo Holborn, "Moltke and Schlieffen: The Prussian–German School," in Earle (ed.), *Makers of Modern Strategy: Military Thought*, pp. 172–205.

185. See Günther E. Rothenberg, "The Thought of Annihilation in the Military Doctrine of Carl von Clausewitz and Count Alfred von Schlieffen," *Operational Thinking in Clausewitz, Moltke, Schlieffen and Manstein* (Bonn: E. S. Mittler & Sohn, 1988), pp. 11–20.

186. See Holborn, "Moltke and Schlieffen," p. 188.

187. See ibid., p. 187.

188. Schlieffen, *Alfred von Schlieffen's Military Writings*, p. 28. Subsequent citations are given in the text.

189. See ibid., p. 188, for a discussion of the "Cannae Studies."

190. Holborn, "Moltke and Schlieffen," p. 201.

191. For a discussion of the origins of World War I, see Paul W. Schroeder, "The Risks of Victory: An Historian's Provocation," *National Interest* 66 (Winter 2001–2), pp. 22–36. See also Holborn, "Moltke and Schlieffen," p. 204.

192. See Foch, *Principles of War*; Basil H. Liddell Hart, *Foch: The Man of Orleans* (Boston: Little, Brown, 1932); Stefan T. Possony and Étienne Mantoux, "Du Picq and Foch: The French School," in Earle (ed.), *Makers of Modern Strategy: Military Thought*, pp. 206–33, at p. 219. Another French strategist, Émile Mayer – a contemporary of Foch at the École Polytechnique – dismissed the idea of rigid principles of war in *The Theory of War and the Study of the Military* (Alger, *Quest for Victory*, p. 128–9).

193. See Foch, *Principles of War*, p. 23.

194. See Possony and Mantoux, "Du Picq and Foch," p. 221.

195. See ibid., p. 222, with the argument that war is "more and more national in its origin and aims, more and more powerful in its means."

196. As quoted in ibid., p. 231: "[F]inal victory cannot depend on the success, however outstanding, of a single attack. That attack must be linked to a certain number of others. It must be part of a whole, not the whole itself."

197. See Foch, *Principles of War*, pp. 281–2. Subsequent citations are given in the text. All emphases shown are in the original.

198. Possony and Mantoux, "Du Picq and Foch," p. 228. Furthermore (Foch, *Principles of War*, p. 290), "No victory is possible unless the commander be energetic, eager for responsibilities and bold undertakings, unless he possess and can impart to all the resolute will of seeing the thing through; unless he be capable of exerting a personal action composed of will, judgment, and freedom of mind in the midst of danger." Victory is held to be related to "moral superiority over the enemy" in French theory of the time because, in its absence, "the

combatant would be discouraged by the suffering that he must endure before gaining victory." Quoted in Alger, *Quest for Victory*, p. 130.

199. Ibid., pp. 206–33.

200. For an excellent analysis of Lyautey, see Douglas Porch, "Bugeaud, Galliéni, Lyautey: The Development of French Colonial Warfare," in Paret (ed.), *Makers of Modern Strategy*, pp. 376–407; Jean Gottmann, "Bugeaud, Galliéni, Lyautey: The Development of French Colonial Warfare," in Earle (ed.), *Makers of Modern Strategy: Military Thought*, pp. 234–59.

201. As Lyautey noted: "A country is not conquered and pacified when a military operation has decimated and terrorized its people. Once the initial shock passes, a spirit of revolt will arise among the masses, fanned by a feeling of resentment which has been created by the application of brutal force" (Gottmann, "Bugeaud, Galliéni, Lyautey," p. 244).

202. See Gottmann (ibid., pp. 234–5), who notes that the objective is to avoid unnecessary destruction during a colonial operation "in order to preserve the productive potential of the theater of operations and thus economize the supplies coming from more distant initial bases; but most important, because the conquered country is to be integrated immediately after the conquest into the 'imperial' whole, politically as well as economically."

203. Ibid., p. 243. For a more recent analysis of Lyautey, see Porch, "Bugeaud, Galliéni, Lyautey."

204. André Maurois, *Lyautey*, trans. Hamish Miles (New York: D. Appleton, 1931), p. 75. This strategy was contrasted by Lyautey with European practices in war (p. 262): "[W]hatever I had to destroy I built up again later, more solidly and durably. Our troops left behind them territory restored to peace, scored with roads, and quickening with life; and commercial exchange preceded the exchange of ideas. . . . What a difference from the wars of Europe, which ravage cathedrals and museums and everything irreplaceable, and annihilate in one day the priceless treasures of centuries."

205. Ibid., pp. 126–7, with respect to Algeria. Lyautey, Maurois continues, wanted "to acquaint the oppressed sedentary peoples with the blessings of peace, and step by step to consolidate the acquired results by setting up outposts which would radiate patrols with wide

range, crossing their beams like those of light-houses."

206. Ibid., pp. 221–2: "He had no absolute doctrine regarding anything. . . . In the realm of action there is no theoretic method true for all times and all places."

207. Quoted in Heinl (comp.), *Dictionary of Military and Naval Quotations*, p. 338.

208. As quoted in Alger, *Quest for Victory*, p. 107.

209. Maurois, *Lyautey*, p. 182.

210. Delbrück, *History of the Art of War*, vols. I–IV. See also Hans Delbrück, *Numbers in History* (London: University of London Press, 1913); Felix Gilbert, "From Clausewitz to Delbrück and Hintze: Achievements and Failures of Military History," *Journal of Strategic Studies* 3,3 (December 1980), pp. 11–20; Peter Paret, "Hans Delbrück on Military Critics and Military Historians," *Military Affairs* 30 (Fall 1966), pp. 148–52; Gordon A. Craig, "Delbrück: The Military Historian," in Earle (ed.), *Makers of Modern Strategy: Military Thought*, pp. 260–83.

211. John Keegan, *The Face of Battle: A Study of Agincourt, Waterloo and the Somme* (New York: Penguin, 1984), p. 53.

212. Delbrück, *History of the Art of War*, vol. IV, p. 432. Subsequent citations are given in the text.

213. Craig, "Delbrück," p. 273.

214. Ibid.

215. Ibid. As an example, Craig wrote that in "the Peloponnesian War, the political weakness of Athens in comparison with that of the League which faced her, determined the kind of strategy which Pericles followed. Had he at tempted to follow the principles of [annihilation,] disaster would have followed automatically" (p. 274).

216. Ibid., p. 275.

217. Ibid.

218. Delbrück is quoted thus in ibid., p. 277: "May God forbid that Germany enter upon the path of Napoleonic policy. . . . Europe stands united in this one conviction: it will never submit to a hegemony enforced upon it by a single state."

219. As quoted in Alger, *Quest for Victory*, pp. 131–2. See also Friedrich Bernhardi, *The War of the Future in the Light of the Lessons of the World War* (London: Hutchinson, 1920) [hereafter cited in the text as *WF*].

220. Friedrich von Bernhardi, *On War of To-day*, vol. I: *Principles and Elements of Modern War*, trans. Karl von Donat (London: Hugh Rees, Ltd., 1912) [hereafter cited in the text as *WT*], pp. 4–5. "I have it in my mind to form the whole matter gradually into a doctrine of modern war, which will in a uniform manner comprehend the manifestations of our time" (p. 6).

221. Ibid., p. 24: "Epaminondas was successful by adopting the oblique battle-order; Hannibal annihilated the Roman legions, formed in deep battle-order by a twofold envelopment; Frederic the Great . . . made use of the oblique battle-order . . . to wipe out his opponent; Napoleon conquered by the shock of the reserves he had held back with the object of bringing about the decision when in the course of the combat he saw the possibility of victory; Moltke preferred envelopment initiated by the operations."

222. Furthermore (p. 173), "we shall strive to obtain victory by breaking through, and either make our main thrust where a rapid success is most probable."

223. Ibid., p. 164 (emphasis in original): "Lastly, the superiority of the offensive lies in the fact that it *alone* can bring the decision. Even a successful defence can only mean superiority when it gives the defender a chance to pass from it and seek a decision by the offensive. . . . [I]t must be probable that so decisive a victory can be won over the enemy that the latter loses his power to bring about a decision which has any prospects of success for him. Such a victory can, as a rule, only be secured by the offensive."

224. He continued (p. 81): "and so the main instrument of the defence will be the counter-attack, which must be planned and organized beforehand."

225. Bernhardi went on to define a defensive strategy as one that "means rather that one side wishes to delay the decision because it no longer feels capable of forcing that decision itself" (p. 162).

226. He also contended (p. 100) that "Napoleon's dictum proves false – that victory is on the side of the big battalions."

227. Bernhardi, *War of the Future*, p. 197: "Diplomacy must therefore confine itself to preparing the way for military victories and exploiting them, but only in accordance with instructions *to be given by the military authorities*" (emphasis in original).

228. Gilbert, "Machiavelli" (Earle version), p. 17.

229. As quoted in Alger, *Quest for Victory,* p. 134, who then remarked that "In order to gain victory, it is necessary to concentrate decidedly superior forces for the main effort by a regrouping of forces and combat means.

3. Modern Origins of Victory

1. See Harvey A. DeWeerd, "Churchill, Lloyd George, Clemenceau: The Emergence of the Civilian," in Edward Mead Earle (ed.), with Gordon A. Craig and Felix Gilbert, *Makers of Modern Strategy: Military Thought from Machiavelli to Hitler* (Princeton: Princeton University Press, 1973), pp. 287–305, who noted the "definite trend toward the mechanization of war, toward the increased size of armies, toward the militarization of population, toward the nationalization of war effort, and toward the intensification of military operations" (pp. 288–9). Also, Gordon A. Craig, "The Political Leader as Strategist," in Peter Paret (ed.), with Gordon A. Craig and Felix Gilbert, *Makers of Modern Strategy: From Machiavelli to the Nuclear Age* (Princeton: Princeton University Press, 1986), pp. 481–509.

2. See DeWeerd, "Churchill, Lloyd George, Clemenceau," p. 291.

3. See ibid., p. 296.

4. As quoted in John I. Alger, *The Quest for Victory: The History of the Principles of War* (Westport, CT: Greenwood, 1982), p. 104. See also Stephen Van Evera, "The Cult of the Offensive and the Origins of the First World War," *International Security* 9.1 (Summer 1984), pp. 58–107.

5. As quoted in Alger, *Quest for Victory,* p. 99.

6. As quoted in ibid., p. 99.

7. J. Colin, *The Transformations of War,* trans. L. H. R. Pope-Hennessy (London: Hugh Rees, Ltd., 1912), p. 347. Compare French military thinker F. Culmann, who proposed after World War I that, while there are principles of war that do not necessarily ensure or guarantee that the state will achieve victory, neglecting these principles will "considerably enhance the chances of defeat [for the state]." Quoted in Alger, *Quest for Victory,* p. 128.

8. Ibid., pp. 348–53. Colin warned about relying "too exclusively" on the "most perfect arms" for victory (p. 349).

9. Ibid., p. 342.

10. For an excellent analysis of Ludendorff, see Hans Speier, "Ludendorff: The German Concept of Total War," in Earle (ed.), *Makers of Modern Strategy: Military Thought,* pp. 306–21.

11. Ludendorff's concept of total war is summarized in ibid., p. 315.

12. Ibid., pp. 315–16.

13. Ludendorff argued that "the nature of total war requires that it be waged only if the whole people is really threatened in its existence, and determined to wage it" (ibid., p. 318). As stated in V. D. Sokolovskii (ed.), *Soviet Military Strategy,* trans. and annot. Herbert S. Dinerstein, Leon Gouré, and Thomas W. Wolfe (Englewood Cliffs, NJ: Prentice–Hall, 1963), p. 365: "Ludendorff's theory of total war . . . envisaged not only the defeat of the enemy's armed forces but also the annihilation of the population, industry, transport, and cities." (A downloadable version of this book is at http://www.rand.org/pubs/reports/R416/.)

14. Erich Ludendorff, *The Nation at War,* trans. A. S. Rappoport (London: Hutchinson, 1936), p. 158. Subsequent citations are given in the text.

15. However, "there is a certain sentimental objection to retreating movements, as retreats are most forced upon the retreating side by tactical decisions" (pp. 158–9).

16. Furthermore (p. 109), "The bombing of the civil population of a country in open cities, and so on, is certainly not in accordance with the laws and usages of war as they have been laid down by international law. . . . [N]o nation, in the struggle for its life, can afford to abstain from using methods which are also directed against it."

17. Compare Foch's comments that "'Small battalions' also have carried off victories" and yet, "Eight more Army Corps at the beginning of the War would have secured us the victory" (pp. 87–8).

18. For an excellent review of the ideas and influence of Haushofer, see Derwent Whittlesey, "Haushofer: The Geopoliticians," in Earle (ed.), *Makers of Modern Strategy: Military Thought,* pp. 388–411.

19. This idea is raised by Whittlesey (p. 392), who cites Edward Mead Earle, "Political and Military Strategy for the United States," an address before the Academy of Political Science, New York, November 13,

1940: *Proceedings of the Academy of Political Science* 19 (1941), pp. 2–9.

20. For an excellent analysis of the influence of Soviet thinkers on war, see Edward Mead Earle, "Lenin, Trotsky, Stalin: Soviet Concepts of War," in Earle (ed.), *Makers of Modern Strategy: Military Thought*, pp. 322–64.

21. For an analysis of the failure of Marxism, see Joshua Muravchik, "Marxism," *Foreign Policy* 133 (November–December 2002), pp. 36–8.

22. See V. I. Lenin, "On the Slogan for a United States of Europe," in Robert C. Tucker (ed.), *The Lenin Anthology* (New York: W. W. Norton, 1975), pp. 200–3, at p. 203.

23. Leon Trotsky, "To: Kremlin, Moscow – Chairman of the Council of People's Commissars Lenin," November 19, 1918, in Jan M Meijer (ed.), *The Trotsky Papers, 1917–1922* (London: Mouton, 1964–71), vol. 1: *1917–1919, pp.* 127–31, at p. 129.

24. V. I. Lenin, "Imperialism, the Highest Stage of Capitalism," in Tucker (ed.), *Lenin Anthology*, pp. 204–74, at p. 207. As Lenin wrote in "A Great Beginning" (pp. 477–88, at pp. 479–80): "In order to achieve victory, in order to build and consolidate socialism, the proletariat must fulfil a twofold or dual task: first, it must, by its supreme heroism in the revolutionary struggle against capital, win over the entire mass of the working and exploited people, it must win them over, organise them and lead them in the struggle to overthrow the bourgeoisie and utterly suppress their resistance. Second, it must lead the whole mass of the working and exploited people . . . toward the creation of a new social bond, a new labour discipline, a new organization of labour."

25. V. I. Lenin, "Report on War and Peace," in ibid., pp. 542–9, at pp. 544–5.

26. Lenin quoted in B. H. Liddell Hart, *The Decisive Wars of History: A Study in Strategy* (London: G. Bell & Sons, Ltd., 1929), p. 146.

27. V. I. Lenin, "Advice of an Onlooker," in "The Revolutionary Taking of Power," in Tucker (ed.), *Lenin Anthology*, pp. 295–414, at pp. 413–14 (emphasis in original).

28. V. I. Lenin, "Immediate Tasks of the Soviet Government," in "The Revolutionary State and Its Policies," in ibid., pp. 438–60, at p. 442. "To suspend the offensive of a victorious army . . . is necessary precisely in order to gain the rest of the enemy's territory." Lenin, "'Left-Wing' Communism," in ibid., pp. 550–618, at p. 556.

29. Lenin, "'Left-Wing' Communism," p. 553. "[A]bsolute centralisation and rigorous discipline in the proletariat are an essential condition of victory over the bourgeoisie" (p. 553).

30. See J. V. Stalin, *Lenin: A Speech Delivered at a Memorial Meeting of the Kremlin Military School, January 28, 1924*, in Stalin, *Works* (Moscow: Foreign Languages Publishing House, 1953), vol. 6, pp. 54–66, at p. 59.

31. See Earle, "Lenin, Trotsky, Stalin," p. 336.

32. Leon Trotsky, "Rough Outline for the Draft of a Programme of the Russian Communist Party," in Meijer (ed.), *The Trotsky Papers*, vol. 1: *1917–1919*, pp. 271–95, at p. 279.

33. Leon Trotsky, "To the Central Committee of the Russian Communist Party," in Meijer (ed.), *Trotsky Papers*, vol. 1, pp. 389–95, at p. 389.

34. Ibid., p. 393 ("To: Kiev – Council of People's Commissars, Rakovskijj").

35. Leon Trotsky, "Char'kov – People's Commissar for Military Affairs, Mezlauk," in Meijer (ed.), *Trotsky Papers*, vol. 1, pp. 471–3, at p. 471.

36. Lenin, "'Left-Wing' Communism," p. 587.

37. See Earle, "Lenin, Trotsky, Stalin," p. 343: "These relatively permanent phenomena must be studied as carefully as transitory conditions at home and abroad."

38. As Earle observed (ibid., p. 350), "these objectives could be attained only by the offensive."

39. Earle argued (ibid.) that "Stalin's regime prepared for total war on a scale which few persons in the outside world even remotely suspected or comprehended."

40. Richard Rhodes, "The General and World War III," *New Yorker* 71.15 (June 19, 1995), pp. 47–59, at p. 47, who quoted General Curtis LeMay with the view that the objective of war is the "complete subjugation of the enemy" (p. 50).

41. Raymond Aron, *The Century of Total War* (Garden City, NY: Doubleday, 1954), pp. 226–7.

42. For Mao's writings and pronouncements, see Mao Tse-tung, *Selected Military*

Writings (Peking: Foreign Languages Press, 1966); Stuart R. Schram, *The Political Thought of Mao Tse-tung* (New York: Frederick A. Praeger, 1966); Mao, *The Writings of Mao Zedong, 1949–1976,* ed. Michael Y. M. Kau and John K. Leung (New York: M. E. Sharpe, 1986).

43. Chen Jian, *Mao's China and the Cold War* (Chapel Hill: University of North Carolina Press, 2001).

44. Mao, *Selected Military Writings,* p. 88.

45. Schram, *Political Thought of Mao Tsetung,* p. 207.

46. Mao, *Selected Military Writings,* p. 78.

47. Schram, *Political Thought of Mao Tsetung,* p. 257. Thus, "This is the historical epoch in which world capitalism and imperialism are going down to their doom and world socialism and democracy are marching toward victory" (p. 281). Mao also observed that "it is possible for China's revolutionary war to develop and attain victory" (p. 203).

48. Mao, *Writings of Mao Zedong,* p. 220: "I hope that the people of our country will solidly unite among themselves as well as with our ally the Soviet Union, solidly unite with all the People's Democracies, with all the nations and people of the world that sympathize with us, and continue to march forward in the direction of victory in the struggle against aggression, victory in constructing our great country, and victory in the defense of lasting peace in the world. Comrades, if we do this, I believe our victory is assured." See also note 47.

49. Mao, *Selected Military Writings,* p. 78.

50. Ibid., p. 130.

51. Ibid., p. 194–5. Later (p. 328), Mao argued that "Unless we reduce the enemy to extreme fatigue and complete starvation, we cannot win final victory."

52. Schram, *Political Thought of Mao Tsetung,* p. 207.

53. Mao, *Selected Military Writings,* p. 129, argued that "Victory or defeat in the first battle has a tremendous effect upon the entire situation, all the way to the final engagement." Subsequent citations are given in the text.

54. Ibid., p. 123: "It [the winning side] will strive to exploit its victory and inflict still greater damage on the enemy, add to the conditions that are in its favor and further improve its situation, and prevent the enemy from succeeding in extricating himself from his unfavourable conditions and unfavourable situation and averting disaster."

55. To this, he added "various principles for winning victory [against Japan]: first, the establishment of an anti-Japanese united front in China; second, the formation of an international anti-Japanese united front; third, the rise of the revolutionary movement of the people of Japan and the Japanese colonies" (ibid., p. 191).

56. "Strategy for the Second Year of the War of Liberation," September 1, 1947 (ibid., p. 329).

57. J. F. C. Fuller, *Tanks in the Great War, 1914–1918* (New York: E. P. Dutton, 1920), p. 298. See J. F. C. Fuller, *On Future War* (London: Sifton Praed, 1928), p. 153: "Tools, or weapons, if only the right ones can be discovered, form 99 per cent. of victory; this is the secret which I intended to divulge. Strategy, command, leadership, courage, discipline, supply, organisation and all the moral and physical paraphernalia of war are nothing as to a high superiority of weapons . . . for given the right tool any war can be won at the smallest cost. . . . [N]o army of 50 years before any date selected would stand 'a dog's chance' against the army existing at this date."

58. See J. F. C. Fuller, *The Reformation of War* (London: Hutchinson, 1923), p. xiii. As Brian Bond and Martin Alexander observed ("Liddell Hart and De Gaulle: The Doctrines of Limited Liability and Mobile Defense," in Paret [ed.], *Makers of Modern Strategy,* pp. 598–623, at p. 602), Fuller had a "wider concern with the impact of science and technology on warfare." See also Fuller, *Armament and History: A Study of the Influence on History from the Dawn of Classical Warfare to the Second World War* (New York: Charles Scribner's Sons, 1945); Fuller, *Decisive Battles: Their Influence upon History and Civilisation* (New York: Charles Scribner's Sons, 1940).

59. Fuller, *Tanks in the Great War,* p. 321.

60. Fuller, *On Future War,* p. 155. Subsequent citations are given in the text.

61. For a discussion of the advantages of tanks, see ibid., p. 189.

62. J. F. C. Fuller, *The Foundations of the Science of War* (London: Hutchinson, 1926), p. 107.

63. Ibid., p. 111, continuing: "for once the enemy's resistance has been overcome the ultimate military objective is won."

64. J. F. C. Fuller, *A Military History of the Western World,* vol. 3: *From the Seven Days Bat-*

tle, 1862, to the Battle of Leyte Gulf, 1944 (New York: Funk & Wagnalls, 1956), p. 381.

65. Fuller, *On Future War*, p. 323.

66. J. F. C. Fuller, *The Conduct of War, 1789–1961: A Study of the Impact of the French, Industrial, and Russian Revolutions on War and Its Conduct* (New Brunswick, NJ: Rutgers University Press, 1961), p. 25.

67. Fuller, *On Future War*, p. 188: "If, in the event of war, an air force can change this policy with less physical destruction than it has been possible to attain by armies and navies in the past, then the air force will not absorb the military purpose of navies and armies which in nature is tactical, but will instead establish a new conception of war" (p. 188).

68. Fuller, *Military History of the Western World*, vol. 3, p. 380.

69. Fuller, *Conduct of War*, p. 76. Cf. p. 256, where victory is "never more than a means toward the end[, which for the statesman] is peace."

70. See Irving M. Gibson, "Maginot and Liddell Hart: The Doctrine of Defense," in Earle (ed.), *Makers of Modern Strategy: Military Thought*, pp. 365–87, at p. 384.

71. B. H. Liddell Hart, *Strategy*, 2d rev. ed. (New York: Frederick A. Praeger, 1967), p. 351. He continued that "there has been a very natural tendency to lose sight of the basic national object, and identify it with the military aim. . . . [P]olicy has too often been governed by the military aim – and this has been regarded as an end in itself instead of a means to the end."

72. See John Shy, "Jomini," in Paret (ed.), *Makers of Modern Strategy*, pp. 143–85, at p. 181: "Against a Clausewitzian conception of warfare – the collision of mass armies, the outcome decided by sheer numbers and will power, but the human cost higher than any imaginable 'victory' could justify – Liddell Hart called for renewed emphasis on mobility, audacity, and skill. His strategy of the indirect approach, elaborated in a series of historical and theoretical books and articles, advocated the war of maneuver to out-think and out-flank the enemy, psychologically as well as geographically, at minimum risk and minimum cost."

73. As quoted in Brian Bond, *Liddell Hart: A Study of His Military Thought* (New Brunswick, NJ: Rutgers University Press, 1977), p. 42.

74. B. H. Liddell Hart, *Thoughts on War* (London: Faber & Faber, 1944), p. 47, which continues: "Wise statesmanship must aim at conserving strength so as to be still strong when peace is settled." Subsequent citations are given in the text.

75. Compare B. H. Liddell Hart, *Strategy: The Indirect Approach* (New York: Frederick A. Praeger, 1954), p. 370: "Victory in the true sense implies that the state of peace, and of one's own people, is better after the war than before. . . .Victory in this sense is only possible if a quick result can be gained or if a long effort can be economically proportioned to the national resources. The end must be adjusted to the means."

76. Ibid., pp. 351–4. See also Bond, *Liddell Hart*, p. 7.

77. Bond, *Liddell Hart*, p. 39: "Clausewitz would not have dissented from Liddell Hart's view that the aim of war is 'to subdue the enemy's will to resist, with the least possible human and economic loss to itself.'"

78. See Edward Mead Earle, "Introduction" to Earle (ed.), *Makers of Modern Strategy: Military Thought*, pp. vii–xi, at p. x, who noted that "since 1870 the Germans have thought in terms of aggressive warfare and military annihilation of the enemy, [while] the British (and more recently the French) in terms of defensive warfare and the long-run consequences of economic attrition."

79. See J. E Kaufmann and H. W. Kaufmann, *The Maginot Line. None Shall Pass* (Westport, CT: Praeger, 1997); Anthony Kemp, *The Maginot Line: Myth and Reality* (New York: Stein & Day, 1982).

80. See Gibson, "Maginot and Liddell Hart," p. 373, for his outline of the notion of firepower: "Fire power produced mainly by artillery would establish a protective cover over the army just as the heavily fortified border [the Maginot Line] would protect the nation."

81. See ibid., p. 381, for the views of Liddell Hart, who proposed that "Britain definitely accept the theory of limited liability in her military obligations and return to her traditional policy of blockade and economic warfare, for which she was eminently suited by her mighty navy and the unlimited resources of her empire." However, a French General Baratier (quoted in ibid.) noted that "If ever Germany attacks our country, she will wage totalitarian war, in the course of which France and England, in order not to succumb, will have to

throw into the balance all their resources on land, on sea and in the air."

82. Erich von Manstein, *Lost Victories* (Chicago: Henry Regnery, 1958), p. 18: "[T]he decisive factor throughout was the self-sacrifice, valour and devotion to duty of the German *fighting soldier,* combined with the ability of *commanders* at all levels and their readiness to assume responsibility. These were the qualities which won us our victories."

83. See Bond, *Liddell Hart,* p. 232.

84. See Reginald T. Paget, *Manstein: His Campaigns and His Trial* (London: Collins, 1951).

85. See Heinz Guderian, *Panzer Leader* (London: Michael Joseph, Ltd., 1952). In the Foreword, Liddell Hart wrote that Guderian "applied the idea of the independent use of armoured forces so fully and decisively that he brought about victories which, measured by any standard, have hardly been matched in the records of warfare" (p. 15).

86. See Bond, *Liddell Hart,* p. 222: "Guderian was in the right stage of development to absorb these ideas [about the nature of tank warfare] and start turning them to practical effect."

87. Guderian, *Panzer Leader,* p. 40.

88. Ibid., p. 41. The argument continues: *"Everything is therefore dependent on this: to be able to move faster than has hitherto been done: to keep moving despite the enemy's defensive fire and thus to make it harder for him to build up fresh defensive positions: and finally to carry the attack deep into the enemy's defences"* (emphasis in original).

89. Ibid., p. 43.

90. Ibid., p. 45.

91. For an analysis of Guderian's intellectual debt to the writings of Liddell Hart, see Bond, *Liddell Hart,* pp. 215–37, esp. p. 221: "So I owe many suggestions of our further development to Captain Liddell Hart." See Guderian, *Panzer Leader,* p. 15: "It was principally the books and articles of the Englishmen, Fuller, Liddell Hart and [tank designer and force leader Gifford] Martel, that excited my interest and gave me food for thought. . . . They envisaged it [the tank] in relationship to the growing motorization of our age, and thus they became the pioneers of a new type of warfare on the largest scale."

92. Guderian, *Panzer Leader,* p. 24: "My historical studies, the exercises carried out in

England and our own experiences with mock-ups had persuaded me that tanks would never be able to produce their full effect until other weapons on whose support they must inevitably rely were brought up to their standards of speed and cross-country performance."

93. Ibid., p. 147.

94. See Kenneth Macksey, *Guderian: Creator of the Blitzkrieg* (New York: Stein & Day, 1975), p. 44, who noted that Guderian had concluded "that tanks working on their own or in conjunction with infantry could never achieve decisive importance." See also Guderian, *Panzer Leader,* pp. 92–4: "The First World War on the Western Front, after being for a short time a war of movement, soon settled down to positional warfare. No massing of war material, on no matter how vast a scale, had succeeded in getting the armies moving again until, in November 1916, the enemy's tanks appeared on the battlefield. With their armour plating, their tracks, their guns and their machine-guns, they succeeded in carrying their crews, alive and capable of fighting, through artillery barrages and wire entanglements, over trench systems and shell craters, in the centre of the German lines. The power of the offensive had come back into its own."

95. Condoleezza Rice, "The Making of Soviet Strategy," in Paret (ed.), *Makers of Modern Strategy,* pp. 648–76, at pp. 662–3. The argument continues: "Tukhachevsky . . . believed in the need for total effort in war . . . [in which] all the economic resources of the Soviet Union had to be mobilized to support the effort in the coming war."

96. Ibid., p. 665, which continues: "Bombers were to be used to interdict enemy reserves and a new type of force, paratroopers, was to be used to seize targets and block the enemy's retreat, allowing a crushing blow to be delivered by the second echelon of forces." The following two quotations in the text are also from ibid., p. 665.

97. Ibid.

98. Ibid., which continues: "The decisive blow leading to ultimate annihilation could then be delivered. But the role of ideology must not be overstated."

99. Ibid., pp. 671, 673: "Tukhachevsky and many others had argued that Russia's strength lay in its vast territory and potential for strategic dispersal of industry." "The Second World War was indeed a victory for the total prepa-

ration of the society for war for which Frunze had lobbied in 1924. . . . The ability to mobilize industry to support a protracted war was decisive."

100. See Bond and Alexander, "Liddell Hart and De Gaulle," p. 600: Fuller and Liddell Hart made "wide-ranging and original contributions to military theory and the conduct of war both in the interwar period and later." Subsequent citations are given in the text.

101. See Brian Bond, *The Pursuit of Victory: From Napoleon to Saddam Hussein* (New York: Oxford University Press, 1996), p. 139: "It seems doubtful if even the theoretical proponents of blitzkrieg such as J. F. C. Fuller and B. H. Liddell Hart fully appreciate what could be achieved by the combination of armoured divisions assisted by tactical air power."

102. Alfred Thayer Mahan, *The Influence of Sea Power on World History, 1660–1783* (Boston: Little, Brown, 1941), pp. 281–94, who wrote that "sea power was crucial to national strength and prosperity and that if a nation could control the world's major waterways and narrow seas or choke points it would be able to operate beyond the frontier of its boundaries." See also Mahan, *Naval Strategy Compared and Contrasted with the Principles and Practice of Military Operations on Land: Lectures Delivered at the Naval War College, Newport, R.I., between the Years 1887 and 1911* (Boston: Little, Brown, 1911); Robert Seager, *Alfred Thayer Mahan: The Man and His Letters* (Annapolis: U.S. Naval Institute Press, 1978).

103. For a review of Mahan's ideas, see Theodore Ropp, "Continental Doctrines of Sea Power," in Earle (ed.), *Makers of Modern Strategy: Military Thought,* pp. 446–56. See Ropp's comments about the control of strategic areas and its implications for the development of modern industrial states, p. 452. Also, Philip A. Crowl, "Alfred Thayer Mahan: The Naval Historian," in Paret (ed.), *Makers of Modern Strategy,* pp. 444–77.

104. Mahan, *Influence of Sea Power,* p. 7.

105. Ibid., p. 22.

106. See Margaret Tuttle Sprout, "Mahan: Evangelist of Sea Power," in Earle (ed.), *Makers of Modern Strategy: Military Thought,* pp. 415–45, at p. 433.

107. Mahan, *Influence of Sea Power,* p. 22.

108. Julian S. Corbett, *Some Principles of Maritime Strategy* (London: Longmans,

Green, 1911), p. 70. Subsequent citations are given in the text.

109. See Sprout, "Mahan: Evangelist of Sea Power," p. 443. And for Tirpitz, a world power was a state with "interests around the globe" (quoted in ibid.).

110. Alfred von Tirpitz, *My Memoirs,* 2 vols. (New York: Dodd, Mead, 1919), vol. II, p. 6. Subsequent citations are given in the text.

111. Raoul Castex, *Strategic Theories,* select., trans., and ed. with intro. Eugenia C. Kiesling (Annapolis: Naval Institute Press, 1994), p. 3. By contrast, he defined tactics as "the world of detail; it governs combat, itself a detail of the greatest importance" (p. 3). Subsequent citations are given in the text.

112. He continued (p. 48): "It will also be essential if the stalemate on the principal front cannot be broken without deploying there personnel and materiel from overseas, in which case the combatants will seek to control the sea both to benefit from reinforcements and to deprive the adversary of them."

113. Bernard Brodie, "The Heritage of Douhet," in his *Strategy in the Missile Age* (Princeton: Princeton University Press, 1959), pp. 71–106, at p. 88. This essay is an excellent analysis of Douhet's ideas and influence.

114. Edward Warner, "Douhet, Mitchell, Seversky: Theories of Air Warfare," in Earle (ed.), *Makers of Modern Strategy: Military Thought,* pp. 485–503, at p. 488.

115. For a detailed analysis of Douhet's ideas about air power and its influence on strategy, see Brodie, "Heritage of Douhet."

116. Giulio Douhet, *The Command of the Air,* trans. Dino Ferrari (Washington, DC: Office of Air Force History, 1983), p. 12. Subsequent citations are given in the text.

117. Ibid., pp. 5–6: "The prevailing forms of social organization have given war a character of national totality – that is, the entire population and all the resources of the nation are sucked into the maw of war. And, since society is now definitely evolving along this line, it is within the power of human foresight to see now that future wars will be total in character and scope."

118. He continued: "Thus, an Independent Air Force which meets only the first condition will nonetheless be able to develop effective action for victory."

119. Brodie, *Strategy in the Missile Age,* pp. 98–9.

120. Ibid.

121. Specifically, Douhet wrote that "aircraft are instruments of offense of incomparable potentialities, against which no effective defense can be foreseen," and "civilian morale will be shattered by bombardment of centers of population." For a useful summary of Douhet's basic arguments, see Warner, "Douhet, Mitchell, Seversky," p. 489. From these ideas, Douhet established a basic theory of air power, which Warner outlines on p. 490.

122. As Brodie summarized Douhet's ideas in *Strategy in the Missile Age* (p. 82), "first, the nature of air power requires that 'command of the air' be won by aggressive bombing action rather than by aerial fighting, and second, an air force which achieves command thereby ensures victory all down the line." However, not all observers agreed with the value of strategic bombing. For example, General Maxwell Taylor, who was President Kennedy's military advisor, wrote that "During World War II, strategic bombing did not have a decisive influence on the destruction of Nazi German military industry. It contributed to the final victory, but was not the decisive factor." See Sokolovskii (ed.), *Soviet Military Strategy*, p. 376.

123. According to Douhet, "the time would soon come when, to put an end to horror and suffering, the people themselves, driven by the instinct of self-preservation, would rise up and demand an end to the war" (Warner, "Douhet, Mitchell, Seversky," p. 491).

124. See David Alan Rosenberg, "The Origins of Overkill: Nuclear Weapons and American Strategy, 1945–1960," *International Security* 7.4 (Spring 1983), pp. 3–71; Peter Pringle and William Arkin, *SIOP: The Secret U.S. Plan for Nuclear War* (New York: W. W. Norton, 1983).

125. See Sokolovskii (ed.), *Soviet Military Strategy*, p. 145.

126. See Warner, "Douhet, Mitchell, Seversky," p. 490.

127. See ibid., p. 498. Subsequent citations are given in the text.

128. See ibid., p. 500, for Mitchell's comment that to "offer a general recipe for victory, applicable to all nations, would be downright presumption on my part."

129. Alexander P. De Seversky, *Victory through Air Power* (New York: Simon & Schuster, 1942), argued that "air power has achieved

primacy in modern warfare," and that "those who do not grasp these elementary truths are unsuited to plan the strategy and the equipment for victory in the present era" (p. 333). See also De Seversky, *Air Power: Key to Survival* (New York: Simon & Schuster, 1950).

130. De Seversky, *Victory through Air Power*, p. 333. The implication is that the "first and decisive arena of modern conflict is neither on land nor on sea but in the skies, in the "air ocean.""

131. Ibid., pp. 330–1; Bernard Brodie (ed.), *The Absolute Weapon: Atomic Power and World Order* (New York: Harcourt, Brace, 1946).

132. De Seversky, *Victory through Air Power*, p. 334. This, he adds, "implies a new type of mind. It calls for leadership by new enthusiastic men rather than by reluctant and disgruntled converts [to air power]."

133. Robert E. Osgood, *Limited War: The Challenge to American Security* (Chicago: University of Chicago Press, 1957), p. 3. For background on total war, see Aron, *Century of Total War*; Paul Kecskemeti, *Strategic Surrender: The Politics of Victory and Defeat* (Stanford: Stanford University Press, 1958), pp. 13–27; Alger, *Quest for Victory*, pp. 97–119; Arthur Marwick, *Britain in the Century of Total War* (Boston: Little, Brown, 1968); Manfred F. Boemeke, Roger Chickering, and Stig Forster (eds.), *Anticipating Total War: The German and American Experiences* (Cambridge: Cambridge University Press, 1999).

134. Franklin D. Roosevelt's "Fireside Chat" of May 2, 1943, at www.mhric.org/fdr/chat24.html.

135. See F. M. Sallagar, *The Road to Total War: Escalation in World War II* (Santa Monica, CA: RAND Corporation, R-465-PR, April 1969), pp. 22–3, who observed that it is "meaningless to define total war as one in which the belligerents employ, literally, their 'total resources.' Mobilization can never be total because of deficiencies in knowledge, skill, and managerial talent, because there is rarely enough time for full conversion, and because, even in an authoritarian country, institutional and social constraints prevent it. It is equally unreasonable to hinge the definition on the use of every weapon available to the belligerents, since there are usually some weapons that turn out to be inappropriate or disadvantageous to the user, no matter what the scale of the war.

What characterizes an all-out, or total, war is that it is fought for such high stakes that the belligerents are willing or compelled to employ, not all weapons they possess, but any weapons they consider appropriate and advantageous to them. It is a war in which no holds are barred, although for one reason or another, not all holds may be used."

136. Bernard Brodie, *A Layman's Guide to Naval Strategy* (Princeton: Princeton University Press, 1942), pp. 3, 6.

137. Ibid., p. viii.

138. Brodie, *Strategy in the Missile Age*, p. 307.

139. Bernard Brodie, "Implications for Military Policy," in Brodie (ed.), *Absolute Weapon*, pp. 70–110, at p. 74.

140. Brodie, *Strategy in the Missile Age*, p. 173. He continued: "Even the frequently-encountered supposition that total war is now impossible, because its mutually annihilistic or 'suicidal' consequences must henceforth be obvious to all."

141. Brodie, *Absolute Weapon*, p. 212.

142. Ibid., p. 85.

143. Bernard Brodie, "War in the Atomic Age," in Brodie (ed.), *Absolute Weapon*, pp. 21–69, at p. 47. For an analysis of deterrence, see Brodie, "The Anatomy of Deterrence," in his *Strategy in the Missile Age*, pp. 264–304.

144. Brodie, *Strategy in the Missile Age*, p. 21.

145. Bernard Brodie, *War and Politics* (New York: Macmillan, 1973), pp. 425–6: "and thus lesser wars that might too easily lead up to the large-scale thermonuclear variety." This reasoning was outlined in a chapter entitled "On Nuclear Weapons: Utility in Nonuse," pp. 375–432.

146. Brodie, "Implications for Military Policy," p. 76: "It [our military establishment] can have almost no other useful purpose."

147. Brodie, *Strategy in the Missile Age*, p. 314.

148. Kecskemeti, *Strategic Surrender*, p. 5. Subsequent citations are given in the text.

149. Ibid., p. 6: "According to Delbrück and his school, however, only the strategy of disruption is appropriate to the objective of total victory."

150. See the discussion of unconditional surrender in "The Allies' Policy in World War II," chap. 7 of ibid., pp. 215–41.

151. Aron, *Century of Total War*, pp. 37, 158.

152. Raymond Aron, *The Great Debate: Theories of Nuclear Strategy*, trans. Ernst Pawel (New York: Doubleday, 1965), pp. 198–9.

153. Ibid., p. 239.

154. Sokolovskii (ed.), *Soviet Military Strategy*, p. 281.

155. Ibid., pp. 312–13. "N. S. Khrushchev has pointed out that 'under present conditions, the most probable wars are not likely to be between capitalist, imperialist countries, although the possibility is not to be excluded. The imperialists are preparing wars mainly against the socialist countries, and primarily against the Soviet Union as the most powerful of the socialist states'" (pp. 355–6). See N. S. Khrushchev, "Toward New Victories of the World Communist Movement," *Kommunist* 1 (1961), pp. 17–18, as cited in *Soviet Military Strategy*, p. 356.

156. Sokolovskii (ed.), *Soviet Military Strategy*, p. 94. Subsequent citations are given in the text.

157. Sokolovskii noted (ibid., p. 71) that "All these and other tasks leading to final victory can only be accomplished by ground forces."

158. From the first edition (May 1924) of Stalin's pamphlet *Foundations of Leninism*, quoted in Leon Trotsky, *Challenge of the Left Opposition (1926–1927)* (New York: Pathfinder, 1980), p. 157.

159. Sokolovskii (ed.), *Soviet Military Strategy*, p. 231. As earlier, subsequent citations are given in the text.

160. Henry A. Kissinger, *Nuclear Weapons and Foreign Policy* (New York: Harper & Brothers, 1957), p. 86.

161. Ibid., 233. See also p. 15: "[G]oing all-out to defeat the enemy may lead to paralysis when total war augurs social disintegration even for the victor."

162. Henry A. Kissinger, *Nuclear Weapons and Foreign Policy*, abridged edition (New York: W. W. Norton, 1969), p. 7. As Kissinger observed (abr., p. 12), "we saw it [the atomic bomb] merely as another tool in a concept of warfare which knew no goal save total victory, and no mode of war except all-out war." Subsequent citations given in this subsection's text are to the abridged edition.

163. Herman Kahn, *On Thermonuclear War: Three Lectures and Several Suggestions*

(Princeton: Princeton University Press, 1961), p. 11, which he described as an outcome that represents a "plausible conviction."

164. Ibid., p. 24, in which he referred to the "old-fashioned concept of victory, as denoting the one who writes the peace treaty, while at the same time making explicit that victory can be costly."

165. Thomas C. Schelling, *Arms and Influence* (New Haven: Yale University Press, 1966), p. 22. "There was a time when the assurance of victory – false or genuine assurance – could make national leaders not just willing but sometimes enthusiastic about war. Not now."

166. Ibid., p. 31, which continues: "Most it wants, in these times, the influence that resides in latent force. It wants the bargaining power that comes from its capacity to hurt, not just the direct consequence of successful military action. Even total victory over an enemy provides at best an opportunity for unopposed violence against the enemy populations. How to use that opportunity in the national interest, or in some wider interest, can be just as important as the achievement of victory itself; but the traditional military suicide does not tell us how to use that capacity for inflicting pain."

167. For a discussion on industrial potential and victory, see Kissinger, *Nuclear Weapons* (unabridged), pp. 88–94.

168. Kecskemeti, *Strategic Surrender*, p. 246.

169. Ibid., p. 128.

170. Richard Rhodes, "The General and World War III," *New Yorker* 71.15 (June 19, 1995), pp. 47–59, at p. 54.

171. Ibid., p. 55.

172. Kecskemeti, *Strategic Surrender*, p. 249. Later (p. 254), he argues that "such wars cannot reasonably be expected to result in complete victory in the political sense. What the winner can reasonably expect is only a relatively modest gain, not departing significantly from the status quo." Kecskemeti also refers to "low-stake" nuclear wars, which "can end in complete victory in the political sense: if the stake is low, the military loser will give it up entirely without much difficulty" (p. 256).

173. Schelling, *Arms and Influence*, p. 23, who noted, "Deterrence rests today on the threat of pain and extinction, not just on the threat of military defeat."

174. See, for example, Bernard Brodie,

"Limited War," in his *Strategy in the Missile Age*, pp. 305–57. Brodie notes (p. 305) that the word "'victorious' . . . is put in quotation marks only to remind ourselves that it has lost its former meaning and needs redefining."

175. Osgood, *Limited War*, p. 29. Kissinger, *Nuclear Weapons* (unabridged), pp. 86–131, made the same argument.

176. Osgood, *Limited War*, p. 25; Robert E. Osgood, *Limited War Revisited* (Boulder, CO: Westview, 1979); Osgood, *The Nuclear Dilemma in American Strategic Thought* (Boulder, CO: Westview, 1988). For a discussion of limited victory, see John J. Mearsheimer, *Conventional Deterrence* (Ithaca, NY: Cornell University Press, 1983), p. 57, who observed that "modern nation-states invariably prefer [decisive victory] to limited victories." Mearsheimer argued that decisive victory was produced by the "natural preference of military officers, the rise of the mass army, the effect of industrialization on warfare, the increasing democratization of societies, and the impact of nationalism" (p. 61).

177. Osgood, *Limited War*, p. 44; also, Benjamin O. Fordham, *Building the Cold War Consensus: The Political Economy of U.S. Security Policy, 1949–51* (Ann Arbor: University of Michigan Press, 1998).

178. For this argument, see Lawrence Freedman, "The First Two Generations of Nuclear Strategists," in Paret (ed.), *Makers of Modern Strategy*, pp. 735–78, at pp. 736–8. See also Freedman, *Evolution of Nuclear Strategy* (London: Oxford University Press, 1981).

179. Michael Howard, "The Influence of Clausewitz," in Carl von Clausewitz, *On War*, ed. and trans. Michael Howard and Peter Paret (Princeton: Princeton University Press, 1976), pp. 27–44, at p. 43, which continues: "The development of atomic weapons by both sides already made it likely that the kind of military solution advocated by General MacArthur might involve a quite unacceptable degree of reciprocal destruction, which the advent of thermonuclear weapons would soon raise to an inconceivable order of magnitude."

180. See Colin S. Gray and Keith B. Payne, "Victory Is Possible," *Foreign Policy* 39 (Summer 1980), pp. 14–27.

181. See Colin S. Gray, *Defining and Achieving Decisive Victory* (Carlisle Barracks, PA: Strategic Studies Institute, U.S. Army War College, April 2002), p. v: "The idea of victo-

ry, let alone decisive victory, was very much out of style during the Cold War."

182. See Freedman, *Evolution of Nuclear Strategy*, pp. 213–42.

183. For a discussion of conventional weapons during the cold war, see ibid., pp. 269–314; Michael Carver, "Conventional Warfare in the Nuclear Age," in Paret (ed.), *Makers of Modern Strategy*, pp. 779–814.

184. Mearsheimer, *Conventional Deterrence*.

185. B. H. Liddell Hart, *Defence of the West* (London: Cassell, 1950).

186. Liddell Hart, *Thoughts on War*, p. 42. Subsequent citations are given in the text.

187. For a discussion of revolutions, see John Shy and Thomas W. Collier, "Revolutionary War," in Paret (ed.), *Makers of Modern Strategy*, pp. 815–62.

188. Henry A. Kissinger, *White House Years* (Boston: Little, Brown, 1979), pp. 195–225.

189. Harry S. Truman, *Memoirs by Harry S. Truman*, 2 vols. (New York: Doubleday, 1955), vol. 2: *Years of Trial and Hope*, p. 345: "Every decision I made in connection with the Korean conflict had this one aim in mind: to prevent a third world war and the terrible destruction that it would bring to the civilized world."

190. Jon Meacham, *Franklin and Winston: An Intimate Portrait of an Epic Friendship* (New York: Random House, 2003), p. 209.

191. Arnold Brecht, *Political Theory: The Foundations of Twentieth-Century Political Thought* (Princeton: Princeton University Press, 1959), p. 428.

192. For an analysis of dealing with war on the Korean Peninsula, see Michael O'Hanlon, "Stopping a North Korean Invasion: Why Defending South Korea Is Easier than the Pentagon Thinks," *International Security* 22.4 (Spring 1998), pp. 135–70.

4. Foundations of Victory

1. *The American Heritage Dictionary of the English Language*, 4th ed., 2000, at www.bartleby.com/61/.

2. Of the vast literature on strategy, see B. H. Liddell Hart, "The Theory of Strategy," in his *Strategy*, 2d rev. ed. (New York: Frederick A Praeger, 1967), pp. 333–46.

3. See V. D. Sokolovskii (ed.), *Soviet Military Strategy*, trans. and annot. Herbert S.

Dinerstein, Leon Gouré, and Thomas W. Wolfe (Englewood Cliffs, NJ: Prentice–Hall, 1963), p. 86. "In ancient Rome and Greece, the first military works bearing on problems of strategy appeared at approximately the same time [and] . . . dealt mainly with the training of troops and the art and mastery of tactics."

4. *American Heritage.*

5. Quincy Wright, *A Study of War*, abr. Louise Leonard Wright (Chicago: University of Chicago Press, 1964), p. 18, for a reference to the "expectation of victory through the use of mutually recognized procedures." Also, there are potential economic gains from victory (pp. 427–8). See also T. N. Dupuy, *Understanding Defeat: How to Recover from Loss in Battle to Gain Victory in War* (New York: Paragon House, 1990), for a discussion of the concept of defeat.

6. Alexander P. de Seversky, *Victory through Air Power* (New York: Simon & Schuster, 1942), p. 334. "A totally new strategy can never be developed and put into effect by those who created the old one which proved fallacious or inadequate."

7. Bernard Brodie, *Strategy in the Missile Age* (Princeton: Princeton University Press, 1959), p. 21.

8. Bernard Brodie, *War and Politics* (New York: Macmillan, 1973), p. 452, who argued that "strategy is a field where truth is sought in the pursuit of viable solutions" (p. 453).

9. According to *Air Force Basic Doctrine: Air Force Doctrine Document 1* (Maxwell AFB, AL: Air University Press, 1997), strategy is defined as "The art and science of developing and using political, economic, psychological, and military forces as necessary during peace and war, to afford the maximum support to policies, in order to increase the probabilities and favorable consequences of victory and to lessen the chances of defeat" (p. 86), whereas doctrine is defined as "Fundamental principles by which the military forces or elements thereof guide their actions in support of national objectives" (p. 81). (The 1997 *AFDD-1* is at www.globalsecurity.org/military/library/policy/usaf/afdd/afdd1.pdf.)

10. There have been discussions about victory but no explicit theory of victory. See John Lewis Gaddis, "Coping with Victory," in Charles W. Kegley Jr. and Eugene R. Wittkopf (eds.), *The Future of American Foreign Policy* (New York: St. Martin's, 1992), pp. 143–53,

who questions the West's victory in the cold war; John I. Alger, *The Quest for Victory: The History of the Principles of War* (Westport, CT: Greenwood, 1982).

11. Colin S. Gray, *War, Peace, and Victory* (New York: Simon & Schuster, 1990), pp. 38–9, argues that a theory of war encompasses a theory of victory, but for reasons that will be discussed in this study, this does not represent an analytically sound theory of victory. He continues (p. 41) by arguing that "If a theory of war, as a particular case of grand strategy, explains with variable plausibility how to win a particular war against a particular enemy at a particular time in history, a doctrine of war explains how to fight."

12. *Webster's Revised Unabridged Dictionary* (1913+1828), at machaut.uchicago.edu/?resource=Webster%27s; s.v. victory.

13. *American Heritage,* s.v. victory.

14. Thomas C. Schelling, *Arms and Influence* (New Haven: Yale University Press, 1966), p. vi, for the observation that "the object of victory has traditionally been described as 'imposing one's will on the enemy,' how to do *that* has typically received less attention than the conduct of campaigns and war."

15. According to *Webster's Revised,* s.v. conquer, "These [synonyms] agree in the general idea expressed by overcome – that of bringing under one's power by the exertion of force. Conquer is wider and more general than vanquish, denoting usually a succession of conflicts. Vanquish is more individual, and refers usually to a single conflict. Subdue implies a more gradual and continual pressure, but a surer and more final subjection. Subjugate is to bring completely under the yoke of bondage."

16. *Webster's Third New International Dictionary Unabridged* (Springfield, MA: Merriam–Webster's, 2002), s.v. www.merriamwebster.com/dictionary/conquer.

17. *American Heritage,* s.v. defeat; *Webster's Revised,* s.v. conquer; www.merriam-webster.com/dictionary/conquer,"defeat or subdue by military force."

18. Ibid., s.v. triumph. According to Roman military tradition, "The general was allowed to enter the city crowned with a wreath of laurel, bearing a scepter in one hand, and a branch of laurel in the other, riding in a circular chariot, or a peculiar form drawn by four horses. He was preceded by the senate and magistrates,

musicians, the spoils, the captives in fetters, etc., and followed by his army on foot in marching order. The procession advanced in this manner to the Capitoline Hill, where sacrifices were offered, and victorious commander entertained with a public feast." The Latin *triumphus* "probably came from the Greek *thriambos,* the name of a procession honouring the god Bacchus"; *Encyclopaedia Britannica Online,* www.britannica.com/eb/article-9073447.

19. *Webster's Third,* s.v. triumph.

20. *American Heritage,* s.v. victory; *WordNet 2.1,* Princeton University, 2005, at wordnet.princeton.edu/perl/webwn, s.v., triumph.

21. *American Heritage,* s.v. defeat.

22. *Webster's Revised,* s.v. prevail.

23. Ibid., s.v. win.

24. *American Heritage,* s.v. success.

25. *Webster's Revised,* s.v. defeat.

26. *American Heritage,* s.v. defeat.

27. *Webster's Revised,* s.v. defeat.

28. *American Heritage,* s.v. defeat.

29. Ibid.

30. *American Heritage,* s.v. surrender; *Webster's Revised,* s.v. surrender.

31. Herman Kahn, *On Thermonuclear War: Three Lectures and Several Suggestions* (Princeton: Princeton University Press, 1961), p. 24: "The word 'prevail' is much used in official statements. It is a carefully chosen word that shows that the user is trying to do the best he can even though he is aware that many deny the old-fashioned distinctions between victory and defeat."

32. See Felix E. Oppenheim, *Political Concepts: A Reconstruction* (Oxford: Basil Blackwell, 1981), p. 1, who argues that "To make political concepts suitable for political inquiry, it seems to me necessary to reconstruct them, i.e., provide them with explicative definitions; these must in certain cases deviate from ordinary language to avoid ambiguities and valuational overtones." The reason is that ordinary language can be "an unsure guide" and "inconsistent" (p. 44). In the present study, as in Oppenheim's, "the expressions to be defined and their defining expressions have been couched in the vocabulary of ordinary language" (p. 180).

33. For a reference to this idea, see Paul Kecskemeti, *Strategic Surrender: The Politics of Victory and Defeat* (Stanford: Stanford University Press, 1958), p. 20.

34. For an analysis of the attempt in the En-

lightenment to develop a general theory of war, see Azar Gat, "The Military Thinkers of the French Enlightenment: The Quest for a General Theory of War," chap. 2 of his *The Origins of Military Thought: From the Enlightenment to Clausewitz* (Oxford: Clarendon, 1991), pp. 25–53.

35. See, for instance, William T. Bluhm, *Theories of the Political System,* 2d ed. (Englewood Cliffs, NJ: Prentice–Hall, 1971); Arnold Brecht, *Political Theory: The Foundations of Twentieth-Century Political Thought* (Princeton: Princeton University Press, 1959); David Easton, *A Systems Analysis of Political Life* (New York: John Wiley & Sons, 1965); Easton, *A Framework for Political Analysis* (Englewood Cliffs, NJ: Prentice–Hall, 1965); Easton, *Varieties of Political Theory* (Englewood Cliffs, NJ: Prentice–Hall, 1966); Easton, *The Political System: An Inquiry into the State of Political Science,* 2d ed. (New York: Alfred A. Knopf, 1971); Oppenheim, *Political Concepts;* James N. Rosenau, "Pre-Theories and Theories of Foreign Policy," in Rosenau, *The Scientific Study of Foreign Policy* (London: Frances Pinter, 1980), pp. 115–69.

36. *American Heritage,* s.v. theory.

37. Bluhm, *Theories of the Political System,* p. 6.

38. Easton, *Systems Analysis of Political Life,* p. 3, which continues: "A theory or generalization that has been well-confirmed would be called a law; one that awaits confirmation through further testing would be an hypothesis."

39. Bluhm, *Theories of the Political System,* p. 6, who proposes that theories "compose the belief systems of ideologies we use to orient ourselves to the world of politics" (p. 7). This construct of theory is "important not only for the conduct of politics but also for the practice of political inquiry." However, no theory provides a "truly comprehensive political science"; rather, it represents "an abstract model to the political order [and] a guide to the systematic collection and analysis of political data" (p. 8).

40. Ibid., p. 6.

41. Oppenheim, *Political Concepts,* p. 189.

42. Anatol Rapoport, "Some System Approaches to Political Theory," in Easton, *Varieties of Political Theory,* p. 132: "In the stronger sense, a theory must contain logically deduced propositions, which, if referring to portions of

the real world, must be in principle verifiable. In its weaker sense, a theory can be simply a preparation of a conceptual scheme in which a theory in the stronger sense will one day be developed. In this sense, a theory is concerned with the singling out of presumably important concepts."

43. Brecht, *Political Theory,* p. 14. Subsequent citations are given in the text.

44. *American Heritage,* s.v. theory; *WordNet 2.1,* Princeton University, 2005, s.v. theory.

45. Easton, *Political System,* p. 52. Easton calls the first "value theory" and the second "causal theory, which is a device for improving the dependability of our knowledge" (p. 53).

46. Ibid., pp. 56–7.

47. Ibid., p. 58. Easton argued (p. 59) that "to pose as an immediate goal of attainment of the methodological rigor and precise formulation of the physical sciences, which are centuries ahead of the social sciences in their theoretical and factual maturity, would be to fall victim to scientism, the premature and slavish imitation of the physical sciences."

48. Easton, *Framework for Political Analysis,* p. 3.

49. Easton, *Varieties of Political Theory,* p. 154.

50. This formulation of the rationale for why we need a theory of victory is paraphrased from Oppenheim, *Political Concepts,* p. 189, who argued that the purpose of "any kind of political inquiry is to *clarify* the various dimensions in terms of which the varying degrees of power or freedom or egalitarianism can be compared; to *illuminate* the connections between power, freedom, and ability; to *distinguish* between self-interest, public, interest, and other political goals" (emphasis added).

51. As Oppenheim noted (ibid., p. 189), "This task seems to me worthwhile, even when a theory in the stronger sense is not likely to be developed in the future."

52. Bernard Crick, *Political Theory and Practice* (New York: Basic Books, 1973), p. 4.

53. Ibid., pp. 11–12.

54. Ibid., pp. 13–14, who interprets ideology as "nominally a theory which claims universal validity, because of a belief that all ideas derive from circumstance, but which then also holds that this truth is deliberately obscured by ruling elites, so that the theory only has to

be asserted in the form of propaganda to the masses."

55. This quote and the next from Carl von Clausewitz, *On War,* ed. and intro. Anatol Rapoport (Baltimore: Penguin Books, 1971), p. 191, which continues: "[I]t lights up the whole road for him, facilitates his progress, educates his judgement, and shields him from error."

56. David Easton, "Alternative Strategies in Theoretical Research," in *Varieties of Political Theory,* pp. 1–14, at p. 2. Theory guides empirical research "by summarizing what has been discovered and by suggesting the relevance of new, proposed investigations" (pp. 3–4).

57. Alternatively, one could build a *model* of victory, defined as a "schematic description of a system, theory, or phenomenon that accounts for its known or inferred properties" (*American Heritage*), and may be a "simplified description of a complex entity or process" (*WordNet 2.0,* Princeton University, 2003, at www.dict.org/bin/Dict?Form=Dict3&Database=wn); both s.v. model.

58. Brecht, *Political Theory,* pp. 20–1.

59. Hans J. Morgenthau, *Politics among Nations: The Struggle for Power and Peace,* 5th ed. (New York: Alfred A. Knopf, 1973), p. 3, argues that a theory "must meet a dual test, an empirical and a logical one: Do the facts as they actually are lend themselves to the interpretation the theory has put upon them, and do the conclusions at which the theory arrives follow with logical necessity from its premises? In short, is the theory consistent with the facts and within itself?"

60. Oppenheim, *Political Concepts,* p. 182.

61. Ibid., p. 195.

62. As Oppenheim observed (ibid., pp. 195–6): "Since different actors, and different ideologies as well, are committed to different moralities and ideologies, it is not possible to come up with definitions embracing such irreconcilable world views."

63. John N. Gray, "On the Contestability of Social and Political Concepts," *Political Theory* 5.3 (1977) pp. 331–48, at p. 339; cited in ibid., p. 195.

64. Ibid., pp. 195–6.

65. For a particularly useful discussion of the application of pretheories and theories, see Suzanne Joseph, "Anthropological Evolutionary Ecology: A Critique," *Journal of Ecological Anthropology* 4 (2000), pp. 6–30, at www.fiu.edu/~jea/joseph1.pdf.

66. Rosenau, "Pre-Theories and Theories," p. 126. However, he observed (p. 126), "Pretheory does not mean the techniques of gathering and handling data. . . . Nor do we have in mind the desirability of orienting foreign policy research toward the use of quantified materials and operationalized concepts." Subsequent citations are given in the text.

67. As Rosenau observed (ibid., p. 129): "To formulate the pre-theory itself one has to assess their *relative potencies.* That is, one has to decide which set of variables contributes most to external behavior, which ranks next in influence, and so on through all the sets. There is no need to specify exactly how large a slice of the pie is accounted for by each set of variables. Such precise specifications are characteristics of theories and not of the general framework within which data are organized. At this pre-theoretical level it is sufficient merely to have an idea of the relative potencies of the main sources of external behavior."

68. Ibid., p. 130: "Some analysts may prefer to use one or another of the rankings to analyze the external behavior of all societies at all times. . . . Whatever the level of complexity, however, the analyst employs a pre-theory of foreign policy when he attaches relative potencies to the main sources of external behavior." However, as Rosenau warns (p. 132): "The author's pre-theory may well exaggerate the potency of some variables and underrate others, in which case the theories which his pre-theory generates or supports will in the long run be less productive and enlightening than those based on pre-theories which more closely approximate empirical reality. Yet, to repeat, this pre-theory is not much more than an orientation and is not at present subject to verification."

69. This is from his n. 44, which continues: "Accordingly, those pre-theories which prove to be the most 'unreal' will be abandoned. Whether the number will ever dwindle down to a single pre-theory espoused by all analysts seems doubtful. . . . More likely is a long-run future in which knowledge of empirical reality becomes sufficiently extensive to reduce the field to several major schools of thought."

70. Ibid., p. 135: "[H]ow will the self-conscious employment of pre-theories of foreign policy allow the field to move beyond its present position? . . . [T]he answer lies in the assumption that the widespread use of explic-

it pre-theories will result in the accumulation of materials that are sufficiently processed to provide the basis for comparing the external behavior of societies." Rosenau offered other caveats: "To think theoretically one must be tolerant of ambiguity, concerned about probabilities, and distrustful of absolutes" (*Scientific Study of Foreign Policy*, p. 27); "To think theoretically one must be constantly ready to be proven wrong" (ibid., p. 30); "[O]ften the more outrageous the theory is, the more it is likely to provoke further investigation" (ibid., p. 30).

71. Brecht, *Political Theory*, p. 14, argues that, "'theory' is always used to designate attempts to 'explain' phenomena, especially when that is done in general and abstract terms."

72. Clausewitz, *On War*, ed. Rapoport, p. 210: "First, the historical investigation and determining of doubtful facts. . . . Secondly, the tracing of effects to causes. This is the *real critical inquiry;* it is indispensable to theory, for everything which in theory is to be established, supported, or even merely explained, by experience can only be settled in this way. Thirdly, the testing of the means employed . . . This is where theory helps history, or rather, the teaching to be derived from it."

73. For a discussion of the complexities of public opinion and war, see John Mueller, *Policy and Opinion in the Gulf War* (Chicago: University of Chicago Press, 1994).

74. Easton, *Political System*, p. 53, defined a *causal theory* as one "which seeks to show the relation among facts. The importance of causal theory lies in the fact that it is an index of the stage of development of any science, social or physical, towards the attainment of reliable knowledge." With respect to prediction, Easton warned (ibid., p. 62) that "Prediction is not the only function of scientific generalization, and the mere fact that social science is unable to offer successful predictions about the course of events need not in itself be proof of its low level of development." Also, as Easton wrote in *Systems Analysis of Political Life*, p. 472, "it would be futile to expect that a single overarching theory is anything but a remote ideal."

75. For the foreseeable future, any theory of victory is limited by our incomplete understanding of the relationship between motives and actions. Oppenheim, *Political Concepts*, pp. 192–3, observes that all actions in the realm of public policy are likely to generate unintended consequences, and that reason and motive are causal determinants of action, and that intention is conceptually part of the meaning of action.

76. The classic approach is to develop a theory of victory that is organized in terms of the aims and means used by policymakers. Let's take *aims* first. Aims can be placed along a continuum from limited to unlimited. In the case of *limited aims,* these might merely amount to minor territorial gains or limited political objectives, such as Japanese war aims in the Russo–Japanese war or the initial war aims of the United States in the Korean War or Vietnam War. These were clearly limited goals that sought not the overthrow of the enemy but merely either specific territorial objectives (in the case of the Russo–Japanese War) or to defend the status quo (in the case of Korea and Vietnam). At the other extreme of the continuum is found the matter of *unlimited aims,* which exists when a belligerent seeks regime change and/or unconditional surrender. In cases such as the two world wars, and more recently in the invasion of Afghanistan in 2001 and of Iraq in 2003, the aims of the United States fit into that category.

The matter of *means* also can be understood in terms of a continuum from partial to maximum means. The case of *partial means* exists when the state uses limited resources and a partial mobilization of its economic and military resources, as seen in the case of the United States with the Vietnam War, Korean War, and invasions of Afghanistan and Iraq in 2001 and 2003, respectively. The category of *maximum means* occurs when the combatant uses all available resources, as seen clearly in the cases of World Wars I and II for the United States, for North Vietnam against the United States in the Vietnam War, and in the case of al-Qaeda in its war against the United States. Typically, maximum means tends to be used when the enemy has chosen unlimited ends, but the United States has fought several wars using only partial means while seeking unlimited aims. This was the case in the cold war and in the recent wars against Afghanistan and Iraq. Ironically, in the current war on terrorism, we have a situation where the United States is seeking unlimited aims with partial means while the enemy is using maximum means for limited ends, if one assumes that bin Laden is merely concerned with eliminating U.S. influence in the Islamic world rather than destroying the United States.

77. The scale is meant to be descriptive of increasing levels of activity or commitment, but is not meant to imply that the progression from left to right is linear in any formal or quantitative sense.

78. See John Bigelow Jr., *The Principles of Strategy: Illustrated Mainly from American Campaigns* (New York: G. P. Putnam's Sons, 1891), pp. 77–9, 139–44, who discussed different kinds of strategy: "Strategy proper, or regular strategy, which aims at depriving the enemy of his supplies . . . tactical strategy, which aims at overmatching him on the field of battle . . . political strategy, which aims at embarrassing his government."

79. For further discussion, see Stephen Van Evera, "What Are Case Studies? How Should They Be Performed?" in his *Guide to Methods for Students of Political Science* (Ithaca, NY: Cornell University Press, 1997), pp. 49–88. For a discussion of grand strategic decisions and political victory, see Avi Kober, "Attrition in Modern and Post-Modern War," in Bradford A. Lee and Karl F. Walling (eds.), *Strategic Logic and Political Rationality: Essays in Honor of Michael I. Handel* (London: Frank Cass, 2003), pp. 74–98, esp. p. 81. Kober notes that "Traditional war has been waged across the entire range of the levels-of-war pyramid, from grand strategy, through strategy and the operational levels all the way down to tactics." (See also note 83 below.)

80. Carl von Clausewitz, *On War*, trans. J. J. Graham (New York: E. P. Dutton, 1918), p. 246: "Strictly speaking, there can be no combat without a decision, consequently without a victory; but the ordinary use of language and the nature of things require that we should only consider those results of combats as victories which have been preceded by very considerable efforts."

81. See Van Evera, "What Are Case Studies?"

82. Kober, "Attrition," p. 87, notes that "Achievements or failures at the tactical level are often directly translated into achievements or failures at the grand-strategic level." Furthermore (pp. 88–9), "A series of decisions at the tactical level may contribute to political achievements, but it is usually outside the ac-

tual battlefield, at the grand-strategic level, where such conflicts are won."

83. John Keegan, *The Face of Battle: A Study of Agincourt, Waterloo and the Somme* (New York: Penguin Books, 1984), p. 18. Subsequent citations are given in the text.

84. He continued (p. 302): "Armies may indeed commit themselves fervently to the cause of bringing about the other's disintegration and utterly fail to achieve it, despite the appalling human loss."

85. However (p. 303), "what battles have in common is human: the behaviour of men struggling to reconcile their instinct for self-preservation, their sense of honour and the achievement of some aim over which other men are ready to kill them."

86. Gat, *Origins of Military Thought*, p. 41.

87. Consider the number of tactical victories that have been achieved in wars that were lost. See George C. Kohn, *Dictionary of Wars* (New York: Facts on File, 1986).

88. For concepts equivalent to political–military victory, see Carl von Clausewitz, *On War*, trans. Graham, p. 62. Clausewitz, *On War*, ed. Rapoport, p. 391, described victories that bring about the overthrow of the enemy: "Dispersion of his Army. . . . Capture of the enemy's capital city. . . . An effectual blow against the principal Ally, if he is more powerful than the enemy himself."

89. Quoted in Chas. W. Freeman Jr., *The Diplomat's Dictionary* (Washington, DC: National Defense University Press, 1996), p. 395.

90. For this definition, see Michael I. Handel, *Masters of War: Classical Strategic Thought*, 3d ed. (London: Frank Cass, 2001), p. xxi.

91. The term "political–military victory" is far less precise than the concept of territorial victories, which by their nature are easily expressed in concrete and measurable terms. But the conquest of territory can represent a political victory if it leads the adversary to change its policy or behavior.

92. See Handel, *Masters of War*, p. 10.

93. See "What Price Deterrence? The Problems of Limited War," and "The Problems of Limited Nuclear War," in Henry A. Kissinger, *Nuclear Weapons and Foreign Policy* (New York: Harper & Brothers, 1957), pp. 132–202.

94. Though the concept of victory involves some relationship between the level of physi-

cal destruction and the *political–psychological* harm that is inflicted on an enemy, this political–psychological dimension of victory is excluded from this study.

95. An important point is that the characteristics of grand strategic victory mirror in many ways the concept of total victory that was witnessed in World War II. However, I want to differentiate these two concepts, arguing that total war is a pathway toward a grand strategy victory, which is a broader and more comprehensive concept.

96. For references to the relationship between victory and moral dimensions, see "Remarks by the President to the George C. Marshall ROTC Award Seminar on National Security at Virginia Military Institute," Lexington, Virginia, April 17, 2002, at www.whitehouse.gov/news/releases/2002/04/20020417-1.html: "[George] Marshall knew that our military victory against enemies in World War II had to be followed by a moral victory that resulted in better lives for individual human beings.... The Marshall Plan, rebuilding Europe and lifting up former enemies, showed that America is not content with military victory alone."

97. Although Bigelow used the term "political strategy," what he described is analogous to strategic victory (*Principles of Strategy*, p. 139): "There are two principal forms of political strategy. The one consists in impairing, destroying, or blocking the machinery of the enemy's Government; the other in coercing his Government, under penalty of dissolution or overthrow."

98. For background on the use of the term "strategic victory," see James P. Parker, *Comparing Strategies of the 2d Punic War: Rome's Strategic Victory over the Tactical/Operational Genius, Hannibal Barca* (Carlisle Barracks, PA: U.S. Army War College, 2001); Gregory W. Powers, *The Civil War Campaigns of 1864: Operational and Tactical Defeat Leading to Strategic Victory* (Ft. Leavenworth, KS: School of Advanced Military Studies, 1988); Alger, *Quest for Victory*.

99. Quoted in Robert Debs Heinl (comp.), *Dictionary of Military and Naval Quotations* (Annapolis, MD: United States Naval Institute, 1988), p. 337.

100. "Jomini's *Art of War*," in *Roots of Strategy, Book 2: 3 Military Classics* (Harrisburg, PA: Stackpole Books, 1987), pp.

389–557, at p. 494: "It is also true that a complete and decided victory may bring similar results even though there may have been no *grand strategic* combinations" (emphasis added). In addition, Clausewitz, *On War*, ed. Rapoport, p. 336.

101. Winston S. Churchill, speech to the House of Commons, May 13, 1940; quoted in Heinl (comp.), *Dictionary of Military and Naval Quotations*, p. 338.

102. See Gat, *Origins of Military Thought*, pp. 41–2: "The conduct of operations was the second branch of the art of war. [Paul Gideon Joly de] Maizeroy [1719–80] gave this branch a new technical term, 'strategy', whose origins in modern military theory also seem to have been lost.... Strategy belongs to the most sublime faculty of mind, to reason.... Strategy... is dependent upon innumerable circumstances – physical, political, and moral." "These rules of strategy (also called the 'military dialectic' by Maizeroy) are: not to do what one's enemy appears to desire; to identify the enemy's principal objective in order not to be misled by his diversions...."

103. Morgenthau, *Politics among Nation*, p. 67.

104. See ibid., pp. 67–8: "A policy that aims at a peace settlement of this kind [Carthaginian peace] must, according to our definition be called imperialistic ... because it tries to replace the prewar status quo ... with a postwar status quo where the victor becomes the permanent master of the vanquished."

105. We should distinguish between the modern concept of regime change and its counterpart at the time of the Roman Empire. In modern times, regime change can occur through democratic elections as well as war, and even in the latter case it is limited by the principles of human rights and international law. The contrasting example is the regime change that occurred when Rome destroyed Carthage in the Third Punic War and annihilated or enslaved the population of Carthage.

106. See "Overview of State-Sponsored Terrorism," *Patterns of Global Terrorism: 1998* (Washington, DC: April 1999), at www.state.gov/www/global/terrorism/1998Report/1998index.html; *Patterns of Global Terrorism: 2003* (Washington, DC: U.S. Department of State, April 2004), at www. state.gov/s/ct/rls/pgtrpt/2003/.

107. For a model of mobilization, see Thomas J. Christensen, *Useful Adversaries, Grand Strategy, Domestic Mobilization, and Sino-American Conflict, 1947–1955* (Princeton: Princeton University Press, 1996), p. 13. Also, James D. Fearon, "Rationalist Explanations for War," *International Organization* 49.3 (Summer 1995), pp. 379–414, esp. pp. 396–8.

108. The sequence of these forms of mobilization for war, and whether it influences or determines the type of victory that is achieved by the state, is an important topic for research – but beyond the scope of this book because it relies heavily on the type and number of forces and military expenditure during peacetime, in addition to military doctrine such as "jointness." This is the area in which policymakers depend most heavily on academic analysis and discussion, as that pertains to the implementation of military doctrine.

109. Jon Meacham, *Franklin and Winston: An Intimate Portrait of an Epic Friendship* (New York: Random House, 2003), p. 177, continuing: "It is on these that they build their practical thought and action. They feel that once the foundation has been planned on true and comprehensive lines all other stages will follow naturally and almost inevitably."

110. Moreover, since the impact of air power is still being hotly debated, a scale with greater nuance is needed to reflect the effect of mobilizing certain combinations of forces with the level and type of victory that is achieved. In the case of mobilization that occurs in Western democracies, we should note that it must have broad public consent. A further point is that wars of national liberation are by definition wars of total national mobilization because they involve a significant fraction of the population in the war.

111. For estimates on the costs of war in various historical periods, see Marc Labonte, "Financing Issues and Economic Effects of Past American Wars," CRS Report for Congress, November 7, 2001, pp. 5–15; at www.911investigations.net/document45.html.

112. See Mueller, *Policy and Opinion;* Eric V. Larson, *Casualties and Consensus: The Historical Role of Casualties in Domestic Support for U.S. Military Operations* (Santa Monica, CA: RAND Corporation, MR-726-RC, 1996), at www.rand.org/pubs/monograph_reports/MR726/index.html; Eric V. Larson and

Bogdan Savych, *American Support for U.S. Military Operations from Mogadishu to Baghdad* (Santa Monica, CA: RAND Corporation, MG-231-A, 2005), at www.rand.org/pubs/monographs/ MG231/index.html.

113. See Ralph J. Begleiter, "Whose Media Are We? Notions of Media and Nationality Challenged by the 'War on Terrorism'," *Brown Journal of World Affairs* 8.2 (Winter 2002), pp. 17–26; at www.udel.edu/communication/web/onlinepubs/whosemedia.pdf.

114. Clive Garsia, *A Key to Victory: A Study in War Planning* (London: Eyre & Spottiswoode, 1940), p. 21: "In the whole chain of cause and effect which leads to victory or defeat there is, in fact, nothing [like the plan of operations] of greater importance."

115. A state's willingness to assume postconflict burdens may be influenced by its ability to mobilize and sustain domestic and international support for victory.

116. See the discussion in Chapter 5 on the level of victory attained by the Allied powers in World War II and the terms of unconditional surrender to which Germany and Japan agreed.

117. See Alfred B. Prados, "Iraq: Former and Recent Military Confrontations with the United States," CRS Issue Brief for Congress, updated September 6, 2002; at fpc.state.gov/documents/organization/14836.pdf.

118. Economic sanctions, although they are at best a questionable instrument, should be included because they have been used as one of the tools for attempting to maintain compliance with the conditions of victory imposed by the victor. See Robert Pape, "Why Economic Sanctions Do Not Work," *International Security* 22.2 (Fall 1997), pp. 90–136.

119. See "Kosovo," chap. 7 in James Dobbins, John G. McGinn, Keith Crane, Seth G. Jones, Rollie Lal, Andrew Rathmell, Rachel M. Swanger, and Anga Timilsina, *America's Role in Nation-Building: From Germany to Iraq* (Santa Monica, CA: RAND Corporation, MR-1753-RC, 2003), pp. 111–28; at www.rand.org/pubs/monograph_reports/MR1753/.

120. For a discussion of nation building in the context of several historical and contemporary cases, see Dobbins et al., *America's Role in Nation-Building.*

121. See ibid.

122. Meacham, *Franklin and Winston,* p. 319.

123. See John Gimbel, *The Origins of the*

Marshall Plan (Stanford: Stanford University Press, 1976), pp. 1–3, 25, 71–9; Imanuel Wexler, *The Marshall Plan Revisited: The European Recovery Program in Economic Perspective* (Westport, CT: Greenwood, 1983); Michael J. Hogan, *The Marshall Plan: America, Britain, and the Reconstruction of Western Europe, 1947–1952* (New York: Cambridge University Press, 1987); "Germany" & "Japan," chaps. 1 and 2 in Dobbins et al., *America's Role in Nation-Building*, pp. 3–23, 25–53; Meacham, *Franklin and Winston*, p. 301.

124. See Jonathan Weisman and Robin Wright, "Funds to Rebuild Iraq Are Drifting Away from Target: State Department to Rethink U.S. Effort," *Washington Post*, October 6, 2004, p. A18, at www.washingtonpost.com/wp dyn/ articles/A9627-2004Oct5.html.

5. America's Theory of Victory

1. See Henry A. Kissinger, *Nuclear Weapons and Foreign Policy* (New York: Harper & Brothers, 1957), p. 28: "It has often been remarked that nothing stultifies military thought so much as a victorious war, for innovation then must run the gamut of inertia legitimized by success. It was no different with United States military thought after World War II. The war had not only been won, but its course had *run true to our notion of what a war should be.* The aggression had been unambiguous and had been directed against United States territory. We had *brought to bear our superior resources and inflicted a terrible retribution.* The enemy had been *utterly defeated by a strategy of attrition unencumbered by political considerations*" (emphasis added).

2. Jacques Ellul, *The Technological Society* (New York: Vintage Books, 1964), p. 16.

3. Ibid.

4. For background on the American Revolution, see John Ferling (ed.), *The World Turned Upside Down: The American Victory in the War of Independence* (Westport, CT: Greenwood, 1988); Jeremy Black, *America as a Military Power: From the American Revolution to the Civil War* (Westport, CT: Praeger, 2002), pp. 5–38; Bradford Perkins, *The Cambridge History of American Foreign Relations,* vol. 1: *The Creation of a Republican Empire: 1776–1865* (Cambridge: Cambridge University Press, 1995); Richard B. Morris, *The American Revolution Reconsidered* (New York: Harper & Row, 1967); Russell F. Weigley, *The American Way of War: A History of United States Military Strategy and Policy* (New York: Macmillan, 1973); Felix Gilbert, *To the Farewell Address: Ideas of Early American Foreign Policy* (Princeton: Princeton University Press, 1961); Richard H. Kohn, *Eagle and Sword: The Federalists and the Creation of the Military Establishment in America, 1783–1802* (New York: Free Press, 1975).

5. See Thomas A. Bailey, *A Diplomatic History of the American People,* 9th ed. (Englewood Cliffs, NJ: Prentice–Hall, 1974), pp. 26–51.

6. As [Bernard Law Montgomery,] Viscount Montgomery of Alamein wrote in *A History of Warfare* (New York: William Morrow, 1983), p. 321, "The decisive factor in the war was the intervention against England in 1778 of France, followed by Spain and the Dutch United Provinces. The reconstructed French navy with its allied fleets could not be contained by the British navy. The war was now another world war, and Britain was desperately pressed to preserve her far flung colonial possessions. With his sea communications cut and Washington's large army behind him, General Cornwallis in command in the main British force in America was compelled to surrender at Yorktown in 1781."

7. Ibid., pp. 320–1: "The logistical problems of fighting at such a distance were considerable. . . . It was above all the complete lack of good military and political leadership which prevented England from quickly crushing what began as thinly supported revolt. . . . [T]he Americans adapted themselves better to fighting in the type of country involved. Whereas the British troops fought in red coats and drill formations, the Americans camouflaged themselves in green and fought largely as irregulars."

8. John Whiteclay Chambers II, ed., *The Oxford Companion to American Military History* (Oxford: Oxford University Press, 1999), p. 849, has 6,824 killed, 8,445 wounded, and some 18,500 noncombat deaths.

9. James L. Stokesbury, *A Short History of the American Revolution* (New York: William Morrow, 1991), p. 112.

10. As President James Monroe would state in his message to Congress of December 2, 1823, "the American continents . . . are hence-

forth not to be considered as subjects for future colonization by any European powers." See Bailey, *Diplomatic History,* p. 183.

11. "Farewell Address," in *George Washington: A Collection,* comp. and ed. W. B. Allen (Indianapolis: Liberty Classics, 1988), pp. 512–27, at p. 524. Also at www.yale.edu/lawweb/avalon/washing.htm.

11. Ibid., p. 516.

12. See Gilbert, *To the Farewell Address,* p. 116. The Proclamation is also at www.yale.edu/lawweb/avalon/neutra93.htm.

13. Ibid., p. 122: "In his draft for the valedictory, Washington elaborated on the dangers of foreign interference in American politics and on the necessity of realizing that in foreign affairs, each nation is guided exclusively by egoistic motives."

14. See Bailey, *Diplomatic History,* pp. 26–51. The Treaty is at www.yale.edu/lawweb/avalon/diplomacy/britain/paris.htm.

15. See Donald R. Hickey, *The War of 1812: A Forgotten Conflict* (Urbana: University of Illinois Press, 1989), p. 301; Black, *America as a Military Power,* pp. 39–74; Bradford Perkins, *Prologue to War: England and the United States, 1805–1812* (University of California Press, 1961); see also Bailey, *Diplomatic History,* pp. 131–62.

16. For background on the causes of the War of 1812, see J. C. A. Stagg, *Mr. Madison's War: Politics, Diplomacy, and Warfare in the Early American Republic, 1783–1830* (Princeton: Princeton University Press, 1983), pp. ix–xii, 3–47. For an alternative view, see Reginald Horsman, *The Causes of The War of 1812* (Philadelphia: University of Pennsylvania Press, 1962), p. 263: "When America went to war in 1812 she was reacting to certain British policies . . . and whether one decides that western expansionists, southern planters, American nationalists, or any other group were responsible for the war, the results are incomplete unless the situation in Europe is taken into consideration. . . . [Therefore,] it is essential to study the motives behind British policy in order to understand the reasons for America going to war in 1812."

17. See George C. Kohn, *Dictionary of Wars* (New York: Facts on File, 1986), p. 507. As Frank A. Updyke, *The Diplomacy of the War of 1812* (Baltimore: Johns Hopkins University Press, 1915), p. 1, observed, "The fundamental cause of the War of 1812 was the irreconcil-

able conflict of the British navigation acts with the commercial development of the United States. The more concrete causes, all of which were connected with the British naval and commercial policy, were the right of search for deserters on neutral vessels and the impressment of American seamen upon the high seas, restrictions upon American trade through the revival by Great Britain of the 'Rule of 1756,' and the promulgation of orders which established the principles of blockade against neutral commerce where, in fact, no legal blockade existed." For the argument that Great Britain was seeking to limit U.S. power, see H. M. Brackenridge, *History of the Late War between the United States and Great Britain* (Philadelphia: James Kay, Jun., & Brother, 1844), p. 13, who argued that, "With the acknowledgement of our independence, Great Britain did not renounce her designs of subjugation. Force had been found unavailing, she next resolved to try what might be done by insidious means. For many years after the peace of 1783, our affairs wore no promising appearance. . . . The cement of our union being thus eaten away, England foresaw what we had to encounter, and prophesying according to her wishes, solaced herself with the hope of seeing us divided, and engaged in civil broils. The seeds of dissension had been abundantly sown; our state of finance was deplorably defective; it might almost be said, that the nation was at an end, for so many jarring interests discovered themselves in the states, as almost to preclude the hope of reducing these discordant elements to harmony and order. A state of anarchy and civil war might restore us to Great Britain."

18. See "Madison's War Message, June 1, 1812, Washington," in Kate Caffrey, *The Twilight's Last Gleaming: Britain vs. America, 1812–1815* (New York: Stein & Day, 1977), pp. 310–13; also at www.theamericanpresidency.us/warmadison.htm. For Madison, "Our moderation and conciliation have had no other effort than to encourage perseverance and to enlarge pretensions. . . . We behold, in fine, on the side of Great Britain a state of war against the United States, and on the side of the United States a state of war toward Great Britain." As Stagg observed (*Mr. Madison's War,* p. 3), "This declaration [of war] was the climax of nearly three decades of troubled relations between the two countries, yet it caught the government of Great Britain unawares and was

seen by Americans as a step of doubtful expediency."

19. Harry L. Coles, *The War of 1812* (Chicago: University of Chicago Press, 1965), pp. 23–5.

20. For an economic analysis of the causes of the war, see Stagg, *Mr. Madison's War*, pp. 48–119.

21. Ibid., p. 3. "The risks involved in discarding the cautious neutrality pursued by successive American administrations since 1789 were undeniably great. The United States was a barely stable republic, untested by the strains of war."

22. Hickey, *War of 1812*, p. 302. In terms of military forces, the number of American troops involved in the war was 130,000, which includes total militia forces of 458,000.

23. See Reginald Horsman, *The War of 1812* (New York: Alfred A. Knopf, 1969), esp. chap. 1, "The Origins of the War," pp. 1–24, who argued that "For the infant United States the initial problem was one of *survival*, and the establishment of a form of government that would hold together thirteen disparate states" (emphasis added).

24. Hickey, *War of 1812*, p. 307: "Another legacy of the war was the enhanced reputation that the United States enjoyed in Europe. Although the nation's performance in this war was mixed, it nonetheless earned the respect of Europe." As one Englishman observed, "the Americans have had the satisfaction of proving their courage – they have brought us to speak of them with respect." And the "war 'had humbled the tone of our ministry and of the nation, and made the United States much more respected in Europe'." See also p. 309, where Hickey notes: "Thus the War of 1812 passed into history not as a futile and costly struggle in which the United States had barely escaped dismemberment and disunion, but as a glorious triumph in which the nation had singlehandedly defeated the conqueror of Napoleon and the Mistress of the Seas."

25. See Coles, *War of 1812*, esp. chap. VII, "Peace without Victory," pp. 237–62. Stagg, *Mr. Madison's War*, p. 503, observed that the United States could not properly mobilize itself for war.

26. See Hickey, *War of 1812*, p. 303: "The nation was unable to conquer Canada or to achieve any of the maritime goals for which it was contending." Horsman, *War of 1812*,

p. 267: "The failure of the United States to conquer Canada both enhanced the sense of Canadian identity and helped to create a long-lasting suspicion of the United States." And Stagg, *Mr. Madison's War*, p. 501, noted: "The purpose of the war was to relieve the Republic from the burdens of British maritime policies."

27. See Alan Lloyd, *The Scorching of Washington: The War of 1812* (Washington, DC: Robert B. Luce, 1974), p. 195, "News of the British defeat at New Orleans reached Washington almost simultaneously with word of peace from Europe." Also, Jack Walsh, "Remembering the Forgotten War," *National Review Online: Weekend*, June 16–17, 2001; at www.nationalreview.com/weekend/history/history-war061601.shtml.

28. The speech, from February 18, 1815, is at www.constitution.org/jm/18150218_peace.htm. See also Lloyd, *Scorching of Washington*, p. 195: "[T]he government had demonstrated the efficiency of its powers of defence . . . and the nation can review its conduct without regret or reproach."

29. Hickey, *War of 1812*, p. 303: "Indeed, these issues [failure to achieve "maritime goals"] were not even mentioned in the peace treaty, which merely provided for restoring all conquered territory and returning to the *status quo ante bellum*." The text of the treaty is at en.wikisource.org/wiki/Treaty_of_Ghent.

30. As Updyke wrote in *Diplomacy of the War of 1812*, p. 460, "Great Britain [was] apprehensive of another war with the United States."

31. Updyke (ibid., p. 437) argued that this interpretation is "true if one looks to the [Ghent] treaty of peace alone to discover results, for the treaty contains not a word as to the settlement of the avowed causes of the war."

32. Coles, *War of 1812*, p. 250.

33. Brackenridge, *History of the Late War*, p. 298: "We have been taught that our best policy is honourable peace, and the preference, in our intercourse with all nations, of justice to profit. We have been taught, and the lesson is worth the sum we paid for the war, that we are weak in conquest, but sufficiently strong for defence."

34. Horsman, *War of 1812*, pp. 266–7.

35. This war is also known as the War between the States, War of the Rebellion, the

War of Secession, the War for Southern Independence, and the War of Northern Aggression. For background, see *The Columbia Encyclopedia*, 6th ed., 2001, at www.bartleby.com/65/ci/CivilWarUS.html; James M. McPherson, *Drawn with the Sword: Reflections on the American Civil War* (New York: Oxford University Press, 1996); Black, *America as a Military Power*, pp. 137–78; Russell F. Weigley, *A Great Civil War: A Military and Political History, 1861–1865* (Bloomington: Indiana University Press, 2000); Brian Holden Reid, *The Origins of the American Civil War* (New York: Longman, 1996); Gabor S. Boritt (ed.), *Why the Civil War Came* (New York: Oxford University Press, 1996); William L. Barney, *Flawed Victory: A New Perspective on the Civil War* (New York: Praeger, 1975).

36. For a discussion of the war's origins, see Shelby Foote, *The Civil War: A Narrative* (New York: Random House, 1974).

37. See Hickey, *War of 1812*, p. 301; Black, *America as a Military Power*, pp. 39–74; Perkins, *Prologue to War*; Bailey, *Diplomatic History*, pp. 131–62.

38. See, for example, William Barney, *The Road to Secession: A New Perspective on the Old South* (New York: Praeger, 1972), pp. 123–60.

39. Mark E. Neely Jr., "Was the Civil War a Total War?" in Stig Forster and Jorg Nagler (eds.), *On the Road to Total War* (Cambridge: Cambridge University Press, 1997), pp. 29–51.

40. See Montgomery, *History of Warfare*, pp. 411, 437.

41. See Richard E. Beringer, Herman Hattaway, Archer Jones, and William N. Still Jr., *Why the South Lost the Civil War* (Athens: University of Georgia Press, 1986); Michael Howard, "When Are Wars Decisive?" *Survival* 41.1 (Spring 1999), pp. 126–35.

42. The contrary view, however, was expressed by Jefferson Davis, who argued that, "We are not fighting for slavery. We are fighting for independence – and that, or extermination, we *will* have." See Dean B. Mahin, *One War at a Time: The International Dimensions of the American Civil War* (Washington, DC: Brassey's, 1999), p. 19.

43. See Bailey, *Diplomatic History*, pp. 339–42; "By the President of the United States of America: A Proclamation," September 22, 1862, at www.archives.gov/exhibits/american_originals_iv/sections/transcript_preliminary_

emancipation.html: "That on the first day of January in the year of our Lord, one thousand eight hundred and sixty-three, all persons held as slaves within any State or designated part of a State, the people whereof shall then be in rebellion against the United States shall be then, thenceforward, and forever free; . . . ."

44. See Richard Taylor, *Destruction and Reconstruction: Personal Experiences of the Late War*, ed. Richard B. Harwell (New York: Longmans, Green, 1955), pp. 293–328.

45. The magnitude of U.S. military and economic power would be demonstrated in a devastating and convincing fashion during the twentieth century with World War I and World War II. Also, Hickey, *War of 1812*, p. 307, quoted in note 24 above. See also Mahin, *One War at a Time*; Frederic Trautman (ed.), *A Prussian Observes the American Civil War: The Military Studies of Justus Scheibert* (Columbia: University of Missouri Press, 2001), who observed that "If martial impulse inspired victory, high-minded sacrifice won the war" (p. 197). Jay Luvaas, *The Military Legacy of the Civil War: The European Inheritance* (Chicago: University of Chicago Press, 1959), p. 226, discussed the influence of the war on European military doctrine, but contended that, "Contrary to popular belief, there never was a time when the Civil War exerted a direct influence upon military doctrine in Europe."

46. See Montgomery, *History of Warfare*, pp. 411, 437.

47. See Harold D. Woodman (ed.), *The Legacy of the American Civil War* (New York: John Wiley & Sons, 1973).

48. For background on World War I, see John Keegan, *The First World War* (New York: Alfred A. Knopf, 1999); Martin Gilbert, *The First World War: A Complete History* (New York: Henry Holt, 1994); Barbara Tuchman, *The Guns of August* (New York: Macmillan, 1962); James Joll, *The Origins of the First World War* (London: Longman, 1992); Hubert C. Johnson, *Break-Through: Tactics, Technology, and the Search for Victory on the Western Front in World War I* (Novato, CA: Presidio, 1994), pp. 281–92.

49. Bailey, *Diplomatic History*, p. 599.

50. Ibid., pp. 575–81.

51. Ibid., pp. 590. The text of this speech is at www.firstworldwar.com/source/peacewithoutvictory.htm. The eventual League's first meeting would be held in New York City in January

1920, where it ratified the Treaty of Versailles, but the United States never joined it.

52. Bailey, *Diplomatic History*, pp. 582–95.

53. Weigley, *American Way of War*, pp. 195, 201. For Wilson's campaign slogan, see Bailey, *Diplomatic History*, pp. 588–9.

54. Bailey, *Diplomatic History*, pp. 563–81.

55. Ibid., p. 593; and see "President Wilson's War Message," April 2, 1917, at coursesa. matrix.msu.edu/~hst203/documents/wilsonwar. html.

56. "President Wilson's War Message." For Wilson, this would involve the "organization and mobilization of all the material resources of the nation in the most abundant and yet the most economical and efficient way possible."

57. See Norman Angell, *The Fruits of Victory* (London: W. Collins Sons, 1921), for his arguments about the futility of war in the "modern" age.

58. Ivan S. Bloch, *Is War Now Impossible? Being an Abridgement of the War of the Future in Its Technical, Economic and Political Relations* (Aldershot, Hampshire, UK: Gregg Revivals, 1991). Bloch's argument that war had become so costly and destructive that it was futile and irrational was articulated a half century before the development of nuclear weapons would force a wider appreciation of his views.

59. See John Keegan, *The Face of Battle: A Study of Agincourt, Waterloo and the Somme* (New York: Penguin Books, 1984), pp. 207–89, for a discussion of the Battle of the Somme, which describes the enormous human losses in a battle in which the lines were effectively fixed.

60. See Adam Gopnik, "The Big One: Historians Rethink the War to End All Wars," *New Yorker* 80.24 (August 23, 2004), pp. 78–85, at p. 82.

61. Ibid. According to T. Harry Williams, *The History of American Wars from 1745 to 1918* (New York: Alfred A. Knopf, 1981), p. 383, "Over 1 million [American] men had been landed by the summer of 1918." Compare Keegan, *First World War*, pp. 372–3: "By March 1918, 318,000 [American] men had reached France, the vanguard of 1,300,000 to be deployed by August, and not one had been lost to the action of the enemy in oceanic transport."

62. James F. Dunnigan and William C. Martel, *How to Stop a War: The Lesson of Two Hundred Years of War and Peace* (New York: Doubleday, 1987), who note that the total number of military deaths for all societies in World War I was on the order of ten million.

63. As will be seen in the course of this discussion, many of these conclusions about victory would emerge as the United States organized itself to fight World War II.

64. Winston S. Churchill, *The Second World War*, 6 vols. (New York: Houghton Mifflin, 1977), vol. 1: *The Gathering Storm*, p. 13. And Marshal Foch, as reported by Churchill (p. 6), said of the Peace Treaty of Versailles, "This is not Peace. It is an Armistice for twenty years."

65. See John Keegan, *The Second World War* (New York: Penguin Books, 1989), pp. 31–2. See also Howard, "When Are Wars Decisive?" (pp. 131–2): "Why was the Allied victory in 1918 not 'decisive'? Were the Germans not sufficiently defeated, or not sufficiently conciliated? Perhaps both. Certainly they had not experienced the horrors of war at first hand, as they did a quarter of a century later; indeed their armies had been everywhere triumphant until the very last three months of the war. The trouble was that the German people did not 'internalize' their defeat."

66. See Gilbert, *First World War*, pp 505–24. Also, see Keegan, *First World War*, p. 423: "The Second World War was the continuation of the First, and indeed it is inexplicable except in terms of the rancours and instabilities left by the earlier conflict."

67. Churchill, *Gathering Storm*, p. 14. "Her fleet had already sunk itself in Scapa Flow. Her vast army was disbanded. By the Treaty of Versailles only a professional long-service army not exceeding one hundred thousand men, and unable on this basis to accumulate reserves, was permitted to Germany for purposes of internal order. The annual quotas of recruits no longer received their training; the cadres were dissolved. Every effort was made to reduce to a tithe the officer corps. No military air force of any kind was allowed. Submarines were forbidden, and the German Navy was limited to a handful of vessels under ten thousand tons."

68. Ibid., pp. 4–5. "There was hardly a cottage nor a family from Verdun to Toulon that did not mourn its dead to shelter its cripples." (Regarding the number of dead, see note 58.)

69. On nationalism, see Hans Kohn, *The Idea of Nationalism: A Study in Its Origins and Background* (New York: Macmillan, 1946). For an analysis of the effects of nationalism, see

Hans J. Morgenthau, *Politics among Nations: The Struggle for Power and Peace*, 5th ed. (New York: Alfred A. Knopf, 1973), pp. 106–11. "With the Napoleonic Wars began the period of national foreign policies and wars; that is, the identification of the great masses by the citizens of a nation with national power and national policies, replacing identification with dynastic interests" (p. 106). Morgenthau also wrote about "small yet powerful profascist groups of intellectual, political, and military leaders in Great Britain and France" (p. 106).

70. Morgenthau, *Politics among Nation,* pp. 109–10: "The first of these events ["that weakened the social fabric of Germany to such an extent as to make it an easy prey for the consuming fire of National Socialism"] was the defeat in the First World War, coinciding with a revolution that was held responsible not only for the destruction of traditional political values and institutions, but for the loss of the war itself. . . . Thus National Socialism was able to identify in a truly totalitarian fashion the aspirations of the individual German with the power objectives of the German nation." See also Alan Bullock, *A Study in Tyranny* (New York: Harper & Row, 1971).

71. See Heinz Guderian, *Panzer Leader* (London: Michael Joseph, Ltd., 1952), p. 432, on "the failure of policy as manifested by the victor nations after the First World War. This policy prepared the ground in which the seeds of National-Socialism were to take root; it gave us unemployment, heavy reparations, oppressive annexation of territory, lack of freedom, lack of equality, lack of military strength. When the victorious nations, in drafting the Versailles Treaty, failed to observe President Wilson's Fourteen Points the Germans lost their trust in the good faith of the Great Powers."

72. A. J. P. Taylor, *The Origins of the Second World War* (New York: Atheneum, 1962), pp. 18–39, 61–86, who stated (p. 19) that "The first war explains the second and, in fact, caused it, in so far as one event causes another".

73. The "Treaty of Versailles" of June 28, 1919, Part VIII, Article 231, stipulated that "The Allied and Associated Governments affirm and Germany accepts the responsibility of Germany and her allies for causing all the loss and damage to which the Allied and Associated Governments and their nationals have been subjected as a consequence of the war imposed

upon them by the aggression of Germany and her allies." For an example of the onerous reparations imposed on Germany, see Article 249: "There shall be paid by the German Government the total cost of all armies of the Allied and Associated Governments in occupied German territory from the date of the signature of the Armistice of November 11, 1918, including the keep of men and beasts, lodging and billeting, pay and allowances, salaries and wages, bedding, heating, lighting, clothing, equipment, harness and saddlery, armament and rolling-stock, air services, treatment of sick and wounded, veterinary and remount services, transport service of all sorts (such as by rail, sea or river, motor lorries), communications and correspondence, and in general the cost of all administrative or technical services the working of which is necessary for the training of troops and for keeping their numbers up to strength and preserving their military efficiency." For the full "Treaty between the Principal Allied and Associated Powers and Poland," signed at Versailles, June 28, 1919, see rpt. in *Treaties, Conventions, International Acts, Protocol and Agreements between the United States of America and Other Powers 1910–1923,* 3 Malloy–Redmond 3714 (1923): history.acusd.edu/gen/text/versaillestreaty/vercontents.html.

74. Churchill, *Gathering Storm,* pp. 6–7. "The economic clauses of the Treaty were malignant and silly to an extent that made them obviously futile. Germany was condemned to pay reparations on a fabulous scale."

75. Ibid., pp. 9–10: "They [the German people] were relieved from the burden of compulsory military service and from the need of keeping up heavy armaments. . . . A democratic constitution, in accordance with all the latest improvements, was established at Weimar. Emperors having been driven out, nonentities were elected. . . . The Weimar Republic, with all its liberal trappings and blessings, was regarded as an imposition of the enemy."

76. Churchill (ibid., p. 16), lamented the failure of democracies to maintain policies consistently: "how the structure and habits of democratic states, unless they are welded into larger organisms, lack those elements of persistence and conviction which can alone give security to humble masses; how, even in matters of self-preservation, no policy is pursued for even ten or fifteen years at a time."

77. Demonstrating that societies can learn from their experiences, the United States and Great Britain after World War II actively sought through their policies to avoid the problems that had led to the outbreak of war in the first place. It is entirely plausible, however, that World War II also might have been limited to a political–military victory had it not been for the Marshall Plan, which invested billions of dollars in rebuilding the economies, societies, and governments of the defeated states.

78. For background on World War II, see Henry Steele Commager, *The Story of the Second World War* (New York: Brassey's, 1991); Martin Gilbert, *The Second World War: A Complete History* (New York: Henry Holt, 1989); Keegan, *Second World War*; J. F. C. Fuller, *The Second World War, 1939–1945: A Strategical and Tactical History* (New York: Duell, Sloan & Pearce, 1949); Stephen E. Pelz, *Race to Pearl Harbor: The Failure of the Second London Naval Conference and the Onset of World War II* (Cambridge, MA: Harvard University Press, 1974).

79. "Beating the Life Out of Germany, October 11, 1943," *The War Speeches of the Rt. Hon. Winston S. Churchill*, 6 vols., comp. Charles Eade (Boston: Houghton Mifflin, 1953), vol. 3: *The End of the Beginning*, pp. 41–2.

80. "Results of the Yalta Conference: A Speech to the House of Commons, February 27, 1945," in ibid., pp. 376–98.

81. Richard Rhodes, "The General and World War III," *New Yorker* 71.15 (June 19, 1995), pp. 47–59, at pp. 47, 53, wrote that this view was consistent with what the Air Force War Plans Division wrote in 1946, which described the nation's "war aim" as the "complete subjugation of the enemy."

82. "Atlantic Charter," at www.yale.edu/lawweb/avalon/wwii/atlantic.htm; "Until Victory Is Won: A Speech to a Conference of Dominion High Commissioners and Allied Countries' Ministers, at St. James's Palace, London, June 12, 1941," *War Speeches of Winston S. Churchill*, vol. 3, p. 444. Moreover, when Churchill was asked at an Oval Office press conference with Roosevelt in December 1941 whether he had "any doubt of the ultimate victory?" his answer was unequivocal: "I have no doubt whatsoever." Jon Meacham, *Franklin and Winston: An Intimate Portrait of an Epic Friendship* (New York: Random House, 2003), p. 144.

83. These "moral" ideas were expressed in the Atlantic Charter (at www.yale.edu/lawweb/avalon/wwii/atlantic.htm), which affirmed the principle of the hope "for a better future for the world." Roosevelt and Churchill declared, among other things, that they "believe that all of the nations of the world, for realistic as well as spiritual reasons must come to the abandonment of the use of force."

84. See ibid., in which Roosevelt and Churchill affirmed: "First, their countries seek no aggrandizement, territorial or other; Second, they desire to see no territorial changes that do not accord with the freely expressed wishes of the peoples concerned; Third, they respect the right of all peoples to choose the form of government under which they will live; and they wish to see sovereign rights and self government restored to those who have been forcibly deprived of them; . . . ."

85. Gordon A. Craig, "The Political Leader as Strategist," in Peter Paret (ed.), with Craig and Felix Gilbert, *Makers of Modern Strategy: From Machiavelli to the Nuclear Age* (Princeton: Princeton University Press, 1986), pp. 481–509, at p. 508.

86. See Kissinger, *Nuclear Weapons*, p. 28 (cited more fully in note 1, above): "[World War II] had not only been won, but its course had run true to our notion of what a war should be. The aggression had been unambiguous and had been directed against United States territory."

87. Ibid., p. 11, discussed the problem of "a theory of war based on the necessity of total victory."

88. Winston S. Churchill, *The Second World War*, vol. 3: *The Grand Alliance*, p. 523, in a speech to the House of Commons on December 11, 1941: "No one must underrate the gravity of the loss which has been inflicted in Malaya and Hawaii, or the power of the new antagonist who has fallen upon us, or the length of time it will take to create, marshal, and mount the great force in the Far East which will be *necessary to achieve absolute victory*. . . . It would indeed bring shame upon our generation if we did not teach them [Japan and Germany] a lesson which will not be forgotten in the records of a thousand years" (emphasis added). See also B. H. Liddell Hart, *History of the Second World War* (London: Cassell, 1970).

89. Harry S. Truman, *Memoirs by Harry*

S. *Truman,* 2 vols. (New York: Doubleday, 1955), vol. 1: *Year of Decisions,* p. 437.

90. Churchill, *Grand Alliance,* pp. 523–5. "The British Empire, the Soviet Union, and now the United States, bound together with every scrap of their life and strength, were, according to my lights, twice or even thrice the force of their antagonists" (p. 511).

91. "Eisenhower Instructs Europeans; Gives Battle Order to His Armies," *New York Times,* June 6, 1944, p. 1.

92. See, e.g., Bullock, *Study in Tyranny.*

93. Churchill, *Grand Alliance,* p. 374; Gilbert, *Second World War,* p. 222. The quotation is from the Atlantic Charter, at www.yale.edu/lawweb/avalon/wwii/atlantic.htm.

94. The so-called Truman Doctrine was expressed in an address by President Truman to a joint session of Congress on March 12, 1947, in which he urged an appropriation of $400 million, plus unspecified civilian and military personnel, to assist Greece and Turkey. Though the short-term goal in Greece was rebuilding after World War II, the stated goal was to prevent the communist takeover of either country. The text of the speech is at www.yale.edu/lawweb/avalon/trudoc.htm.

95. Bernard Brodie, "Implications for Military Policy," in Brodie (ed.), *The Absolute Weapon: Atomic Power and World Order* (New York: Harcourt, Brace, 1946), pp. 70–110. For a discussion of limited war, see Robert E. Osgood, *Limited War: The Challenge to American Security* (Chicago: University of Chicago Press, 1957); Osgood, *Limited War Revisited* (Boulder, CO: Westview, 1979), pp. 15–32; Kissinger, *Nuclear Weapons,* pp. 174–202.

96. Lawrence Freedman, *The Evolution of Nuclear Strategy* (New York: St. Martin's, 1989), pp. 60–1.

97. Kissinger, *Nuclear Weapons,* p. vi, wrote that, given "a fear that any strong action on the part of the United States anywhere in the world may ignite a full-scale nuclear war, we find ourselves more and more reluctant to frame a strong foreign policy or implement it so as to preserve the vital interests of the free world."

98. Bernard Brodie, *War and Politics* (New York: Macmillan, 1973), p. 21, who observed that in the nuclear age, "we cannot go on blithely letting one group of specialists decide how to wage war and another decide when and to what purpose, with only the most casual and spasmodic communication between them."

99. Kissinger, *Nuclear Weapons,* pp. xi–xii.

100. Thomas C. Schelling, *Arms and Influence* (New Haven: Yale University Press, 1966), p. 34.

101. This realization eventually undermined the consensus in the government and public about the value of civil defense.

102. For arguments regarding limited-war options with nuclear weapons, see Osgood, *Limited War Revisited,* p. 6; Colin S. Gray, "Nuclear Strategy: The Case for a Theory of Victory," *International Security* 9.4 (Summer 1979), pp. 54–87; Colin S. Gray and Keith B. Payne, "Victory Is Possible," *Foreign Policy* 39 (Summer 1980), pp. 14–27.

103. See Bernard Brodie, "The Weapon," in Brodie (ed.), *The Absolute Weapon: Atomic Power and World Order* (New York: Harcourt, Brace, 1946), pp. 21–69.

104. For arguments about the absolutist American view of using force, see Kissinger, *Nuclear Weapons;* Robert E. Osgood, *The Nuclear Dilemma in American Strategic Thought* (Boulder, CO: Westview, 1988); Herman Kahn, *On Thermonuclear War* (Princeton: Princeton University Press, 1961). The United States first tested a hydrogen bomb in 1952; the USSR, in 1953. Both had more powerful and deployable versions within two years. Bernard Brodie, *Strategy in the Missile Age* (Princeton: Princeton University Press, 1959), p. 154; Osgood, *Limited War,* p. 227.

105. See Michael Mandelbaum, "The Bomb, Dread, and Eternity," *International Security* 5.2 (Fall 1980), pp. 3–23. In view of the threat of nuclear annihilation, "Death, and the threat of death, are central and perennial features of human existence, and death on a large scale was scarcely unknown before 1945. But nuclear weapons bring to social life something else, which is new. They threaten the cultural mechanisms for coming to terms with human mortality. Ceremonies and doctrines that provide some cultural context for death are universal features of organized social existence. Their purpose is to emphasize what continues even as an individual life ends; they connect death to life. The need for 'symbolic immortality' that they provide seems to be basic to human beings. . . . Nuclear weapons could destroy all those things that make symbolic immortality possible. The difference between past wars and a full-scale nuclear conflict is the difference between destruction and an-

nihilation. It is the difference between the end of an era and the end of a culture. Nuclear weapons, unlike other weapons known to man, have 'the power to make everything into nothing'" (pp. 3–4).

106. For argument about this conclusion, see Gray, "Nuclear Strategy"; Gray and Payne, "Victory Is Possible."

107. Kissinger, *Nuclear Weapons,* p. 3.

108. Ibid., p. 11, described a stalemate in which the United States "never succeeded in translating our military superiority into a political advantage."

109. Gray, "Nuclear Strategy," p. 71.

110. Bernard Brodie, "Implications for Military Policy," in Brodie (ed.), *Absolute Weapon,* pp. 70–110, at p. 74. He argued further that "The main war goal upon the beginning of a strategic nuclear exchange should surely be to terminate it as quickly as possible and with the least amount of damage possible – on both sides." Cited in Gray, "Nuclear Strategy," p. 75. Citing Kissinger, Gray noted (p. 67) that "Every calculation with which I am familiar indicates that a general nuclear war in which civilian populations are the primary target will produce casualties exceeding 100 m[illion]. Such a degree of devastation is not a strategic doctrine: it is an abdication of moral and political responsibility. No political structure could survive it."

111. Kissinger, *Nuclear Weapons,* p. 20.

112. See Dinesh D'Souza, "Russian Revolution: How Reagan Won the Cold War," *National Review* 49.2 (November 24, 1997), pp. 36–41, at www.vakkur.com/hx/cold_war_reagan.htm. Reagan's full "Address at Commencement Exercises at the University of Notre Dame" of May 17, 1981, is at www.reagan.utexas.edu/archives/speeches/1981/51781a.htm.

113. Kissinger, *Nuclear Weapons,* pp. 196–8, on catalytic nuclear war.

114. See Peter Schweizer, *Victory: The Reagan Administration's Secret Strategy That Hastened the Collapse of the Soviet Union* (New York: Atlantic Monthly Press, 1994).

115. For background, see Russell F. Weigley, "Old Strategies Revisited: Douglas MacArthur and George C. Marshall in the Korean War," in his *American Way of War,* pp. 382–98; Kohn, *Dictionary of Wars,* pp. 251–2. It was already June 25 in Korea when the initial predawn attack occurred.

116. See Allen S. Whiting, *China Crosses the Yalu: The Decision to Enter the Korean War* (New York: Macmillan, 1960), p. 112.

117. Ibid., pp. 103–4.

118. Kissinger, *Nuclear Weapons,* pp. 27–8, who remarked that, "the Korean War revealed . . . our almost exclusive concern with all-out war and with the most destructive type of strategy." Note that China would not conduct its first nuclear test until 1964.

119. Weigley, "Old Strategies Revisited," p. 383. Weigley also referred to the "ingrained . . . American habit of thinking of war in terms of annihilative victories" (p. 382).

120. See Sergei N. Goncharov, John W. Lewis, and Xue Litai, *Uncertain Partners: Stalin, Mao and the Korean War* (Stanford: Stanford University Press, 1993), p. 191.

121. The prospect of strategic defeat was a prominent example of the condition that superpowers avoid because of fears that they will be forced to fight in order to preserve their credibility and, ultimately, deterrence.

122. Truman, *Memoirs,* vol. 2: *Years of Trial and Hope,* p. 415: "But a fearful difficulty lay in the fact that the course advocated by MacArthur might well mean all-out, general world war – atomic weapons and all."

123. See Bailey, *Diplomatic History,* pp. 819–28.

124. See James T. Laney and Jason T. Shaplen, "How to Deal with North Korea," *Foreign Affairs* 82.2 (March–April 2003), pp. 16–30; at www.mrs.umn.edu/~joos/kh/e/laney_howtoNK.pdf.

125. See Herman Kahn, "On the Possibilities for Victory or Defeat," in Frank E. Armbruster, Raymond D. Gastil, Herman Kahn, William Pfaff, and Edmund Stillman, *Can We Win in Vietnam?* (New York: Frederick A. Praeger, 1969), pp. 178–204. Also, Guenter Lewy, *America in Vietnam* (New York: Oxford University Press, 1978), esp. "Could the United States Have Won in Vietnam?" pp. 430–41.

126. For background on the Vietnam War, see Daniel Ellsberg, *Papers on the War* (New York: Simon & Schuster, 1972); Leslie H. Gelb with Richard K. Betts, *The Irony of Vietnam: The System Worked* (Washington, DC: Brookings Institution, 1979); Marc J. Gilbert, *Why the North Won the Vietnam War* (New York: Palgrave, 2002); David Halberstam, *The Best and the Brightest* (New York: Random House,

1972); George C. Herring, *America's Longest War: The United States and Vietnam, 1950–1975* (New York: John Wiley & Sons, 1979); David Kaiser, *American Tragedy: Kennedy, Johnson, and the Origins of the Vietnam War* (Cambridge, MA: Belknap, 2000); Stanley Karnow, *Vietnam: A History* (New York: Viking, 1983); David W. Levy, *The Debate over Vietnam* (Baltimore: Johns Hopkins University Press, 1995); Lewy, *America in Vietnam;* Robert E. Osgood, "The Lessons of Vietnam" and "Post-Vietnam Refinements of Limited War Strategy," in *Limited War Revisited,* pp. 33–51 and 52–66, respectively; Lewis Sorley, *A Better War: The Unexamined Victories and Final Tragedy of America's Last Years in Vietnam* (New York: Harcourt Brace, 1999); Harry G. Summers Jr., *On Strategy: A Critical Analysis of the Vietnam War* (Novato, CA: Presidio, 1982); Robert Thompson, *No Exit from Vietnam* (New York: David McKay, 1969).

127. Jeffrey Record, "Vietnam in Retrospect: Could We Have Won?" *Parameters* 26.4 (Winter 1996–7), pp. 51–65, at p. 61; at www.carlisle.army.mil/usawc/Parameters/96winter/record.htm.

128. For a discussion of North Vietnam's strategy for victory, see Cecil B. Currey, *Victory at Any Cost: The Genius of Viet Nam's Gen. Vo Nguyen Giap* (Washington, DC: Brassey's, 1997).

129. Quoted in Record, "Vietnam in Retrospect," p. 52, who added: "In the end, the United States failed either to avert a communist takeover of South Vietnam, or to avoid humiliation, loss of prestige, and domestic recrimination." On the campaign's design, see Weigley, *American Way of War,* pp. 460–4.

130. For arguments about whether the United States could win the Vietnam War, see William Colby, *Lost Victory: A Firsthand Account of America's Sixteen-Year Involvement in Vietnam* (Chicago: Contemporary Books, 1989); Armbruster et al., *Can We Win in Vietnam?;* C. Dale Walton, *The Myth of Inevitable U.S. Defeat in Vietnam* (London: Frank Cass, 2002); Mark W. Woodruff, *Unheralded Victory: The Defeat of the Viet Cong and the North Vietnamese Army 1961–1973* (Arlington, VA: Vandamere, 1999); Record, "Vietnam in Retrospect," who asks (p. 51), "Was the United States in fact defeated?" For a discussion of the dilemmas of fighting guerrilla wars, see John Shy and Thomas W. Collier, "Revolutionary

War," in Paret (ed.), *Makers of Modern Strategy,* pp. 815–62.

131. For a discussion of insurgency warfare, see Shy and Collier, "Revolutionary War." For a review of how technological forces have changed the conduct of guerrilla wars, see Martin van Creveld, "Real War," chap. 20 in *Technology and War: From 2000 B.C. to the Present* (New York: Free Press, 1991), pp. 297–310.

132. Eric V. Larson, *Casualties and Consensus: The Historical Role of Casualties in Domestic Support for U.S. Military Operations* (Santa Monica, CA: RAND Corporation, MR-726-RC, 1996), at www.rand.org/pubs/monograph_reports/MR726/index.html.

133. Ibid., pp. 29–89.

134. Bradley Graham and Vernon Loeb, "U.S. Still Letting Local Opposition Man Ground War," *Washington Post,* December 4, 2001, p. A12; Vernon Loeb, "U.S. to Beef Up Units Probing Afghan Caves," *Washington Post,* December 22, 2001, p. A17.

135. See *ABC News–Washington Post Poll,* October 30–November 2, 2005, accessed via www.pollingreport.com/iraq.htm.

136. Van Creveld, "Computerized War," chap. 16 in *Technology and War,* pp. 235–50.

137. Robert S. McNamara, *In Retrospect: The Tragedy and Lessons of Vietnam* (New York: Times Books, 1995), p. 6.

138. E. S. Quade and W. I. Boucher, "Introduction," in their *Systems Analysis and Policy Planning* (New York: American Elsevier, 1968), pp. 1–19; Charles J. Hitch and Alain C. Enthoven, "Systems Analysis," in Samuel A. Tucker (ed.), *A Modern Design for Defense Decision* (Washington, DC: Industrial College of the Armed Forces, 1966), pp. 119–95; Charles J. Hitch and Roland N. McKean, *The Economics of Defense in the Nuclear Age* (Cambridge, MA: Harvard University Press, 1961); Weigley, *American Way of War,* p. 459.

139. Michael Beschloss, *Reaching for Glory: Lyndon's Johnson's Secret White House Tapes, 1964–1965* (New York: Simon & Schuster, 2001), p. 194 (emphasis added). While Johnson rejected victory, he said (p. 238): "I don't believe I can walk out. . . . If I did, they'd take Thailand. . . . They'd take Cambodia. . . . They'd take Burma. . . . They'd take Indonesia. . . . They'd take India. . . . They'd come right back and take the Philippines. . . . I'd be another Chamberlain and . . . we'd have another Munich."

140. Ibid., p. 343. Cf. p. 378: "I don't

know whether those [Pentagon] men have ever [calculated] whether we can win with the kind of training we have, the kind of power."

141. Ibid., p. 382, which continues: "We must increase it [forces] if we're going to win, and [with] this limited term that we define [and] limited way we define 'win,' it requires additional troops."

142. Ibid., p. 406.

143. Henry A. Kissinger, *White House Years*, pp. 226–311.

144. George [H. W.] Bush and Brent Scowcroft, *A World Transformed* (New York: Alfred A. Knopf, 1998), p. 486.

145. Thom Shanker, "Defense Minister from Vietnam Meets Rumsfeld," *New York Times*, November 11, 2003, p. A11.

146. See Freedman, *Evolution of Nuclear Strategy*, pp. 216, 271–2.

147. For background and analyses of the policy of unconditional surrender, see Anne Armstrong, *Unconditional Surrender: The Impact of the Casablanca Policy upon World War II* (New Brunswick, NJ: Rutgers University Press, 1961); Raymond G. O'Connor, *Diplomacy for Victory: FDR and Unconditional Surrender* (New York: W. W. Norton, 1971); Paul Kecskemeti, *Strategic Surrender: The Politics of Victory and Defeat* (Stanford: Stanford University Press, 1958); Leon V. Sigal, *Fighting to a Finish: The Politics of War Termination in the United States and Japan, 1945* (Ithaca, NY: Cornell University Press, 1988). For excellent analyses of the influence of unconditional surrender during the American Civil War, see John Y. Simon, "Grant, Lincoln, and Unconditional Surrender," in Gabor S. Boritt (ed.), *Lincoln's Generals* (New York: Oxford University Press, 1994), pp. 161–98; James M. McPherson, "Lincoln and the Strategy of Unconditional Surrender," in Gabor S. Boritt (ed.), *Lincoln, the War President* (New York: Oxford University Press, 1992), pp. 29–62.

148. Armstrong, *Unconditional Surrender*, p. 14, cites a historical study by Lord Hankey.

149. *Webster's Revised Unabridged Dictionary* (1913+1828), at machaut.uchicago.edu/?resource=Webster%27s.

150. *The American Heritage Dictionary of the English Language*, 4th ed., 2000, at www.bartleby.com/61/.

151. Everett Holles, *Unconditional Surrender* (New York: Howell, Soskin, 1945), p. 21, where he continued: "Surrender 'at discretion' is another military way of saying essentially the same thing, since the 'discretion' is always that of the victor."

152. Armstrong, *Unconditional Surrender*, p. 14.

153. Gerhard von Glahn, *Law among Nations: An Introduction to Public International Law*, 3d ed. (New York: Macmillan, 1976), p. 574; Glahn discusses the legal roots of unconditional surrender on pp. 573–4.

154. See Hugo Grotius, *The Law of War and Peace*, trans. Francis W. Kelsey (New York: Bobbs–Merrill, 1963), p. 740.

155. Ibid., pp. 825–6.

156. Ibid., pp. 826–8.

157. See McPherson, "Lincoln and the Strategy," p. 34.

158. Simon, "Grant, Lincoln, and Unconditional Surrender," p. 188. Grant's "Unconditional Surrender" letter called for "No terms except unconditional and immediate surrender can be accepted. I propose to move immediately upon your works." See www.civilwarhome.com/grantdon.htm.

159. See *Personal Memoirs of U.S. Grant*, 2 vols. (New York: Charles L. Webster, 1885–6), vol. I, p. 368, as cited in McPherson, "Lincoln and the Strategy," p. 45.

160. See McPherson, "Lincoln and the Strategy," p. 34, who gives President Lincoln principal "responsibility for the unconditional victory of Union forces." For an excellent discussion of how Lincoln's strategy for the war shifted toward total war and unconditional surrender, see pp. 40–62. In addition (p. 58), when Jefferson Davis said, "We are fighting for independence – and that, or extermination, we *will* have," Lincoln responded: "Between him and us the issue is distinct, simple, and inflexible. It is an issue which can only be tried by war, and decided by victory."

161. Black, *America as a Military Power*, p. 169, quoted Davis from a proclamation on the merits of a proposed guerrilla war: "Relieved from the necessity of guarding cities and particular points . . . with an army free to move from point to point . . . operating in the interior of our own country, where supplies are more accessible, and where the foe will be far removed from his own base . . . nothing is now needed to render our triumph certain but the exhibition of our own unquenchable resolve." See Jay Winik, *April 1865: The Month That Saved America* (New York: HarperCollins,

March 2001); Daniel Sutherland, "A Civil Ending?" review of William C. Davis, *An Honorable Defeat: The Last Days of the Confederate Government*, in *New York Times Book Review*, July 8, 2001, p. 26, who observed that "Jefferson Davis insisted that victory alone could save the South, and he meant to achieve it, even if he had to disperse his armies and wage a guerrilla war." However, "His unrealistic predictions of ultimate victory bordered on the 'delusional,' William Davis says, but for Jefferson Davis, an honorable defeat – if, indeed, defeat must come – meant going down swinging." Also, Michael Fellman, *Inside War: The Guerrilla Conflict in Missouri during the American Civil War* (New York: Oxford University Press, 1989), p. xvii: "Missouri exploded into a devastating, demoralizing, deteriorating guerrilla war in 1861." See Beringer et al., *Why The South Lost*, p. 327, who observed that "Confederate victory had never depended on military successes; a national resistance in a vast, thinly settled country would have sufficed."

162. See "Lincoln's Meeting with Members of the Confederate Government at Hampton Roads, Va.," February 3, 1865, www. civilwarhome.com/Lincoln%20at%20Hampton% 20Roads.htm, in which President Lincoln met with a three-man commission appointed by Jefferson Davis to discuss the end of the war. Also quoted in McPherson, "Lincoln and the Strategy," pp. 60–1, who observed (p. 61): "Lincoln grasped the necessity of adopting a strategy of total war to overthrow the enemy's social and political system."

163. As Grant wrote, "To have peace 'on any terms' the South would demand the restoration of their slaves already freed. They would demand indemnity for losses sustained, and they would demand a treaty which would make the North slave hunters for the South." This, in the end, "would be the beginning of war" (Simon, "Grant, Lincoln, and Unconditional Surrender," pp. 189–90). Although earlier in the war Grant had sought "to protect the property of the citizens whose territory was invaded," he later believed that "we are not only fighting hostile armies, but a hostile people, and must make (them) feel the hard hand of war" (McPherson, "Lincoln and the Strategy," p. 46).

164. Michael Barone, "War Is Too Important to Be Left to the Generals," *Weekly Standard* 7.38 (June 10, 2002), p. 31, who observed

that Lincoln kept strict control over the course of the war; at www.weeklystandard.com/Content/ Public/Articles/000/000/001/308rifdm.asp.

165. "Surrender at Appomattox, 1865," Eye-Witness to History, at www.eyewitnessto history.com/appomatx.htm (1997).

166. Armstrong, *Unconditional Surrender*, pp. 14–15.

167. See "10 November 1918, The Armistice Demands, Official Release by the German Government, published in the *Kreuz-Zeitung*, November 11, 1918," at www.lib.byu.edu/~rdh/wwi/1918/armistice.html.

168. Ibid.

169. For an excellent analysis of unconditional surrender in World War II, see Kecskemeti, *Strategic Surrender*, pp. 215–41.

170. "Franklin D. Roosevelt's Pearl Harbor Speech" to Congress, December 8, 1941; at www.history.navy.mil/branches/teach/pearl/infamy/infamy6.htm. Shortly thereafter, Roosevelt said in a radio address that the United States would seek "final and complete" victory. Armstrong, *Unconditional Surrender*, p. 16.

171. See "Congressional Declaration of War on Germany," December 11, 1941, at www. law.ou.edu/hist/germwar.html.

172. "Declaration by United Nations, Signed January 1, 1942," *Foreign Relations of the United States: Diplomatic Papers, 1942 – General; the British Commonweath; the Far East* (Washington, DC: U.S. GPO, 1960), pp. 1–38, at pp. 25–6; at digicoll.library.wisc.edu/ cgi-bin/FRUS/FRUS-idx?type=article&did=FRUS. 0001.0158.0004&isize=M. The reasoning was that complete victory "is essential to defend life, liberty, independence, and religious freedom" (p. 25). See Meacham, *Franklin and Winston*, p. 157.

173. Weigley, *American Way of War*, p. 238; "Casablanca Decisions: A Speech to the House of Commons, February 11, 1943," *War Speeches of Winston S. Churchill*, vol. 3, pp. 407–23.

174. Armstrong, *Unconditional Surrender*, p. ix (citing Robert E. Sherwood, *Roosevelt and Hopkins: An Intimate History*, rev. ed. [New York: Harper & Row, 1950], pp. 693–4), and p. 11; Kecskemeti, *Strategic Surrender*, p. 216. For Japan's governmental deliberations about ending the war, see *The United States Strategic Bombing Survey [USSBS], Summary Report, Pacific War*, July 1, 1946 (Washington, DC: U.S. GPO; rpt., Maxwell AFB, AL:

Air University Press, 1987), pp. 103–7; this is available for download, together with the *Summary Report, European War,* September 30, 1945, at aupress.au.af.mil/Books/USSBS/ USS-BS.pdf.

175. Meacham, *Franklin and Winston,* p. 209.

176. Armstrong, *Unconditional Surrender,* pp. 42–3. "[C]ables on file at the British Foreign Office show that the British Cabinet had been consulted about the decision to demand unconditional surrender. The cable file contains a message from Churchill at Casablanca dated January 19, 1943, to Clement Attlee requesting the War Cabinet's views on the inclusion of a demand for the unconditional surrender of Germany and Japan in the Casablanca press release and stating, 'the President liked this idea and it would stimulate our friends in every country'" (p. 42).

177. "Visit to Cyprus: A Speech to a Representative Gathering of the Islanders, February 1, 1943," *War Speeches of Winston S. Churchill,* p. 397.

178. *Department of State Bulletin* 8.190 (February 13, 1943), p. 146, as quoted in Osgood, *Limited War,* p. 291.

179. "Allied Armies Land in France in the Havre–Cherbourg Area; Great Invasion is Under Way," *New York Times,* June 6, 1944, p. 1. In an hour-long "Fireside Chat" radio address, Roosevelt said that "the victory still lies some distance ahead. That distance will be covered in due time – we have no fear of that. But it will be tough and it will be costly." "Address of the President on the Fall of Rome," June 5, 1944, at www.mhric.org/fdr/chat29.html.

180. This is the "Proclamation Defining Terms for Japanese Surrender," or Postdam Proclamation of July 26, 1945, published as "Proclamation Calling for the Surrender of Japan," *Department of State Bulletin* 13.318 (July 29, 1945); at www.ibiblio.org/pha/policy/1945/450726a.html. Truman's secretary of war, Henry Stimson, had written in a memorandum to the president "that a carefully timed warning be given to Japan by the chief representatives of the United States, Great Britain, China and, if then a belligerent, Russia, calling upon Japan to surrender and permit the occupation of her country in order to insure its complete demilitarization for the sake of the future peace. This warning should contain the

following elements: • The varied and overwhelming character of the force we are about to bring to bear on the islands. • The inevitability and completeness of the destruction which the full application of this force will entail. • . . ." Henry L. Stimson, "Memorandum for the President: Proposed Program for Japan," July 2, 1945, www.nuclearfiles.org/menu/library/correspondence/stimson-henry/corr_stimson_1945-07-02.htm.

181. "Address before a Joint Session of the Congress, April 16, 1945," at www.trumanlibrary.org/whistlestop/tap/41645.htm.

182. Quoted in Sigal, *Fighting to a Finish,* p. 94, who notes (p. 94): "Public opinion polls consistently registered the appeal of unconditional surrender."

183. Ibid., p. 115. The full speech is at www.jewishvirtuallibrary.org/jsource/ww2/truman060145.html.

184. Holles, *Unconditional Surrender,* p. 11. Generaloberst (Colonel General) Alfred Jodl, who signed the surrender for Germany, said, "With this signature, the German people and armed forces are, for better or worse, delivered into the victors' hands" (ibid.).

185. The text of the September 2 "Instrument of Surrender" appears within the "Formal Surrender" signed at Seoul a week later; at www.yale.edu/lawweb/avalon/wwii/j1.htm.

186. For background, see Lester Brooks, *Behind Japan's Surrender: The Secret Struggle That Ended an Empire* (New York: McGraw-Hill, 1968); Robert J. C. Butow, *Japan's Decision to Surrender* (Stanford: Stanford University Press, 1954); Robert A. Pape, "Why Japan Surrendered," *International Security* 18.2 (Fall 1993), pp. 154–201; USSBS, *Pacific War,* pp. 103–7; see Montgomery, *History of Warfare,* p. 545: "But the removal of the obstacle of unconditional surrender would of itself have saved those lives [lost at Hiroshima and Nagasaki], because, I consider, Japan would then have surrendered earlier."

187. Kecskemeti, *Strategic Surrender,* p. 216, argues that "The policy of unconditional surrender was specifically designed to make sure that the winners, in accepting surrender, would not unwittingly permit the survival of potential forces of aggression."

188. See USSBS, *European War,* p. 14.

189. Kecskemeti, *Strategic Surrender,* p. 216. See Bradford A. Lee, "Winning the War but Losing the Peace? The United States and

the Strategic Issues of War Termination," in Bradford A. Lee and Karl F. Walling (eds.), *Strategic Logic and Political Rationality: Essays in Honor of Michael I. Handel* (London: Frank Cass, 2003), pp. 249–73, at p. 259: "In World War II in Europe, the basic political objective was to achieve the unconditional surrender of Germany, but if possible in such a way that the United States and Great Britain could shape an overall postwar European balance of power favorable to the West."

190. See *USSBS, European War,* pp. 7–34, *Pacific War,* pp. 67–92. In terms of Japan's shipbuilding program (p. 74): "the aggregate tonnage sunk increased far more rapidly than could be matched by the expansion of the Japanese shipbuilding program."

191. Franklin D. Roosevelt, "State of the Union Address," January 7, 1943; at www.thisnation.com/library/sotu/1943fdr.html.

192. See Ronald H. Spector, *Eagle against the Sun* (New York: Free Press, 1985), p. 418; see Joint Chiefs of Staff, "Strategic Plan for the Defeat of Japan," May 8, 1943, at www.fdrlibrary.marist.edu/psf/box2/a18j01.html.

193. Thomas B. Allen and Norman Polmar, *Code-Name Downfall* (New York: Simon & Schuster, 1995), p. 126. See also *Unconditional Surrender*, Federation of the American Scientists, www.fas.org/irp/eprint/arens/ chap1. htm [on through /chap5.htm], for a discussion of two subordinate operations: Operation Olympic, which was an invasion of the island of Kyushu in the fall of 1945, and Operation Coronet, which was an invasion of the island of Honshu in the spring of 1946.

194. To express the absolute scale of the war, Lincoln warned in 1862 that "the people have not yet made up their minds that we are at war with the South. They have not buckled down the determination to fight this war through." In describing Lincoln's view of the war, Carl Sandburg wrote that "Lincoln had warned nearly a year back that the contest might develop into 'remorseless, revolutionary warfare'." Sandburg, *Abraham Lincoln: The Prairie and the War Years,* one-volume edition (New York: Harcourt, Brace, 1954), pp. 311, 321; Weigley, *American Way of War,* p. 281, who observed that, "If the American people were to remain patient enough to see the Pacific war through to the unconditional surrender of Japan, then the pace of the war must not be allowed to lag."

195. George C. Marshall, "Memorandum for the Secretary of War [Henry L. Stimson], Subject: Basic Objective in the Pacific War," June 9, 1945, at www.historyhappens.net/archival/ hironag/hiroshimashad/marshallmemo.htm. Marshall concluded, however, by observing that "the suppression of the statement 'unconditional surrender' will have little practical effect on the final result."

196. See Armstrong, *Unconditional Surrender,* pp. 109–224. A related issue is that while the decision by a defeated state to surrender unconditionally brings an end to war, the policy of unconditional surrender does not establish or impose any legally binding requirement on the parties to stop the war.

197. For a discussion of these competing national strategies for war, see McPherson, "Lincoln and the Strategy," p. 38, who describes these as, "absolute or ideal types" whereas "in the real world some wars are a mixture of both types."

198. *American Heritage; Webster's Revised.*

199 . Dagobert D. Runes (ed.), *Dictionary of Philosophy,* rev. ed. (New York: Philosophical Library, 1983), pp. 70–1; at www.ditext.com/ runes/c.html.

200. As Wittgenstein argues in *Philosophical Investigations,* "there may be more than one criterion for the same state of affairs." See Paul Edwards (ed.), *The Encyclopedia of Philosophy,* 8 vols. in 4 (New York: Macmillan & Free Press, 1967), vol. 2, p. 258. See also Edward Craig (ed.), *Routledge Encyclopedia of Philosophy,* 10 vols. (New York: Routledge, 1998), vol. 2, p. 712, which states that, "it is through a careful description of our actual employment of expressions that we come to understand the nature of . . . phenomena." It noted that Wittgenstein "does not believe that the understanding which a grammatical investigation achieves can be expressed in the form of a clear, unambiguous description of the structure and function of language in general." The reason is that "the criteria governing our concepts are much more complicated, our language games much more subtle and involved than at first appears."

201. Holles, *Unconditional Surrender,* p. 17; Martin Gilbert, *The Day the War Ended: May 8, 1945 – Victory in Europe* (New York: Henry Holt, 1995).

202. Holles, *Unconditional Surrender,* p. 11.

203. Although this debate has never been resolved, see Armstrong, *Unconditional Surrender,* chap. 3 ("The Effects of the Policy of Unconditional Surrender on the Military Conduct of the War"), pp. 109–67, and chap. 4 ("The Effect of the Policy of Unconditional Surrender on the German Anti-Nazi Resistance Movement"), pp. 167–224; Kecskemeti, *Strategic Surrender.* pp. 155–211; Sigal, *Fighting to a Finish,* 87–157; Montgomery, *History of Warfare,* p. 545.

204. See Winik, *April 1865,* pp. 146–72, for the argument that leaders of the Confederacy debated whether to conduct a guerrilla war after it became clear that the South would lose the conventional war on the battlefield.

205. In estimating the total resources that would be necessary to defeat Germany and Japan, General Albert C. Wedemeyer wrote that "Wars are won on sound strategy implemented by well-trained forces which are adequately and effectively equipped" and not simply through economic production. See Weigley, *American Way of War,* pp. 316–17.

206. Truman, *Memoirs,* vol. 1, p. 422, which continues: "It was to spare the Japanese people from utter destruction that the ultimatum of July 26 was issued at Potsdam. Their leaders promptly rejected that ultimatum. If they do not now accept our terms, they may expect a rain of ruin from the air, the like of which not has been seen on this earth. Behind this air attack will follow sea and land forces in such numbers and power as they have not yet seen and with the fighting skill of which they are already well aware." Truman's full statement is at www.atomicarchive.com/Docs/Hiroshima/PRHiroshima.shtml.

207. Ibid., p. 427.

208. See Sigal, *Fighting to a Finish,* p. 246, for a discussion of options for occupying Japan and questions about how to "discredit militarism 'completely and permanently'." See also Stanley Weintraub, *The Last Great Victory: The End of World War II, July/August 1945* (New York: Truman Talley Books, 1995).

209. See John Campbell, *The Experience of World War II* (New York: Oxford University Press, 1989); Peter Liberman, *Does Conquest Pay? The Exploitation of Occupied Industrial Societies* (Princeton: Princeton University Press, 1996).

210. See Truman, *Memoirs,* vol. 1, pp. 397–8, with Truman arguing that "the United States could not spend money to rehabilitate Italy just to enable her to pay reparations to other countries."

211. David E. Sanger and Eric Schmitt, "U.S. Has a Plan to Occupy Iraq, Officials Report," *New York Times,* October 11, 2002, pp. A1, A14, at p. A14.

212. See Earl F. Ziemke, *The U.S. Army in the Occupation of Germany, 1944–1946* (Washington, DC: U.S. Army, Center of Military History, 1990). In effect, the Potsdam Agreement not only transferred authority in Germany to military commanders from the United States, Russia, Britain, and France in their zones of occupation, but it also established control over Germany and coordinated Allied policy. According to the Potsdam Declaration, "The Allied armies are in occupation of the whole of Germany. . . . Agreement has been reached at this conference on the political and economic principles of a coordinated Allied policy toward defeated Germany during the period of Allied Control." See "The Potsdam Declaration," August 2, 1945, at www.ibiblio.org/pha/policy/1945/450802a.html. See also Allen W. Dulles, "That Was Then: Allen W. Dulles on the Occupation of Germany," *Foreign Affairs* (November–December 2003), at www.freerepublic.com/focus/f-news/1003379/posts. The Allies' "Agreement on Control Machinery in Germany" of November 14, 1944, had established three zones of influence – later changed to four to include one for France – and an Allied Control Council, which would serve as the military occupation governing body.

213. See "Potsdam (Berlin) Conference, 17 July–2 August 1945," at www.taiwandocuments.org/potsdam.htm; John Curtis Perry, *Beneath the Eagle's Wings: Americans in Occupied Japan* (New York: Dodd, Mead, 1980); William Manchester, *American Caesar: Douglas MacArthur 1880–1964* (New York: Dell, 1978); Edwin O. Reischauer, *The Japanese* (London: Belknap Press, 1977).

214. Edwin M. Martin, *The Allied Occupation of Japan* (New York: American Institute of Pacific Relations, 1948), p. 3. This language is found in the "U.S. Initial Post-Surrender Policy for Japan," White House News Release, September 6, 1945, at www.ibiblio.org/pha/policy/1945/450906b.html.

215. "Fourth Inaugural Address, January 20, 1945," in Davis Newton Lott, *The Presi-*

dents Speak: The Inaugural Addresses of the American Presidents, from Washington to Clinton (New York: Henry Holt, 1994), p. 290; at www.yale.edu/lawweb/avalon/presiden/inaug/froos4.htm.

216. As noted, the United States shared its German occupation authority with England, France, and the Soviet Union. The occupation of Japan was mostly a U.S. affair, though the British Commonwealth Occupation Force assisted in demilitarization, and the USSR occupied some Japanese territories, including North Korea. See Campbell, *Experience of World War II;* James Dobbins, John G. McGinn, Keith Crane, Seth G. Jones, Rollie Lal, Andrew Rathmell, Rachel M. Swanger, and Anga Timilsina, *America's Role in Nation-Building: From Germany to Iraq* (Santa Monica, CA: RAND Corporation, MR-1753-RC, 2003), at www.rand.org/pubs/monograph_reports/MR1753/; Martin, *Allied Occupation of Japan,* pp. 3–13; Armstrong, *Unconditional Surrender,* pp. 239–49.

217. Sanger and Schmitt, "U.S. Has a Plan to Occupy Iraq," p. A14.

218. Armstrong, *Unconditional Surrender,* p. 16. The quote is from Roosevelt's "State of the Union Address," January 6, 1942; at www.thisnation.com/library/sotu/1942fdr.html.

219. Martin, *Allied Occupation of Japan,* p. 14. This language too is found in the "U.S. Initial Post-Surrender Policy for Japan."

220. Holles, *Unconditional Surrender,* p. 24. FDR's remark is from his "Fireside Chat" of December 12, 1943, at www.mhric.org/fdr/chat27.html.

221. Martin, *Allied Occupation of Japan,* p. 20. See also "The Potsdam Declaration," at www.ibiblio.org/pha/policy/1945/450802a.html.

222. Ibid., p. 51, which then cites Truman's "U.S. Initial Post-Surrender Policy for Japan": "High officials of the Japanese Imperial General Headquarters and General Staff, other high military and naval officials of the Japanese Government, leaders of ultra-nationalist and militarist organizations and othe important exponents of militarism and aggression will be taken into custody and held for future disposition."

223. See Campbell, *Experience of World War II;* Liberman, *Does Conquest Pay?*

224. Armstrong, *Unconditional Surrender,* p. 16, citing Roosevelt's "State of the Union Address" of January 6, 1942. FDR's ultimate objective was to eliminate the sources of militarism in Germany, Italy, and Japan. As Roosevelt said in ending that speech, "Only total victory can reward the champions of tolerance, and decency, and faith."

225. There were reports as early as the fall of 2002 that American government officials, following the World War II model, planned to occupy Iraq after a war, install an interim governing authority, and rebuild its government on the basis of popular elections. Sanger and Schmitt, "U.S. Has a Plan to Occupy Iraq."

226. Armstrong, *Unconditional Surrender,* p. 251.

227. See Martin, *Allied Occupation of Japan,* p. 3: "The authority of the Emperor and the Japanese Government will be subject to the Supreme Commander, who will possess all powers necessary to effectuate the surrender terms and to carry out the policies established for the conduct of the occupation and control of Japan." (This too is from the "U.S. Initial Post-Surrender Policy for Japan.")

228. Martin, *Allied Occupation of Japan,* p. 4. Subsequent citations are given in the text.

229. See Armstrong, *Unconditional Surrender,* pp. 248–9, who noted that "the United States [had] come to an appreciation of the danger to American national interest and to Western Europe of further Soviet expansion, either physical or political. . . . The very Americans who had once criticized Churchill and the British chiefs [of staff] for narrow nationalism, imperialism, and for thoughts of power politics had begun themselves to think in terms of the balance of power and began hastily to reconstruct German economic, political, and finally military power as a bastion of the West." Armstrong then addressed the implications of this: "The realities of the Cold War destroyed the last official vestiges of the policy and mentality of Unconditional Surrender."

230. This criterion of political and governmental reform was thus even more pragmatic that it seemed, because it helped the United States build two powerful allies for the cold-war struggle against the Soviet Union.

231. See Dobbins et al., *America's Role in Nation-Building,* pp. 2–23, 25–53.

232. See R. Bosworth Smith, *Rome and Carthage: The Punic Wars* (New York: Scribner's, 1889); Brian Caven, *The Punic Wars* (New York: St. Martin's Press, 1980); T. A. Dorey and D. R. Dudley, *Rome against Carthage* (London: Secker & Warburg, 1971); William O'Connor, *Hannibal, Soldier, States-*

man, *Patriot, and the Crisis of the Struggle between Carthage and Rome* (New York: G. P. Putnam's Sons, 1897).

233. Truman, *Memoirs,* vol. 1, p. 388. The whole chapter in which this appears is online at www.mtholyoke.edu/acad/intrel/truman24.htm.

234. For data on extent of devastation in Germany and Japan, see *USSBS, European War,* pp. 20–37, *Pacific War,* pp. 86–92. This figure is a rough and hence unreliable estimate. Accuracy would entail a detailed study of the effects of damage on each sector of the economy, including, oil, electric power, steel, and railways in addition to consumer goods.

235. Armstrong, *Unconditional Surrender,* pp. 230–1. Cf. Michael J. Hogan, *The Marshall Plan: America, Britain, and the Reconstruction of Western Europe, 1947–1952* (New York: Cambridge University Press, 1987), p. 30: "in 1946–47 the average calorie intake per day was only 1,800, an amount insufficient for long-term health."

236. John Gimbel, *The Origins of the Marshall Plan* (Stanford: Stanford University Press, 1976). President Truman, in his "Address before the Canadian Parliament in Ottawa," June 11, 1945, described the moment as "this critical point in history, . . . this trying period, between a war that is over and a peace that is not yet secure"; at trumanlibrary.org/publicpapers/viewpapers.php?pid=2134. Turkey also received Marshall Plans funds in accordance with the Truman Doctrine (see note 94).

237. See Dobbins et al., *America's Role in Nation-Building,* pp. 2–23, 25–53.

238. Howard W. French, "100,000 People Perished, but Who Remembers?" *New York Times,* March 14, 2002, p. A4.

239. "U.S. Initial Post-Surrender Policy for Japan."

240. See Martin, *Allied Occupation of Japan,* pp. 138–40, 93–5, quotation at p. 95.

241. See Bullock, *Study in Tyranny,* pp. 121–86. Also, Taylor, *Origins of the Second World War,* pp. 18–39.

242. The Allies had the legal authority to impose martial law because representatives of the German and Japanese governments had accepted the terms of unconditional surrender.

243. Hogan, pp. 340–3. U.S. Secretary of State J. F. Byrnes, in a speech given in Stuttgart on September 6, 1946, stated that "Germany must be given a chance to export goods in order to import enough to make her economy self-sustaining. Germany is a part of Europe and recovery in Europe, and particularly in the states adjoining Germany, will be slow indeed if Germany with her great resources of iron and coal is turned into a poorhouse." "Restatement of Policy on Germany," at usa.usembassy.de/etexts/ga4-460906.htm.

244. Bailey, *Diplomatic History,* pp. 816–17.

245. It is interesting, however, to compare how the United States acted after the Gulf War in 1991, and its failure to respond in any fashion to Iraqi suffering. In large measure this is explained by the failure to defeat Iraq's government decisively, and by later Iraqi intransigence in resisting United Nations mandates to inspect nuclear, chemical, biological, and missile programs in Iraq.

246. Martin, *Allied Occupation of Japan,* p. 45, quoting "U.S. Initial Post-Surrender Policy for Japan."

247. This formulation sounds remarkably similar to a policy of imperialism. For a discussion of the goals of imperialism, see Morgenthau, *Politics among Nation,* pp. 56–9, who defines the three goals of imperialism as "world empire," "continental empire," and "local preponderance."

248. To quote the "Atlantic Charter," at www.yale.edu/lawweb/avalon/wwii/atlantic.htm: "Sixth, after the final destruction of the Nazi tyranny, they hope to see established a peace which will afford to all nations the means of dwelling in safety within their own boundaries, and which will afford assurance that all men in all the lands may live out their lives in freedom from fear and want."

249. See Stimson's "Memorandum for the President" of July 2, 1945.

250. "Basic Initial Post-Surrender Directive to Supreme Commander for the Allied Powers for the Occupation and Control of Japan," November 3, 1945, quoted in Martin, *Allied Occupation of Japan,* p. 123; at www.ndl.go.jp/constitution/e/shiryo/01/036/036tx.html.

251. Truman, *Memoirs,* vol. 1, pp. 431–2: In terms of "our position on the postwar control of Japan . . . [w]e wanted Japan controlled by an American commander, acting on behalf of the Allies."

252. See "Germany to Oppose Iraq War in U.N.," *Deutsche Welle,* January 22, 2003, at www.dw-world.de/dw/article/0,,761326,00. html.

6. 1986 Raid on Libya

1. For background on Operation El Dorado Canyon, see Brian L. Davis, *Qaddafi, Terrorism, and the Origins of the U.S. Attack on Libya* (New York: Praeger, 1990), esp. pp. 133–80; Joseph T. Stanik, *El Dorado Canyon: Reagan's Undeclared War with Qaddafi* (Annapolis, MD: Naval Institute Press, 2003); Robert E. Venkus, *Raid on Qaddafi* (New York: St. Martin's Press, 1992); David C. Martin and John Walcott, *Best Laid Plans: The Inside Story of America's War against Terrorism* (New York: Harper & Row, 1988), pp. 258–322; "Briefing by Shultz and Weinberger on Strikes against Libya," *New York Times,* April 15, 1986, p. A13.

2. For the transition from "rogue states" to "states of concern," see Steven Mufson, "What's in a Name? U.S. Drops Term 'Rogue State'," *Washington Post,* June 20, 2000, p. 16.

3. For background, see Daniel Benjamin and Steven Simon, *The Age of Sacred Terror* (New York: Random House, 2002); Harvey W. Kushner (ed.), *Essential Readings on Political Terrorism: Analyses of Problems and Prospects for the 21st Century* (Lincoln, NE: Gordian Knot Books, 2002); Paul K. Davis and Brian Michael Jenkins, *Deterrence and Influence in Counterterrorism: A Component in the War on al-Qaeda* (Santa Monica, CA: RAND Corporation, MR-1619-DARPA, 2002), at www.rand.org/pubs/monograph_reports/MR1619/index.html; Bruce Hoffman, "Holy Terror: The Implications of Terrorism Motivated by a Religious Imperative" (Santa Monica, CA: RAND Corporation, P-7834, 1993), rpt. in *Studies in Conflict and Terrorism* 18.4 (Winter 1995), pp. 271–84, at nwcitizen.com/publicgood/reports/holywar3.htm; Brian Michael Jenkins, *New Modes of Conflict* (Santa Monica, CA: RAND Corporation, R-3009-DNA, 1983).

4. Walter Laqueur, "Reflections on Terrorism," *Foreign Affairs* 65.1 (Fall 1986), pp. 86–100; Robert B. Oakley, "International Terrorism," *Foreign Affairs* 65.3 (special issue, *America and the World 1986*), pp. 611–29.

5. See Scott McConnell's interview with Robert Pape, "The Logic of Suicide Terrorism," *American Conservative* 4.10 (July 18, 2005), pp. 17–22; at www.amconmag.com/2005_07_18/article.html.

6. Terrorism was not responsible for the "blackout" that occurred in the eastern United States and parts of Canada on August 14, 2003, and left millions without electrical power. See "Power Surge Blacks Out Northeast, Hitting Cities in Canada and 8 States; Midday Shutdowns Disrupt Millions," *New York Times,* August 15, 2003, p. A1. See also U.S. Department of Homeland Security, *National Strategy for the Physical Protection of Critical Infrastructures and Key Assets* (Washington, DC: U.S. GPO, 2003).

7. Spain's decision to withdraw its forces from Iraq in the aftermath of the al-Qaeda attack against the railroads in Madrid on March 11, 2004, is cause for concern. See "Spain Plans Quick Pullout of Iraq," *CNN,* April 19, 2004, at www.cnn.com/2004/WORLD/europe/04/18/spain.withdraw/index.html.

8. *The 9/11 Commission Report: Final Report of the National Commission on Terrorist Attacks upon the United States* (Washington, DC: U.S. GPO, 2004), pp. 115–19.

9. See, e.g., Bruce Hoffman, "Terrorist Targeting: Tactics, Trends, and Potentialities" (Santa Monica, CA: RAND Corporation, P-7801, 1992); rpt. in *Terrorism and Political Violence* 5.2 (Summer 1993), pp. 12–27.

10. See Bruce Hoffman and Donna Kim Hoffman, *The RAND–St. Andrews Chronology of International Terrorist Incidents: 1995* (Santa Monica, CA: RAND Corporation, RP-666, 1998), originally published in *Terrorism and Political Violence* 8.3 (Autumn 1996), pp. 87–127; Bruce Hoffman, *Inside Terrorism* (New York: Columbia University Press, 1998).

11. In "The President's State of the Union Address," January 29, 2002, President Bush used the phrase "axis of evil" to describe the policies of Iran, Iraq, and North Korea that support terrorism: "States like these, and their terrorist allies, constitute an axis of evil, arming to threaten the peace of the world. By seeking weapons of mass destruction, these regimes pose a grave and growing danger. They could provide these arms to terrorists, giving them the means to match their hatred. They could attack our allies or attempt to blackmail the United States. In any of these cases, the price of indifference would be catastrophic." Online at www.whitehouse.org/news/2002012902-SOTU.asp.

12. N. Browne, "U.S. Attack on Libya,"

Strategic Analysis 12 (July 1989), pp. 417–38; William Broyles, "The Real Strategy in the Libya Bombing," *U.S. News & World Report* 100 (May 12, 1986), p. 14; Davis, *Qaddafi, Terrorism;* George P. Shultz, *Turmoil and Triumph: My Years as Secretary of State* (New York: Charles Scribner's Sons, 1993), pp. 677–87; Edward Schumacher, "The United States and Libya," *Foreign Affairs* 65.2 (Winter 1986–7), pp. 329–48, esp. p. 335; Stanik, *El Dorado Canyon;* Caspar Weinberger, *Fighting for Peace: Seven Critical Years in the Pentagon* (New York: Warner Books, 1990), chap. 7, pp. 175–201; "Documentation: American Bombing of Libya," *Survival* 28.5 (September October 1986), pp. 446–60; David M. North, "Air Force, Navy Brief Congress on Lessons from Libya Strikes," *Aviation Week & Space Technology* 124.22 (June 2, 1986), p. 63; "Reagan, Officials Statements on Libya," *Congressional Quarterly Weekly Report* 44 (April 19, 1986), pp. 881–3; Ronald Reagan, "The Fight against Terrorism," *Vital Speeches of the Day* 52 (May 1, 1986), pp. 418–19; Reagan, "Libyan Sanctions," *Department of State Bulletin* 86.2108 (March 1986), pp. 36 9; Mihailo Stevović, "American Aggression against Libya: Causes and Effects," *Review of International Affairs (Belgrade)* 37.(May 5, 1986), pp. 6–8; "U.S. Exercises Right of Self-Defense against Libyan Terrorism," *Department of State Bulletin* 86.2111 (June 1986), pp. 1–27; Frederick Zillian, "The U.S. Raid on Libya – and NATO," *Orbis* 30.3 (Fall 1986), pp. 499–524.

13. In *The National Security Strategy of the United States of America* (Washington, DC: White House, September 2002), at www.whitehouse.gov/nsc/nss.pdf, the Bush administration stated, "Our enemies have openly declared that they are seeking weapons of mass destruction," notably those "terrorist organizations of global reach and any terrorist or state sponsor of terrorism which attempts to gain or use weapons of mass destruction" (pp. v, 6). The CIA reported to Congress that "We also know that al-Qa'ida has ambitions to acquire or develop nuclear weapons and has been receptive to any outside nuclear assistance that might become available." See Central Intelligence Agency, "Unclassified Report to Congress on the Acquisition of Technology Relating to Weapons of Mass Destruction and Advanced Conventional Munitions, 1 Jan-

uary through 30 June 2002" (Washington, DC: CIA, April 2003), at www.cia.gov/cia/reports/721_reports/jan_jun2002.html. See also Matthew Bunn, Anthony Wier, and John P. Holdren, *Controlling Nuclear Warheads and Materials: A Report Card and Action Plan* (Cambridge, MA: Kennedy School of Government, Belfer Center for Science and International Affairs, March 2003), p. viii: "For at least a decade, Osama bin Laden and his al-Qaeda terrorist network have been attempting to get stolen nuclear weapons or nuclear materials and the nuclear expertise to make a bomb." Available at www.nti.org/e_research/cnwm/cnwm.pdf.

14. "Whether terrorist tactics are used in the course of revolutionary violence is largely a matter of indifference to the Soviets. . . . [They] provide arms and other assistance to a wide spectrum of revolutionary groups. . . . Much of this support is readily utilizable in terrorist activities. The Soviets support certain allied or friendly governments   notably Libya . . . which in turn directly or indirectly support the terrorist activities of a broad spectrum of violent revolutionaries." Central Intelligence Agency, "Soviet Support for International Terrorism and Revolutionary Violence," Special National Intelligence Estimate (SNIE) 11-2-81 (Washington, DC: CIA, May 27, 1981), pp. 1–3; these "key judgments" (only) are at www.cia.gov/csi/books/princeton/snie_11_2_81.pdf.

15. For background on terrorism, see Michelle L. Malvesti, "Explaining the United States' Decision to Strike Back at Terrorists," *Terrorism and Political Violence* 13.2 (Summer 2001), pp. 85–106; Richard H. Shultz Jr., "Can Democratic Governments Use Military Force in the War against Terrorism?" *World Affairs* 148.4 (Spring 1986), pp. 57–62. Edwin Meese III, *With Reagan: The Inside Story* (Washington, DC: Regnery Gateway, 1992), p. 202, wrote that "Qaddafi had vowed to bring about the assassination of President Reagan."

16. See Malvesti, "Explaining the United States' Decision"; Robert E. Osgood, "The Revitalization of Containment," in William G. Hyland (ed.), *The Reagan Foreign Policy* (New York: Meridian, 1987), pp. 19–56, at p. 45.

17. For background on Libya, see Ali Abdullatif Ahmida, *The Making of Modern Libya: State Formation, Colonization and Resistance,*

1830–1932 (Albany, NY: SUNY Press, 1994); J. A. Allan (ed.), *Libya since Independence: Economic and Political Development* (New York: St. Martin's Press, 1982); Lisa Anderson, *The State and Social Transformation in Tunisia and Libya, 1830–1980* (Princeton: Princeton University Press, 1986); Anderson, "Assessing Libya's Qaddafi," *Current History* 84.502 (May 1985), pp. 197–200, 226–7; Jonathan Bearman, *Qadhafi's Libya* (London: Zed Books, 1986); David Blundy and Andrew Lycett, *Qaddafi and the Libyan Revolution* (Boston: Little, Brown, 1987); Edward P. Haley, *Qaddafi and the U.S. since 1969* (New York: Praeger, 1984); Stanik, *El Dorado Canyon,* pp. 23–5, 66–107.

18. U.S. Department of State, "Background Note: Libya," November 2005, at www.state.gov/r/pa/ei/bgn/5425.htm; Geoffrey M. Levitt, *Democracies against Terror: The Western Response to State-Sponsored Terrorism* (New York: Praeger, and Washington, DC: Center for Strategic and International Studies, 1988), p. 1; Granville Austin, "The Libya Raid and the Arab–Israeli Dispute," *Journal of Palestine Studies* 15.4 (Summer 1986), pp. 99–111; Lillian Craig Harris, "America's Libya Policy Has Failed," *Middle East International* 285 (October 10, 1986), pp. 14–15; Davis, *Qaddafi, Terrorism,* pp. 33–55, 57–100.

19. "U.S. Presses Allies on Libya and Weighs Military Action," *World News Digest,* April 11, 1986.

20. "Reagan Ordered Air Strikes to Preempt Libyan Terrorists," *Aviation Week & Space Technology* 12.6 (April 27, 1986), pp. 22–3.

21. Steven Erlanger, "4 Guilty in 1986 Disco Bombing, Linked to Libya, in West Berlin," *New York Times,* November 14, 2001, p. A5.

22. See Gerald M. Boyd, "Genesis of a Decision: How the President Approved Retaliatory Bombing," *New York Times,* April 15, 1986, p. A11; Davis, *Qaddafi, Terrorism,* pp. 81–8.

23. James Reston, "Leave It to the People?" *New York Times,* April 20, 1986, p. D25; "Americans Sanction More Raids if Libyan Terrorism Continues," *Gallup Report* no. 247 (April 1986), pp. 2–12; "Qaddafi and Terrorism: Sampling Global Opinion on the U.S. Raid and the Future," *World Press Review* 33.6 (June 1986), pp. 21–6.

24. Ronald Reagan, "Address to the Nation on the United States Air Strike against Libya," in *Public Papers of the Presidents of the United States: Ronald Reagan, 1986, Book I* (Washington, DC: U.S. GPO, 1988), p. 469 (online at www.reagan.utexas.edu/archives/speeches/1986/41486g.htm). The same speech insists that "Self-defense is not only our right, it is our duty . . . [and] consistent with Article 51 of the United Nations Charter."

25. Reagan, "Address . . . on the United States Air Strike against Libya," p. 469; Boyd, "Genesis of a Decision."

26. See Davis, *Qaddafi, Terrorism,* pp. 81–8.

27. Shultz, *Turmoil and Triumph,* pp. 197–8.

28. Davis, *Qaddafi, Terrorism,* p. 81.

29. Reagan, "Address . . . on the United States Air Strike against Libya," p. 469.

30. Davis, *Qaddafi, Terrorism,* pp. 85–8.

31. Ronald Reagan, "Remarks at the Welcoming Ceremony for the Freed American Hostages," in *Public Papers of the Presidents of the United States: Ronald Reagan, 1981* (Washington, DC: U.S. GPO, 1982), p. 42 (online at www.reagan.utexas.edu/archives/speeches/1981/12781b.htm). See also Bernard Gwertzman, "Administration Assails Making of Hostage Deal," *New York Times,* February 19, 1981, p. A1.

32. For background on the NSDD, see Christopher Simpson, *National Security Directives of the Reagan and Bush Administrations: The Declassified History of U.S. Political and Military Policy, 1981–1991* (Boulder, CO: Westview, 1995), pp. 405–6. See also "Reagan Signs Policy Aimed at Terrorism," *San Diego Union–Tribune,* April 15, 1984, p. 00; "U.S. Plans Tough Policy on Terrorism," *New York Times,* April 17, 1984, p. A3; David Hoffman and Don Oberdorfer, "Secret Policy on Terrorism Given Airing," *Washington Post,* April 18, 1984, p. A1.

33. Davis, *Qaddafi, Terrorism,* p. 66.

34. "Egyptian Troops Storm Hijacked Jet in Malta . . . Libyan-Backed Palestinians Blamed; Other Developments," *World News Digest,* November 23, 1985.

35. "Palestinian Terrorists Hit Rome and Vienna Airports . . . El-Al Counters Targeted," *World News Digest,* December 27, 1985.

36. "Libya: Qaddafi Denies Backing Terrorism," *World News Digest,* September 1, 1985; "Facts on Muammar el-Qaddafi," *World News Digest,* 2003; Davis, *Qaddafi, Terrorism,* p. 90.

37. Hosmer, *Operations against Enemy*

Leaders, p. 17; "Reagan Ordered Air Strikes."

38. Margaret Thatcher, *The Downing Street Years* (New York: HarperCollins, 1993), p. 444, who quoted a private communication from President Reagan, as cited in Stephen T. Hosmer, *Operations against Enemy Leaders* (Santa Monica, CA: RAND Corporation, MR-1385-AF, 2001), p. 17, which is at www.rand.org/pubs/monograph_reports/MR1385/index.html.

39. Davis, *Qaddafi, Terrorism*, pp. 83, 101–13.

40. Shultz, *Turmoil and Triumph*, pp. 643–68, who, after the attack, hoped that "we had shown that we possessed the will to take military action against a state found to be directly supporting terrorism" (p. 688).

41. Davis, *Qaddafi, Terrorism*, pp. 81–4.

42. Ibid.

43. Tim Zimmerman, "Coercive Diplomacy and Libya," in Alexander L. George and William E. Simons (eds.), *The Limits of Coercive Diplomacy*, 2d ed. (Boulder, CO: Westview, 1994), pp. 201–28, at p. 204, noted that the U.S. strike on Libya was "consciously designed in a way that made Qaddafi's death possible." See Shultz, *Turmoil and Triumph*, p. 688, for Shultz's comment during a press conference about Qaddafi: "You've had it, pal."

44. "Iran Frees U.S. Hostages after Signing of Pact Unfreezing Teheran's Assets; Americans Fly to U.S. Base in West Germany, Tell Carter of 'Acts of Barbarism' during Imprisonment," *World News Digest*, January 23, 1981.

45. Ronald Reagan, "Address to the Nation: United States Air Strike against Libya," *Weekly Compilation of Presidential Documents* 22.16 (April 21, 1986), pp. 491–2, at p. 491 (and see note 24 above).

46. Shultz, *Turmoil and Triumph*, pp. 677–8.

47. Ibid., p. 679.

48. Davis, *Qaddafi, Terrorism*, p. 102.

49. "Libya: Anniversary of U.S. Raid Marked; Other Developments," *World News Digest*, May 1, 1987, reported: "U.S. officials had cited figures purporting to show that the U.S. raid on Libya – combined with increased security measures in Europe – had caused a distinct drop in terrorist incidents in 1986, according to reports March 20–April 12." Empirically, however, Libya's support for terrorism seems not to have decreased immediately after the 1986 raid. See Karen Gardela-Treverton and Bruce Hoffman, *The RAND Chronology of International Terrorism for 1988* (Santa Monica, CA: RAND Corporation, R-4180-RC, 1992). The situation has clearly improved since then, according to the U.S. Department of State, *Country Reports on Terrorism 2004* (Washington, DC, April 2005), p. 89: "In 2004, Libya held to its practice in recent years of curtailing support for international terrorism. . . . Libya has provided cooperation in the global war on terrorism, and [Qaddafi] continued his efforts to identify Libya with the international community in the war on terrorism." Yet, as the report makes clear, "Libya remains designated as a state sponsor of terrorism and is still subject to the related sanctions." Online at www.state.gov/documents/organization/45313.pdf.

50. W. Hays Parks, "Lessons from the 1986 Libya Airstrike," *New England Law Review* 36.4 (2002), pp. 755–66, at p. 758; online at www.nesl.edu/lawrev/vol36/4/parks.pdf.

51. Shultz, *Turmoil and Triumph*, p. 680.

52. "U.S. Response to Libyan Attack," *Department of State Bulletin* 86.2110 (May 1986), p. 80; "U.S. Navy Hits Libyan Ships, Missile Site in Gulf of Sidra," *World News Digest*, March 26, 1986.

53. "Briefing by Shultz and Weinberger," p. A13.

54. See George J. Church, "Hitting the Source," *Time* 127.17 (April 28, 1986), pp. 16–20, at p. 26; Seymour Hersh, "Target Qaddafi," *New York Times Magazine*, February 22, 1987, pp. 16–26; "Operation El Dorado Canyon," originally accessed at Federation of American Scientists, but now residing at www.globalsecurity.org/military/ops/el_dorado canyon.htm, for background on the strike; "U.S. Attack Met No Libyan Aircraft," *Defense Daily*, April 16, 1986, p. 257.

55. See the "Operation El Dorado Canyon" Web site.

56. See Stephen E. Anno and William E. Einspahr, *Command and Control Lessons Learned: Iranian Rescue, Falklands Conflict, Grenada Invasion, Libya Raid* (Montgomery, AL: Air War College, 1988), pp. 49–50.

57. "Operation El Dorado Canyon" Web site.

58. Ibid.; see also Neil A. Lewis, "Paris Barred Jets: Weinberger Says Rebuff Added 1,200 Miles to Flight from Britain," *New York Times*, April 15, 1986, p. A1.

59. Hosmer, *Operations against Enemy Leaders,* pp. 13–14, 27–8.

60. "U.S. Libya Raid Aftermath; Qaddafi Said to Be Depressed; Other Developments," *World News Digest,* June 11, 1986; cited in Hosmer, p. 28.

61. Hosmer, *Operations against Enemy Leaders,* pp. 29–30.

62. Anthony H. Cordesman, "After the Raid: The Emerging Lessons from the U.S. Attack on Libya," *Armed Forces* 5 (August 1986), pp. 355–60; Henry W. Prunckun, "Military Deterrence of International Terrorism: An Evaluation of Operation El Dorado Canyon," *Studies in Conflict and Terrorism* 20.3 (July–September 1997), pp. 267–80; Tim Zimmerman, "American Bombing of Libya: A Success for Coercive Diplomacy?" *Survival* 29.3 (May–June 1987), pp. 195–214.

63. Shultz, *Turmoil and Triumph,* p. 687, who wrote that after the U.S. attack, Qaddafi "quieted down and retreated into the desert."

64. *Proliferation: Threat and Response* (Washington, DC: Office of the Secretary of Defense, November 1997), p. 25, which states that, while "Qadhafi [*sic*] has retreated from supporting subversion, destabilization, and terrorism in hopes of having the UN sanctions against Libya lifted, Libya has retained a significant infrastructure to support terrorist activities against Western interests." Online at www.defenselink.mil/pubs/prolif97/.

65. Stanik, *El Dorado Canyon,* pp. 146–7.

66. John Eldridge, "Reassessing Libya: An Analysis from Jane's NBC Defence," online at www.janes.com/security/international_security/news/nbcd/nbcd031223_1_n.shtml. See also Schumacher, "United States and Libya," pp. 345–6.

67. See Stanik, *El Dorado Canyon,* pp. 15, 26–7, 146–75; Hosmer, *Operations against Enemy Leaders,* pp. 27–31; Davis, *Qaddafi, Terrorism,* pp. 33–100; Zimmerman, "American Bombing of Libya"; Schumacher, "United States and Libya," pp. 330–1.

68. For an analysis of attacks against enemy leadership, see Hosmer, *Operations against Enemy Leaders;* George J. Church, "Targeting Gaddafi" [*sic*], *Time* 127.16 (April 21, 1986), pp. 18–22; Mark Whitaker and John Walcott, "Getting Rid of Kaddafi [*sic*]: Reagan's Policy Raises Some Troubling Questions," *Newsweek* 107.12 (April 28, 1986), pp. 18–25, at pp. 20–5.

69. Meese, *With Reagan,* p. 205, described Reagan's "direct involvement" in targeting. The unintentional killing of civilians or destruction of facilities that have no military function is known as *collateral damage.*

70. See Stanik, *El Dorado Canyon,* p. 109.

71. Meese, *With Reagan,* p. 203, wrote that in "military terms, it was a great success."

72. George Lardner Jr., "Terrorist Incidents Down 15%, State Dept. Says," *Washington Post,* May 1, 1991, p. A22.

73. James Gertzenzang, "'Major Damage' Reported on All Libyan Targets," *Los Angeles Times,* April 18, 1986, p. 1; Bernard Weinraub, "U.S. Calls Libya Raid a Success," *New York Times,* April 16, 1986, p. A1; David Ignatius, "Bombing Qadhafi [*sic*] Worked," *Washington Post,* July 13, 1986, p. B5.

74. See "U.S. Libya Raid Aftermath; Qaddafi Said to Be Depressed; Other Developments."

75. For a discussion of the rules of engagement that governed the raid, see Stanik, *El Dorado Canyon,* pp. 46–8, 127–8; Venkus, *Raid on Qaddafi,* pp. 12, 49, 74, 84–5, 144–6.

76. See Venkus, *Raid on Qaddafi,* pp. 84–5, 144–6.

77. See Lou Cannon, *President Reagan: The Role of a Lifetime* (New York: Simon & Schuster, 1991), p. 654. See also Shultz, *Turmoil and Triumph,* p. 685: "President Mitterrand of France was equivocating about granting overflight rights."

78. As noted by Federation of American Scientists (and now posted at www.globalsecurity.org/military/ops/ssc.htm), "The 1997 Quadrennial Defense Review (QDR) report explicitly establishes Small-scale contingencies (SSCs) as a new mission for military operational requirements and a major consideration in deciding on force structure: '[S]wift intervention by military forces may be the best way to contain, resolve, or mitigate the consequences of a conflict that could otherwise become far more costly and deadly. These operations encompass the full range of joint military operations beyond peacetime engagement activities but short of major theater warfare and include: show-of-force operations, interventions, limited strikes, noncombatant evacuation operations, no-fly zone enforcement, peace enforcement, maritime sanctions enforcement, counterterrorism operations, peacekeeping, humanitarian assis-

tance, and disaster relief.'" This QDR itself is at www.fas.org/man/docs/qdr/.

79. Erlanger, "4 Guilty in 1986 Disco Bombing."

80. Felicity Barringer, "Libya Set to Take Responsibility for Pan Am Blast, Envoys Say," *New York Times,* August 13, 2003, p. A11. The final $540 million, which was to be disbursed if the United States removed Libya from its list of state sponsors of terrorism, was withdrawn from escrow by Libya early in April 2005. James Kirkup, "Libya Takes Back Its £500m Fund for Lockerbie Bereaved," *The Scotsman,* April 11, 2005, at thescotsman.scotsman.com/international.cfm?id=380332005.

81. Steven R. Weisman, "U.S. Will Keep Penalties against Libya, Officials Say," *New York Times,* August 15, 2003, p. A12; "US Concerned about Libyan Chemical Weapons Program," *Associated Press,* December 2, 1997; "CIA Can't Stop Libyan Chemical Weapons Plant," *Reuters World Service,* March 24, 1996.

82. For an analysis of Libya's decision, see International Institute for Strategic Studies, "The Libyan Disarmament Model: Aberration or Precedent?" *Strategic Comments* 10.4 (May 2004): pp. 1–2, accessed via www.iiss.org/stratcom.

83. Ronald Reagan, *An American Life: The Autobiography* (New York: Simon & Schuster, 1990), pp. 518–19: "We believe a large part of Libya would like to get rid of the colonel. . . . The attack was not designed to kill Qaddafi; that would have violated our prohibition against assassination [Exec. Order 12333]. The objective was to let him know yhat we weren't going to accept his terrorism anymore, and that if he did it again he could expect to hear from us again. It was impossible, however, to know exactly where he would be at the time of the attack. We realized that it was possible, perhaps probable, that he might be at or near the intelligence center when our planes struck."

7. 1989 Invasion of Panama

1. See "The Attack; U.S. Troops Gain Wide Control in Panama; New Leaders Put In, but Noriega Gets Away," *New York Times,* December 21, 1989, p. A1, for Noriega's claim that "the 'bodies of our enemies' would float down the Panama Canal and the people of Panama would win complete control over the waterway." As quoted in *Operation Just Cause: The*

Planning and Execution of Joint Operations in Panama, February 1988–January 1990 (Washington, DC: Joint History Office, Office of the Chairman of the Joint Chiefs of Staff, 1995), p. 27; at www.dtic.mil/doctrine/jel/ history/ justcaus.pdf.

2. See "Presidential Address," December 20, 1989, *Weekly Compilation of Presidential Documents,* vol. 25, pp. 1974–5; "Transcript of the President's Speech," *New York Times,* December 22, 1989; "Address to the Nation Announcing United States Military Action in Panama," at bushlibrary.tamu.edu/research/ papers/1989/89122000.html. See Bob Woodward, *The Commanders* (New York: Simon & Schuster, 1991), p. 90, who quoted President Bush as saying, "I've asserted what my interest is at this point. It is democracy in Panama; it is protection of the life of Americans in Panama."

3. For background on Panama and the military invasion, see Colin L. Powell, with Joseph E. Persico, *My American Journey* (New York: Random House, 1995); Thomas Donnelly, Margaret Roth, and Caleb Baker, *Operation Just Cause: The Storming of Panama* (New York: Lexington Books, 1991); Edward M. Flanagan, *Battle for Panama: Inside Operation Just Cause* (Washington, DC: Brassey's, 1993); Kevin Buckley, *Panama: The Whole Story* (New York: Simon & Schuster, 1991); *Operation Just Cause: Planning and Execution,* pp. 1–2; James A. Baker III, with Thomas M. Defrank, *The Politics of Diplomacy: Revolution, War and Peace, 1989–1992* (New York: G. P. Putnam's Sons, 1995), pp. 177–94; Margaret E. Scranton, *The Noriega Years* (Boulder, CO: Lynne Rienner Publishers, 1991); Linda Robinson, "Dwindling Options in Panama," *Foreign Affairs* 68.5 (Winter 1989–90), pp. 187–205, at p. 190; Thomas Donnelly, "Lessons Unlearned: A Comparison of Three American Wars," *National Interest* 60 (Summer 2000), pp. 76–82.

4. Woodward, *Commanders,* p. 133. Powell also said that "the massive use of force was less risky than a smaller effort" (p. 168).

5. Thomas A. Bailey, *A Diplomatic History of the American People,* 9th ed. (Englewood Cliffs, NJ: Prentice–Hall, 1974), p. 184; excerpts of the speech are at www.yale.edu/ lawweb/avalon/monroe.htm. In a letter dated October 24, 1823, Thomas Jefferson had written to President Monroe that "we aim not at the acquisition of any of those possessions,"

but that "we will oppose, with all our means, the forcible interposition of any other power." See "Thomas Jefferson on the Monroe Doctrine," at www.mtholyoke.edu/acad/intrel/thomas.htm.

6. Michael L. Conniff, *Panama and the United States: The Forced Alliance* (Athens: University of Georgia Press, 1992). U.S. work on the canal began after a French attempt had recently failed.

7. Anne Patterson, Deputy Assistant Secretary for Inter-American Affairs, "Strategic Interests in Panama," *U.S. Department of State Dispatch* 6.12 (March 20, 1995), p. 229; at dosfan.lib.uic.edu/ERC/briefing/dispatch/1995/html/Dispatchv6no12.html.

8. For an excellent review of Mahan's ideas about naval power, see Margaret Tuttle Sprout, "Mahan: Evangelist of Sea Power," in Edward Mead Earle, *Makers of Modern Strategy* (Princeton: Princeton University Press, 1973), pp. 415–45, at p. 426.

9. The U.S. Southern Command calls this situation highly unlikely. (See Chapter 10.)

10. Baker, *Politics of Diplomacy*, p. 179.

11. Scranton, *Noriega Years*, p. 202. Noriega had been a critical U.S. ally, permitting the United States to establish listening posts, coordinating diplomacy between Washington and Cuba, allowing the exiled Shah of Iran to seek refuge in Panama, and channeling American money to the insurgencies in El Salvador and Nicaragua. This relationship ended when the DEA indicted Noriega on February 5, 1988, on federal drug charges. Woodward, *Commanders*, p. 83, notes: "Although he once had been one of the CIA's key Latin American assets, the administration now viewed him as an outlaw and an enemy of U.S. interests." For Noriega and the CIA, see Institute for Policy Studies, "A Tangled Web," *Congressional Record*, 105th Congress, May 7, 1998, pp. H2955–6, which notes (p. H2955): "In 1976, CIA Director George Bush pays Noriega $110,000 for his services, even though as early as 1971 U.S. officials agents had evidence that he was deeply involved in drug trafficking. . . . The general is rewarded handsomely . . . collecting $200,000 from the CIA in 1986 alone." Online at www.fas.org/irp/congress/1998_cr/980507-l.htm. Also see Donnelly et al., *Operation Just Cause*, p. 10; Eytan Gilboa, "The Panama Invasion Revisited: Lessons for the Use of Force in the Post Cold War Era," *Political Science Quarterly* 110.4 (Winter

1995–6), pp. 539–62, at www.mtholyoke.edu/acad/intrel/gilboa.htm.

12. Patterson, "Strategic Interests in Panama," p. 228.

13. See Conniff, *Panama and the United States*, pp. 116–53.

14. Baker, *Politics of Diplomacy*, p. 178.

15. See "Fighting in Panama: The White House; Text of Statement by Fitzwater," *New York Times*, December 21, 1989, p. A19.

16. Baker, *Politics of Diplomacy*, pp. 193–4. "Just Cause was an exercise in supporting democracy and the rule of law in the hemisphere. . . The United States was simply enforcing the will of the Panamanians by restoring the legitimately elected government to authority."

17. Ibid., p. 178. "His [Noriega's] corrupt and repressive military regime undermined our efforts both to promote democracy in the hemisphere and to combat narcotics trafficking." See also Henry A. Kissinger, *National Bipartisan Commission on Central America* (Washington, DC: U.S. GPO, 1984).

18. Baker, *Politics of Diplomacy*, p. 179.

19. For a discussion of relations with Panama and the broader context of imperialist policies toward Latin America, see Conniff, *Panama and the United States;* Jorge I. Dominguez, *The Future of Inter-American Relations* (New York: Routledge, 2000); David Malone and Yuen Foong Khong (eds.), *Unilateralism and U.S. Foreign Policy: International Perspectives* (Boulder, CO: Lynne Rienner Publishers, 2003); Kissinger, *National Bipartisan Commission on Central America*.

20. Buckley, *Panama: Whole Story*, pp. 185–7. See also Woodward, *Commanders*, p. 170, on Baker's view that OAS would "denounce the interference. . . . [but] privately most of these governments would send back-channel word that they were neutral or even pleased." On December 22, 1989, the OAS condemned the U.S. invasion of Panama harshly by a vote of 20 to 1. It had earlier condemned Noriega for election fraud, declaring his rule unconstitutional, after the aborted May elections. Ian Vasquez, "Washington's Dubious Crusade for Hemispheric Democracy," *Policy Analysis* 201 (January 12, 1994), at www.cato.org/pubs/pas/pa-201.html. In June 1991 the OAS adopted the U.S.-drafted Santiago Declaration, committing it to defend regional democracy. Baker, *Politics of Diplomacy*, p. 194.

21. George [H. W.] Bush and Brent Scowcroft, *A World Transformed* (New York: Alfred A. Knopf, 1998), p. 62, wrote that sending troops "to restore democratic rule . . . would have provoked a firestorm of outrage from Latin American leaders sensitive to foreign, especially Yankee, intervention."

22. *Operation Just Cause: Planning and Execution*, p. 5.

23. As cited in ibid., p. 29. See also Powell, *My American Journey*, pp. 418–21.

24. See Stephen T. Hosmer, *Operations against Enemy Leaders* (Santa Monica, CA: RAND Corporation, MR-1385-AF, 2001), p. 12: "CIA personnel were apparently barred from providing advice to dissident Panamanian officers who were plotting a coup in October 1989 because of the possibility that the coup might lead to Noriega's death." (This report is at www.rand.org/pubs/monograph_reports/MR1385/index.html.) See also Stephen Engelberg, "CIA Seeks Looser Rules on Killings during Coups," *New York Times*, October 17, 1989, p. A8.

25. See Bush and Scowcroft, *World Transformed*, p. 62. In *My American Journey* (New York: Random House, 1995), Powell described meetings with President Bush's "clear intention to restore democracy" (p. 419). See also Baker, *Politics of Diplomacy*, p. 178.

26. *Operation Just Cause: Planning and Execution*, pp. 6–7.

27. Baker, *Politics of Diplomacy*, p. 191; Donnelly et al., *Operation Just Cause*. According to Powell (*My American Journey*, pp. 420–1), the "existing plan, code-named Blue Spoon, was beefed up to include taking out the entire PDF as well as removing Noriega. . . . [T]his force was to seize all PDF installations, put down PDF resistance, and help bring the legitimately elected Endara government to power."

28. See Donnelly et al., *Operation Just Cause*, pp. 381–91, and see pp. 395–6: "To the extent Just Cause eliminated the PDF as an institution – although former PDF troops make up a majority of the restructured public forces – it offered Endara and his country a blank page upon which to compose a new, more democratic and just society."

29. See Bush and Scowcroft, *World Transformed*, p. 23.

30. Baker, *Politics of Diplomacy*, p. 178.

31. William M. Leogrande, "An Anachronism – but It Works," *Los Angeles Times*, December 28, 1989, p. B7, cites an "80% public-approval rating for the invasion"; at american.edu/faculty/leogrande/panama-anachronism.htm.

32. See Powell, *My American Journey*, pp. 413–34, for a discussion of U.S. policy.

33. *Operation Just Cause: Planning and Execution*, p. 21, which described General Powell's support for using overwhelming force. (As mentioned in note 27 above, Operation Just Cause was originally code-named Operation Blue Spoon [ibid., p. 32].)

34. Powell, *My American Journey*, pp. 420–1; Woodward, *Commanders*, pp. 117–18. As Donnelly et al., *Operation Just Cause*, noted (p. 399): "[General] Stiner's analysis of the role of the PDF in Panamanian society meshed neatly with the intention to use swift, overpowering force to accomplish the Bush Administration's goals in Panama."

35. Also see Martin van Creveld, *Technology and War: From 2000 B.C. to the Present* (New York: Free Press, 1991), for thoughts on how guerrilla warfare and terrorism can undermine a society, and its parallels with the disintegration of Panama under Noriega.

36. See Donnelly et al., *Operation Just Cause*, pp. 104–34; *Operation Just Cause: Planning and Execution*, pp. 37–44.

37. Powell, *My American Journey*, pp. 433, 415; Baker, *Politics of Diplomacy*, pp. 84, 89, 188–91.

38. *Operation Just Cause: Planning and Execution*, p. 2.

39. There were reports that Noriega might escape into the woods to conduct guerrilla warfare against U.S. military forces. See, e.g., Woodward, *Commanders*, p. 89: "the Southern Command had learned that Noriega had two plans to put into effect if he was attacked personally or sought by U.S. forces. One was to go to the hills and conduct guerrilla operations; the second was to take American hostages."

40. Baker, *Politics of Diplomacy*, pp. 193–4, outlined this argument: "The salutary effects of Just Cause went well beyond the isthmus. It made a crucial difference in Colombia. . . . It also convinced the Sandinista government that there were consequences to stealing an election."

41. Powell, *My American Journey*, p. 431–2: "Near the center of Panama City stood a radio tower. Every armchair strategist knows that you have to knock out the enemy's capacity to communicate."

42. See Donnelly et al., *Operation Just Cause,* pp. 135–213; *Operation Just Cause: Planning and Execution,* pp. 37–44.

43. Baker, *Politics of Diplomacy,* pp. 177–8; Eytan Gilboa, "The Panama Invasion Revisited: Lessons for the Use of Force in the Post Cold War Era," *Political Science Quarterly* 110.4 (Winter 1995–6), pp. 539–62. Donnelly et al., *Operation Just Cause,* noted (p. 399): "More than strictly a military organization, the PDF permeated every aspect of Panamanian life. It was organized along provincial lines, acting as the agent of the central government. . . . It served also as a police force, down to the function of writing traffic tickets. Most importantly, it was a sort of Mafia, distributing the spoils of bribery and corruption to its members."

44. Donnelly et al., *Operation Just Cause,* pp. 383–91.

45. For background on the air operation, see *Operation Just Cause: Planning and Execution,* p. 33; see also p. 23. Interestingly, Secretary of Defense Dick Cheney questioned whether the air defense threat was sufficiently serious to merit using the F-117A stealth fighter, but he approved its use against Rio Hato and suspected Noriega hideouts La Escondida and Boquete (p. 31). John Morrocco, "F-117A Fighter Used in Combat for First Time in Panama," *Aviation Week & Space Technology* 132.1 (January 1, 1990), pp. 32–3.

46. Donnelly et al., *Operation Just Cause,* p. 139: "Even the PDF seemed to sense something was up."

47. Ibid., p. 340; Woodward, *Commanders,* p. 140: "The plan called for the Air Force's new F-117A stealth fighters to drop 2,000-pound bombs around the barracks, stunning and disorienting the PDF troops inside . . . [and] would provide the best, most accurate nighttime bombing capability."

48. Donnelly et al., *Operation Just Cause,* p. 399.

49. *Operation Just Cause: Planning and Execution,* pp. 20, 33. As General Powell noted, "air refuelers did not just make a difference in this operation – they made it possible." Cited at "Operation Just Cause," first accessed at the Federation of American Scientists Web site, but now residing at www.globalsecurity. org/military/ops/just_cause.htm.

50. Noriega had recently turned to Cuba and Nicaragua for economic and military assis-

tance. They "funneled Communist bloc weapons and instructors to Panama and helped Noriega to develop civilian defense committees . . . for intelligence collection and population control." Ibid., p. 6.

51. Ibid., p. 23.

52. Ibid., p. 8.

53. Baker, *Politics of Diplomacy,* p. 177: "From the start of my tenure, I was privately concerned that one trouble spot confronting our new administration might eventually require a military solution: the Isthmus of Panama. . . . An erstwhile ally of the United States, Noriega had become increasingly dangerous as his collusion with international drug trafficking deepened, and assaults by his armed forces against American servicemen and their families in Panama escalated."

54. See ibid., Bush and Scowcroft, *World Transformed;* Powell, *My American Journey;* Woodward, *Commanders.*

55. Colin Powell, one of the principal architects of the Persian Gulf War, drew what we called a "bedrock" principle from Operation Just Cause. As he wrote in *My American Journey,* p. 434: "The lessons I had absorbed from Panama confirmed all my convictions over the preceding twenty years, since the days of doubt over Vietnam. Have a clear political objective and stick to it. Use all the force necessary, and do not apologize for going in big if that is what it takes. Decisive force ends wars quickly and in the long run saves lives. Whatever threats we faced in the future, I intended to make these rules the bedrock of my military counsel."

56. *Operation Just Cause: Planning and Execution,* p. 65–6; Donnelly, "Lessons Unlearned." Some Central American and Panamanian organizations put the civilian death toll as high as two to four thousand, as did an independent Commission of Inquiry led by former U.S. Attorney General Ramsey Clark; see "Operation Just Cause," at www.globalsecurity. org/military/ops/just_cause.htm.

57. "Presidential Statement, January 3, 1990," *Weekly Compilation of Presidential Documents* 26, pp. 8–9; online as "Remarks Announcing the Surrender of General Manuel Noriega in Panama," at bushlibrary.tamu. edu/research/papers/1990/90010305.html.

58. For a discussion of rebuilding Panama, see *Operation Just Cause: Planning and Execution,* pp. 51–6.

59. Few observers would have predicted

that the United States would launch a military invasion of Panama so soon after the November 9 opening of the Berlin Wall (a cold-war breakthrough in more ways than one). Baker, *Politics of Diplomacy*, p. 194: "[I]n breaking the mind-set of the American people about the use of force in the post-Vietnam era, Panama established an emotional predicate that permitted us to build the public support so essential to the success of Operation Desert Storm thirteen months later."

60. This issue would reemerge during the Persian Gulf War, when there was considerable speculation whether the United States might capture or kill Saddam Hussein; see Chapter 8.

61. See Hosmer, *Operations against Enemy Leaders*, pp. 9–47.

62. Merle D. Kellerhals Jr., "Rumsfeld Discusses Emerging U.S. Defense Strategy," August 17, 2001, at www.iwar.org.uk/news-archive/2001/national-security/08-17-01.htm: "U.S. Defense Secretary Donald Rumsfeld says the newly emerging U.S. war fighting strategy will focus on winning one major regional conflict decisively, while at the same time being capable of carrying on smaller-scale deployments in areas like the Balkans, Haiti and Somalia."

63. On rebuilding Panama, see Donnelly et al., *Operation Just Cause*, pp. 350–79. In mid-1990, a group of Panamanian businesses filed a $30 million lawsuit against the United States for damages resulting from looting that followed the invasion. "Panama Companies Sue U.S. for Damages," *New York Times*, July 21, 1990. For a skeptical view of Panama's progress in the late 1990s, see Steve C. Ropp, "Panama: Tailoring a New Image," *Current History* 96.607 (February 1997), pp. 55–60.

64. The 1982 deployment to Lebanon and the 1983 invasion of Grenada had earlier signaled that the United States could at least alter a government's policies and actions through the use of military force – lessons applied in 1986 in Libya (see Chapter 6).

65. For an analysis of the Goldwater–Nichols Act, which aimed to limit interservice rivalry, see James R. Locher III, *Victory on the Potomac: The Goldwater–Nichols Act Unifies the Pentagon* (College Station: Texas A&M University Press, 2002).

8. The 1991 Persian Gulf War

1. See Rick Atkinson, *Crusade: The Untold Story of the Persian Gulf War* (New York: Houghton Mifflin, 1993); Lawrence Freedman and Efraim Karsh, *The Gulf Conflict, 1990–1991: Diplomacy and War in the New World Order* (Princeton: Princeton University Press, 1995); Norman Friedman, *Desert Victory: The War for Kuwait* (Annapolis, MD: Naval Institute Press, 1991); Philip H. Gordon, Martin Indyk, and Michael O'Hanlon, "Getting Serious about Iraq," *Survival* 44.3 (Autumn 2002), pp. 9–22; Richard P. Hallion, *Storm over Iraq: Air Power and the Gulf War* (Washington, DC: Smithsonian Institution Press, 1992). See also Jeffrey Record, *Hollow Victory: A Contrary View of the Gulf War* (New York: Brassey's, 1993), pp. 155–60, for his discussion of a "pyrrhic victory."

2. For arguments that the Bush administration did not intend to impose a "total" victory on Iraq, see George [H. W.] Bush and Brent Scowcroft, *A World Transformed* (New York: Alfred A. Knopf, 1998), p. 412.

3. See ibid., p. 399, for a statement of U.S. security and economic interests. See also Greg Seigle, "Iraq Could Have Caught Up with WMD Production," *Jane's Defence Weekly* 30.21 (November 25, 1998), p. 4; Thalif Deen, "Iraq May Still Have the Talent to Produce Nuclear Weapons," *Jane's Defence Weekly* 30.5 (August 5, 1998), p. 6. See Central Intelligence Agency, "Unclassified Report to Congress on the Acquisition of Technology Relating to Weapons of Mass Destruction and Advanced Conventional Munitions: 1 January through 30 June 2001" (Washington, DC: CIA, January 2002), for discussion on Iraq's programs; at www.cia.gov/cia/reports/721_reports/jan_jun2001.htm.

4. George [H. W.] Bush, "Address to the Nation Announcing the Deployment of United States Armed Forces to Saudi Arabia," August 8, 1990, at bushlibrary.tamu.edu/research/papers/1990/90080800.html (also at www. meij. or.jp/text/Gulf%20War/US9008062.htm). On the U.S. response, see Department of Defense, *Conduct of the Persian Gulf War: Final Report to Congress* (Washington, DC: U.S. GPO, 1992), pp. 58–9; at www.ndu.edu/library/epubs/cpgw.pdf.

5. See Zbigniew Brzezinski, *Power and Principle: Memoirs of the National Security*

Advisor, 1977–1981 (New York: Farrar, Straus, Giroux, 1983), pp. 178, 456; Joshua M. Epstein, *Strategy and Force Planning: The Case of the Persian Gulf* (Washington, DC: Brookings Institution, 1987), for an analysis of the dynamics of U.S. responses to a Soviet invasion. (That such concerns were present even in the Bush administration is clear from the ensuing note.)

6. National Security Directive 26, October 2, 1989, p. 1; at www.fas.org/irp/offdocs/nsd/nsd26.html. The quotation immediately continues by stating that such force may be used "against the Soviet Union or any other regional power with interests inimical to our own."

7. Ibid., p. 2. See also Bush and Scowcroft, *World Transformed*, p. 306; DoD, *Conduct of the Persian Gulf War*, p. 369.

8. Bob Woodward, *The Commanders* (New York: Simon & Schuster, 1991), p. 226. See DoD, *Conduct of the Persian Gulf War*, p. 19, for estimates that Saudi Arabia accounts for roughly 20 percent of the world's oil reserves.

9. Woodward, *Commanders*, p. 226.

10. See Bush and Scowcroft, *World Transformed*, p. 322, who quote CIA Director William Webster as briefing President Bush as follows: "He [Saddam Hussein] will stay if not challenged within the next year. This will fundamentally alter the Persian Gulf region. He would be in an inequitable position, since he would control the second- and third-largest proven oil reserves with the fourth-largest army in the world. He would also have Kuwaiti financial assets, access to the Gulf, and the ability to pour money into his military." In terms of international support, Secretary of State James Baker wrote that, "from the very beginning, the President recognized the importance of having the express approval of the international community if at all possible." James A. Baker III, with Thomas M. Defrank, *The Politics of Diplomacy: Revolution, War and Peace, 1989–1992* (New York: G. P. Putnam's Sons, 1995), p. 304. For a general discussion of U.S. diplomatic efforts to build an international coalition against Iraq, see Baker, *Politics of Diplomacy*, pp. 300–20. Moreover, Woodward, *Commanders*, p. 226, reported that "Iraq now held about 20 percent of the world's known oil reserves. If Saddam were to take over Saudi Arabia, he would have 40 percent."

11. DoD, *Conduct of the Persian Gulf War*,

p. 19, quoting Bush, "Address . . . Announcing the Deployment . . . to Saudi Arabia." Although Iraq had invaded Kuwait on August 2, it did not proclaim Kuwait's annexation until August 8.

12. See William Safire, "The Time Has Come," *New York Times*, July 13, 1995, p. A23, who continued by noting that the "presumption of weakness guarantees that you will be tested."

13. Woodward, *Commanders*, p. 225, notes that "Kuwait had been overrun by more than 100,000 troops, well beyond what was needed. The Iraqi forces in Kuwait were being resupplied and reorganized, in some cases just ten miles from the Saudi border. They could easily continue their march and punch through meager Saudi defenses."

14. See Janice Gross Stein, "Deterrence and Compellence in the Gulf, 1990–91," *International Security* 17.2 (Fall 1992), pp. 147–79, for the argument that Hussein failed to understand U.S. resolve because the United States did not clearly express its intention to defend Kuwait.

15. DoD, *Conduct of the Persian Gulf War*, p. 6.

16. On Iraq's military forces see F. Gregory Gause III, "Iraq's Decisions to Go to War, 1980 and 1990," *Middle East Journal* 56.1 (Winter 2002), pp. 47–70. By January 1991, Iraqi ground strength overall was estimated at "1.2 million men, 69–71 divisions and forces commands, 5,800 tanks, 5,100 armored personnel carriers, and 3,850 artillery pieces." DoD, *Conduct of the Persian Gulf War*, p. 83.

17. See Efraim Karsh, *The Iran–Iraq War: A Military Analysis* (Adelphi Paper no. 20, London: International Institute for Strategic Studies, 1987), p. 62, who writes: "This [Iran's strategic ambitions] is precisely what is rallying widespread international support for Iraq and allows Saddam Hussein to claim that Iraq is *the* front-line state in a war between the whole Arab nation and revolutionary Iran" (emphasis in original).

18. As Woodward noted (*Commanders*, p. 206), "Iraq had been complaining bitterly that Kuwait was exceeding its oil production quotas set by the Organization of Petroleum Exporting Countries (OPEC), driving the prices down." See DoD, *Conduct of the Persian Gulf War*, p. 5: "On 17 July, Saddam accused Kuwait and the United Arab Emirates of complicity with the United States to cheat on oil

production quotas. He blamed this overpro-
duction for driving down the price of oil, causing losses of billions of dollars to Iraq."

19. See Stein, "Deterrence and Compellence."

20. See Woodward, *Commanders,* pp.
211–15, for a description of Glaspie's conversation with Saddam Hussein. In Bush and
Scowcroft, *World Transformed,* pp. 310–11,
Bush wrote that "Glaspie, a veteran diplomat
in whom I had full confidence, has been
much criticized for what happened in her
meeting with Saddam. She was lied to by him,
and she clearly spelled out that we could not
condone settlement of disputes by other than
peaceful means. It is a total misreading of this
conversation to conclude that we were giving
Saddam Hussein a green light to seize his
neighbor. No one, especially Saddam Hussein, could doubt that the U.S. had strong interests in the Gulf and did not condone aggression."

21. See Bush and Scowcroft, *World Transformed,* pp. 302–33; see p. 333 for Bush's
observation that "I never wavered from the
position that I would do whatever it took to
remove Iraq from Kuwait."

22. These points were enumerated by Bush
in National Security Directive 45; at www.
fas.org/Irp/offdocs/nsd/nsd_45.htm. See Bush and
Scowcroft, *World Transformed,* p. 341.

23. "A puppet regime imposed from the
outside is unacceptable. The acquisition of territory by force is unacceptable. No one, friend
or foe, should doubt our desire for peace; and
no one should underestimate our determination to confront aggression. . . . [S]oon after
the Iraqi invasion, the United Nations Security Council, without dissent, condemned Iraq,
calling for the immediate and unconditional
withdrawal of its troops from Kuwait." Bush,
"Address . . . Announcing the Deployment
. . . to Saudi Arabia."

24. For instance, U.N. Security Council
Resolution (UNSCR) 660 (August 2, 1990)
demanded that "Iraq withdraw immediately
and unconditionally all its forces *to the positions
in which they were located* on 1 August 1990"
(emphasis added); at www.fas.org/news/un/
iraq/sres/sres0660.htm. UNSCR 678 (November 29), discussed later in this section, "Au-
thorizes Member States co-operating with the
Government of Kuwait . . . to use *all necessary
means* to uphold and implement resolution
660" (emphasis added) if Iraq has not fully

withdrawn by January 15, 1991; at www.
fas.org/news/un/iraq/sres/sres0678.htm.

25. Bush and Scowcroft, *World Transformed,* p. 379, which continues: "The Senate
quickly approved similar resolutions supporting the deployment of troops and our actions
in the Gulf." The two resolutions were HJ
Res. 658 and S. Con. Res. 147. Though each
was referred to the other house, neither was
adopted by the full Congress. See Richard F.
Grimmett, "The War Powers Resolution: After Thirty Years," CRS Report for Congress,
March 11, 2004, section "Persian Gulf War,
1991," pp. 1, 11; at www.fas.org/man/crs/
RL32267.html.

26. "The sovereign independence of Saudi
Arabia is of vital interest to the United States.
. . . U.S. forces will work together with those of
Saudi Arabia and other nations to preserve the
integrity of Saudi Arabia and to deter further
Iraqi aggression." Bush, "Address . . . An-
nouncing the Deployment . . . to Saudi Arabia."

27. See, e.g., UNSCR 661 (August 6,
1990); at www.fas.org/news/un/iraq/sres/
sres0661.htm.

28. Bush and Scowcroft, *World Transformed,* p. 364, articulated this view in discussions with General Secretary of the Soviet
Union, Mikhail Gorbachev.

29. Bush and Scowcroft, *World Transformed,* p. 333; and see the Webster briefing
cited in note 10 above.

30. See International Institute for Strategic
Studies, *The Military Balance, 1990–1991*
(London: Brassey's, 1990); Karsh, *Iran–Iraq
War;* DoD, *Conduct of the Persian Gulf War,*
pp. 9–16.

31. DoD, *Conduct of the Persian Gulf War,*
p. 143.

32. Ibid., pp. 15, 97.

33. Lawrence Freedman and Efraim Karsh,
"How Kuwait Was Won: Strategy in the Gulf
War," *International Security* 16.2 (Fall 1991),
pp. 5–41.

34. See William Safire, "Protecting Saddam," *New York Times,* March 18, 2002, p.
A27.

35. See Jon Lee Anderson, "The Unvanquished," *New Yorker* 76.38 (December 11,
2000), pp. 76–89, for background on the inspections, which notes (p. 79): "A U.N. Security Council Resolution stipulated that sanctions would not be withdrawn until Iraq was
disarmed, but the UNSCOM inspectors reported that the Iraqis lied about what they had

destroyed, continued to conceal weapons and weapons-making systems, and, in general, refused to cooperate with them."

36. George [H. W.] Bush, "A Nation Blessed," adapted from a commencement address to the Naval War College, June 15, 2001, *Naval War College Review* 54.4 (Autumn 2001), pp. 135–40, at p. 139; at www.nwc.navy.mil/press/review/2001/autumn/rtoc-au1.htm. See Shlopah, Stillim, et al., *A Global Access Strategy for the U.S. Air Force*, p. 3.

37. Bush and Scowcroft, *World Transformed*, p. 414. Also, UNSCR 678 is online at www.fas.org/news/un/iraq/sres/sres0678.htm.

38. DoD, *Conduct of the Persian Gulf War*, pp. 21–4. Neither the Soviet Union nor China joined the U.S.-led coalition to expel Iraq, but China did agree to suspend arms deliveries. Iran denounced Iraq's invasion but immediately thereafter announced its neutrality.

39. Ibid., p. 20.

40. Bush, "Nation Blessed," p. 136.

41. See William J. Perry, "Desert Storm and Deterrence," *Foreign Affairs* 70.4 (Fall 1991), pp. 66–82.

42. In addition to the nonbinding resolutions cited earlier (see note 25), both houses of Congress passed the "Authorization for Use of Military Force against Iraq Resolution" (P.L. 102-1) on January 12, 1991. See Grimmett, "War Powers Resolution," p. 15.

43. See Charles Krauthammer, "Backdown on Iraq," *Washington Post*, August 26, 1998, p. A19, who refers to "the total surrender of the Clinton administration in the face of Saddam's determination to rebuild his weapons of mass destruction." See Thalif Deen, "Iraq Attaches Conditions as It Agrees to Join Sanctions Review," and Ed Blanche and Greg Seigle, "Showdown for Iraq and USA," both in *Jane's Defence Weekly* 30.14 (October 7, 1998), pp. 5 and 37, respectively; David Ruppe, "The U.N.: Going Back to Iraq?" *Jane's Defence Weekly* 31.10 (March 10, 1999), p. 51; William M. Arkin, "UNSCOM R.I.P.," *Bulletin of the Atomic Scientists* 55.2 (March–April 1999), p. 64, at www.thebulletin.org/article.php?art_ofn=ma99arkin; Thom Shanker, "Rumsfeld Denounces Iraq for Rejecting Further Arms Inspections," *New York Times*, August 14, 2002, p. A5.

44. "Is Iraq Just Waiting for 'Go' on New Weapons?" *Associated Press*, September 4, 1998. Testimony presented to the Senate For-

eign Relations Committee and the House Armed Services Committee reported that the "United States and Britain systematically had undermined efforts by U.N. inspectors to get to the bottom of Iraq's arsenal of mass weapons, which Iraq is barred from having." It also noted that the "lack of resolve would enable Iraq to keep these weapons and could lead Saddam to expel the inspectors."

45. See Alfred B. Prados, "Iraq: Former and Recent Military Confrontations with the United States," CRS Issue Brief for Congress, updated September 6, 2002; at fpc.state.gov/documents/organization/14836.pdf.

46. The term "campaign" describes the air, land, and naval operations of the war. The Joint Chiefs of Staff define a campaign as "a series of related operations aimed at accomplishing a strategic or operational objective within a given time and space." See *Department of Defense Dictionary of Military and Associated Terms, Joint Publication 1-02* (Washington, DC: U.S. GPO, as amended May 7, 2002), p. 61, which also refers to a "campaign plan."

47. For background on military operations, see Anthony H. Cordesman and Abraham R. Wagner, *The Lessons of Modern War*, vol. IV: *The Gulf War* (Boulder, CO: Westview, 1996); DoD, *Conduct of the Persian Gulf War; Gulf War Air Power Survey*, 5 vols. (Washington, DC: U.S. GPO, 1993); at www.airforcehistory.hq.af.mil/Publications/Annotations/gwaps.htm.

48. Woodward, *Commanders*, p. 225. "Kuwait had been overrun by more than 100,000 troops, ... Saudi Arabia had a military of less than 70,000 and only one small unit stood between the Iraqi units and the vast Saudi oil fields."

49. See Stephen Biddle, "Victory Misunderstood," *International Security* 21.2 (Fall 1996), pp. 139–79, who wrote (p. 142): "This unprecedentedly low loss rate came as a major surprise, despite great effort before the war to predict losses. These efforts attracted many of the country's foremost scholars and policy analysts, and exploited the best available net assessment methods. The results were way off. All published results radically overestimated casualties: the best got no closer than a factor of three; the next best missed by a factor of six. The majority were off by more than an order of magnitude; official estimates were reportedly high by at least that much, while

some official projections were reportedly off by more than a factor of 200."

50. See Eric V. Larson, *Casualties and Consensus: The Historical Role of Casualties in Domestic Support for U.S. Military Operations* (Santa Monica, CA: RAND Corporation, MR-726-RC, 1996), esp. pp. 30–40, 91–4 on the Persian Gulf War; at www.rand.org/pubs/monograph_reports/MR726/index.html. This study addresses "the willingness of the American public to accept casualties in U.S. military operations" and notes that "there is often a great deal of ambiguity in these data, which makes policy-quality public-opinion analysis a subtle, complex, and often frustrating enterprise" (pp. 1–2). Still, Larson found that "[A] plurality of those polled believed that the Gulf situation was worth going to war and that, at every level of expected war dead from 3,000 to 40,000, those believing the situation was worth going to war outnumbered those who did not" (p. 38). He notes "a Pentagon estimate that had predicted that 30,000 Americans would be killed if a ground war were started" (p. 35, n. 77).

51. Bush and Scowcroft, *World Transformed*, p. 439.

52. John Mueller, *Policy and Opinion in the Gulf War* (Chicago: University of Chicago Press, 1994), pp. 69–79.

53. Bush, "Nation Blessed," p. 139.

54. See Stephen Biddle, "Learning the (Wrong) Lessons from the Gulf War," *Wall Street Journal*, September 3, 1997, p. A22.

55. See Richard J. Newman, "Getting Ready for the Wrong War?" *U.S. News & World Report* 122.18 (May 12, 1997), pp. 31–5, at p. 31.

56. For background on the air campaign, see *Gulf War Air Power Survey*, vol. 1; James A. Winnefeld, Preston Niblack, and Dana J. Johnson, *A League of Airmen: U.S. Air Power in the Gulf War* (Santa Monica, CA: RAND Corporation, MR-343-AF, 1994); Benjamin S. Lambeth, "Desert Storm Revisited," chap. 4 of his *The Transformation of American Air Power* (Ithaca, NY: Cornell University Press, 2000), pp. 103–80.

57. DoD, *Conduct of the Persian Gulf War*, pp. 100–1.

58. "Operation Desert Storm," first accessed at the Federation of American Scientists Web site, but now residing at www.globalsecurity.org/military/ops/desert_storm.htm. See also

Richard Pyle, "Gulf War II to Be Much Quicker," *Washington Times*, January 29, 2003, p. 1, at www.frontpagemag.com/Articles/ReadArticle.asp?ID=5827.

59. DoD, *Conduct of the Persian Gulf War*, pp. 114–15, 118–19, 675.

60. Christian Lowe, "Deadly Accurate Bombs Require Sophisticated Gear on the Ground," *Marine Corps Times* 4.31 (August 2002), p. 15.

61. William H. Arkin, "Baghdad: The Urban Sanctuary in Desert Storm?" *Airpower Journal* 11.1 (Spring 1997), pp. 4–20, at p. 13; Williamson Murray, "Part I: Operations," in *Gulf War Air Power Survey*, vol. II: *Operations and Effects and Effectiveness*, p. 241; DoD, *Conduct of the Persian Gulf War*, p. 96.

62. Bush and Scowcroft, *World Transformed*, p. 463: "None of us minded if he [Saddam] was killed in the course of an air attack. Yet it was extremely difficult to target Saddam, who was known to move frequently and under tight security. Saddam was far more elusive and better protected [than Manuel Noriega]."

63. DoD, *Conduct of the Persian Gulf War*, pp. 95–8.

64. Ibid., p. 97.

65. Ibid., pp. 154, 159. The Tuwaythah site had been bombed by Israel in 1981; see "Timeline of Iraq: 1932–2003," at usinfo.state.gov/mena/Archive_Index/Timeline_of_Iraq_19322003.html.

66. See "U.N.'s Iraq Inspection Program," *Associated Press*, December 16, 1997, which described the inspection regime that the United Nations imposed on Iraq. The United Nations Special Commission on Iraq was tasked with determining Iraq's compliance with U.N. Security Council orders to destroy long-range missiles, chemical weapons, and biological weapons. Furthermore, the International Atomic Energy Agency (IAEA) ensures that Iraq has dismantled its nuclear weapons program. See also, "Chief U.N. Weapons Inspector: Iraq Putting Up New Roadblocks," *CNN*, September 3, 1998, which notes that the U.N. sanctions against Iraq, including an oil embargo, cannot be ended "until U.N. weapons inspectors certify that Iraq has destroyed all of its nuclear, chemical and biological weapons, as well as any ballistic missiles." What remained controversial even after the U.S.-led invasion of Iraq in March 2003 is what happened to

these Iraqi programs. See Charles J. Hanley, "U.N.: Arms Expert Warning Had Bad Premise," *Associated Press,* October 24, 2004, for a discussion of the Duelfer Report on Iraq's WMD; at www.aboutmytalk.com/t153357/s&.html. For more on UNSCOM, see www.un.org/depts/unscom/.

67. DoD, *Conduct of the Persian Gulf War,* pp. 13–15.

68. See Eric Schmitt with Philip Shenon, "New Mobile Radar System Looking Out for Iraqi Missile Launchings in the Gulf," *New York Times,* December 26, 2002, p. A14. For a discussion of "Scud-hunting," see DoD, *Conduct of the Persian Gulf War,* pp. 97, 156, 165, and particularly the section on "The Counter-Scud Effort," pp. 166–8: "The Scud-hunting effort in southeast Iraq was similar to that in the west. The search area was nearly as large, and *the mobile Scud launchers were difficult to find.* . . . By early February, the counter-Scud effort seemed to be having an effect, although *no destruction of mobile launchers had been confirmed.* . . . When the war ended, intelligence analysis showed that Iraqis had fired 88 modified Scuds, 42 towards Israel and 46 at Saudi Arabia and other Persian Gulf states" (p. 168, emphasis added). See also Richard H. Van Atta and Michael J. Lippitz, with Jasper C. Lupo, Robert B. Mahoney, and Jack Nun, *Transformation and Transition: DARPA's Role in Fostering an Emerging Revolution in Military Affairs,* vol. 1: *Overall Assessment* (Alexandria, VA: Institute for Defense Analyses, 2003), p. 22, which argued that the Scud hunt "showed that Iraqi Scud missiles could not be found and destroyed with manned aircraft in spite of a massive sortie rate." Online at www.darpa.mil/body/pdf/P3698_DARPA_VolII.pdf.

69. DoD, *Conduct of the Persian Gulf War,* p. 98. By January 15, 1991, Iraq had amassed in the Kuwaiti theater of operations an army of 545,000 troops; these were equipped with more than four thousand tanks, three thousand artillery pieces, and three thousand armored personnel carriers. Ibid., p. 254.

70. Ibid., p. 135: "During the war, more than 35,000 attack sorties were flown against KTO targets, including 5,600 against Republican Guard forces."

71. DoD, *Conduct of the Persian Gulf War,* p. 98. See also p. 158: "In less than six weeks, a combat experienced army of several hundred thousand troops, with thousands of tanks, other armored vehicles, and artillery pieces, dug into well-sited and constructed defensive positions, was severely degraded and weakened from the air." Regarding Iraqi casualties, see "Gulf War Facts," www.cnn.com/specials/2001/gulf.war/facts/gulfwar.

72. See Thomas G. Mahnken and Barry D. Watts, "What the Gulf War Can (and Cannot) Tell Us about the Future of Warfare," *International Security* 22.2 (Fall 1997), pp. 151–62, at pp. 152–3. "No previous army was ever subjected to an air campaign of this scale before the onset of ground operations. By the beginning of the ground campaign, Coalition air power had blinded, bloodied, pinned down, and frustrated a force of some fifty divisions. Those Iraqi units that did survive to fight were irrelevant to the outcome of the conflict because they were simply no match for their Coalition adversaries" (p. 159). Also see John Mueller, "The Perfect Enemy: Assessing the Gulf War," *Security Studies* 5.1 (Autumn 1995), pp. 77–117.

73. See Winnefeld et al., *League of Airmen,* pp. 132–4, 166–7, 269.

74. For background on the land war, see Robert H. Scales Jr., *Certain Victory: The U.S. Army in the Gulf War* (Washington, DC: Brassey's, 1997).

75. DoD, *Conduct of the Persian Gulf War,* p. 227.

76. Bush and Scowcroft, *World Transformed,* p. 462. In a conversation with President Bush, Dutch Prime Minister Ruud Lubbers said, "I don't think air power alone will do the job, but from a political point of view it is better to start a ground attack later" (p. 467). On the 1990s air-power debate, see Chapter 12, note 142.

77. Woodward, *Commanders,* pp. 243, 250. For General Norman Schwarzkopf, air power is particularly important when four factors exist (ibid., p. 251): "One, it's a target-rich environment – easy to see things. Secondly, Iraq has no experience operating under air attack. Three, we have sophisticated munitions with more precision than ever before. Four, there could be quite a significant morale effect on the Iraqis in the rear who have never been subjected to danger in the past."

78. DoD, *Conduct of the Persian Gulf War,* pp. 227, 268–70.

79. Andrew Leyden, *Gulf War Debriefing*

Book: An After Action Report (Central Point, OR: Hellgate, 1997), p. 39.

80. DoD, *Conduct of the Persian Gulf War,* pp. 233, 236–7. It is worth noting that on January 14, the day before the UNSCR 678 deadline for Iraq's withdrawal from Kuwait, the Iraqi flag was changed to include the words "Allahu Akbar" (God is Great) between the stars of it's central white band. See Amatzia Baram, "Broken Promises," *Wilson Quarterly* 27.2 (Spring 2003), pp. 41–51, at www.wilsoncenter.org/index.cfm?fuseaction= wq. essay&essay_id=32223.

81. Ibid., p. 240.

82. Ibid., pp. 229–30.

83. See H. Norman Schwarzkopf, with Peter Petre, *The Autobiography: It Doesn't Take a Hero* (New York: Bantam Books, 1993), pp. 451–72. For details regarding the "Highway of Death," see "Appendix 2: Iraqi Combatant and Noncombatant Fatalities in the 1991 Gulf War" in Carl Conetta, *The Wages of War: Iraqi Combatant and Noncombatant Fatalities in the 2003 Conflict,* Project on Defense Alternatives Research Monograph 8, October 20, 2003; at www.comw.org/pda/0310rm8ap2. html.

84. DoD, *Conduct of the Persian Gulf War,* p. 294.

85. For background on U.S. naval operations, see Office of the Chief of Naval Operations, *The United States Navy in "Desert Shield"/"Desert Storm"* (Washington, DC: Department of the Navy, May 15, 1991); at www.history.navy.mil/wars/dstorm/index.html.

86. DoD, *Conduct of the Persian Gulf War,* pp. 136–7, 184–5, 189–90, 196, 222.

87. Ibid., p. 183.

88. Ibid., pp. 200–2, 206–8.

89. Williamson Murray and Robert H. Scales Jr., *The Iraq War: A Military History* (Cambridge, MA: Belknap, 2003), pp. 1–4, discuss how the superior U.S. intelligence system, combined with precision weapons and stealth, provided a highly effective instrument. *Conduct of the Persian Gulf War* noted (p. 176) that "The war with Iraq was the first conflict in history to make comprehensive use of space systems support. . . . Space systems communications played a central role in the effective use of advanced weapon systems. . . . The largely featureless KTO terrain made precise electronic navigation crucial to many missions and functions." For a discussion of accomplishments and shortcomings with respect to space, see ibid., "Observations," p. 346.

90. Woodward, *Commanders,* p. 249.

91. It was Defense Secretary Dick Cheney who remarked, when addressing the American Legion on February 27, 1991, "It looks like what's happened is that the mother of all battles has turned into the mother of all retreats." Regarding the highway, see note 83 above.

92. For comparison, Iraq had one million people in its armed forces in 1990, but only 389,000 as of 2002; and in terms of military equipment, Iraq's force of 5,000 main battle tanks in 1990 had dwindled to 2,600 in 2002. IISS, *Military Balance, 1990 1991,* p. 105; International Institute for Strategic Studies, *The Military Balance, 2002–2003* (Oxford: Oxford University Press 2002), p. 105.

93. DoD, *Conduct of the Persian Gulf War,* p. 634; the same summary table is also at www.globalsecurity.org/military/ops/desert_storm-finan.htm. For a discussion of the cost of the Persian Gulf War, see Marc Labonte, "Financing Issues and Economic Effects of Past American Wars," CRS Report for Congress, November 7, 2001, pp. 12–13, who notes a lower coalition figure: "In effect, foreign governments financed a large part of the war effort by the United States – contributions from foreign governments equaled $48 billion, while the overall cost of the war was $61 billion in current dollars." Online at fpc.state. gov/documents/organization/6271.pdf.

94. See Perry, "Desert Storm and Deterrence," pp. 66–82.

95. The first part is from Bush's "Address . . . Announcing the Deployment . . . to Saudi Arabia"; the second is from his "Remarks and an Exchange with Reporters on the Iraqi Invasion of Kuwait," August 5, 1990, at bushlibrary. tamu.edu/research/papers/1990/90080502.html; both are quoted by Woodward, *Commanders,* pp. 277, 260, who also notes (p. 319), "Cheney saw no willingness on Bush's part to accept anything less than the fulfillment of this stated objective, the liberation of Kuwait."

96. Bush, "Nation Blessed," p. 138.

97. Baker, *Politics of Diplomacy,* p. 435. "Powell and Cheney had reported that the Iraqis were being routed at will. U.S. intelligence reported that the once-feared Republican Guard had been decimated, and thousands of tanks and artillery pieces destroyed or captured. The American-led military coalition had

achieved both its war aims and political objectives" (pp. 435–6).

98. Ibid., p. 436, where Baker added: "It had been a spectacularly successful victory."

99. As Colin Powell states in *My American Journey* (p. 36), "I was not advocating either route, war or sanctions, on this day. I simply believed that both options had to be considered fully and fairly. No decision would be required from the President for weeks. . . . In our democracy it is the president, not generals, who make the decisions about going to war. . . . The sanctions clock was ticking down. If the President was right, if he decided that it must be war, then my job was to make sure we were ready to go in and win."

100. DoD, *Conduct of the Persian Gulf War*, p. 294.

101. Baker, *Politics of Diplomacy*, p. 436.

102. See Biddle, "Victory Misunderstood," quoted in note 49 above.

103. Bush, "Nation Blessed," p. 139.

104. Baker, *Politics of Diplomacy*, p. 331.

105. Bush and Scowcroft, *World Transformed*, pp. 469, 364, 382. Bush had also used the word "prevail" in his " Address to the Nation Announcing Allied Military Action in the Persian Gulf," January 16 [already 17 in Iraq], 1991, at bushlibrary.tamu.edu/research/papers/1991/91011602.html: "I instructed our military commanders to take every necessary step to prevail as quickly as possible. . . . I am convinced not only that we will prevail but that out of the horror of combat will come the recognition that no nation can stand against a world united."

106. President George H. W. Bush, "Address to the Nation on the Suspension of Allied Offensive Combat Operations in the Persian Gulf," February 27, 1991, at bushlibrary. tamu.edu/research/papers/1991/91022702.html; quoted in Bush and Scowcroft, *World Transformed*, p. 486.

107. Melissa Healy, "Campaign 2000 – A Historical Perspective: 100 Hours in March 1991 Shaped Cheney's Place in History," *Los Angeles Times*, August 27, 2000, p. A3.

108. Bush and Scowcroft, *World Transformed*, p. 487.

109. Baker, *Politics of Diplomacy*, p. 437: "By the time the cease-fire was announced on February 28, the vast bulk of Iraq's military machine, including most of its nuclear, chemical, and biological weapons programs, was de-

stroyed." Colin Powell, "U.S. Forces: Challenges Ahead," *Foreign Affairs* 71.5 (Winter 1992–3), pp. 32–45, at p. 37, argued that "All wars are limited. As Carl von Clausewitz was careful to point out, there has never been a state of absolute war. Such a state would mean total annihilation. The Athenians at Melos, Attila the Hun, Tamerlane, and Romans salting the fields of the Carthaginians may have come close, but even their incredible ruthlessness gave way to pragmatism before a state of absolute war was achieved."

110. Robert S. Greenberger and Thomas E. Ricks, "Clinton and Pentagon Plan Less Obsessive Stance toward Iraq, with Big Troop and Ship Pullback," *Wall Street Journal*, May 13, 1998, p. A24.

111. Bush and Scowcroft, *World Transformed*, p. 488.

112. See Jane Mayer, "The Manipulator," *New Yorker* 80.15 (June 7, 2004), pp. 58–68, at p. 61; online at www.newyorker.com/fact/content?040607fa_fact1.

113. See Bush and Scowcroft, *World Transformed*, pp. 488–90; Baker, *Politics of Diplomacy*, pp. 436–8.

114. Woodward, *Commanders*, p. 274. For example, Defense Secretary Cheney questioned whether Saddam had a different vision of victory in the war.

115. "Saddam Claims Victory in Gulf War," *CNN*, January 17, 2001, at archives. cnn.com/2001/WORLD/meast/01/17/iraq.hussein/.

116. See Mark Bowden, "Tales of the Tyrant," *The Atlantic* 289.5 (May 2002), pp. 35–53, who observed (p. 48), "Saddam's vision was clouded by a strong propensity for wishful thinking." After being "[d]efeated militarily, Saddam has in the years since responded with even wilder schemes and dreams, articulated in his typically confused, jargon-laden, quasi-messianic rhetoric" (p. 50). Online at www.iraqwatch.org/perspectives/atlantic-bowden-saddam.htm.

117. Anderson, "Unvanquished," which suggests that "Saddam Hussein seems to think he can still win the Gulf War – and, with his oil reserves, he just might" (p. 76).

118. "Saddam Claims Victory in Gulf War"; also, see Chapter 11 on the campaign against Iraq in 2003.

119. T. D. Allman, "Saddam Wins Again," *New Yorker* 72.16 (June 17, 1996), pp. 60–5, at p. 60.

120. For background on U.S. policy toward Iraq after the Persian Gulf War, see Daniel Byman and Matthew Waxman, *Confronting Iraq: U.S. Policy and the Use of Force since the Gulf War* (Santa Monica, CA: RAND Corporation, MR-1146-OSD, 2000), pp. 37–76 (at www.rand.org/pubs/monograph_reports/MR1146/index.html); Thomas Donnelly, "Lessons Unlearned: A Comparison of Three American Wars," *National Interest* 60 (Summer 2000), pp. 76–82, who calls the Gulf War an "incomplete" one "whose outcome continues to bedevil policymakers." See also Mackubin Thomas Owens, "With Eyes Wide Open: A Strategy for War with Iraq," *National Review Online*, August 14, 2002, for arguments that the United States, because of pressure from General Colin Powell, stopped the Persian Gulf War too soon; at www.nationalreview.com/owens/owens081402.asp. See William Safire, "Like Father, Unlike Son," *New York Times*, September 2, 2002, p. A17, who argued that "Gen. Colin Powell promised to 'kill' Saddam's army but then killed our victory instead by quitting too soon."

121. Ahmed Hashim, "Iraq: Fin de Régime?" *Current History* 95.597 (January 1996), pp. 10–15.

122. "Drifting to a New Iraq Policy," *New York Times*, August 12, 1998, p. A18.

123. See Chapter 5, which drew a similar conclusion regarding the political–military victory attained in World War I.

9. Bosnia–Kosovo, 1992–1999

1. Following established practice, "Bosnia" is often used herein as shorthand for "Bosnia and Herzegovina," the country's full name.

2. See Charles G. Boyd, "Making Peace with the Guilty: The Truth about Bosnia," *Foreign Affairs* 74.5 (September–October 1995), pp. 22–38, at p. 26, which continues by noting that "For some, the war in Bosnia has become a tragedy of proportions that parallel the Holocaust, an example of plain good against stark evil. . . . Regrettably, that behavior is not unprecedented in Balkan conflicts, and to say that it is peculiarly Serb behavior says more about the observer than the Balkans." See also "Responses," *Foreign Affairs* 74.6 (November–December 1995), pp. 148–55; Anthony Lewis, "Shame, Eternal Shame," *New York Times*, December 2, 1994, p. A15.

3. On the "endgame strategy," see Derek Chollet, *The Road to Dayton: U.S. Diplomacy and the Bosnia Peace Process, May–December 1995* (U.S. Department of State, Dayton History Project, May 1997), pp. 25–48; at www.gwu.edu/~nsarchiv/NSAEBB/NSAEBB171/ch2.pdf. On the Congressional vote, see Elaine Sciolino, "Senate Vote to End Embargo May End as Pyrrhic Victory," *New York Times*, July 28, 1995, pp. A1, A4; Craig R. Whitney, "Allies Condemn Vote," *New York Times*, July 28, 1995, p. A4.

4. For a review of this shift, see Daniel Williams, "Grim Balkans Outlook Affected U.S. Position; Policy Based on Emotion, Not Broad Principle," *Washington Post*, August 19, 1993, p. A1; Michael R. Gordon, "U.S. and Bosnia: How a Policy Changed," *New York Times*, December 4, 1994, p. A1. On intervention's inevitability, see Sabrina Petra Ramet, "The Bosnian War and the Diplomacy of Accommodation," *Current History* 93.586 (November 1994), pp. 380–5. On civilian deaths, see George Kenney, "The Bosnia Calculation," *New York Times Magazine*, April 23, 1995, pp. 43–5, at www.balkan-archive.org.yu/politics/war_crimes/srebrenica/bosnia numbers.html; Emir Suljagic with Mirsad Tokaca, "Genocide Is Not a Matter of Numbers," at www.bosnia.org.uk/news/news_body.cfm?newsid=2139.

5. Sam Fulwood III, "Clinton Steps Up His Support for Military Action in Bosnia," *Los Angeles Times*, August 6, 1992, p. 8; John Steinbruner, "The Quagmire of Caution: Only Bold Moves in Bosnia Will Stop the Bloodshed," *Washington Post*, April 25, 1993, p. C1. Regarding U.S. relations with Serbia, see Albrecht Schnabel and Ramesh Thakur, *Kosovo and the Challenge of Humanitarian Intervention: Selective Indignation, Collective Action, and International Citizenship* (New York: U.N. University Press, 2000), esp. G. John Ikenberry, "The Costs of Victory: American Power and the Use of Force in the Contemporary Order," pp. 85–100. In late December 1992, outgoing President Bush had sent President Milošević of Serbia a warning that "in the event of conflict in Kosovo caused by Serbian action, the U.S. will be prepared to employ military force against Serbians in Kosovo and in Serbia proper." See "'Christmas Warning' Cable from President Bush to Serbian President Milošević, December 24,

1992," in Philip E. Auerswald and David P. Auerswald (eds.), *The Kosovo Conflict: A Diplomatic History through Documents* (Cambridge, MA: Kluwer Law International, 2000), p. 65; Barton Gellman, "Slaughter in Racak Changed Kosovo Policy," *Washington Post*, April 18, 1999, p. A1, at www.washingtonpost.com/wp-srv/national/longterm/policy041899.htm.

6. For background on the war and intervention, see Misha Glenny, *The Fall of Yugoslavia* (New York: Penguin Books, 1996); Warren Christopher, *In the Stream of History: Shaping Foreign Policy for a New Era* (Stanford: Stanford University Press, 1998); Richard Holbrooke, *To End a War: From Sarajevo to Dayton – and Beyond* (New York: Random House, 1998); John Zametica, *The Yugoslav Conflict* (Adelphi Paper no. 270, London: International Institute for Strategic Studies, 1992); Dana H. Allin, *NATO's Balkan Interventions* (Adelphi Paper no. 347, London: International Institute for Strategic Studies, 2002); Ivo H. Daalder, "Decision to Intervene: How the War in Bosnia Ended," *Foreign Service Journal* 75.12 (December 1998), pp. 24–31, at www.brookings.org/views/articles/daalder/199812.htm; Daalder, *Getting to Dayton: The Making of America's Bosnia Policy* (Washington, DC: Brookings Institution, 2000); David Owen, *Balkan Odyssey* (New York: Harcourt Brace, 1995); Bob Woodward, *The Choice* (New York: Simon & Schuster, 1996); Wayne Bert, *The Reluctant Superpower: United States' Policy in Bosnia, 1991–95* (New York: St. Martin's Press, 1997); V. P. Gagnon Jr., "Yugoslavia: Prospects for Stability," *Foreign Affairs* 70.3 (Summer 1991), pp. 17–35; Michael Kelly, "Surrender and Blame," *New Yorker* 70.42 (December 19, 1994), pp. 44–51; Kelly, "Damage Control," *New Yorker* 71.25 (August 21–28, 1995), pp. 62–6.

7. For a discussion of ethnic separatism, see Kamal S. Shehadi, *Ethnic Self-Determination and the Break-up of States* (Adelphi Paper no. 283, London: International Institute for Strategic Studies, 1993); Misha Glenny, "The Age of the Parastate," *New Yorker* 71.11 (May 8, 1995), pp. 45–53, at p. 53: "Neither the Serbs nor Muslims nor the Croats are strong enough to win this war. Nor are any of them weak enough to lose it. The parastates are again preparing for battle. Clearly, no parastate can achieve final victory unless it

persuades its reluctant patrons to invest substantial political and military capital in its dubious endeavor."

8. On the deterioration of parts of the region, see Wesley Clark, *Waging Modern War: Bosnia, Kosovo and the Future of Combat* (New York: Public Affairs, 2001); on Bosnia, see Noel Malcolm, *Bosnia: A Short History* (New York: New York University Press, 1994); David Rieff, *Slaughterhouse: Bosnia and the Failure of the West* (New York: Simon & Schuster, 1995); David Rohde, *Endgame: The Betrayal and Fall of Srebrenica, Europe's Worst Massacre since World War II* (New York: Farrar, Straus, Giroux, 1997); on Kosovo, see Malcolm, *Kosovo: A Short History* (New York: New York University Press, 1998); Tim Judah, "Kosovo's Road to War," *Survival* 41.2 (Summer 1999), pp. 5–18; John Daniszewski, "Evidence Details Systematic Plan of Killings in Kosovo," *Los Angeles Times*, August 8, 1999, p. 1, online at www.freeserbia.net/Articles/1999/Genocide.html. For a comparison of Kosovo to Kashmir, see William Safire, "For 3K Freedom," *New York Times*, July 9, 1999, p. A15, at www.kurdistanica.com/english/politics/analysis/analysis-014.html.

9. Christopher, *In the Stream of History*, p. 362: "If the [Bosnia] conflict continues, so would the worst atrocities Europe has seen since World War II." See also Roger Cohen, "Bosnia's Army Emerges as a Formidable Enemy," *New York Times*, June 15, 1995, p. A1; William Safire, "Break the Siege," *New York Times*, June 15, 1995, p. A17.

10. Madeleine Albright, with Bill Woodward, *Madam Secretary: A Memoir* (New York: Miramax, 2003), p. 180: "In June 1993, the Clinton administration approved a new policy toward Central and East Europe designed to bolster democracy, reduce trade barriers, and reward nations undertaking economic reform." See also Gregory L. Schulte, "Former Yugoslavia and the New NATO," *Survival* 39.1 (Spring 1997), pp. 19–42.

11. Albright, *Madam Secretary*, p. 180: "During the first months of the Clinton presidency, our foreign policy team held numerous rambling and inconclusive meetings about the [Balkan] crisis we had inherited, without achieving consensus."

12. The best discussion of the historical roots of the antagonism is Misha Glenny, *The Balkans: Nationalism, War, and the Great Powers, 1804–1999* (New York: Viking, 2000).

13. Susan L. Woodward, *Balkan Tragedy: Chaos and Dissolution after the Cold War* (Washington, DC: Brookings Institution, 1995), pp. 21–46.

14. See ibid., pp. 223–72. Also Christopher, *In the Stream of History*, p. 343: "The primary cause of the [six constituent republics'] separation was nationalism, stoked more by cynical, power-hungry leaders than by ancient ethnic hatreds." Regarding Serbian motives elsewhere in the region, see Barry R. Posen, "The War for Kosovo: Serbia's Political–Psychological Strategy," *International Security* 24.4 (Spring 2000), pp. 39–84.

15. For a discussion of its origins, see Glenny, *Balkans*, pp. 545–633. Woodward, *Balkan Tragedy*, p. 333, argues that "this was a civil war, ingrained in the history and temperament of the Balkans, particularly Bosnia, and inclining its populations inevitably toward ethnic conflict and war over territory whenever an imperial or dictatorial protection collapsed." See also James Gow, *Triumph of the Lack of Will: International Diplomacy and the Yugoslav War* (New York: Columbia University Press, 1997), pp. 1–45; Karl Mueller, "The Demise of Yugoslavia and the Destruction of Bosnia: Strategic Causes, Effects, and Responses," in Robert C. Owen (ed.), *Deliberate Force: A Case Study in Effective Air Campaigning – Final Report of the Air University Balkans Air Campaign Study* (Montgomery, AL: Air University Press, 2000), pp. 1–36, at www.au.af.mil/au/aul/aupress/Books/Owen/Owen.pdf.

16. For the origins of the possibility of national and religious sources of hostility, see Samuel P. Huntington, "The Clash of Civilizations?" *Foreign Affairs* 72.3 (Summer 1993), pp. 22–49; Huntington, "If Not Civilizations, What?" *Foreign Affairs* 72.5 (November–December 1993), pp. 186–94; Fouad Ajami, "The Summoning," *Foreign Affairs* 72.4 (September–October 1993), pp. 2–9.

17. Elaine Sciolino, "U.S. Policy Shift in Bosnia Creates a Muddle with Allies," *New York Times*, November 30, 1994, pp. A1, A6, particularly in terms of how the allies would end the war. See also Richard Stevenson, "Britain and France Criticize U.S. on Bosnia Positions," *New York Times*, November 29, 1994, p. A4. See also Sciolino, "U.S. and NATO Say Dispute on Bosnia War Is Resolved," *New York Times*, December 2, 1994, p. A4, on the rift between the United States

and its NATO allies over the Clinton administration's reversal on whether to use air power to coerce the Serbs to end the war in Bosnia. As Daalder, *Getting to Dayton*, p. 5, observed, "When the Clinton administration came to office in January 1993, it inherited a U.S. – indeed Western – Bosnia policy that was in complete disarray."

18. See Katherine Q. Seelye, "Many in Congress Reluctant to Widen U.S. Role in Bosnia," *New York Times*, June 2, 1995, p. A1; Elaine Sciolino, "Clinton's Policy on Bosnia Draws Criticism in Congress," *New York Times*, June 8, 1995, p. A8; Alison Mitchell, "Dole Rebuffs Clinton on Bosnia Arms Ban," *New York Times*, July 11, 1995, p. A5; Woodward, *Choice*, p. 255: "The Republican majority in both the House and Senate was behind Dole on this one, pushing legislation aimed right at the heart of the United Nations' and the Clinton administration's policy. Dole wanted the United States to break with the United Nations and unilaterally lift the arms embargo on the besieged Bosnian Muslims."

19. Craig R. Whitney, "A Testing of NATO: U.S. and Europe Adrift in Balkans," *New York Times*, November 24, 1994, p. A6; Anthony Lewis, "The End of NATO?" *New York Times*, November 28, 1994, p. A15; William Safire, "Robust or Bust," *New York Times*, November 28, 1994, p. A15.

20. For a discussion of refugee movements, see Gil Loescher, *Refugee Movements and International Security* (Adelphi Paper no. 268, London: International Institute for Strategic Studies, 1992); Claudena M. Skran, *Refugees in Inter-war Europe: The Emergence of a Regime* (New York: Oxford University Press, 1995).

21. See "Statement by the NATO Foreign Ministers, December 17, 1992" (in Auerswald and Auerswald [eds.], *Kosovo Conflict*, p. 64), who were "deeply concerned about possible spillover of the [Bosnian] conflict"; at www.nato.int/docu/comm/49-95/c921217b.htm. On the refugee problem and its implications for Europe, see Hanns W. Maull, "Germany in the Yugoslav Crisis," *Survival* 37.4 (Winter 1995–6), pp. 99–130; Pauline Neville-Jones, "Dayton, IFOR and Alliance Relations in Bosnia," *Survival* 38.4 (Winter 1996–7), pp. 45–65, at p. 58.

22. Bosnia had been occupied in 1878 by Austria-Hungary; the population of Hungary is 94 percent Magyar. On Hungary and refu-

gee concerns, see Sabrian Petra Ramet, "War in the Balkans," *Foreign Affairs* 71.4 (Fall 1992), pp. 79–88, esp. pp. 79–80. For Germany's reunification costs, see Charles Wolf Jr. and Kamil Akramov, "Is Germany's Reunification Experience Relevant?" *North Korean Paradoxes: Circumstances, Costs, and Consequences of Korean Unification* (Santa Monica, CA: RAND Corporation, 2005, MG-333-OSD), pp. 51–8; at www.rand.org/pubs/monographs/2005/RAND_MG333.pdf .

23. Christopher, *In the Stream of History,* pp. 361–2. The context was the opening of the Balkan Proximity Peace Talks in Dayton, Ohio, on November 1, 1995; at dosfan.lib.uic.edu/ERC/bureaus/eur/releases/951101ChristopherBalkan.html.

24. See Owen, *Balkan Odyssey,* pp. 84–5. As Christopher (ibid., pp. 360–1), at the Dayton talks, phrased the problem: "We are here to prevent a wider war that would undermine the security of Europe at a time when the whole continent should finally be at peace. . . . As this region is engulfed in flames and violence, a new Europe is being built around it."

25. See Woodward, *Balkan Tragedy,* p. 399: "The issues of Bosnia and former Yugoslavia could not be isolated from those affecting U.S.–Russian relations, the expansion of NATO, and stability in eastern Europe."

26. See Albright, *Madam Secretary,* p. 179: "Initially the crisis was viewed by Europeans and the senior Bush administration alike as a European problem that should and could be settled by Europeans." And yet, as Woodward noted in *Balkan Tragedy,* p. 396, "both the Bush and the Clinton administrations were also unwilling to remain uninvolved, leaving the situation entirely to Europeans." See also Craig R. Whitney, "Europeans Debate Options for a U.N. Force in Bosnia," *New York Times,* July 13, 1995, p. A6.

27. Christopher, *In the Stream of History,* pp. 360–1.

28. Gow, *Triumph of the Lack of Will,* pp. 90–1.

29. See "Address by President Clinton, October 6, 1995" (Freedom House, Washington, DC), in Philip Auerswald, Christian Duttweiler, and John Garafano, *Clinton's Foreign Policy: A Documentary Record* (New York: Kluwer Law International, 2003), pp. 38–46, at p. 40; at dosfan.lib.uic.edu/ERC/briefing/dispatch/1995/html/Dispatchv6no42.html.

30. Woodward, *Balkan Tragedy,* pp. 388–90. See "Address by President Clinton, February 26, 1999" (Grand Hyatt Hotel, San Francisco), in Auerswald et al., *Clinton's Foreign Policy,* pp. 67–78, at p. 71; at www.mtholyoke.edu/acad/intrel/clintfps.htm: "But if we don't stop the [Kosovo] conflict now, it clearly will spread. And then we will not be able to stop it, except at far greater cost and risk."

31. Daalder, *Getting to Dayton,* p. 108: "The issue was not one state or two, three, or none. Rather, the issue was U.S. credibility as a world leader, its credibility in NATO, the United Nations, and at home." See also Christopher, *In the Stream of History,* p. 369.

32. See "Address by President Clinton, September 21, 1999" (U.N. General Assembly), in Auerswald et al., *Clinton's Foreign Policy,* pp. 78–83, at p. 81; at www.un.int/usa/99_059.htm. Clinton also said, with respect to the role of the United Nations in "preventing mass slaughter and dislocation," that the "international community had a compelling interest in seeing them end" (p. 82). Also, Albright, *Madam Secretary,* p. 192; Michael Mandelbaum, "Foreign Policy as Social Work," *Foreign Affairs* 75.1 (January–February 1996), pp. 16–32.

33. Woodward, *Balkan Tragedy,* p. 397: "Neither U.S. administration facing the Yugoslav conflict considered it a matter of U.S. vital interests, although the Clinton administration did refine its categories in response to the war in Bosnia to allow a middle category of national interest." For a general discussion of U.S. policy toward Bosnia, see pp. 395–400.

34. James A. Baker III, with Thomas M. Defrank, *The Politics of Diplomacy: Revolution, War and Peace, 1989–1992* (New York: G. P. Putnam's Sons, 1995), pp. 648–51.

35. Christopher, *In the Stream of History,* p. 12.

36. See Woodward, *Balkan Tragedy,* p. 397: "This category did not justify risking soldiers' lives but was sufficient to justify diplomatic attention."

37. Daalder, *Getting to Dayton,* p. 108.

38. "Majority Would Back Military Effort in Bosnia," *Gallup Poll Monthly* 329 (February 1993), p. 12, while 16 percent said that no U.S. interest is at stake in Bosnia.

39. See "Americans Split over Air Strikes in Bosnia," *Gallup Poll Monthly* 341 (February 1994), p. 15. And the respondents in that poll

were split pretty evenly – 47 percent said "yes," 45 percent said "no" – over whether the United States had a moral obligation to be involved in Bosnia.

40. See "Americans Want to Keep at Arm's Length from Bosnian Conflict," *Gallup Poll Monthly* 345 (June 1995), p. 16: "And less than one-third of the public believe that the United States has any moral obligation to protect the citizens of Bosnia against Serbian attacks – 63 percent disagree that such an obligation exists."

41. "Majority of Americans Want U.S. Troops Out of Bosnia," *Gallup Poll*, July 25, 1997, accessed July 2004 at www.gallup.com/poll/news/970725.htm.

42. As Clinton would write, ten years after Dayton: "After the genocide of 1995, when more than 7,000 men were murdered in Srebrenica, it was clear that only NATO under America's leadership could ensure peace. . . . [T]he United States and our European allies should have acted in Bosnia earlier. But when America did act, with bombings followed by the diplomatic initiative that culminated in Dayton, we made a decisive difference." Bill Clinton, "American Engagement," *Wall Street Journal*, November 23, 2005; at economistsview.typepad.com/economistsview/2005/11/bill_clinton_am.html.

43. President Clinton admitted that he had "underestimated the difficulty of getting broad agreement through NATO and then getting the U.N. to use the NATO force." See "Remarks by President Clinton, May 3, 1994" (Carter Center, Atlanta), in ibid., pp. 22–37, at p. 31; online at www.clintonfoundation.org/legacy/050394-remarks-by-president-on-cnn-telecast-of-a-global-forum-with-clinton.htm. In October 1995, he added that, "in instances from Bosnia to Haiti, working out how we can lead and still maintain our alliances and cooperate through the United Nations and through NATO is sometimes frustrating and almost always difficult. But it is very important. We don't want to run off into the future all by ourselves. And that means we have to work responsibly through these international organizations." See "Address by President Clinton, October 6, 1995," p. 45.

44. See Christopher, *In the Stream of History*, pp. 337–42.

45. William J. Clinton, *A National Security Strategy of Engagement and Enlargement*

(Washington, DC: White House, July 1994), p. 21. For senior policymakers in the Clinton administration, NATO was also to play a constructive role in integrating Russia and other states in Eastern Europe into the West; see Christopher, *In the Stream of History*, pp. 547–9, who wrote: "The heart of our European policy is strengthening NATO, already the greatest military alliance in history. . . . It sets standards for behavior, encourages cooperation, and prevents conflict among its members."

46. Roger Cohen, "Balkan War May Spread into Croatia," *New York Times*, December 2, 1994, p. A4; Roger Cohen, "In Balkans, Power Shift," *New York Times*, August 18, 1995, pp. A1, A4.

47. See Daalder, *Getting to Dayton*, pp. 30, 41.

48. Ibid., pp. 15–19. On May 22, 1993, the United States and its allies agreed on a policy, which was known as the Joint Action Plan, "to protect the six 'safe areas' with force, if necessary . . . ; establish an international war crimes tribunal; place monitors on the Serbian border to ensure that Belgrade was honoring the international embargo of the Bosnian Serbs; [and] increase the international presence in Kosovo and Macedonia to help contain the conflict." Christopher, *In the Stream of History*, p. 346: "This effort [to rearm Bosniaks and Croats] ran into trouble from the moment I landed in Europe on May 2. Our central concept of lifting the arms embargo was adamantly opposed at several key stops, especially London, Paris, and Moscow."

49. See Allin, *NATO's Balkan Interventions*, pp. 13–33.

50. Christopher, *In the Stream of History*, p. 347. Early in 1995, the United States began overriding the embargo to rearm the Bosniaks through covert airdrops of military supplies, including (at Tuzla) "Anti-tank guided weapons to counter Bosnian Serb armour, Stinger surface-to-air missiles to ward off helicopters, night vision goggles and, most importantly, Motorola radio sets." See BBC News, *Correspondent*, Friday, June 22, 2001, "Allies and Lies," at news.bbc.co.uk/1/hi/audiovideo/programmes/correspondent/1390536.stm.

51. Ibid., pp. 345.

52. Colin L. Powell, with Joseph E. Persico, *My American Journey* (New York: Random House, 1995), p. 566.

53. See Glenny, *Balkans,* pp. 485–95, esp. p. 486: "Yet uniquely in occupied and fascist Europe, armed resistance organizations mounted a challenge to the Nazi's New World Order from the very beginning."

54. Powell, *My American Journey,* p. 566.

55. For troop strength, see "Three Paths in Bosnia," *New York Times,* July 14, 1995, p. A4: "NATO has long determined that its forces could destroy the Bosnian Serbs but it would take an army of more than 200,000 troops." Also see Peter Maass, "Paying for the Powell Doctrine," *Dissent* 49.1 (January 2002), pp. 49–59, at pp. 49, 59: "In the early days of the Bosnian War, Colin Powell, who at the time chaired the Joint Chiefs of Staff, came to the conclusion that stopping the fighting would require the use of 250,000 troops. . . . It is not surprising that [he] threw around inflated force estimates in the early 1990s." Online at www.petermaass.com/core. cfm?p=1&mag=81&magtype=1.

56. For background on the Dayton Accords, see Daalder, *Getting to Dayton;* Albright, *Madam Secretary,* pp. 264–71; Holbrooke, *To End a War;* Lenard J. Cohen, "Bosnia and Herzegovina: Fragile Peace in a Segmented State," *Current History* 95.599 (March 1996), pp. 103–12.

57. See Chris Hedges, "Bosnian Serbs Capture Town in U.N. 'Safe Area'," *New York Times,* July 12, 1995, pp. A1, A4; Roger Cohen, "As Usual, Serbs Call the Shots," *New York Times,* July 12, 1995, p. A4.

58. For a detailed analysis of the air campaign, see John A. Tirpak, "Deliberate Force," *Air Force Magazine* 80.10 (October 1997), pp. 36–43, online at www.afa.org/magazine/Oct1997/1097deli.asp.

59. Thomas E. Ricks, "U.S. Troops May Extend Bosnia Mission," *Wall Street Journal,* October 1, 1996, p. A19.

60. See Glenny, *Balkans,* pp. 634–62.

61. William J. Clinton, *A National Security Strategy of Engagement and Enlargement* (Washington, DC: White House, February 1995) [hereafter, *NSS 1995*], p. 25; at www.maxwell.af.mil/au/awc/awcgate/nss/nss-95. pdf. "While that war does not pose a direct threat to our security or warrant unilateral U.S. involvement, U.S. policy is focused on five goals."

62. Kelly, "Surrender and Blame," p. 47; Clinton continued, "I would begin with air

power against the Serbs to try to restore the basic conditions of humanity."

63. See Albright, *Madam Secretary,* pp. 186–9; Daalder, *Getting to Dayton,* p. 67, who writes that the "Bosnian Serbs . . . engaged in the worst war crimes in Europe since the end of World War II. . . . [A]lmost 8,000 men and boys were summarily executed en masse." Also Stephen Kinzer, "Bosnia Lets Refugees Leave Camp but 20,000 Others Are Missing," *New York Times,* July 16, 1995, p. A1; Stephen Engelberg, Tim Weiner, Raymond Bonner, and Jane Perlez, "Srebrenica: The Days of Slaughter," *New York Times,* October 29, 1995, p. A1; Boyd, "Making Peace with the Guilty."

64. "Americans Oppose Air Strikes against Bosnia," *Gallup Poll Monthly* 332 (May 1993), p. 13. In terms of moral obligations, 17 percent agreed that the United States has a very "good reason," and 46 percent said a "good" reason, to stop the atrocities.

65. See Woodward, *Balkan Tragedy,* p. 9: "The Bosnian war was particularly conducive to such a policy, based on a liberal perspective of individual rights and political arrangement guaranteeing those rights."

66. Ibid., p. 398: "U.S. efforts to take a position on the conflict in terms of systemic norms – that borders not be changed by force and that fundamental human rights not be violated."

67. Clinton, *NSS 1995,* p. ii. "Our global interests and our historic ideals impel us to oppose those who would endanger the survival or well-being of their peaceful neighbors. Nations should be able to expect that their borders and their sovereignty will always be secure. At the same time, this does not mean we or the international community must tolerate gross violations of human rights within those borders."

68. Christopher, *In the Stream of History,* p. 360: "We are here to prevent a wide war that would undermine the security of Europe at a time when the whole continent should finally be a peace." Daalder, *Getting to Dayton,* p. 4.

69. Clinton, *NSS 1995,* p. 25; see Albright, *Madam Secretary;* Holbrooke, *To End a War;* Daalder, *Getting to Dayton;* Woodward, *Balkan Tragedy.*

70. See Woodward, *Balkan Tragedy,* p. 369, Table 10–1, "Refugees from Yugoslavia by Country of Destination, Selected Coun-

tries, 1992–94." By April 1994, almost seven hundred thousand refugees were reported to be in Europe.

71. This refers, of course, to the assassination by a Serbian nationalist of Archduke Ferdinand of Austria and his wife in Sarajevo on June 28, 1914, during Bosnia's occupation by Austria-Hungary.

72. See Clinton, *NSS 1995*, p. 25; Jeffrey Record, *Perils of Reasoning from Historical Analogy: Munich, Vietnam, and American Uses of Force since 1945*, Occasional Paper no. 4, Center for Strategy and Technology (Montgomery, AL: Air War College, 1998).

73. See Craig R. Whitney, "For European Leaders, Some Agonizing Reminders of the Vietnam War," *New York Times*, May 30, 1995, p. A5, for a discussion of the Vietnam quagmire that occupied American policymakers.

74. See "Majority Would Back Military Effort in Bosnia," pp. 12–13.

75. See Christopher, *In the Stream of History*, p 361: "If war in the Balkans is reignited, it could spark a wider conflict like those that drew American soldiers in huge numbers into two European wars in this century." See Maynard Glitman, "U.S. Policy in Bosnia: Rethinking a Flawed Approach," *Survival* 38.4 (Winter 1996–7), pp. 67–8, notably the realization that the "forces of nationalism and separatism would ultimately prevail."

76. Ivo H. Daalder, "Bosnia after SFOR: Options for Continued U.S. Engagement," *Survival* 39.4 (Winter 1997–8), pp. 5–21.

77. See "Operation Provide Promise," first accessed at the Federation of American Scientists site, but now residing at www.globalsecurity.org/ military/ops/provide_promise.htm; "History's Longest Airlift Ends with Delivery to Sarajevo," *USA Today*, January 10, 1996, p. 1, at www.usatoday.com/news/index/bosnia/jan96/ nbos069.htm; Louis A. Arana-Barradas, "A 'Promise' of Peace," *Airman* 40 (March 1996), pp. 42–5, at www.af.mil/news/airman/0396/promise.htm; Jordan S. Chroman, "Operation Provide Promise – Resupplying the Bosnians," *Quartermaster Professional Bulletin* (Summer 1993), at qmfound.com/ bosnians.htm.

78. "Operation Provide Promise" Web site; for mention of truck convoys, see "U.S. Department of State Daily Briefing #127," September 14, 1992, at dosfan.lib.uic.edu/erc/briefing/ daily_briefings/1992/9209/127.html.

79. In addition to the sources cited in note 77, see "435th Airlift Wing," at www. military.com/HomePage/UnitPageFullText/ 0,13476,735627,00.htm; Brian L. Williams, Ken K. Studer, and Nancy E. Studer, "Operation Provide Promise: The Airdrop Phase," *Quartermaster Professional Bulletin* (Autumn 1993), at qmfound.com/operation_provide_ 1promise.htm.

80. These threats were real despite the fact that many aircraft were equipped with missile-warning and radar-warning gear. For background, see Lambeth, *NATO's Air War for Kosovo: A Strategic and Operational Assessment* (Santa Monica, CA: RAND Corporation, MR-1365-AF, 2001), pp. 17–66; at www. rand.org/pubs/monograph_reports/MR1365/.

81. "Operation Provide Promise" Web site.

82. For a discussion of coalition problems, see Lambeth, *NATO's Air War*, pp. 184–9.

83. Roger Cohen, "Allies Resolve to Bolster U.N. Peacekeeping in Bosnia: U.S. Weighs a Combat Role; How NATO Air Strikes Put U.N. Troops in Harm's Way," *New York Times*, May 30, 1995, pp. A1, A4.

84. UNSCR 816 is online at www.un.org/ Docs/scres/1993/scres93.htm. The U.N. Security Council passed a number of resolutions dealing with the various Yugoslav wars; UNSCR 781 (October 9, 1992) established the no-fly zone. See "Appendix: Key U.N. Resolutions," *Survival* 37.4 (Winter 1995–6), pp. 131–2, at p. 132.

85. See "Operation Deny Flight," first accessed at the Federation of American Scientists site, but now residing at www.globalsecurity. org/military/ops/deny_flight.htm.

86. This and the other UNSCRs mentioned are at www.un.org/Docs/scres/1993/ scres93.htm and www.un.org/Docs/scres/ 1994/ scres94.htm. Srebrenica had earlier been declared a safe area by UNSCR 819 (April 16, 1993).

87. Regarding Sarajevo, see the sources in note 63. For Tuzla, see these CNN articles of October 9, 1995: Jackie Shymanski, "Cease-fire Looking More Unlikely," at www.cnn.com/ WORLD/Bosnia/updates/oct95/10-09/index.html, and Jamie McIntyre, "NATO Warplanes Strike Serb Positions," at www.cnn.com/WORLD/ Bosnia/updates/oct95/10-09/airstrikes/index.html (and see also note 50 above).

88. "Operation Deny Flight" Web site.

89. Art Pine, "NATO Planes Attack Air

Base, Artillery Sites," *Los Angeles Times,* November 22, 1994, p. 2; Whitney, "For European Leaders, Some Agonizing Reminders"; Daniel Williams, "NATO Continues Extensive Bombing across Bosnia," *Washington Post,* August 31, 1995, p. A1; Elaine Sciolino, "NATO Raids Are Increased against Serbs," *New York Times,* September 8, 1995, p. A5.

90. These UNSCRs, dated May 31, 1995, are at www.un.org/Docs/scres/1995/ scres95.htm.

91. See Eric Schmitt, "Wider NATO Raids on Serbs Expose Rifts in Alliance," *New York Times,* September 12, 1995, pp. A1, A4.

92. Michael O. Beale, *Bombs over Bosnia: The Role of Airpower in Bosnia–Herzegovina* (Montgomery, AL: School of Advanced Airpower Studies, Maxwell AFB, August 1997), pp. 19–30, at www.au.af.mil/au/aul/aupress/ SAAS_Theses/Beale/beale.pdf; John N. T. Shanahan, "No-Fly Zone Operations: Tactical Success and Strategic Failure," in Mary A. Sommerville (ed.), *Essays on Strategy XIV* (Washington, DC: National Defense University, 1997), pp. 3–25, at www.ndu.edu/ inss/books/Books%20-%202000/essa/essastfa. html; Robert C. Owen, "The Balkans Air Campaign Study: Part I," *Airpower Journal* 11.2 (Summer 1997), pp. 4–24, at p. 23 n. 25.

93. For an analysis of Operation Deliberate Force, see John A. Tirpak, "Deliberate Force," *Air Force Magazine* 80.10 (October 1997), pp. 36–43, online at www.afa.org/magazine/ Oct1997/1097deli.asp; "Operation Deliberate Force," first accessed at the Federation of American Scientists site, but now residing at www.globalsecurity.org/military/ops/deliberate_ force.htm; Owen (ed.), *Deliberate Force.*

94. The NAC also identified events that would trigger future NATO responses.

95. See Daalder, *Getting to Dayton,* p. 130.

96. Roger Cohen, "Western Powers Approve Attacks against Bosnian Serbs," *New York Times,* August 30, 1995, pp. A1, A8. NATO declared that the "air operations were initiated after the U.N. military commanders concluded, beyond reasonable doubt, that Monday's brutal mortar attack in Sarajevo came from Bosnian Serb positions." See "Operation Deliberate Force," www.globalsecurity. org/military/ops/deliberate_force.htm.

97. Ibid.

98. Ronald M. Reed, "Chariots of Fire: Rules of Engagement in Operation Deliberate Force," in Owen (ed.), *Deliberate Force,* pp.

397–445, at p. 406, citing NATO NAC Notice C-N(95)65, 26 July 1995 (AFHRA, CAOC-06) and MCM-KAD-057-95, "NATO Air Operations to Stabilize Bosnia–Herzegovina beyond Gorazde," 31 July 1995 (AFHRA, CAOC-06-03).

99. Ibid., pp. 406–7, quoting MCM-KAD-057-95.

100. Ibid., pp. 289–90

101. "Operation Deliberate Force," www. globalsecurity.org/military/ops/deliberate_force.ht m.

102. For discussion of the Dayton Accords, see the following essays in *Survival* 39.4 (Winter 1997–8): Daalder, "Bosnia after SFOR"; Carl Bildt, "There Is No Alternative to Dayton," pp. 19–21; Pauline Neville-Jones, "Washington Has a Responsibility Too," pp. 22–4; Robert A. Pape, "Partition: An Exit Strategy for Bosnia," pp. 25–8; see also Jane M. O. Sharp, "Dayton Report Card," *International Security* 22.3 (Winter 1997–8), pp. 101–37. The text of the Accords is at www.ohr.int/dpa/default. asp?content_id=380 and www.state.gov/www/ regions/eur/bosnia/bosagree.html.

103. See "Operation Joint Endeavor," at www. globalsecurity.org/military/ops/joint_endeavor.htm, and "Operation Joint Guard," at www. globalsecurity.org/military/ops/joint_guard.htm.

104. See William Joseph Buckley (ed.), *Kosovo: Contending Voices on Balkan Interventions* (Grand Rapids, MI: William B. Eerdmans, 2000); Michael Ignatieff, "Counting Bodies in Kosovo," *New York Times,* November 21, 1999, p. A15. For the resurgence of violence in 2004, see Nicholas Wood, "NATO Expanding Kosovo Forces to Combat Violence," *New York Times,* March 19, 2004, p. A3. The FRY, the confederation that survived SFR Yugoslavia, comprised Serbia and Montenegro (for which it was renamed in 2002).

105. For background on Operation Allied Force, see Adam Roberts, "NATO's 'Humanitarian War' over Kosovo," *Survival* 41.3 (Autumn 1999), pp. 102–23; Ivo H. Daalder and Michael E. O'Hanlon, *Winning Ugly: NATO's War to Save Kosovo* (Washington, DC: Brookings Institution, 2000); Michael Mandelbaum, "A Perfect Failure: NATO's War against Yugoslavia," *Foreign Affairs* 78.5 (September–October 1999), pp. 2–8; Benjamin S. Lambeth, "NATO's Air War for Kosovo," chap. 6 of his *The Transformation of American Air Power* (Ithaca, NY: Cornell University Press,

2000), pp. 181–232; Lambeth, *NATO's Air War for Kosovo*; Stephen T. Hosmer, *The Conflict over Kosovo: Why Milošević Decided to Settle When He Did* (Santa Monica, CA: RAND Corporation, MR-1351-AF, 2001), at www.rand.org/pubs/monograph_reports/MR1351/index.html. See also the RAND Research Brief "Operation Allied Force: Lessons for the Future" (Santa Monica, CA: RAND Corporation, 2001), at www.rand.org/pubs/research_briefs/RB75/index1.html. For estimates of the number of displaced people, see Arthur C. Helton, "We're Seeing Refugees as Weapons," *Washington Post,* April 18, 1999, p. B1. Ian Fisher, "Ex-Commander in Yugoslavia Will Surrender to U.N. Tribunal," *New York Times,* April 15, 2002, p. A3, cites eight hundred thousand, whereas "Operation Allied Force, Operation Noble Anvil" – first accessed at the Federation of American Scientists site, but now residing at www.globalsecurity.org/military/ops/allied_force.htm – cites three hundred thousand.

106. Mike O'Connor, "NATO Jets Patrol Skies near Serbia in Show of Force," *New York Times,* June 16, 1998, pp. A1, A6.

107. See the "Operation Allied Force, Operation Noble Anvil" Web site. (Though this series of air strikes is usually called by its NATO name, Operation Allied Force, the American air operation was known as Noble Anvil.)

108. UNSCR 1199, adopted September 23, 1998, is online at www.un.org/Docs/scres/1998/scres98.htm.

109. For operational background, see the "Operation Allied Force, Operation Noble Anvil" Web site.

110. See Lambeth, *NATO's Air War;* Daniel L. Byman and Matthew C. Waxman, "Kosovo and the Great Air Power Debate," *International Security* 24.4 (Spring 2000), pp. 5–38; Andrew L. Stigler, "A Clear Victory for Air Power: NATO's Empty Threat to Invade Kosovo," *International Security* 27.3 (Winter 2003), pp. 124–57; "A View from the Top" – an unpublished briefing to the secretary of defense (SECDEF), 21 October 1999, by Admiral James O. Ellis, the commander of Joint Task Force Noble Anvil during Operation Allied Force (and commander, Allied Forces Southern Europe) – described the operation as the "most precise and lowest collateral damage air campaign in history" (emphasis in original); see presentation materials at www.

d-n-i.net/fcs/ppt/ellis_kosovo_aar.ppt. See also RAND's "Operation Allied Force: Lessons for the Future," p. 1.

111. "Operation Allied Force: NATO Air Campaign in FRY," 1999, unpublished briefing; online at www.kosovo.mod.uk/account/ intro.htm as Lord Robertson of Port Ellen, Secretary of State for Defence, "Kosovo: An Account of the Crisis" [and so cited hereafter], see esp. the section "NATO Air Strikes." See also Lambeth, *NATO's Air War,* pp. 219, 239.

112. See Daalder and O'Hanlon, *Winning Ugly,* p. 18. "NATO's policy of keeping aircraft above 15,000 feet above sea level, which limited the effectiveness of the tactical bombing . . . was primarily due to Washington's preference to avoid casualties at nearly any cost." Compare "Operation Allied Force, Operation Noble Anvil": "Flying at or above 15,000 feet, attack aircraft were flying only at night and were instructed not to make multiple passes or other maneuvers that would entail unnecessary risks." See also Lambeth, *NATO's Air War,* pp. 17–66.

113. RAND's "Operation Allied Force: Lessons for the Future," p. 2.

114. See "Operation Allied Force, Operation Noble Anvil," www.globalsecurity.org/military/ops/allied_force.htm; Robertson, "Kosovo." See also Dana Priest and William Drozdiak, "NATO Struggles to Make Progress from the Air," *Washington Post,* April 18, 1999, p. A1. It was during this stage, on May 7, that the Chinese Embassy was bombed, allegedly by mistake. (However, see John Sweeney, Jens Holsoe, and Ed Vulliamy, "NATO Bombed Chinese Deliberately," *The Observer,* October 17, 1999: "According to senior military and intelligence sources in Europe and the U.S. . . . NATO electronic intelligence [Elint] detected it sending army signals to Milošević's forces." At www.guardian.co. uk/Kosovo/Story/0,2763,203214,00.html.

115. See Dana Priest , "NATO Struggles to Make Progress from the Air," *Washington Post,* April 18, 1999, p. A1. NATO forces used munitions that were specifically designed to shut down rather than physically destroy electrical production and oil-refining facilities.

116. See Steven Erlanger, "Yugoslavia's Opposition Leader Claims Victory over Milošević," *New York Times,* September 26, 2000, p. A1. For an analysis of Milošević, see Dusko Doder and Louise Branson, *Milošević:*

Portrait of a Tyrant (New York: Free Press, 1999).

117. See Richard K. Betts, "Compromised Command: Inside NATO's First War," *Foreign Affairs* 80.4 (July–August 2001), pp. 126–32, at p. 126, who noted that many assets were left unstruck, "'held hostage' as 'incentives' for the Serbs to halt." (Online at www.foreignaffairs.org/20010701fareviewessay4999//.html.) For critiques of the air campaign, see Mandelbaum, "Perfect Failure"; "Kosovo Air Operations: Need to Maintain Alliance Cohesion Resulted in Doctrinal Departures," General Accounting Office, Report to Congressional Requesters, GAO-01-784, July 27, 2001, at www.gao.gov/cgi-bin/getrpt?GAO-01-784; Priest, "NATO Struggles to Make Progress"; Dana Priest, "Air Chief Faults Kosovo Strategy," *Washington Post*, October 22, 1999, p. A14; *Joint Statement on the Kosovo After Action Review* (Washington, DC: Department of Defense, October 14, 1999), at www.defenselink.mil/releases/1999/b10141999_bt478-99.html; John A. Tirpak, "Short's View of the Air Campaign," *Air Force Magazine* 82.9 (September 1999), pp. 43–7, at www.afa.org/magazine/sept1999/0999watch.asp; Mackubin [T.] Owens, "Kosovo and the Future of U.S. Air Power," *Washington Times*, July 5, 1999, p. 17.

118. Lambeth, *NATO's Air War*, pp. 231–4.

119. See ibid. See also Byman and Waxman, "Kosovo and the Great Air Power Debate"; Stigler, "Clear Victory for Air Power."

120. See Michael R. Gordon and Eric Schmitt, "Shift in Targets Let NATO Jets Tip the Balance," *New York Times*, June 5, 1999, p. A1, as cited in Lambeth, *NATO's Air War*, p. 61.

121. See Lambeth, *NATO's Air War*, p. 132: "In the later aftermath of Allied Force, on-site surveys of bomb damage effects by KFOR observers and other inspectors further confirmed that NATO's attacks against VJ [Yugoslav army] forces had accomplished far less than had initially been assumed."

122. Allied Force Munitions Assessment Team, *Kosovo Strike Assessment Final Report*, "Operation Allied Force, Kosovo 1999," October 14, 1999, unpublished briefing; statistical presentation at fs.huntingdon.edu/jlewis/Outlines/MidE/Kosovo-DesStmAirWarStatistics-7pp/index.htm. See also John Barry and Evan Thomas, "The Kosovo Cover-up," *Newsweek*

135.20 (May 15, 2000), pp. 23–6, at mujweb.atlas.cz/www/kutija/nw000515.htm; see Dembart, "U.S. Allows Precise Civilian Use: Satellite Locator Get New Niche," *IHT*, p. 1; *International Herald Tribune*, May 11, 2000.

123. Lambeth, *NATO's Air War*, p. 125. "Operation Allied Force, Kosovo 1999," citing a Joint Intelligence Team survey, states that 56 percent of the sorties planned "were aborted due to weather" and that 33 percent of the three thousand "executed sorties were adversely affected by weather."

124. Barry and Thomas, "Kosovo Cover-up," pp. 24–5; John D. Morrocco, "Kosovo Conflict Highlights Limits of Airpower and Capability Gaps," *Aviation Week & Space Technology* 150.20 (May 17, 1999), pp. 31–3.

125. For a discussion of approval for air strikes, see Lambeth, *NATO's Air War*, pp. 181, 186–8, 191–2. See also Lambeth, *Transformation of American Air Power*, p. 204: "Also in many cases, the recommended bomb size was reduced to minimize or preclude any chance of causing unintended damage. For example, of every five LGBs [laser-guided bombs] dropped by an F-117 during the campaign's opening night, one was a 500-lb GBU-12 instead of a 2,000-bomb GBU-24, offering a lower likelihood of destroying the intended target but also less chance of causing collateral damage."

126. Paul Mann, "Kosovo Lessons Called Ambiguous," *Aviation Week & Space Technology* 150.26 (June 28, 1999), pp. 32–6.

127. The so-called Kumanovo Agreement was signed on June 9 and is online at www.nato.int/kosovo/docu/a990609a.htm. See Lambeth, "Why Milošević Gave Up When He Did," in *NATO's Air War*, pp. 67–86, esp. p. 76: "Milosevic asked Chernomyrdin directly on June 3 in response to NATO's ultimatum: 'Is this what I have to do to get the bombing stopped?'"

128. UNSCR 1244, date June 10, 1999, is online at www.un.org/Docs/scres/1999/ scres99.htm.

129. Alexandros Yannis, "Kosovo under International Administration," *Survival* 43.2 (Summer 2001), pp. 31–48; P. H. Liotta, "After Kosovo: Terminal Ambiguity," *Problems of Post-Communism* 49.3 (May–June 2002), pp. 23–32.

130. See Lambeth, *NATO's Air War*, chaps. 5–7.

131. For a comparison of U.S. responses to Darfur and Bosnia, see Tom Malinowski, "Repeating Clinton's Mistakes," *Washington Post*, May 3, 2005, p. A21; at www.washingtonpost.com/wp-dyn/content/article/2005/05/02/AR2005050201262.html.

132. See Daalder, *Getting to Dayton*, p. 108.

133. "Congress and the Country Consider Post-Conflict Bosnia," *CSCE Digest* 18.12 (December 1995), pp. 1, 5–6.

134. See "Remarks by President Clinton, May 3, 1994," p. 30. Also see Bill Clinton, *My Life* (New York: Alfred A. Knopf, 2004), pp. 509–13, 848–51.

135. Ibid. pp. 17–18, 108.

136. See Lambeth, *NATO's Air War*, pp. 8–11, 24–5, 81–2. For criticism about Clinton administration policy toward Bosnia as the U.S. Senate exercised greater influence on policy, see George Melloan, "Why Congress Took Over Bosnian Policy," *Wall Street Journal*, July 31, 1995, p. A15.

137. Albright, *Madam Secretary*, p. 192. For the views of additional participants in the policymaking process, see also Christopher, *In the Stream of History*; Richard Holbrooke, *To End a War*; Powell, *My American Journey*.

138. For this argument, see Ted Galen Carpenter, "Introduction: A Great Victory?" in his *NATO's Empty Victory: A Postmortem on the Balkan War* (Washington, DC: Cato Institute, 2000), pp. 1–8. See also Dana Priest, "Fear of Casualties Drives Bosnia Debate," *Washington Post*, December 2, 1995, p. 1.

139. Boyd, "Making Peace with the Guilty," pp. 37–8. Regarding the possible use of ground forces, see Steven Engelberg and Alison Mitchell, "Seesaw Week for U.S. Tactics in the Balkans," *New York Times*, June 5, 1995, p. A1: "[Clinton] made clear that he intended to make no permanent commitment of American troops to Bosnia. . . . But the President and his national security advisor, Anthony Lake, also felt that the United States needed to reassure its allies by offering to contribute American ground forces to move the embattled United Nations troops to more defensible positions."

140. For a view of why air power was necessary, see Albert Wohlstetter, "Bosnia: Air Power, Not Peacekeepers," *Wall Street Journal*, December 9, 1994, p. A16. For some observers this limited case of military intervention had "no more than a near-term effect": Boyd, "Making Peace with the Guilty," pp. 35, 37–8. For Bosnia, Clinton's policy was based on three principles: reluctance to "unilaterally lift the arms embargo," and unwillingness both to "divide the NATO alliance by unilaterally bombing Serb military positions" and "to send American troops there, putting them in harm's way under a UN mandate I thought was bound to fail." For Kosovo, his policy was "to oppose ethnic cleansing," which is equivalent to political-military victory. See Clinton, *My Life*, pp. 513, 681.

141. Daalder, *Getting to Dayton*, pp. 185–6. Using force under these circumstances would "lead to calls either for early termination or for further escalation" (p. 186).

142. On many levels, this issue has not yet been resolved, as evidenced by the American debate in 2006 about intervention in Iraq.

143. For a discussion of Congressional opposition to U.S. involvement in the war in Bosnia, in particular, Kosovo, see Daalder and O'Hanlon, *Winning Ugly*, pp. 161–2.

144. This issue is discussed in detail in the section "Air Power and Victory" in Chapter 12. For the debate about the increasing value of air power over ground forces, see Jeffrey Record, "Operation Allied Force: Yet Another Wake-Up Call for the Army?" *Parameters* 29.4 (Winter 1999–2000), pp. 15–23, at p. 15, who notes "the growing relative attractiveness of air power alone as a vehicle for the very kind of value-driven U.S. military interventions that have dominated the Pentagon's operational agenda since the Soviet Union's disappearance"; online at www.carlisle.army.mil/usawc/Parameters/99winter/record.htm. See also Earl H. Tilford Jr., "Operation Allied Force and the Role of Air Power," *Parameters* 29.4 (Winter 1999–2000), pp. 24–38, at www.carlisle.army.mil/usawc/Parameters/99winter/tilford.htm.

145. For Clinton, the fear was that failure in Bosnia "would destroy the Clinton presidency." See Daniel Williams, "Ex-Official Accuses U.S. of Being Soft on Serbs," *Washington Post*, February 4, 1994, p. A24; Thomas L. Friedman, "Getting In, Getting Out: Any War in Bosnia Would Carry a Domestic Price," *New York Times*, May 2, 1993, p. D1.

146. See Lambeth, *NATO's Air War*, pp. 67–86, for a discussion of why the air cam-

paign persuaded Milošević to capitulate to NATO.

147. Lambeth, *Transformation of American Air Power*, p. 204: "Measures imposed to avoid causing noncombatant casualties were uncompromisingly exacting, and NATO pilots were instructed to return home with their weapons unless their target could be positively identified." As noted by Lambeth, *NATO's Air War*, p. 136: "Pressures to avoid civilian casualties and unintended damage to nonmilitary structures were greater in Allied Force than in any previous campaign involving U.S. forces. Nevertheless, despite rules of engagement characterized by USAF Major General Charles Wald as being 'as strict as I've seen in my 27 years in the military,' there were more than 30 reported instances throughout the air war of unintended damage caused by errant NATO munitions or mistakes in targeting, including a dozen highly publicized incidents in which civilians were accidentally killed." See also Joel Haverman, "Convoy Deaths May Undermine Moral Authority," *Los Angeles Times*, April 15, 1999, p. A1.

148. Zametica, *Yugoslav Conflict*, p. 78. "The Yugoslav crisis had given countless early warnings that it could easily escalate into violent conflict, and yet the international community did not begin to move until it was too late." Also see the discussion on the lessons from the war for the international community, pp. 76–9.

149. For the argument that NATO won the war in Kosovo, see Daalder and O'Hanlon, *Winning Ugly*, pp. 183–4, 192–8.

150. "Special Report: Kosovo – the Data," *Gallup Poll Monthly* 402 (March 1999), p. 16.

151. For data on U.S. public opinion support for intervention, see ibid., p. 12.

152. Ibid., pp. 17–18.

153. Daalder and O'Hanlon, *Winning Ugly*, p. 183.

154. See Nicholas Wood, "Kosovo Torn by Widest Violence since U.N. Took Control in '99," *New York Times*, March 18, 2004, p. A1; Wood, "NATO Expanding Kosovo Forces"; International Institute for Strategic Studies, "Ethnic Violence in Kosovo: A New Downward Spiral?" *Strategic Comments* 10.2 (March 2004), pp. 1–2, accessed via www.iiss.org/stratcom.

155. Wood, "NATO Expanding Kosovo Forces."

156. Regarding the first set of talks in Vienna, see "UN Positive after Kosovo Meeting," *BBC News*, February 21, 2006, at news.bbc.co.uk/1/hi/world/europe/4731142.stm. A fourth round began on May 4; www.unmikonline.org/news.htm#0305.

157. See Nicholas Wood, "Kosovars Survey the Damage of Ethnic Violence," *New York Times*, March 21, 2004, p. 4.

158. Regarding the Dayton Accords, see note 102.

159. The regime change, not declared as an initial objective, complicated the political balance for U.S. and European policymakers by creating the perception that the United States and its NATO allies were committed to a dramatic change that their public might not have supported.

160. Marlise Simons, "Court Looks for Ways to Speed Milošević Trial," *New York Times*, July 28, 2004, p. A11; Simons, "Milosevic's Trial Ends but Inquiries Continue," *New York Times*, March 15, 2006.

161. See Alan Vick, Richard Moore, Bruce R. Pirnie, and John Stillion, *Aerospace Operations against Elusive Ground Targets* (Santa Monica, CA: RAND Corporation, MR-1398-AF, 2001), particularly chap. 2, "The Kosovo Experience," pp. 11–28; at www.rand.org/pubs/monograph_reports/MR1398/.

162. For more on UNMIK, see "UNMIK at a Glance," at www.unmikonline.org/intro.htm.

163. For background on EUFOR, see "EU Military Operation in Bosnia and Herzegovina," at www.euforbih.org/mission/mission.htm. See also Nick Hawton, "EU Troops Prepare for Bosnia Swap," *BBC News*, October 23, 2004, at news.bbc.co.uk/1/hi/world/europe/3944191.stm; "EU military operation in Bosnia and Herzegovina," at www.euforbih.org/mission/mission.htm.

164. For KFOR, see "KFOR Objectives/Mission," at www.nato.int/kfor/kfor/objectives.htm.

165. "Reconstruction and Economic Development [are] led by the European Union": see "UNMIK at a Glance."

10. 2001 Invasion of Afghanistan

1. While there were many general warnings about a possible attack against the United States, there was no specific detailed warning that an attack was imminent on the morning

of 9/11. See Richard A. Clarke, *Against All Enemies: Inside America's War on Terror* (New York: Free Press, 2004); *The 9/11 Commission Report: Final Report of the National Commission on Terrorist Attacks upon the United States* (Washington, DC: U.S. GPO, 2004), in particular chaps. 5 ("Al Qaeda Aims at the American Homeland," pp. 145–73), 6 ("From Threat to Threat," pp. 174–214), 7 ("The Attack Looms," pp. 215–53), and 8 ("'The System Was Blinking Red'," pp. 254–77). For the attack times, see pp. 8–14; fatalities are summarized on p. 311.

2. See *9/11 Commission Report*, p. 38: After receiving warnings of an attack against the Pentagon and a possible attack against the White House, "The White House requested (1) the implementation of continuity of government measures. . . ." See also, Bob Woodward, *Bush at War* (New York: Simon & Schuster, 2002), p. 18: "Cheney immediately clicked into the possibility that the terrorists might be trying to decapitate the government, to kill its leaders. He said they had a responsibility to preserve the government, its continuity of leadership." Ibid., p. 57: "Card said the vice president would be moved to an undisclosed location as a precaution against having the president and vice president together in the event of another attack. Continuity in government – ensuring the survival of someone in the constitutional line of succession to the presidency – was an essential priority." See also discussions on pp. 270, 272.

3. "The official death count was 2,976" according to "Most 9/11 Families Opt For Fund," an AP story dated Jan. 16, 2004, at www.cbsnews.com/stories/2004/06/15/national/main623139.shtml. Some twenty-four hundred died at Pearl Harbor: "Pearl Harbor: Day of Infamy," at www.military.com/Resources/History-SubmittedFileView?file=history_pearlharbor.htm. Hawaii was then a U.S. territory.

4. For background on al-Qaeda and the Taliban in Afghanistan, see Rohan Gunaratna, *Inside Al Qaeda: Global Network of Terror* (New York: Columbia University Press, 2002).

5. For background on this operation, see Anthony H. Cordesman, *The Lessons of Afghanistan: War Fighting, Intelligence, and Force Transformation* (Washington, DC: CSIS Press, 2002); "Afghanistan: Current Issues and U.S. Policy (Washington, DC: Report for

Congress, Congressional Research Service, April 1, 2003), pp. 1–5; Benjamin S. Lambeth, *Air Power against Terror: America's Conduct of Operation Enduring Freedom* (Santa Monica, CA: RAND Corporation, MG-166-CENTAF, 2005), at www.rand.org/pubs/monographs/2005/RAND_MG166.

6. George W. Bush, "Presidential Address to the Nation," October 7, 2001, at www.whitehouse.gov/news/releases/2001/10/20011007-8.html.

7. See Nicholas Lemann, "The War on What?" *New Yorker* 78.27 (September 16, 2002).

8. George W. Bush, "Address to a Joint Session of Congress and the American People," September 20, 2001, at www.whitehouse.gov/news/releases/2001/09/20010920-8.html.

9. One key exception was Operation Infinite Reach, discussed briefly below in this section.

10. Norman Friedman, *Terrorism, Afghanistan, and America's New Way of War* (Annapolis, MD: Naval Institute Press, 2003); M. Hassan Kakar, *Afghanistan: The Soviet Invasion and the Afghan Response, 1979–1982* (Berkeley: University of California Press, 1995); Anthony H. Cordesman and Abraham R. Wagner, *The Lessons of Modern War*, vol. 3: *The Afghan and Falklands Conflicts* (Boulder, CO: Westview, 1990).

11. On the Mujahideen and the Soviet–Afghan War see Lester W. Grau and Michael A. Gress, eds. and trans., *The Soviet–Afghan War: How a Superpower Fought and Lost* (Lawrence: University Press of Kansas, 2002); Lester W. Grau and Ali A. Jalali, *Afghan Guerrilla Warfare: In the Words of the Mujahideen Fighters* (Minneapolis: MBI Publishing, 2001); Richard H. Shultz Jr. and Andrea J. Dew, *Insurgents, Terrorists, and Militias: The Warriors of Contemporary Combat* (New York: Columbia University Press, 2006).

12. See Alan J. Kuperman, "The Stinger Missile and U.S. Intervention in Afghanistan," *Political Science Quarterly* 114.2 (Summer 1999), pp. 219–63, at p. 219; Grau and Gress (eds.), *Soviet–Afghan War*, pp. 211–13: "The Mujahideen acquisition of the American-manufactured 'Stinger' shoulder-fired air-defense missile gave them the ability to hit an aircraft out to a distance of 4,800 meters and up to 2,000 meters in elevation. The Soviet command had to severely limit the employment of helicopters especially during daylight." The

Pentagon worried that Stingers left over from that conflict would be used to down U.S. aircraft. "Once the Soviet occupation ended, the CIA tried to buy back the remaining Stingers left in Afghanistan without much success." Jean-Michel Stoullig, "U.S. Fears Stinger Missiles Can Be Used against Its Own in Afghanistan," *Agence France Presse,* December 4, 2001, at www.globalsecurity.org/org/news/2001/011204-attack01.htm.

13. The rise of Islamic fundamentalism during the 1980s and early 1990s in Afghanistan is outside the scope of this chapter; however, see discussion in William Maley (ed.), *Fundamentalism Reborn? Afghanistan and the Taliban* (New York: New York University Press, 1998); Olivier Roy, *The Failure of Political Islam* (Cambridge, MA: Harvard University Press, 1996); Roy, *Afghanistan: From Holy War to Civil War* (Princeton, NJ: Darwin, 1995); Shultz and Dew, *Insurgents, Terrorists, and Militias.*

14. Ahmed Rashid, *Taliban: Militant Islam, Oil and Fundamentalism in Central Asia* (New Haven, CT: Yale University Press, 2000); Maley (ed.), *Fundamentalism Reborn?*

15. Rashid, *Taliban;* Larry P. Goodson, *Afghanistan's Endless War: State Failure, Regional Politics, and the Rise of the Taliban* (University of Washington Press, 2001).

16. See Gunaratna, *Inside Al Qaeda,* pp. 39–53, for background on Osama bin Laden, and pp. 54–69 for a discussion of links to al-Qaeda. The word *jihad* does not really mean "holy war," as explained by Ahmed Hashim, "The World According to Usama [*sic*] bin Laden," *Naval War College Review* 54.4 (Autumn 2001), pp. 11–35, at p. 18: "The phrase meaning 'holy war' is *harb mukaddasah; jihad* conveys striving or exertion (that is, fighting) in the way of God – against the evil in oneself, against Satan, against apostates (*murtadd*) within one's society, or against infidels."

17. See *9/11 Commission Report,* pp. 55–7, 63–7; Woodward, *Bush at War,* p. 32.

18. *9/11 Commission Report,* pp. 47, 59. It also noted (pp. 48, 59), that bin Laden issued a similar public fatwa in August 1996.

19. John L. Esposito, *Unholy War: Terror in the Name of Islam* (Oxford: Oxford University Press, 2002), pp. 3–21.

20. *9/11 Commission Report,* p. 70.

21. Barton Gellman and Dana Priest, "U.S.

Strikes Terrorist-Linked Sites in Afghanistan, Factory in Sudan," *Washington Post,* August 21, 1998, p. A1, at www.washingtonpost.com/wp-srv/inatl/longterm/eafricabombing/stories/strikes082198.htm; Vernon Loeb and Michael Grunwald, "Officials Refuse to Detail Bin Laden Links," *Washington Post,* August 21, 1998, p. A19; at www.washingtonpost.com/wp-srv/inatl/longterm/eafricabombing/stories/evidence082198.htm. See also *9/11 Commission Report,* pp. 116–18; Woodward, *Bush at War,* p. 5.

22. Shah Alam, "Bin Laden Revenge Vow over U.S. Missile Raid Irks Taliban Chief," *Agence France Presse,* August 24, 1998. See also *9/11 Commission Report,* p. 117.

23. Loeb and Grunwald, "Officials Refuse," p. A19: "Clinton instantly put bin Laden in the pantheon of global menaces occupied by the likes of Iraq President Saddam Hussein, calling the Saudi in an Oval Office address to the nation 'perhaps the preeminent organizer and financier of international terrorism in the world today'." See also "President Clinton's Oval Office Remarks on Anti-terrorist Attacks" (August 20, 1998), at usinfo.state.gov/is/Archive_Index/President_Clintons_Oval_Office_Remarks_on_Antiterrorist_Attacks.html; James Bennet, "U.S. Cruise Missiles Strike Sudan and Afghan Targets Tied to Terrorist Network," *New York Times,* August 21, 1998, p. A1, at partners.nytimes.com/library/world/africa/082198attack-us.html.

24. On the connection with Somalia, see *9/11 Commission Report,* pp. 59–60.

25. Gunaratna, *Inside Al Qaeda,* p. 67.

26. See the discussion in Chapter 6.

27. For background, see the works cited in Chapter 6, note 3, as well as R. Kim Cragin and Scott Gerwehr, *Dissuading Terror: Strategic Influence and the Struggle against Terrorism* (Santa Monica, CA: RAND Corporation, MG-184-RC, 2005), p. 5, at www.rand.org/pubs/monographs/MG184/index.html.

28. In addition to the discussion in Chapter 6, see ibid.; Walter Laqueur, "Reflections on Terrorism," *Foreign Affairs* 65.1 (Fall 1986), pp. 86–100; Robert B. Oakley, "International Terrorism," *Foreign Affairs* 65.3 (special issue, *America and the World 1986*), pp. 611–29.

29. Title 22 of the U.S. Code, chap. 38, sec. 2656f(d); at www4.law.cornell.edu/uscode/html/uscode22/usc_sec_22_00002656---f000-.html.

30. Cindy C. Combs, *Terrorism in the Twenty-first Century* (Englewood Cliffs, NJ: Prentice–Hall, 1997); see also Martha Crenshaw, "The Causes of Terrorism," in Charles Kegley (ed.), *International Terrorism: Characteristics, Causes, Controls* (New York: St. Martin's Press, 1990), pp. 113–26.

31. For example, Osama bin Laden, in an interview conducted by journalist Rahimullah Yusufzai late in December 1998, stated: "Acquiring weapons for the defense of Muslims is a religious duty. If I have indeed acquired these weapons, then I thank God for enabling me to do so. And if I seek to acquire these weapons, I am carrying out a duty." "Wrath of God," *Time Asia* 153.1 (January 11, 1999), at www.time.com/time/asia/asia/magazine/1999/990111/osama1.html. In a report to the Congress, the CIA noted that "al-Qa'ida has ambitions to acquire or develop nuclear weapons and has been receptive to any outside nuclear assistance that might become available." See Central Intelligence Agency, "Unclassified Report to Congress on the Acquisition of Technology Relating to Weapons of Mass Destruction and Advanced Conventional Munitions, 1 January through 30 June 2002" (Washington, DC: CIA, April 2003), at www.cia.gov/cia/reports/721_reports/jan_jun2002.html. For a discussion of intelligence about al-Qaeda's pursuit of nuclear devices, see *The Commission on the Intelligence Capabilities of the United States Regarding Weapons of Mass Destruction*, Report to the President of the United States (Washington, DC: March 31, 2005) [aka *Robb–Silberman Report*; at www.wmd.gov/report/], pp. 271–6.

32. See Matthew Bunn, Anthony Wier, and John P. Holdren, *Controlling Nuclear Warheads and Materials: A Report Card and Action Plan* (Cambridge, MA: Kennedy School of Government, Belfer Center for Science and International Affairs, March 2003), pp. vii, 179; at www.nti.org/e_research/cnwm/ cnwm.pdf.

33. See Woodward, Bush at War, p. 137. Also Graham Allison, *Nuclear Terrorism: The Ultimate Preventable Catastrophe* (New York: Times Books, 2004).

34. For background on this pattern of terrorist attacks, see *9/11 Commission Report*, chaps. 2–6, pp. 47–214.

35. *9/11 Commission Report*, p. 254. Subsequent citations are given in the text. For a detailed analysis of those threats and the reactions within the U.S. government, see the report's chap. 8 ("'The System Was Blinking Red'"), pp. 254–77.

36. "Other reports' titles warned, 'Bin Ladin [*sic*] Attacks May Be Imminent' and 'Bin Ladin [*sic*] and Associates Making Near-Term Threats'" (ibid., p. 257).

37. A "man identified as one of the Sept. 11 hijackers" had said in a videotape that "It is time to kill Americans in their own homeland, among their sons, and near their forces and intelligence." Tim Golden, "Videotape Links Al Qaeda with Sept. 11 Hijackers," *New York Times*, April 16, 2002, p. A20.

38. After 9/11, the president established the White House Office of Homeland Security and the Homeland Security Council and "directed Homeland Security Advisor Tom Ridge to study the federal government as a whole to determine if the current structure allows us to meet the threats of today while anticipating the unknown threats of tomorrow. After careful study of the current structure – coupled with the experience gained since September 11 and new information we have learned about our enemies while fighting a war – the President concluded that our nation needs a more unified homeland security structure." The new security structure created in 2002 was the Department of Homeland Security. See *The Department of Homeland Security*, June 2002, at www.dhs.gov/interweb/assetlibrary/book.pdf, p. 2.

On the role the Department of Homeland Security should play in intelligence gathering and overhauling the national intelligence apparatus, see *9/11 Commission Report*, chap. 13 ("How to Do It? A Different Way of Organizing the Government"), pp. 399–428.

39. *The National Security Strategy of the United States of America* (Washington, DC: White House, September 2002) [hereafter, *NSS 2002*], p. 14; at www.whitehouse.gov/nsc/nss.pdf.

40. See ibid., p. 15: "The United States has long maintained the option of preemptive actions to counter a sufficient threat to our national security. The greater the threat, the greater is the risk of inaction – and the more compelling the case for taking anticipatory action to defend ourselves, even if uncertainty remains as to the time and place of the enemy's attack. To forestall or prevent such hos-

tile acts by our adversaries, the United States will, if necessary, act preemptively."

41. George W. Bush, "The President's State of the Union Address," January 29, 2002, at www.whitehouse.gov/news/releases/2002/01/20020129-11.html.

42. *NSS 2002*, p. 5.

43. See *9/11 Commission Report*, p. 380. The report also noted (p. 60) that "Bin Laden sought the capability to kill on a mass scale."

44. Woodward, *Bush at War*, p. 137: "Cheney's biggest concern was still the possibility that bin Laden or other terrorists would acquire and use weapons of mass destruction. Nothing had suggested that al-Qaeda possessed any nuclear devices, but there was a concern about biological and chemical weapons."

45. Woodward, *Bush at War*, p. 192: "The overriding lesson from the 1990s in Afghanistan was: Don't leave a vacuum. The abandonment of Afghanistan after the Soviets were ousted in 1989 had created conditions for the rise of the Taliban and the virtual takeover of the country by bin Laden and al-Qaeda."

46. Ibid., p. 167.

47. Ibid., p. 81.

48. On September 20, the president had demanded that the Taliban immediately turn all al-Qaeda leaders over to the United States, release all imprisoned foreign nationals, close all terrorist training camps, allow the United States full access to inspect those camps, and surrender all terrorists and supporters to "appropriate authorities." Bush, "Address to a Joint Session . . ." Abdul Salam Zaeef, the Taliban ambassador to Pakistan, replied: "Our position on this is that if America has proof, we are ready for the trial of Osama bin Laden in light of the evidence." "Taliban Won't Turn Over Bin Laden," *CBS News*, Sept. 21, 2001, at www.cbsnews.com/stories/2001/09/11/world/main310852.shtml, which notes that "Afghanistan's Islamic clerics urged bin Laden to leave the country on his own accord." Later, as U.S. forces amassed for the invasion, "Zaeef said the Taliban would detain bin Laden and try him under Islamic law if the United States makes a formal request and presents them with evidence." This too was rejected, as was an offer "to release Western aid workers on trial in Afghanistan if the United States withdraws its threat of military strikes against Afghanistan." "U.S. Rejects Taliban Offer to Try bin Laden," *CNN*, archives.

cnn.com/2001/US/10/07/ret.us.taliban/. A week after the invasion began, an offer to yield bin Laden to a third country was refused, with the president saying, "I told them exactly what they need to do, and there's no need to discuss innocence or guilt. We know he's guilty." "Bush Rejects Taliban's Offer to Turn Over bin Laden to Third Party," October 14, 2001, *CNN*, transcripts.cnn.com/TRANSCRIPTS/0110/14/sun.03.html.

49. See Bush, "Presidential Address to the Nation," October 7, 2001, for the statement that, "The United States of America is a friend to the Afghan people, and we are the friends of almost a billion worldwide who practice the Islamic faith."

50. Woodward, *Bush at War*, p. 147. The president would echo this point in a Veterans Day speech: "We have no territorial ambitions, we don't seek an empire." "President Bush Salutes Veterans at White House Ceremony," November 11, 2002, at www.whitehouse. gov/news/releases/2002/11/20021111-2.html. Woodward (ibid., p. 128) also quoted Tenet as saying, "We want to structure it as Afghanistan versus the outsiders. . . . We are not invading. We are not occupying. Mullah Omar betrayed the Afghan people. He let in those outsiders."

51. Ibid., pp. 191–3.

52. Bush, "Presidential Address to the Nation," October 7, 2001. As Defense Secretary Rumsfeld put it, "we need to start creating an environment in which Afghanistan becomes inhospitable to the al-Qaeda and the Taliban." Woodward, *Bush at War*, p. 124.

53. Bush, "Address to a Joint Session . . . ," September 20, 2001. Bush continued: "Our war on terror begins with al-Qaeda, but it does not end there. It will not end until every terrorist group of global reach has been found, stopped, and defeated."

54. "Transcript: Rumsfeld, Myers Brief on Military Operation in Afghanistan," October 7, 2001, at www.globalsecurity.org/military/library/news/2001/10/mil-011007-usia04.htm.

55. Woodward, *Bush at War*, pp. 35–6, for pre-9/11 discussions of plans to destabilize the Taliban.

56. Bush, "Address to a Joint Session . . . ," September 20, 2001. Other examples include Bush's 2002 State of the Union Address and the 2002 U.S. *National Security Strategy*.

57. Bush, "Address to a Joint Session . . . ," September 20, 2001.

58. Woodward, *Bush at War*, p. 102.

59. Bush, "Address to a Joint Session . . . ," September 20, 2001.

60. Ibid.

61. Vernon Loeb, "Rumsfeld Voices Caution about Success," *Washington Post,* October 19, 2001; at www.washingtonpost.com/ac2/wp-dyn/A22311-2001Oct19.

62. This discussion draws heavily from "Operation Enduring Freedom – Afghanistan" – first accessed at the Federation of American Scientists Web site, but now at www.globalsecurity.org/military/ops/enduring-freedom.htm – which provides an excellent review of the military operations against Afghanistan.

63. See ibid.

64. Tommy Franks, with Malcolm McConnell, *American Soldier* (New York: HarperCollins, 2004), pp. 321–536.

65. Thomas E. Ricks, "U.S. to Set Up New Bases to Help Afghanistan Rebuild," *Washington Post,* December 20, 2002, p. 45: "The troops are expected to engage in small-scale construction projects, such as digging wells, building schools and fixing minor bridges."

66. Woodward, *Bush at War,* p. 124, where Rumsfeld continues: "But we need to start creating an environment in which Afghanistan becomes inhospitable to the al-Qaeda and the Taliban."

67. See James Carney and John F. Dickerson, "Inside the War Room," *Time* 158.28 (December 31, 2001–January 7, 2002; double issue), pp. 112–21.

68. See "Operation Enduring Freedom – Deployments," at www.globalsecurity.org/military/ops/enduring-freedom_deploy.htm: "C-130 cargo planes are reported to have landed in Uzbekistan at a former Soviet air field located near Tashkent. . . . Combat Search and Rescue Units were prepared for deployment, reportedly to Uzbekistan or Tajikistan. . . . At least one thousand troops from the 10th Mountain Division . . .were deployed to Uzbekistan." See also Elizabeth Skinner, "Enduring Freedom for Central Asia?" *Strategic Insights* 1.2 (April 2002), at www.ccc.nps.navy.mil/si/apr02/russia.asp: "Uzbekistan's border with Afghanistan is now one of the chief staging areas for U.S. operations as part of Enduring Freedom, . . . Tajikistan also has offered a dilapidated military airfield located near the capital Dushanbe. . . . Turkmenistan's president, Saparmurat Niyazov, supports the transportation of humanitarian aid into Afghanistan through his country, but so far has stood by his government's pledge of 'positive neutrality', refusing any military cooperation."

69. "Operation Enduring Freedom – Afghanistan."

70. Vernon Loeb, "Second Day of Strikes Includes Searching for Mobile Targets: U.S. Seeks Taliban Troops on the Run," *Washington Post,* October 9, 2001, p. A8.

71. "Presidential Address to the Nation," October 7, 2001. The morning before the attack, there were media reports that U.S. military operations were about to begin. Woodward, *Bush at War,* p. 208.

72. "Operation Enduring Freedom – Afghanistan."

73. Woodward, *Bush at War,* p. 210.

74. Ibid., p. 200.

75. See Dan Balz and Mike Allen, "Bush Declares Al Qaeda Is 'On the Run': Campaign Could Last 'Year or Two'," *Washington Post,* October 12, 2001, p. A1; at www.library.ohiou.edu/indopubs/2001/10/12/0029.html.

76. Woodward, *Bush at War,* p. 52. Regarding the nature of the cave facilities, see Matthew Forney, "Inside the Tora Bora Caves," December 11, 2001 (Web exclusive) at www.time.com/time/world/article/0,8599,188029,00.html.

77. See Molly Moore and Susan B. Glasser, "Afghan Militias Claim Victory in Tora Bora," *Washington Post,* December 18, 2001, p. A1; Karl Vick, "For U.S., Attack on Kandahar Was a Victory on Two Fronts," *Washington Post,* December 26, 2001, p. A6.

78. "Operation Enduring Freedom – Afghanistan."

79. Vernon Loeb, "Rumsfeld Announces End of Afghan Combat," *Washington Post,* May 2, 2003, p. A16.

80. "Operation Enduring Freedom – Afghanistan." On the detainment facilities at Bagram, see Tim Golden and Eric Schmitt, "A Growing Afghan Prison Rivals Bleak Guantánamo," *New York Times,* February 26, 2006, p. A1.

81. See, e.g., James Risen with Judith Miller, "Bin Laden's Trail Is Lost, but Officials Suspect He Is Alive," *New York Times,* February 4, 2002, p. A8.

82. U.S. Central Command, "International Contributions to the War on Terrorism," at www.centcom.mil/sites/uscentcom1/Shared%20Documents/Coalition.aspx; see also "Operation Enduring Freedom: One Year of Accom-

plishments" (October 7, 2002), at www.white-house.gov/infocus/defense/enduringfreedom.html. NATO's International Security Assistance Force (ISAF), established in December 2001, has enlarged its purview from Kabul and Bagram Air Base to cover northern and western Afghanistan, and is expected to extend its activities southward; see ISAF's "Primary Role" Web page, at www.afnorth.nato.int/ISAF/mission/mission_role.htm. See also "International Security Assistance Force," at www.globalsecurity. org/military/ops/oef_orbat_isaf6.htm.

83. Woodward, *Bush at War,* p. 133, quoted Bush as arguing, in a National Security Council meeting at the White House on September 25, 2001, that "We can't define the success or failure in terms of capturing UBL [i.e., bin Laden]." Still, three months later the president said, "Listen, a while ago I said to the American people, our objective is more than bin Laden. But one of the things for certain is we're going to get him running and keep him running, and bring him to justice." "President, General Franks Discuss War Effort," December 28, 2001, at www.whitehouse.gov/news/releases/2001/12/20011228-1.html.

84. Ibid., p. 220.

85. This discussion draws heavily from "Operation Enduring Freedom – Operations," at www.globalsecurity.org/military/ ops/enduring-freedom-ops.htm, which provides an excellent overview of the military operations.

86. "Operation Enduring Freedom – Deployments." For more on Djibouti's role, see "Operation Enduring Freedom – Horn of Africa/Djibouti," at www.globalsecurity.org/military/ops/oef-djibouti.htm.

87. See Glenn W. Goodman Jr., "Terminal Accuracy: Smart Munitions Knock Out Ground Targets with Fewer Weapons, Less Collateral Damage," *Armed Forces Journal International* 140.3 (October 2002), pp. 64–72, at p. 64: "During the first two months of the strikes on al-Qaeda and Taliban targets in Afghanistan last fall, 4,600 of the 7,200 air-delivered PGMs expended were JDAMs, while the rest were laser-guided bombs and Tomahawk cruise missiles." Available online at www.armedforcesjournal.com/AFJI/Mags/2002/Oct/terminal.html.

88. "Operation Enduring Freedom – Operations."

89. Ibid. These figures include both Air Force bombers and Navy fighters. By contrast, 9 percent of the munitions used in the Persian Gulf War were precision guided, and 35 percent were in Operation Allied Force in Kosovo. See John A. Tirpak, "Enduring Freedom," *Air Force Magazine* 85.2 (February 2002), pp. 32–9, at www.afa.org/magazine/Feb2002/0202airwar.asp; Williamson Murray, "Part I: Operations," in *Gulf War Air Power Survey,* vol. II: *Operations and Effects and Effectiveness* (Washington, DC: U.S. GPO, 1993), at www.airforcehistory.hq.af. mil/Publications/Annotations/gwaps.htm; Department of Defense, *Conduct of the Persian Gulf War: Final Report to Congress* (Washington, DC: U.S. GPO, 1992), at www.ndu.edu/library/epubs/cpgw.pdf.

90. "Operation Enduring Freedom – Operations."

91. Woodward, *Bush at War,* p. 208: "'I've told them they have whatever authority they need,' Bush said, 'as long as it abides by the rule of low collateral.' . . . Commanders and pilots had discretion to hit targets as long as they expected it would only cause minimal damage to civilians."

92. This is the total for "eleven locations where civilians were said to be killed by American strikes": "Operation Enduring Freedom – Operations."

93. "Operation Enduring Freedom – Deployments." See also "Forward Operating Base Rhino," at www.globalsecurity.org/military/world/afghanistan/rhino.htm.

94. See "Operation Enduring Freedom – Afghanistan" and ". . . – Operations."

95. Woodward, *Bush at War,* p. 175.

96. Ibid.: "[T]he CIA experts said it was important to make the war Afghan versus Arab, not some Westerners versus Afghans."

97. Woodward, *Bush at War,* p. 230: "He [Tenet] said they had put their fate in the hands of the Afghan tribals, who were to act at a time, place and pace of their choosing."

98. See Scott M. Britten, "Directing War from Home," in William C. Martel (ed.), *The Technological Arsenal: Emerging Defense Capabilities* (Washington, DC: Smithsonian Institution Press, 2001), pp. 199–219.

99. See Elsa Walsh, "Learning to Spy: Can Maureen Baginski Save the FBI?" *New Yorker* 80.34 (November 8, 2004), pp. 96–103, for a discussion of new targeting approaches.

100. See Bush, "President's State of the Union Address," January 29, 2002; International Institute for Strategic Studies, "Towards Stability in Afghanistan: Qualified Progress?" *Strategic Comments* 10.4 (May 2004), pp. 1–2, accessed via www.iiss.org/stratcom.

101. See "Operation Enduring Freedom: One Year of Accomplishments."

102. See Woodward, *Bush at War,* p. 334. Some two dozen Afghans, meeting under U.N. auspices, would produce the Bonn Agreement of December 5, 2001, regarding setting up a new government; at www.afghan-web.com/politics/bonn_agreement_2001.html.

103. Woodward, *Bush at War,* p. 81.

104. Bush, "Presidential Address to the Nation," October 7, 2001.

105. See Carney and Dickerson, "Inside the War Room," p. 115: "Untroubled by doubt, uninterested in nuance, Bush has been relentlessly focused."

106. Bush, "Presidential Address to the Nation," October 7, 2001

107. Woodward, *Bush at War,* p. 275.

108. Ibid., p. 241, who quoted Bush as saying this.

109. Cited in ibid., p. 189; *9/11 Commission Report,* esp. chap. 4 ("Responses to Al Qaeda's Initial Assaults"), pp. 108–43; Richard H. Shultz Jr., "Showstoppers: Nine Reasons Why We Never Sent Our Special Operations Forces after al-Qaeda before 9/11," *Weekly Standard* 9.19 (January 26, 2004), pp. 25–33; at www.weeklystandard.com/content/public/articles/000/000/003/613twavk.asp.

110. Bush, "Presidential Address to the Nation," October 7, 2001.

111. See "Operation Enduring Freedom (OEF) U.S. Casualty Status," updated daily at www.defenselink.mil/news/casualty.pdf.

112. See "President Pledges Assistance for New York in Phone Call with Pataki, Giuliani," transcript, televised phone call, September 13, 2001, at www.whitehouse.gov/news/releases/2001/09/20010913-4.html; see also Mike Allen, "Bush Says He Is Preparing for War," *Washington Post,* September 13, 2001, p. A1, at www.washingtonpost.com/ac3/ContentServer?pagename=article&articleid=A24813-2001Sep13&node=nation/specials/attacked/archive; David Von Drehle, "Bush Pledges Victory; Reagan National Closed Indefinitely," *Washington Post,* September 14, 2001, p. A1.

113. Von Drehle, "Bush Pledges Victory."

114. See Seymour M. Hersh, "The Other War: Why Bush's Afghanistan Problem Won't Go Away," *New Yorker* 80.19 (April 12, 2004), pp. 40–9, at p. 40; at www.newyorker.com/fact/content/?040412fa_fact. Rumsfeld continued: "There are people who are throwing hand grenades and shooting off rockets and trying to kill people, but there are people who are trying to kill people in New York or San Francisco. So it's not going to be a perfectly tidy place."

115. David Montgomery, "In This War, 'V' May Be for Vague Victory," *Washington Post,* December 18, 2001, p. C1.

116. Woodward, *Bush at War,* pp. 189–90, refers to Secretary of Defense Donald Rumsfeld's "Campaign against Terrorism: Strategic Guidance for the U.S. Department of Defense," as the basis for the Department of Defense's actions in the global war against terrorism.

117. As noted in a study commissioned to advise on postconflict reconstruction generally: "U.S. democracy and governance programs have four principal objectives: (1) to strengthen the rule of law and respect for human rights; (2) to develop more genuine and competitive political processes; (3) to foster the development of a politically active civil society; and (4) to promote more transparent and accountable government institutions." See Center for Strategic and International Studies and the Association of the U.S. Army, "Play to Win: Final Report of the Bi-Partisan Commission on Post-Conflict Reconstruction," January 2003 (n.p.), in the section "Governance and Participation"; at www.reliefweb.int/rw/lib.nsf/db900SID/LGEL-5JVD76?OpenDocument.

118. See Carlotta Gall, "Afghan Council Gives Approval to Constitution," *New York Times,* January 5, 2004, p. A1.

119. This quotation is from Bush's speech at the Pentagon memorial service on October 11, 2001: "President Pays Tribute at Pentagon Memorial," at www.whitehouse.gov/news/releases/2001/10/20011011-1.html.

120. Woodward, *Bush at War,* p. 314.

121. Richard Morin and Claudia Deane, "Poll: Strong Backing for Bush, War," *Washington Post,* March 11, 2002, p. A1.

122. See Eric V. Larson and Bogdan Savych, *American Support for U.S. Military Operations from Mogadishu to Baghdad* (Santa Monica, CA: RAND Corporation, MG-231-

A, 2005), pp. 91–127, at www.rand.org/
pubs/monographs/MG231/index.html.

123. Ricks, "U.S. to Set Up New Bases."

124. See Timothy L. O'Brien, "U.S. Treasury Chief Pledges $1.2 Billion in Afghan Aid," *New York Times,* September 19, 2003, p. A10.

125. For a discussion of contested ideas, see Felix E. Oppenheim, *Political Concepts: A Reconstruction* (Oxford: Basil Blackwell, 1981), pp. 195–6.

126. See Carlotta Gall, "Taliban Threat Is Said to Grow in Afghan South," *New York Times,* May 3, 2006, p. A1: "The fact that American troops are pulling out of southern Afghanistan in the coming months, and handing matters over to NATO peacekeepers . . . has given a lift to the insurgents, and increased the fears of Afghans. . . . The arrival of large numbers of Taliban in the villages, flush with money and weapons, has dealt a blow to public confidence in the Afghan government, already undermined by lack of tangible progress and frustration with corrupt and ineffective leaders. . . . Uruzgan, the province where President Hamid Karzai first rallied support against the Taliban in the months after the Sept. 11 attacks, is now, four years later, in the thrall of the Islamic militants once more, and the provincial capital is increasingly surrounded by areas in Taliban control, local and American officials acknowledge. . . . The Bush administration is alarmed, according to a Western intelligence official close to the administration. He said that while senior members of the administration consider the situation in Iraq to be not as bad as portrayed in the press, in Afghanistan the situation is worse than it has been generally portrayed."

127. See Carlotta Gall, "Afghan Lawmakers Review Court Nominees," *New York Times,* May 17, 2006, p. A10: "In a move that drew Western criticism, Mr. Karzai reappointed Fazel Hadi Shinwari as chief justice and head of the Supreme Court. He is a 73-year-old religious conservative who was neither a trained judge nor a recognized Islamic scholar. He has also been accused of corruption and nepotism in recent months. . . . 'The international community would have preferred someone more qualified, or someone who has respect for the rule of law,' said one Western diplomat in Kabul. . . . Mr. Karzai has sought to placate Western donors financing judicial

reform by removing the other eight Supreme Court judges, and by appointing well-qualified judges beneath Mr. Shinwari. . . . Government officials said that the new Supreme Court had been appointed with a clear message from the president to end corruption, and that progress would be closely watched." See also Gall, "Taliban Threat Is Said to Grow," quoted in note 126 as to "public confidence in the Afghan government."

11. 2003 Invasion of Iraq

1. "President Bush Addresses the Nation," March 19, 2003, at www.whitehouse.gov/news/releases/2003/03/20030319-17.html. It was predawn, March 20, in Baghdad.

2. Ibid.

3. Bruce Hoffman, "Plan of Attack: Insurgents in Iraq are Forging Improbable Alliances to Fight What Some Analysts Call a 'Netwar'," *Atlantic Monthly* 294.1 (June–July 2004), pp. 42–3, at p. 42; at www.theatlantic.com/doc/200407/hoffman.

4. "Excerpts from Bush Speech on American Strategy in Iraq," *New York Times,* May 25, 2004, p. A12: "The rise of a free and self-governing Iraq will deny terrorists a base of operations, discredit their narrow ideology and give momentum to reformers across the region. This will be a decisive blow to terrorism at the heart of its power, and a victory for the security of America and the civilized world." The full text of the speech, delivered at the United States Army War College in Carlisle, Pennsylvania, is at www.whitehouse.gov/news/releases/2004/05/20040524-10.html.

5. See David Ignatius, "Achieving Real Victory Could Take Decades," *Washington Post,* December 26, 2004, p. B1, quoting Central Command's General John Abizaid: "Victory will be hard to measure, he says, because the enemy won't wave a white flag and surrender one day." Larry Diamond, "What Went Wrong in Iraq," *Foreign Affairs* 83.5 (September–October 2004), pp. 34–56, at www.foreignaffairs.org/20040901faessay83505/larry-diamond/what-went-wrong-in-iraq.html; Michael W. Isherwood, "U.S. Strategic Options for Iraq: Easier Said than Done," *Washington Quarterly* 25.2 (Spring 2002), pp. 145–59, at www.twq.com/02spring/isherwood.pdf; David Isby, "Saddam's Last Stand? A Besieged Baghdad Would Turn on Itself," *Washington Times,*

November 7, 2002, at intelmessages.org/
messages/nationalsecurity/www/board.messages-
02/2392.html.

6. See Eric Schmitt, "Rapid Pullout from
Iraq Urged by Key Democrat," *New York
Times*, November 18, 2005, p. A1.

7. "President Bush Addresses the Nation,"
March 19, 2003.

8. Ibid. Earlier, Secretary of State
Madeleine Albright argued that the purpose of
bombing Iraq in 1998 was to "diminish the
ability of Saddam Hussein to make weapons of
mass destruction." See George Melloan, "A
Case for Bombing Iraq Exists; Why Not Make
It?" *Wall Street Journal*, February 10, 1998, p.
A19.

9. See Raymond W. Copson (coord.),
"Iraq War: Background and Issues Overview,"
CRS Report for Congress, April 22, 2003),
pp. 1–4, at www.fas.org/man/crs/RL31715.pdf
and www.maxwell.af.mil/au/awc/awcgate/crs/
rl31715.pdf; Patrick E. Tyler, "Bush Signal:
Time Is Now," *New York Times*, November 8,
2002, p. A1. Some date the onset of planning
from Defense Secretary Rumsfeld's demand on
9/11 for "best info fast. Judge whether good
enough hit S.H. [Saddam Hussein] at same time.
Not only UBL [bin Laden]." See "Plans for Iraq
Attack Began on 9/11," *CBS News*, Sept. 4,
2002, at www.cbsnews.com/stories/2002/09/04/
september11/main520830.shtml.

10. "We know he's been developing weapons of mass destruction." "President Holds
Prime Time News Conference," October 11,
2001, at www.whitehouse.gov/news/releases/
2001/10/20011011-7.html; Dan Balz and Mike
Allen, "Bush Declares Al Qaeda Is 'On the
Run': Campaign Could Last 'Year or Two',"
Washington Post, October 12, 2001, p. A1, at
www.library.ohiou.edu/indopubs/ 2001/
10/12/0029.html. Compare "President's State
of the Union Message to Congress and the
Nation," *New York Times*, January 29, 2003,
pp. A12–13: "The world has waited 12 years
for Iraq to disarm. America will not accept a
serious and mounting threat to our country,
our friends and our allies." Richard W. Stevenson, "Bush Warns Iraq It Has Only Weeks to
Yield Weapons," *New York Times*, January 31,
2003, p. A1; "Powell's Address, Presenting
'Deeply Troubling' Evidence on Iraq," *New
York Times*, February 6, 2003, p. A14: "Indeed, the facts and Iraq's behavior show that
Saddam Hussein and his regime are conceal-

ing their efforts to produce more weapons of
mass destruction." Also, David E. Sanger,
"U.S. Plans to Pressure Iraq by Encouraging
Scientists to Leak Data to Inspectors," *New
York Times*, November 9, 2002, p. A10; "Inspectors Say Their Work in Iraq Is Far from
Complete," *New York Times*, January 27,
2003, p. A1. But see Matt Kelley, "U.S. Sup-
plied the Kinds of Germs Iraq Later Used for
Biological Weapons," AP story, September 30,
2002, at www.usatoday.com/news/world/2002-
09-30-iraq-ushelp_x.htm: "The CDC and a biological sample company . . . sent strains of all
the germs Iraq used to make weapons, including anthrax, the bacteria that make botulinum
toxin and the germs that cause gas gan-
grene. . . . Iraq also got samples of other deadly pathogens, including West Nile virus. The
transfers came in the 1980s, when the United
States supported Iraq in its war with Iran."

11. Bob Woodward, *Plan of Attack: The
Definitive Account of the Decision to Invade
Iraq* (New York: Simon & Schuster, 2004), p.
1. As President Bush asked Rumsfeld, "What
kind of a war plan do you have for Iraq? How
do you feel about the war plan for Iraq?" Also,
see Glenn Kessler, "U.S. Decision on Iraq Has
Puzzling Past," *Washington Post*, January 12,
2003, p A1; Douglas Jehl, "British Memo on
U.S. Plans for Iraq War Fuels Critics," *New
York Times*, May 20, 2005, p. A8; Daniel Byman, "Iraq after Saddam," *Washington Quarterly* 24.4 (Autumn 2001), pp. 151–62, at
www.twq.com/01autumn/byman.pdf; George C.
Wilson, "Toppling Saddam with Quick
Strikes," *National Journal*, December 21,
2002, pp. 37–42.

12. See *The National Security Strategy of the
United States of America* (Washington, DC:
White House, September 2002), available at
www.whitehouse.gov/nsc/nss.pdf, p. 14; George
W. Bush, "The President's State of the Union
Address," January 29, 2002, at www.
whitehouse.gov/news/releases/2002/01/
20020129-11.html.

13. Ibid. Earlier in the speech he'd noted,
"The Iraqi regime has plotted to develop anthrax, and nerve gas, and nuclear weapons for
over a decade. . . . This is a regime that agreed
to international inspections – then kicked out
the inspectors."

14. "Vice President Speaks at VFW 103rd
National Convention," August 26, 2002, at
www.whitehouse.gov/news/releases/2002/08/

20020826.html: "After his defeat in the Gulf War in 1991, Saddam agreed under U.N. Security Council Resolution 687 to cease all development of weapons of mass destruction. He agreed to end his nuclear weapons program. He agreed to destroy his chemical and his biological weapons. He further agreed to admit U.N. inspection teams into his country to ensure that he was in fact complying with these terms. In the past decade, Saddam has systematically broken each of these agreements. The Iraqi regime has in fact been very busy enhancing its capabilities in the field of chemical and biological agents. And they continue to pursue the nuclear program they began so many years ago. These are not weapons for the purpose of defending Iraq; these are offensive weapons for the purpose of inflicting death on a massive scale, developed so that Saddam can hold the threat over the head of anyone he chooses, in his own region or beyond." See Stephen Fidler and David White, "Intelligence Report Says Baghdad Is Ready to Use Chemical and Biological Weapons," *Financial Times,* September 25, 2002, p. 2.

15. For the CIA's view of Iraq's noncompliance with specific UNSCRs, see "Iraq's Weapons of Mass Destruction Programs" (Washington, DC: CIA, October 2002), at www.cia.gov/cia/reports/iraq_wmd/Iraq_Oct_2002.pdf. For a U.N. view of U.S. noncompliance with the Security Council, see "Iraq War Illegal, Says Annan," *BBC News,* September 16, 2004, at news.bbc.co.uk/1/hi/world/middle_east/3661134.stm.

16. "Security Council, 15–0, Votes a Tough Resolution Telling Hussein to Disarm," *New York Times,* November 9, 2002, p. A1. See also UNSCR 1441 (November 8, 2002), at daccess-ods.un.org/TMP/893004.1.html.

17. "President Says Saddam Hussein Must Leave Iraq within 48 Hours; Remarks by the President in Address to the Nation," March 17, 2003, at www.whitehouse.gov/news/releases/2003/03/20030317-7.html; see also Copson (coord.); "Iraq War," pp. 6–7.

18. See Amatzia Baram, "An Analysis of Iraqi WMD Strategy," *Nonproliferation Review* 8.2 (Summer 2001), pp. 25–39, available at cns.miis.edu/pubs/npr/vol08/82/82baram.pdf; David E. Sanger, "U.S. Disputes Iraqi Denial That It Has Weapons Banned by U.N.," *New York Times,* November 14, 2002, p. A15; Ju-

lia Preston, "Iraq Tells the U.N. Arms Inspections Will Be Permitted," *New York Times,* November 14, 2002, p. A1; Steven R. Weisman with Julia Preston, "Powell Says Iraq Raises Risk of War by Lying on Arms," *New York Times,* December 20, 2002, p. A1; "The U.S. Catalogs 'Material Omissions'," *New York Times,* December 20, 2002, p. A14; Condoleezza Rice, "Why We Know Iraq Is Lying," *New York Times,* January 23, 2003, p. A27; Sanger, "U.S. Plans to Pressure Iraq"; "Powell's Address"; "Iraq's Response: 'Incorrect Allegations'," *New York Times,* February 6, 2003, p. A17; Madeleine Albright, "Where Iraq Fits in the War on Terror," *New York Times,* September 13, 2002, p. A27: "If Baghdad persists in its defiance, the president has rightly placed the burden on those who oppose the use of force to explain how else compliance may be assured." On the unexpected nature of the war, see Thom Shanker, "Regime Thought War Unlikely, Iraqis Tell U.S.," *New York Times,* February 12, 2004, p. A1.

19. See Rice, "Why We Know Iraq Is Lying"; *The Commission on the Intelligence Capabilities of the United States Regarding Weapons of Mass Destruction,* Report to the President of the United States (Washington, DC: March 31, 2005), pp. 8–11 [hereinafter, *Robb–Silberman Report;* at www.wmd.gov/report/].

20. See the *Robb–Silberman Report,* p. 3: "While the intelligence services of many other nations also thought that Iraq had weapons of mass destruction, in the end it was the United States that put its credibility on the line, making this one of the most public – and most damaging – intelligence failures in recent American history." Regarding the earlier final report of the Iraq Survey Group, whose WMD search had begun on May 30, 2003, see "Report Concludes No WMD in Iraq," October 7, 2004, *BBC News,* at news.bbc.co.uk/1/hi/world/middle_east/3718150.stm. For earlier, post–Gulf War difficulties in verifying Iraqi WMD, see Neil King Jr., "Lack of Smoking Gun Weakens Stance on Iraq," *Wall Street Journal,* February 10, 1998, p. A14; Robert S. Greenberger and Thomas E. Ricks, "Clinton and Pentagon Plan Less Obsessive Stance toward Iraq, with Big Troop and Ship Pullback," *Wall Street Journal,* May 13, 1998, p. A24.

21. As noted in Chapter 10, this phrase, used regarding the 2001 Afghanistan coali-

tion, is now usually applied to the 2003 war in Iraq.

22. See "Joint Resolution to Authorize the Use of United States Armed Forces against Iraq," October 2, 2002, at www.whitehouse.gov/news/releases/2002/10/20021002-2.html; also "Statement by the President," October 16, 2002 (the date this became Public Law 107–243), at www.whitehouse.gov/news/releases/2002/10/20021016-11.html. According to that joint resolution, "The President is authorized to use the Armed Forces of the United States as he determines to be necessary and appropriate in order to (1) defend the national security of the United States against the continuing threat posed by Iraq; and (2) enforce all relevant United Nations Security Council resolutions regarding Iraq."

23. "President Bush Discusses Iraq; Remarks by President Bush and Polish President Kwaśniewski in Photo Opportunity," January 14, 2003, at www.whitehouse.gov/news/releases/2003/01/20030114-2.html. "That's the question: Is Saddam Hussein disarming? He's been given 11 years to disarm. And so the world came together and we have given him one last chance to disarm. So far, I haven't seen any evidence that he is disarming. Time is running out on Saddam Hussein. He must disarm. I'm sick and tired of games and deception. And that's my view of timetables." Also, Stevenson, "Bush Warns Iraq."

24. See International Institute for Strategic Studies, "France, America and Iraq: On the Brink," Strategic Comments 9.2 (March 2003), pp. 1–2, accessed via www.iiss.org/stratcom.

25. "President Says Saddam Hussein Must Leave Iraq." See also Steven R. Weisman, "Exile for Hussein May Be an Option, U.S. Officials Hint," New York Times, January 20, 2003, p. A1; Christopher Marquis, "Saudi Prince Encourages Exile Agreement for Hussein's Departure," New York Times, January 30, 2003, p. A11, at www.nytimes.com/2003/01/30/international/middleeast/30SAUD.html; Thom Shanker and James Risen, "Hussein Tells Interrogators He Didn't Direct Insurgency," New York Times, December 16, 2003, p. A1.

26. Barton Gellman and Dana Priest, "CIA Had Fix on Hussein," Washington Post, March 20, 2003, at www.washingtonpost.com/wp-dyn/articles/A58177-2003Mar20.html; "U.S. Launches Cruise Missiles at Saddam; Saddam

Denounces Attack as 'Criminal'," CNN, March 20, 2003, at www.cnn.com/2003/WORLD/meast/03/19/sprj.irq.main. Although President Reagan, in a similar situation, noted "our prohibition against assassination" (see Chapter 6, note 83), it appears that "no criminal penalties automatically attach to its violation, and any punishment would be at the prerogative of the president." Walter Pincus, "Saddam Hussein's Death Is a Goal, Says Ex-CIA Chief," Washington Post, February 15, 1998, p. A36, at www.washingtonpost.com/wp-srv/inatl/longterm/iraq/keyplayers/saddam021598.htm, which continues: "When it comes to bombing, the executive order [12333] is bypassed because military action is targeted on buildings; leaders of the targeted country are considered potential collateral damage."

27. The extent to which Saddam Hussein has supported international terrorism has been much questioned, in particular whether there was any connection with al-Qaeda (see note 9). See, e.g., Douglas Jehl, "The Reach of War: Intelligence; Qaeda–Iraq Link U.S. Cited Is Tied to Coercion Claim," New York Times, December 9, 2005, p. A1: "The Bush administration based a crucial prewar assertion about ties between Iraq and al-Qaeda on detailed statements made by a prisoner [al-Qaeda leader Ibn al-Shaykh al Libi] while in Egyptian custody who later said he had fabricated them to escape harsh treatment, according to current and former government officials." The 9/11 Commission Report: Final Report of the National Commission on Terrorist Attacks upon the United States (Washington, DC: U.S. GPO, 2004), p. 66: "[T]o date we have seen no evidence that these [brief, exploratory 1999] contacts ever developed into a collaborative operational relationship. Nor have we seen evidence indicating that Iraq cooperated with al-Qaeda in developing or carrying out any attacks against the United States." The lack of a credible Qaeda–Iraq link was purportedly indicated in a PDB on September 21, 2001; Murray Waas, "Key Bush Intelligence Briefing Kept From Hill Panel," November 22, 2005, at nationaljournal.com/about/njweekly/stories/2005/1122nj1.htm. There is, however, evidence of indirect support for regional terrorism, such as funds provided to the families of Palestinian suicide bombers. See, e.g., "Palestinians Get Saddam Funds," BBC News, March 13, 2003, at news.bbc.co.

uk/2/hi/middle_east/2846365.stm, and the ex-
purgated CIA report online at www.globalsecu-
rity.org/intell/library/congress/2004_rpt/iraq-wmd-
intell_chapter12-i.htm. For more on prewar
Iraq and terrorism, see the sources cited below
in note 39.

28. Quoted in Woodward, *Plan of Attack,*
pp. 154–5. A working draft was reviewed at
a principals meeting on August 14, 2002.
Bush signed it on August 29, 2002 (ibid., p.
228).

29. Ibid., p. 155. In terms of regime
change, "The final element of the strategy was
to 'demonstrate that the United States is prepared to play a sustained role in the
reconstruction of a post-Saddam Iraq with
contributions from and participation by the international community.'"

30. Copson (coord.), "Iraq War," p. 7. For
the speech see "President Discusses the Future of
Iraq," February 26, 2003, at www.whitehouse.
gov/news/releases/2003/02/20030226-11.html.

31. "President Bush Addresses the Nation," March 19, 2003; "President Discusses
Beginning of Operation Iraqi Freedom,"
March 22, 2003, at www.whitehouse.gov/
news/releases/2003/03/20030322.html.

32. Woodward, *Plan of Attack,* p. 10. See
also "President Bush Outlines Iraqi Threat,"
October 7, 2002, at www.whitehouse.gov/
news/releases/2002/10/20021007-8.html, where
Bush notes that "two administrations – mine
and President Clinton's – have stated that
regime change in Iraq is the only certain
means of removing a great danger to our nation." Cf. "Transcript: Confronting Iraq
Threat 'Is Crucial to Winning War on Terror'," *New York Times,* October 8, 2002, p.
A12.

33. Woodward, *Plan of Attack,* p. 150. On
whether Saddam should have been removed during the Persian Gulf War, see Mark Strauss, "Attacking Iraq," *Foreign Policy* 129 (March–April
2002), pp. 14–19, at www.keepmedia.com/
pubs/ForeignPolicy/2002/03/01/6313?ba=a&bi=1&
bp=97.

34. See United Nations resolution UNSCR
1483 of May 22, 2003 (daccess-ods.un.org/
TMP/2168214.html) as well as UNSCR 1511 of
October 16, 2003 (daccess-ods.un.org/
TMP/8918564.html), which establishes the
United States as the temporary occupying
power of Iraq.

35. Copson (coord.), "Iraq War," p. 6: "In

January 2003, the Administration revived as-
sertions that it had made periodically since the
September 11, 2001, attacks that the Baghdad
regime supported and had ties to the al-Qaeda
organization and other terrorist groups." On
Saddam Hussein and terrorist organizations,
see note 27 above. See L. Paul Bremer, III,
with Malcolm McDavere, *My Year in Iraq: The
Struggle to Build a Future of Hope* (New York:
Simon & Schuster, 2006), pp. 13, 87–104.

36. Woodward, *Plan of Attack,* p. 120. Cf.
Bob Woodward, "President Broadens Anti-
Hussein Order," *Washington Post,* June 16,
2002, p. A1, at www.library.cornell.edu/ colldev/
mideast/antihuss.htm. For the full interview, see
The White House, Office of the Press Secretary, "Interview of the President by Sir Trevor
Mcdonald of Britain's ITV Television Network," April 4, 2002, at www.usembassy.
it/file2002_04/alia/a2040709.htm.

37. George W. Bush, "Address to a Joint
Session of Congress and the American People," September 20, 2001, accessed via
www.whitehouse.gov/news/releases/2001/09/
20010920-8.html. As quoted in Chapter 10,
Bush said that "we will pursue nations that
provide aid or safe haven to terrorism. . . .
From this day forward, any nation that continues to harbor or support terrorism will be regarded by the United States as a hostile
regime."

38. "President Says Saddam Hussein Must
Leave Iraq."

39. For the administration's case, see Eric
Schmitt, "Rumsfeld Says U.S. Has 'Bullet-
proof' Evidence of Iraq's Links to Al Qaeda,"
New York Times, September 28, 2002, p. A9;
James Harding, "Rumsfeld Details Iraq's
Links to Al-Qaeda Network," *Financial
Times,* September 27, 2002, p. 1; Michael R.
Gordon, "Bush Says New Intelligence Data
Shows Baghdad Helps and Protects Terror-
ists," *New York Times,* January 29, 2003, p.
A1. For discussions of alleged connections be-
tween Iraq and al-Qaeda, see Richard A.
Clarke, *Against All Enemies: Inside America's
War on Terror* (New York: Free Press, 2004),
pp. 30–3; Jeffrey Goldberg, "The Unknown:
The CIA and the Pentagon Take Another
Look at Al Qaeda and Iraq," *New Yorker*
78.46 (February 10, 2003), pp. 40–7, at www.
newyorker.com/fact/content/articles/030210fa_fact.
The *9/11 Commission Report,* pp. 228–9, dismissed as unsupported the "allegation that

[9/11 terrorist Mohammed] Atta met with an Iraqi intelligence officer in Prague in April 2001." Ironically, as Jessica Stern reports in "How America Created a Terrorist Haven," *New York Times*, August 20, 2003, p. A21 (at www.ksg.harvard.edu/news/opeds/2003/stern_terrorism_nyt_082003.htm): "Even before the coalition troops invaded, a senior United States counterterrorism official told reporters that 'an American invasion of Iraq is already being used as a recruitment tool by Al Qaeda and other groups.'"

40. Copson (coord.), "Iraq War," p. 6: "In making its case for confronting Iraq, the Bush Administration characterized the regime of Saddam Hussein in Iraq as a grave potential threat to the United States and to peace and security in the Middle East." Also, Woodward, *Plan of Attack*, pp. 42, 56.

41. *Robb–Silberman Report*, p. 3.

42. Woodward, *Plan of Attack*, p. 13; Anthony H. Cordesman, *The Iraq War: Strategy, Tactics, and Military Lessons* (Westport, CT: Praeger, 2003), pp. 433–41.

43. As Woodward, *Plan of Attack*, p. 13, summarized: "The inspectors had helped to dismantle Iraq's chemical, biological, and surprisingly advanced nuclear programs, but suspicious accounting of destroyed munitions and elaborate concealment mechanisms left many unanswered questions." Ironically, as was revealed in 2005, "In the weeks after Baghdad fell . . . , looters systematically dismantled and removed . . . equipment capable of making parts for missiles as well as chemical, biological and nuclear arms . . . from 8 or 10 sites that were the heart of Iraq's dormant program on unconventional weapons. . . . [This] raises the possibility that the specialized machinery from the arms establishment that the war was aimed at neutralizing had made its way to the black market or was in the hands of foreign governments." James Glanz and William J. Broad, "Looting at Weapons Plants Was Systematic, Iraqi Says," *New York Times*, March 13, 2005, p. A1.

44. Neela Banerjee, "Stable Oil Prices Are Likely to Become a War Casualty, Experts Say," *New York Times*, October 2, 2002, p. A13.

45. Woodward, *Plan of Attack*, p. 99.

46. See Cordesman, *Iraq War: Strategy, Tactics*, pp. 544–50.

47. See "President Bush Addresses the Nation," March 19, 2003. Bush reaffirmed that

"we will accept no outcome but victory" in his March 22 radio address; "President Discusses Beginning of Operation Iraqi Freedom."

48. Woodward, *Plan of Attack*, p. 225, who noted that "The president, in particular, liked to have something that could be called a victory." Also, quoting Bush, p. 260: "Maybe one year from now we will be toasting victory and talking about the transition to freedom."

49. Harlan Ullman and James P. Wade, with L. A. "Bud" Edney, Fred M. Franks, Charles A. Horner, and Jonathan T. Howe, *Shock and Awe: Achieving Rapid Dominance* (Washington, DC: Institute for National Strategic Studies, National Defense University, 1996), pp. 19, 33: "In the Clausewitzian view, 'shock and awe' were necessary effects arising from application of military power and were aimed at destroying the will of an adversary to resist. . . . [T]he targets . . . include military, civilian, industrial, infrastructure, and societal components of a country or group." Online at www.dodccrp.org/publications/ pdf/ Ullman_Shock.pdf.

50. For a review of the planning, see T. Michael Moseley, Assessment and Analysis Division, "Operation Iraqi Freedom – By the Numbers" (Shaw AFB, SC: U.S. Central Air Forces, April 30, 2003), at www.globalsecurity.org/military/library/report/2003/uscentaf_oif_report_30apr2003.pdf; Thomas E. Ricks, "Timing, Tactics on Iraq War Disputed," *Washington Post*, August 1, 2002, p. A1; Thom Shanker, "Rumsfeld Favors Forceful Actions to Foil an Attack," *New York Times*, October 14, 2002, p. A1; Vernon Loeb, "Buildup Accelerates for Invasion of Iraq," *Washington Post*, January 6, 2003, p. A1; Tommy Franks, with Malcolm McConnell, *American Soldier* (New York: HarperCollins, 2004), pp. 321–536; International Institute for Strategic Studies, "Invading Iraq: U.S. Battle Plans Take Shape," *Strategic Comments* 8.10 (December 2002), pp. 1–2, accessed via www.iiss.org/stratcom (and at www.mafhoum.com/press4/131P1.pdf).

51. For an excellent review of the operational aspects of the war, see Cordesman, *Iraq War: Strategy, Tactics*, pp. 57–147, from which this discussion draws.

52. See ibid., p. 61; Woodward, *Plan of Attack*, pp. 383–99. See also the sources cited in note 26 above. Dora Farm was "a farm south of Baghdad that Saddam's wife used"; see "Woodward Shares War Secrets," *CBS News*,

April 18, 2004, www.cbsnews.com/stories/
2004/04/15/60minutes/main612067.shtml.

53. Cordesman, *Iraq War: Strategy, Tactics,*
p. 61, notes that several Iraqi missiles were
launched against coalition forces but were intercepted by Patriot missile defense forces.

54. Woodward, *Plan of Attack,* p. 330;
Cordesman, *Iraq War: Strategy, Tactics,* p. 59.

55. See "President Discusses Beginning of
Operation Iraqi Freedom." Bush noted, however, that "Iraqi officials have placed troops
and equipment in civilian areas, attempting to
use innocent men, women and children as
shields for the dictator's army."

56. Woodward, *Plan of Attack,* p. 158; the
other three were target significance, description and critical elements, and appropriate
weaponry. See also the "Background Briefing
on Targeting" of March 5, 2003, at www.
globalsecurity.org/wmd/library/news/iraq/2003/
iraq-030305-dod01.htm.

57. Williamson Murray and Robert H.
Scales Jr., *The Iraq War: A Military History*
(Cambridge, MA: Belknap, 2003), pp. 167–8.

58. Woodward, *Plan of Attack,* p. 401.

59 Franks, *American Soldier,* p. 440:
"Communications intercepts had revealed that
the Iraqis would not destroy the oil fields any
sooner than necessary, because they were earn-
ing about fifty million dollars a day from those
wells through the U.N.'s oil-for-food program. But I was also certain that Saddam
would order the sabotage when air operations
against regime leadership targets made it obvious that war had begun."

60. Murray and Scales, *Iraq War,* pp.
74–5.

61. Woodward, *Plan of Attack,* p. 54,
which also states: "Franks noted that in the
Afghanistan war he had tried to move away
from the classic military plan of an air campaign of massive bombing followed by ground
operations." According to Franks, *American
Soldier,* p. 337, the Central Command "would
apply the necessary lines of operation to attack
or influence what Clausewitz had described
more than one hundred years before as the enemy's 'centers of gravity' – the slices." The
purpose of these lines of operation was to
"create a critical mass that would reduce the
amount of conventional combat power that
would be needed" (Woodward, *Plan of Attack,* p. 54; and see p. 55). Franks described
the concept this way (*American Soldier,* pp.

395–6): "By applying military mass simultaneously at key points, rather than trying to push
a broad, slow conventional advance, we throw
the enemy off balance." The meanings of
"lines of operation" used by Jomini and
Franks are contrasted by Philipp Eder and Johann Fischer, "A Solution for the Confusing
Application of Lines of Operation," *Campaigning (JAWS)* (Spring 2006), pp. 50–
60, who note (p. 56): "Currently . . . the term
lines of operation has a double meaning and
is seen differently in the western world's mili-
taries. On one hand we apply lines of operation accordingly to Jomini focused on the factor space, on the other hand we use this term
as a part of his basic concept of operational design. This can be separated by introducing the
term 'operational alignment' to cover the factor space while defining lines of operation as
part of an operational design."

62. Woodward, *Plan of Attack,* p. 54. Cf.
Murray and Scales, *Iraq War,* p. 94: "Centcom's plan called for the main ground and air
offensive to commence simultaneously. The
plan presumed that an attack conducted in
many dimensions – air, land, and sea – and
timed to strike the Iraqis from many directions
would achieve system-overload in Iraqi military and political organizations in which everything flowed from the center." See also Greg
Jaffe, "War Plan Aims to Balance Roles of
Ground Forces, New Weapons," *Wall Street
Journal,* November 27, 2002.

63. See Cordesman, *Iraq War: Strategy,
Tactics,* p. 57, which provides an excellent description and analysis of the Iraq War.

64. One consequence of the fact that this
represents a new strategy for war is that the
discussion in this study of the military campaign in Operation Iraqi Freedom is organized
chronologically rather than in terms of the discrete land, air, and maritime components that
wasused in earlier chapters.

65. Murray and Scales, *Iraq War,* pp. 64,
89–90.

66. See ibid., pp. 129–53, for a discussion
of British operations in the southern region of
Iraq. Also Cordesman, *Iraq War: Strategy,
Tactics,* pp. 58–60.

67. Cordesman, *Iraq War: Strategy, Tactics,*
p. 62.

68. Cordesman (ibid., p. 64) offered four
explanations for the Iraqi people not rising in
support of the coalition: "(1) its failure to sup-

port the uprising in 1991, (2) its failure to conduct a meaningful public diplomacy campaign to explain that it was not responsible for the suffering of the Iraqi people under U.N. sanctions, (3) Iraqi and Arab hostility to the United States because of U.S. support for Israel and the Arab portrayal of the Second Intifada, and (4) the coalition's failure to convincingly rebut conspiracy theories that its goals were 'neo-imperialist' and focused on seizing Iraqi oil."

69. Murray and Scales, *Iraq War,* pp. 74–5. *Close air support* was defined in Chapter 9 as "air strikes on behalf of and directed by ground forces."

70. Franks, *American Soldier*, pp. 391, 510, on "rats leaving a ship" quote on prospects for regime collapse.

71. Murray and Scales, *Iraq War,* p. 75.

72. Cordesman, *Iraq War: Strategy, Tactics,* pp. 66–7.

73. Ibid., p. 143.

74. Murray and Scales, *Iraq War,* p. 72.

75. Cordesman, *Iraq War: Strategy, Tactics,* p. 67. Subsequent citations are given in the text.

76. Ibid., p. 77: "The resulting combination of air operations, direct land-based attack, and precision special operations created a synergy that was key to the coalition strategy."

77. These attacks "showed that the coalition could defeat Iraq's remaining forces, and they proved to the Iraqi defenders that the regime's claims about coalition defeats were false" (ibid., p. 94).

78. "In practice, however, no such mobilization [of a Popular Army] occurred. Cadres of regime loyalists did fight and presented a serious problem in terms of urban warfare in many cities in the south, but only as cadres – not as forces backed by large-scale popular support" (ibid., p. 96). Also see the detailed discussion in Richard H. Shultz Jr. and Andrea J. Dew, *Insurgents, Terrorists, and Militias: The Warriors of Contemporary Combat* (New York: Columbia University Press, 2006), chap. 7.

79. Murray and Scales, *Iraq War,* pp. 71–7.

80. Ibid., pp. 69–71.

81. See the sections on JSOTFs in "Isolation of the Regime," chap. 5 of Gregory Fontenot, E. J. Degen, and David Tohn, *On Point: The United States Army in Operation Iraqi Freedom* (Ft. Leavenworth, KS: Center for Army Lessons Learned, 2004), at www.

globalsecurity.org/military/library/report/2004/onpoint/ch-5.htm. For a U.S. view of Ansar al-Islam from shortly before the war, see Walter Pincus, "Alleged Al Qaeda Ties Questioned," February 7, 2003, p. A21, at www.washingtonpost.com/ac2/wp-dyn/A38235-2003Feb6.

82. Murray and Scales, *Iraq War,* p. 93–4: "Experience in Afghanistan convinced Franks that the presence of special operations forces would increase the combat effectiveness of his command enormously. Thus, unlike the Gulf War, where [General Norman] Schwarzkopf had refused to integrate special forces into the overall campaign plan, in the Iraq War Franks was delighted to involve special ops alongside his conventional forces." See also Franks, *American Soldier,* p. 260.

83. See International Institute for Strategic Studies, "The UN and Iraq: A 'Fork in the Road'?" *Strategic Comments* 9.7 (September 2003), pp. 1–2, accessed via www.iiss.org/stratcom (and also at www.mafhoum.com/press6/164P53.htm). See also Bremer, *My Year in Iraq,* pp. 61–9.

84. Cordesman, *Iraq War: Strategy, Tactics,* p. 141.

85. Ibid., p. 143; and see "Operation Iraqi Freedom (OIF) U.S. Casualty Status," updated daily at www.defenselink.mil/news/casualty.pdf.

86. Woodward, *Plan of Attack,* p. 155.

87. For criticisms that the Gulf War produced an incomplete victory, see Jeffrey Record, *Hollow Victory: A Contrary View of the Gulf War* (New York: Brassey's, 1993), pp. 155–60; Michael Sterner, "Closing the Gate: The Persian Gulf War Revisited," *Current History* 96.606 (January 1997), pp. 13–19; Melissa Healy, "Campaign 2000 – A Historical Perspective: 100 Hours in March 1991 Shaped Cheney's Place in History," *Los Angeles Times*, August 27, 2000, p. A3; Joe Klein, "Closework," *New Yorker* 77.29 (October 1, 2001), pp. 44–9, at p. 46, online at faculty.virginia.edu/usdiphis/readings/Klein,%20Closework.pdf. See also the sources in Chapter 8, note 120.

88. See Lawrence F. Kaplan, "Phase Two: Why the Bush Administration Will Go After Iraq," *New Republic* 4534 (December 10, 2001), pp. 21–3; "Thom Shanker and David E. Sanger, "U.S. Envisions Blueprint on Iraq Including Big Invasion Next Year," *New York Times*, April 28, 2002, p. A1; Woodward,

Plan of Attack, pp. 9–51, on the debate in Bush administration about dealing with Iraq once and for all.

89. See Toby Dodge, *Iraq's Future: The Aftermath of Regime Change* (Adelphi Paper no. 372, London: International Institute for Strategic Studies, 2005), pp. 25–42.

90. See Diamond, "What Went Wrong in Iraq," pp. 37–42; Dodge, *Iraq's Future,* pp. 9–24. CIA veteran Milt Bearden, in "Iraqi Insurgents Take a Page from the Afghan 'Freedom Fighters'," *New York Times,* November 9, 2003,p. D7, noted that "the Iraqi resistance has taken a page from a sophisticated insurgency playbook in their confrontations with the American-led coalition. The insurgents' strategy could have been crafted by Sun Tzu, . . . [who wrote] that the highest realization of warfare is to attack the enemy's strategy." For recent looks at the insurgency, see "Iraqi Insurgency Groups," at www.globalsecurity.org/military/ops/iraq_insurgency.htm; *The Insurgency,* prod. and dir. Tom Roberts, *Frontline,* aired Feb. 21, 2006, at www.pbs. org/wgbh/pages/frontline/insurgency/; Jonathan Finer, "Iraq's Insurgents: Who's Who," *Washington Post,* March 19, 2006, p. B3, at www.washington-post.com/wp-dyn/content/article/2006/03/17/AR2006031702087_pf.html. See also Bremer, *My Year in Iraq,* pp. 178–209.

91. See Patrick E. Tyler and Amy Waldman, "G.I. Is Killed in Grenade Attack on Convoy; Another Blast Starts Fire on Oil Pipeline," *New York Times,* June 23, 2003, p. A12; James Glanz and Tom Shanker, "Reports in Iraq Show Attacks in Most Areas," *New York Times,* September 29, 2004, p. A1. See also Douglas Jehl and David E. Sanger, "Prewar Assessment on Iraq Saw Chance of Strong Divisions," *New York Times,* September 28, 2004, pp. A1, A11: "The [intelligence] assessments predicted that an American-led invasion of Iraq would increase support for political Islam and would result in a deeply divided Iraq society prone to violent internal conflict." For a recent analysis of the insurgency, see Anthony H. Cordesman, "Iraq's Evolving Insurgency: The Nature of Attacks and Patterns and Cycles in the Conflict" (Washington, DC: CSIS Press, Working Draft, revised: February 3, 2006), at www.csis.org/media/csis/ pubs/060203_iraqicombattrends.pdf: "[Multi-National Force–Iraq] intelligence estimates that the

number of insurgent attacks on coalition forces, Iraqi forces, and Iraqi civilians; and acts of sabotage; rose by 29% in 2005. The total rose from 26,496 in 2004 to 34,131 in 2005. These attacks have had a relatively consistent average success rate of 24% (attacks that cause damage or casualties)" (p. ii).

92. In anticipation of the January elections, see International Institute for Strategic Studies, "Elections in Iraq: A Crucial Test," *Strategic Comments* 10.9 (November 2004), pp. 1–2, accessed via www.iiss.org/stratcom; David E. Sanger and Richard W. Stevenson, "Bush Casts Iraqi Vote as Step in Global March to Freedom," *New York Times,* January 27, 2005, p. A1; Bakhtiar Dargali, "The Long Road to a Vote," *New York Times,* January 29, 2005, p. A19. For the election itself, see Dexter Filkins, "Iraqis Vote Amid Tight Security and Scattered Attacks," *New York Times,* January 30, 2005, p. A1; Dexter Filkins, with John F. Burns, James Glanz, Edward Wong, and Christine Hauser, "Defying Threats, Millions of Iraqis Flock to Polls," *New York Times,* January 31, 2005, p. A1; John F. Burns and James Glanz (with Edward Wong), "The Outcome: Iraqi Shiites Win, but Margin Is Less than Projection," *New York Times,* February 14, 2005, p. A1.

93. Edward Wong, "Turnout in the Iraqi Election Is Reported at 70 Percent," *New York Times,* December 22, 2005, p. A10. For the December elections generally, see Dexter Filins, "Will It Be Different Now?" *New York Times,* December 18, 2005, p. D1; Filkins, "Iraqis Urging Unity, but Rifts May Be Too Deep," *New York Times,* January 22, 2006, p. A4.

94. See Diamond, "What Went Wrong in Iraq."

95. See., e.g., the earlier cited NSPD "Iraq: Goals, Objectives and Strategy," which planned to "assist [the Iraqi people] in creating a society based on moderation, pluralism and democracy." Woodward, *Plan of Attack,* pp. 154–5.

96. For an analysis of postwar planning failures, see Diamond, "What Went Wrong in Iraq"; Shultz and Dew, *Insurgents, Terrorists, and Militias,* chap. 7. Also, Nadia Schadlow, "War and the Art of Governance," *Parameters* 33.3 (Autumn 2003), pp. 85–93, which discusses "the apparent failure of the United

States to plan adequately for the restoration of political and economic order once major combat operations had ended [which stems from the reluctance] of civilian and military leaders . . . to consider the establishment of political and economic order as *a part of war itself*" (emphasis in original); at www.carlisle.army.mil/usawc/Parameters/03autumn/schadlow.pdf.

97. See Cordesman, "Iraq's Evolving Insurgency," p. 1: "[T]he US failed to come to grips with the Iraqi insurgency during the first year of US occupation in virtually every important dimension. It was slow to react to the growth of the insurgency in Iraq, to admit it was largely domestic in character, and to admit it had significant popular support. . . . For all of 2003, and most of the first half of 2004, senior US officials and officers . . . kept referring to the attackers as 'terrorists,' kept issuing estimates that they could not number more than 5,000, and claimed they were a mixture of outside elements and diehard former regime loyalists . . . that had little popular support."

98. See *Foreign Policy* and Carnegie Endowment for International Peace, "From Victory to Success: Afterwar Policy in Iraq," special report in *Foreign Policy* 137 (July–August 2003), pp. 49–72; at www.foreignpolicy.com/issue_julaug_2003/afterwar.pdf.

99. For data on casualties, see "War in Iraq – Forces: U.S. & Coalition/Casualties," *CNN*, at www.cnn.com/SPECIALS/2003/iraq/forces/casualties/. See also note 85.

100. Regarding National Intelligence Estimates, see *Robb–Silberman Report*, pp. 8–11. Also, Woodward, *Plan of Attack*, pp. 194–9.

101. See Kathleen T. Rehm, "U.S. Not Interested in Iraqi Oil, Rumsfeld Tells Arab World," *American Forces Press Service*, February 26, 2003, for Rumsfeld's rejection as "utter nonsense" that the United States is seeking to acquire Iraqi oil; at www.defenselink.mil/news/Feb2003/n02262003_200302267.html. See also Woodward, *Plan of Attack,* pp. 322–4. For a contrary view, see Neil Mackay, "Official: US Oil at the Heart of Iraq Crisis," *Sunday Herald* (Glasgow), October 6, 2002, at www.sundayherald.com/ 28285. On Iraq's oil and the U.N. Oil for Food program, see "Iraq's Oil," *Online NewsHour,* April 24, 2003, at www.pbs.org/newshour/bb/middle_east/iraq/oil_4-24-03.html.

102. See International Institute for Strategic Studies, "Iraq's Role in Oil Markets: A Complicating Factor," *Strategic Comments* 9.7 (September 2003), pp. 1–2, accessed via www.iiss.org/stratcom (and at www.menavista.com/Iraq_oil_market.pdf); Vijay V. Vaitheeswaran, "Pipe Dreams in Iraq," *Foreign Policy* 138 (September–October 2003), pp. 70–1; Neela Banerjee, "A Revival for Iraq's Oil Industry, as Output Nears Prewar Levels," *New York Times,* March 1, 2004, p. A1: "[T]he country is producing 2.3 million to 2.5 million barrels a day, compared with 2.8 million barrels a day before the war." See also Bremer, *My Year in Iraq,* pp. 109–12.

103. For a discussion of technological advances in the war, see International Institute for Strategic Studies, "Winning a War in Iraq: The Application of Technology," *Strategic Comments* 9.2 (March 2003), pp. 1–2, accessed via www.iiss.org/stratcom; Murray and Scales, *Iraq War,* pp. 156–7.

104. Murray and Scales, *Iraq War,* pp. 160–1.

105. Ibid., p. 172, regarding "the inherent difficulty in assessing fully the extent of the contribution that air power made to the Coalition's victory."

106. For a recent cost–benefit analysis see Linda Bilmes and Joseph E. Stiglitz, "The Economic Costs of the Iraq War," paper prepared for the Allied Social Science Associations meetings, Boston, January 2006, at www2.gsb.columbia.edu/faculty/jstiglitz/cost_of_war_in_iraq.pdf. See also Louis Uchitelle, "When Talk of Guns and Butter Includes Lives Lost," January 15, 2006, p. C3.

107. Woodward, *Plan of Attack,* p. 162. Subsequent citations are given in the text.

108. For Cheney and Libby (ibid., p. 402), "World War I . . . had been settled with an armistice and some Germans felt they had not been beaten. In this war, it was crucial they make certain there would be no ambiguity about victory."

109. "President Discusses 2006 Agenda," February 1, 2006, at whitehouse.gov/news/releases/2006/02/20060201-5.html.

110. Ibid.

111. "President Bush Addresses the Nation," March 19, 2003. He also noted that "the only way to limit its duration is to apply decisive force."

112. "In Bush's Words: 'We Will Do What Is Necessary' in the Fight against Terror," *New York Times,* September 8, 2003, p. A10. For the full speech, see "President Addresses the Nation," September 7, 2003, at www.whitehouse.gov/news/releases/2003/09/20030907-1.html.

113. Woodward, *Plan of Attack,* pp. 154–5.

114. Ibid., p. 412.

115. Ibid., p. 413.

116. This exit strategy is discussed in Eric Schmitt, "Top Pentagon Aide Who Bore Much of the Blame for Contentious Policies Is Stepping Down," *New York Times,* January 27, 2005, p. A13. See also Bremer, *My Year in Iraq,* pp. 105–6, 269–70.

117. See Todd S. Purdum, "After 12 Years, Sweet Victory: The Bushes' Pursuit of Hussein," *New York Times,* December 16, 2003, p. A1; and see John F. Burns, "Surprise. Hussein Acts as if He's on Trial," *New York Times,* May 21, 2006, p. D3, who wrote: "[T]he chief judge . . . confirmed that Mr. Hussein and the other seven defendants would face formal charges of crimes against humanity for their role in a 'widespread and systematic attack' on the people of Dujail, a mainly Shiite town, . . . As for holding the trial during an insurgency, the death toll tells its own story: a drumbeat of unsolved assassinations has killed five tribunal employees, including a judge, as well as two defense lawyers."

118. This is, of course, still a highly tendentious issue. See, e.g., Stern, "How America Created a Terrorist Haven." For the argument that the timing of the war was optional, see Clarke, *Against All Enemies,* pp. 247–87.

119. See Elizabeth Bumiller, "White House Cuts Estimate of Cost of War with Iraq," *New York Times,* December 31, 2002, p. A1; International Institute for Strategic Studies, "Challenges for the Defence Industry," *Strategic Comments* 9.4 (June 2003), pp. 1–2, and "Paying for Iraq and the War on Terror," *Strategic Comments* 9.7 (September 2003), pp. 1–2, both accessed via www.iiss.org/stratcom. More recent estimates are much higher: "The Congressional Budget Office has now estimated that in their central, mid-range scenario, the Iraq war will cost over $266 billion more in the next decade, putting the direct costs of the war in the range of $500 billion. . . . We estimate that the total costs of the Iraq war is in the range of $750 billion to $1.2 trillion, assuming that the US begins to withdraw troops in 2006 and maintains a diminishing presence in Iraq for the next five years." Bilmes and Stiglitz, "Economic Costs of the Iraq War," pp. 2, 5.

120. Although claiming reliable numbers were hard to come by, "US Forces Order of Battle – 28 April [2003]," at www.globalsecurity.org/military/ops/iraq_orbat_030428.htm, noted: "Excluding forces deployed in direct support of Operation Enduring Freedom, there are probably about 219,000 military personnel in the CENTCOM area of responsibility."

121. See Pew Research Center poll, "Do you think the U.S. made the right decision . . . in using military force against Iraq?" accessed via www.pollingreport.com/iraq.htm.

122. See ibid.; cf. ABC News–*Washington Post* poll, "[D]o you think the war with Iraq was worth fighting, or not?" at the same Web site. A third poll at that site, by CBS News–*New York Times,* "[D]o you think the United States did the right thing in taking military action against Iraq. . . ?" shows a majority in favor through March 2004. See also "Iraq Support Steady in Face of Higher Casualties; Most Say Al Qaeda Is Weaker than Before 9/11," Pew Research Center Survey Report, September 17, 2004, at people-press.org/reports/display.php3?ReportID=225.

123. See Pew and ABC News–*Washington Post* polls. The CBS News–*New York Times* poll shows a clear majority against as of January 2005. A recent CNN poll at the same site (conducted by Opinion Research Corp., May 5–7, 2006) show 58 percent now "disapprove of the United States' decision to go to war with Iraq in March 2003."

124. Woodward, *Plan of Attack,* p. 155; Cordesman, *Iraq War: Strategy, Tactics,* pp. 127–8; Kenneth M. Pollack, "After Saddam: Assessing the Reconstruction of Iraq" (Washington, DC: Brookings Institution, Saban Center for Middle East Policy, January 7, 2004), *Foreign Affairs* 83.1 (January–February 2004), at www.brookings.edu/views/papers/pollack/20040107.pdf.

125. Ibid., pp. 61–2: "For Iraq, Franks said, the assumptions were: . . . 8. The Department of State would promote creation of a broad-based, credible provisional government as had been done in Afghanistan through the Bonn Conference earlier in the month."

126. It is Feith who is featured in the previously cited Schmitt, "Top Pentagon Aide."

127. Woodward, *Plan of Attack,* p. 328. Once again, subsequent citations are given in the text.

128. Interestingly, Franks noted (ibid., p. 62) that "The military did not do nation building very well."

129. Ibid., p. 339, quoted Frank Miller of the NSC: "A successful establishment of rule of law in the immediate post-conflict environment is critical to ensuring stability, allowing for relief and reconstruction, and rapidly rebuilding Iraqi society." See also Bremer, *My Year in Iraq,* pp. 87–103.

130. See Jon Lee Anderson, "Out on the Street," *New Yorker* 80.35 (November 15, 2004), pp. 72–9, at p. 76; and Shultz and Dew, *Insurgents, Terrorists, and Militias,* chap. 7.

131. For the political system, see Max Boot, "Think Again: Neocons," *Foreign Policy* 83.1 (January–February 2004), pp. 20–8; Warren Hoge, "U.N. Chief Says Iraq Elections Could Be Held Within a Year," *New York Times,* February 24, 2004, p. A6; Dexter Filkins, "Iraqis Receive U.S. Approval of Constitution," *New York Times,* March 2, 2004, p. A1. For the economy, see Bremer, *My Year in Iraq,* pp. 77, 116; Neil King Jr., "Bush Officials Draft Broad Plan for Free-Market Economy in Iraq," *Wall Street Journal,* May 1, 2003, p. A1. Also, James Dao and Eric Schmitt, "Rift over Plan to Impose Rule on Iraq," *New York Times,* October 10, 2002, p. A16; David E. Sanger and Eric Schmitt, "U.S. Has a Plan to Occupy Iraq, Officials Report," *New York Times,* October 11, 2002, pp. A1, A14, at p. A1: The occupation plan "would put an American officer in charge of Iraq for a year or more while the United States and its allies searched for weapons and maintained Iraq's oil fields." Also, David E. Sanger and James Dao, "U.S. Is Completing Plan to Promote a Democratic Iraq," *New York Times,* January 6, 2003, p. A1: "The proposals . . . would amount to the most ambitious American effort to administer a country since the occupations of Japan and Germany at the end of World War II." James Fallows, "The Fifty-first State?" *Atlantic Monthly* 290.4 (November 2002), pp. 53–64, at www.theatlantic.com/doc/200211/fallows.htm.

132. For discussions about the problems of limiting collateral damage, see, e.g., Woodward, *Plan of Attack,* pp. 148, 158–9.

133. See "The Office of Reconstruction and Humanitarian Assistance (ORHA), Statement by Douglas J. Feith, Undersecretary of Defense for Policy, Senate Committee on Foreign Relations, February 11, 2003," at www.sourcewatch.org/index.php?title=Office_of_Reconstruction_and_Humanitarian_Assistance.

134. See "The Price of Building a New Iraq," *New York Times,* September 25, 2003, p. A10; Jeff Gerth, "Report Urges Iraqis to Steer Reconstruction after Hussein," *New York Times,* December 18, 2002, p. A15; Jonathan Finer, "Head of Iraq Reconstruction Says Unexpected Security Costs Eating into Budget," *Washington Post,* May 22, 2005, p. A28. On this effect of corruption on the budget, see, e.g., James Glanz, "Army to Pay Halliburton Unit Most Costs Disputed by Audit," *New York Times,* February 27, 2006, p. A1.

135. See Ellen Knickmeyer, "U.S. Has End in Sight on Iraq Rebuilding," *Washington Post,* January 2, 2006, p. 1: "Since the reconstruction effort began in 2003, midcourse changes by U.S. officials have shifted at least $2.5 billion from the rebuilding of Iraq's decrepit electrical, education, water, sewage, sanitation and oil networks to build new security forces for Iraq and to construct a nationwide system of medium- and maximum-security prisons and detention centers that meet international standards. . . . Many of the changes were forced by an insurgency more fierce than the United States had expected when its troops entered Iraq." Online at www.washingtonpost.com/wp-dyn/content/article/2006/01/02/AR2006010200370.html.

136. As of this writing, violence is on the risea mong Shiite political militias in Basra; see, e.g, Sabrina Tavernis and Qais Mizher, "Iraq's Premier Seeks to Control a City in Chaos," *New York Times,* June 1, 2006, p. A1.

137. See, e.g., Richard A. Oppel Jr. and Mona Mahmoud, "Iraqis' Accounts Link Marines to the Mass Killing of Civilians," *New York Times,* May 29, 2006, p. A1; John F. Burns, "U.S. Troops Kill 2 Women, and Iraqi Death Toll Grow," *New York Times,* June 1, 2006, p. A14.

138. See, e.g., David E. Sanger and Eric Schmitt, "Hot Topic: How U.S. Might Disengage in Iraq," *New York Times,* January 10,

2005, p. A1; "U.S. Is Sending Reserve Troops to Iraq's West," *New York Times,* May 30, 2006, p. A1.

139. See, e.g., Richard A. Oppel Jr., "More Than 40 Are Killed in Iraqi Insurgent Attacks," *New York Times,* May 30, 2006, p. A12. A Congressional Research Service report, discussing the range of figures cited by various sources using different methodologies, notes that "The Department of Defense has not released an estimate of Iraqi civilian deaths during OIF." Hanna Fischer, "Iraqi Civilian, Police, and Security Forces Casualty Estimates," CRS Report for Congress, May 8, 2006, p. 2, at www.fas.org/sgp/crs/mideast/RS22441. pdf. One source for ongoing updates is iCasualties: OIF Iraqi Death, at icasualties.org/oif/ IraqiDeaths.aspx, which draws on accounts in the media; but civilian deaths recorded here are not all attributed to insurgents. See also "Iraq Death Toll in Third Year of Occupation Is Highest Yet," Iraq Body Count Press Release 13, 9th March 2006, at ww.iraqbodycount. org/press/pr13.php, which lists "20 [civilian deaths] per day in Year, 31 per day in Year 2, and 36 per day in Year 3" – this last based on incomplete data and thus projected as 40.

140. See Diamond, "What Went Wrong in Iraq."

141. See International Institute for Strategic Studies, "Insurgency in Iraq: Deteriorating Security," *Strategic Comments* 9.8 (October 2003), pp. 1–2, accessed via www.iiss.org/ stratcom.

142. See Anderson, "Out on the Street," p. 76: "On May 16, 2003, Bremer issued a sweeping ban of the Baath Party: all senior members were barred from public life; lower-level members were also barred, but some could appeal. . . . A week later, he disbanded the Iraqi Army." On rectifying the excesses of de-Baathification in the name of stability, see Fareed Zakaria, "Exploit Rifts in the Insurgency," *Newsweek* 146.16 (October 17, 2005), pp. 44.

143. See Robert F. Worth, "Shiite–Kurd Bloc Falls Just Short in Iraqi Election," *New York Times,* January 21, 2006, p. A1: "Along with the results, election officials released statistics showing that voter turnout among Sunni Arabs, who largely boycotted the January elections, was even higher in December than previously disclosed. In Salahuddin Province, which is mostly Sunni, turnout was 96 percent, the highest in the country. Anbar

Province, which is overwhelmingly Sunni, had an 86 percent turnout."

144. International Institute for Strategic Studies, "Transnational Terrorism after the Iraq War: Net Effect," *Strategic Comments* 9.4 (June 2003), pp. 1–2, accessed via www.iiss.org/stratcom; Stern, "How America Created a Terrorist Haven."

145. See Daniel L. Byman, "Building the New Iraq: The Role of Intervening Forces," *Survival* 45.2 (Summer 2003), pp. 57–71; at www.brookings.edu/views/articles/fellows/ byman20030601.htm.

12. Military Power and Victory

1. See Russell F. Weigley, *The American Way of War: A History of United States Military Strategy and Policy* (New York: Macmillan, 1973), pp. 3–53, for the section on "Waging War with Limited Resources, 1775–1815." Lee Kennett, *A History of Strategic Bombing* (New York: Charles Scribner's Sons, 1982), pp. 180–1, observes that "A strategic bombing fleet of any size was a rich nation's weapon, and that nation had to be rich not only in money but in men and technology as well." He notes that "Only the Americans could afford to offer themselves a bomber like the B-29, which cost over $800,000 . . . and gulped six thousand gallons of aviation gasoline on a single mission. And only the Americans could build them by the thousands and maintain them in style. In the summer of 1944, XX Bomber Command had fifty B-29s operational – and twenty thousand men working to keep them that way." Also see Max Boot, "The New American Way of War," *Foreign Affairs* 82.4 (July–August 2003), pp. 41–58; online at www.foreignaffairs.org/ 20030701faessay15404/max-boot/the-new- american-way-of-war.html.

2. See *The United States Strategic Bombing Survey [USSBS], Summary Report, Pacific War,* July 1, 1946 (Washington, DC: U.S. GPO; rpt., Maxwell AFB, AL: Air University Press, 1987), p. 52; downloadable, together with the *Summary Report, European War,* September 30, 1945, at aupress.au.af.mil/ Books/USSBS/USSBS.pdf.

3. Alain C. Enthoven and Wayne K. Smith, *How Much Is Enough? Shaping the Defense Program, 1961–1969* (New York: Harper & Row, 1971).

4. The notion that different forms of mil-

itary power have unique capabilities was discussed by B. H. Liddell Hart. See Brian Bond, *Liddell Hart: A Study of His Military Thought* (New Brunswick, NJ: Rutgers University Press, 1977), p. 40: "Just as land power and sea power have their peculiar powers and also their inherent limitations, so air power has its necessary limitations."

5. See Martin Blumenson, "A Deaf Ear to Clausewitz: Allied Operational Objectives in World War II," *Parameters* 23.2 (Summer 1993), pp. 16–27, at p. 16: "According to Clausewitz and common sense, an army in wartime succeeds by defeating the enemy army. Destroying the ability of the opponent's uniformed forces to function effectively eliminates what stands in the way of military victory." As noted by Philip S. Meilinger, "Ten Propositions Regarding Air Power" (Working Paper no. 36, Fairbairn, Australia: RAAF Air Power Studies Centre, September 1995), p. 3: "Armies become tactical instruments that ground away at the enemy army, hoping that an accumulation of battlefield victories would position them for decisive, strategic operations." Online as "Ten Propositions. Emerging Airpower," *Airpower Journal* 10 (Spring 1996), pp. 1–18, at www.airpower.airuniv.edu/airchronicles/apj/apj96/spr96/meil.pdf.

6. For background on the role of ground forces in strategy, see Russell F. Weigley, *History of the United States Army* (New York: Macmillan, 1967); Richard K. Betts, "Conventional Strategy: New Critics, Old Choices," *International Security* 7.4 (Spring 1983), pp. 140–62; Joshua M. Epstein, "The 3:1 Rule, the Adaptive Dynamic Model, and the Future of Security Studies," *International Security* 13.4 (Spring 1989), pp. 90–127; John W. R. Lepingwell, "The Laws of Combat? Lanchester Reexamined," *International Security* 12.1 (Summer 1987), pp. 89–134; John J. Mearsheimer, "Assessing the Conventional Balance: The 3:1 Rule and Its Critics," *International Security* 13.4 (Spring 1989), pp. 54–89. For discussions of changes in ground forces, see Frederick Kagan, "Army Doctrine and Modern War: Notes toward a New Edition of FM 100-5," *Parameters* 27.1 (Spring 1997), pp. 134–51, at p. 135 (online at www.carlisle.army.mil/usawc/Parameters/97spring/kagan.htm) for the argument that the function of war at the operational level is to "achieve strategic victory." David Jablonsky, "Army Transforma-

tion: A Tale of Two Doctrines," *Parameters* 31.3 (Autumn 2001), pp. 43–62 (at www.carlisle.army.mil/usawc/Parameters/01autumn/Jablonsk.htm); Kip P. Nygren, "Emerging Technologies and Exponential Change: Implications for Army Transformation," *Parameters* 32.2 (Summer 2002), pp. 86–99 (at www.carlisle.army.mil/usawc/Parameters/02summer/nygren.htm); Peter A. Wilson, John Gordon IV, and David E. Johnson, "An Alternative Future Force: Building a Better Army," *Parameters* 33.4 (Winter 2003–4), pp. 19–39 (at www.carlisle.army.mil/usawc/Parameters/03winter/wilson.htm).

7. "The Army Vision recognizes explicitly that in future operations, Army forces will perform missions as part of a larger joint-combined-multinational force." See Thomas S. Szayna, Frances M. Lussier, Krista Magras, Olga Oliker, Michele Zanini, and Robert Howe, *Improving Army Planning for Future Multinational Coalition Operations* (Santa Monica, CA: RAND Corporation, MR-1291-A, 2001), p. xi; at www.rand.org/pubs/monograph_reports/MR1291/.

8. See Brian Caven, *The Punic Wars* (New York: St. Martin's Press, 1980).

9. See Lynn E. Davis and Jeremy Shapiro, "Introduction," in Davis and Shapiro, eds., *The U.S. Army and the New National Security Strategy* (Santa Monica, CA: RAND Corporation, MR-1657-A, 2003), pp. 1–5, at p. 1, at www.rand.org/pubs/monograph_reports/MR1657/. They argue that the "primary role of the U.S. Army is, and will remain, to achieve dominance on the ground and thereby contribute to deterring the use and even creation of large-scale land forces on the part of adversaries."

10. Ibid.

11. See Misha Glenny, *The Fall of Yugoslavia* (New York: Penguin Books, 1996).

12. See Richard Holbrooke, *To End a War: From Sarajevo to Dayton – and Beyond* (New York: Random House, 1998); Marta Dassu and Nicholas Whyte, "America's Balkan Disengagement?" *Survival* 43.4 (Winter 2001), pp. 123–36.

13. Meilinger, "Ten Propositions," p. 12, argued that "Surface warfare is largely a linear affair defined by terrain and figures on a map." Accordingly, "ground forces still have a primarily tactical focus and tend to be concerned

primarily with an enemy or obstacles to their immediate front."

14. For Meilinger (ibid., p. 9), "the army can be used for such things as occupation and administrative duties. But that is not its main purpose; in any event, police or other paramilitary forces can effectively conduct such tasks."

15. Walter Perry, Bruce Pirnie, and John Gordon IV, *The Future of Warfare: Issues from the 1999 "Army After Next" Study Cycle* (Santa Monica, CA: RAND Corporation, MR-1183-A, 2001), pp. xiii–xx; at www.rand.org/pubs/monograph_reports/MR1183/. This report used terminology from the *Army After Next* study (see note 36 below) to define the challenges that ground forces must be able to manage in the future, including "strategic preclusion," dealing with nuclear armed opponents, the exploitation of space, sea control, air superiority, sustainment, urban terrain, refugees during conflicts, air mobility, survivability, training soldiers, and "hybrid" forces (which refer to combinations of "air, naval, and coalition ground forces").

16. See International Institute for Strategic Studies, *The Military Balance, 2003–2004* (Oxford: Oxford University Press, 2003), pp. 14, 173–4.

17. See "Adding It Up: The Price of Rebuilding a New Iraq," *New York Times*, September 9, 2003, p. A10. The rebuilding of Iraq is being dominated by private-sector firms, and involves significant efforts to reestablish public safety, notably the police, border enforcement, and the protection of facilities as well as rebuilding the judicial system. It also includes the establishment and training of a new Iraqi Army and a civil defense corps.

18. "Endurance" here is used in a looser sense than that of the *Department of Defense Dictionary of Military and Associated Terms, Joint Publication 1-02* (Washington, DC: U.S. GPO, as amended November 30, 2004), p. 182, which defines it as the "time an aircraft can continue flying, or a ground vehicle or ship can continue operating, under specified conditions, e.g., without refueling."

19. Compare Napoléon's disastrous invasion of Russia in 1812 with the need for logistics in war; he "found conditions with which he was unfamiliar – a vast country with few good roads and without supplies." See [Bernard Law Montgomery,] Viscount

Montgomery of Alamein, *A History of Warfare* (New York: William Morrow, 1983), p. 365.

20. See International Institute for Strategic Studies, "The U.S. Army: Stretched Too Thin?" *Strategic Comments* 9.9 (November 2003), pp. 1–2, accessed via www.iiss.org/stratcom: "Ideally, it takes five units or individuals to keep one overseas indefinitely, while simultaneously ensuring adequate training and readiness to meet other contingencies."

21. David E. Sanger and Thom Shanker, "As Calls for an Iraq Pullout Rise, 2 Political Calendars Loom Large," *New York Times*, November 28, 2005, p. A1.

22. For a discussion of the revolution in military affairs, see Andrew F. Krepinevich Jr., "Cavalry to Computer," *National Interest* 37 (Fall 1994), pp. 30–42, at www.findarticles.com/p/articles/mi_m2751/is_n37/ai_16315042; Andrew Bacevich, "Preserving the Well-Bred Horse," *National Interest* 37 (Fall 1994), pp. 43–9, at www.findarticles.com/p/articles/mi_m2751/is_n37/ai_16315044; Joseph S. Nye Jr. and William A. Owens, "America's Information Edge," and Eliot A. Cohen, "A Revolution in Warfare," both in *Foreign Affairs* 75.2 (March–April 1996), pp. 20–36 and 37–54, respectively; Richard J. Harknett and the JCISS Study Group, "The Risks of a Networked Military," *Orbis* 44.1 (Winter 2000), pp. 127–43. For a discussion of the RMA in the context of the Gulf War, see these four essays in *International Security* 22.2 (Fall 1997): Daryl G. Press, "Lessons from Ground Combat in the Gulf: The Impact of Training and Technology," pp. 137–46; Thomas A. Keaney, "The Linkage of Air and Ground Power in the Future of Warfare," pp. 147–50; Thomas G. Mahnken and Barry D. Watts, "What the Gulf War Can (and Cannot) Tell Us about the Future of Warfare," pp. 151–62; Stephen Biddle, "The Gulf War Debate *Redux:* Why Skill *and* Technology Are the Right Answer," pp. 163–74.

23. William C. Martel (ed.), *The Technological Arsenal: Emerging Defense Capabilities* (Washington, DC: Smithsonian Institution Press, 2001); Michael O'Hanlon, "Modernizing and Transforming U.S. Forces: Alternative Paths to the Force of Tomorrow," in Michele A. Flournoy (ed.), *QDR 2001: Strategy-Driven Choices for America's Security* (Washington, DC: National Defense University Press,

2001), pp. 293–318, at www.ndu.edu/inss/press/QDR_2001/sdcascont.html.

24. Ann M. Florini, "The Opening Skies: Third-Party Imaging Satellites and U.S. Security," *International Security* 13.2 (Fall 1988), pp. 91–123; Vipin Gupta, "New Satellite Images for Sale," and Irving Lachow, "The GPS Dilemma: Balancing Military Risks and Economic Benefits," both from *International Security* 20.1 (Summer 1995), pp. 94–125 and 126–48, respectively.

25. See United States Army, *Field Manual 100-5: Operations* (Washington, DC: Department of the Army, 1993), p. 28; at www.fprado.com/armorsite/US-Field-Manuals/FM-100-5-Operations.pdf.

26. See, e.g., Richard Holbrooke, "Bold Stroke in Bosnia," *New York Times*, July 11, 1997, p. A21, who, in arguing that "Those who most wish to withdraw our troops next year must understand that . . . the troops must be used more vigorously in the time remaining before this arbitrary deadline," identified the "paradox of the current situation."

27. On the U.S. intervention in Somalia – which, like that in Bosnia, began late in the administration of George H. W. Bush – see Walter Clarke and Jeffrey Herbst, "Somalia and the Future of Humanitarian Intervention," *Foreign Affairs* 75.2 (March–April 1996), pp. 70–85; Chester A Crocker, "The Lessons of Somalia: Not Everything Went Wrong," *Foreign Affairs* 74.3 (May–June 1995), pp. 2–8; John R. Bolton, "Wrong Turn in Somalia," *Foreign Affairs* 73.1 (January–February 1994), pp. 56–66.

28. For criticism by the Bush administration on using the military for nation building, see Condoleezza Rice, "Foundation for a Nation," *Washington Post*, October 29, 2001, p. A17. For a historical look at the United States and nation building, see James Dobbins, John G. McGinn, Keith Crane, Seth G. Jones, Rollie Lal, Andrew Rathmell, Rachel M. Swanger, and Anga Timilsina, *America's Role in Nation-Building: From Germany to Iraq* (Santa Monica, CA: RAND Corporation, MR-1753-RC, 2003), at www.rand.org/pubs/monograph_reports/MR1753/.

29. See Steven R. Weisman, "The Shape of a Future Iraq: U.S. Entangled in Disputes," *New York Times*, January 9, 2004, p. A1; Andrew F. Krepinevich Jr., "How to Win in Iraq," *Foreign Affairs* 84.5 (September–October

ber 2005), pp. 87–104, at www.cfr.org/publication/8847/how_to_win_in_iraq.html; Adeed Dawisha and Karen Dawisha, "How to Build a Democratic Iraq," *Foreign Affairs* 82.3 (May–June 2003), pp. 36–50, at www.foreignaffairs.org/20030501faessay11218/adeed-i-dawisha-karen-dawisha/how-to-build-a-democratic-iraq.html.

30. Apparently, the term was introduced in the context of Somalia, well before the Battle of Mogadishu: Jim Hoagland, "Prepared for Non-Combat," *Washington Post*, April 15, 1993, p. A29. For discussions of mission creep, see Rachel Bronson, "When Soldiers Become Cops," *Foreign Affairs* 81.6 (November–December 2002), pp. 122–32, at www.markville.ss.yrdsb.edu.on.ca/politics/rachelbronson.html; Eliot A. Cohen, *Supreme Command: Soldiers, Statesmen, and Leadership in Wartime* (New York: Free Press, 2002); Warren Bass, "The Triage of Dayton," *Foreign Affairs* 77.5 (September–October 1998), pp. 95–109. The Korean War has been called a case of mission creep *avant la lettre*. See Steven William Nerheim, "NSC-81/1 and the Evolution of U.S. War Aims in Korea, June–October 1950" (Carlisle Barracks, Pa.: U.S. Army War College, April 10, 2000, Report A973873).

31. See Neil Sheehan, Hedrick Smith, E. W. Kenworthy, and Fox Butterfield, *The Pentagon Papers* (New York: Bantam Books, 1971), pp. 510–88. On Vietnam, see Chapter 5, note 126.

32. See Eugene C. Gritton, Paul K. Davis, Randall Steeb, and John Matsumura, *Ground Forces for a Rapidly Employable Joint Task Force: First-Week Capabilities for Short-Warning Conflicts* (Santa Monica, CA: RAND Corporation, MR-1152-OSD/A, 2000), p. 1; at www.rand.org/pubs/monograph_reports/MR1152/. In their view, "uncertainties about threat and scenario details will require highly flexible military capabilities and – we believe – the ability for substantial action within *hours and days* rather than many days and even weeks." More important, the study authors observe that the "early use of *ground forces* . . . would be quite different from the Marine Corps and Army forces feasible in the near to mid term" (pp. 1–2; emphasis in original). For criticisms of the Army's technological transformation, see Wilson et al., "An Alternative Future Force."

33. Department of Defense, *Conduct of the Persian Gulf War: Final Report to Congress* (Washington, DC: U.S. GPO, 1992), pp. 34–7, 77–80.

34. See Thomas L. McNaugher, "Redefining Army Transformation," in Davis and Shapiro (eds.), *U.S. Army and the New National Security Strategy*, pp. 293–307. As McNaugher notes, there are "significant impediments to realizing transformation as it is currently described, crucial areas in which the basic concepts of Army Transformation are in need of significant refinement." For a discussion of the implications of the U.S. Army's modernization, see Vernon Loeb, "A Force Changes, from the Inside Out," *Washington Post*, September 26, 2002, p. 31; "Army Has a Comprehensive Plan for Managing its Transformation but Faces Major Challenges," General Accounting Office, Report to Congressional Committees, GAO-02-96, November 16, 2001, at www.gao.gov/cgi-bin/getrpt?GAO-02-96; "Army Transformation Faces Weapon Systems Challenges," General Accounting Office, Report to Congressional Committees, GAO-01-311, May 21, 2001, at www.gao. gov/cgi-bin/getrpt?GAO-01-311; *"Leap Ahead" Technologies and Transformation Initiatives within the Defense Science and Technology Program,* Hearing before the Subcommittee on Emerging Threats and Capabilities of the Committee on Armed Services, United States Senate, 107th Congress, First Session, June 5, 2001 (Washington, DC: U.S. GPO, 2002); "Army Transformation May Require More Trade-offs, GAO Says," *Defense Daily* 210.43 (May 31, 2001), pp. 1–3; Andrew F. Krepinevich Jr., "The Army and Land Warfare: Transforming the Legions," *Joint Forces Quarterly* 32 (Autumn 2002), pp. 76–82, at jdeis.cornerstoneindustry.com/jdeis/jel/jel/jfq_pubs/1432.pdf.

35. See Thom Shanker, "New Chief Sets Out to Redesign a Stretched-Thin Army," *New York Times*, January 26, 2004, p. A19, who notes that Army Chief of Staff Schoomaker seeks to make the Army lighter and leaner without encountering the political and economic costs increasing its size.

36. To understand these challenges, see John Matsumura, Randall Steeb, Thomas Herbert, Scot Eisenhard, John Gordon, Mark Lees, and Gail Halverson, *The Army After Next: Exploring New Concepts and Technologies*

for the *Light Battle Force* (Santa Monica, CA: RAND Corporation, DB-258-A, 1999), at www.rand.org/pubs/documented_briefings/DB258/; Gritton et al., *Ground Force*, pp. 23–50; Perry et al., *Future of Warfare*, who note that the Army chief of staff in 1996 assigned the Training and Doctrine Command to "explore the nature of warfare thirty years into the future and to help develop a long-term vision of the Army" (p. xi).

37. See John D. Mayer, *Rapid Deployment Forces: Policy and Budgetary Implications* (Washington, DC: Congressional Budget Office, 1983); at www.cbo.gov/ftpdoc.cfm?index=5057&type=1.

38. Bob Woodward, *The Commanders* (New York: Simon & Schuster, 1991), p. 230.

39. For instance, the decision by Colonel Muammar Qaddafi to dismantle Libya's WMD program was arguably influenced by the U.S. invasion of Iraq. See William Safire, "Spinning into Control," *New York Times*, January 12, 2004, p. A23: "Colonel Qaddafi took one look at our army massing for the invasion of Iraq and decided to get out of the mass-destruction business."

40. See Michael J. Hogan, *The Marshall Plan: America, Britain, and the Reconstruction of Western Europe, 1947–1952* (New York: Cambridge University Press, 1987), pp. 1–25. See also point 4 in the section "American Criteria for Victory" in Chapter 5.

41. For background on maritime forces, see A. T. Mahan, *The Interest of America in Sea Power* (Boston: Little, Brown, 1898), pp. 3–27; Mahan, *From Sail to Steam: Recollections of Naval Life* (New York: Harper & Brothers, 1907); Mahan, *The Influence of Sea Power on World History, 1660–1783* (Boston: Little, Brown, 1941); Bernard Brodie, *A Layman's Guide to Naval Strategy* (Princeton: Princeton University Press, 1942), pp. 3–115; Julian S. Corbett, *Some Principles of Maritime Strategy* (New York: Longmans, Green, 1911), pp. 87–127; John B. Hattendorf, *The Evolution of the U.S. Navy's Maritime Strategy, 1977–1987* (Newport, RI: Naval War College Newport Papers, 2004), pp. 3–100; George W. Baer, *One Hundred Years of Sea Power: The U.S. Navy, 1890–1990* (Stanford: Stanford University Press, 1994); Frank W. Lacroix and Irving N. Blickstein, *Forks in the Road for the U.S. Navy: Documented Briefing* (Santa Monica, CA: RAND Corporation, DB-

409-NAVY, 2003), pp. vii–ix, for a discussion of future roles for maritime forces (at www.rand.org/pubs/documented_briefings/DB409/).

42. *DoD Dictionary*, p. 323.

43. See Meilinger, "Ten Propositions," p. 4: "After one has gained command of the sea, a fleet can then bombard fortresses near shore, enforce a blockade, or conduct amphibious operations. In the first case, however, the results are limited by the range of the ships' guns; in the second, the enemy feels the results only indirectly and over time. Certainly a blockade can deprive a belligerent of items needed to sustain the war effort; however, the blockaded party can substitute and redistribute its resources to compensate for what has been denied. In short, indirect economic warfare takes much time; indeed, only rarely has a blockade brought a country to its knees. In the last instance amphibious operations are generally only a prelude to sustained land operations, but this action merely takes us back to the cycle of army versus army."

44. "Forward . . . From the Sea" (Washington, DC: Department of the Navy, 1994), p. 7 [hereafter, "FFTS94"], at www.dtic.mil/jv2010/navy/b014.pdf.

45. William J. Clinton, *A National Security Strategy of Engagement and Enlargement* (Washington, DC: White House, July 1994), p. 7. For related definitions of presence – notably "permanent presence," "mission presence," or "limited access" – see David A. Shlapak, John Stillion, Olga Oliker, and Tanya Charlick-Paley, *A Global Access Strategy for the U.S. Air Force* (Santa Monica, CA: RAND Corporation, MR-1216-AF, 2002), pp. 16–17; at www.rand.org/pubs/monograph_reports/MR1216/.

46. "FFTS94," p. 10.

47. See "Vision . . . Presence . . . Power: A Program Guide to the U.S. Navy – 2000 Edition" (Washington, DC: Department of the Navy, 2000), p. 1, at www.news.navy.mil/palib/policy/vision/vis00/v00-ch1b.html; Robert L. Pfaltzgraff Jr. and Richard H. Shultz Jr., *Naval Forward Presence and the National Military Strategy* (Annapolis, MD: Naval Institute Press, 1993).

48. *DoD Dictionary*, p. 323.

49. "Vision . . . Presence . . . Power," p. 1.

50. See Corbett, *Some Principles of Maritime Strategy;* Donald M. Schurman, *Julian S. Corbett, 1854–1922: Historian of British Mar-*

itime Policy from Drake to Jellicoe (London: Royal Historical Society, 1981).

51. See *Naval Doctrine Publication 1: Naval Warfare* (Washington, DC: Department of the Navy, March 28, 1994), p. 45. The concept of mobility (also called *maneuver*) is directly related to *mass*, which describes the ability to "concentrate combat power at the decisive time and place" (ibid., p. 44).

52. *DoD Dictionary*, p. 346.

53. See Brodie, *Layman's Guide*, pp. 3–115; Corbett, *Some Principles of Maritime Strategy*, pp. 87–127; Mahan, *Interest of America in Sea Power*, pp. 3–27.

54. Donald Kagan, *On the Origins of War and the Preservation of Peace* (New York: Doubleday, 1995), pp. 15–79.

55. "Forward . . . From the Sea: The Navy Operational Concept" (Washington, DC: U.S. GPO, March 1997), p. 2 [hereafter, "FFTS97"]; at www.news.navy.mil/palib/policy/fromsea/ffseanoc.html. It continues, "These are the places where American influence and power have the greatest impact and are needed most often. For forward-deployed naval forces, the littorals are a starting place as well as a destination."

56. Vernon Clark, "Sea Power 21: Operational Concepts for a New Era," remarks delivered at U.S. Naval War College's Current Strategy Forum, Newport, RI, June 12, 2002, pp. 1, 3, at www.navyleague.org/public_relations/cno_speech_at_current_strategy_forum_2002.pdf. Clark called this projection of sovereignty "Sea Basing," noting (p. 3) "it uses the 70% of the earth's surface that is covered with water as a vast maneuver space to aid in the warfighting effort." See also Clark, "Sea Power 21: Projecting Decisive Joint Capabilities," *U.S. Naval Institute Proceedings* 128.10 (October 1, 2002), pp. 32–41.

57. See "Vision . . . Presence . . . Power," p. 6; "FFTS94," p. 5, "U.S. naval forces . . . are therefore free of the political encumbrances that may inhibit and otherwise limit the scope of land-based operations in forward theaters."

58. Les Aspin, "A Defense Strategy for the New Era," sec. 2 of *Report on the Bottom-Up Review* (Washington, DC: Office of the Secretary of Defense, October 1993); at fas.org/man/docs/bur/part02.htm. It also includes decisions about "whether to signal America's interest in resolving a crisis, evacuate American

citizens from danger, render humanitarian assistance, or conduct strikes against countries supporting terrorism or defying U.N. resolutions."

59. As described in "FFTS97," p. 1, "A key operational advantage of forward-deployed naval forces is that we provide on-scene capabilities for executing simultaneously all three components of the *National Military Strategy*, and do so without infringing on any nation's sovereignty. This advantage exists because we operate in international waters."

60. "FFTS94," p. 5.

61. See Patrick E. Tyler, "War Games Play Well for Taiwan's Leader," *New York Times*, March 22, 1996, p. A1; also, Elaine Sciolino, "White House Snubs China over Military Maneuvers," *New York Times*, March 23, 1996, sec. 1, p. 5.

62. See note 18 above.

63. *DoD Dictionary*, p. 517, defines "sustainment" as the "provision of personnel, logistics, and other support required to maintain and prolong operations or combat until successful accomplishment or revision of the mission or of the national objective."

64. Aspin, *Report on the Bottom-Up Review*, sec. 2.

65. Aspin's report noted (ibid.): "By stationing forces abroad we also improve our ability to respond effectively to crises or aggression when they occur. Our overseas presence provides the leading edge of the rapid response capability that we would need in a crisis."

66. See "Vision . . . Presence . . . Power," p. 8.

67. *DoD Dictionary*, p. 205. Beyond its general meaning, the term "flexible response" has a long lineage in the nuclear debate. See Lawrence Freedman, *The Evolution of Nuclear Strategy* (New York: St. Martin's Press, 1989), pp. 228, 285–6.

68. See Anthony H. Cordesman, *The Iraq War: Strategy, Tactics, and Military Lessons* (Westport, CT: Praeger, 2003), p. 57.

69. As described in "FFTS94," p. 2: "Naval Forces are particularly well-suited to the entire range of military operations in support of our national strategy."

70. See Ronald O'Rourke, "Navy CVNX Aircraft Carrier Program: Background and Issues for Congress," CRS Report for Congress, updated February 19, 2002), p. 2, which

warns that "The Navy recently has experienced cost growth in its aircraft carrier construction programs" (p. 6); at www.thememoryhole. org/crs/more-reports/RS20643.pdf. See also *Options for Funding Aircraft Carriers* (Santa Monica, CA: RAND Corporation, MR-1526-NAVY, 2002), p. xii; at www.rand.org/pubs/monograph_reports/MR1526/. And see John Birkler, Michael Mattock, John F. Schank, Giles K. Smith, Fred Timson, James Chiesa, Bruce Woodyard, Malcolm MacKinnon, and Denis Rushworth, *The U.S. Aircraft Carrier Industrial Base: Force Structure, Cost, Schedule, and Technology Issues for CVN 77* (Santa Monica, CA: RAND Corporation, MR-948-NAVY/OSD, 1998), which notes that, in terms of its cost, "An aircraft carrier requires several escort ships to provide defense against air, missile, and submarine attack. It requires auxiliary ships to deliver supplies and aviation fuel. Aircraft carriers today deploy approximately 50+ strike aircraft (F/A-18s and F-14s)" (p. 19). The report (online at www.rand.org/pubs/monograph_reports/MR948/) continues by arguing that "Carriers represent too big a target."

71. See Assessments of Selected Major Weapons Programs (Washington, DC: US Government Accountability Office, March 2006), pp. 47–8. See also Paul L. Francis, Director, Acquisition and Sourcing Management, "Multiyear Procurement Authority for the Virginia Class Submarine Program," letter to Jerry Lewis, Chairman, Subcommittee on Defense, House Committee on Appropriations, June 23, 2003; General Accounting Office, Report, GAO-03-895R, p. 1, at www.gao.gov/cgi-bin/getrpt?GAO-03-895R; John Birkler, John F. Schank, Giles K. Smith, Fred Timson, James Chiesa, Marc Goldberg, Michael Mattock, and Malcolm MacKinnon, *The U.S. Submarine Production Base: An Analysis of Cost, Schedule, and Risk for Selected Force Structures – Executive Summary* (Santa Monica, CA: RAND Corporation, MR-456/1-OSD, 1994), at www.rand.org/pubs/monograph_reports/MR456.1/.

72. See Daniel Gouré, "Pity the Poor PLA Navy," letter in section "In My View," *Naval War College Review* 57.1 (Winter 2004), pp. 131–2: "Attacking a U.S. aircraft carrier, particularly one steaming in harm's way, is one of the most difficult tasks that can confront any hostile power. . . . [The study] *Aircraft Car-*

rier (In)vulnerability . . . concludes that U.S. aircraft carriers are extremely difficult to find and target, but that even were it possible for an adversary to do so, the defensive firepower available in the carrier battle group and the inherent resilience of the platform itself would make it highly unlikely that the aircraft carrier could be attacked successfully." (The full letter is online at www.nwc.navy.mil/press/Review/2004/Winter/imv-w04.htm.) Yet, as observed in Birkler et al., *U.S. Aircraft Carrier Industrial Base*, p. 19, "The loss of an aircraft carrier would be a major political blow to the United States and a tragic event in its own right. A carrier and the air wing deployed on the ship have a crew of approximately 5,000 persons."

73. For an analysis of emerging technologies, see John Stillion and David T. Orletsky, "Emerging Threat Technologies," in *Airbase Vulnerability to Conventional Cruise-Missile and Ballistic-Missile Attacks: Technology, Scenarios, and U.S. Air Force Responses* (Santa Monica, CA: RAND Corporation, MR-1028-AF, 1999), pp. 5–17; at www.rand.org/pubs/monograph_reports/MR1028/index.html. To understand technological advances planned for the U.S. Navy, see National Research Council, Naval Studies Board, *Technology for the United States Navy and Marine Corps, 2000–2035: Becoming a 21st Century Force*, 9 vols. (Washington, DC: National Academy Press, 1997), vol. 1: *Overview;* entire report at newton.nap.edu/html/tech_21st/tfnf.htm.

74. See Federation of American Scientists, "FFG-7 Oliver Hazard Perry-class," at www.fas.org/man/dod-101/sys/ship/ffg-7.htm.

75. Michael O'Hanlon, "A Few Tanks for Iran," *Washington Post*, December 5, 2000, p. A43, at brook.edu/Views/Op-Ed/OHanlon/20001205.htm. The risks of this proliferation of advanced technologies are not confined to maritime forces alone. In January 2004 a U.S. Blackhawk helicopter was shot down near the town of Falluja in Iraq. Perhaps more ominously, a C-5 transport aircraft was hit by ground fire, probably a surface-to-air missile, which forced it to return to Baghdad International Airport. See Neela Banerjee, "9 Soldiers Dead in Crash in Iraq," *New York Times,* January 9, 2004, p. A1.

76. See *Naval Doctrine Publication 4: Naval Logistics* (Washington, DC: Department of the Navy, February 20, 2001), p. 5. The functional areas of logistics include supply, maintenance, transportation, engineering, health services, and other logistics services, which operates as an "intricate network of *materiel, facilities, transportation, technical support, and information*" (p. 5; emphasis in original).

77. To estimate the transit times for ships in days and nautical miles, the Defense Mapping Agency produced a guide that is based on estimated transit speeds of eighteen and twenty-five knots. Defense Mapping Agency, *Distances between Ports,* 8th ed. (Pub. 151, Bethesda, MD: DMA Hydrographic/Topographic Center, 1995); a 2006 edition is at pollux.nss.nima.mil/pubs/pubs_j_show_sections.html?dpath=DBP&ptid=5&rid=189.

78. Cf. the section "Maritime Warfare and Victory" in Chapter 3.

79. This is the reason for transforming the U.S. Navy's ability to use overseas basing. See "Sea Basing: Poised for Take-Off," Office of Force Transformation, Department of Defense, Arlington, VA, February 15, 2005; at www.oft.osd.mil/library/library_files/trends_372_Transformation_Trends_15_February_2005%20Issue.pdf. The Sea Basing Joint Integrating Concept defines sea basing as "the rapid deployment, assembly, command, projection, reconstitution and re-employment of joint combat power from the sea." For more on sea basing, see note 56.

80. See Brodie, *Layman's Guide;* Corbett, *Some Principles of Maritime Strategy;* Mahan, *Interest of America in Sea Power;* Donald Kagan, *Pericles of Athens and the Birth of Democracy* (New York: Free Press, 1991), pp. 112–15, 117, 203; Kagan, *The Peloponnesian War* (New York: Viking, 2003).

81. Henry A. Kissinger, *White House Years* (Boston: Little, Brown, 1979), p. 910.

82. Ibid., pp. 318–19. With respect to aircraft carriers that were stationed in South Korea, "No doubt subconsciously, everyone drew comfort from the fact that it would take the aircraft carriers three days to get to where they could launch planes. Hawks could tell themselves that we were doing something; doves could console themselves that we still had a cushion of time. . . . In this context the decision to move the carriers was essentially time-wasting; it looked tough but implied inaction."

83. "FFTS94," p. 7. Notably, "Our national strategy calls for the individual services to

operate jointly to ensure both that we can operate successfully in all warfare areas and that we can apply our military power across the spectrum of foreseeable situations."

84. The obvious exception to this argument is the use of nuclear weapons, but the defense establishment has essentially written off this scenario now that the cold war is over (see Chapter 1). Nuclear weapons have not been relevant to maritime planning since President George H. W. Bush changed the alert status of nuclear forces in September 1991 and removed these weapons from U.S. ships – with the exception of ballistic missile submarines (SSBNs or "boomers").

85. See Bob Woodward, *Plan of Attack: The Definitive Account of the Decision to Invade Iraq* (New York: Simon & Schuster, 2004), p. 54.

86. For background on the debate about whether air power wins wars, see Robert A. Pape, "Coercive Air Power in the Vietnam War," *International Security* 15.2 (Fall 1990), pp. 103–46; Pape, *Bombing to Win: Air Power and Coercion in War* (Ithaca, NY: Cornell University Press, 1996); John Buckley, *Air Power in the Age of Total War* (Bloomington: Indiana University Press, 1999); Daniel L. Byman, Matthew C. Waxman, and Eric Larson, *Air Power as a Coercive Instrument* (Santa Monica, CA: RAND Corporation, MR-1061-AF, 1999), available at www.rand.org/pubs/monograph_reports/MR1061/index.html; Benjamin S. Lambeth, *The Transformation of American Air Power* (Ithaca, NY: Cornell University Press, 2000), p. 1, who examines the "potential ability of conventional air power to achieve strategic effects independently of ground action."

87. For background on air power, see Kennett, *History of Strategic Bombing*; USSBS, *European War,* July 1, 1946, *Pacific War,* September 30, 1945; Mark A. Clodfelter, *The Limits of Air Power: The American Bombing of North Vietnam* (New York: Free Press, 1989); Pape, "Coercive Air Power in the Vietnam War"; DoD, *Conduct of the Persian Gulf War;* Meilinger, "Ten Propositions"; John Gooch (ed.), *Airpower Theory and Practice* (London: Frank Cass, 1995); Charles M. Perry, Robert L. Pfaltzgraff Jr., and Joseph C. Conway, *Long-Range Bombers & the Role of Airpower in the New Century* (Cambridge, MA: Institute for Foreign Policy Analysis, 1995); Pape,

Bombing to Win; Buckley, *Air Power in the Age of Total War;* Byman et al., *Air Power as a Coercive Instrument;* Lambeth, *Transformation of American Air Power; Air Warfare: Air Force Doctrine Document 2-1,* January 22, 2000, at www.dtic.mil/doctrine/jel/service_pubs/afd2_1.pdf and www.doctrine.af.mil/Library/Doctrine/afdd2-1.pdf; Phillip S. Meilinger, *Airmen and Air Theory: A Review of the Sources* (Maxwell Air Force Base, Montgomery, AL: Air University Press, 2001).

88. Lambeth, *Transformation of American Air Power,* p. 9, defines air power as a "complex amalgam of hardware and less tangible but equally important ingredients bearing on its effectiveness, such as employment doctrine, concepts of operations, training, tactics, proficiency, leadership, adaptability, and practical experience." Meilinger, "Ten Propositions," p. 6, argues that "air power is targeting; targeting is intelligence; and intelligence is analyzing the effects of air operations."

89. Missiles are included in the category of air power because of their aerodynamic properties and operating characteristics.

90. See ibid., pp. 9–10, for "three bounding rules . . . [on] what is meant by *air power*" (emphasis in original): "First, *air power* does not refer merely to combat aircraft or to the combined hardware assets of an air arm. . . . Second, air power is inseparable from battlespace information and intelligence. . . . Third, air power, properly understood, knows no color of uniform."

91. For a discussion of the strengths of air power, see Meilinger, "Ten Propositions," p. 1, who defines the attributes of air power as range, speed, elevation, lethality, and flexibility. He also argues that "the speed, range, and flexibility of airpower grant it ubiquity" (p. 6). See also Lambeth, *Transformation of American Air Power,* pp. 1–11; Pape, *Bombing to Win.*

92. Meilinger, "Ten Propositions," p. 9.

93. For a discussion of the 1991 Persian Gulf War, see Chapter 8.

94. See Lambeth, *Transformation of American Air Power,* pp. 103–52, for a discussion of the use of air power in the 1991 Persian Gulf War. Lambeth observes (p. 104) that the "contribution of U.S. air power to the allied victory in *Desert Storm* constituted enough of a departure from past experience to suggest that a new relationship between air and surface forces in joint warfare may be in the offing."

95. See "Pentagon Report: Military Wants Nukes to Penetrate Buried Targets," *Associated Press*, March 15, 2002, at www.military.com/ContentFiles/FC_buried_031402.htm; Michael Sirak, "Massive Bomb to MOP Up Deeply Buried Targets," *Jane's Defence Weekly* 41.29 (July 21, 2004), p. 10, at forum.keypublishing.co.uk/showthread.php?t=34339; Eric A. Miller, "Bunker-Busting Nuke Expands U.S. Options," *Defense News*, September 16–22, 2002, p. 21, which reports: "According to a joint 2001 Department of Defense and Department of Energy report to Congress on hard and deeply buried targets, more than 10,000 underground targets exist worldwide, with more than 1,400 known or suspected to be sheltering weapons of mass destruction, ballistic missiles, or other military command facilities."

96. Benjamin S. Lambeth, *NATO's Air War for Kosovo: A Strategic and Operational Assessment* (Santa Monica, CA: RAND Corporation, MR-1365-AF, 2001), p. 20; at www.rand.org/pubs/monograph_reports/MR1365/.

97. For Meilinger, "Ten Propositions," p. 6, "In air war, one cannot afford a mobilization that takes weeks or months – the conflict may be over before it can take effect."

98. See Byman et al., *Air Power as a Coercive Instrument*, p. 5.

99. Byman et al. (ibid., p. iii) argue that it is "effective against adversaries with diverse economics, cultures, political institutions, and military capabilities."

100. See *USSBS, European War*, p. 18.

101. Michael Dugan, "The Air War," *U.S. News & World Report* 110.5 (February 11, 1991), pp. 24–31, at p. 27.

102. Kennett, *History of Strategic Bombing*, p. 183: "The costly raids on the ball-bearing works at Schweinfurt did not slow down the German war machine." Albert Speer, *Inside the Third Reich: Memoirs* (New York: Macmillan, 1970), p. 285, reported that "After this attack the production of ball bearings dropped by 38 percent." *USSBS, European War*, p. 15, notes that "In this attack 36 of the 200 attacking planes were lost." Regarding modern precision attacks, see "Deadly Accurate Bombs Require Sophisticated Gear on the Ground," *Marine Corps Times*, August 12, 2002.

103. See Paul K. Davis, *Effects-Based Operations (EBO): A Grand Challenge for the Analytical Community* (Santa Monica, CA: RAND Corporation, MR-1477-USJFCOM/AF, 2001); at www.rand.org/pubs/monograph_reports/MR1477/.

104. A separate issue is whether the remnants of the defeated state's political and military leadership are able to organize and sustain an insurgency against the victorious, occupying power. An important contemporary example is that of Iraq in the aftermath of the coalition's military victory in April 2003.

105. For a discussion of the history of economic targeting before 1945, see Benjamin S. Lambeth and Kevin N. Lewis, *Economic Targeting in Modern Warfare* (Santa Monica, CA: RAND Corporation, P-6735, July 1982), pp. 5–12. "Concepts governing economic targeting for aerial bombardment offensives developed hand in hand with the use of aircraft for military purposes. . . . Strategic air attack came to describe strikes that reached above and beyond the defended perimeter of a nation in order to destroy the fundamental resources on which an enemy's war potential relied."

106. Speer, *Inside the Third Reich*, p. 346. "Until then [May 8, 1944] we had managed to produce approximately as many weapons as the armed forces needed, in spite of their considerable losses. But with the attack of nine hundred and thirty-five daylight bombers of the American Eighth Air Force upon several fuel plants in central and eastern Germany, a new era in the air war began. It meant the end of German armaments production." See Russell F. Weigley, *The American Way of War: A History of United States Military Strategy and Policy* (New York: Macmillan, 1973), p. 358, quoting Albert Speer: "The American [air] attacks, which followed a definite system of assault on industrial targets, *were by far the most dangerous. It was in fact these attacks which caused the breakdown of the German armaments industry*" (Weigley's emphasis).

107. See *USSBS, European War*, p. 14. The conference established as the objective of the strategic air forces the "destruction and dislocation of the German Military, industrial, and economic system and the undermining of the morale of the German people to the point where their capacity for armed resistance is fatally weakened" (p. 14). Subsequent citations are given in the text.

108. Ibid., p. 10: "In the spring and early summer of 1944, all air forces based on England were used to prepare the way for the invasion."

109. This discussion draws on Clodfelter, *Limits of Air Power*. For Meilinger, "Ten Propositions," p. 1, the limitations of air power include gravity, the ephemeral nature of air strikes, weather and night, political restrictions, and inability to hold ground.

110. In the 2003 invasion, the strategy was to avoid signaling the Iraqi leadership with the expected full-scale air campaign.

111. For an analysis of airbase vulnerabilities, see Stillion and Orletsky, *Airbase Vulnerability*, p. iii, which warns that "Both emerging technologies and the proliferation of existing capabilities will give adversaries pursuing anti-access strategies a variety of new options against U.S. airbases, ports, troop concentrations, and ships at sea." See also Albert Wohlstetter, Fred Hoffman, R. J. Lutz, and Henry S. Rowen, *Selection and Use of Strategic Air Bases* (Santa Monica, CA: RAND Corporation, R-0266, 1954); Albert Wohlstetter, "The Delicate Balance of Terror," *Foreign Affairs* 37.2 (January 1959), pp. 211–34.

112. Woodward, *Commanders*, pp. 273–4.

113. See, e.g., Scott McConnell's interview with Robert Pape, "The Logic of Suicide Terrorism," *American Conservative* 4.10 (July 18, 2005), pp. 17–22; at www.amconmag.com/2005_07_18/article.html.

114. "DoD News Briefing – Secretary Rumsfeld and Gen. Myers," February 19, 2003, at www.defenselink.mil/transcripts/2003/t02192003_t0219sd.html. See also Safire, "Spinning into Control"; "U.S. vs. Iraq: The 1991 Gulf War," *San Francisco Chronicle*, September 24, 2002, at www.sfgate.com/cgi-bin/article.cgi?f=/c/a/2002/09/24/MN168392.DTL.

115. See "Operation Iraqi Freedom – April 2; Day Fourteen," at www.globalsecurity.org/military/ops/iraqi_freedom_d14.htm.

116. Of the five most expensive military modernization programs as of May 2006, the most expensive is the Joint Strike Fighter program and the fifth is the F-22A fighter aircraft – which together account for a total projected cost of $271 billion. See *Defense Acquisitions: Assessments of Selected Major Weapon Programs*, GAO-06-391 (Washington, DC: General Accountability Office, March 2006), at www.gao.gov/new.items/d06391.pdf. See also Donald Stevens, John Gibson, and David Ochmanek, "Modernizing the Combat Forces: Near-Term Options," in Zalmay Khalilzad and Jeremy Shapiro (eds.), *Strategic Appraisal: United States Air and Space Power in the 21st Century* (Santa Monica, CA: RAND Corporation, MR-1314, 2002), pp. 85–141, at www.rand.org/pubs/monograph_reports/2005/MR1314/MR1314.ch4.pdf.

117. In the summary to their study on the future of air power, Perry et al. (*Long-Range Bombers*, p. ix) observed: "Perhaps the most important set of choices confronted by American defense planners in the post–Cold War era centers on striking a balance in the allocation of scarce defense resources among three overarching objectives: sustaining readiness; bringing on line the next generation of weapons systems; and maintaining a force structure adequate to meet a range of military contingencies."

118. See National Defense Budget Estimates for FY 2006 (Washington, DC: Office of Secretary of Defense [Comptroller], April 2005), p. 26, at www.dod.mil/comptroller/defbudget/fy2006/fy2006_greenbook.pdf.

119. Global defense spending in 2004 was roughly $950 billion annually of which U.S. spending was $466 billion. See "World Wide Military Expenditures," at www.globalsecurity.org/military/world/spending.htm. For the B-2, see United States Air Force, "B-2 Bomber Factsheet," at www.af.mil/factsheets/factsheet.asp?fsID=82.

120. See Bernard Fox, Michael Boito, John C. Graser, and Obaid Younossi, *Test and Evaluation Trends and Costs for Aircraft and Guided Weapons* (Santa Monica, CA: RAND Corporation, MG-109-AF, 2004); at www.rand.org/pubs/monographs/MG109/.

121. Marc Selinger, "Airborne Laser's Overruns Could Reach $2 Billion, Senator Says," *Aerospace Daily & Defense Report* 209.47 (March 12, 2004), p. 3; at www.aviationnow.com/avnow/news/channel_aerospacedaily_story.jsp?id=news/abl03124.xml. A prototype of this new weapon is presently scheduled for testing in 2008; see *Defense Acquisitions: Assessments*, pp. 19–20.

122. Cf. the section "Air Warfare and Victory" in Chapter 3.

123. See Eliot A. Cohen, "The Meaning and Future of Air Power," *Orbis* 39.2 (Spring 1995), pp. 189–200.

124. *USSBS, European War*, p. 5. See ibid., pp. 37–40, for conclusions regarding the employment of air power during the European campaign of World War II.

125. *USSBS, Pacific War*, p. 57.

126. *USSBS, European War,* p. 6. In Japan, according to *USSBS, Pacific War,* p. 92, "Total civilian casualties . . . as a result of 9 months of air attack, including those from the atomic bombs, were approximately 806,000. Of these, approximately 330,000 were fatalities."

127. See Andrew L. Stigler, "A Clear Victory for Air Power: NATO's Empty Threat to Invade Kosovo," *International Security* 27.3 (Winter 2003), pp. 124–57.

128. Meilinger, *Airmen and Air Theory,* p. 9.

129. Ibid., p. 104.

130. Lambeth, *Transformation of American Air Power,* p. 7.

131. See Gian P. Gentile, *How Effective Is Strategic Bombing? Lessons Learned from World War to Kosovo* (New York: New York University Press, 2001).

132. See Meilinger, "Ten Propositions," p. 4: "[A]lthough an invasion of Japan proper was unnecessary, the evidence was not clear-cut – it took four years and the combined operations of all the services to set the stage for the final and decisive air phase."

133. *USSBS, Pacific War,* has "60,000 to 70,000" killed in Hiroshima (p. 100) and "40,000 . . . killed or missing" in Nagasaki (p. 101); but when aftereffects (e.g., radiation poisoning) are included, some 140,000 deaths in Hiroshima and 70,000 in Nagasaki by the end of 1945 have been attributed to the atomic bombs – death rates of 54 percent. Richard Rhodes, *The Making of the Atomic Bomb* (New York: Simon & Schuster, 1986), pp. 734, 740, 742. See also *USSBS, Pacific War,* p. 107: "Based on a detailed investigation of all the facts, and supported by the testimony of the surviving Japanese leaders involved, it is the Survey's opinion that certainly prior to 31 December 1945, and in all probability prior to 1 November 1945, Japan would have surrendered even if the atomic bombs had not been dropped."

134. Meilinger, *Airmen and Air Theory,* p. 131; Kennett, *History of Strategic Bombing;* Steven T. Ross, *American War Plans, 1945–1950* (London: Frank Cass, 1996); Stephen Possony, *Strategic Air Power: The Pattern of Dynamic Security* (Washington, DC: Infantry Journal Press, 1949).

135. Bernard E. Trainor, "American Arms vs. Iraq," *New York Times,* February 13, 1998, p. A1.

136. Lambeth, *NATO's Air War,* p. v.

137. See Peter J. Boyer, "A Different War: Is the Army Becoming Irrelevant?" *New Yorker* 78.17 (July 1, 2002), pp. 54–67, at www.newyorker.com/archive/content/?030407fr_archive04. The article was quoting an interview of a couple weeks before; see "Deputy Secretary Wolfowitz Interview with the *New Yorker,*" Tuesday, June 18, 2002, at www.defenselink.mil/transcripts/2002/t07022002_t0618ny.html. Lambeth, *Transformation of American Air Power,* p. 297, noted that "It would be a pointless exaggeration to suggest that air power can now win wars single-handedly."

138. Phillip S. Meilinger, "Proselytizer and Prophet: Alexander P. de Seversky and American Airpower," in Gooch (ed.), *Airpower Theory and Practice,* pp. 7–35, at p. 23; Lambeth, *Transformation of American Air Power,* p. 1.

139. Meilinger, *Airmen and Air Theory,* p. 145, who argued against "any monocausal factor in victory [because] war is simply too complex to become that reductive." For Lambeth, *Transformation of American Air Power,* p. 10, "[A]ir power entails a creative harnessing of all of the diverse combat and combat-supported elements of the U.S. armed forces, including space and information warfare adjuncts, that exploit the medium of air and space to visit fire and steel (or, as it may be in the case of information operations, ones and zeros) on enemy targets." He also noted (p. 297) that "recent developments have dramatically increased the relative combat potential of air power in comparison to that of other force elements. That, in turn, has made possible the application of new concepts of operation in joint warfare."

140. Meilinger, "Proselytizer and Prophet," p. 18; see also p. 30: "Air power does not have to win wars alone in order to be decisive any more than does an army." Meilinger also argues ("Ten Propositions," p. 2) that "Seldom is one service used to wage a campaign or war, although one service may dominate such conflicts."

141. Ibid., pp. 28–9.

142. To understand this debate, see Benjamin S. Lambeth, "Bounding the Airpower Debate," *Strategic Review* 25.4 (Fall 1997): pp. 42–55 (repr. Santa Monica, CA: RAND Corporation, RP-660, 1997), available via www.rand.org/pubs/reprints/RP660/; Byman et al., *Air Power as a Coercive Instrument,* pp.

3–5 on "The Role of the USAF" and chap. 7, "Implications and Recommendations," pp. 129–39. For those who argue that air power is not the decisive instrument of military power, see Pape, *Bombing to Win;* Clodfelter, *Limits of Air Power;* Eliot A. Cohen, "The Mystique of Air Power," *Foreign Affairs* 73.1 (January–February 1994), pp. 109–24. For those who support the idea that air power is a new and decisive form of military power, see John Warden, "Success in Modern War: A Response to Robert Pape's *Bombing to Win,*" *Security Studies* 7.2 (Winter 1997–8), pp. 172–90; Meilinger, "Ten Propositions"; Lambeth, *Transformation of American Air Power.*

143. Boot, "New American Way of War"; Williamson Murray and Robert H. Scales Jr., *The Iraq War: A Military History* (Cambridge, MA: Belknap, 2003), pp. 88–128.

144. Regarding the Key West agreement, see James W. Canaan, "The Coming Flap on Roles and Missions," *Air Force Magazine* 75.10 (October 1992), pp. 10–12, at www.afa.org/magazine/1992/1092watch.asp; David D. Dyche, "Military Reorganization: Challenge and Opportunity" (Quantico, VA: Marine Corps University, Command Staff College, 1990), at www.globalsecurity.org/military/library/report/1990/DDD.htm.

145. Kissinger, *Nuclear Weapons,* p. 407.

146. See *USSBS, Pacific War,* p. 50.

147. See ibid., p. 115, for the observation that "atomic weapons will not have eliminated the need for ground troops, for surface vessels, for air weapons, or for the full coordination among them, the supporting services and the civilian effort, but will have changed the context in which they are employed." This is useful guidance for those who believe that any one form of military power is more important than the rest.

148. Headquarters United States Marine Corps, *Marine Corps Strategy 21* (Washington, DC: Department of the Navy, November 3, 2000), p. 1: "The Marine Corps will enhance its strategic agility, operational reach, and tactical flexibility to enable joint, allied, and coalition operations and interagency coordination . . . [and thereby] shape the international environment, respond quickly to the complex spectrum of crises and conflicts, and gain access or prosecute forcible entry operations." See also Michael O'Hanlon, "A Marine's Lessons for Europe," *Japan Times,* August 1,

2002, at www.brookings.edu/views/op-ed/ohanlon/20020801.htm.

149. See Gerry J. Gilmore, "Army to Develop Future Force Now, Says Shinseki," *Army News Service,* October 13, 1999, at www.fas.org/man/dod-101/army/unit/docs/a19991013shinvis.htm; Michael O'Hanlon, "History Will Credit Shinseki," *Japan Times,* June 19, 2003, at brookings.edu/views/op-ed/ohanlon/20030618.htm.

150. See Ronald O'Rourke, "Navy Role in Global War on Terrorism (GWOT) – Background and Issues for Congress" (Washington, DC: Congressional Research Service, CRS Report for Congress, February 2, 2006), pp. 4–5, at www.fas.org/sgp/crs/natsec/RS22373.pdf; James W. Crawley, "'Brown Water' Navy Takes Shape," *Media General News Service,* January 10, 2006, at www.militaryphotos.net/forums/showthread.php?t=68395; as well as Sandra I. Erwin, "Shrewd Tactics Underpin Navy Strategy to Defeat Diesel Submarines," *National Defense,* March 2005, at www.nationaldefensemagazine.org/issues/2005/Mar/UF-Shrewd_Tactics.htm.

151. O'Hanlon, "A Few Tanks for Iran."

152. For background on how air power is adapting to modern conditions in war, see the following RAND Reports (Santa Monica, CA: RAND Corporation): Alan Vick, David T. Orletsky, Abram N. Shulsky, and John Stillion, *Preparing the U.S. Air Force for Military Operations Other than War* (MR-842-AF, 1997), at www.rand.org/pubs/monograph_reports/MR842/; Alan Vick, David T. Orletsky, John Bordeaux, and David A. Shlapak, *Enhancing Air Power's Contribution against Light Infantry Targets* (MR-697-AF, 1996); Alan Vick, John Stillion, David R. Frelinger, Joel S. Kvitsky, Benjamin S. Lambeth, Jeff Marquis, and Matthew C. Waxman, *Aerospace Operation in Urban Environments: Exploring New Concepts* (MR-1187-AF, 2000), at www.rand.org/pubs/monograph_reports/MR1187/; Alan Vick, Richard Moore, Bruce R. Pirnie, and John Stillion, *Aerospace Operations against Elusive Ground Targets* (MR-1398-AF, 2001), at www.rand.org/pubs/monograph_reports/MR1398/.

13. Conclusions

1. John Keegan, *A History of Warfare* (New York: Alfred A. Knopf, 1994), p. 17.

2. For a particularly useful discussion of

the application of pretheories and theories, see Suzanne Joseph, "Anthropological Evolutionary Ecology: A Critique," *Journal of Ecological Anthropology* 4 (2000), pp. 6–30; at www.fiu.edu/~jea/joseph1.pdf. See also the discussion in Chapter 4 of the present volume.

3. James N. Rosenau, "Pre-Theories and Theories of Foreign Policy," in Rosenau, *The Scientific Study of Foreign Policy* (London: Frances Pinter, 1980), pp. 115–69, at p. 129; at www.ub.unimaas.nl/ucm/e-readers/ss337/rosenau1.pdf. See the section "Toward a Pretheory of Victory" in Chapter 4, where Rosenau's views are examined in more detail.

4. Ibid., p. 130 and its n. 44.

5. Rosenau, *Scientific Study of Foreign Policy*, p. 30.

6. On prediction and causality, see Chapter 4, n74.

7. Rosenau, "Pre-Theories and Theories," pp. 132, 135.

8. *The American Heritage Dictionary of the English Language*, 4th ed., 2000, at www.bartleby.com/61/: "A rule in science and philosophy stating that entities should not be multiplied needlessly. This rule is interpreted to mean that the simplest of two or more competing theories is preferable and that an explanation for unknown phenomena should first be attempted in terms of what is already known."

9. Rosenau, "Pre-Theories and Theories," p. 135.

10. See John Mueller, *Policy and Opinion in the Gulf War* (Chicago: University of Chicago Press, 1994); Eric V. Larson, *Casualties and Consensus: The Historical Role of Casualties in Domestic Support for U.S. Military Operations* (Santa Monica, CA: RAND Corporation, MR-726-RC, 1996); at www.rand.org/pubs/monograph_reports/MR726/index.html.

11. For example, see Marc Labonte, "Financing Issues and Economic Effects of Past American Wars," Congressional Research Service Report for Congress, November 7, 2001, pp. 5–15; at www.911investigations.net/document45.html.

12. See Michael I. Handel, *Masters of War: Classical Strategic Thought,* 3d ed. (London: Frank Cass, 2001), p. 37.

13. See Carlotta Gall, "Afghan Legislators Get Crash Course in Ways of Democracy," *New York Times,* December 19, 2005, p. A14;

Gall, "Cheney and Afghan Milestone," *New York Times,* December 20, 2005, p. A14; Gall, "Afghan Parliament Opens, and Finds Democracy Is a Bit Untidy," *New York Times,* December 21, 2005, p. A14. Also, Eric Schmitt, "U.S. to Cut Force in Afghanistan," *New York Times,* December 20, 2005, p. A14. The Bonn Agreement of December 5, 2001, is online at www.afghan-web.com/politics/bonn_agreement_2001.html.

14. For these texts, see "Atlantic Charter," at www.yale.edu/lawweb/avalon/wwii/atlantic.htm; "The Yalta Conference," at www.yale.edu/lawweb/avalon/wwii/yalta.htm.

15. On the resurgent Taliban threat, see Chapter 10, note 126.

16. "Bush's View: 'Work Is Not Done'," *New York Times,* December 19, 2005, p. A12. For the speech, see "President's Address to the Nation," December 18, 2005, www.whitehouse.gov/news/releases/2005/12/20051218-2.html.

17. See *National Strategy for Victory in Iraq* (Washington, DC: National Security Council, November 2005), p. 4; at www.whitehouse.gov/infocus/iraq/iraq_national_strategy_20051130.pdf.

18. See the section "Interpreting Victory" in Chapter 10; see also Dexter Filkins, "As Iraqis Vote for a Parliament, an Islamist–Secular Split Is Seen," *New York Times,* December 16, 2005, p. A1; Richard A. Oppel Jr., "Sunni Group Near Deal with Kurds on Iraqi Government," *New York Times,* January 3, 2006, p. A9.

19. See *National Strategy for Victory in Iraq,* p. 1.

20. See ibid., p. 13. As the report notes (pp. 23–4), oil production increased from 1.58 million barrels per day (bpd) in 2003 to 2.25 million bpd in 2004; Iraq's GDP increased from $13.6 billion in 2003 to $25.5 billion in 2004, with projected growth rates of 3.7 percent in 2005 and 17 percent in 2006. For the estimate that Iraq's 2005 (estimated) GDP is $24.3 billion, see U.S. Department of State, "Background Note: Iraq," at state.gov/r/pa/ei/bgn/6804.htm#econ.

21. "Bush's View: 'Work Is Not Done'," where, in his speech of December 18, 2005, the president noted that "Reconstruction efforts and the training of Iraqi security forces started more slowly than we hoped."

22. International Institute for Strategic Studies, "Transnational Terrorism after the Iraq War: Net Effect," *Strategic Comments* 9.4

(June 2003), pp. 1–2, accessed via www.iiss.org/stratcom; Stern, "How America Created a Terrorist Haven." While the present study was in press, militant leader Abu Musab al-Zarqawi, "the figurehead of the Sunni insurgency" and "leader of al-Qaeda in Iraq," was killed in an air strike on a safe house. See "Zarqawi Killed in Iraq Air Raid," *BBC News,* Thursday, June 8, 2006, at news.bbc.co.uk/2/hi/middle_east/5058304.stm; "What's Next After Zarqawi's Death?" *CBS News,* Thursday, June 8, 2006, at www.cbsnews.com/stories/2006/06/08/iraq/main1692753.shtml.

23. *National Strategy for Victory in Iraq,* p. 5. President Bush, in his address of June 8, 2005, at Fort Bragg, North Carolina, quoted Osama bin Laden as saying that a "third world war is raging" in Iraq and will end in "either victory and glory, or misery and humiliation"; see "President Addresses Nation, Discusses Iraq, War on Terror," at www.whitehouse.gov/news/releases/2005/06/20050628-7.html.

24. See Edward Wong, "Turnout in the Iraqi Election Is Reported at 70 Percent," *New York Times,* December 22, 2005, p. A10. This turnout significantly exceeded the 58 percent turnout in January 2005, largely because Sunnis voted in larger numbers rather than boycotting the election. See Robert F. Worth, "Shiite–Kurd Bloc Falls Just Short in Iraqi Election," *New York Times,* January 21, 2006, p. A1. It also exceeds the 63 percent turnout in the constitutional referendum held in October 2005.

25. See Sabrina Tavernise, "U.N.'s Observer in Baghdad Calls the Voting Valid: Election Rerun Unlikely," *New York Times,* December 29, 2005, p. A1.

26. "President Discusses War on Terror and Rebuilding Iraq," December 7, 2005, at www.whitehouse.gov/news/releases/2005/12/20051207-1.html.

27. "Senate Rejects Democratic Call to Begin Withdrawing Troops in Iraq," *New York Times,* June 22, 2006, p. A1.

28. "President Discusses War on Terror and Rebuilding Iraq."

29. Although the interventions in Somalia and Haiti were excluded, those share important similarities to others in this study, notably Bosnia and Kosovo, where armed intervention was mixed with humanitarian and peacekeeping operations, and Panama.

30. It took more than two years after the 2003 invasion of Iraq before the Bush administration specifically defined what it meant by victory and what postwar conditions would constitute victory achieved. See *National Strategy for Victory in Iraq,* pp. 11–12.

31. On the revolution in military affairs, see the sources in Chapter 12, note 22.

Index